W9-ANP-222

Percentage of persons who were foreign born, 2000

Percent
- 1.1–3.1
- 3.6–5.9
- 7.1–9.8
- 10.4–15.8
- 16.7–26.2

The top states in percentage of people who were foreign born in California, New York, Hawaii, New Jersey, and Florida. Most of the Hawaiian immigrants were Asian; most of Florida's immigrants were Hispanic; and the other three states had a mixture of immigrants.

Percentage of persons who reported that they were of two or more races, 2000

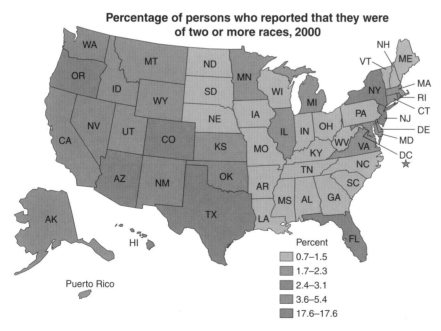

Percent
- 0.7–1.5
- 1.7–2.3
- 2.4–3.1
- 3.6–5.4
- 17.6–17.6

For the first time, the Census Bureau allowed people to choose more than one race. Hawaii had the highest percentage who did so. On the mainland, a higher percentage of people in the West chose two or more races.

Public & Private Families

AN INTRODUCTION

ANDREW J. CHERLIN
Johns Hopkins University

5e

Boston   Burr Ridge, IL   Dubuque, IA   New York   San Francisco   St. Louis
Bangkok   Bogotá   Caracas   Kuala Lumpur   Lisbon   London   Madrid   Mexico City
Milan   Montreal   New Delhi   Santiago   Seoul   Singapore   Sydney   Taipei   Toronto

For Claire and Reid

The McGraw·Hill Companies

PUBLIC AND PRIVATE FAMILES: AN INTRODUCTION

Published by McGraw-Hill, a business unit of The McGraw-Hill
Companies, Inc., 1221 Avenue of the Americas, New York, NY, 10020.
Copyright © 2008, 2005, 2002, 1999, by The McGraw-Hill Companies,
Inc. All rights reserved. No part of this publication may be reproduced
or distributed in any form or by any means, or stored in a database or
retrieval system, without the prior written consent of The McGraw-
Hill Companies, Inc., including, but not limited to, in any network or
other electronic storage or transmission, or broadcast for distance
learning.
Some ancillaries, including electronic and print components, may not
be available to customers outside the United States.

This book is printed on acid-free paper.

1 2 3 4 5 6 7 8 9 0 DOW/DOW 0 9 8 7 6

ISBN   978-0-07-352808-3
MHID 0-07-352808-0

Vice president and editor in chief: *Emily Barrosse*
Sponsoring editor: *Gina Boedeker*
Senior developmental editor: *Jennie Katsaros*
Senior marketing manager: *Lori DeShazo*
Senior project manager: *Diane M. Folliard*
Art editor: *Katherine McNab*
Senior photo research coordinator: *Alexandra Ambrose*
Lead designer: *Gino Cieslik*
Media project manager: *Stacy Dorgan Bentz*
Production supervisor: *Janean A. Utley*
Composition: *Carlisle Publishing Services*
Printing: *R.R. Donnelley, Willard*

Credits: The credits section for this book begins on page 553 and is
considered an extension of the copyright page.

Library of Congress Cataloging-in-Publication Data

Cherlin, Andrew J., 1948–
    Public & private families: an introduction / Andrew J. Cherlin. – 4th ed.
        p. cm.
    Includes bibliographical references and index.
    ISBN-13: 978-0-07-352808-3 (alk. paper)
    ISBN-10: 0-07-352808-0 (alk. paper)
        1. Family—United States. 2. Family. 3. Family policy. I. Title. II. Title:L Public and
    private families.
    HQ536.C44 2008
    306.85—dc22

                                                                    2006046734

The Internet addresses listed in the text were accurate at the time of publication. The
inclusion of a Web site does not indicate an endorsement by the authors or McGraw-
Hill, and McGraw-Hill does not guarantee the accuracy of the information presented at
these sites. www.mhhe.com

About the Author

Andrew J. Cherlin is Benjamin H. Griswold III Professor of Public Policy and Sociology at Johns Hopkins University. He received a B.S. from Yale University in 1970 and a Ph.D. in sociology from the University of California at Los Angeles in 1976. His books include *Marriage, Divorce, Remarriage* (revised and enlarged edition, 1992), *Divided Families: What Happens to Children When Parents Part* (with Frank F. Furstenberg, Jr., 1991), *The Changing American Family and Public Policy* (1988), and *The New American Grandparent: A Place in the Family, A Life Apart* (with Frank F. Furstenberg, Jr., 1986). In 1989–1990 he was chair of the Family Section of the American Sociological Association. In 1999 he was president of the Population Association of America, the scholarly organization for demographic research.

Courtesy of Will Kirk, Johns Hopkins University.

In 2005 Professor Cherlin was awarded a John Simon Guggenheim Memorial Foundation Fellowship. He received the Distinguished Career Award in 2003 from the Family Section of the American Sociological Association. In 2001 he received the Olivia S. Nordberg Award for Excellence in Writing in the Population Sciences. He has also received a Merit Award from the National Institute of Child Health and Human Development for his research on the effects of family structure on children. His recent articles include "The Deinstitutionalization of American Marriage," in the *Journal of Marriage and Family;* "The Influence of Physical and Sexual Abuse on Marriage and Cohabitation," in the *American Sociological Review;* and "American Marriage in the Early Twenty-First Century," in *The Future of Children.* He also has written many articles for *The New York Times, The Washington Post, The Nation, Newsweek,* and other periodicals. He has been interviewed on *ABC News Nightline,* the *Today Show,* network evening news programs, National Public Radio's *All Things Considered,* and other news programs and documentaries.

Contents in Brief

Contents

v

Part Two   Gender, Class, and Race-Ethnicity   77

Chapter 3   Gender and Families, 79

Chapter 4 Social Class and Families, 111

Chapter 5 # Race, Ethnicity, and Families, 143

Part Three   Sexuality, Partnership, and Marriage,   183

Chapter 6   Sexualities, 185

Boxed Features

Chapter 8 # Work and Families, 257

Boxed Features

Chapter 10 # The Elderly and their Families, 329

Part Five   Conflict, Disruption, and Reconstitution,   365

Chapter 11 Domestic Violence, 367

Chapter 12 Divorce, 401

Chapter 13 # Remarriage and Stepfamilies, 437

Part Six	Family and Society, 467

Chapter 14 # The Family, the State, and Social Policy, 469

List of Boxes

How Do Sociologists Know What They Know?

Preface

The sociology of the family is deceptively hard to study. Unlike, say, physics, the topic is familiar (a word whose very root is Latin for "family") because virtually everyone grows up in families. Therefore, it can seem "easy" to study the family because students can bring to bear their personal knowledge of the subject. Some textbooks play to this familiarity by mainly providing students with an opportunity to better understand their private lives. The authors never stray too far from the individual experiences of their readers, focusing on personal choices such as whether to marry and whether to have children. To be sure, giving students insight into the social forces that shape their personal decisions about family life is a worthwhile objective. Nevertheless, the challenge of writing about the sociology of the family is also to help students understand that the significance of families extends beyond personal experience. Today, as in the past, the family is the site of not only private decisions but also activities that matter to our society as a whole.

These activities center on taking care of people who are unable to fully care for themselves, most notably children and the elderly. Anyone who follows social issues knows of the often-expressed concern about whether, given developments such as the increases in divorce and childbearing outside of marriage, we are raising the next generation adequately. Anyone anxious about the well-being of the rapidly growing elderly population (as well as the escalating cost of providing financial and medical assistance to the elderly) knows the concern about whether family members will continue to provide adequate assistance to them. Indeed, rarely does a month pass without these issues appearing on the covers of magazines and the front pages of newspapers.

In this textbook, consequently, I have written about the family in two senses: the *private family*, in which we live most of our personal lives, and the *public family*, in which adults perform tasks that are important to society. My goal is to give students a thorough grounding in both aspects. It is true that the two are related— taking care of children adequately, for instance, requires the love and affection that family members express privately toward each other. But the public side of the family deserves equal time with the private side.

■ Organization

This book is divided into 6 parts and 15 chapters. Part One ("Introduction") introduces the concepts of public and private families and examines how sociologists and other social scientists study them. It also provides an overview of the history of the family. Part Two ("Gender, Class, and Race-Ethnicity") deals with the three key dimensions of social stratification in family life: gender, social class, and race-ethnicity. In Part Three ("Sexuality, Partnership, and Marriage"), the focus shifts to the private family. The section examines the emergence of the modern concept of sexuality, the formation of partnerships, and the degree of persistence and change in the institution of marriage. Finally, it covers the complex connections between work and family.

Part Four ("Links across the Generations") explores how well the public family is meeting its responsibilities for children and the elderly. Part Five ("Conflict, Disruption, and Reconstitution") deals with the consequences of conflict and disruption in family life. It first studies violence against wives and children. Then divorce, remarriage, and stepfamilies are discussed. Finally, in Part Six ("Family and Society") social and political issues involving the family and the state are discussed, and then the text concludes with a chapter on the meaning of the great social changes in family life over the past century.

■ Special Features

Public and Private Families is distinguishable from other textbooks in several important ways.

First and foremost, it explores both the public and the private family. The public/private distinction that underlies the book's structure is intended to provide a more balanced portrait of contemporary life. Furthermore, the focus on the public family leads to a much greater emphasis on government policy toward the family than in most other textbooks. In fact, every chapter except the first and last includes a short, boxed essay under the general title, "Families and Public Policy," to stimulate student interest and make the book relevant to current political debates.

In addition to this unique emphasis on both the *Public and Private Families,* the text:

- **Highlights family life in other cultures.** Although the emphasis in the book is on the contemporary United States and other Western nations, no text should ignore the important historical and cross-cultural diversity of families. Consequently, in addition to relevant material in the body of the text, I have also included in every chapter except the first and last a boxed essay under the title, "Families in Other Cultures."
- **Includes distinctive chapters.** The attention to the public family led me to write several chapters that are not included in some sociology of the family textbooks. These include Chapter 14, "The Family, the State, and Social Policy," Chapter 9, "Children and Parents," and Chapter 10, "The Elderly and Their Families." These chapters examine issues of great current interest, such as income assistance to poor families, the effects of out-of-home child care, the costs of the Social Security and Medicare programs, and the extension of marriage to same-sex couples. Throughout these and other chapters, variations by race, ethnicity, and gender are explored.
- **Gives special attention to the research methods used by family sociologists.** To give students an understanding of how sociologists study the family, I include a section in Chapter 1 titled, "How Do Family Sociologists Know What They Know?" This material explains the ways that family sociologists go about their research. Then in other chapters, I include boxed essays under a similar title on subjects ranging from national surveys to feminist research methods to archival research.
- **Features "Families on the Internet" sections.** Since I wrote the first edition of this textbook, the World Wide Web has changed from a pleasant diversion to an essential information-gathering tool. Almost every chapter contains information that I gathered from the Web, including the most up-to-date demographic statistics from government statistical sites such as the Bu-

reau of the Census Web pages. But the Internet is also a powerful instructional tool. Consequently, at the end of each chapter is a section titled "Families on the Internet," in which I list Web sites that students may find useful.

- **Includes new photo essay features to engage the reader and enliven the text.** I have added a photo essay about Hurricane Katrina, "Poverty and Altitude," in Chapter 5, about skipped-generation households, "Grandparents as Parents," in Chapter 10, and about same-sex marriages/partnerships, "The Boundaries of Marriage," in Chapter 14.

■ Pedagogy

Each chapter begins in a way that engages the reader: the neither-men-nor-women berdaches of many Native American tribes; the story of American men who fly to Russia in search of brides; the case of Danny Henrikson, taken from a stepfather who raised him and awarded by a judge to a father he did not know; and so forth. And each of the six parts of the book is preceded by a brief introduction that sets the stage.

- I have added several *Quick Review* boxes in each chapter that include bulleted, one-sentence summaries of the key points of the preceding sections.
- Each chapter includes the following types of questions:

  - *Looking Forward*—Questions that preview the chapter themes and topics.
  - *Ask Yourself*—Two questions, which appear at the end of each of the three types of boxes.
  - *Looking Back*—Looking Forward questions reiterated at the end of each chapter, around which the chapter summaries are organized.
  - *Thinking about Families*—Two questions, which appear at the end of each chapter and are designed to encourage critical thinking about the "public" and the "private" family.

- *Cross-reference icons:* These icons, embedded in the text, point readers to the exact page where an important concept was introduced in an earlier chapter.

■ What's New in Each Chapter?

As always, this edition contains numerous new citations to recent articles and books in every chapter; and all statistics have been updated if newer data exist. In addition, the following changes have been made.

CHAPTER 1. PUBLIC AND PRIVATE FAMILIES

- Updated information on same-sex marriage.

CHAPTER 2. THE HISTORY OF THE FAMILY

- Expanded "Life Course" section including a new subsection on the emergence of "early adulthood" as a stage of life.
- New *Families in Other Cultures* essay on Cai Hua's (2001) ethnography, *A Society without Fathers or Husbands: The Na of China*.

- Citations and a quotation from Stefanie Coontz's (2005) book, *Marriage, A History*.
- New subsection on diversity in colonial American families.

CHAPTER 3. GENDER AND FAMILIES

- New material on how most researchers now see parental socialization of children as a bidirectional process, with children influencing parents as well as being influenced by them.
- Description of a study showing how the division of household labor is shaped not only by couple's own preferences but by gender inequality at the national level.

CHAPTER 4. SOCIAL CLASS AND FAMILIES

- New section on evidence of the diverging demographics of family life by educational attainment.
- Consistent with this new section, I introduce a three-category model of social standing (college degree, high school degree, no high school degree) based on Weber's idea of status groups, in addition to presenting the standard four-class model (upper, middle, working, lower).
- I have deleted the discussion of the Marxist theory of class because I did not subsequently use it and because of the new status-group model I am presenting.
- New chapter opener on imports from China.
- Deletion of material on "working-class kinship," which is quite dated and no longer applicable.

CHAPTER 5. RACE, ETHNICITY, AND FAMILIES

- Summary of the "natural experiment" of African American marriage rates in the military.
- Discussion of the black feminist concept of "intersectionality."
- Completely rewritten section on Mexican Americans emphasizing the role of immigration in producing distinctive family patterns (high birthrates, early marriage, more extended family households), the much lesser distinctiveness of their U.S.-born descendants, and the substantial role of the Mexican-origin population in U.S. population growth.
- New section on "Racial and Ethnic Intermarriage," reviewing recent scholarship on the rates of intermarriage for the major racial and Hispanic groups. Discussion of possible effects of high rates of intermarriage and multiracial self-identification on racial and ethnic group boundaries in the future, including the possibility of a new black/nonblack divide.
- New photo essay about Hurricane Katrina, "Poverty and Altitude."

CHAPTER 6. SEXUALITIES

- Reflecting the comments of several instructors who use this book, the focus is now on sexuality, and the title has been changed from "Sexuality and Love" to "Sexualities."
- Rewritten and expanded section on "Sexual Identities." It brings together material that had been in separate sections of the chapter.
- New discussion of the strengths and limitations of "queer theory," the growing and influential body of thought which claims that sexual life is artificially

organized into categories that reflect the power of heterosexual norms and which argues against the use of the concept of sexual identities.

- New data on sexual activities, attractions, and orientations from the 2002 National Survey of Family Growth.
- New section, "Beyond the Family," which discusses two kinds of living arrangements that blur the boundaries between family living and nonfamily living: families of choice and living-apart-together (LAT) relationships.

CHAPTER 7. COHABITATION AND MARRIAGE

- New section on "The Current Context of Marriage" that draws upon my 2004 article, "The Deinstitutionalization of American Marriage," in the *Journal of Marriage and Family*. I have not used the word "deinstitutionalization," however, in this section; and I have tried to clarify and simplify the language of the article in several places.
- New material based on several important recent articles on cohabitation, including growing evidence that for many cohabitors, especially childless young adults, cohabitation seems like an alternative way of being single rather than a stage in the marriage process.
- New *Families in Other Cultures* essay on "The Rise of the Love Marriage."
- Updated information for the *Families and Public Policy* box, "Domestic Partnerships," which focuses on legal rights for heterosexual couples. (Civil unions and marriage for same-sex couples are discussed in other chapters.)

CHAPTER 8. WORK AND FAMILIES

- Data from 1998 and 2000 American time-use studies suggesting further narrowing of the gap between women's and men's housework.
- Theories of why care workers are paid low wages.
- Exchange theory and gender theory perspectives on the association between the share of housework done by wives and wives' earnings.
- New scholarship on difference in the quality, rather than quantity, of women's and men's leisure time.

CHAPTER 9. CHILDREN AND PARENTS

- New section on "Religion and Socialization."
- First national statistics on adoption from the 2000 Census.
- Updated presentation of studies on children of lesbian and gay parents.
- New statistics on parents' use of time from Bianchi et al (2006), *Changing Rhythms of American Family Life*.

CHAPTER 10. THE ELDERLY AND THEIR FAMILIES

- New chapter opener on the increased prevalence of grandparents and step-grandparents in children's lives.
- New discussion of active life expectancy (a new key term).
- Updated policy box on financing Social Security and Medicaid.
- Expanded subsection on multigenerational households (new key term), including information on skipped-generation households.
- Expanded and updated section on public and private provision of care for the elderly.
- New photo essay about skipped-generation households, "Grandparents as Parents."

CHAPTER 11. DOMESTIC VIOLENCE

- New section on the growing movement among researchers to distinguish two kinds of intimate partner violence, both of which are new key terms: "situational couple violence," a less serious kind initiated by both men and women, and "intimate terrorism," a more serious kind, perpetrated almost entirely by men seeking to control women's actions. A chart summarizes the distinctions.

CHAPTER 12. DIVORCE

- New section on recent trends that covers the apparent divergence of divorce rates since 1980 on the basic of educational attainment, with the rates rising for people without high school degrees and falling for college graduates.
- New subsection on behavioral genetic studies of the effects of divorce on children.

CHAPTER 13. REMARRIAGE AND STEPFAMILIES

- New material (e.g., stepparents as "affinity-seekers") from Lawrence H. Ganong and Marilyn Coleman's (2004) book, *Stepfamily Relationships: Development, Dynamics, and Interactions*.

CHAPTER 14. THE FAMILY, THE STATE, AND SOCIAL POLICY

- Discussion of 2006 bill that established marriage promotion programs.
- Discussion of alternative policies for assisting children (previously discussed in Chapter 15).
- Expanded discussion of same-sex marriage.
- New photo essay about same-sex marriages/partnerships, "The Boundaries of Marriage."

CHAPTER 15 SOCIAL CHANGE AND FAMILIES

- At the suggestion of several instructors, I have shortened this chapter by moving some material to prior chapters.

■ Supplements Package

McGraw-Hill creates and publishes an extensive array of print, digital, and video supplements for students and instructors. This edition of *Public and Private Families* is accompanied by a comprehensive package:

FOR THE STUDENT

- *Public and Private Families: A Reader, 5th Edition*—Edited by the text's author and keyed to text chapters, this Reader includes articles and book excerpts by family sociologists and other writers on a variety of issues facing families today. A special discount is available when the textbook and Reader are ordered as a package.
- *Reel Families CD-ROM*—This unique interactive movie enables students to take on the role of one of the story's characters and influence key plot turns by making choices for that character. The movie allows students to explore course concepts and terminology in a relevant and meaningful context. Movie segments are augmented by an array of review and assessment features. With

this learning tool, students can explore a wide variety of family issues firsthand and master course concepts more completely than they could by just reading any text.

- *Online Learning Center Web Site*—This provides innovative, text-specific resources including quizzes with feedback that students can use to study for exams, flashcards that can be used to master vocabulary, and more.

FOR THE INSTRUCTOR

- The *Online Instructor's Resource* manual—provides access to a wide array of important ancillaries:
  - *Instructor's Manual/Testbank*—includes detailed chapter outlines, key terms, overviews, lecture notes, and a complete testbank
  - *Reel Families Instructor's Guide*—teaching tips and notes that make it easy to integrate the *Reel Families CD* into your course
  - *Computerized Testbank*—easy-to-use computerized testing program for both Windows and Macintosh computers
  - *PowerPoint Slides*—complete, chapter-by-chapter slideshows featuring text, art, and tables
- *Reel Families Lecture Launcher Videotape*—so even if you can't require students to use the CD, you can use the movie footage to jumpstart lectures in a unique and exciting fashion
- *Full-Length Videotapes*—a wide variety of videotapes from the *Films for the Humanities and Social Sciences* series is available to adopters of the text.
- *Course Management Systems*—whether you use WebCT, Blackboard, e-College, or another course management system, McGraw-Hill will provide you with a cartridge that enables you to either conduct your course entirely online or supplement your lectures with online material. And if your school does not yet have one of these course management systems, we can provide you with PageOut, an easy-to-use tool that allows you to create your own course Web page and access all material on the Online Learning Center.
- *Primis Online*—a unique database publishing system that allows instructors to create their own custom text from material in this text or elsewhere and deliver that text to students electronically as an e-book or in print format via the bookstore.

■ Acknowledgments

To write a book this comprehensive requires the help of many people. At McGraw-Hill, sponsoring editor Sherith Pankratz provided initial support, senior development editor Jennie Katsaros provided valuable editorial guidance, and Diane Folliard smoothly managed the production process. In addition, the following people read the fourth edition and provided me with helpful suggestions for this revision:

Vernon Bates, Pacific University

Gina Carreno, Florida Atalnatic University

Mary Ann Czamezki, University of Wisconsin–Milwaukee

Debra Levy, UNC–Wilmington

Norma Ojeda, San Diego State University

Michele Parker, Glendale Community College

Debra Peterson, Bemidji State Universtiy

Cathie Robertson, Grossmont–Cuyamaca Community College

Bahira Sherif Trask, University of Delaware

Nicholas Wolfinger, University of Utah

Andrew J. Cherlin

Visual Preview

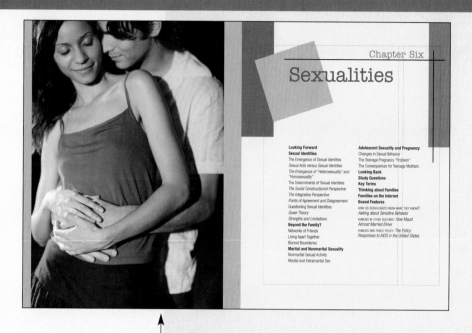

Explores the Public and Private Family

Thorough coverage of both the private, personal aspects of families—sexuality, companionship, choosing a spouse or partner—and the public, societal aspects of families—policies to support employed parents, concern about adolescent childbearing, debates over poverty and welfare programs.

Highlights Family Life in Other Cultures

Although the emphasis in the book is on the contemporary United States and other Western nations, every chapter features a boxed essay entitled "Families in Other Cultures" that highlights cross-cultural similarities and differences.

Spotlights Research Methods Used by Family Sociologists

Many chapters include a boxed section entitled "How Do Sociologists Know What They Know?" that explains the ways that family sociologists go about their research.

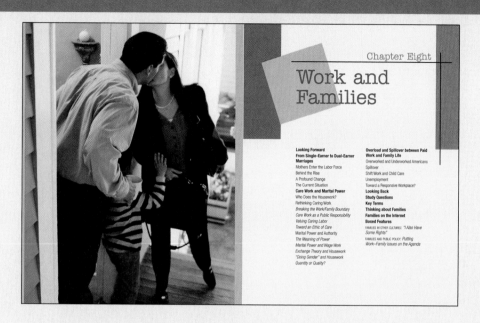

Chapter-Opening Previews

Detailed chapter-opening outlines and "Looking Forward" questions draw students in and help them focus on the chapter's most critical concepts.

NEW Photo Essays

Three photo essays invite students to visually examine topics such as poverty, skipped-generation households, and same-sex marriages.

"Quick Review" Summaries

Each chapter features several internal section summaries in addition to the one at the end of the chapter, ensuring that students stay on track as they read.

Complete End-of-Chapter Reviews

Clear, concise chapter summaries, key terms lists, review questions, critical thinking exercises, and Internet activities provide students with essential study materials.

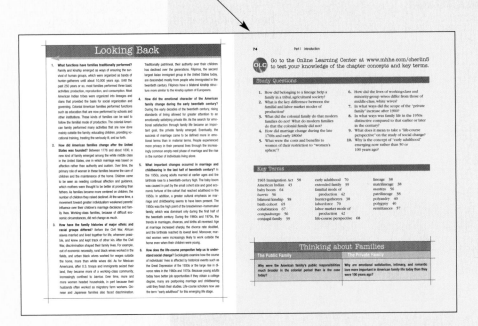

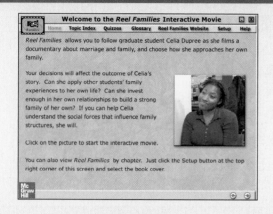

Reel Families
Interactive Movie
CD-ROM

This unique interactive movie takes the concept of active learning to a whole new level, enabling students to take on the role of one of the story's characters and influence key plot turns by making choices for that character. With this breakthrough learning tool, students can explore a wide variety of family issues firsthand and master course concepts more completely than they could by just reading a text.

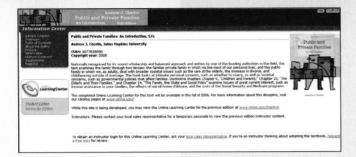

Online Learning Center Web Site

This unique, book-specific Web site features access to flashcards that can be used to master vocabulary, quizzes with feedback, and many other chapter review tools.

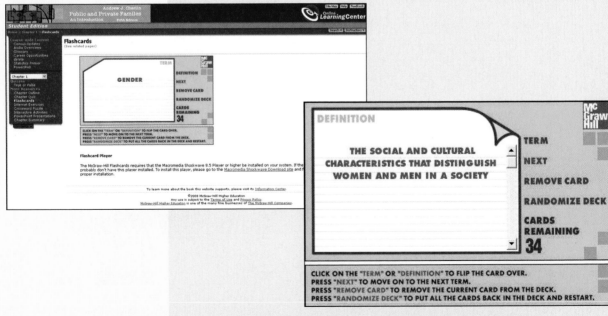

Part One

Introduction

The family has two aspects. It is, first, the place where we experience much of our private lives. It is where we give and receive love, share our hopes and fears, work through our troubles, and relax and enjoy ourselves. Second, it is a setting in which adults perform tasks that are of importance to society, particularly raising children and assisting elderly parents. To be sure, people undertake these tasks not to perform a public service but rather to express love, affection, and gratitude. Nevertheless, family caretaking benefits us all by raising the next generation and by reducing our collective responsibility for the elderly. Indeed, people today frequently express concern over whether changes in the family have reduced parents' abilities to raise their children well. This book is about both the private and public aspects of families. It examines the contributions of family life not only to personal satisfaction but also to public welfare. The first two chapters provide an introduction to this perspective.

• **Chapter 1** explores the most useful ways to think about families. It reviews the debates about family life today, and it examines the approaches that sociologists and other social scientists use to study families. • **Chapter 2** provides an overview of the history of the family. Over the past few decades, family historians have produced many studies that provide useful insights. A knowledge of family life in the past can help us to understand families today.

Public and Private Families

Looking Forward

1. How do Americans feel about marriage and families?

2. What do families do that is important for society? What do families do that is important for the individuals in them?

3. How do sociologists go about studying families?

4. What are the leading theoretical approaches to studying families?

On October 3, 1954, a half-century ago, CBS broadcast the first episode of *Father Knows Best.* It humorously depicted the daily dilemmas of a middle-class family: Jim Anderson, an amiable insurance salesman in Springfield; his stay-at-home wife Margaret; and their three children, Princess, Bud, and Kitten. Jim, it turns out, didn't always know best. Often, Margaret intuited the solution to life's little problems and guided Jim toward the right decision. But she never challenged his position as king of the family, serving rather as the power behind the throne. And she rarely stepped out of the house. Along with shows such as *The Adventures of Ozzie and Harriet* and *Leave It to Beaver, Father Knows Best* launched a new genre: the family situation comedy.

The families on these 50s sitcoms looked similar. They were headed by what was often called the **breadwinner–homemaker family**—a married couple with children in which the father worked for pay and the mother did not. These portrayals reflected the times. Like their TV counterparts, most families—poor or middle class—were headed by married couples in the 1950s, and the average woman gave birth to three children. However, the TV families didn't accurately reflect the racial and ethnic diversity of the nation. A study of 85 families depicted on television in the 1950s found that 82 were white, 2 were Hispanic, 1 was American Indian, and none were African American (Robinson & Skill, 2001).

Contrast these staid families with some examples of the households found on TV during the mid-2000s:

> **breadwinner–homemaker family** a married couple with children in which the father worked for pay and the mother did not

- *Will and Grace:* A single woman whose friend is a gay man. Two other main characters are an alcoholic socialite and a gay sidekick.
- *The George Lopez Show:* George learns in the first episode that his father, whom his mother has always insisted is dead, is still alive.
- *The New Adventures of Old Christine:* A divorced mother who tells her brother, "My divorce is better than most people's marriages."

Moreover, by the early 1990s, one in six TV families was headed by a divorced or separated parent, and one in seven was African American (Robinson & Skill, 2001). In addition, the vast majority of TV mothers worked outside the home (Douglas, 2003).

It's no accident, of course, that television families are much more diverse now than in the 1950s. Real-life families are much more diverse, as we will learn in the following chapters. Families in which married couples raise their biological children, although still common, do not dominate family life the way they did in the past. It's more acceptable to live with a partner or have children without marrying, to be divorced or remarried, or to be childless. In addition, as the political and economic power of racial and ethnic minorities has grown, and as immigration has increased, the media have increasingly targeted minority audiences; no network today would field an all-white lineup of family shows.

Some observers embrace the diversity of American family life at the start of the twenty-first century, others tolerate it, and still others are concerned about it. Over the past two decades, a political debate about family life has emerged: On one side is the "marriage movement"—a loose group of conservative and centrist activists, religious leaders, and social scientists who want to strengthen the institution of marriage. Sometimes called "traditionalists" (although the 1950s family was not traditional, as we will learn in the next chapter), they view childrearing as the central purpose of marriage. They bemoan changes in family life such as the increases in divorce, in childbearing outside of marriage, and in couples who live together outside of marriage. They charge that parents today are doing a poorer job of bringing up children due to the increase in single-parent families and a higher percentage of mothers working outside the home.

On the other side are what we might call the "diversity defenders": liberal activists, feminists, and like-minded social scientists, who focus less on childrearing and more on the personal rewards that family life provides to adults. They believe that adults should be free to choose the style of life they find most satisfying. They argue that society can adjust to the new family forms, such as two-earner couples and single-parent households, by changing the ways in which the workplace and the school are organized. They assert that there is little evidence to back up the claim that having a working mother hurts children. And they argue that single-parent families can be just as good for children as married-couple families if they receive the support they need. (In Chapter 9 we will study children's well-being, in Chapter 12 we will take a close look at single-parent families, and in Chapter 14 we will examine the policy debates in detail.)

The members of the marriage movement, on the other hand, favor public policies that encourage marriage. In 2006 Congress passed a welfare bill that included $150 million per year for promoting marriage. Supporters argued that activities such as relationship-skills training and high school course modules could help increase marriage rates and therefore benefit children. Opponents argued that marriage promotion programs were unlikely to be successful and could encourage bad marriages that would hurt children (Cherlin, 2003).

The diversity defenders counter that public policies should support families of all types, whether they include a married couple or not. For instance, many favor extending the legal protections of marriage to same-sex couples because they believe that gay and lesbian couples experience the same kind of intimacy and commitment as opposite-sex couples and therefore deserve the same kind of rights and recognition. In May 2004, Massachusetts became the first state to legalize same-sex marriage, and in 2005, Canada and Spain became the third and fourth nations (after Belgium and the Netherlands) to legalize it. During the 2004 presidential election campaign, President George W. Bush pledged to uphold the "sanctity of marriage" by supporting a constitutional amendment that would restrict marriage to opposite-sex unions. Suddenly, same-sex marriage became a front-burner political issue.

Confetti rains on Stephane Chapin and Bertrand Charpentier, who were married by the mayor of Bègles, France, in 2004 even though gay marriage is prohibited in France. An appeals court later declared the marriage null and void.

Although the political activists have taken sides, most Americans are more ambivalent about the great changes in family life over the past half-century. This chapter will begin by examining the sources of that ambivalence. It will then consider fundamental questions raised by the debate: What is a family? What do families do that is important to society? What do families do that is meaningful to individuals? It will present the main research methods sociologists use to study the family. And it will conclude with a brief survey of the main theoretical perspectives that sociologists and other social scientists use to help explain how families do what they do.

Individualism and Families

A family life centered on marriage remains the preference of most Americans. When young adults are asked their plans for the future, the overwhelming majority respond that they plan to marry and to have children. Yet Americans are much more tolerant than they used to be of those who aren't married. When Alan Wolfe (1998, p. 110) conducted interviews to learn whether Americans could be divided into "traditionalists" and "modernists" in their beliefs about family life, he concluded that they could not. Rather, he found that many people agreed with some of what both the marriage movement and the diversity defenders were saying. "The divisions over the family do not take place between camps of people," he wrote; "instead, they take place within most individuals." That is to say, many of us hold parts of both positions.

individualism a style of life in which individuals pursue their own interests and place great importance on developing a personally rewarding life

utilitarian individualism a style of life that emphasizes self-reliance and personal achievement, especially in one's work life

Our tolerance of those who choose differently from us derives from the individualistic way Americans approach personal life. By **individualism,** I mean a style of life in which individuals pursue their own interests and place great importance on developing a personally rewarding life. Individualism in American life is of two types (Bellah, Marsden, Sullivan, Swidler, & Tipton, 1985). The older, more-established type is **utilitarian individualism:** a style of life that emphasizes self-reliance and personal achievement, especially in one's work life. Benjamin Franklin was the quintessential utilitarian individualist. In his *Poor Richard's*

Almanack he advised that "Early to bed and early to rise, makes a man healthy, wealthy, and wise" and that "God helps them that help themselves." Today, this is the style of the person determined to succeed on his or her own or to get to the top of the corporate ladder. The second type, newer on a large scale, is **expressive individualism:** a style of life that emphasizes developing one's feelings and emotional satisfaction. This is the style of the person who wants to connect emotionally with a romantic partner, express his or her innermost thoughts to a trusted friend, and develop a good body at the health club.

expressive individualism
a style of life that emphasizes developing one's feelings and emotional satisfaction

The 2003 Supreme Court decision overruling a Texas law against gay sexual acts exemplifies American individualism and its tolerance of diverse lifestyles. Writing for the majority, Justice Anthony Kennedy stated:

> *Liberty presumes an autonomy of self that includes freedom of thought, belief, expression, and certain intimate conduct. (Lawrence v. Texas, 2003)*

An autonomy of self: Kennedy argues that liberty cannot be attained unless individuals can maintain an independent sense of who they are. *Freedom of thought, belief, expression, and certain intimate conduct:* Individuals must also be free to express their feelings through their intimate lives. This sentence seems to say that expressive individualism is an essential component of liberty.

The individualistic outlook of Americans has influenced what they think of marriage and parenthood. In 1999, the editors of the *New York Times Magazine* asked me to help design a national telephone survey about Americans' most important values (Cherlin, 1999b). We presented randomly selected adults with a list of value statements and asked how important each one was to them. The list is displayed in Figure 1.1 in order of the percentage replying "very important." What is most interesting is the relative ranking of these value statements. The first four reflect either utilitarian individualism ("Being responsible for your actions," "Being able to stand up for yourself") or expressive individualism ("Being in good health," "Being able to communicate your feelings"). Note that "Having children" ranked sixth and "Being married" ranked tenth. In fact, the proportion of people who replied that "Being married" was very important was less than the proportion who replied that "Being a good neighbor" was very important. Overall, the rankings suggest that Americans value independent action and self-expression more highly than playing the roles of parent or spouse.

This is not to say that Americans don't value family life. In the same survey, people often reported that family and children were the most fulfilling and satisfying aspects of their lives. But in an individualistically oriented society, adults are expected to construct their family lives in ways that are consistent with their self-development. Today, most Americans still want to marry, but they have less of a need to do so than in the past. Marriage must compete with alternatives such as staying in school longer to obtain a higher degree, taking more time to develop a career, living with a partner without marrying, or having children outside of marriage. Some people may be ambivalent about marriage, at once drawn by its promise of intimacy and wary of its commitments and constraints. Family life therefore becomes much more diverse than it was a half-century ago. Even though most Americans choose to marry and a majority choose to have children within a marriage, they tend to respect the choices that other, freely acting individuals may make.

FIGURE 1.1
Percentage of adults replying "very important" when asked how important each of these values is to them. (*Source:* Cherlin, 1999)

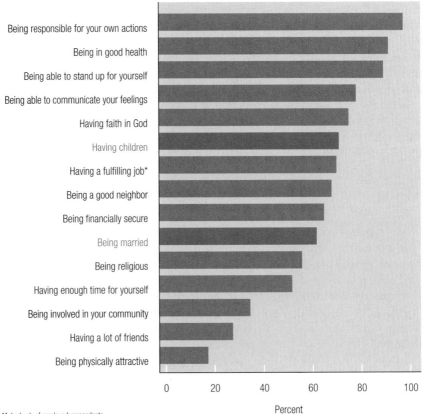

Being responsible for your own actions
Being in good health
Being able to stand up for yourself
Being able to communicate your feelings
Having faith in God
Having children
Having a fulfilling job*
Being a good neighbor
Being financially secure
Being married
Being religious
Having enough time for yourself
Being involved in your community
Having a lot of friends
Being physically attractive

Percent

*Asked only of employed respondents

Quick Review

- Families have become much more diverse over the past half-century.
- Some observers are concerned about the increasing proportion of children who are not being raised by two married, biological parents.
- Others argue that the alternative family forms are just as good as lifelong marriage.
- Americans tend to take individualistic perspectives on adult life.
- Utilitarian individualism emphasizes self-reliance and personal achievement.
- Expressive individualism emphasizes one's feelings and emotional satisfaction.

■ What Is a Family?

The growing diversity of families and the widespread ambivalence about marriage raise the fundamental question of how to define a family. At one extreme, some observers claim that families are so diverse that the concept may not even be useful anymore. At the other extreme are those who press politicians to use the singular form "family" (instead of the plural "families") to signify that there is only one proper kind of family—the married couple living with their biological children.

The definition of the family is also important economically. Rules specifying who is a "family member" determine billions of dollars of government and corporate benefits. For example, I am eligible for health insurance coverage through my employer for my "family," which is defined as a spouse and children under 18. If I were unmarried but living with a woman who was the mother of my children, I could insure the children but not the mother. If I had been living for years with a man whom I considered my lifelong partner, I probably could not insure him. Moreover, how one defines a family plays an important role in the debate over whether the family has declined.

The definition of the family also varies from culture to culture. This book is primarily about families in the **Western nations,** the countries of Western Europe and the overseas English-speaking countries of the United States, Canada, Australia, and New Zealand. The main focus is on the family in the United States, but there are strong similarities between the American family and the family in other Western nations (Cherlin & Furstenberg, 1988). The primary unit in all these countries is the small, household-based family of parents and children. Young adults choose their spouses with modest input from their parents, and marriage is monogamous. (**Monogamy** is a marriage system in which persons cannot have more than one spouse.) Substantial proportions of married women work for pay outside the home (although that was not the case earlier in the twentieth century). Over the past few decades, nearly all the Western nations have undergone similar increases in cohabitation, childbearing outside of marriage, and divorce.

Nevertheless, we can draw important lessons by studying families elsewhere in the world. Therefore, this book will include numerous examples of family patterns in non-Western countries, including the developed nations of East Asia such as Japan and Taiwan, and developing countries throughout the world. In many of these countries, ties to parents and other kin play a larger part in the structure of the family. Often, parents provide substantial guidance to children in choosing spouses. In some countries, women rarely work outside the family home or compound. In many countries in Africa, Arabic Asia, and other areas, polygamous marriage is allowed. (**Polygamy** is a marriage system in which men or women [or both] are allowed to have more than one spouse at a time.) At the same time, significant changes have occurred in family patterns in much of the developing world over the past several decades; examining these changes can help us better understand the changes that have occurred closer to home. Similar insights can be drawn from studying the changes in family life in Western history. Each of the subsequent chapters of this book will include a separate, short essay on families in other cultures, with "other cultures" occasionally defined to include earlier periods in Western history.

For the United States and other Western nations, I would argue that there is no single definition of a family that is adequate for all purposes. Rather, how you define a family depends on what questions you want to answer. Two key questions are

1. How well are family members taking care of children, the chronically ill, and the frail elderly?
2. How well are families providing the emotional satisfaction people value so highly—intimacy, love, personal fulfillment?

These questions address, respectively, the public responsibilities and the private pleasures the family is called upon to meet. For each of these questions, I submit, one of two definitions of the family will be helpful; I will call them the public family and the private family. These definitions provide two useful ways of looking at

Western nations the countries of Western Europe and the overseas English-speaking countries: the United States, Canada, Australia, and New Zealand

monogamy a marriage system in which people are allowed only one spouse

polygamy a marriage system in which men or women (or both) are allowed to have more than one spouse

U.S. families are more diverse today than in earlier times because of the great changes that have occurred since the middle of the twentieth century. Single-parent families, extended families, and complex families formed by remarriages are among the kinds of families with which the two-parent, first-marriage family must share its spotlight.

externalities benefits or costs that accrue to others when an individual or business produces something

negative externalities the costs imposed on other individuals or businesses when an individual or business produce something of value to itself

the same reality—and often the very same group of adults and children. Some observers may impose their own theological definitions of what constitutes a family from religious works such as the Bible or the Koran. But social science cannot determine the moral essence of the family, nor need it do so.

THE PUBLIC FAMILY

In examining the concept of the public family, it's useful to borrow a few terms from the field of economics. Economists who specialize in public welfare have introduced the notion of **externalities,** of which there are two types.[1] First, **negative externalities** occur when an individual or a business produces something

---

[1] A standard treatment of these topics can be found in Stiglitz (1988).

that is beneficial to itself but imposes costs on other individuals or businesses. For example, factories that release sulfur dioxide through smokestacks impose a cost on everyone else by polluting the air. The factory gains by producing goods without having to install expensive smokestack scrubbers, but everyone else loses. Second, **positive externalities** occur when an individual or business produces something that benefits others but for which the producers are not fully compensated. For example, a corporation may start an expensive job-training program in order to obtain qualified workers; but some of the workers may take jobs with rival firms after completing the training. The other firms obtain skilled workers without paying the cost of their training.

> **positive externalities** benefits received by others when an individual or business produces something, but for which the producer is not fully compensated
>
> **public goods** things that may be enjoyed by people who do not themselves produce them

Some positive externalities involve the production of what are called **public goods.** These goods have a peculiar property: It is almost impossible to stop people who don't produce them from enjoying them. As a result, public goods are often produced in smaller quantities than is socially desirable. Suppose a town raises taxes to build a water filtration plant that cleans a polluted river. It cannot stop residents of other towns downstream from enjoying the cleaner water; yet these fortunate residents have paid nothing for the cleanup. In a situation like this, it is clearly in each town's interest to have some other town farther up the river produce the public good—the treatment plant. Yet if no town builds the plant, no one will enjoy cleaner water. One solution to this dilemma is for the county or state government to raise taxes in all the towns and then build the plant. Another is for the towns to reach an agreement whereby one will build the plant but all will contribute to the costs. Either solution compensates the producer of the public good for the benefits that others obtain.

Although it may seem like a long leap from factories to families, the concepts of externalities and public goods still apply. Families do produce valuable public goods—most notably, children (England & Folbre, 1999). For example, when I retire, I hope to receive a Social Security check from the government each month, just as retired people do today. The funds for those checks will come from payroll taxes paid by workers. After 2010, the many men and women born during the post–World War II baby boom will begin to reach retirement age; I hope to be one of them. Currently, there are about five persons of working age for each retired person; but by 2030 there may be only three persons of working age for every retired person.[2] This means that the burden of supporting the elderly will increase greatly. It's in my interest, then, for families to have and rear children today who will pay taxes when they grow up.

More generally, it's in society's interest that today's children become good citizens with traits such as obeying the law, showing concern about others, and being informed voters. It's also in society's interest that they be productive workers who are willing and able to fill the needs of the economy. To be sure, critics charge that families often raise children in ways that reproduce existing inequalities between women and men (see Chapter 3) or between the working class and middle class (see Chapter 4). Nevertheless, what they do is of great public value. They are greenhouses growing the workers and citizens of tomorrow.

But children are costly to raise, and I will receive the same Social Security check whether or not the workers were raised by me. Therefore, it's in my economic interest to remain childless and to have every other family except mine

---

[2] Considering 20 to 64 as working age and 65 or older as retirement age. See *U.S. Interim Projections by Age, Sex,* U.S. Bureau of the Census (2006a).

free-rider problem the tendency for people to obtain public goods by letting others do the work of producing them—metaphorically, the temptation to ride free on the backs of others

raise children. Yet if everyone followed this strategy there would be no next generation. This dilemma is sometimes known as the **free-rider problem:** the tendency for people to obtain public goods by letting others do the work of producing them—metaphorically, the temptation to ride free on the backs of others. Luckily, people have children for reasons other than economic self-interest. At the moment, however, they are barely having enough to replace the current generation of parents. Everyone benefits from the child rearing that parents do.[3]

In addition, families provide other services that have the character of public goods. As will be noted in Chapter 10, adult children still provide the bulk of the care for the frail elderly. If I am old and ill, I will benefit if I have adult children who will care for me. But others will also benefit from the care that my family provides. Without them, I would need more assistance from the government-funded medical insurance programs for the elderly (Medicare) and for the poor (Medicaid). Consequently, the care my family provides will keep government spending, and hence taxes, lower for everyone. The same logic applies to care that family members provide for the chronically ill.

The first definition, then, concerns the view of the family you take when you are concerned about the family's contribution to the public welfare—the useful services family members provide by taking care of one another. It is a definition of what I will call the **public family:** *one adult, or two adults who are related by marriage, partnership, or shared parenthood, who is/are taking care of dependents, and the dependents themselves.* Dependents are defined as children, the frail elderly, and the chronically ill. The family members usually reside in the same household, but that is not essential. For example, an elderly woman may live in her own apartment but still receive daily assistance from her daughter or son. Nor is it essential that the family members be married or of the opposite sex. The important fact is that they are taking care of dependents and, in doing so, producing public goods. This definition would include, of course, a married couple and their children or their elderly parents. But it would also include a divorced (or never-married) mother and her children, a cohabiting couple with children, a lesbian couple who are jointly raising a child who was born to one of them, or a gay man caring for a partner with AIDS. Note also who would be excluded by this definition: a childless married couple with no dependent or elderly relatives, or opposite-sex or same-sex cohabitors without children, the elderly, or ill dependents.

public family one adult, or two adults who are related by marriage, partnership, or shared parenthood, who is/are taking care of dependents, and the dependents themselves

The boundaries of the public family are sometimes unclear. Suppose that after a divorce a father makes regular child support payments to his ex-wife and sees his children often. You might argue that he is still sharing parenthood and therefore part of the family under this definition. If the mother remarries, her new husband could also be considered part of the family. As will be discussed in later chapters, divorce, remarriage, and childbearing outside of marriage have made older notions of family boundaries unsatisfactory. Yet no social or legal consensus exists on what new boundaries should be accepted.

The production of public goods invites public scrutiny, and public families are easily identifiable to outsiders by the presence of dependents. Because society

---

[3] This example holds only, however, for developed countries such as the United States, where the birthrate is at or below the level needed to replace the population. In developing countries with very high birthrates, children can impose negative externalities. Given the high death rates in the poorest developing countries, it is in the interest of a peasant farmer to have many children to ensure that at least one or two will still be alive when the farmer is too old to work. But if every family follows that logic, the land may become overpopulated and the country's development may slow. See Cain (1983).

has an interest in how well families manage the care of dependents, the law allows for some regulation of these families—despite strong sentiment in the United States against intervening in family matters. For example, we require families to send their children to school until age 16. And state social welfare agencies have the power to remove children from homes judged to be harmful. More recently, several states have required medical personnel to report suspected cases of physical abuse of children. The public family, then, is about caretaking and dependency. It points us toward the kinds of kinship ties that are important for nurturing the young and caring for the elderly and the ill. It is a useful perspective for answering questions such as: How adequately will our society raise the next generation? How will we care for the growing number of elderly persons?

THE PRIVATE FAMILY

At the same time, the family is much more than a public service institution. It also provides individuals with intimacy, emotional support, and love. Indeed, most people today think of the family and experience it in these private terms. Although some of the intimacy is expressed sexually, the family is also where we get hugs as children and back rubs as adults. It is where children form first attachments, teenagers take steps toward autonomy, and adults share their inner selves with someone else. The public family is not the most useful perspective in this regard because the central question is not how we will care for dependents or reproduce the workforce but, rather, how we will obtain the intimacy and emotional support we desire.

An appropriate definition of the private family must, therefore, encompass intimate relationships whether or not they include dependents. Yet if we are to maintain our focus on families, the definition still must encompass some rules for defining what kinds of intimate relationships constitute a family. It is difficult to know where to draw the line between private families and other kinds of intimate relationships, such as two people who live in separate apartments and see each other a few times a week. Where exactly is the boundary between family life and less intensive forms of intimacy? Rapid change has undermined the consensus among Americans about the norms of family life—the social rules about what constitutes a family and how people should behave when they are in one. Let me offer, then, a definition of the **private family** not as an authoritative statement but rather as a starting point for analyzing this uncertainty: *two or more individuals who maintain an intimate relationship that they expect will last indefinitely—or, in the case of a parent and child, until the child reaches adulthood—and who live in the same household and pool their incomes and household labor.* This definition allows for children to be part of the private family, although the character of the intimacy between parents and children is clearly different from that between adult partners. It does not require that the individuals be of opposite sexes. The relationship must be one in which the commitment is long term, in which the expectation is that the adult partners will stay together indefinitely. I do not require that they expect to stay together for life because it's not clear how many married couples even expect as much, given that about half of all marriages now end in divorce. The definition also includes the notion that the partnership usually is household-based and economic as well as intimate—shared residence, common budgets. This reflects my sense that intimate relationships in families are not merely erotic and emotionally supportive but also involve sharing the day-to-day details of managing one's life.

private family two or more individuals who maintain an intimate relationship that they expect will last indefinitely— or in the case of a parent and child, until the child reaches adulthood—and who live in the same household and pool their incomes and household labor

The private family:
Americans seek intimacy and emotional support from their spouses and partners.

To be sure, individuals also receive emotional support and material assistance from kin with whom they are not in an intimate relationship. The word "family" is sometimes used in the larger sense of relationships with sisters, uncles, grandmothers, and so forth. These broader kinship ties are still an important part of the setting in which people embed their intimate relations to spouses, partners, and children. The usual definition of "kin" is the people who are related to you by descent (through your mother's or father's line) or marriage. Yet the concept of kinship is also becoming broader and harder to define, as this book will show. In settings as varied as sharing networks among low-income African Americans, friend-based support networks among lesbians and gay men, and middle-class networks of adults who are related only through the ties of broken marriages and remarriages, people are expanding the definition of kinship, creating kin, as it were, out of relationships that don't fit the old mold. In fact, throughout the book I will distinguish between what I will call **created kinship**—kinship ties that people have to construct actively—and **assigned kinship**—kinship ties that people more or less automatically acquire when they are born or when they marry. And I will return in the final chapter to the changing nature of kinship and its implications for family life.

created kinship kinship ties that people have to construct actively

assigned kinship kinship ties that people more or less automatically acquire when they are born or when they marry

TWO VIEWS, SAME FAMILY

No matter which perspective—public or private—you choose, many, perhaps most, family units will fit that perspective. That is to say, both perspectives may apply to the same family unit. A married couple may be providing each other with love and intimacy and also raising children. Indeed, the public and private dimensions of the family often overlap. For example, it's difficult for families to provide good child care without love and emotional support. Moreover, even the private family is influenced by the larger society. As will be discussed in Chapter 2,

Table 1.1 Two Ways of Looking at the American Family		
	THE PUBLIC FAMILY	**THE PRIVATE FAMILY**
Examples	Married couple, cohabiting couple, or single parent with children	Married or cohabiting couples without children
		Gay or lesbian couples without children
	Single person caring for ailing parent	
	Gay person caring for partner with AIDS	
Main Functions	Raising the next generation	Providing love and intimacy
	Caring for the elderly	Providing emotional support
	Caring for the ill and disabled	
Key Challenge	Free-rider problem	Boundary problem

the development of the private family depended upon, among other things, the availability of wages high enough so that family members no longer needed to focus their attention on day-to-day subsistence. The two perspectives, then, can be thought of as complementary and sometimes overlapping ways of looking at the same reality: the institution of the family.

Table 1.1 reviews the basic distinction between these two perspectives. The first row shows examples of families as seen through the public and private family perspectives. The second row shows the main functions of the family in the public and private domains. In raising the next generation of children—the workers, citizens, and parents of the future—parents and other caregivers are best viewed as carrying out the functions of the public family. The same can be said for caregivers of the frail elderly or for disabled individuals. In contrast, when providing love, intimacy, and emotional support, family members are carrying out the functions of the private family. The third row shows the key challenges families face in these two guises. It's in people's narrow self-interests to let others do the hard work of raising children or caring for the elderly—activities that benefit society as a whole. (And much of this care is provided by women outside of the paid workforce. See Chapter 8.) But if too many people try to ride free, our society may not invest enough time and effort in producing the next generation or in caring for the elderly. In fact, some social critics believe American society has already reached this point. As for the private family, its key challenge is maintaining its dominant position as the setting where people experience emotional gratification. With the decline of marriage, there are many kinds of relationships that provide intimacy, love, and sex. Will the private family continue to cohere as a social institution, or will its boundaries collapse into a sea of diverse, limited personal relationships?

In sum, to examine the contributions of families to the public welfare is to look at relationships through the lens of the public family. To examine the family's provisions of intimacy, love, and fulfillment is to look through the lens of the private family. Sometimes, both lenses apply to the same situation, as when a parent derives great emotional satisfaction from raising a child. Both perspectives are embedded in each of the chapters that follow. Which is better? Neither. They are two takes on the same reality. Many textbooks emphasize the private family by focusing primarily on interpersonal relationships in courtship, cohabitation, and marriage. In doing so, they pay less attention to the socially valuable work that families do. Although this book, too, will have much to say about the private family, it will also emphasize the public family. In addition to the essays on families in other cultures, each

Quick Review

- The primary family unit in the United States and most other Western nations is the small, household-based unit of parents and children.
- No single definition of the family is adequate for all purposes.
- This book takes two perspectives and proposes two definitions:
  - The "public family," which focuses on the care that family members provide for dependents.
  - The "private family," which focuses on the love and emotional satisfaction family members provide for each other.
- Both definitions can be applied to the same family unit because most families have both a public and a private dimension.

subsequent chapter will include a short essay on families and public policy; and chapters such as "The Family, the State, and Social Policy," "Children and Parents," and "The Elderly and Their Families" will be directed primarily toward public issues.

How Do Family Sociologists Know What They Know?

objectivity the ability to draw conclusions about a social situation that are unaffected by one's own beliefs

Sociologists collect and analyze data consisting of observations of real families and the people in them. For the most part, they strive to analyze their data using objective, scientific methods. **Objectivity** means the ability to draw conclusions about a social situation that are unaffected by one's own beliefs. But it is much more difficult for a sociologist to be objective than it is for a natural or physical scientist. Sociologists not only study families, but they also live in them. They often have strong moral and political views of their own (indeed, strong views about social issues are what lead many people to become sociologists), and it is difficult to prevent those views from influencing one's research. In fact, there are some sociologists who argue that objectivity is so difficult to achieve that sociologists shouldn't try. Rather, they argue, sociologists should acknowledge their values and predispositions so that others can better interpret their work (see *How Do Sociologists Know What They Know?:* Feminist Research Methods, in Chapter 3).

scientific method a systematic, organized series of steps that ensures maximum objectivity and consistency in researching a problem

hypothesis a speculative statement about the relationship between two or more variables

But most sociologists, although aware that their views can influence the way they interpret their data, model their research on the scientific method. For a detailed examination of the scientific method in sociology, consult any good introductory sociology textbook. For example, Schaefer (2007, p. 29) defines the **scientific method** as "a systematic, organized series of steps that ensures maximum objectivity and consistency in researching a problem." The essence of the scientific method is to formulate a hypothesis that can be tested by collecting and analyzing data. (A **hypothesis,** Schaefer writes, is "a speculative statement about the relationship between two or more variables" [p. 45].) It's easy to come up with a hypothesis (God is a woman), but the trick is to find one that can be shown to be true or false by examining data. Sociologists therefore tend to formulate very specific hypotheses about family life that can be confirmed or disconfirmed by observation. For example, sociologists have hypothesized that having a first child as a teenager lowers, on average, the amount of education a woman attains; and statistical data are consistent with this claim.

Even so, there are inherent limitations in how well social scientists can use the scientific method. The best way to confirm or disconfirm a relationship between two factors is to conduct an experiment in which all other factors are held constant. Scientists do this by randomly assigning subjects to one of two groups: an experimental group and a control group. For example, doctors will study whether a new drug speeds recovery from an illness by assembling a group of volunteers, all of whom have the illness, and then randomly giving half of them (the experimental group) the new drug. By randomizing, the doctors hope that all other confounding factors (such as past medical history) will be equalized between the two groups. Then they compare the average recovery times of the experimental group and the control group (those who did not receive the drug).

But it is rarely possible for sociologists to conduct randomized experiments on families. Without randomization, there is always the possibility that another, unobserved factor, lurking just beneath the surface, is causing the relationship we see. Consider again teenage childbearing. Women who have a first child as a teenager tend to come from families that have less education and less money, on average, than do other women. So the reason that teenage mothers attain less education may reflect their disadvantaged family backgrounds rather than having a child; in others words, they might have had less education even if they hadn't had children as teenagers. To truly settle this issue, a truth-seeking but cold-blooded sociologist would want to obtain a list of all families with teenage girls in the United States and then to assign *at random* some of the girls to have children and others to remain childless until their twenties. Because of the random assignment, teenage childbearing would be about as likely to occur in middle-class families as in poor families. In this way, the social scientist could eliminate family background as a cause of any differences that emerge between teenage mothers and nonmothers.

For very good ethical and legal reasons, of course, sociologists simply cannot conduct this type of study. Without random assignment, we can't be sure that

An interviewer goes door-to-door during the 2000 Census. Social scientists frequently use survey research to study families.

having a child as a teenager *causes* a woman to have less education. Still, the lack of randomized experiments does not mean that sociologists should abandon the scientific method. Astronomers, after all, can't do experiments either. But this limitation makes the task of deciding whether a sociological study confirms or disconfirms a hypothesis more difficult.

If not from experiments, where does the data that family sociologists use come from? Generally, from one of two research methods. The first is the **survey,** a study in which individuals or households are randomly selected from a larger population and asked a fixed set of questions. Sociologists prepare a questionnaire and give it to a professional survey research organization. The organization then selects a sample of households randomly from an area (a city, a state, or the entire nation) and sends interviewers to ask the questions of one or more family members in the households. The responses are coded numerically (e.g., a "yes" answer is coded 1 and a "no" is coded 0), and the coded responses for all individuals are made available to the sociologists as a computer file.

The random selection of households is done to ensure that the people who are asked the questions are representative of the population in the area. This kind of random selection of households shouldn't be confused with conducting a randomized experiment. A random-sample survey is not an experiment because the households that are selected are *not* divided into an experimental group and a control group. Nevertheless, data from surveys provides sociologists with the opportunity to examine associations among characteristics of a large number of individuals and families. (See *How Do Sociologists Know What They Know?:* The National Surveys, in this chapter.)

The advantage of the survey method (assuming that the households are randomly selected) is that its results are representative not only of the sample that was interviewed but also of the larger population in the area. The main disadvantage is the limited amount of information that can be gathered on each person or family. Most people won't participate in an interview that takes more than an hour or two. Moreover, the same set of questions is asked of everyone, with little opportunity to tailor the interview to each participant. Another disadvantage is that it's difficult to determine whether the people in the sample are responding honestly, especially if the questions touch upon sensitive issues. (See *How Do Sociologists Know What They Know?:* Asking about Sensitive Behavior, in Chapter 6.)

The second widely used research method is the **observational study,** also known as *field research,* in which the researcher spends time directly observing each participant in the study—often much more time than an interviewer from a survey organization spends. The researcher may even join the group she or he is studying for a period of time. The individuals and families to be studied are not usually selected randomly; rather, the researcher tries to find families that have a particular set of characteristics he or she is interested in. For example, in a classic observational study of a low-income area of Boston, Herbert Gans (1982) moved into an Italian neighborhood for eight months and got to know many families well. He was able to argue that the stereotype of slum families as "disorganized" was not true. The strength of the observational method is that it can provide a much more detailed and nuanced picture of the individuals and families being studied than can the survey method. Sociologist-observers can view the full complexity of family behavior and can learn more about it.

The disadvantage of observational studies is that it is hard to know how representative the families being studied are of similar families. Because it takes a great

survey a study in which individuals from a geographic area are selected, usually at random, and asked a fixed set of questions

observational study (also known as field research) a study in which the researcher spends time directly observing each participant

Table 1.2 Comparing Survey Studies and Observational Studies			
WHO IS STUDIED	**HOW THEY ARE STUDIED**	**STRENGTHS**	**LIMITATIONS**
Survey Study			
Large, random sample of individuals or familes	An interviewer asks questions from a predesigned questionnaire and records the answers	Results can be generalized to the population of interest	Only limited knowledge can be obtained; hard to judge honesty of responses
Observational Study			
Small, purposefully chosen sample of individuals or families	A researcher observes them in depth over a long period of time, sometimes participating in their daily activities	Detailed knowledge is obtained	Findings may not be representative of other, similar individuals or families

deal of time to study a family in depth, observational studies typically are carried out with far fewer families than are surveys. Moreover, sociologists who do observational studies usually can't choose their families randomly by knocking on doors or calling on the telephone because they must win a family's cooperation and trust before the family will agree to be studied in such detail. So although observational studies may yield a great deal of information about a small number of families, we may be unsure that we can generalize this knowledge to other similar families that weren't in the observational study.

Surveys and observational studies, consequently, have complementary strengths and limitations. If the knowledge from sociological studies could be stored in a lake, a survey-based lake would be wide (because of the large number of people reached) but shallow (because of the limited time spent with each family), whereas an observationally based lake would be narrow but deep. Ideally, it would be best to employ both methods to study a problem, and some research projects attempt to do so. But to choose a large number of families randomly and then to send in sociologists to observe each family intensively over weeks and months is too expensive to be feasible. Moreover, the set of skills necessary to do survey research versus observational research is so distinct that sociologists tend to specialize in one or the other.

Sociologists sometimes use other research methods as well. For some topics, it is useful to examine historical sources. Chapter 7 describes a study in which magazine articles from 1900 to 1979 were used to study changing conceptions of marriage. Occasionally, it is even possible to do an experiment. In the 1960s and 1970s, the Federal government sponsored experiments to learn about the consequences of providing families with a guaranteed minimum income. In several communities, families were selected and randomly divided into experimental and control groups. Families in the experimental group received checks from the experimenters if their incomes fell below a threshold. The results indicated that a guaranteed income produced some reduction in work effort and possibly an increase in marital disruption (Robins, Spiegelman, Weiner, & Bell, 1980).

These are the major methods that sociologists use to study families. In several of the chapters of this book, we will examine the methodology of key studies so that you may better understand how family sociologists develop their research findings.

longitudinal survey a survey in which interviews are conducted several times at regular intervals

primary analysis analysis of survey data by the people who collected the information

secondary analysis analysis of survey data by people other than those who collected it

The National Surveys

Sociologists who study the family in the United States draw many of their findings from a series of national surveys that have been conducted over the past few decades. These surveys interview randomly selected samples of the U.S. population. They are similar to the opinion-poll surveys you see in the newspapers (e.g., what percent of the public thinks the president is doing a good job?), but they differ in several important ways:

- *They are larger* The surveys in the newspapers typically interview 500 to 1,500 individuals. The social scientific surveys typically interview 5,000 to 10,000 individuals or more. Because of this larger size, the social scientific surveys can provide reliable information on subgroups of the population, such as couples who are living together outside of marriage, currently divorced individuals, and never-married adults.
- *They are carried out using in-person interviews* In contrast, most of the newspaper polls are conducted by randomly dialing telephone numbers and speaking to people over the telephone. In-person interviews can be longer and more detailed (because people tire of telephone conversations more quickly than in-person conversations) and can be more flexible (e.g., the interviewer can give the subject a self-administered questionnaire for her husband or partner to fill out). But in-person interviews are also much more expensive to carry out.
- *They are longitudinal* Whereas the typical newspaper poll is a one-time activity, social scientists prefer a **longitudinal survey,** meaning a survey in which interviews are conducted several times at regular intervals. This design allows social scientists to study social change. The surveys typically select families or individuals at random and then reinterview them annually or biennially about how their lives are changing.
- *They are intended to be public resources* Most newspaper polls are meant for **primary analysis,** meaning they are analyzed by the people who collected the information. The data from these polls are then forgotten. The social scientific studies are designed for **secondary analysis,** meaning analysis of the data by people other than the group that collected it. The questionnaires are intentionally broad so that the interviewers can collect a wide range of information that will be of interest to many researchers. The results are coded numerically into electronic files and made available to anyone who wants to analyze them.
- *They are conducted by academic research centers rather than by commercial polling firms* The academic centers, such as the National Opinion Research Center at the University of Chicago and the Survey Research Center at the University of Michigan, typically take extra steps in designing and carrying out a survey so that the results are of better quality (e.g., the data conforms better to

Quick Review

- Survey research and observational research are the two methods most commonly used by sociologists.
- The two methods have complementary strengths and limitations.
- Table 1.2 summarizes the differences between the two methods.

Sociological Theory and Families

The methods sociologists use and the questions they ask are influenced by sociological theory. Let me present a brief introduction to the theoretical perspectives that have been most commonly applied to studying families. I will present them in two groups: "classical" perspectives that formed the core of sociological theory during the twentieth century and "contemporary" perspectives that have emerged during the past few decades. I will draw upon these perspectives often in this book.

the statistical theory underlying random-sample surveys; a greater percentage of the selected subjects are reached and interviewed).

Because of the large sample size, longitudinal design, use of in-person rather than telephone interviews, and extra care in the fieldwork, the social scientific surveys are very expensive. Most are sponsored by U.S. government agencies such as the National Institutes of Health, the National Science Foundation, or the Bureau of Labor Statistics. The agencies support those large surveys to provide information on many research questions so that hundreds of researchers can analyze the data.

One such study is the National Survey of Families and Households. Interviews were first conducted during 1987 and 1988 with a randomly selected sample of 13,007 individuals, including over-samples of African Americans, Puerto Ricans, Mexican Americans, single-parent families, families with stepchildren, cohabiting couples, and re-cently married persons. A broad range of questions about personal background and family life were asked. From 1992 to 1994, reinterviews were conducted with 10,007 of these individuals. A round of interviews was conducted by telephone from 2001 to 2002.

Another study is the Panel Study of Income Dynamics. In 1968, researchers at the University of Michigan interviewed 5,000 American households selected at random. They have reinterviewed the members of these households every year since then. When children grew up and left home, or adults divorced and moved out, the study followed them and interviewed them in their new households. The Panel Study of Income Dynamics greatly increased our knowledge of the economic fortunes of families over time. For example, the results indicate that few families are poor every year, but over the course of a decade many families, perhaps one-fourth, experience at least a year in which they are poor (Duncan, 1984).

Throughout the book, findings from these and other national surveys will be presented. Although not without limitations (see Chapter 6, *How Do Families Know What They Know?* Asking about Sensitive Behavior), they constitute a valuable resource to everyone interested in families, households, parents, and children. The "Families on the Internet" feature at the end of this chapter lists the World Wide Web addresses at which information about these surveys can be obtained.

Ask Yourself

1. Besides researchers, who else might be interested in the results of social scientific surveys? Can you think of any practical use for this information?
2. Why do you think researchers would want to see survey results for particular racial and ethnic groups or specific types of families?

www.mhhe.com/cherlin5

CLASSICAL PERSPECTIVES

The Functionalist Perspective   The dominant sociological perspective in the 1950s was **functionalist theory.** The functionalist theorists tried to determine the functions, or uses, of the main ways in which a society is organized. Functionalism had been developed earlier in the century by anthropologists who undertook field research among tribes and small societies in Africa, Asia, and Latin America. The anthropologists wanted to show that seemingly strange customs in other cultures had important uses and were valid, alternative ways of organizing a society—in other words, they wished to demonstrate that our culture was not superior to others. Their books documented the roles, relations, and practices of particular societies and then explained how these systems were able to maintain their societies' existences.

Beginning in the 1940s and continuing through the 1950s, numerous sociologists employed the functionalist approach to explain aspects of the ways social

functionalist theory a sociological theory that attempts to determine the functions, or uses, of the main ways in which a society is organized

groups, including families, were organized. The foremost practitioner of functionalism in sociology was Talcott Parsons, whose theoretical writings profoundly influenced other sociologists. Ironically, the effect of Parsons's writings about the American family was the opposite of the anthropologists' writings about exotic cultures. Whereas the anthropologists' message seemed to be that there were many valid ways of organizing family life, Parsons's message—whether intentional or not—seemed to be that the breadwinner–homemaker family of the 1950s was the natural, superior form.

Robert Bales, a psychologist and colleague of Parsons on the Harvard faculty, had conducted a series of experiments with small groups, in which they were observed discussing how to go about some task. Bales claimed that in each group, one person emerged as the "instrumental" leader who led the group discussion about how to accomplish the task they had been assigned. A different person emerged as the "expressive" or "socioemotional" leader who kept up the group's spirit with warm, supportive remarks and jokes. This general tendency of small groups to divide the leadership tasks between two people, according to Bales, was functional in the sense that the coexistence of both kinds of leadership contributed to a better performance by the group.

Parsons and Bales then leaped to the assumption that since the family was a small group, it was functional for one adult member to specialize in instrumental leadership and for the other to specialize in expressive leadership. Lo and behold, that was how the middle-class 1950s family was organized. The husband, they wrote, was the instrumental leader because his labor provided the financial support for the family; and the stay-at-home wife was the expressive leader because she provided emotional support to her husband and children. Consequently, Parsons and Bales argued that the breadwinner–homemaker family was well organized to fulfill the tasks that society assigned to it: providing the material goods necessary for a decent living, providing emotional support to adults, and raising children (Parsons & Bales, 1955). Although they never said it was superior to other ways of organizing families, by implication it was, for if wives worked outside the home there would no longer be a full-time expressive specialist.

But work outside the home they did. Although Parsons and Bales seemed to view the breadwinner–homemaker family of the 1950s as if it were timeless, it was, in fact, unusual in historical perspective. As married women poured into the workforce in the 1960s and 1970s, the breadwinner–homemaker family lost its dominant position (see Chapter 2). Much of the sociological writing about the family in the 1960s, 1970s, and 1980s was devoted to refuting Parsons's implicit conclusion that this change in the family was for the worse. This antifunctionalist viewpoint was congenial to the growing body of sociological research influenced by the resurgence of the feminist movement in the 1960s. Still, no single theoretical perspective has dominated the post-1950s literature. Rather, most writers have borrowed eclectically from several theoretical traditions, which are examined briefly.

conflict theory a sociological theory that focuses on inequality, power, and social change

The Conflict Perspective   One of these is **conflict theory.** Whereas functionalism focuses on stability and cooperation among members of a group, conflict theory focuses on inequality, power, and social change. Conflict theorists study how individuals, or groups of individuals, come to dominate others and the circumstances under which those who are dominated are able to reduce or eliminate the disadvantages they face. When analyzing the family, conflict theorists see men as more powerful and women as less powerful. For example, Randall Collins states that male dominance rests on two sources of coercion: physical force and control of economic resources. In societies in which men's use of physical force is curtailed by the state or by custom, men cannot be as dominant; nor can they be as dominant in societies in which women produce valuable goods and services outside the household (Collins, 1971). Conflict theorists have a much less favorable view of the 1950s family than did Parsons because of what they see as women's domination by men, due, in large part, to women's lack of economic resources.

Conflict theorists also see other groups as subject to domination. Marxist writers, for example, have emphasized the conflicting interests of capitalists—the people who own factories and businesses—and the workers in those enterprises. The owners obtain their incomes by paying workers less than the value of the goods the factory or business sells and keeping the difference. Some Marxist-influenced writers on the family claim that women's unpaid work in the home benefits employers in two ways. First, the housework women do allows employers to pay workers less than what would be required if workers had to pay for household services. Second, the emotional support wives provide to husbands eases the burdens of the often alienating and monotonous work that employers require them to do (Zaretsky, 1986).

The Exchange Perspective   A third classical perspective is **exchange theory.** This sociological approach is similar to the model of human behavior that economists use. People are viewed as rational beings who decide whether to exchange goods or services by considering the benefits they will receive, the costs they will incur, and the benefits they might receive if they chose an alternative course of action. In the rational choice-based theory of the family that won Gary Becker the 1992 Nobel Memorial Prize in economics, women often choose rationally to exchange the performance of household and child care services in return for receiving the benefits of a man's income. If men are more "efficient" at market production—meaning they can earn higher wages—and women are more "efficient" at home production—meaning they are better at raising small children— then both partners gain from this exchange, argues Becker (1991). Thus, Becker's model is consistent with the Parsonian analysis of the family.

But in the hands of others, exchange theory can shade into conflict theory and lead to very different conclusions. Many sociologists maintain that exchanges take on a different character if the two actors come to the exchange with unequal resources. Richard Emerson and his colleagues developed a version of exchange theory that is useful in studying families (Cook, O'Brien, & Kollock, 1990; Emerson, 1972). According to Emerson, if person A values goods or services person B has to offer, and if person A has few alternative sources of obtaining these goods or services, then person A is said to be dependent on person B. The degree of dependency is greater the more highly A values these goods or services and the fewer alternative sources A has. And the more A is dependent on B, the greater is B's power over A. When one person is more powerful than another, he or she may be able to shape the exchange so that he or she receives greater benefits and incurs fewer costs than does the other person. Husbands, many writers have suggested, are in a stronger bargaining position when they are the sole earners in their families because their wives have fewer alternative sources of income. According to exchange theory, when wives earn money on their own, their dependence decreases and therefore their husbands' power over them decreases (Scanzoni, 1972).

exchange theory a sociological theory that views people as rational beings who decide whether to exchange goods or services by considering the benefits they will receive, the costs they will incur, and the benefits they might receive if they were to choose an alternative course of action

symbolic interaction theory a sociological theory that focuses on people's interpretations of symbolic behavior

The Symbolic Interactionist Perspective   Also important is the distinctive perspective of **symbolic interaction theory.** The major figure in symbolic interaction theory was philosopher George Herbert Mead, who taught at the University of Chicago early in the twentieth century.[4] Among all animals, only human beings, the symbolic interactionists point out, do not merely react instinctively to what others of their species do but rather *interpret* what others do. We interpret symbols—gestures, words, appearances—whose meanings we have come to understand. This interpretation occurs in situations in which we interact with someone. It is this process of the interpretation of symbols during social interaction that the symbolic interactionists study. Some symbols are so clear and uniform that interpretation is straightforward; thus, we all know that the traffic officer's raised hand, palm facing the driver, means stop. But some symbols are harder to interpret. Symbols involving differences between women and men, it has been argued recently, are particularly problematic and in need of continual affirmation (see Chapter 3). For example, husbands who don't want to change their babies' diapers may make a grand display of fumbling at the changing table when called upon by their wives, thus exhibiting their male "inferiority" at the task. The interactionist perspective is also useful in analyzing situations where family relations

Sociologists use multiple theoretical perspectives to understand contemporary families such as this dual-career couple.

[4] For an account of Mead's viewpoint by his foremost interpreter in sociology, see Blumer (1962).

seem less institutionalized, less set in concrete—such as in newly formed stepfamilies or dual-career marriages. It helps sensitize us to the ways in which people create shared understandings of how family members should act toward one another. These shared understandings become the bases of the social roles people play in families—spouse, parent, breadwinner, homemaker, child, and so forth.

CONTEMPORARY PERSPECTIVES

During the last few decades of the twentieth century, social theorists developed new perspectives that have become influential in scholarship on the family. These theorists tend to be critical of the functionalist views of Parsons in sociology, Becker in economics, and their followers. Instead, they focus more on inequalities in families and on the ways that individuals can act in their daily lives to shape and reshape family life. Because of these emphases, they tend to draw on the classical perspectives of conflict, exchange (in the power and inequality version), and symbolic interactionism.

The Feminist Perspective   **Feminist theory** is a perspective developed to better understand, and to transform, inequalities between women and men. The central concept in feminist theory is **gender,** which is usually defined as the social and cultural characteristics that distinguish women and men in a society (see Chapter 3). Feminist theorists argue that nearly all the gender differences we see in the roles of women and men are of cultural origin and have been socially constructed. By socially constructed, they mean arising not from biological differences but rather from culturally accepted rules, from relationships of power and authority, and from differences in economic opportunities. For example, the culture might include a rule that women should not work outside the home (as was the case among the American middle class from the mid-nineteenth to the mid-twentieth centuries). Or the opportunities for women might be limited to jobs that tend to pay less than comparable jobs in which most workers are men.

Moreover, feminist theorists assert that these cultural differences are constructed in ways that maintain the power of men over women (Thorne, 1992). For instance, feminist theorists criticize the idea that the breadwinner-homemaker family provided an exchange that was equally beneficial to women and men. Rather, they note that women's direct access to money through paid employment was restricted in this type of family, which maintained women's dependence on men. They also note that men's relationships with their children were often limited. The cultural belief that "women's place is in the home" and the lower wages paid to women employed outside the home compelled married women to give up the idea of paid employment. Under these constraints, their best strategy may indeed have been to trade household services for a male income; but it was a forced choice set up by a social system that favored men.

Some feminist theorists maintain that the family is itself an artificial creation that has been organized to maintain male dominance. They would deny that there are any deep-seated predispositions among people that would lead to the formation of the kinds of families that we see. In fact, some would argue that we shouldn't even try to study the family anymore because to do so accepts as "natural" the inequalities built into it. Rather, we should merely study households and the relations among people within them. Needless to say, these critics would reject the contention that there is any biological basis for the ways in which men

feminist theory a sociological theory that focuses on the domination of women by men

gender the social and cultural characteristics that distinguish women and men in a society

and women act in families. At the extreme, some maintain that even sexual intercourse, pregnancy, and giving birth are best viewed as, in the words of two anthropologists, "cultural facts, whose form, consequences, and meanings are socially constructed in any society" (Yanagisako & Collier, 1987).

Whether or not you think it's useful to study the family (as I obviously do), there is an important insight to be gained from feminist theory. It makes us aware that the experience of living in a family is different for women than it is for men. Arrangements that make men happiest don't necessarily make women happiest. A husband might prefer that his wife stay home to care for their children and do household work full time. His wife might prefer to combine a paying job with housework and child care, and she might wish that he would share more of the household tasks. In other words, women's interests in the family are not necessarily the same as men's interests. The breadwinner-homemaker bargain may have been great for men (except for those who wanted an active role in raising their children), and it may have been great for women who wished to raise children and do housework full time, but it frustrated other women by restricting the possibility of developing a satisfying career outside the home. Feminist theory urges us to view families through a prism that separates the experiences of men and women rather than just considering what's best for the family as a whole. It is a view that I will take repeatedly in this book.

The Modernity Perspective   A number of theorists of modernity claim that personal life has changed fundamentally over the last several decades. They argue that the modern era—the long period that began with the spread of

Family life is changing so much that no clear rules govern how husbands and wives should divide the household chores.

industrialization in the mid-to-late nineteenth century—effectively ended in the last half of the twentieth century. It has been replaced, they state, by what they call the **late modern era** (Giddens, 1991) or sometimes the postmodern era. Looking back at the modern era, they emphasize that individuals moved through a series of roles (student, spouse, parent, housewife, breadwinner) in a way that seemed more-or-less natural. Choices were constrained. In mill towns, two or three generations of kin might work at the same factory. Getting married was the only acceptable way to have children, except perhaps among the poor. Young people often chose their spouses from among a pool of acquaintances from their neighborhood, church, or school. Life's stages flowed in a way that one accepted and didn't have to question.

But in the late modern era, the modernity theorists maintain, individuals must make choices about nearly all aspects of their lives (Beck & Beck-Gernsheim, 2002). You can't get a job in the factory where your father and grandfather worked because overseas competition has forced it to close, so you must choose another career. You get little help from relatives in finding a partner, so you sign on to an Internet dating service and review hundreds of personal profiles. As other lifestyles become more acceptable, you must choose whether to get married and whether to have children. In ways such as these, your identity in the late modern age is transformed from a "given" to a "task" (Bauman, 1992, 2002).

As these choices are made, it is said, questions of personal identity become more important. People do the work of developing their identities through **reflexivity,** the process through which individuals take in knowledge, reflect on it, and alter their behavior as a result (Beck, Giddens, and Lash, 1994). In other words, people pay attention to their experiences and regularly ask themselves: How am I feeling? Do I find my life fulfilling? How do I want to live the rest of it? The development of one's identity in the late modern era is a continual, lifelong process of reflection and making choices.

Modernity theory is consistent with a view of families as diverse, changing, and developing in unpredictable directions. It can help us make sense of family life at a time when individuals must continually make choices in uncertain circumstances, for which there are no clear rules. For instance, two-career marriages are new enough that no general agreement exists on how spouses should divide up the tasks of work at home and in the labor market. (We will examine the work/family dilemma in Chapter 8.) Divorce and remarriage are new enough on a large scale that stepparents and stepchildren have little guidance on who is part of their family and how they should act toward them. (We will examine stepfamilies in Chapter 13.) These new circumstance bring both opportunities for fashioning mutually beneficial arrangements but also the costs of the anxiety and conflict that working out new rules can bring. We will return to the implications of the modernity perspective in Chapter 15.

Perspectives from Evolutionary Psychology   Nearly all sociologists believe that most of the differences in the roles men and women play and in the behaviors they show are social and cultural in origin. Yet some also think that the institution of the family has biological roots and, correspondingly, that the differences between women and men have both social and biological origins; they also believe that a person's sexual orientation (heterosexual or homosexual) probably has a substantial biological component. For example, a number of studies build a plausible case that the greater aggressiveness shown, on average, by

late modern era the period between the last few decades of the twentieth century and the present day

reflexivity the process through which individuals take in knowledge, reflect on it, and alter their behavior as a result

men may be biologically based in part.[5] The evidence is suggestive but less solid that women, on average, may be more adept at enabling and maintaining relationships[6] (Rossi, 1984), and that men may be more inclined to pursue sex outside of lasting relationships.[7] As will be discussed in later chapters, the existence of these biological differences could account, in part, for the persistent differences in how women and men interact and in how they care for young children.

Why might biology underlie some of the differences in the ways that women and men go about finding partners and building family lives? Scholars from the emerging subdiscipline of **evolutionary psychology** claim that some of the differences are the result of the same evolutionary pressures that Charles Darwin recognized in plants and animals (Buss, 1994; Pinker, 1997; Symons, 1979). The basic argument is that animals, including humans, tend to behave in ways that maximize the chances that they will be able to reproduce themselves. These tendencies are rooted in the genes that the animals carry. Animals that are successful have offspring, whereas animals that are not die off. Over eons of time, therefore, genes that lead to behavior that increases the chance of bearing offspring spread through the species.

But why might men, on average, have genes that predispose them to different reproductive strategies than women? Here the evolutionary psychologists and like-minded sociologists note the different roles that men and women played in the hunter-gatherer bands in which most humans and their evolutionary predecessors lived until about 8,000 B.C. These differences will be noted in more detail in Chapter 2. In particular, women not only bore children but also cared for them while young and breast-fed them for several years. Under these conditions, the evolutionists hypothesize, women maximized their chances of having and raising children by finding men who would provide resources and protection exclusively to them for at least the first several years of pregnancy and child care. Men, on the other hand, may have maximized their reproductive potential by impregnating several women; and they benefited from being aggressive enough to dominate other males and therefore control sexual access to many women. Thus, it is said, women, on average, came to value sex in the context of relationships and commitment more than men, whereas men were more likely to value sex outside of lasting relationships and to behave aggressively.

However, biological differences between men and women cannot explain changes in the family over the past few decades or even over the past few centuries because evolution occurs so slowly (Udry, 1994). For the same reason, the theory of evolution cannot explain the great changes in sexual behavior over the past few decades.[8] Nor can it explain the numerous differences in family behavior across nations and cultures today.

What is more, even if evolution and genes are important, they do not imply that any particular form of the family is biologically rooted. For example, there is little reason to believe that a family in which the wife stays home to raise the children and the husband works for pay outside the home is more biologically "natural" than one in which they both work outside the home. In fact, in the hunter-gatherer societies that existed for so much of our past, women tended to

evolutionary psychology
the view that human behavior can be explained in terms of evolutionary pressure to behave in ways that maximize the chances of reproduction

[5] See Chapter 3.

[6] See also Chapter 3.

[7] See Chapter 6.

[8] See Chapter 6.

Table 1.3 Theoretical Perspectives on the Family		
THEORETICAL PERSPECTIVE	**MAIN THEME**	**APPLICATION TO FAMILIES**
Classical		
Functionalist	Family life is organized in ways that are useful (functional) for society.	The breadwinner–homemaker family is an efficient way to organize family life.
Conflict	Political and economic systems serve the interest of the wealthy and powerful.	Family life is organized in ways that benefit the interests of the owners of businesses and factories.
Exchange	Individuals with greater resources and more alternatives can drive better bargains.	Husbands' power over wives is greater when wives do not earn money on their own.
Symbolic interaction	Individuals interpret the actions of others and act in ways consistent with their interpretations.	Individuals give, and look for, symbolic cues about how to conduct the activities of everyday family life.
Contemporary		
Feminist	Society is organized in ways that privilege men over women.	A system of male dominance gives husbands more power than their wives.
Modernity	Individuals reflexively influence their social environments.	Individuals choose how they will act in new family forms such as stepfamilies.
Evolutionary psychology	Humans' evolutionary past affects how they think and behave.	Men and women may differ, on average, in how they interact and how they care for young children.

provide half or more of the food that was consumed. They did so through the gathering of edible plants—all the while caring for young children without much help from men. This picture of early human society, as some authors have noted, seems more similar to contemporary single-parent families than to nuclear families (Tanner & Zihlman, 1976).[9] Many people mistakenly assume that the "traditional" family fits the breadwinner-homemaker mold. To the contrary, as will be demonstrated in the next chapter, the breadwinner–homemaker family is historically unusual.

Evolutionary psychologists believe that our biological makeup creates predispositions toward some behaviors and away from others. Whether we, in fact, exhibit these behaviors depends on the social circumstances of our lives: the upbringing we received from our parents; the cultural influences we absorbed from peers, neighbors, ministers, and the media; and the economic constraints or racial prejudices we may have faced. These social factors may exaggerate whatever biological differences there may be between women and men, so that the differences we see are greater than biology alone would create. Moreover, evolutionary perspectives can lead us to overlook the substantial similarities between men's and women's approaches to sexuality and family life (Schwartz & Rutter, 1998). Biological predispositions, then, would not determine a person's behavior. Rather, they would create tendencies and leanings. On average, a group of people who share a predisposition (toward, say, aggressive behavior) would be likely to show more of it than would a group who does not share it; but it is difficult to predict how any single member of the group would behave.

_____

[9] See also Chapter 2.

Quick Review

- Four "classical" theories formed the core of sociological theory during the twentieth century: functionalist, conflict, exchange, and symbolic interactionist.
- Three contemporary theoretical perspectives, developed over the past few decades, are influencing how researchers view family life: feminist, modernity, and evolutionary psychology.
- Table 1.3 summarizes the main theme of each perspective and its application to studying families.

A Sociological Viewpoint on Families

As noted earlier, some sociologists would argue that no one can conduct completely objective research. Therefore, they say, one must examine, reflexively, how one approaches the subject. Only by frankly examining and stating one's viewpoint can one provide a framework others can use to properly evaluate one's own research. In that spirit, let me briefly discuss the viewpoint I bring to the writing of this textbook. In reading this book, you should keep these convictions in mind. I believe that families perform services of value to society and therefore should be publicly supported when necessary. Despite their increasing diversity, families, in my opinion, still constitute a coherent social category worth studying. I believe that, other things being equal, stable, long-term partnerships—opposite-sex or same-sex—provide the best environment for raising children. These partnerships need not be marriages, but getting married seems to enhance the chances of long-term stability and to increase the investments parents make. I also believe that alternative family forms, with adequate support, can provide good environments for children. I think it is likely that our evolutionary history has produced some inherent differences between women and men, although I think these differences are exaggerated by the way our culture and social structure are organized. But I don't believe these inherent differences, if any, are large enough to prevent equality for women and men in family life, which is the goal that I think we should strive for in the early twenty-first century.

In this book, I will use the singular form "the family" rather than the plural form "families" when discussing the family as a **social institution.** This term refers to a set of roles and rules that define a social unit of importance to society. The roles give us positions such as parent, child, spouse, ex-spouse, stepfather, partner, and so forth. The rules offer us guidance about how to act in these roles. But the use of the singular is not meant to imply that there is only one kind of family. On the contrary, there are many forms. Similarly, one might write about "the corporation" in a textbook on social organizations without implying that there is no difference between General Motors and a chain of grocery stores. Or an author might discuss "the hospital" in a text on medical sociology while recognizing the difference between a giant teaching hospital in a central city and a community hospital out in the suburbs. In addition, referring to "the family" is not meant to imply that the interests of wives, husbands, and children are always identical—any more than that the interests of workers and managers in corporations are identical.

In all of these cases, the use of the singular would signal the study of a social institution rather than just a set of relationships. An institution can grow stronger or weaker over time; it can take on somewhat different forms at different times and

social institution a set of roles and rules that define a social unit of importance to society

places; and it can be difficult to define at its margins. But it is a visible structure that people can recognize and understand. It also does something important for society. I think the "family" still fits this description. Its important functions include rearing children, caring for the elderly, and providing comfort and emotional support to its members. Nevertheless, people's actions are greatly changing the family and eroding some of its institutional basis. Stability and change in the family are the subject matter of this book.

Currently, most Americans seem to view the family primarily in emotional, personal terms—the terms of the private family—and to pay less attention to the commitments and obligations of the public family. This emphasis on sentiment and self-fulfillment might lead one to assume that the private family is the older, more established perspective. But that isn't so. The emergence of the private family is a relatively new development in history. Its origins lie in the upper-class and merchant families of Western Europe in the 1600s and 1700s. It did not spread to the masses until the late 1800s and 1900s. Most people have used the public perspective in thinking about families throughout most of history. The historical development of the family is the subject of the next chapter.

Looking Back

1. **How do Americans feel about marriage and families?** Some people are concerned about the diversity of American families, while others are pleased by it. Those who are concerned support public policies that support marriage, whereas those who defend diversity urge support for all types of families. Many Americans are ambivalent and agree with some of the positions taken by both sides. In general, Americans take an individualistic perspective toward family life, which emphasizes self-reliance and achievement but also feelings and emotional satisfaction.

2. **What do families do that is important for society? What do families do that is important for the individuals in them?** Families contribute to society by raising the next generation and caring for the ill and the elderly. On an individual level, families are settings in which people give and receive love, intimacy, and social support. This book proposes two definitions of the family—one for each of these questions. The public family perspective defines the family in terms of the presence of caregivers and dependents. The private family perspective defines the family in terms of an indefinite, intimate relationship between two or more individuals who live in the same household and share the fruits of their labor. These two perspectives constitute different views of the same reality; a given family unit might fit both of them.

3. **How do sociologists go about studying families?** Sociologists observe real families and the people in them, and for the most part, they try to analyze their data objectively using the scientific method. Sociologists formulate hypotheses that can be tested, although there are limits to their use of the scientific method. The two most common research methods sociologists use are (1) the survey, a study in which a randomly selected group of individuals or families are asked a fixed set of questions; and (2) the observational study, in which the researcher spends time directly observing each participant in the study.

4. **What are the leading theoretical approaches to studying families?** Four classical perspectives are functionalist theory, which emphasizes the useful ways in which families are organized; conflict theory, which claims that families are organized in ways that benefit the powerful; exchange theory, which examines how family members bargain based on their resources and their alternatives; and symbolic interaction, which focuses on how individuals interpret the social world. More recent perspectives include feminist theory, which analyzes systems of male dominance; modernity theory, which emphasizes the choices individuals must make in constructing family lives; and evolutionary theory, which claims that humans' evolutionary history affects how they think and behave.

Go to the Online Learning Center at www.mhhe.com/cherlin5 to test your knowledge of the chapter concepts and key terms.

Study Questions

1. How do television programs reflect the changes that have occurred in American family life?
2. What are the two components of American individualism?
3. Why might children be considered a "public good"?
4. What kinds of daily activities are better analyzed by thinking of the family as a public rather than a private institution?
5. Conversely, what daily activities are better analyzed by thinking of the family as a private institution?
6. Are there daily activities that could be viewed as having both a public and a private component?
7. Why can't sociological research be as objective as research in physics or chemistry?
8. Why have many subsequent theorists been critical of the functionalist perspective on families?
9. Give an example of a social institution other than the family.

Key Terms

assigned kinship   14
breadwinner–homemaker family   4
conflict theory   22
created kinship   14
evolutionary psychology   28
exchange theory   23
expressive individualism   7
externalities   10
feminist theory   25
free-rider problem   12
functionalist theory   21
gender   25
hypothesis   16
individualism   6
late modern era   27
longitudinal survey   19
monogamy   9
negative externalities   10
objectivity   16
observational study   18
polygamy   9
positive externalities   11
primary analysis   19
private family   13
public family   12
public goods   11
reflexivity   27
scientific method   16
secondary analysis   19
social institution   30
survey   18
symbolic interaction theory   24
utilitarian individualism   6
Western nations   9

Thinking about Families

The Public Family	The Private Family
What are some of the ways that your family has carried out its "public" functions?	How has your family carried out its "private" functions?

Families on the Internet   www.mhhe.com/cherlin5

Note: While all the URLs listed were current as of the printing of this book, these sites often change. Please check our Web site (http://www.mhhe.com/cherlin5) for updates.

The Internet is a great source of information about family issues. Throughout this book, the "Families on the Internet" section will provide you with suggested World Wide Web sites. Keep in mind that Web sites come and go on the Internet and that the contents of each Web site change often. This flux means that you might occasionally not find a Web site or specific piece of information within a site that is listed in this section. I will attempt, however, to suggest sites that are likely to be long-lived.

In addition, the publishers of this book have established a Web site where up-to-date links to useful sites will be posted.

The first way to obtain information on the family is to enter a phrase in a search engine such as Google. As you know, the phrase can't be too broad: Entering "family" will cause the search engine to return a blizzard of links. But a more focused entry can be useful: Typing "feminist theory" or "gay marriage," for example, should return a number of useful links. It may also, however, return some not-so-useful links; and it can be difficult and time-consuming to distinguish the good sites from the bad, or simply irrelevant, sites.

Consequently, it helps to have some suggested links to broader Web sites that provide issue-oriented information on a number of topics. For almost any public issue involving the family, two such "umbrella" sites are good places to start. The first is the Moving Ideas Network, www.movingideas.org, a site that provides links to many liberal and moderate organizations and publications. The second umbrella site is www.townhall.com, which has links to many conservative organizations and publications. Try to find a topic for which both sites have information and compare their perspectives.

The organizations that maintain the major national surveys have Web sites. Information on the National Survey of Families and Households is available at www.ssc.wisc.edu/nsfh/. Information on the Panel Study of Income Dynamics is available at www.psidonline.isr.umich.edu.

Chapter Two

The History of the Family

Looking Forward

1. What functions have families traditionally performed?

2. How did American families change after the United States was founded?

3. How have the family histories of major ethnic and racial groups differed?

4. How did the emotional character of the American family change during the early twentieth century?

5. What important changes occurred in marriage and child-bearing in the United States in the last half of the twentieth century?

6. How does the life course perspective help us to understand social change?

The serious study of the history of the family began in 1960, when the manager of a tropical fruit importing firm in France, a self-described "Sunday historian," published a book about the history of childhood (Ariès, 1960). Philippe Ariès, curious about family life in the Middle Ages, had examined works of art dating back 1,000 years. Any artist will tell you that children's heads are larger in proportion to the rest of their bodies than adults' heads. Yet many early medieval artists used adult proportions when painting children's heads and bodies, as if their subjects were, in fact, small adults. Moreover, the artists dressed children in the same clothes as adults. From such evidence Ariès concluded that the concept of childhood was a modern invention.

Of course, there always had been children, but until the 1700s, wrote Ariès, the long stage of life we call childhood wasn't recognized by most people. American historian John Demos put forth a similar argument about the Puritans in Plymouth Colony in the 1600s: "Childhood as such was barely recognized in the period spanned by Plymouth Colony. There was little sense that children might somehow be a special group, with their own needs and interests and capacities" (Demos, 1970). According to historians such as Ariès and Demos, parents withheld love and affection from infants and toddlers because so many of them died. The great French essayist Montaigne wrote in the late 1500s, "I have lost two or three children in their infancy, not without regret, but without great sorrow."[1] *Two or three*—Montaigne couldn't even remember how many. If children survived, wrote Ariès and Demos, they were treated as little adults. By age seven, boys and girls performed useful work—helping fathers in the fields or mothers at the hearth—and played the same games and attended the same festivals as adults.

Ariès argued that it was only with the spread of schooling and the decline in child deaths—neither of which occurred on a large scale until the 1800s outside the noble and middle classes—that the notion of a protected, extended stage of childhood emerged.

Ariès's influential book launched a new generation of historians who studied ordinary families rather than royal families. His contribution is still respected even though many historians now believe that he underestimated parents' appreciation of childhood as a stage of life. For every Montaigne, the revisionist historians have found a Martin Luther, who wrote in the 1500s after the death of his infant daughter,

---

[1] From vol. 2, no. 8, of Montaigne's *Essais*. Quoted on p. 39 of Ariès (1960).

Marriage of Giovanni Arnolfini and Giovanna Cenami, Jan van Eyck's famous painting of the wedding vows of a wealthy couple in 1434, shows a late medieval view of marriage. Wives were valued primarily for their childbearing and domestic roles: The bride is shown holding her long gown over her womb, as if she were pregnant. In back of her is a statuette of St. Margaret, the patron saint of childbearing women. Arnolfini stands straight, his facial expression stern, as if ready to assume his role as head of the household. His wife's pose is more submissive: her head slightly bowed, her eyes slightly downcast. A dog symbolizes the faithfulness expected of the couple.

"I so lamented her death that I was exquisitely sick, my heart rendered soft and weak; never had I thought that a father's heart could be so broken for his children's sake."[2] When historian Linda Pollock located and read 68 diaries written by American and British parents in the 1600s and 1700s, she found that most of them were aware that children were different from adults and that they needed parental guidance and support. The diarists frequently referred to their children as "comforts" and showed pride in their accomplishments. "I doe not think one child of 100 of his age durst doe so much," wrote one proud father (Pollock, 1983). (See also Nicholas [1991], Ozment [2001].) Nevertheless, parents of this period did seem less saddened by the death of an infant than of an older child.

The family history industry that Ariès spawned has produced thousands of books and articles. During the same period, a related field, the history of women and gender, has grown just as fast. Together, these fields provide an anchor for the study of the contemporary family. They describe the context in which the contemporary family has developed. Among other things, they tell us that the public family is as old as human civilization but that the private family blossomed only during the past few hundred years. For the sociologist studying the contemporary family, the historical literature is a wonderful source of insights. This chapter will provide a brief guided tour of that literature. Of necessity, it will be a highly selective tour, one that provides a foundation for the detailed study of the modern family in the remaining chapters of this book.

[2] Quoted in Ozment (1983).

First, we must go back even further in time than the historians have traveled in order to understand the origins of family and kinship. Then we will look at what the colonial and American Indian families were like prior to 1776. Afterward, we will follow the changes in the American family that took place between 1776 and the start of the twentieth century. We will then study the diversity of racial and ethnic American families in the twentieth century and the rise of what I call "the private family." Then we will consider the changing "life course" and an emerging life stage, early adulthood.

What Do Families Do?

THE ORIGINS OF FAMILY AND KINSHIP

We have all seen pictures of a new colt, minutes after birth, standing on its four legs. My local newspaper printed a photograph of a one-day-old dolphin swimming with its mother. In contrast, the average human baby cannot sit up until about six months and cannot walk until about age one. This difference in maturation time between humans and other animals is not an accident of nature; rather, it reflects the evolution of our species. Throughout most of their existence, human beings have been **hunter-gatherers:** They wandered through the forests in small bands, hunting animals and gathering edible plants. According to the theory of evolutionary biology, humans evolved from four-legged primates to beings that could walk upright and hunt or gather with two arms. But humans are born smaller (relative to their adult size) than most other mammals and need prolonged, intensive care in order to survive. In hunter-gatherer societies, as in nearly all other known societies, mothers provide most of the care during the first few years of children's lives. Anthropologists who have studied the few remaining hunter-gatherer societies report that mothers carry their young with them during the first year and continue to breastfeed them for several years (Howell, 1979). As a result, women specialize in finding plants and hunting small animals within a limited area, whereas men range farther afield in search of larger animals.

hunter-gatherers people who wander through forests or over plains in small bands, hunting animals and gathering edible plants

About 10,000 years ago, humans discovered the advantage of remaining in one place and planting crops. Settled agriculture revolutionized human organization because it allowed humans to accumulate surpluses of grain that could support larger kinship groups than was possible in hunter-gatherer societies. Indeed, human societies were often organized around large kinship groups. In societies in which a tribe ruled a territory and no other strong government existed, people often traced descent through either the father's or the mother's line, but not both. What resulted were kinship groups called **lineages: patrilineages** if descent is traced through the father's line; **matrilineages** if traced through the mother's line. These groups seem odd, at first, to people in Western nations, who trace descent through both the father's and mother's line; but the structure serves a purpose. Among other virtues, lineages limit the number of people who are related to a person and with whom that person must share land, water, animals, and other resources. In a patrilineage, my sons will marry women from outside the lineage; then the couples will live near me (sometimes with me) and remain in my lineage. My grandsons will do the same. But my daughters and granddaughters will marry men from other lineages, move to their land, and leave my lineage. Consequently, I need to share my resources with, and to defend, only those

lineage a form of kinship group in which descent is traced through either the father's or the mother's line

patrilineage a kinship group in which descent is through the father's line

matrilineage a kinship group in which descent is through the mother's line

Multigenerational households have been more common in China than in the West.

persons related to me through my father, my brothers, and my sons. If a maternal uncle needs assistance, that's his lineage's problem; I am not my mother's brother's keeper.

Kinship, as one anthropologist has written, developed as "a weapon in the struggle for survival" (Fox, 1967). In tribal societies, family ties provide the structure that holds the society together: You are a member of the tribe not because you are a citizen (a concept that can't exist without a state) but rather because you are related to the other members. You obey rules set by the tribal elders, not laws set by a government. You tend farmland not because you purchased it but because the tribe lets you use it. Kinship groups ensure order, recruit members from outside the group (usually through marriage), defend against other outsiders, provide labor at harvesttime, and assist the less fortunate. Anthropologists who study social organization in tribal societies focus on family and kinship because, to a large extent, that *is* social organization.

In most societies, kinship groups are made up of smaller family units, consisting of a mother and children always, a husband usually, and other household members sometimes. In many of the Western nations [➡ p. 9] the larger kinship groups have been weak, and the smaller husband-wife-children unit has dominated. This smaller unit of husband, wife, and children is referred to as the **conjugal family** (the word "conjugal" is from the Latin term for joining together in marriage). If any other relatives—such as a grandparent or uncle—are present in the household, it is said to contain an **extended family**. Many Americans assume that in the past Grandma, Grandpa, Mom, Dad, and the kids sat around the hearth,

conjugal family a kinship group comprising husband, wife, and children

extended family a kinship group comprising the conjugal family plus any other relatives present in the household, such as a grandparent or uncle

swapping stories, and enjoying one another's company. To be sure, there were substantial numbers of extended families in many European nations (Kertzer, 1991). But there were fewer families like that in the United States, England, and northern France, for two reasons. First, young people in those areas typically waited until they could start a new household before they married. That might mean waiting for the father to retire and turn over his land or moving to the city to work for a merchant. Second, Grandma and Grandpa often didn't live long enough to share a household with their grandchildren, although most elderly people continued to live with one child, often unmarried at first, who remained at home (Ruggles, 1994).

In other parts of the world, larger family units have been more common. The traditional Chinese family was patrilineal, and the cultural ideal was for five male generations (and their wives and children) to live under one roof, ruled by the oldest male. There, too, few families reached the ideal, because the oldest generations rarely lived long enough, and because a family had to be affluent to support such a large dwelling. Nevertheless, households containing extended families were more common in China than in Western nations. In many African societies, men were allowed (and in some countries still are allowed) to have more than one wife, a practice known as **polygyny** (literally, in Greek, "many women"). A wealthy man might take a second or third wife and establish each of them in separate dwellings in the same compound. All the wives and children might cook and eat together, under the direction of the senior wife. In a much smaller number of societies, women were allowed to practice **polyandry,** having more than one husband. In nearly all societies, some form of marriage has existed. But there are a few exceptions. (See *Families in Other Cultures*: "To Leave Your Mother and Sisters for a Wife, That Would Be Shameful.")

In sum, family and kinship systems were developed to provide for people's fundamental needs, such as producing sufficient food and defending against outsiders. Although kin often shared strong emotional bonds, families did not develop primarily out of people's desire for love and intimacy; rather, they developed out of their will to survive, prosper, and raise children. Thus the origins of family and kinship are best analyzed from the perspective of the public family introduced in Chapter 1: the view of families as settings in which people take care of one another and depend on one another. In contrast, the perspective of the private family, which emphasizes intimacy and personal fulfillment, is less useful; its utility is greater for analyzing contemporary families, as will be noted later.

MODES OF PRODUCTION

Until the past 250 years or so, most families performed three basic activities:

1. *Production*   They produced much of the food, clothes, and other goods and services they used.
2. *Reproduction*   They bore and raised children.
3. *Consumption*   They consumed food, firewood, and other essentials as a unit.

Today, in the United States and other Western countries, families still reproduce and consume, but few families produce many of the goods and services they use. Instead, they exchange their labor for money, which they use to buy goods and services. Even farmers are no longer self-sufficient producers. Rather, they grow one or two crops, sell them on the market, and buy most of the food they eat. The

polygyny a form of polygamy in which a man is allowed to have more than one wife

polyandry a form of polygamy in which a woman is allowed to have more than one husband

"To Leave Your Mother and Sisters for a Wife, That Would Be Shameful."

Anthropologists have long maintained that marriage has been present in every known society. In addition to the plain, one-husband-to-one-wife version, some societies have allowed polygynous marriages in which a husband could have many wives or, more rarely, polyandrous marriages in which one wife could have many husbands. But whatever the precise rules, marriage was thought to be a basic building block of family and society. Only one counter-example was known: the Nayar of India, among whom women could receive sexual visits from multiple "husbands" who had little responsibility for the children their liaisons produced (Gough, 1959). But the Nayar were a special case: the men tended to work as soldiers, so they had long absences from home. Now we have an anthropological study of a society in China—a minority group called the Na who live in Yunnan and Sichuan provinces—whose way of organizing family and kinship is stunningly different from any society previously studied. They are, as anthropologist Cai Hua titles his book, *A Society without Fathers or Husbands* (Hua, 2001).

Here's how Na kinship worked, at least until recently. Brothers and sisters live in their mother's household throughout their lives. Instead of taking wives, men visit women in other households, primarily at night, arriving around midnight and leaving at dawn, supposedly without the members of the women's households knowing. Men appear to be free to visit any Na woman who will consent to have sex with them. Hau calls these liaisons "furtive visits" because they are ostensibly done in secret: The man throws pebbles on the woman's roof or knocks on the door an agreed-upon number of times. But given the number of visits and

the close quarters in most households, it's hard to imagine that "secret" means much more than a tacit agreement that others will not pay attention. In fact, mothers often monitor these visits, and everyone in the village, Hua reports, seems to know who is partnering with whom. If a man and a woman are particularly attracted to each other they may become lovers and have sex mostly with each other for a few months or even a few years. But both women and men may have sex with partners other than their lovers.

When children are born, they remain with their mothers and their maternal uncles and aunts in a small compound consisting of three or four buildings made of clay and wood. Their social organization resembles that of matrilineal societies in which children remain with their mothers and their maternal uncles become father figures. But in nearly all other matrilineal societies, the fathers of the children are known and socially recognized. They may not live with their children, but they are presences in their lives nevertheless. The Na, however, do not recognize fatherhood. A man is not expected to take any responsibility for children he may have sired, and a woman may not be sure who the father is. Traditionally, the Na believed that the fetus exists in a woman's womb prior to intercourse and that all men do through sex is water the fields of the womb, enabling the fetus to grow. "It makes no difference," Hua writes of the villagers' beliefs, "who does the watering."

After the Communist revolution in China, the government began a campaign to promote monogamy among the Na. For example, a 1974 decree withheld rations of grain from children born outside of marriage until the mother said who the father was. The Na

resisted these measures. Men felt loyal to their sisters, whose children they jointly raised and with whom they exchanged support throughout their adult lives. They did not want to cohabit with the mothers of their children. One man told the anthropologist, "To leave your mother and sisters for a wife, that would be shameful." The government eventually backed down, although some penalties remain. By the 1990s, furtive visits were still common and marriage rare, but the percentage of people engaging in open, public sexual relationships had increased. The old ways were still visible but weakening as the Na received more education. Schoolchildren read standard Chinese textbooks in which all children had fathers; and they sometimes had to fill out forms asking for the name of their father. They took biology classes which taught that the fetus is created by the union of the man's sperm and the woman's egg. The message was clear: Children should have fathers.

The existence of the Na teaches us that marriage is not the only basis for organizing family life. It is possible to have a society without fathers and husbands, a society in which men have virtually no relationship—legal or social—with their children. And it is possible to have a society in which sexual freedom is valued over stable romantic ties. Even if humans have a propensity toward stable, long-term bonds, the Na demonstrate that humans are capable of creating social systems that can override that propensity. Yet the rather jaw-dropping uniqueness of the Na system also reinforces the fact that marriage, or at least a stable, long-term sexual partnership between women and men, has been the overwhelmingly common way of organizing human family systems throughout history.

familial mode of production a means of production in which the family produces nearly all its own food, makes most of its own clothes, and with the help of others, builds its own dwelling

shift from producing most of what the family consumes to buying most of what the family consumes is the most fundamental change in the Western family over the past few centuries. A typical family under the old system, referred to as the **familial mode of production**,[3] would be a largely self-sufficient farming family whose members grow grain, tend a vegetable garden, keep animals for milk or meat or eggs, make most of the clothes they wear, and with the help of other kin, build their own dwellings.

In the mid-1700s the familial mode of production began to decline in the American colonies and England, and in the early 1800s elsewhere in the Western nations. A new system took hold in which most men, and many unmarried women, worked for wages. Families purchased more clothing and made less of it at home. In the expanding cities, families could not easily grow their own food, so they had to buy it. Consequently, they produced less at home and bought and sold more on the market. The advent of this new system of production for exchange (working for wages to exchange for goods) rather than for use (working to grow food and eat it) accelerated in the 1800s, as more and more men began to work for wages. This system, referred to as the **labor market mode of production**, had solidified by the late 1800s, when working for wages in factories became a widespread way for men, immigrant and working-class women, and even their children to make a living.

labor market mode of production a means of production in which people work for pay and thus produce less for their own use at home and buy and sell more on the market

The transition from the familial to the labor market mode of production had two important consequences for family life. First, it separated the workplace from the home. Before, husbands, wives, and children had worked together in a common family enterprise. Then in the 1800s, as more and more husbands began to work in factories or offices, a gap opened between the world of work and the world of the family. Second, the transition eroded the authority of fathers over their children, because fathers no longer controlled a key resource—land—that sons needed to attract a wife. In the next two sections we will trace these themes in the history of the American family.

Quick Review

- For most of our history, humans were hunter-gatherers.
- Lineages offered a number of advantages to humans after settled agriculture began.
- In the Western nations, the smaller, conjugal family has dominated.
- Under the familial mode of production, families produced most of what they consumed.
- Under the labor market mode of production, families purchased most of what they consumed.

The American Family before 1776

There were several American families prior to the Revolution. There were, first of all, the families of the indigenous people who would become known as American Indians. There were the families of the European colonists. And there were the families of the African slaves, who were transported involuntarily to the Americas beginning in the 1500s. I will discuss the history of African American families

---

[3] Some authors refer to the familial mode of production as the "domestic mode of production" or the "family economy" and to the labor market mode of production as the "capitalist mode of production" or the "family wage economy." I follow the usage in Caldwell (1982).

later in this chapter. For now, let us examine the American Indian family and the European colonists' family before 1776.

AMERICAN INDIAN FAMILIES: THE PRIMACY OF THE TRIBE

Although there is little direct evidence about American Indian societies before the 1800s, scholars think that most American Indians lived in tribal societies based on lineages. (The term **American Indian** is often used for a subset of the original, indigenous people who had settled in North America thousands of years before Columbus, namely those who had settled in the territory that later became the 48 contiguous United States [Snipp, 1989]. Indeed, it was because Columbus mistakenly believed that he had reached India that he gave this aboriginal population the misnomer "Indian.") We do know that the American Indian population was devastated by diseases brought by Europeans, such as smallpox—diseases to which the native population had developed no immunities. Moreover, we know that large numbers of American Indians were killed in wars and massacres (Shoemaker, 1991). How these catastrophic events modified family and kinship is unclear. In the absence of direct evidence, scholars have assumed that the numerous accounts of American Indian societies in the 1800s and early 1900s can be generalized back in time. Although the assumption that present arrangements accurately reflect the past ignores the historical changes that occurred to American Indian societies after the arrival of the Europeans, the outlines of American Indian family and kinship seem clear.

Both patrilineal and matrilineal tribes existed. Related lineages were often organized into larger clans that provided the basis for social organization and governing. In matrilineal tribes such as the Hopi, for example, a person traced his or her

American Indian the name used for a subset of all Native Americans, namely, those who were living in the territory that later became the 48 contiguous United States

In most American Indian tribes, families were organized into lineages in which descent was traced through either the father's or the mother's line.

relatives through his or her mother's line.[4] If you were a child, your father was a guest in your mother's home. Although strong bonds existed between wives and husbands, a woman's ties to her maternal kin—her mother, her mother's brothers, her maternal cousins—were generally stronger. Consequently, your maternal uncles played an important role in your upbringing. They, not your father, had to approve your choice of spouse. Still, if you were a boy, you did learn many of the skills of an adult male—growing crops, herding animals—from your father. It was as if you had two kinds of fathers: a biological father who taught you skills and an uncle-father who held greater authority over you. If you were a girl, you spent less time with your father.

When Hopi boys reached puberty, they moved out of the household, sleeping in the men's ceremonial house and eventually marrying into another clan. Girls, on the other hand, remained in or near their mothers' homes throughout their lives, bringing husbands from other clans into their dwellings. In general, American Indian children were more independent than European American children: they were given more freedom and experienced less physical punishment (Mintz, 2004). In all tribal societies, the common requirement that individuals marry someone outside their clan forged alliances across clans. If clan A and clan B frequently exchanged young adults as marriage partners, the two clans would likely consider themselves as allies in any disputes with other clans in the tribe. Thus, the lineage and clan organization of American Indian societies served to strengthen the social order and to protect individuals against unfriendly outsiders.

Kinship was also matrilineal among the Apache of Arizona. Soon after a girl's first menstruation (which probably occurred several years later in her life than is the case today), her lineage held a four-day Sun Rise ceremony, after which she was eligible to marry (Joe, Sparks, & Tiger, 1999). Marriages were typically arranged by elders from the prospective bride's and groom's lineages. (Marrying someone from the same lineage was forbidden.) A series of gifts was exchanged by the bride's and groom's families, which culminated in the groom's family bringing him to the home of the bride. The bride's family then constructed a separate home for the couple. The gifts between families symbolized the importance of establishing an alliance with a family in another lineage. It's not that love between the young couple was necessarily lacking, but their marriage also served the larger purpose of tying together members of two lineages who could provide assistance in times of trouble or need.

EUROPEAN COLONISTS: THE PRIMACY OF THE PUBLIC FAMILY

Among the European colonists, there were no lineages. But the conjugal family of husband, wife, and children provided services that were of great value to the community. Consider education. In Plymouth Colony, children received their basic education from their parents or, if they were working as servants, in another family's home. Parents and masters were required by law to teach reading to their children and young servants, so they could at least "be able to duely read the scriptures" (Demos, 1970). Why weren't these children learning to read in school? Because there was no school—or rather, because the family *was* school. In addition to providing schooling, all Plymouth Colony families were expected to provide vocational training. Through apprenticeship and service, working next to

---

[4] This account of Hopi kinship draws from Queen, Habenstein, and Quadagno (1985).

an adult, children and youths learned the skills they needed to farm, trade, garden, cook, and make clothes. All families were also expected to supplement church services by engaging in "family worship," praying and meditating daily.

Selected Plymouth Colony families also functioned as

- *Hospitals*   Some adults who supposedly had specialized knowledge took sick persons into their homes for treatment.
- *Houses of correction*   Judges ordered some idle or criminal persons to live in the homes of upstanding families to learn how to change their ways.
- *Orphanages*   Children whose parents had died—a far more common occurrence than today—were taken in by a relative or family friend.
- *Nursing homes*   Frail elderly parents were cared for in their homes by their children.
- *Poorhouses*   Families sometimes took in poor relatives who needed food and shelter. (Demos, 1970)

Today, all these activities, with the exception of caring for the elderly, are carried out primarily outside the home, mostly by publicly supported institutions. In Plymouth Colony, then, the family's public role was much broader than it is now.

In contrast, the family's private role was much smaller. The kind of privacy that Westerners today take for granted hardly existed a few hundred years ago, as is apparent to anyone who visits the Puritan houses that still stand in Massachusetts. The downstairs area of a typical house contained one or two rooms. The larger of them was an all-purpose room called the "hall," in which the members of the household spent most of their indoor waking hours. It was dominated by a huge fireplace used for heating and cooking. In smaller houses, the second downstairs room would contain little except bedding. Most houses also had one or two second-story lofts with beds. Often, only the hall contained furniture for any activity other than sleeping. In this one room, fathers, mothers, children (Plymouth families had an average of seven or eight children), servants or apprentices, and perhaps a grandparent ate, cooked, talked, prayed, sewed clothing, relaxed, and received visitors. Individuals simply could not find a place to get away from other household members.

Not only did individuals have difficulty maintaining privacy but the conjugal family also had difficulty maintaining privacy from other households. The colonists did not regard the conjugal family as separate from society, but rather as an integral part of it. To a great extent, a family's affairs were considered public business. For example, Puritan laws required that married couples maintain harmonious relations and raise their children properly—and imposed fines on those who didn't. Friends and neighbors commonly called at one another's houses without advance notice. Given all the ways in which privacy was prevented, the idea of a private, conjugal family with its own separate space—and of individual privacy within the family—may not have been in the mind-set of most people. At best, privacy was probably dismissed as unattainable.

FAMILY DIVERSITY

But not all colonial families fit the ideal of two married, biological parents and their children. Particularly outside of New England, families were diverse. For one thing, death rates were so high that children commonly lost a parent and lived in a stepfamily after their remaining parent remarried (Unlenberg, 1980). In addition, people sometimes proclaimed themselves married in front of family or friends, without the participation of clergy, and were accepted as married by their communities. Europeans, it turns out, had a long tradition of informal marriage. Until the Council of Trent in 1563, the Catholic Church accepted as a marriage any public statement by a couple that they considered themselves married to each other, as long as neither partner coerced the other and their marriage did not violate church laws about who could marry whom. Until 1753 the Church of England, which had broken with the Catholic Church during the reign of Henry VIII, recognized informal marriage (Therborn, 2004). Even as late as 1850, informal marriage was common in England among the poorer classes (Gillis, 1985). People used the phrase "living tally" to describe couples living as married but who had never wed in the church.

Informal marriage was particularly common in the Middle Colonies (New York, New Jersey, Pennsylvania, Delaware, and Maryland) and Southern Colonies (Virginia, North Carolina, South Carolina, and Georgia), where the Anglican Church (the American wing of the Church of England) did not provide enough clergy, and in frontier areas where social control was looser. An Anglican minister in eighteenth-century Maryland said, "if . . . no marriage should be deemed valid that had not been registered in the parish book, it would I am persuaded bastardize nine-tenths of the People in the Country."[5] As in England, informal marriage persisted into the nineteenth century. In 1833, the Chief Justice of the State of Pennsylvania wrote that if the state truly enforced its marriage laws, the "vast majority" of the state's children would be considered illegitimate. A form of bigamy also sometimes occurred: A man who left his wife and migrated to a faraway state or territory was unlikely to be followed, so he could marry anew without much fear of prosecution (Hartog, 2000). In the nineteenth and early twentieth centuries, in contrast, families probably became *less* diverse over time, as churches established control of marriage and as fewer parents died while their children were young.

Quick Review

- Lineages and clans constituted the main social organization of American Indian tribal societies.
- In American colonial society, families had many public functions but a smaller private role than today.
- Parental death and informal marriage produced diverse types of families.

The Emergence of the "Modern" American Family: 1776–1900

Pinpointing the beginnings of social change is always difficult; rarely can we discern a great divide between an older way of life and an emerging one. Nevertheless, the decades surrounding the American Revolution seem to have been a watershed in the history of the American family. In an overview of the history of women and the family in the United States, Carl Degler (1980) claims that between

[5] Quoted in Cott (2000). The Anglican minister is quoted on p. 32, the Chief Justice, on p. 39.

1776 and 1830, the outlines emerged of a kind of family that would remain prominent well into the twentieth century. Clearest among the white middle class, it had four new characteristics:

- Marriage was increasingly based on affection and mutual respect rather than on male authority and custom. As a consequence, women experienced increasing autonomy in the family. (But, I would add, they were increasingly restricted to the home.)
- The primary role of the wife became the care of children and the maintenance of the home. Women came to be seen as morally superior to men, and the home came to be seen as "women's sphere."
- The attention and energy of the husband and wife were increasingly centered on their children. Children came to be seen as needing not only discipline and economic support, but also attention, affection, and loving care.
- The number of children per family declined, in part as a consequence of the greater investment of emotion and time that they were seen to need.

Moreover, some historians believe that the idea of individualism gained greater currency during the 1700s. Lawrence Stone's (1977) influential account of British family history claims that individualism gained ground among the British middle and upper classes in the 1700s. Individualism, Stone wrote, had two meanings where the family was concerned. The first was a greater consideration of one's own self and, in particular, one's own sense of self-satisfaction. This led, in turn, to an increased emphasis on personal gratification in family relationships. The second meaning was of autonomy—individual freedom from constraints imposed by

Under the ideology of "separate spheres" that developed in the 1800s, caring for children was seen as a central part of women's lives.

others. Consequently, Stone called this phenomenon the rise of "affective individualism," a concept very similar to "expressive individualism," defined in chapter 1. [➡ p. 7] Since the work of Stone, Ariès (whose theory of childhood was described at the beginning of the chapter), and other historians of what has become known as the "sentiments school" appeared, however, many historians have argued that sentiment and affection had been present for centuries prior to the 1700s (Cooper, 1999; Ozment, 2001).

Nevertheless, there probably was a movement toward greater individualism and sentiment in American family life in the 1700s and early 1800s. In 1776 Americans had begun a war of independence dedicated, as every schoolchild knows, to the values of "life, liberty, and the pursuit of happiness." That young adults successfully freed themselves from the control of their elders, and relations between husbands and wives and between parents and children became more affectionate, probably was not a coincidence.

Despite these changes, marriage retained a moral basis in custom and law through the nineteenth century. According to historian Nancy Cott (2000), political philosophers argued that lifetime marriage with the husband as the head was similar to American governance: It involved democratic rule by a leader (the husband) with the voluntary consent of the governed (the wife). Preserving marriage was seen as essential to maintaining a democratic moral order. Consequently, government support for marriage—such as laws that made obtaining a divorce difficult—was viewed as necessary and proper. Cott's thesis suggests that the family's contribution to public welfare was conceived more broadly than today. I defined the "public family" in terms of its valuable care for dependents. [➡ p. 12] Prior to the twentieth century, many Americans also thought that marriage served as the foundation of national morality. This view of marriage as the moral and political backbone of society would erode during the twentieth century, although it has reemerged among some members of the marriage movement [➡ p. 5] in the twenty-first.

FROM COOPERATION TO SEPARATION: WOMEN'S AND MEN'S SPHERES

Another spur to family change was the transition from the familial mode of production to the labor market mode of production. It began sometime in the 1700s and early 1800s, with the growth of commercial capitalism—an economic system that emphasizes the buying, selling and distribution of goods such as grain, tobacco, or cotton. Commercial capitalism created jobs for merchants, clerks, shippers, dockworkers, wagon builders, and others like them, who were paid money for their labor. The opportunity to earn money outside the home undermined the authority of fathers. Because sons had alternatives to farming, fathers no longer had a near monopoly on the resources needed to make a living. This greater economic independence facilitated the growth of individualism. The transition accelerated in the mid-1800s with the spread of industrial capitalism, which created factory work for the great masses of immigrants and their descendants.

The heart of this change was the movement of men's work out of the home. Instead of working together in a common household enterprise, husbands and wives now worked on separate enterprises—he exchanging his labor for wages, she maintaining the home and raising the children. Instead of working in close proximity, the two were physically separated during the workday. Moreover, wage work held no intrinsic value for most men, and in nineteenth-century factories it was frequently exhausting and dangerous.

The sharp split between a rewarding home life and an often alienating work life led to the emergence of the idea of "separate spheres": men's sphere being the world of work and, more generally, the world outside the home; and women's sphere being the home, relatives, and children. Whereas men's sphere was seen as being governed by the rough ethic of the business world, women's sphere came to be seen as morally pure, a place where wives could renew their husbands' spirituality and character. And whereas men's sphere was seen as providing no reward other than a paycheck, women's sphere was the center of affection and nurturing, the emotional core for husbands and children.

Thus developed a nineteenth-century ideology, a set of beliefs, which historian Barbara Welter named "the cult of True Womanhood" (Welter, 1966). The True Woman was, first of all, a pious upholder of spiritual values. She was also pure: She was to have no sexual contact before marriage—although men might try to tempt her—and none afterward except with her husband. Moreover, the True Woman was submissive to men, particularly her husband. And finally, she was domestic: Her proper place was in the home, comforting her husband, lovingly raising her children.

Woman's sphere at once limited women's opportunities and glorified their domestic role. It was a more restricted role than wives in the colonial era had experienced. To be sure, the Puritan wife was also home most of the day, but she was collaborating with her husband in the family economy; without her contribution, her husband might not have been able to feed and clothe their children. Then the movement to wage labor separated women from paid work. Men went out every morning into the wider social world, but their wives could not follow. In a culture that had begun to celebrate individualism, women were supposed to give up much of their individualism to care for their husbands and children. Seen from this vantage point, one might argue that women's lives were worse than they had been before the Revolution—more restricted, less productive, more dependent and more isolated. Indeed, many historians have argued as much.

But other historians, while acknowledging the restrictions and dependency inherent in the domestic sphere, argue that it nevertheless offered some benefits. Appointing women the guardians of moral values and giving them the major role in rearing children provided them with substantial influence. However circumscribed, it may have allowed wives to counter the authority of their husbands, which had been so pervasive in the colonial period. Moreover, the ideology of women's sphere may have created a self-consciousness of, and an identification with, women as a group. Women established and maintained deep friendships with other women, reinforced by the segregation of their lives and by female rituals surrounding childbirth, weddings, illnesses, and funerals (Smith-Rosenberg, 1975). Some joined together in public associations to promote values consistent with domesticity, such as greater devotion to religion, assistance for the poor, or enlightened child-rearing. These friendships and associations may have been a prerequisite for the development of feminist organizations in the nineteenth and twentieth centuries. Historian Nancy Cott captured the dual nature of women's sphere in the title of her book, *The Bonds of Womanhood* (Cott, 1977), for the bonds that tied women to the domestic sphere also bound them together in a subculture of sisterhood that prefigured their social and political movements decades later.

WORKING-CLASS FAMILIES

This was the picture for the white middle class. But life was different for the working class, especially for the tens of millions of immigrants who poured into American

Members of a working-class family sew garments, for which they were paid by the piece, in 1913.

cities. Between 1850 and World War I, the scale of immigration was simply massive. Even in 1850, 10 percent of the population had been born in another country (U.S. Bureau of the Census, 1975). Then began a sustained increase in immigration. By 1900, 15 percent of the population was foreign born. The percentage then fell to 5 percent in 1960 before rising again to 12 percent in 2003 (U.S. Bureau of the Census, 2004c).

The migrants to the country's growing cities from overseas or from rural America worked long hours for low wages and lived in crowded, often unsanitary conditions. In Homestead, Pennsylvania, in the 1890s, workers labored at one of Andrew Carnegie's steel mills from 7:00 A.M. to 5:30 P.M., six days a week, for less than $15 a week. Some worked longer night shifts or all seven days. According to one report, half of the African American and Slavic workers in the town lived in one- or two-room shanties without indoor plumbing or toilets (Mintz & Kellogg, 1988).

Living between Modes   Working-class families may or may not have aspired to the breadwinner-homemaker model, but in either case, it was a style of life they could not afford. Instead, they needed to pool the economic contributions of more than one family member in order to subsist. Before stricter child labor laws were passed, children as young as 10 or 11 often worked alongside their fathers and older siblings at a factory. Steven Mintz (2004) writes of one girl in the 1830s:

> *Hannah Borden, a young Fall River, Massachusetts, textile worker, was required to have her looms running at five in the morning. She was given an hour for breakfast and a half hour for lunch. Her workday ended at half past seven, fourteen and a half hours after it had begun. For a six-day workweek, she received between $2.50 and $3.50. (pp. 140–141)*

Unmarried older sons and daughters contributed their wages to the family fund. To be sure, few wives worked for wages outside the home—just 2.5 percent of white married women (of all classes combined) did so in 1890 (Goldin, 1977). For a wife to work outside the home was such a sign of economic failure that white families avoided it unless there was no alternative except extreme hardship (Robinson, 1993). Instead, working-class wives made important economic contributions at home. Some earned money by doing laundry; others did piecework—literally, work for which they were paid by the piece—such as stitching shoes. Often they took into their households a kind of resident that has now almost disappeared—the boarder or lodger.

A boarder is someone who pays to live in a room and to eat meals in someone's household; a lodger is someone who pays for a room but does not eat in the household. Let me use the term "boarder" for both. In the nineteenth and early twentieth centuries, boarding was the most common living arrangement for unmarried adults who were not living with their parents. Very few people lived alone; as recently as 1900, only 5 percent of all households contained one person (Kobrin, 1976). Rather than live alone, unmarried people boarded for several reasons. First, few could afford to live alone, because wages were too low. Second, the surge of immigrants had created a housing shortage, which drove rents up further. Third, preparing meals required much more time and effort than is the case today. Since there were no refrigerators or freezers, people had to shop for food almost daily. There were no microwave meals, no TV dinners, no inexpensive fast-food restaurants. Fourth, having grown up in households larger than ours today, people may have preferred to live in the company of others. By one estimate, 15 to 20 percent of all urban households contained boarders at any given time (Modell & Hareven, 1973); the proportion of households that ever took in boarders was certainly much higher than that. In a sense, boarders were a replacement for grown children in the household's economy. When an older child who had contributed part of his or her earnings left home, a bed was freed and a hole was left in the family's budget. Families typically took in a boarder in response.

Working-class families did not correspond neatly to either the familial or the labor market mode of production. Like families operating in the familial mode, they pooled the efforts of several members in a common family enterprise: The husband and his teenage son might work for wages, the wife might take in boarders and do piecework, and an unmarried older sister might contribute her wages so her brother could go to college. But unlike families in the familial mode, most members exchanged their labor for wages. More accurately, from the mid-1800s to the early 1900s, working-class families were living between modes. These families were still producing for their own use, even though some members worked for wages some of the time. Many urban working-class families, for instance, grew vegetables and baked bread (Coontz, 1999). Parents and children still contributed the fruits of their labor, be it cash or crops, to a common family fund. Individuals subordinated their own desires to the good of the family. And what was good for the family was decided by the parents, particularly the father.

Although living between modes was an admirable way for families to manage on limited resources, it was an unstable system. Once older children decided that they needn't turn over most of their earnings to their parents, the authority of the father eroded. Once the husband's wages increased enough that his wife could cut back on piecework and boarding, the family became heavily dependent on his wages. In such families, parents got smaller economic returns from children and were forced to expend more time and energy educating and rearing them. Families such as these were likely to decide that having fewer children and investing more in each was preferable to having many children. The result was a smaller, more isolated conjugal family—the kind we are familiar with today.

Quick Review

- In the late 1700s and early 1800s, American marriage seemed to change.
  - Greater importance was given to affection and mutual respect rather than male authority.
  - Increasing attention was paid to the loving care of (a declining number of) children.
- Under the emerging doctrine of "separate spheres," men's sphere was the world outside the home, women's the home, relatives, and children.
- Women's sphere restricted their opportunities but also fostered friendships and participation in public organizations.
- Men's and women's spheres were less separate among working-class families, and wives made important economic contributions.

African American, Mexican American, and Asian Immigrant Families

Europeans, of course, were not the only immigrants to the United States. Three other groups were present early in the nation's history. Africans had been forced to immigrate—captured or bought in West Africa, transported across the ocean under horrible conditions that killed many, and sold as slaves upon arrival. Mexicans, in search of grazing land, had pushed north into the area that is now the Southwest. Asian immigrants first arrived in large numbers in the mid-nineteenth century, when they were used as laborers by the railroads and other enterprises. The family lives of all three groups differed from those of the Europeans. Like white working-class women, those from racial and ethnic minority groups had to contribute economically outside, as well as inside, the home (Dill, 1988).

AFRICAN AMERICAN FAMILIES

An African Heritage?   As later chapters will document, African American families have long been distinct from white families: Historically, they have maintained stronger ties to extended kin such as uncles, aunts, and cousins and have borne a higher percentage of children outside marriage. The extent to which these differences reflect the lasting influence of African culture has been hotly debated (Herskovits, 1990). But the similarities between the old and the new cultures are striking enough to consider whether some continuities may exist.

Traditionally, African society was organized by lineages, which I have defined as large kinship groups that trace their descent through the male or female line. Members of the lineage cooperated and shared resources with others, and adults carefully controlled and monitored courtship and marriage among the young. What mattered most was not the happiness of the married couple, but the birth of children who could be retained by the lineage. In the Western nations, we are used to thinking of marriage as an event that occurs at a particular time: On the appointed date, two people participate in a ceremony and register their intentions with the state government. But in Africa, marriage was much more of a process, a series of steps that occurred over a long period of time (Bledsoe, 1990). Childbearing could occur before the ceremony, but the clear expectation was that marriage would follow within a few years.

Historically, African American families have placed more emphasis on ties to extended kin than have European American families.

When Africans brought these cultural patterns to the United States, the institution of slavery stripped their elders of authority over the marriage process. Their lineages, as anthropologist Niara Sudarkasa (1980, 1981) has written, were reduced to extended families. In Africa, elders had had substantial authority over individuals because they controlled crucial resources, most notably land. An African who was disowned by a lineage faced a terrible future. But in the United States, the wider kinship group no longer controlled the allocation of land, livestock, or jobs. Thus, among many African Americans, the extended kinship groups were limited to serving as social support networks. Extended families were important to individuals who belonged to them, but they had less control over their members' actions.

The Impact of Slavery   Until the appearance of new scholarship in the 1970s, in fact, most historians thought that the oppression and harsh conditions of slavery had destroyed most of the culture African slaves brought with them, leaving little in its place. The writings of both white and black scholars emphasized the losses imposed by slavery: the uprooting from Africa, the disruption of families through sales of family members to new owners, the inability of fathers to protect their families from the abuses imposed by masters. In an influential 1939 book, E. Franklin Frazier, a sociologist and an African American, argued that white masters had destroyed all social organization among the slaves. As a result, he wrote, slave family life was disorganized; the only stable bond was between mothers and their children:

> *Consequently, under all conditions of slavery, the Negro mother remained the most dependable and important figure in the family. (Frazier, 1939)*

From Frazier and others, then, came the idea that both during and after slavery, most African American families were headed by women and that African American men were relatively powerless in and outside the home. But in 1976, historian Herbert Gutman published a comprehensive study of plantation, local government,

A family history chart from about 1880, "designed for the colored people of America" according to the artist, W. H. Cowell, shows scenes from before and after the Civil War.

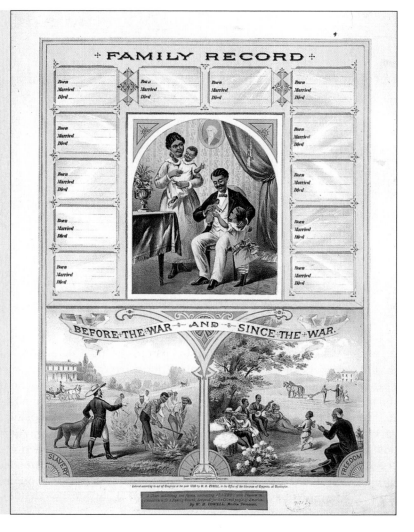

and census records that suggested a much different picture (Gutman, 1976). Gutman found substantial evidence that whenever possible, slaves had married and lived together for life and that they knew and kept track of uncles, aunts, cousins, and other kin. He cited letters such as one the field hand Cash sent to relatives on a Georgia plantation after he, his wife, Phoebe, and some of their children were sold away:

> *Clairissa your affectionate Mother and Father sends a heap of love to you and your Husband and my Grand Children. Mag. & Cloe. John. Judy. My aunt sinena ... Give our Love to Cashes brother Porter and his Wife Patience. Victoria sends her Love to her Cousin Beck and Miley. (Gutman, 1976)*

Moreover, Gutman argued, before and after slavery, in both the North and the South, most African American families included two parents. These family ties were forged despite the frequent sale of husbands, wives, and children to other masters, despite the sexual abuse of slave women by owners, and despite high rates of disease and death.

Still, there were some differences, both before and after the Civil War, between black and white families. For example, young slave women often had a first child before marrying; if so, they were usually married within a few years, although not necessarily to the father (Jones, 1985). This pattern may have occurred in part because slave owners valued women who had many children, increasing the owner's wealth. Yet as we have seen, it is also consistent with custom in Africa. Moreover, the disruption of slave families may have been more severe on smaller plantations. In the Appalachian area, where landowners had fewer slaves, the frequent hiring out of slaves to other landowners disrupted marriages. Sales of slaves—often to cotton farmers in the lower South—may have been more common than in the larger plantations, with perhaps one-third of Appalachian slave marriages broken by sales (Dunaway, 2003).

Another difference between black and white families was that after the Civil War, wives in rural black families worked seasonally in the fields, whereas rural white women didn't. According to 1870 Census figures for the Cotton Belt states, about 4 in 10 African American wives had jobs, almost all as field workers. In contrast, 98 percent of white wives said they were "keeping house" and had no other job (Jones, 1985). Here again, the differences reflect a mixture of economic pressure and culture. The plots of land African American sharecroppers farmed in the late nineteenth century provided such a marginal standard of living that men and women (and often children) were needed in the fields, at least at harvesttime. Historian Jacqueline Jones has also noted that "the outlines of African work patterns endured among the slaves" (Jones, 1985), in that African women often bore the major responsibility for cultivating food.

Moreover, although most black families still had two parents, black mothers were more likely to be living without a male partner than white mothers. This racial difference stemmed partly from the high mortality rates of black men; by one estimate, 42 percent of black wives were widowed by ages 45 to 50 around 1900 (Preston, Lim, & Morgan, 1992). But a difference still remains after mortality is taken into account (Morgan, McDaniel, Miller, & Preston, 1993). A much larger racial difference in household structure would emerge after about 1960 (see Chapter 5).

When black families migrated to Northern cities in the twentieth century, black women continued to work outside the home in larger numbers than white women. About one-third of married nonwhite women worked outside the home in the 1920s and 1930s, compared with less than one-tenth of married white women (Goldin, 1977). Because of discrimination, black men were offered only low-paying, physically challenging jobs that couldn't support a family, such as stoking a blast furnace in a steel factory. Staying home simply was not an option for most black wives, who also faced discrimination and found work mainly as domestic servants. Not until the 1960s did black women break out of domestic service into occupations previously reserved for white women. Today, women of both races still lag behind men in earnings, and black men's employment situation, though improved, remains difficult.

MEXICAN AMERICAN FAMILIES

Like African Americans, Mexican Americans established a presence early in the history of what is now the United States—although unlike African Americans, the descendants of these early residents are now vastly outnumbered by recent immigrants. In the early nineteenth century, well before migrants from the eastern United States arrived, Mexicans settled the frontier of what was then northern Mexico (Moore & Cuèllar, 1970). These pioneers crossed deserts and fought with American Indians to reach as far west as California and as far north as Colorado. Their early settlements generally included an elite landowning family and poorer farmer-laborer settlers. The landowning elite tended to be (or claimed to be) of nearly pure Spanish descent. Some owned vast tracts of land on which they grazed cattle or sheep. They arranged their children's marriages with care and celebrated elaborate weddings and feasts, so as to preserve or merge their holdings with other wealthy families or with wealthy Anglo (non-Mexican) immigrants (Griswold del Castillo, 1979).

More numerous were the laborers who worked the great estates or farmed or grazed animals on their own smaller holdings. They tended to be **mestizos,** people whose ancestors included both Spanish settlers and Native Americans from Mexico. There is some evidence that informal marriages were more common among this group (Griswold del Castillo, 1979). Informal marriages allowed couples to evade the control of their parents and other kin; and with fewer resources to protect than among the elite, the *mestizo* classes had less reason to control who married whom. These small landholders and laborers attempted to enlist the sponsorship and support of the well-to-do through the tradition of **compadrazgo,** a godparent relationship in which a wealthy or influential person outside the kinship group became the *compadre,* or godparent, of a newborn child, particularly at its baptism. The godfather and godchild were expected to retain a special relationship, and the godparent was supposed to assist his godchild, for example, by providing or finding a job (Camarillo, 1979).

This social structure was disrupted by a series of wars, revolts, and land grabs by U.S. troops and immigrants during the 1830s and 1840s. When it was over, the United States had acquired, by conquest, the current Southwest. Soon thereafter, most of the Spanish elite lost their land to taxes, drought, and Anglo squatters. Instead of ranchers and farmers, Mexicans became more of a working-class community, employed by the growing numbers of Anglos (Camarillo, 1979). Census statistics for the Los Angeles district in the last half of the nineteenth century show a rising number of households headed by women (Griswold del Castillo, 1979). Some of these women were probably married to men who migrated from harvest to harvest, picking crops; others were informally married. But many were probably unmarried, their numbers reflecting the economic changes of the time. Mexican American women, like African American women, could find low-paying but steady work as domestics and launderers for wealthier Anglos, whereas Mexican American men were losing their established positions as small ranchers and farmers.

As the number of Anglo immigrants rose, Mexican Americans were forced into **barrios,** segregated neighborhoods in the city. Residents of the *barrios* faced high unemployment or low income if they provided low-wage labor to Anglo employers. During economic expansions, waves of new Mexican immigrants were drawn into the country, further depressing their wages (Camarillo, 1979). Mexican immigrant families often were highly male-dominant: Husbands were supposed to be powerful, respected, and in charge; wives were supposed to submit to their authority (Queen et al., 1985). But the traditional male dominance eroded under the low wages of urban employment and the separation of migrant workers from their families. Today, Mexican American families in the barrios still show the effects of poverty and unemployment. Yet they remain distinctive in other respects, such as their high birthrates (see Chapter 5).

ASIAN IMMIGRANT FAMILIES

The Asian Heritage   Before the middle of the twentieth century, most Asian American families in the United States consisted of immigrants from China and Japan and their descendants. Family systems in East Asia (where China and

mestizo a person whose ancestors include both Spanish settlers and Native Americans

compadrazgo in Mexico, a godparent relationship in which a wealthy or influential person outside the kinship group is asked to become the *compadre*, or godparent, of a newborn child, particularly at its baptism

barrio a segregated Mexican-American neighborhood in a U.S. city

Japan are located) were sharply different from those in the United States and other Western countries, although these differences are currently diminishing (Goode, 1963; Hong, 1999; Queen et al., 1985). In the traditional East Asian family, fathers had more authority over family members than is true in the West. For example, fathers usually controlled who their children would marry and when. In addition, kinship was patrilineal, or traced through the father's line. In China, the ideal was that a man's sons (and eventually his grandsons) would bring their wives into his growing household. Daughters would be sent at marriage to live in their in-laws' households. When parents grew old, sons and their wives were expected to live with them and care for them. In Japan, the oldest son carried the main responsibility for the care of elderly parents. Thus, East Asian cultures placed a greater emphasis on children's loyalty to their parents than Western culture. For a son or daughter, happiness in marriage was less important than fulfilling obligations to parents and other kin.

Asian Immigrants

Chinese immigrants first began to arrive during the California gold rush in the 1850s. After the Civil War, they were hired to build the railroads of the Southwest. Because the vast majority of these immigrant laborers were men, relatively few new families were formed. In fact, about half left wives behind (Glenn, 1983). Many of the men fulfilled the obligations they felt toward kin by sending **remittances,** or cash payments, to family members such as spouses or elderly parents in their country of origin. In California and most other western states, laws prohibited Chinese (and later Japanese) immigrants from marrying white Americans or becoming citizens. In fact, American sentiment against Chinese immigrants was so strong that in 1882 Congress passed the Chinese Exclusion Act, which restricted Chinese immigration until after World War II (Olson, 1979). By the mid-twentieth century, Chinese immigrants could more easily bring over their wives. Many immigrant families started small businesses such as laundries or restaurants in which all family members worked (Glenn, 1983).

remittances cash payments sent by immigrants to family members in their country of origin

In the 1880s, significant numbers of Japanese immigrants began to arrive in Hawaii (which the United States would soon annex) and the mainland United States. The ratio of women to men was more balanced among the Japanese than among Chinese immigrants, so more families were formed. Both Chinese and Japanese families were patrilineal. The father's authority was strong, and ties to extended family members were important. Traditionally, parents or other relatives arranged their children's marriages (Wong, 1988). Since immigrants usually left their extended families behind, they developed other ways of building family-like ties in the United States. For example, people from the same region of China or Japan formed mutual aid societies, and wealthy merchants sometimes played the supervisory roles village elders had in Asia (Olson, 1979).

Like the Chinese, Japanese immigrants faced discrimination. After the war with Japan began in 1941, some Americans warned that Japanese immigrants might be disloyal, even though many had lived in the United States for decades. Bowing to these fears, the government rounded up Japanese immigrants, most of whom lived in California, and sent them to internment camps. Aside from the imprisonment, humiliation, and economic losses the Japanese suffered there, the camps eroded the traditional authority of Japanese parents (Kitano, 1988). They had little to offer children who were exposed to American activities such as dancing to the music of the latest bands. Young Japanese American men could even volunteer to join a much-decorated U.S. Army unit that fought in Europe.

After the war, the autonomy children had experienced in the camps contributed to sharp changes in Japanese American marriage patterns. Whereas the older generation's marriages had been arranged by relatives who stressed obligations to kin and emotional restraint, the younger generation much more often chose their own spouses based on romantic love and companionship (Yanagisako, 1985).

1965 Immigration Act act passed by the U.S. Congress which ended restrictions that had blocked most Asian immigration and substituted an annual quota

Overall, Asian immigration was modest until Congress passed the **1965 Immigration Act,** which ended restrictions that had blocked most Asian immigration and substituted an annual quota of 170,000. Since then, the Asian population of the United States has expanded rapidly. The 2000 Census counted 11.9 million Americans of Asian origin in 2000. (The census, for the first time, allowed individuals in 2000 to list more than one race, and 10.2 million people listed *only* Asian. See Chapter 5, *Families and Public Policy:* How Should Multiracial Families Be Counted?) The two largest groups were Chinese (23 percent) and Filipinos (20 percent). Asian Indians constituted 16 percent and three other groups each constituted 10 percent: Japanese, Korean, and Vietnamese (U.S. Bureau of the Census, 2002c).

bilateral kinship a system in which descent is reckoned through both the mother's and father's lines

Filipino immigration began as a small stream of mostly students after the United States captured the Philippines in the Spanish-American War of 1898. After 1965, many Filipino immigrants were professionals, most notably nurses. Unlike Chinese and Japanese families, Filipino families trace descent through both the father's and mother's line, a system called **bilateral kinship** (the system followed in the United States). Such a system usually provides women more independence than patrilineal kinship, so Filipino American women have been more likely to work outside the home than women in Chinese or Japanese families (Kitano & Daniels, 1988).

Quick Review

- The family lives of groups that emigrated from Africa (through slavery), Mexico, and Asia differed from the family lives of European immigrants.
- The women in all immigrant families were more likely to contribute economically than were middle-class women.
- African American families have maintained stronger ties to extended kin and borne a higher percentage of children outside of marriage than have European American families.
- Most African American families had two parents, even during slavery.
- Early Mexican settlers included a landed elite and a larger population of *mestizos.*
- Mexican families use the tradition of *compadrazgo* to obtain assistance for children.
- Chinese immigration was heavily male at first, and immigrants sent home remittances to family.
- Japanese families were sent to internment camps during World War II.
- Both Chinese and Japanese families were traditionally patrilineal, with arranged marriages.

The Rise of the Private Family: 1900–Present

THE EARLY DECADES

An increase in premarital sex. A drop in the birthrate. A new youth culture rebelling against propriety, dressing outrageously, and indulging in indecent dance steps. And a rapidly rising divorce rate. Sound familiar? No, this is not a description of the present, or even of the 1960s and 1970s. Rather, these were the concerns of American moralists, politicians, and social scientists during the first few decades of the twentieth century. The flourishing new youth culture was exemplified in the 1920s by the "flapper" girls. Independent, often employed outside the home, and brazen enough to bob their hair and wear lipstick and eyeliner in public, the flappers patronized dance halls and movie theaters with their male companions. Historian Stephanie Coontz (2005) notes that interest in and openness about sexuality grew during this period. A good marriage, people increasingly thought, required a good sex life, although the husband's satisfaction still seemed to matter more than the wife's. By the 1920s, birth control pioneers such as Margaret Sanger had opened clinics, and public discussion about ways to prevent births was widespread.

Perhaps the greatest source of concern, the divorce rate had risen to the point where a marriage begun in 1910 had about a 1-in-7 chance of ending in divorce. This may seem like a small risk today, but it represented a substantial increase over the 1-in-12 chance in 1880 or the 1-in-20 chance at the end of the Civil War (Cherlin, 1992). Yet the period from the 1890s through the 1920s was generally one of increasing prosperity—which raises the question of why an increase in divorce would occur. In part, it was made possible by the growing economic independence of women, who were now better educated, had fewer children, had likely worked outside the home before marrying, and therefore had greater potential to find work outside the home if their marriages ended (O'Neill, 1967). But that is not the whole story, for the marriage rate kept rising right along with the divorce rate. What had occurred, in addition, is that both women and men came to expect a greater amount of emotional satisfaction from marriage (May, 1980). More than ever before, they sought happiness, companionship, and romantic love in marriage. If they found their marriages fell short of their expectations, they

In the 1920s, greater numbers of independent young women were employed outside the home.

Families and Public Policy

Divorce Reform: Have We Been Here Before?

At current rates, about one out of two marriages begun in the United States today will end in divorce (Bramlett & Mosher, 2002). As noted, the divorce rate has been increasing since at least the Civil War. The most recent burst occurred between the early 1960s and mid-1970s, during which time the probability that a marriage would end in divorce doubled. Since then, the rate has declined slightly (Cherlin, 1992). Nevertheless, the rise in divorce has alarmed some commentators, who fear that it is undermining the institution of the family. (The effects of divorce will be discussed in detail in Chapter 12.)

Some writers have called for a toughening of divorce laws, which were relaxed in the 1970s and 1980s, when all states enacted "no fault" divorce legislation. Yet this is not the first time a debate has emerged about the consequences of divorce, and restrictive legislation has been proposed. In fact, the divorce debates of the Progressive Era (1890–1930) bear an uncanny resemblance to the current discourse. As in the 1960s and 1970s, a rise

in the divorce rate during that era caused concern. So did a fall in the birthrate among native-born whites. John Watson, a leading psychologist, voiced the fears of many when he predicted that "in fifty years there will be no such thing as marriage" (Mintz & Kellogg, 1988). Arthur Calhoun, the leading historian of the family, acknowledged the sweeping changes, but wrote approvingly that "We are in the midst of a social revolution" which would make a new, more democratic family "inevitable" (Calhoun, 1919).

Divorce had been available in most states since the colonial era but at first on a very restricted basis. Through most of the 1800s, it was stigmatizing and granted only on limited grounds such as adultery. According to a legal historian, "Divorce was not a right, only a remedy for a wrong" (Hartog, 2000). Nevertheless, in the 1890s and 1900s, rising divorce rates led many legislatures, especially in the eastern states, to tighten divorce laws. According to historian Elaine Tyler May, between 1889 and 1906 state legislatures enacted

more than 100 restrictive marriage and divorce laws. For instance, 15 states forbade remarriage until one or two years after a final divorce decree, and 6 eliminated certain grounds for divorce. New York permitted divorce only in the event of adultery, and South Carolina prohibited it altogether (May, 1980).

The Progressive Era was also a time of great and varied action by groups seeking reform in order to increase democracy, governmental efficiency, and the quality of life. So-called social progressives sought improvements in industrial working conditions and in the lives of parents and children (Skocpol, 1992). Many social progressives, including those interested in the family, sought reform through the passage of new laws. For example, an Inter-Church Conference led by Episcopal Bishop William Doane convinced President Theodore Roosevelt to order the Bureau of the Census to carry out a new study on marriage and divorce.

In Roosevelt's message to Congress in 1905, he wrote:

were more likely to ask for a divorce. (See *Families and Public Policy:* Divorce Reform: Have We Been Here Before?) As Coontz (2005) writes, the trend had begun in the latter part of the 1800s:

> *The people who took idealization of love and intimacy to new heights during the nineteenth century did not intend to shake up marriage or unleash a new preoccupation with sexual gratification.... In the long run, however, they weakened it. The focus on romantic love eventually undercut the doctrine of separate spheres for men and women and the ideal of female purity, putting new strains on the institution of marriage.*

The emphasis on love and companionship, and the accompanying strain on marital bonds, spread in the early 1900s.

And so women and men came to see marriage and family as central to their quest for an emotionally satisfying private life. Before the twentieth century, emotional satisfaction had been less important to both husbands and wives, but not

There is widespread conviction that the divorce laws are dangerously lax and indifferently administered in some of the states, resulting in a diminished regard for the sanctity of the marriage relation.[1]

To eliminate overly liberal state laws, Roosevelt called for uniform divorce legislation in all states.

Yet despite all this activity, despite numerous conferences on uniform divorce laws and attempts in Congress to tighten state provisions, little was accomplished, and the divorce rate continued to rise. Why did reformers have so little success? Historians who have studied the era argue that the reformers were fighting against powerful cultural changes in the nature of marriage. Marriage was becoming more of a companionship, more of a relationship among equals. Increasingly, people sought personal satisfaction through marriage.[2] I would add that the rising standard of living in the early decades of the twentieth century allowed people to focus less on food and shelter and more on emotional satisfaction. Because of this new emphasis, people who found their marriages lacking in satisfaction were more likely to consider divorce (see Chapter 12). Moreover, the increasing employment of women decreased their economic dependence on men, making marriage less necessary.

Given the strength of these cultural and economic forces, the social progressives were unable to enact their program of divorce reform. Advances in one state would be stymied by setbacks in others. Resistance to more restrictive divorce legislation remained firm. The failures of the reformers may hold lessons for those who today urge public action to reduce the divorce rate. The same cultural and economic forces have continued to influence marriage and divorce throughout the twentieth century. Indeed, one could argue that they are more powerful now: The quest for personal fulfillment has led to widespread cohabitation outside of marriage; the loosening of cultural constraints has led to a toleration of childbearing outside of marriage; and the economic independence of women has grown as a majority of wives now work outside the home. A look backward at the entire century, and particularly at the Progressive Era, suggests that today's divorce reformers have few promising strategies to follow. Lowering the divorce rate through political action and moral suasion is a very difficult task.

Ask Yourself

1. Think back over the last two or three generations in your family. Has the divorce rate increased from one generation to the next? What about marital happiness and personal fulfillment—does it seem to have increased?

2. Should the law be changed so it is more difficult to obtain a divorce? From the family's point of view, what might be the advantages and disadvantages of doing so?

[1]Quoted in O'Neill (1967).
[2]Mintz and Kellogg, May, and O'Neill all present arguments along these lines.

www.mhhe.com/cherlin5

because they were ignorant of the concept—no Ariès-like claim is made here that people of the twentieth century discovered happiness. Rather, before the twentieth century the standard of living had been so low that most people needed to concentrate on keeping themselves clothed, housed, and fed. Before 1900, pursuing personal pleasure was a luxury few could indulge in. Most were too busy just trying to get by.

Even after 1900, large segments of the American population—immigrants and racial and ethnic minorities—had little time to invest in private life. My grandparents immigrated from Eastern Europe just after the turn of the century, started a grocery store, and raised 10 children. Had I been around to ask them whether their marriage was satisfying, they would have said of course—they were raising a big family. They would not have answered in terms of companionship, romance, sexual pleasure, excitement, or personal growth. Yet these were the ways in which more and more Americans came to define a successful marriage in the twentieth century.

Still, Americans (and the citizens of other Western nations) were gradually enlarging the scope of the *private family*. They were defining marital success in emotional terms, not material terms, and were beginning to derive their greatest satisfaction not from the roles they played (breadwinner, homemaker, father, mother) but from the quality of the relationships they had with their spouses and children. This process had certainly begun long ago among the more prosperous classes, and it continued throughout the twentieth century. But in some eras its ascendancy was more noticeable than in others, and the first few decades of the twentieth century were such an era.

As these developments were occurring, the family was becoming less of a dominant force in people's lives. The many public goods the colonial family had provided gradually diminished: Compulsory schooling replaced education at home; hospitals replaced sickbeds; department stores replaced home crafts; and so forth. As marriage became less necessary economically and materially, it was redefined as a means of gaining emotional satisfaction. A well-known text on the family described this transformation as a shift "from institution to companionship" (Burgess & Locke, 1945). (See Chapter 7.) In this process, marriage became more fragile, for the bonds of sentiment were weaker than the ties forged by working a family farm or the unchallenged authority of the patriarch. Soon, an institution that had been designed to enhance survival and security began to creak under the weight of expectations that it provide so much emotional satisfaction. One result was a more or less continuous increase in the divorce rate, which reached a high plateau about 1980.

Privacy also increased after 1900. Two demographic trends contributed to this increase. First, the birthrate declined, which meant, among other things, fewer persons per room. Second, adult life expectancy increased due to advances in medicine and a rising standard of living. As a result of these trends, parents were younger when they finished the child rearing stage of life, and they lived longer after their last child left home. Consequently, a new stage of family life, the "empty nest" phase, became common. Before the twentieth century, far fewer married couples ever witnessed the departure of all their children (Cherlin & Furstenberg, 1992).

Greater prosperity also meant that more apartments were built, and more people could afford to live on their own. And the rise in individualism probably made more unmarried people *wish* to live on their own. Consequently, boarding and lodging went from commonplace to rarity during the first half of the century (Laslett, 1973). In 1950, 9 percent of all households contained one person; by 1970 the figure was 17 percent; and by 2000 it was 26 percent (Kobrin, 1976; U.S. Bureau of the Census, 2001d). Even so, during the first few decades of the century, about two-thirds of young women and perhaps 40 percent of young men did not leave home until they married. If they did, it was often because their parents lived in rural areas, where young adults couldn't find jobs. Later, in the 1940s and 1950s, the age at which young adults left home fell sharply, both because of earlier marriage and because many young men left home to join the military during World War II and the Korean War (Goldscheider & Goldscheider, 1994).

The first few decades of the twentieth century, then, were an important time of change in the American family. The basis for marriage moved away from an economic partnership and toward emotional satisfaction and companionship. Men and women became more economically independent of each other. As a result of these developments, the bonds of marriage became weaker, and divorce became more common. In addition, prosperity, lower birthrates, and longer life expectancy accelerated the trend toward privacy, as exemplified by child-free older couples and people living alone.

THE DEPRESSION GENERATION

The prosperity of the early decades of the century was interrupted by the Great Depression, which began in 1929 and continued until the late 1930s. In addition to its severe effects on family finances, the Depression also undermined the authority and prestige of the father. If he lost his job, his family might view him as having failed in his role as breadwinner. If his wife or his children were forced to find jobs, as many were, their labor was a constant reminder of his inability to fulfill their expectations. We might expect that the divorce rate would have risen as a result of these difficulties, but instead it fell temporarily. Couples stayed together not because they were happier—many were less happy—but because they couldn't afford to get a divorce and live in two households. Years later, after the worst of the Depression was over, the divorce rate surged among couples who had married at the start of the Depression, had developed serious problems, but hadn't been able to separate until it was over (Cherlin, 1992).

These economic hardships also forced many young adults to postpone marriage and childbearing. The Depression was so long and so severe that some couples never had the opportunity to have children. As a result, lifetime childlessness was more common among women who reached their peak childbearing years in the 1930s than in any other generation of women in the twentieth century: About one in five never had a child (Rindfuss, Morgan, & Swicegood, 1988). In contrast, only about 1 in 10 of the women who reached their peak reproductive years during the 1950s baby boom never had a child.

As fathers and mothers struggled to make a living, their children helped out. Teenage boys took whatever jobs they could find; teenage girls took over more of the household work for mothers who were forced to work outside the home.

The hardships of the Great Depression strained many families in the 1930s. The family of farm laborer William Jones was photographed at "home"—blankets thrown over fence posts and containers—along a rural Missouri highway.

The result was what Glen Elder, Jr., called "the downward extension of adultlike experience": Girls took on the role of homemaker; boys took on the role of bread-winner. Elder (1974) examined the records of a group of children who were first observed in 1932, at age 11, and then followed through adulthood. He found that when they reached adulthood, the men and women in the group who came from economically deprived families valued marriage and family life more highly than those whose families hadn't experienced hardship. Women from deprived fami-lies married at younger ages than other women. Perhaps the difficulties their fami-lies had faced when they were adolescents made the deprived group eager for a secure marriage, or perhaps they viewed families as an important resource in hard times. In any event, when they reached adulthood, these young men and women turned inward to build their own family lives.

Quick Review

- In the twentieth century, people increasingly viewed family life through the perspective I have called the *private family*.
  - People began to derive their greatest pleasure from the quality of their personal relationships.
  - People increasingly viewed marriage primarily as a means of obtaining emotional satisfaction.
  - Divorce became more common.
  - Privacy itself increased as standards of living rose, birthrates dropped, and life expectancy rose.
- The hardship of the Great Depression forced a generation to alter their family lives by, for example, delaying or forgoing marriage and childbearing.

THE 1950S

In fact, when the young adults of the Depression generation began to marry and have children after World War II, they created the most unusual and distinctive fam-ily patterns of the century. They married younger and had more children than any other twentieth-century generation. Figure 2.1 shows the percentage of 20- to 24-year-old men and women who had never been married, from 1890 to 2004. This is the age group that is most sensitive to variations in age at marriage. Note the per-centage is highest at the beginning and end of this chart, indicating that young men and women were most likely to be single (and therefore to marry at an older age) in the late 1800s and the current era. The percentage who had never been married declined slowly during the first half of the twentieth century and then plunged to its lowest point during the 1950s. After 1960, it rose sharply especially for women, who by the turn of the century were marrying later than at any time in the previous 100 years.

baby boom the large number of people born during the late 1940s and 1950s

The years after World War II were also the time of the great **baby boom**. Cou-ples not only married at younger ages but also had children faster—and had more of them—than their parents' generation or, as statistics would later show, than even their children's generation. Indeed, the late 1940s through the 1950s was the only period in the past 150 years during which the American birthrate rose substantially. It spiked dramatically just after the war, as couples had babies they had postponed

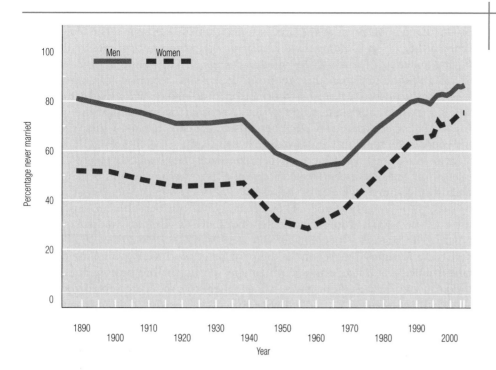

FIGURE 2.1
Percentage never married among men and women aged 20 to 24, 1890 to 2004. (*Sources:* for 1890–1960, *U.S. Bureau of the Census, 1995, Historical Statistics of the United States, Colonial Times to 1970,* pp. 20–21; for 1970–2002, *U.S. Bureau of the Census, Current Population Reports,* Series P20, various issues.)

having during the war. After a few years it dropped, but then began to climb again, peaking in 1957. Women who married during the 1950s had an average of slightly more than three children, the highest fertility rate of the century (Evans, 1986).

Although the causes of the baby boom are not fully clear, a strong post–World War II economy and a renewed cultural emphasis on marriage and children were certainly contributing factors. One explanation focuses on the unique circumstances of the young adults who married during the 1950s. Since most of them were born during the Depression, when birthrates were low, they constituted a relatively small **birth cohort**, as demographers call all the people born during a given year or period of years. After the bad luck of growing up during the Depression and the war, they had the good fortune to reach adulthood just as the economy was growing rapidly. The Allied victory in World War II had left the United States with the strongest economy in the world. Employers needed more workers, but the small size of the cohort meant there were fewer workers to hire (especially given the widespread preference during the 1950s that married women forgo work outside the home). In this tight labor market wages rose for young men, allowing them to support larger families.[6]

This explanation, however, is incomplete. Birthrates rose not only among newlyweds in their early twenties but also among women in their thirties who had been married for years (Rindfuss et al., 1988). These older women belonged to larger cohorts, so the small-cohort-size theory can't account for their behavior. Rather, the pervasiveness of the rise in births suggests that the preferred family size shifted during the baby boom. The cultural emphasis on getting married and having children seems to have been greater than was the case before or since— perhaps as a result of the trauma of the Depression and the war. The shift had a broad effect on women and men in their twenties, thirties, and even early forties.

birth cohort all people born during a given year or period of years

[6] The relative-cohort-size theory was expounded by Easterlin (1980).

Together, the strong economy and the marriage-and-childbearing orientation produced the high point of the breadwinner–homemaker family. The federal government helped by granting low-interest mortgages to armed forces veterans, allowing millions of families to purchase single-family homes in the growing suburbs. For the first time, the "American dream" of marriage, children, and a single-family home was within reach of not only the middle class, but many in the working class as well (Laslett, 1973). Yet some homemakers missed the world of paid work and school they had left behind and felt constrained by their economic dependence on their husbands (Weiss, 2000).

In any case, the breadwinner–homemaker family faded quickly. Figure 2.2, compiled from census data by Donald Hernandez, shows the rise and decline of the breadwinner-homemaker family from 1790 to 1989, from the perspective of children aged 0–17. As the graph makes clear, the breadwinner–homemaker family is not the "traditional" American family. The figure divides all children into four groups. The first is the percentage who were living with neither parent—a small number at all times. The second is the percentage who were living in two-parent farm families. As noted earlier, farm families do not fit the breadwinner-homemaker model, because farm wives typically help to produce essential goods and services by tending livestock, growing vegetables, making clothing, harvesting, and so forth. Note that living on a farm was the experience of a majority of children until the mid-1800s.

The third group is the percentage of children living in breadwinner-homemaker families, defined there as two-parent, single-earner families not living on farms. This percentage was small early in the nation's history, but began to rise sharply in the mid-1800s, reaching a temporary peak in 1930. It fell briefly during the Depression, then peaked again in 1960. Data show that this family form was dominant only in the first half of the twentieth century, reaching its zenith during the 1950s. After 1960, as the figure shows, its dominance ended.

FIGURE 2.2
Percentage of children aged 0–17 living in each of four types of families, 1790–1989. (*Source:* Donald J. Hernandez, *America's Children: Resources from Family, Government, and the Economy,* New York: Russell Sage Foundation, 1993.)

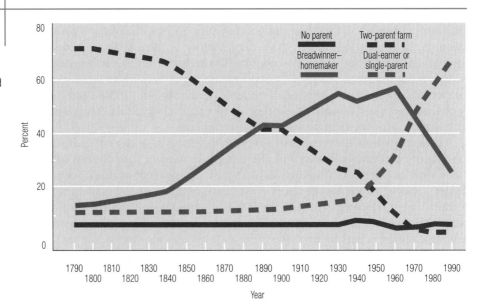

The fourth group is nonfarm families that do not fit the breadwinner–home-maker mold, either because both parents work or because only one parent is present in the home. Only about 10 percent of children lived in these kinds of families before 1900, but after 1940 the percentage rose dramatically. By 1989, the last year shown in the chart, these families were by far the largest group, greatly exceeding the declining breadwinner–homemaker group. The reasons for the rise in single-parent and dual-earner families, and the consequences of this rise, will be discussed extensively in later chapters. Still, the breadwinner–homemaker family has not disappeared; in 2002, about one-fifth of all children lived in such a family (U.S. Bureau of the Census, 2003b).

Moreover, overlooked during the 1950s because of all the attention given to the baby boom was a countercurrent that would loom large later in the century. Increasingly, homemakers went back to work outside the home after their children were of school age. They took jobs that had been typed as women's work—jobs that were relatively low paying, but still required some education, such as secretary, nurse, or salesclerk. And some urged their daughters to postpone marriage in order to pursue higher education and professional careers (Weiss, 2000).

THE 1960S AND BEYOND

Just as social commentators confidently announced a return to large families, the roller-coaster car reached the top of its track and hurtled downward. The birthrate plunged from the heights of the baby boom to an all-time low in the 1970s, from which it has risen only slightly since then. Women who were in their childbearing years in the 1970s and 1980s had an average of only about 2.0 children (Evans, 1986). The baby boom had begotten the baby bust. In addition, young women and men were marrying at later and later ages; between the mid-1950s and 2000, the age at which half of all first marriages occur increased by about five years for men and women (U.S. Bureau of the Census, 2005n). So the percentage of young adults who had never married, as Figure 2.1 shows, surpassed the levels of the early twentieth century. One might expect that because they were marrying later, young adults would also have left home later. Yet the average age of leaving home has not increased much since the 1970s. The reason is that more and more young adults are now leaving home not to marry or even to attend college, but rather to live independently—to get a job, find an apartment, and be on their own (Goldscheider & Goldscheider, 1994).

Moreover, the divorce rate doubled between the early 1960s and the late 1970s and has declined just slightly since then. At current rates, about one in two marriages will end in divorce (Bramlett & Mosher, 2002). As at the beginning of the twentieth century, there is great concern about the consequences of this high divorce rate. At the beginning of the 1900s, optimists could at least argue that the marriage rate was increasing right along with the divorce rate; but that was not the case during the 1960s and 1970s. Young adults postponed marrying, and divorced adults postponed remarrying, although **cohabitation**—the sharing of a household by unmarried persons in a sexual relationship—accounted for some of that postponement (Bumpass, Sweet, & Cherlin, 1991).

cohabitation the sharing of a household by unmarried persons who have a sexual relationship

There was one important continuity with the 1950s: Married women continued to work outside the home in ever larger numbers. Even women with pre-school-aged children joined the workforce in large numbers. By 2004, about three-fourths of all married women with school-aged children and about two-thirds of married women with pre-school-aged children were working outside the home (U.S. Bureau of the Census, 2005l). Whereas in the 1950s, married women tended to drop out of the paid workforce when they were raising small children, today married women are much more likely to remain at their jobs throughout the child rearing years. This change in women's work lives has had a powerful effect on the family.

The most recent period in the history of the family—from about 1960 to the present—will be the main subject matter of this book. As a prelude to understanding the present, future chapters will examine in detail the recent history of marriage, childbearing, divorce, cohabitation, and women's labor force participation in the United States and elsewhere in the Western nations. These discussions will also be informed by studies of non-Western countries, which can deepen our understanding of the nature of contemporary family patterns.

Quick Review

- The 1950s produced the most distinctive family patterns of the twentieth century, notably early marriage and larger numbers of children.
- Rising wages and a cultural shift toward home and family may have caused the 1950s baby boom.
- Family trends reversed in the 1960: Young adults married later, birthrates fell, divorce rates rose.
- In addition, married women with young children began to enter the workforce in large numbers in the 1960s.

The Changing Life Course

We have seen that family and personal life changed greatly during the twentieth century. One way to understand these changes is to compare the experiences of groups of individuals who were born in different time periods. This approach is known as the **life-course perspective:** the study of changes in individuals' lives over time and how those changes are related to historical events.

life-course perspective
the study of changes in individuals' lives over time, and how those changes are related to historical events

SOCIAL CHANGE IN THE TWENTIETH CENTURY

Consider Figure 2.3. In the middle of the figure is a time line for the twentieth century, divided into 10-year intervals. The top half shows the time lines for three different birth cohorts born 30 years apart. The first group was born in 1920; I have labeled them the "depression cohort" because they were nine years old when the Great Depression began in 1929. The second group, "the baby boom cohort," was born in 1950, at the start of the baby boom. The third group, born in 1980, is more difficult to label. Some social commentators have noted that people born in the 1980s and 1990s are very roughly the tenth generation of Americans born since the country was founded. I will call the third group the "tenth generation cohort." The bottom half of Figure 2.3 shows time lines for the occurrence of major historical events and trends that have changed family and personal life. For example, the Great Depression lasted from 1929 until about 1940, and the baby boom occurred from the late 1940s to the early 1960s.

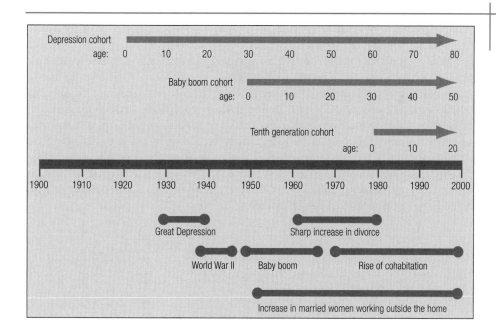

FIGURE 2.3
A life-course perspective on social change in the twentieth century.

One can think of the top and bottom halves of Figure 2.3 as showing two kinds of time. The top half displays what we might call "individual time": the passing of time in people's lives as they age. This is the usual way we think of time. The bottom half displays what might be called "historical time": the beginning and ending of key events and social trends that have influenced family life during the century. The figure's usefulness is that it allows a comparison of individual time and historical time; or put another way, it places the course of an individual's life in historical context.

For example, the figure shows that in 1950, as the baby boom started, members of the depression cohort were still in their childbearing years; therefore, they became the parents of the baby boomers. The figure also shows that by the time the baby boom cohort reached age 30 in 1980, a sharp rise in divorce had occurred. As a result, the baby boomers have had a much higher rate of divorce than the depression cohort. In addition, the figure shows that the tenth generation cohort is the first to have lived their early childhood years after the sharp rise in divorce. That is why far more tenth generation cohort members have experienced the breakup of their parents' marriages than have previous cohorts.

This way of looking at changes in family and personal life is an example of the life-course perspective. Rather than study families as an undifferentiated group, sociologists and historians who use this perspective tend to study the lives of individuals within families. They examine how historical developments affect the course of these individuals' personal and family lives. Elder's work on the depression cohort (defined in his case as people born in 1921) is probably the most influential study of this genre (Elder, 1974). The life-course perspective is particularly attractive to scholars who wish to study social change over time. And as this chapter has made clear, the twentieth century was a time of great change in the kinds of family lives individuals led.

THE EMERGENCE OF EARLY ADULTHOOD

Recently, sociologists have used the life-course perspective to suggest the emergence of a new stage of life: **early adulthood** (Settersten, Furstenberg, & Rumbaut, 2005). I will define it as the period between the mid-teens and about age 30 when individuals finish their education, enter the labor force, and begin their own families. (The **labor force** is defined as all people who are working for pay or who are looking for paid work.) It is the stage of life when one makes the transition from adolescence (itself only a century old, as we will see in Chapter 7) to adulthood. As I noted earlier in this chapter, most young people made the transition to adulthood quickly in the mid-twentieth century, marrying at historically young ages and having children soon afterwards. Today, this transition has become longer and more varied and complex.

The Role of Education   The main factor in the lengthening of early adulthood is education. Changes in the labor force have put a premium on schooling: Employment opportunities have improved much more for the college-educated than for those without a college degree. Consequently, early adults are increasingly pursuing higher education. Some are enrolling in graduate and professional schools that promise great rewards but take additional years of study. Others are completing college, even if that means years of part-time study. In the early 1990s, it was unusual for a twenty-five-year-old to still be in school; but today perhaps one out of six whites and one out of eight blacks of that age are enrolled at least part-time (Fussell & Furstenberg, 2005). Early adults who are still in school are more likely to defer decisions about careers and families. Given the increasing acceptance of cohabitation, they may live with a partner until they finish their educations rather than marry. Or they may marry but postpone having children. Although they may be working for pay to help defray the costs of their education, they delay starting on a career ladder until after they have the appropriate degree in hand.

Constrained Opportunities   Early adults with more limited education take other, usually shorter, paths to reach the traditional markers of adulthood. Most of those who don't graduate from high school, or who graduate but don't go on to college, enter the job market well before their college-bound peers. Some take college courses but don't achieve a bachelor's degree. Their opportunities are more constrained than were the opportunities of similarity educated individuals a half-century ago (Hill & Yeung, 1999). As I will explain in Chapter 4, the movement of manufacturing jobs overseas and the growth of automation have reduced the demand for non-college-educated workers. The kinds of decent-paying blue-collar factory jobs that sustained a generation of workers and their families a half-century ago are in short supply. Sociologists argue that non-college-educated entrants into the labor force often must take "stopgap jobs"—short-term, often part-time jobs such as working at a fast-food restaurant—that give them a modest income for a short time but don't help to develop a career (Oppenheimer, Kalmijn & Lim, 1997).

Consequently, some non-college-educated adults are postponing marriage not because they are still studying but rather because they (or their prospective marriage partners) don't think their economic prospects are good enough to support a marriage. But forgoing marriage no longer means one must forgo having children because childbearing outside of marriage has become more acceptable. So some early adults father, or give birth to, children without marrying. These

early adulthood period between mid-teens and about age 30 when individuals finish their education, enter the labor force, and begin their own families

labor force all people who are working for pay or who are looking for paid work

unmarried mothers and fathers form a group one study labels "parents without careers" (Osgood, Ruth, Eccles, Jacobs, & Barber, 2005). In 2000, 5 percent of white 25-year-olds and 28 percent of black 25-year-olds were unmarried parents. They have made more progress toward traditional markers of adulthood than their childless contemporaries still in school because they have had children and are often working. But their work lives are erratic and usually consist of a series of low- and moderate-paying jobs rather than a career. And they may not marry for a long time, if ever.

Many early adults are living independently of their parents, a situation we will examine more closely in Chapter 7. But the probability that an independent early adult will move back in with his or her parents—if, for example, he or she loses a job or breaks up with a partner—has increased since the mid-twentieth century (Goldscheider, 1997). This trend toward returning to the nest is another reason why early adults often achieve lasting independence—and full adulthood—in fits and starts over a longer period of time. Nevertheless, by age 30 the differences between the college-educated and the less-educated in marriage, parenthood, and employment are smaller. Most have married, most are working, and a majority have children. What education does is make a difference in how they get there—how they experience early adulthood.

Declining Parental Control   A century ago, when most people lived with their parents until they married, parents had more control over their young adult children. Today, when most early adults live separately, parents have less control. As a result, parents have less influence over whom their children marry or live with. For example, Rosenfeld and Kim (2005) hypothesized that early adults who have moved away from their parents will have marriages and cohabiting unions that are less conventional because their parents aren't around to object. They examined records for 20- to 29-year-olds from the U.S. Census, which asks people not only for their current state of residence but also for the state where they were born. They found that the more unconventional the marital or cohabiting union that early adults were in, the more likely they were to have moved away from the state where they were born. People who were cohabiting were a bit more likely to have moved away than people who were married. People who were in interracial unions, married or cohabiting, were more likely to have moved away than people in same-race unions; people in same-sex unions were even more likely to have moved away; and those in interracial same-sex unions most likely of all to have moved away.

EARLY ADULTHOOD AND THE LIFE-COURSE PERSPECTIVE

The growing literature on early adulthood is a good example of the life-course perspective for several reasons. It focuses on a key transition in the lives of individuals—in this case the lengthening period from adolescence to adulthood. It demonstrates the substantial social changes that have occurred in this stage of life. And importantly, it places that transition in historical perspective by showing the influences of the decline in manufacturing jobs, the growing employment opportunities for the well-educated, and the greater acceptance of cohabitation and childbearing outside of marriage. As they make the transition today, early adults steer a course in a different sea than was sailed in the past. Many reach their destinations later, and by different routes, than their parents and grandparents.

Quick Review

- The life-course perspective seeks to study the course of individual lives in historical context.
- Early adulthood is the term for an emerging life stage between adolescence and adulthood.
- The pursuit of higher education is the main factor lengthening early adulthood.
- Early adults without college degrees start the transition to full adulthood sooner.

WHAT HISTORY TELLS US

The history of the family tells us that Americans come from regions of the world that have different family traditions. To some extent, the American mixing bowl blends those traditions together and reduces the differences. The result is that the family lives of today's ethnic and racial groups have more in common than not. Still, the historical record can help us understand some of the variation we see today.

Americans of European ancestry hail from a system that has emphasized the conjugal unit of the married couple and children more than have family systems in other regions of the world. In the nineteenth and early twentieth centuries, European-American conjugal families developed a sharp division of labor between the husband, who worked outside the home, and the wife, who by and large worked inside the home. That sharp division, however, broke down in the last half of the twentieth century as more married women entered the workforce. And during the twentieth century, Americans placed increasing weight on personal satisfaction as the standard people should use in judging the quality of their relationships. European-American family traditions are important because they have been the basis for American law and custom. For example, American law gives parents nearly exclusive rights over children and gives far less authority to grandparents or other kin. (See Chapter 9, *Families and Public Policy:* Elián, the Troxels, and Parents' Rights.)

The family systems of American Indians and of Americans from other regions (such as Latin America, Asia, and Africa) have traditionally placed more emphasis on kin beyond the conjugal family. Sometimes these family systems consisted of tightly organized lineages. Think of the matrilineal tribes of the Hopi. At other times and places, they consisted of extended families in which grandparents, uncles, aunts, and others from both sides of a person's family might contribute to her or his well-being and even share a home. And as the Mexican tradition of *compadrazgo* showed, sometimes individuals without any ties of blood or marriage were recruited into a person's kin network.

Marriage was still central to most of these systems, although less so in Africa. But married couples were embedded in larger family structures that could provide assistance and support. This tradition of support is important because marriage declined among all American racial and ethnic groups during the last half of the twentieth century. The weakening of marriage left European-American families in a particularly vulnerable position because they had less of a tradition of extended family support to fall back on. The story of recent changes in marriage and family life, and their impact on Americans with different heritages, will be told in subsequent chapters.

Looking Back

1. **What functions have families traditionally performed?** Family and kinship emerged as ways of ensuring the survival of human groups, which were organized as bands of hunter-gatherers until about 10,000 years ago. Until the past 250 years or so, most families performed three basic activities: production, reproduction, and consumption. Most American Indian tribes were organized into lineages and clans that provided the basis for social organization and governing. Colonial American families performed functions such as education that are now performed by schools and other institutions. These kinds of families can be said to follow the familial mode of production. The colonial American family performed many activities that are now done mainly outside the family: educating children, providing vocational training, treating the seriously ill, and so forth.

2. **How did American families change after the United States was founded?** Between 1776 and about 1830, a new kind of family emerged among the white middle class in the United States, one in which marriage was based on affection rather than authority and custom. Over time, the primary role of women in these families became the care of children and the maintenance of the home. Children came to be seen as needing continual affection and guidance, which mothers were thought to be better at providing than fathers. As families became more centered on children, the number of children they raised declined. At the same time, a movement toward greater individualism weakened parents' influence over their children's marriage decisions and family lives. Working-class families, because of difficult economic circumstances, did not change as much.

3. **How have the family histories of major ethnic and racial groups differed?** Before the Civil War, African slaves married and lived together for life, wherever possible, and knew and kept track of other kin. After the Civil War, discrimination shaped their family lives. For example, out of economic necessity, rural black wives worked in the fields, and urban black wives worked for wages outside the home, more than white wives did. As for Mexican Americans, after U.S. troops and immigrants seized their land, they became more of a working-class community, increasingly confined to *barrios*. Over time, more and more women headed households, in part because their husbands often worked as migratory farm workers. Chinese and Japanese families also faced discrimination.

Traditionally patrilineal, their authority over their children has declined over the generations. Filipinos, the second largest Asian immigrant group in the United States today, are descended mostly from people who immigrated in the twentieth century. Filipinos have a bilateral kinship structure more similar to the kinship system of Europeans.

4. **How did the emotional character of the American family change during the early twentieth century?** During the early decades of the twentieth century, rising standards of living allowed for greater attention to an emotionally satisfying private life. As the search for emotional satisfaction through family life became an important goal, the private family emerged. Eventually, the success of marriage came to be defined more in emotional terms than in material terms. People experienced more privacy in their personal lives through the increasingly common empty-nest phase of marriage and the rise in the number of individuals living alone.

5. **What important changes occurred in marriage and childbearing in the last half of twentieth century?** In the 1950s, young adults married at earlier ages and the birthrate rose to a twentieth-century high. The baby boom was caused in part by the small cohort size and good economic fortune of the cohort that reached adulthood in the 1950s. In addition, a greater cultural emphasis on marriage and childbearing seems to have been present. The 1950s was the high point of the breadwinner–homemaker family, which was dominant only during the first half of the twentieth century. During the 1960s and 1970s, the trends in marriages, divorces, and births all reversed: Age at marriage increased sharply, the divorce rate doubled, and the birthrate reached its lowest level. Moreover, married women were increasingly likely to work outside the home even when their children were young.

6. **How does the life-course perspective help us to understand social change?** Sociologists examine how the course of individuals' lives is affected by historical events such as the Great Depression of the 1930s or the large rise in divorce rates in the 1960s and 1970s. Because young adults today have better job opportunities if they obtain a college degree, many are postponing marriage and childbearing until they finish their studies. Life-course scholars now use the term "early adulthood" for this emerging life stage.

Go to the Online Learning Center at www.mhhe.com/cherlin5
to test your knowledge of the chapter concepts and key terms.

Study Questions

1. How did belonging to a lineage help a family in a tribal, agricultural society?
2. What is the key difference between the familial and labor market modes of production?
3. What did the colonial family do that modern families do not? What do modern families do that the colonial family did not?
4. How did marriage change during the late 1700s and early 1800s?
5. What were the costs and benefits to women of their restriction to "women's sphere"?

6. How did the lives of working-class and minority-group wives differ from those of middle-class, white wives?
7. In what ways did the scope of the "private family" increase after 1900?
8. In what ways was family life in the 1950s distinctive compared to that earlier or later in the century?
9. What does it mean to take a "life-course perspective" on the study of social change?
10. Why is the concept of "early adulthood" emerging now rather than 50 or 100 years ago?

Key Terms

1965 Immigration Act   58
American Indian   43
baby boom   64
barrio   56
bilateral kinship   58
birth cohort   65
cohabitation   67
compadrazgo   56
conjugal family   39

early adulthood   70
extended family   39
familial mode of
  production   42
hunter-gatherers   38
labor-force   70
labor market mode of
  production   42
life-course perspective   68

lineage   38
matrilineage   38
mestizo   56
patrilineage   38
polyandry   40
polygyny   40
remittances   57

Thinking about Families

The Public Family	The Private Family
Why were the American family's public responsibilities much broader in the colonial period than is the case today?	Why are emotional satisfaction, intimacy, and romantic love more important in American family life today than they were 100 years ago?

Families on the Internet   www.mhhe.com/cherlin5

Note: While all the URLs listed were current as of the printing of this book, these sites often change. Please check our Web site (http://www.mhhe.com/cherlin5) for updates.

Although it's the most modern of media, the Internet is also a great resource for historians. In fact, it is transforming historical research by providing access to millions of sources. For example, the Library of Congress maintains the Web site, "American Memory" (http://lcweb2.loc.gov/). It contains searchable links to more than 9 million digital items—photos, pamphlets, films, etc.—from over 100 collections. A search on "marriage" returned 1,734 items such as a 1923 letter from anthropologist Margaret Mead to her grandmother explaining why she intended to retain her maiden name after marrying.

"History Matters" (http://americanhistory.about.com) is a Web site maintained for high school and college students too. Clicking on "eras of American history" and then "Great Depression photos" returns harrowing photographs of families enduring the hardships of the Depression.

The University of Rochester has placed online several monthly issues of *Godey's Lady's Book* from 1850, one of the most popular magazines of the nineteenth century. You can view articles, poems, and engravings (www.history.rochester.edu/godeys). Go to the February 1850 issue and read "The Elopement," a story about a young woman whose father saves her from a tragic elopement at the last minute. What is the message to young women about obeying family versus their own hearts when choosing a husband?

Part Two

Gender, Class, and Race-Ethnicity

Families are affected by the larger social structures in which they are embedded. Three main axes of social stratification are gender, class, and race-ethnicity. How gender is structured greatly affects the ways that men and women relate to each other in families. Social class differences influence the ways that family life is organized. Racial and ethnic groups also differ in their family lives. Moreover, gender, class, and race-ethnicity are linked because all three are structures in which a more powerful group (men, the wealthier classes, whites) dominate the less powerful; and all three can affect a family simultaneously. Consequently, the content of the next three chapters should be seen as overlapping and interlocking, even though for educational purposes it is useful to have one chapter focus on each of the these core constructs of sociology. • **Chapter 3** examines the construction and maintenance of gender differences, a core source of differentiation in family life. It presents several different approaches to understanding gender. • **Chapter 4** explores differences in family life among social classes. It includes an examination of how trends in the economy have affected families. • **Chapter 5** considers the consequences for families of the divisions in society along racial-ethnic lines. The distinctive family patterns of African Americans are discussed. The chapter also examines commonly used categories such as "Hispanic" and "Asian," which include groups that vary greatly in their family patterns.

Gender and Families

Looking Forward

1. How might fetal development affect the behavior of women and men?

2. How do sociologists distinguish between the concepts of "sex" and "gender"?

3. How do children learn the gender roles of women and men?

4. How does everyday life reinforce gender differences?

5. Are gender differences built into the structure of society?

6. What have been the contributions of gender studies to our understanding of the family?

The Berdache

berdache in Native American societies, a man or woman who dressed like, performed the duties of, and behaved like a member of the opposite sex

In 1841, the American traveler and artist George Catlin published his monumental *Manners, Customs, and Conditions of the North American Indians*. The result of his eight years of traveling among Native Americans in the West, it included about 300 engravings. One of them, entitled "Dance to the Berdache," is shown on page 81. It depicts warriors of the Sauk and Fox Indians dancing around a man wearing women's clothing. "For the extraordinary privileges he is known to possess," wrote Catlin of the man, "he is . . . looked upon as medicine and sacred, and a feast is given to him annually." Men like him, who dressed like women, performed women's occupations, and behaved like women, were called **berdaches** by French colonists. They existed in more than 100 Native American cultures (Callendar & Kochems, 1983).[1] In a smaller number of these cultures, female berdaches, who dressed and worked like men, were also found.

Most individuals became berdaches in one of two ways. First, some children displayed what their parents thought were berdache-like characteristics. In some of the Native American cultures, parents might develop a male child as a berdache if he showed "a gentle, androgynous [having characteristics of both sexes] nature" and showed great interest in the work of the other sex (Williams, 1986). Second, some men and women experienced spiritual visions at adolescence or even later that they took as signs to become berdaches. These visions usually involved some supernatural intervention, such as instructions from the female moon deity. Berdaches were generally accepted members of adult society; anthropologists report that attitudes toward them "varied from awe and reverence through indifference to scorn and contempt" (Callendar & Kochems, 1983). In many cultures they were credited with supernatural powers and exceptional skill at carrying out the other sex's work. The dance at the annual feast that Catlin sketched indicated that the Sauk and Fox respected the powers of the berdache. As neither ordinary men nor ordinary women, berdaches could undertake special tasks that women and men could not perform as easily, such as negotiating a marriage bargain between a woman's family and a man's family or settling a dispute between a man and a woman.

---

[1] According to a commentary by Sue-Ellen Jacobs appended to this article, the word *berdache* came from the Arabic *bardaj,* which in turn came from the Persian *bardah,* meaning "kept boy" or "male prostitute." This term represented the colonists' preconceptions and was inappropriate; nevertheless, it became common usage.

George Catlin's "Dance to the Berdache," from Catlin's *Manners, Customs, and Conditions of the North American Indians,* 1841. Original sketch at the National Museum of American Art, Smithsonian Institution, Washington, DC.

In many cultures, a berdache could marry a person of the same sex who was not a berdache. Male berdaches typically engaged in homosexual intercourse, while the sexual relations of married female berdaches were lesbian. But many berdaches also had heterosexual relations; the Navaho, for example, permitted male berdaches any form of sexual intercourse with either sex (Callendar & Kochems, 1983). Moreover, a male berdache could renounce his role and return to being an ordinary male. By some accounts, non-berdache males could have sex with a berdache without being considered primarily homosexual.[2]

Female berdaches, who were less common, were found in Native American cultures in which relationships between men and women were relatively egalitarian and in which women owned and distributed the goods they produced. But in cultures with strong lineages, they were very rare. For instance, in matrilineal cultures, the children of a man's sister remained in his lineage under his control. Under these circumstances, females of reproductive age were too valuable to the men of the lineage to be allowed to take on the berdache role. But in less hierarchical cultures, some women could take on a male role without threatening the male social order (Blackwood, 1984). Put simply, female berdaches were more likely to be found in societies in which men had less control over women.

As the influence of European culture on Native Americans grew during the nineteenth century, the number of berdaches declined rapidly; by the end of the century there were very few. Nevertheless, the story of the berdaches can help to answer some important questions that will be addressed in this chapter.

1. *What is the difference between sex and gender?* The social situation of the berdaches illustrates the distinction sociologists make between sex and gender. In most sociological writing, **sex** refers to the biological characteristics

sex the biological characteristics that distinguish men and women

[2] See the interpretation in Williams (1986).

that distinguish women and men: sex chromosomes, reproductive organs, sex-specific hormones, and physical characteristics (Richardson, 1977). A very small number of people are born with ambiguous sex characteristics, but for the vast majority there is a clear sexual identification as either woman or man. **Gender,** in most sociological writing, refers to the social and cultural characteristics that distinguish women from men (Richardson, 1977). In our society, such characteristics include the different clothing that men and women wear or the expectation that boys shouldn't cry when they are hurt. Gender is said to be a social creation; sex is said to be a biological creation.

> **gender** the social and cultural characteristics that distinguish women and men in a society

The distinction between sex and gender will be useful in examining many of the topics in this book. Nevertheless, drawing a line that separates the two is occasionally more difficult than this definition at first suggests. For example, the literature on the berdaches indicates that parents sometimes perceived qualities in their young sons that were more typical of daughters and then raised them as berdaches. If sexual orientation is partly biologically determined, as evidence suggests (see Chapter 6), these parents may have recognized a predisposition in their sons toward a homosexual orientation. Indeed, some students of the berdaches phenomenon have advanced this interpretation. Walter Williams wrote:

> *Indian societies constructed an alternative gender and put their emphasis on the berdache's character and social role rather than on only sexual behavior. This is certainly a social construction.... Yet, the berdache does have an identity, which seems much more a reflection of the individual's innate character. (Williams, 1986)*

If correct, this view implies that the gender parents chose for their sons—the berdache—was socially assigned on the basis, in part, of innate, biological characteristics. In other words, a berdache's gender was influenced both by culture and by biology. On the other hand, in contemporary American society, there are examples of people whose biological sex is, in part, socially created. As will be discussed later in the chapter, transsexuals, individuals who think of themselves as having the opposite sex, sometimes undergo hormone treatments to change their body's characteristics and have surgery to remove or alter their sexual organs. In some real-world situations, then, separating sex and gender neatly may not be possible.

2. *How many genders are there?* The story of the berdaches shows that gender need not be confined to two sexes. Just what gender were the berdaches? Did a male berdache who dressed, acted, and married like a woman take on the female gender? Not quite, for he could not give birth, often had greater physical strength, was sometimes taken along on hunts, and differed in other ways from women (Williams, 1986). Rather, the berdache appears to have occupied an intermediate position between male and female—a third gender, of sorts. He was called not a "man" or a "woman" but a "halfman-halfwoman," a "man-woman," or a "would-be-woman." Reflecting this mixture, the Zuni buried male berdaches in women's dress but men's trousers, on the men's side of the graveyard (Callendar & Kochems, 1983).

In the blurring of the difference between male and female, the status as an in-between gender, the berdache demonstrates how society and culture created gender categories. Recently, a number of adults who were born with ambiguous sexual organs have formed an organization, calling themselves **intersexuals** (Cowley, 1997). As children, most had surgery and long-term treatments with sex hormones to make their genitals and secondary sex characteristics more like those of males or females (see below). Their goal is to convince doctors and parents not to reassign a child's sex until the individual is old enough to make an informed choice.

intersexual a person who is born with ambiguous sexual organs

Still, even though the berdache's story and the emergence of intersexual activists show that female versus male is not the only possible gender distinction, the two-gender model is the typical manner in which people have made sense out of sex. Consequently, the assumption throughout most of this chapter will be that there are two genders.

3. *Can a person's gender identity be modified?* In some tribes Native American men were allowed to become berdaches in adolescence or even later if a supernatural event guided them to do so. They were also allowed to shed the status and return to the male gender. Clearly, under some cultural circumstances, gender identity can be established after middle childhood and modified in adulthood. Yet even in this extraordinary case, the modification is not from male to female, but rather from male to an in-between third gender. Research shows that most children develop a gender identity during their preschool years, that it is reinforced during middle childhood and adolescence, that it becomes a central part of the child's self-definition, and that it is altered in only a handful of exceptional cases.

A recent report illustrates the difficulty of completely overriding a biological predisposition toward being a woman or man. During infancy, a boy's penis was accidentally cut off during surgery. His parents accepted the recommendation of doctors that he undergo further surgery to feminize his genitals and be raised as a girl. Early medical reports indicated that the child was behaving in appropriately feminine ways, and the case was widely cited as showing that gender identity can be socially assigned (Colapinto, 2000; Money & Tucker, 1975). However, a 30-year followup told a different story (Diamond & Sigmundson, 1997). As a child the boy rebelled continually against the clothing and play styles suggested to him and, as an adolescent, simply refused to be a girl. After being informed of his history, he elected to have further surgery and hormone treatments in order to masculinize himself. He lived his adult life as a man and married before committing suicide in 2004 at age 38. In an editorial accompanying the medical journal report on the case, a physician writes, "the organ that appears to be critical to psychosexual development and adaptation is not the external genitalia, but the brain" (Reiner, 1997, p. 225). And the brain appears to form a gender identity in response to both biological and social cues.

4. *How much do gender differences reflect men's attempts to retain power over women?* We have learned that male berdaches were tolerated in many Native American cultures throughout western North America, but female berdaches were more restricted. Women had the freedom to modify their gender only in cultures in which they had substantial resources relative to men and in which the power of male-dominated lineages was weak. In cultures in which men had greater control over women, they blocked women's moves toward a male role. Do similar forces still operate today? As a social creation, notions of gender are likely to reflect the existing

power relationships in a society. In fact, some scholars would restrict the definition of gender to sex-linked characteristics that reflect male power over women or would argue even more broadly that all gender differences reflect gender politics (Scott, 2000). Others would argue for a looser connection between gender and power. We will examine the connection between gender differences and male domination later in this chapter.

Overall, the story of the berdaches shows a flexibility and variability in gender that is unusual. Yet even in this unusual instance, as well as in the current controversy over sex reassignment, we can see evidence that both cultural norms and biological predispositions may influence a person's gender identity, that a shift in gender identity from male to female or vice versa occurs only rarely, and that gender differences can be influenced by the degree of power men have over women. Although the berdaches and the intersexuals show that alternative ways of organizing the culture and biology of sex and gender are possible, their rarity underscores how widespread is the familiar two-sex, two-gender model most of us take for granted.

The distinction between women and men, female and male, is basic to the study of the family because of the sharp differentiation, in nearly all societies, between what women and men do in families. Exactly what they do differs from one society to the next, but almost universally, they tend to do different things. To understand families, we must understand gender. And to understand gender, we must begin before birth, for the paths of male and female begin to diverge in the womb. The origins and consequences of gender differences in childhood, and their maintenance in adulthood through social interaction and male domination, constitute the subject of this chapter. (A more general examination of how parents raise their children will be the subject of Chapter 9.)

The Gestational Construction of Gender

When a sperm and an egg unite to form a human embryo, each contributes a sex chromosome—the genetic material that determines which sex the embryo will turn out to be. The egg always contributes an X chromosome. If the sperm also contributes an X chromosome, the embryo will normally develop into a girl. If the sperm contributes a Y chromosome, the embryo will normally develop into a boy. So at the moment of conception, the developing child's genetic sex is determined. But the story of sex and gender is far from over.

gestation the nine-month development of the fetus inside the mother's uterus

For the first several weeks of **gestation** (the term for the nine-month development of the fetus inside the mother's uterus), the external sex organs of soon-to-be girls and boys are identical. These primitive genitals can develop into either a clitoris, vagina, and ovaries or a penis, scrotum, and testes. But soon male embryos begin to develop testes. In the second trimester (the middle three months) of gestation, the testes in soon-to-be boys produce male sex hormones called androgens. These hormones cause the genitals to develop into the male form. In the absence of high levels of androgens, the genitals develop into the female form. After only a few months, then, the developing child's genital sex is determined by the level of male sex hormones.

HORMONAL INFLUENCES

So far the story is uncontroversial. But some scientists believe that the androgens that circulate in male fetuses do more than cause the genitals to take on the male form. They claim that parts of the fetus's brain develop differently depending on the level of androgen that is present. In other words, the brains of males and females may be organized somewhat differently because of the presence or absence of high levels of male sex hormones during the second trimester of gestation. If so, then some of the gender differences we recognize in women and men could be the result of differences in prenatal (before birth) hormone levels.

There is some evidence for this theory. Studies of girls who were exposed to abnormally high levels of male sex hormones while in their mother's wombs have found that they showed higher levels of interest in strenuous physical activity—climbing trees, biking, playing football—and lower levels of doll play and infant care than girls with normal hormonal histories. Similarly, boys who were exposed to abnormally high levels of female sex hormones showed lower levels of physical activity and more doll play and infant care than boys with normal hormonal histories. These findings suggest that prenatal hormone levels may influence behavior in ways consistent with gender stereotypes (Ehrhardt, 1985). Yet we cannot be sure that they reflect the effect of prenatal sex hormones on the brain. Skeptics note that the girls also had somewhat male-like genitals, which may have caused them to think differently about themselves or their parents to treat them differently from normal girls (Bem, 1993).

Further support for the hormone/brain organization thesis comes from a 30-year study of mothers who gave birth between 1960 and 1963 and their daughters. Blood samples were taken from the mothers-to-be during each trimester of pregnancy and stored for later analysis. In 1990, the blood samples were tested for male and female sex hormones, both of which are normally present in women's blood. At the same time, blood samples were taken from the daughters, who were

Biosocial theorists believe that a biological basis may exist for the higher levels of physical aggression that boys, on average, show compared to girls.

by then aged 27 to 30. Their sex-hormone levels were measured, and they were asked a detailed series of questions about gender-typed behaviors and values, such as the importance of a career and of marriage, the number of gender-typed activities they engaged in, whether they liked caring for babies, and the number of births they had had. The responses to all these indicators were combined into a single measure of "gendered behavior." (Critics note that this measure is time- and culture-bound because gender-typed activities differ over time and across societies [Kennelly, Merz, & Lorber, 2001].) The researchers found that the higher the level of male sex hormones in the mothers' blood in the second trimester of pregnancy (when hormones cause sexual differentiation), the more masculine was the gendered behavior of their daughters 27 to 30 years later. This was true even after adjusting for the level of male sex hormones in the daughter's own blood. Still, the researchers noted that hormone levels accounted for about one-fourth of the variation in gendered behavior; social and cultural influences could have accounted for most of the other three-fourths (Udry, Morris, & Kovenock, 1995).

BIOSOCIAL INFLUENCES

This study suggests that gendered behavior may be a result of both biological predispositions (e.g., prenatal hormone levels) and social experiences (e.g., parents' pressure to behave in gender-typed ways). Sociologists who believe that both biology and society have important influences on gender differences are said to be taking the **biosocial approach** to human behavior (Rossi, 1977, 1984). The biosocial perspective does not suggest that hormones and chromosomes are destiny nor that biology always wins out over social influences. In fact, those who believe biological influences do affect gendered behavior would add at least three qualifications.

biosocial approach (to gender differences) the theory that gender identification and behavior are based in part on people's innate biological differences

First, biologically based differences in gendered behavior exist only "on average"; individuals can show a wide range of behavior. If we were to select a large group of women and another large group of men at random and measure the incidence of some biologically influenced behavior, we would find the behavior occurred more frequently among one group than the other. For example, if the behavior were physical aggression, we might find that, on average, aggression levels were higher among the men than among the women. But not all men, nor all women either, would show the same level of aggression. A modest number of women would be very aggressive, and a modest number of men not at all aggressive. To take another example, even if, on average, women are more predisposed than men to engage in nurturing behavior, as some observers suggest, in any randomly selected group, some women will not be very nurturing and some men quite nurturing.

Second, whether biological predispositions lead to actual behaviors depends on the environment in which a person is raised. For example, a child who is predisposed to be physically aggressive may not behave aggressively if his or her parents provide supportive but firm guidance and control. But a comparably predisposed child might behave very aggressively if his or her parents are neglectful. Biology and environment—nature and nurture—work together to produce behavior. It makes little sense, therefore, to attempt to determine how much of children's observed behavior is "genetic" or "environmental" because the interaction of nature and nurture is what produces the behaviors we see (Maccoby, 2000).

Third, social influences can counteract biological predispositions. For instance, even if, on average, men are predisposed to be more physically aggressive than women, our society can control overly aggressive behavior through moral education, public pressure, and, for extreme aggression, law enforcement. Why, then, should biological predispositions matter at all? Because counteracting the influence of genes or hormones on human behavior is a bit like rolling a stone uphill: It can be done, but it takes continuing effort. If society were to decide that all biologically based gender differences in behavior should be eliminated, strong, deliberate steps would need to be taken to achieve that goal. And the stronger the biological predisposition, the stronger those steps would need to be. Understanding the biological bases of behavior, then, can help us estimate the ease or difficulty of bringing about social change.

Quick Review

- Some researchers think that the brains of male and female fetuses may be organized somewhat differently by the presence or absence of high levels of male sex hormones.
- Sociologists taking the biosocial approach to human behavior believe that both biologically based predispositions and social experiences influence gendered behavior.
- Biologically based differences, if any, exist only "on average."
- Social influences can counteract biologically based predispositions.

The Childhood Construction of Gender

Once born, children face multiple influences on their behavior. Sociologists, who have borrowed the concept of roles from the theater, often write about the social roles people play. A **social role** is a pattern of behaviors associated with a position in society (e.g., parent, teacher, supervisor, elected official).

The term **gender roles** can be defined as the different sets of behaviors that are commonly exhibited by women and men. Gender roles usually occur in pairs, one for each gender. For example, in many marriages during the first half of the twentieth century, men tended to play the gender role of "breadwinner," the person who earns all the income for the family, whereas women tended to play the role of "homemaker," the person who specializes in caring for the children and keeping house. Many sociologists think gender roles are entirely socially created, although a minority allow for biological influences. Moreover, the gendered division of labor is said to reflect men's interests more than women's. This power relationship will be discussed later in the chapter.

The first wave of feminist scholarship in the sociology of gender relied heavily on the concept of gender roles. Sociologists used role theory to demonstrate ways in which parents, the media, and peer groups influenced children's ideas of proper behavior for a girl or boy. Other sociologists studied the ways in which society reinforced the roles of breadwinner and homemaker. Role-theory research in the 1970s and 1980s produced important findings that will be reviewed in this section. Beginning in the 1980s and continuing in the 1990s, many gender scholars became dissatisfied with the concept of gender roles. They argued that the simple dichotomy between men's roles and women's roles shouldn't be taken for granted. Instead, argued the revisionists, scholars should examine the tenuous, changing, socially constructed nature of the very idea of a "male role" and a "female

social role a pattern of behaviors associated with a position in society

gender roles the different sets of behaviors that are commonly exhibited by women and men

As part of the socialization process, children learn appropriate gendered behavior from their parents.

role." For example, Ferree, Lorber, and Hess (2000) wrote, "Given the variety and multiplicity of human differences and the many similarities among people regardless of what gender categories they might be assigned to," researchers should ask the question, "What creates the categories of 'men' and 'women' and makes them socially meaningful?" These scholars tend to favor the interactionist approach and the sex–gender system approach to studying gender differences, both of which will be presented later in the chapter. Nevertheless, virtually all gender scholars would agree that society gives children powerful messages about what gender means and how women and men should behave.

PARENTAL SOCIALIZATION

socialization the way in which one learns the ways of a given society or social group so that one can function within it

socialization approach (to gender differences) the theory that gender identification and behavior are based on children's learning that they will be rewarded for the set of behaviors considered appropriate to their sex but not for those appropriate to the other sex

Researchers in the role-theory tradition have argued that people first acquire gender roles through socialization during childhood. **Socialization,** according to the definition in one widely cited book, is "the process by which we learn the ways of a given society or social group so that we can function within it" (Elkin & Handel, 1984). It is how individuals learn to take on the attitudes and behaviors considered culturally appropriate for them. The emphasis in the **socialization approach** to gender differences is on conscious, social learning: Children are rewarded for behavior adults think is appropriate for their gender and admonished or punished for behavior that is not considered appropriate. By watching parents, teachers, television actors, and others, children learn the behavior of both genders, but they soon learn that they will be rewarded for one set of behaviors and not for the other. For example, although at first little boys cry as much as little girls, they are admonished not to, so that as men they cry less often than women. More generally, men are encouraged to be competitive and independent, whereas women are encouraged to be more nurturing to children and adults, and better at enabling and maintaining personal relationships.

In the standard role-theory model of socialization, children passively learn lessons from their parents. Many researchers now think this model is too simplistic and that, in reality, both children and parents influence each other's behavior as socialization proceeds (Maccoby, 2003; McHale & Crouter, 2003). A brother and sister may respond differently to their parents' attempts at discipline because they have different predispositions for disruptive behavior or merely because the younger child is acting differently from the older one in order to compete for the parents' attention. The parents may then respond differently to the two children, perhaps becoming stricter with one than the other. This response, in turn, may encourage the two children to become even more different in their actions. Or parents may buy a toy building set as a birthday present for a son in response to his interest in playing with blocks; and this present may make him even more interested in stereotypically male toys than his sister. In other words, a feedback loop is created in which differences in siblings' predispositions, whether biologically based or based on earlier treatment, may make parents respond differently to each of them, which in turn will make their behaviors even more distinctive from each other.

THE MEDIA

Nor is gender socialization confined to parents; children learn lessons from books and television, among other sources. As recently as the 1960s, schools made little effort to balance the gender content in the books children were assigned to use. Publishers produced stories and histories that focused mainly on boys and men. Then, spurred by the feminist movement, school systems began to demand more balanced literature. Today, in most children's books, girls and boys receive much more equal treatment. Still, inequities remain. A study of all illustrated fiction books for children up to age nine published in France in 1994 (one-fourth of which were translations of English-language books) found that the main characters were more likely to be male. In addition, male characters were more likely than female characters to be shown working outside the home. And parents, when included, were more likely to be mothers than fathers (Brugeilles, Cromer, & Cromer, 2002).

Over the past few decades books have lost ground to television and computer software as a source of information for children. The average 4-year-old watches two hours of television per day; the average 12-year-old watches four hours (Comstock & Scharrer, 2001). Studies have shown that at least through the early 1980s, more of the characters in children's programming were male than female, and the characters undertook mostly gender-stereotyped activities (Barcus, 1983). Moreover, the cable channels children and adolescents watch also show gender imbalances. A study of randomly selected music videos on Music Television (MTV) found that men appeared twice as often as women and engaged in significantly more aggressive and dominant behavior. Women were shown engaging in more implicitly sexual and subservient behavior and more often were objects of men's sexual advances (Sommers-Flanagan, Sommers-Flanagan, & Davis, 1993).

EARLY PEER GROUPS

Researchers also suspect that much of the development of gender-specific behavior occurs from an early age in children's **peer groups**—similar-age children who play or perform other activities together. Between the ages of two and

peer group a group of people who have roughly the same age and status as one another

three, children begin to sort themselves into same-sex peer groups. Psychologist Eleanor Maccoby argues that these same-sex peer groups strongly influence the distinctive behavior patterns of boys and girls (Maccoby, 1998). In observing pairs of children who were on average 33 months old, Maccoby and her colleagues found that these youngsters were far more likely to show social behavior—offering or grabbing a toy, hugging or pushing, vocally greeting or protesting, and so forth—to children of the same sex than to children of the opposite sex. When girls were paired with other girls, they were just as active as boys who were paired with boys; but when girls were paired with boys, they frequently stood back and let the boys monopolize the toys. Observers suggest that the rough-and-tumble play style and focus on competition and dominance among boys are unattractive to girls. Moreover, they argue, young girls have difficulty influencing boys. Between ages three and five, girls increasingly attempt to influence other children by making polite suggestions, but boys increasingly make direct demands (Serbin, Sprafkin, Elman, & Doyle, 1984).

Maccoby suggests that boys' peer groups reinforce a competitive, dominance-oriented interaction style that carries over into such adult male communication tactics as interrupting, boasting, contradicting, and threatening tactics that restrict conversation. Girls' groups, she suggests, reinforce a different style that carries over into adult female communication. Through expressing agreement or support, asking questions rather than making statements, and acknowledging other persons' comments, girls continue interactions rather than restricting them. These styles, Maccoby asserts, may influence adult, mixed-sex interactions in school, at the office, and in families. Same-sex peer groups emerge so early, she suggests, that both parental influence and biological predispositions may shape them (Maccoby, 1990).

LATER PEER GROUPS

Symbolic interactionists say that children develop a sense of self through activities such as peer group play—a "gendered" sense of self, in this instance. As a girl (or a boy) formulates what she will say or do in the group, she imagines how the others are likely to respond. This process of imagining how others will respond is what George Herbert Mead called "taking the role of the other" (Blumer, 1962). It is, interactionists say, how children develop an internalized sense of appropriate behavior.

Consider the same-sex peer groups that are formed in school settings by children somewhat older than the ones we have been considering. Children are socialized, in part, through playing games and sports in same-sex, school-age peer groups. In these groups, children learn the behaviors expected of them, try out these behaviors with their peers, get feedback on how well they are performing, and try again. Sociologists have studied how this interactive process produces and reinforces different behavior patterns in boys and girls. In a study of Little League baseball teams, Gary Alan Fine observed that boys were concerned with impression management—behaving in a way that met with approval from the other boys—as well as with winning or losing. They learned to control their emotions and not to cry; otherwise they would risk ridicule from their peers. They also learned to value competition. Once, when an opposing team showed up with too few players, a coach offered his first-place team the options of winning by forfeit or playing the game anyway and taking the small risk that they would lose. All the best players argued for taking the forfeit; only two players argued in favor of going ahead with the game because they were supposed to be playing for fun. When the team voted overwhelmingly to take the forfeit, the boys learned a lesson about valuing competition over cooperative play—a lesson that is consistent with the expected behavior of men (Fine, 1987).

In the past, elementary school girls tended to play indoors more than boys, to engage more often in noncompetitive activities without a goal, and to play in smaller groups. These play settings reinforced the relational and emotional skills women are expected to have. In these small groups, girls showed more affection than boys and learned to pick up on nonverbal cues about their friends' moods. The traits that were reinforced by girls' play were consistent with an adult life that emphasized home, family, emotional closeness, and cooperation (Lever, 1976). But since the passage in 1972 of a law prohibiting discrimination against women and girls in federally funded athletic programs, women's participation in high school varsity sports has expanded dramatically (Harrison & Lynch, 2005). One would expect that the character of girls' play would now be different, but we still await a good study on the subject.

In any case, not all girls and boys follow these stereotypical scripts when at play. When Barrie Thorne (1993) observed children in elementary schools, she found that most play groups comprised either all girls or all boys. But a modest number of girls and boys played in groups with the other gender, and there was much crossing of the gender border—for example, when boys and girls chased one another or invaded the other gender's space. The degree of separation between girls' and boys' worlds, Thorne concluded, was overstated. Thorne's approach to her study reflects many of the principles of feminist research methods (see *How Do Sociologists Know What They Know?* Feminist Research Methods).

In sum, studies of young children's preferences and activities suggest numerous influences on the different behaviors of girls and boys. Society's expectations about how to behave are transmitted to children through channels such as parents, books, television, and peer groups. In these ways, cultural differences between women and men are reproduced in the next generation. Yet the evidence also suggests that children may have innate predispositions that affect gender differences in their behavior. These predispositions appear to be stronger for boys than for girls. Boys seem to prefer blocks, trucks, and rough play more than girls, on average, regardless of their parents' opinions about how they should play. Thus the influence of same-sex peer groups may reflect both socialization and biological predispositions.

UNCONSCIOUS INFLUENCES

Another perspective on the reproduction of gender differences, the psychoanalytic approach to gender differences, has been developed by social scientists who don't think biology has much effect on gender, yet are puzzled by the tenacity of the gender stereotypes acquired in childhood and surprised by how hard they are to change. Its foremost proponent in sociology is Nancy Chodorow, who draws on it to explain why women do the mothering in nearly all societies (Chodorow, 1978).

The **psychoanalytic approach** to gender differences is based on the psychoanalytic theory of children's development first put forth by Austrian psychiatrist Sigmund Freud at the turn of the twentieth century. Freud thought that children become like their same-sex parent by internalizing—unconsciously incorporating— a representation of that parent into their own personalities. So Freud's theory stresses unconscious mental processes, whereas the socialization approach

psychoanalytic approach (to gender differences) the theory that gender identification and behavior are based on children's unconscious internalization of the qualities of their same-sex parent

How Do Sociologists Know What They Know?   Feminist Research Methods

Sociologist Barrie Thorne (1993) begins her book about children's play groups, *Gender Play: Girls and Boys in School*, by writing not about her subject but about herself. She recalls that the segregation of girls and boys on the playgrounds of the elementary school she attended was considered "natural." She tells the reader that her views on gender were transformed by the women's movement of the 1970s and 1980s, which argued that the differences between the genders are not natural but rather a social construction. She describes her commitment to raise her own children in a nonsexist way.

Thorne then discusses how, in her own research, she took pains to learn the terminology that the subjects themselves used: "kids" rather than "children." She explained, "I found that when I shifted to 'kids' in my writing, my stance toward the people in question felt more side-by-side than top-down" (p. 9). Using "kids" helped her to adopt the viewpoint of her subjects, as opposed to the viewpoint of an adult feminist scholar.

In fact, Thorne's entire first chapter consists of preliminary material about herself and her relationship with her subjects. The chapter illustrates an orientation that is called *feminist research methods*. It

emerged from the feminist movement of the 1970s and 1980s and is linked to feminist theory [➡ p. 25] and to the modernity perspective [➡ p. 26] that is sometimes called "postmodernism." Researchers are encouraged to *reflexively* [➡ p. 27] examine the nature of the research process that they are undertaking. Two feminist methodologists write approvingly of "the tendency for feminists to reflect on, examine critically, and explore analytically the nature of the research process" (Fonow & Cook, 2005, p. 2218).

Researchers are also encouraged to learn the point of view of the subjects they are studying. This emphasis on entering into the subjects' perspective is known as "connected knowing" in feminist research methods (Belenky, Clinchy, Goldberger, & Tarule, 1997). They are also encouraged to minimize power differences between researchers and the groups they study (Harding & Norberg, 2005). That is why Thorne sought to use language and methods that made her more of a "side-by-side" observer than a "top-down" observer.

Researchers are also encouraged to conduct socially engaged research that may create social change, particularly by reducing the oppression of women—and

also by ending the gender constraints placed on men (Reinharz, 1992; Harding & Norberg, 2005). Feminist researchers explicitly acknowledge this political agenda. More important, they argue that *all* social scientific research reflects the social and political beliefs of the researchers but that most social scientists hide their beliefs—sometimes even from themselves.

In contrast, most sociologists try to follow the *scientific method.* [➡ p. 16] A key assumption of the scientific method as it is often practiced is that researchers are neutral figures who stand outside the phenomena they study. The researcher's point of view, it is said, should not influence the methods she or he uses or the conclusions that she or he makes. In this way, social scientists strive for objectivity—a way of viewing the social world that is independent of personal beliefs. Feminist methodologists sometimes describe this orientation as "separated knowing" because of the distant and impartial stance it implies (Belenky et, al., 1997).

But feminist researchers argue that objectivity is nearly impossible to achieve (Ruddick, 1996). They argue that much supposedly "objective" social scientific

stresses conscious processes. And whereas the central mechanism of the socialization approach is learning, the corresponding mechanism in psychoanalytic theory is internalization. Children become like a parent through a process that is beyond their conscious control and not even evident to them at the time.

The version of psychoanalytic theory borrowed by Chodorow asserts that the first several years of life are crucial to a person's gender identity and sense of self (Chodorow, 1978). After birth, the infant unconsciously experiences itself as merged and continuous with its first caretaker, who is almost always a woman. The young child, whether girl or boy, becomes deeply attached to the all-encompassing, comforting female figure and internalizes her image. There soon comes a time, however, when boys realize they must establish their gender identities as males. To do so, they must transfer their attachment and identity from their mothers to their fathers (or to other males, if the father is not present). This event is research actually reflects male bias. The very categories that social scientists use often reflect prevailing political agendas (Harding & Norberg, 2005). For example, they note that not long ago, the U.S. Bureau of the Census, in its surveys, defined the husband as the "head of household" in a married-couple family, no matter what the family's situation was. Similarly, violence against women by husbands and partners was greatly underreported in crime statistics until feminists focused attention on the problem (Reinharz, 1992).

Proponents of feminist research methods frequently try to show that there is substantial variation from person to person in the ways in which women and men act. They do so because they oppose generalizations about women that might be used to restrict their independence and equality (for example, the belief, prevalent at mid-century, that the husband should earn the money and the wife should stay home and care for the children). They sometimes carry out research with the intent of demonstrating that generalizations about women are wrong. Thorne warns, for instance: "One should be wary of what has been called 'the tyranny of averages,' a misleading practice of referring to average differences as if they are absolute" (pp. 57–58).

So Thorne ventured out to the elementary school playground to disprove the idea that boys and girls are inherently different in their play styles—boys more aggressive, more concerned with dominance in groups; girls more concerned with relationships with a small number of friends. On the playground, girls and boys did separate, for the most part, in the ways the generalizations about them predict. They were not, however, completely separate. Thorne provided an insightful analysis of contact between girls and boys during the "border work" that maintained their separation, such as invading the other gender's spaces and chasing one another. She also found that a few children defied the stereotype, such as a boy who played jump rope and an athletic girl who played sports with the boys. And she documented occasional mixed games of dodgeball and the like.

From evidence such as this, Thorne concluded that gender "has a fluid quality" (p. 159) and that the claim that boys and girls have separate cultures "has outlived its usefulness" (p. 108). However, as one reviewer noted, the number of times that boys and girls cross the gender boundaries "are a tiny minority of her observations" (England, 1994, p. 283). Consequently, claiming that the average differences between boys and girls aren't important because some individuals cross the boundaries may be an overstatement.

Even if one is not always convinced by the conclusions of researchers like Thorne, one can find useful lessons in feminist research methods. Perhaps the main lesson is that researchers should pay more attention to where they are coming from: the reasons they choose to study a particular topic, the assumptions they have going into a research project, and the beliefs they hold that might influence their conclusions. Feminist researchers have made a convincing case that in the study of family and gender, objectivity has its limits.

Ask Yourself

1. Does your gender affect the way you react to Barrie Thorne's research? Explain.

2. What are the advantages and disadvantages of feminist research methods and of the scientific method? Why?

www.mhhe.com/cherlin5

said to be a traumatic break for boys, who must do the difficult work of distancing themselves from their mothers to protect their gender identities. Consequently, the theorists argue, boys build psychological barriers between themselves and their mothers; they put fences around their gender identities. In the psychoanalytic language, they create rigid ego boundaries as a way of protecting their emerging identities. Girls, on the other hand, need not distance themselves from their mothers to establish their gender identities. They remain connected to their first attachment in life, and they enjoy a longer, more continuous period of attachment as they come to identify themselves as female.

As a result, Chodorow argues, women tend to have a greater capacity for relating to others and an easier time establishing close relationships. They are also better, on average, at relating to infants than men, because of their greater ability to respond to a small being who cannot verbally express its needs.

Quick Review

- Sociologists have used the concept of "gender roles" (now somewhat out of fashion) to examine the different messages girls and boys receive about how they should behave.
- Sociologists who take the socialization approach to gender differences believe that children learn they will be rewarded for some types of behavior but not others.
- Parents both act and respond to their children by rewarding them for behavior they think appropriate and withholding rewards for behavior they think inappropriate.
- The media—television, books, magazines, commercial Web sites—often portray boys and girls, and men and women, behaving in gender-stereotypical ways.
- Children's same-gender peer groups often reinforce gender-stereotypical behavior.
- Sociologists who take the psychoanalytic approach to gender differences believe that children's early experience of being cared for by women may affect their personality development.
- Feminists have developed research methods that challenge key assumptions of the standard social scientific model. (See *How Do Sociologists Know What They Know?:* Feminist Research Methods.)

The Continual Construction of Gender

As noted earlier, over the past decade or two, sociological research on the construction of gender differences has moved away from studying socialization or predispositions formed in childhood. In this recent way of thinking, gender is more fluid, more fragile, more in need of constant reinforcement, than role theory or psychoanalytic theory suggests. Scholars also maintain that gender is a master identity, far too broad to be considered just one of life's roles, like the role of professor or student. They argue instead for an approach that focuses on the continual construction and maintenance of gender differences throughout adulthood.

DOING GENDER

interactionist approach (to gender differences) the theory that gender identification and behavior are based on the day-to-day behavior that reinforces gender distinctions

Candace West and Don H. Zimmerman (1987) developed this approach in "Doing Gender," perhaps the most influential article on the sociology of gender in the past two decades. To develop their framework, which is commonly known as the **interactionist approach,** they hearkened back to symbolic interaction theory (Blumer, 1962). [➥ p. 24]. "We argue," West and Zimmerman (1987, p. 129) wrote, "that gender is not a set of traits, nor a role, but the product of social doings of some sort." These social doings occur through "situated conduct"—interactions between men and women in particular settings (such as a kitchen or a job interview). Gender is an achieved property that is created through countless social interactions that reinforce gender differences.

For example, how do a wife and husband come to understand that she should do most of the housework? Socialization theory suggests that doing the housework is part of the gender role women learn beginning with the dolls and teacups they are given in childhood and the praise they get for helping their mothers wash the dishes. But the symbolic interactionists, while not denying that socialization occurs, emphasize that questions such as who does the housework

The interactionists suggest that gendered behavior is not only learned in childhood but also reinforced day after day in adulthood.

are settled again and again in daily life. For example, in a study conducted by Sarah Fenstermaker Berk (1985), a woman who was asked "What household work does your husband do?" replied:

> *He tries to be helpful. He tries. He's a brilliant and successful lawyer. It's incredible how he smiles after he sponges off the table and there are still crumbs all over.*

Here the husband's smile—the symbol—indicates to his wife that he is incapable of sponging all the crumbs off the table, despite having enough brains to be a brilliant and successful lawyer. It is a way for the husband to express a feigned helplessness, which he and his wife both interpret as meaning that she's the only one who can do a good job of cleaning up after dinner. Daily scenes such as this, Berk and others argue, not only produce clean tables but also produce—and reproduce—gender distinctions. The interactionists focus on people's actions in concrete situations such as this one in order to determine how social meanings—in this case the shared understanding of who should do the housework—are produced.

In a sense, the interactionist approach turns the logic of role theory on its head. The role-theory view is that men offer to carry packages for women because men and women are taught to believe that women aren't strong enough to manage on their own; the interactionist view is that men and women believe that women can't manage on their own because men keep offering to carry their packages. The setting is a woman walking to her car in a supermarket parking lot carrying a manageable load of groceries; the interaction is that a male friend of hers approaches and offers to carry the bags for her; she smiles politely and accepts his offer with thanks, even though she could have made it to the car herself. The achievement is reinforcing and, in effect, re-creating gender differences—in other words, doing gender. You can think of many other daily situations that have similar properties; add them up and multiply by the thousands of days in the average life, say the interactionists, and you get a powerful mechanism for reproducing a society with gender differences so strong that people think they are natural.

PRECARIOUS GENDER DIFFERENCES

Implicit in the interactionist approach is the premise that gender differences are fragile enough that they need to be reinforced and reproduced day after day; otherwise, there would be no need to keep reproducing them. Is this premise valid? Socialization theorists and evolutionary theorists would say no. However, interactionists claim that the social order we take for granted in everyday life is much more precarious, much more house-of-cards–like, than we think. People must spend a lot of time, they assert, creating and re-creating a shared sense of social order in their everyday lives. According to this line of reasoning, people must continually "do" gender—do the work of creating a shared sense of what the relations between men and women should be (West & Zimmerman, 1987). Gender becomes a verb, usually in the passive voice: Housework is gendered, work for wages is gendered, child care is gendered, over and over in hundreds of situations. The household, in Berk's phrase, becomes a gender factory that produces the shared reality of gender relations along with crumb-free tables (Berk, 1985).

Quick Review

- Sociologists who take the interactionist approach believe that gender is not a fixed role or trait but rather a social construction that must be actively maintained throughout adulthood.
- Through situated conduct—interaction in concrete settings—in everyday life, women and men unthinkingly reproduce and sustain gender differences.
- People decide a person's sex based on socially recognized characteristics, which don't always reflect biological sex.

Gender and Male Domination

Another body of writing about the construction and maintenance of gender differences focuses not on social interaction or socialization, but on the very structure of society: its hierarchies of dominance and power and its economic and political systems. According to this line of reasoning, gender differences are social creations deeply imbedded in the way society is organized (Risman, 1998). More specifically, in the United States and most other nations, inequalities between women and men are said to be built into their social systems through **patriarchy**. In most general terms, patriarchy is a social order based on the domination of women by men. But following some scholars, I prefer to reserve the term for conditions that are more common in agricultural societies, in which older men control their families and family groups are the main economic units. In industrialized societies, in which the family or lineage is no longer the main economic group, I prefer the simpler term "male domination" (Thorne, 1992; Orloff, 1993). But no matter which term one uses, the main point of this scholarship is that men exercise power over women in ways that are similar to how the wealthy exercise power over the poor and whites exercise power over blacks. Like class (see Chapter 4) and race (see Chapter 5), gender is said to be one of the basic ways in which a society is stratified into more and less powerful groups.

patriarchy a social order based on the domination of women by men, especially in agricultural societies

For instance, a recent study of 22 countries suggests that how a couple divides the housework is not just a matter of their personal beliefs about gender roles. Rather, how much gender equality exists at the national level also influences them. Consider two couples, A and B, who both believe that ideally housework should be divided equally. Suppose couple A lives in a country such as Russia or Japan, where few women are in parliament, few have powerful or prestigious occupations, and few earn high salaries. Suppose couple B, in contrast, lives in a country such as Sweden or Canada, where women have much more political and economic power at the national level. Then couple B will tend to divide the housework more equally than will couple A, even though their personal beliefs are the same. How they live their home lives, the study suggests, is influenced by the power and influence that women have in their national political and economic systems (Fuwa, 2004).

THE SEX–GENDER SYSTEM

Put another way, societies often take the biological sex differences between women and men and use them as the basis for a comprehensive social order in which men have advantages over women. Specific, limited sex differences become the basis for pervasive gender differences. Gender theorists refer to this transformation of biological differences into a social order that supports male domination as a **sex–gender system** (Rubin, 1975).

Consider the economy, for example. In Western nations, people must purchase the goods they need with money (as opposed to making their own clothes and building their own houses). Western societies are organized so that men have access to more money than women: Men are more likely to work for pay, and when they do, most earn considerably higher wages and salaries than women (see Chapter 8). To be sure, men tend to have more education and work experience than women, in part because many women withdraw from the paid workforce to bear and rear children. Gender theorists argue, however, that the wage gap is far wider than differences in education and work experience would predict—and recent economic studies suggest that their argument is correct. (See *Families and*

sex–gender system the transformation of the biological differences between women and men into a social order that supports male domination

Women still earn less than men in comparable jobs, on average, despite modest progress in the past decade or two.

| Families and Public Policy | The Earnings Gap |

In 2004, women who worked full-time as financial managers earned 60 percent as much as men who worked full-time as financial managers. Women bus drivers earned 75 percent as much as men who worked as bus drivers. And women computer programmers earned 87 percent as much as men made (U.S. Bureau of Labor Statistics, 2005a). Why in nearly all occupations did women earn less than men? And why were women workers concentrated in lower-paying jobs? Do employers discriminate against women workers? Or are other factors responsible for the earnings gap?

In the 1960s and 1970s, some labor economists argued that the earnings gap reflected the different social roles women choose. That is, they assumed that women preferred to devote a larger share of their lives to raising children than did men. Economists such as Solomon Polachek argued that women intentionally chose the kinds of jobs they could leave for a period of time and then reenter, and they left voluntarily when they had young children (Polachek, 1979). Women earned less than men, according to this argument, because, on average, they had less work experience and invested less in their careers (for example, by taking fewer job-training courses).

The evidence, however, has not supported this model—at least not as the sole explanation for the earnings gap. Numerous studies of the wage differences between women and men found that even after controlling for education, work experience, and other factors, a substantial portion of the gap remains. Robert Michael, a labor economist and chair of a National Academy of Sciences panel on Pay Equity Research, wrote in 1989:

there exist sizeable and systematic wage differences between women and men that cannot be explained by measured differences in skill, experience, effort, job commitment, or most any other attribute of workers that has been studied. Some argue that the unexplained differences constitute a serious inequity that should be addressed by public and private policy. (Michael, Hartmann, & O'Farrell, 1989)

Why might the earnings gap still exist? One possibility is that some employers may engage in "statistical discrimination." They may note, accurately, that women have slightly higher rates of leaving jobs than men. Consequently, they may hesitate to

Public Policy: The Earnings Gap.) In a number of ways—such as when parents encourage sons more than daughters to have careers, when employers discriminate against women in hiring or pay, and when long-established rules provide men with higher pay than women for comparable work—society creates and reinforces men's economic domination. Therefore, most women must depend on men if they wish to live in a household with a substantial income.

Just how men have achieved their dominant position in society is a subject of some debate. Many writers of this genre link male domination to capitalism—the economic system of the United States and most other nations (Shelton & Agger, 1993). **Capitalism,** which will be discussed (along with socialism) in detail in Chapter 14, is an economic system in which goods and services are privately produced and sold on a market for profit. Gender theorists have maintained that economic inequalities between women and men benefit capitalists, the owners of businesses, in at least three ways. First, employers save money by hiring women at lower wages than they would have to pay men. During the twentieth century, the sector of the economy that produces services, such as medical care, communications, insurance, restaurant meals, and the like, expanded faster than the factory sector. During this expansion, women—especially unmarried women—were hired as nurses (but less often as doctors), secretaries (but not managers), and telephone operators (but not supervisors), as well as for other service jobs (Oppenheimer, 1970). Their wages tended to be substantially lower than the wages of men with comparable responsibility, providing employers with considerable savings. Second, the lower wages paid to women tend to create divisions between

capitalism an economic system in which goods and services are privately produced and sold on a market for profit

hire women for jobs that require expensive training and therefore tend to pay well. When they interview a woman, they may be wary of hiring her because they know that as a group, women have higher turnover rates—even though the specific woman they are interviewing might never quit (England & Farkas, 1986). Their statistical discrimination, in turn, can affect how parents socialize the next generation, and so on. Consequently, discrimination tends to linger, even though employers' attitudes toward women in the workplace may have become more positive.

A subtler issue is **comparable-worth discrimination:** a situation in which women and men in the same company do different jobs of equivalent value, but the women are paid less than the men. A remedy for this problem is to have an expert body classify jobs according to their "worth," as defined by attributes such as skill, effort, responsibility, and working conditions. Then wages or wage guidelines would be set according to the job rankings, usually by a government body. To be sure, deciding how much value a given job produces relative to another is difficult. Yet in Australia and Great Britain, where government influence over wage levels is greater than in the United States, similar actions have reduced the earnings gap (Gregory et al., 1989).

Over the past decade or two, modest progress has been made in closing the earnings gap. In 1979, the median weekly earnings of women who worked full-time were about 63 percent of men's earnings; in 2004 the figure had increased to 80 percent (U.S. Bureau of Labor Statistics, 2005a). Still, women's earnings lag behind men's in nearly every occupation. And some of the progress in narrowing the gap has occurred because the wages of men without college educations have gone down, rather than because the wages of women have risen (Bernhardt, Morris, & Handcock, 1995). We will return to this topic in Chapter 8.

Ask Yourself

1. Have you ever compared notes with your coworkers and discovered that the women in your group were being paid less than the men? If so, how did you and the other employees interpret the earnings gap?

2. Besides statistical discrimination and comparable worth discrimination, what other explanations can you think of for the earnings gap?

www.mhhe.com/cherlin5

male and female workers, which prevent them from joining together and organizing to protect their interests against the interests of capitalists.

Third, the unpaid work of housewives, gender theorists argue, allows families to subsist on the often modest wages men earn. Employers count on their male workers being married to women who will wash their clothes, cook their meals, and raise their children at no cost. Thus, employers gain greater profits by paying their workers less than the full cost of raising a family. Indeed, in the first half of the twentieth century, this division of labor was enshrined as the "family wage system," in which husbands were supposed to earn enough so that their wives did not need to work for pay (see Chapter 14). Wives' unpaid work was, and still is, invisible economically: Government statisticians do not count housework and childrearing as part of the gross national product—the annual accounting of the total amount of goods and services produced in the country. Yet wives' unpaid work is economically valuable. In recent decades, as more married women have taken jobs outside the home, millions of families have discovered how expensive it is to pay someone else to care for their children while they work.

Still, the nature of the connection between male domination and capitalism is unclear. Most feminist theorists have maintained that the two work well together, but are at least partially distinct. For example, some have described the social and economic organization of the United States as "patriarchal capitalism," arguing that male domination of women and capitalists' domination of workers are intertwined, with each reinforcing the other (Hartmann, 1976). Male domination is said to have emerged before capitalism, but to have broadened and strengthened

comparable-worth discrimination a situation in which women and men do different jobs of equivalent value in the same company but the women are paid less

once capitalism was established. An implication of this line of thought is that male domination would be reduced if capitalism were replaced by another economic system, such as socialism.

This implication, however, is undercut by cross-national research. Several scholars have studied the position of women in countries with a socialist economic system. Under **socialism,** the number and type of goods produced, and who they are distributed to, are decided by the government rather than by the market. Theoretically, a socialist system should eliminate the economic disparities between women and men, because there are no business owners who could profit from paying women lower wages or from having unpaid housewives subsidize the wages employers pay men. In fact, in socialist countries such as the former Soviet Union and its Eastern European satellites, nearly all urban women worked outside the home. Many of the Eastern European states reserved a set portion of government and parliamentary positions for women. East Germany and others provided benefits for mothers, such as very inexpensive day care and generous maternity leaves (Haney, 2002).

But women did not achieve equality with men in East Germany or elsewhere in Eastern Europe. They were paid less than men, on average, and became segregated in certain kinds of jobs. Husbands still expected their wives to do nearly all the housework and child care, even though their homes lacked time-saving devices such as refrigerators and automatic washing machines and dryers. The government also expected mothers to take care of the home: Female workers in East Germany were granted one paid "housework day" off per month. Men's domination of women, in other words, is not just a function of the economic system; it may even be largely independent of it. Although there are differences between the status of women in capitalist and socialist societies, male domination seems to be built into the social structures of most nations in ways that are compatible with either capitalism or socialism.

socialism an economic system in which the number and types of goods produced, and who they are distributed to, are decided by the government rather than by the actions of a market

In socialist countries nearly all the women, like these cigarette factory workers in Bulgaria in 1963, worked outside the home, but gender inequality did not disappear.

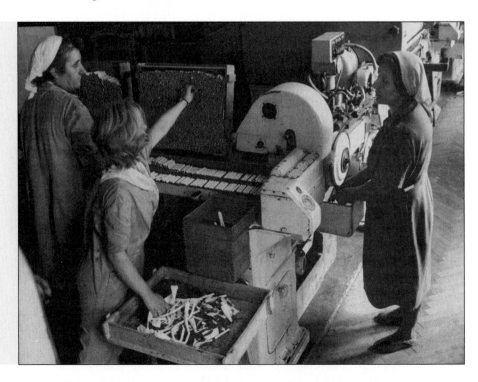

GENDER, CLASS, AND RACE

The scholars who established the sociology of gender as a field of study in the 1960s and 1970s maintained that gender is not reducible to class differences, as earlier scholars had argued. They maintained that gender should be thought of in the same way scholars think of race and class—namely, as a primary basis of social stratification. By the 1980s, this view was widely accepted, and it remains so today. But in the 1980s and 1990s, some sociologists who studied minority groups criticized gender theorists for not linking gender with race (and its close cousin ethnicity) and class—essentially, for focusing heavily on the lives of white, middle-class women (Acker, 2000; Glenn, 2000b). The critics agreed that gender is as much a part of social stratification as race and class, but they noted that members of minority groups experience gender and race together, and often in combination with class. Therefore, one often needs to study a situation from these three overlapping lenses—gender, race, and class—at the same time in order to fully understand it.

For example, the number of workers who provide support and caring to middle-class families has increased in the past decade or two. (And, in fact, a new subfield of *care work studies* has developed around these workers, as we will discuss in Chapter 8.) They include nannies, house cleaners, home health care aides, day care center staff, and others. These jobs tend to be typed as women's work (when's the last time you saw a male nanny?), so issues of gender are clearly important in understanding their growth. But it is also true that a substantial number are African American, Hispanic, or Asian and that most are lower-class or working-class. A recent immigrant woman from Mexico or Jamaica who lacks proper documents may be channeled into the nanny business, where she will accept low pay and quite possibly send home part of her earnings to pay someone to care for her own children (Parreñas, 2002). To understand her story, you will need to see how her gender, ethnicity, and class position intersect to place her in a suburban American home.

GENDER: THE MALE POINT OF VIEW

Sociological writings on gender have commonly focused on the conditions under which women and girls live their lives. This orientation reflects the roots of gender studies in the feminist movement that began in the 1960s. Although men have not been absent from gender studies, they tended to be included mainly because of the ways in which they influence or control women. Beginning in the 1980s, however, both a scholarly and a popular literature emerged that was focused on men. This body of literature grew greatly in the 1990s, as social movements aimed at men gained strength. The main topic of these writings was **masculinity**—the set of personal characteristics that society defines as being typical of men.

The popular writings on masculinity have sought to define its essence and to build a more positive image of men. In part, the authors were reacting to what they saw as an overly negative feminist view of men. Poet Robert Bly (1990) became the best-known writer and movement leader through the publication of *Iron John: A Book about Men.* In it, Bly used a Grimm brothers fairy tale about a young man's encounter with a "wild man" to illustrate the need for men to get in touch with their forceful, hard, even fierce maleness. Unless men could find this inner essence, Bly and others argued, they were unlikely to be successful in their work or family lives. The leaders of this wing of the men's movement were careful to state that they were not encouraging violent or irresponsible

masculinity the set of personal characteristics that society defines as being typical of men

behavior, however. "The kind of energy I'm talking about is not the same as macho, brute strength which men already know enough about," Bly told an interviewer (Thompson, 1991). "It's forceful action undertaken, not without compassion, but with resolve." Soon groups such as Promise Keepers filled sports stadiums for rallies at which men were urged to be good, responsible fathers and husbands and to remain true to their masculinity.

Still, it was clear that in this version of masculinity, men were supposed to bring their forcefulness to their family lives and to remain the dominant partners in marriage. Male dominance in marriage, of course, is precisely what feminists object to. Thus, a second, feminist-influenced branch of men's studies emerged in opposition to the first. Although less prominent than the first in the popular culture (but see Pollack [1998] on the problems of "real boys"), it is quite prominent in sociological writing. Writers in this feminist-influenced tradition of men's studies accept the position that male dominance must be eliminated from marriage (and in the larger society as well) (Brod & Kaufman, 1994).

Moreover, these writers reject the idea that masculinity has a singular essence (Coltrane, 1994). Instead, they argue that what we often think of as the "essence" of masculinity—aggressiveness, attempts to dominate, emotional detachment, aversion to homosexuality, and so forth—is merely a social construction. The sex-gender system, these authors think, subordinates women in part by instilling in men characteristics that lead them to dominate women. If the sex-gender system were changed, they argue, masculinity might take a different form: more egalitarian, nurturing, and emotionally connected, and less exclusively heterosexual. These authors write not of masculinity but of *masculinities,* the title of an influential book by R. W. Connell (1995) that implies that there is more than one way to be masculine. Connell and others argue that the social influences that prop up the Western version of masculinity are so pervasive they become invisible to us. Consequently, we assume incorrectly that the current version of masculinity is the way men naturally are.

Some writers are attempting to bridge the gap between the more traditional brand of the men's movement and the feminist-influenced branch. Nock (1998) argues that marriage is the setting in which men finally separate from their parents and do what is expected of successful men: provide for and protect a family. Because most men rise to the challenge, he writes, marriage improves men's lives. Nock acknowledges that people's expectations about marriage have traditionally benefited men and disadvantaged women. Nock's solution is to restructure the institution of marriage so that women and men benefit equally from it. For instance, he favors reducing the economic dependence of wives on husbands. To stabilize marriage, he would give increased tax credits to some married couples. Yet giving more benefits to married couples would keep marriage in a privileged position compared to other family forms—a move strongly opposed by many liberals and feminists. How (and whether) to support both gender equity and marriage remains a contentious social issue.

The Contributions of Gender Studies

We have reviewed several approaches to the study of gender differences (see Table 3.1). The socialization approach emphasizes conscious learning and interpretation by children of the world around them—their parents, peers, television, and so forth. The lessons very young children learn allow them to construct a

Quick Review

- Many sociologists argue that gender differences are built into the structure of society in ways that support male domination.
- Sociologists who take the sex–gender system approach believe that societies transform modest biological differences into pervasive gender differences that disadvantage women.
- Some theorists have argued that capitalists benefit from inequalities between women and men because they pay women lower wages and benefit from women's unpaid housework services.
- But the inequalities between women and men under socialism suggest that systems of male domination may be independent of whether a nation is capitalist or socialist.
- Women from minority racial and ethnic groups often experience inequalities that simultaneously involve their gender, class, and racial/ethnic position.
- Feminist sociologists argue that the characteristics that comprise "masculinity" as we know it are socially constructed rather than natural.
- Table 3.1 summarizes the differences among the approaches to studying gender differences discussed in this chapter.

sense of what society expects a girl or a boy to be like. The sex–gender system approach emphasizes the dominance men maintain over women through political and economic systems, customs, and traditions. (See *Families in Other Cultures: China's Missing Girls* on p. 104) The biosocial and psychoanalytic approaches

Table 3.1 Approaches to the Study of Gender Differences		
APPROACH	**HOW GENDER IS CONSTRUCTED**	**EXAMPLES**
Socialization	Through learning from adults, the media, peers, and the like what kinds of behavior are expected of women and men.	Boys are given trucks and tools for birthday presents; girls are given dolls and stuffed animals. Boys are admonished not to cry; girls are allowed to cry.
Sex–gender system	Through the constraints of an economic and social system that restricts women's behavior in ways that favor men.	Women are paid less than men for working at the same job. Women who work outside the home are still expected to be the primary caregivers to children, even if they are married.
Biosocial	Through biologically based (e.g., genetic, hormonal) differences that have evolved over the history of the human existence.	Boys will sometimes insist on playing with trucks and tools even if they are given dolls and stuffed animals.
Psychoanalytic	Through relations with women caregivers early in life, which cause women to internalize a sense of connectedness to others and men to internalize a sense of separateness.	Women, on average, may find it easier to form close relationships with others; men may find it easier to be separate from others.
Interactionist	Through continual reinforcement of gender differences because of the everyday behaviors of women and men.	Husbands who are very competent outside the home will claim they're not good at washing dishes or changing diapers, and their wives will agree with them and do these tasks.

| China's Missing Girls

American parents may have a slight preference for sons over daughters—although this preference has weakened over time (Pollard & Morgan, 2002). But most expectant couples are very happy if the woman gives birth to a healthy child of either gender. This is not as true in some other cultures. Consider China: Its families traditionally were patrilineal [➥ p. 38], defined as a kinship system in which descent is traced solely through the father. In such a system, a father transmitted his family line through his sons. His daughters, upon marrying, become part of their husbands' family lines. Moreover, China's families were also **patrilocal,** meaning that a young wife goes to live in her husband's parents' home. As a result, from the parents' perspective, daughters neither continue the family line nor contribute to the family's well-being as adults. Sons on the other hand, continue the family line and are expected to remain at home to care for their elderly parents. Especially in rural areas where help with farm labor is highly valued, this patriarchal system created a distinct preference for sons over daughters. If a newly married man's wife gave birth to a girl, his relatives would console him with the saying that having a daughter brings in a son.

Many other cultures also have strong son preferences (see Das Gupta & Bhat, 1997, on India). But when the continuing preference for sons in China collided with the government's desire to reduce its rate of population growth, the consequences for girls—and for gender relations in general—were dramatic. China is the most populous nation on earth, making up one-fifth of humankind. In 1979, it instituted a "one-child policy," which limited urban families to one child and allowed most rural families only two. Because the state controlled people's access to jobs, housing, land, and consumer goods, it could—and did—penalize families that exceeded the limit.[1]

Under this rule, having a daughter precluded having a son. Consequently, the strict policy evoked resistance. In a normal population, women give birth to about 106 boys for every 100 girls. (Because males have higher death rates, these numbers even out as the boys and girls age.) In China the sex ratio was very close to 106 to 100 in the 1960s and 1970s, before the one-child policy (Zeng et al., 1993). But China's 2000 census showed a sex-ratio at birth of 120 to 100 (Banister, 2003). For second births, the ratio is even higher: 152 to 100. Clearly, many fewer girl babies are

being reported than would ordinarily have been born; they have become known as the millions of "missing girls" (Riley, 2004).

No one knows for sure what is responsible for this discrepancy. One factor is underreporting of girl babies who are hidden, sent to live with friends or relatives elsewhere, or given up for adoption (Zeng et al., 1993). In some cases, families abandon newborn girls, often in places where they can be found and placed in overburdened orphanages, brimming with girls but bare of boys. But recent reports suggest that sex-selective abortions may be an important cause. The number of sophisticated ultrasound scanners, which can determine the sex of a fetus, increased greatly in China in the 1980s and 1990s. Some parents are learning the sex of fetuses through ultrasound tests and then selectively aborting females (Riley, 2004). And finally, a small number of parents may be allowing their infant daughters to die of neglect—not breastfeeding them as long as boys, for xample—or even killing them.

Moral questions aside, the one-child policy has helped China's economic development by reducing population growth. But it is beginning to cause problems: As the first one-child generation reaches adulthood, young men are finding a shortage of young

patrilocal a kinship system in which newly married couples live with the husband's parents

both suggest that girls and boys may have deep-seated predispositions toward certain types of behaviors. The biosocial approach emphasizes genetic and hormonal influences, while the psychoanalytic approach emphasizes the children's experiences with women caregivers. Finally, the interactionists argue that gender is too problematic to be created merely through childhood socialization; rather, it must be created and re-created in the everyday lives of adults. Throughout life, they argue, people construct and maintain gender differences through their everyday interactions with others.

Despite their different perspectives—or perhaps because of them—sociologists who have studied gender (along with their colleagues in anthropology, history, and psychology) have made important contributions to our understanding of the family. First, they have demonstrated that the roles men and women play in

In a one-child system, Chinese couples are often happier if they have a boy than a girl.

women to marry because of the sex-ratio imbalance. The elderly, who traditionally in China have relied on their children—especially their sons—for support, find they have fewer children, and often no sons, to care for them. The Chinese government is realizing that it will have to increase its support of the elderly greatly as a result. News reports suggest that it is easing up on enforcing the policy and allowing exemptions in some areas, but couples who want to have a third child must pay a fine (Eckholm, 2002).

Ask Yourself

1. Has anyone in your family ever expressed disappointment at the birth of a girl? If so, what was the reason for desiring a boy?
2. Aside from the patrilineal nature of Chinese culture, what other reasons might account for China's missing girls?

[1]Market-oriented economic reforms in China have reduced the power of the government to enforce the one-child family policy because more people now obtain jobs themselves through the labor market.

www.mhhe.com/cherlin5

families are in part socially and culturally constructed. Indeed, many sociologists would argue that such differences are almost entirely constructed by conscious social forces. But even those who believe that there is a psychoanalytic or biological component to gender-role distinctions would agree that our society greatly exaggerates these distinctions. That is, even if one believes that on average women are predisposed to relate somewhat better to infants and small children than men, that does not explain why so few husbands share the care of older children. Biology cannot explain why a brilliant lawyer is unable to clean a table. Psychoanalytic theory cannot explain why the great 1950s liberal Adlai Stevenson told the 1955 graduating class of Smith College (a private liberal arts college for women) that their place in politics was to "influence man and boy" through the "humble role of housewife" (Chafe, 1972). Moreover, biology can't explain the social changes in gender roles and family life that have occurred over the past few decades, or even the past few centuries, because evolutionary change is slow. Consequently, the biological and psychoanalytic approaches may not be very useful to a sociologist who is trying to explain social change—although they might be helpful in determining the difficulty of bringing about social change. In this book the social and cultural construction of gender will be relevant to discussions of changing conceptions of sexuality (Chapter 6), patterns of courtship, dating, and spouse choice, and the relationships between married or cohabiting couples (Chapter 7).

Second, sociologists of gender have taught us that gender distinctions sometimes (some would say *always*) reflect differences in power between men and women. Adlai Stevenson's speech was meant to convey to the Smith graduates how important their restricted political role was. But women whose only political influence is through their husbands are not equal in political power to men. After the rise of the feminist movement in the 1960s and 1970s and the increases in the number of women elected to political office, no male politician would make Stevenson's statement. Feminist scholars argue, moreover, that power differences do not stop at the family's front door; rather, the roles women play within marriages often reflect their husbands' greater power—in particular, his greater economic power. Said differently, the lesson is that families are not islands isolated from the rest of society; rather, the relations of power and inequality that hold outside the home can also extend within it. Differences in power and the allocation of work within the household will be examined in Chapter 8. Other chapters will include discussions of the effects of male domination on domestic violence against women (Chapter 11), the economic circumstances of divorced women (Chapter 12), and family law and policy (Chapter 14).

Looking Back

1. **How might fetal development affect the behavior of women and men?** There is some evidence that biological differences in the development of male and female fetuses could account for some of the gender differences in children's and adults' behavior. Studies have found a correlation between gender-typical behavior and exposure to higher levels of male sex hormones before birth. Biologically based differences only exist "on average"; individuals can show a wide range of behavior. And social influences such as parental upbringing and education can counteract biological predispositions.

2. **How do sociologists distinguish between the concepts of "sex" and "gender"?** Sociologists use the term *sex* to refer to biologically based differences between women and men and *gender* to refer to differences that are social and cultural, and therefore constructed by society. Gender differences often reflect male domination

over women. Nevertheless, in some instances social and biological influences on gender differences are difficult to disentangle. In practice, people assign to a person a "sex category" based on socially accepted characteristics, not biological markers.

3. **How do children learn the gender roles of women and men?** According to the socialization approach, young children learn stereotypical gender roles from parents, peers, teachers, and the media. The emphasis in this approach is on conscious, social learning. In general, children are taught to think that boys and men are aggressive, competitive, and independent, whereas girls and women are less aggressive, more nurturing, and better at enabling and maintaining personal relationships. From these lessons, children mentally construct the concept of gender. In fact, some scholars argue that gender is such a broad and central identity it should not be considered merely a social role.

4. **How does everyday life reinforce gender differences?** Sociologists who take the interactionist approach believe that gender roles need continual reinforcement throughout life. In their view gender differences are reproduced in daily interactions between women and men in settings such as the home and the workplace. Without being conscious of it, individuals do the work of maintaining gender differences.

5. **Are gender differences built into the structure of society?** Many gender theorists argue that gender differences are built into the structure of nearly all societies through patriarchy, a social order based on the domination of men over women. Society, they charge, turns limited sex differences into pervasive gender differences and enshrines them in a sex–gender system. Gender the-

orists argue that gender should be seen as a basic source of social stratification, as important as race and class. Minority- group women often experience gender, class, and racial or ethnic inequality simultaneously.

6. **What have been the contributions of gender studies to our understanding of the family?** Sociologists who study gender have demonstrated that the roles men and women play in families are in part socially and culturally constructed. Indeed, many sociologists would argue that gender differences are almost entirely social constructions. Sociologists have also shown that gender-role distinctions often reflect differences in power between women and men.

 Go to the Online Learning Center at www.mhhe.com/cherlin5 to test your knowledge of the chapter concepts and key terms.

Study Questions

1. What does the story of the berdaches teach us about sex and gender?
2. Let us suppose for the moment that prenatal male hormone levels influence aggressive behavior. Would we then expect all boys to be aggressive and all girls to be unaggressive?
3. The newest medium to which children and adolescents are exposed is the Internet. Do frequently visited Web sites impart messages about women's and men's proper behavior?
4. What are the limitations of the concept of "gender roles"?
5. Is "doing gender" in daily life—the daily reinforcement of gendered behavior through social interaction—strong enough to maintain the gender differences we see in society?
6. Do you agree, as many feminist researchers do, that "connected knowing" is preferable to "separated knowing"?
7. What are the arguments for and against the proposition that women's oppression is closely linked to capitalism?
8. If the Chinese patrilineal kinship system were to weaken with economic modernization, how might the preferences of Chinese parents for the sex of their children change?

Key Terms

berdache   80
biosocial approach (to gender
   differences)   86
capitalism   98
comparable-worth
   discrimination   99
gender   82
gender roles   87
gestation   84

interactionist approach
   (to gender differences)   94
intersexual   83
masculinity 101
patriarchy   96
patrilocal   104
peer group   89
psychoanalytic approach
   (to gender differences)   91

sex   81
sex-gender system   97
socialism   100
socialization   88
socialization approach
   (to gender differences)   88
social role   87

Thinking about Families

The Public Family	The Private Family
Do parents, peers, and teachers prepare boys for success in the work world more than they prepare girls?	Does everyday life reinforce gender differences in families in ways we usually don't notice?

Families on the Internet   www.mhhe.com/cherlin5

Note: While all the URLs listed were current as of the printing of this book, these sites often change. Please check our Web site (http://www.mhhe.com/cherlin5) for updates.

Information on gender and on women's issues abounds on the Internet. On the liberal side, the Feminist Majority Foundation Online Web site (www.feminist.org) provides links to many sources of information. Click on "feminist research center" and you will find a list of women's studies programs, feminist journals, and feminist magazines. A conservative perspective is available from Concerned Women for America (www.cwfa.org).

For an abundance of factual information on labor force issues such as earnings differences between women and men, go to the home page of the Women's Bureau at the U.S. Department of Labor (www.dol.gov/wb). The Women's Bureau is concerned with working conditions, including equal pay, for women employed outside the home. Click on "Statistics" (under "Resources & Info") to see their list of leading occupations for women. In how many of these occupations are 80 percent or more of the workers women? The Census Bureau maintains a list of news releases about reports on women's statistics (http://www.census.gov/Press-Release/www/releases/archives/women/index.html).

Social Class and Families

Looking Forward

1. How have changes in the American economy since the 1970s affected families?

2. What factors determine the social class position of families?

3. How have the family lives of people at the top and bottom of the social order diverged recently?

4. Are there social class differences in kinship?

5. Are there differences across classes in how parents raise children?

As I was revising this chapter in Miami, on leave from my university, I saw a huge freighter steaming slowly toward the harbor with hundreds of trailer-truck-sized containers stacked on its broad-beamed deck. In 2005 the port of Miami imported 155,664 tons of alcoholic beverages, 136,105 tons of clothing and textiles, 126,403 tons of refrigerated fruits and vegetables, 76,021 tons of nonalcoholic beverages, 62,682 tons of lumber and wood, 62,556 tons of furniture and other wood products, 57,459 tons of iron, steel, and other metal products, and 42,304 tons of paper (Port of Miami, 2006). A half-century ago, most of these goods would have been brewed, woven, sewn, grown, harvested, milled, built, or processed in the United States. The factories and farms that used to make these goods employed millions of American workers, most of whom did not have college degrees. On the side of the freighter, I saw "China Shipping Lines" painted in large letters; and in fact the port of Miami received more tons of commodities from China than from any other country in 2005—almost 50 percent more than from the number 2 country, Italy. The flood of Chinese goods shows how the globalization of production has reduced the employment opportunities for people without college degrees in the United States.

Automation has also eliminated jobs. When I call Amtrak to make a train reservation, a perky voice answers by saying, "Hi, I'm Julie, Amtrak's automated agent," and continues to give me options until I yell "operator" several times and am finally connected to a human being. Julie could not function without a voice recognition system that depends upon fast, powerful computers and complex software that did not exist until about a decade ago. Before then, sales agents, most of whom did not have college degrees, answered the phones. Jobs like theirs are also disappearing. At the same time, jobs for the well-educated people who design systems like Amtrak's are increasing. The U.S. Bureau of Labor Statistics predicts that the nation will employ an additional 750,000 computer specialists of various kinds between 2004 and 2014, the vast majority of whom will have bachelor's degrees (U.S. Bureau of Labor Statistics, 2006).

In fact, since the 1960s, average wages have stayed the same or decreased for workers without college degrees because of globalization and automation. Only the college-educated have experienced substantial wage growth since then (Katz & Autor, 1999). How changes in the economy have affected families—and, more generally, how social class position, education, and income affect families—are the topics that will be addressed in this chapter.

■ Families and the Economy

Every old city has seen the closing of factories that had formerly provided full-time jobs at good wages to workers without college educations. For example, clothing imported from China and elsewhere has displaced clothing that used to be made in the United States on American sewing machines. The Singer Sewing Machine Company dominated Elizabeth, New Jersey, from its founding in 1873 until it closed in 1982—its market reduced by ready-to-wear clothes and its competitive edge lost to plants in developing countries that paid workers far lower wages. One longtime worker told anthropologist Katherine Newman:

> *I worked there forty-seven years and one month. I was one of many people in my family. My niece worked there. My two brothers, my father. You see, Singer's in the old days, it was a company that went from one generation to the other. (Newman, 1988)*

THE IMPACT OF ECONOMIC RESTRUCTURING

Young workers without a college education have been particularly hard hit by the changes in the U.S. economy. The growth of semiskilled and skilled manufacturing jobs has slowed because of two factors. The first is technological change, such as growing use of computers in offices and factories; the new technologies allow firms to replace workers with machines. The second factor is the movement of factory production to developing nations such as Taiwan and Mexico, where wages are much lower. Due to these changes in the economy, there is a growing shortage of full-time jobs, with fringe benefits, that pay substantially above the minimum wage and yet are available to persons without a college degree. These were the kinds of jobs that used to allow high school–educated young adults in this country to support a family. Even during the strong economy of the late 1990s, the wages of these men hardly rose (Richer, Frank, Greenberg, Savner, & Turetsky, 2003).

More and more, what's available to young workers without a college education are low-paying service and unskilled manual-labor jobs. In addition, the employment arrangements available to these workers are changing. The older, "standard" job that dominated American industry until recently involved full-time work that continued indefinitely and was performed under the supervision of the employer. But since the 1970s, there has been a sharp increase in **nonstandard employment:** jobs that do not provide full-time, indefinite work directly for the firm that is paying for it (Kalleberg, 2000). Nonstandard employment includes part-time work, work for temporary help agencies, work for subcontractors who perform services (such as maintenance) for larger firms, and short-term contract work. By 2001, 23 percent of the workforce was composed of part-time or temporary workers (U.S. Bureau of Labor Statistics, 2001, 2002). Most of these jobs offer low or moderate wages, but even middle-class jobs are not immune to the trend. As corporations downsize their managerial workforce to save money, middle-aged white-collar workers can find themselves replaced by temporary or contract workers.

In contrast, the 1950s and 1960s were prosperous times for American families. Between 1945 and 1973, the average income of full-time workers, adjusted for inflation, doubled (Levy & Michel, 1991). Young men and women growing up in the 1950s and 1960s expected that they would eventually earn more than their parents, just as their parents were earning more than their grandparents. In the

nonstandard employment jobs that do not provide full-time, indefinite work directly for the firm that is paying for it

early 1970s, however, wages stopped increasing. Particularly hard hit were the kinds of entry-level jobs for which young parents tend to be qualified. The impact of the economic slump was so great that in 1996, the average 30-year-old husband with a high school degree earned 20 percent less than a comparable man in 1979 (Levy, 1998). Consequently, the gap between the wages of more-educated and less-educated male workers has widened considerably since the 1970s. To make matters worse, housing prices have risen substantially; and in the 1980s and 1990s a small but growing number of homeless families began to draw concern. (See *Families and Public Policy*: Homeless Families: The Tip of the Iceberg.)

UNEQUAL DISTRIBUTION OF INCOME

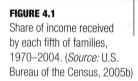

distribution of family income the proportion of the total income of all families in the nation that each family receives

As wages have failed to grow for workers without college degrees, earnings have become more unequal. Suppose that every family in the nation tossed its annual income into one huge pot and then they all lined up, one family in back of the other. If we wanted the **distribution of family income**—the proportion of the total income of all families in the nation that each family receives—to be equal, we would simply give each family in line the same amount of money from the pot. If we wanted the distribution to be unequal, we might give, say, 35 percent of all the money in the pot to the first one-fifth of families in the line, 30 percent to the next one-fifth, 20 percent to the next one-fifth, 10 percent to the next one-fifth, and just 5 percent to the last one-fifth. In fact, the actual distribution of family income in the United States is even more unequal than this hypothetical experiment would create. Moreover, inequality has increased since the early 1970s. Figure 4.1 shows the income shares of each fifth of families from 1970 to 2004. During this period, the share of income that went to the bottom fifth declined from 5.4 to 4.0 percent. Although this does not look like a substantial change, it means that the bottom fifth's income share dropped by about 25 percent.

FIGURE 4.1
Share of income received by each fifth of families, 1970–2004. (*Source:* U.S. Bureau of the Census, 2005b)

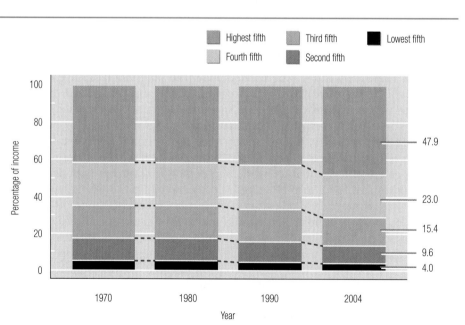

The second- and third-lowest fifths also saw their shares shrink. Even the next-to-highest fifth had a modest decrease. Only the top fifth of all families increased its income share substantially; it rose from 40.9 to 47.7 percent. During this period, then, the wealthy were getting wealthier while the poor were getting poorer and those in the middle were struggling to keep up.

Income inequality among families has increased for three reasons:

- The growing inequality in the earnings of men.
- The growth of single-parent families.
- The movement of middle-class wives into the workforce.

As for the first reason, men with less education and few skills have seen their incomes drop, on average, whereas men with more education have seen their incomes rise.[1] Consequently, the gap has widened between families with husbands who do not have college degrees and families with husbands who do have college degrees. The second reason is important because families with only one parent must rely on the earnings of one wage earner. And women's earnings are, on average, lower than men's. [→pp. 98–99] So the growth of single-parent families has widened inequality by creating a larger number of low- and moderate-income families.

The third reason is perhaps more subtle. A few decades ago, most of the married women who worked for pay came from less affluent families. In contrast, most well-off married women did not work for pay. As a result, the net effect of wives' employment was to boost the incomes of low-income families; and this effect reduced family income inequality. Over the last few decades, however, many wives from more affluent families have taken jobs outside the home. Their employment raised the incomes of families in which the husband already was earning a good income. Therefore, the rise in married women's employment since about 1970 has actually increased family income inequality (Burtless & Karoly, 1995).

Trends in Poverty   Poverty decreased in the United States during the prosperous 1950s and 1960s, then increased from the 1970s through the mid-1990s. Since the mid-1990s, a strong economy has reduced poverty again. How do sociologists know this? Each year the U.S. government calculates an official **poverty line** and publishes statistics on the number of families with incomes below the line. The poverty line is a strange concoction that no one likes but no analyst can do without. It was established in the mid-1960s, when federal officials figured out how much it would cost to buy enough food to meet the Agriculture Department's standard for an "economy" diet—and then, on the assumption that families spend one-third of their income on food, simply multiplied by three (Katz, 1989). To account for inflation, this standard (which is adjusted for the number of people in the family) is multiplied every year by the increase in the cost of living. Advocates for the poor claim it is too low and therefore underestimates the low-income population; many conservatives claim it is too high. Its main virtue is that it can be used to examine changes over time in the percentage of families that fall above or below it. In 2004, the line stood at $19,157 for a family of two adults and two children under 18 and at $15,219 for a family of one adult and two children (U.S. Bureau of the Census, 2005h).

poverty line a federally defined income limit defined as the cost of an "economy" diet for a family, multiplied by three

[1] There is disagreement, however, among economists about the role of men's earnings in the rise of income inequality. Some economists argue that declines in the number of men who work full-time or who work at all are more important than differences in the earnings of employed men (Haveman, 1996).

FIGURE 4.2
Percent of families with
children under 18 that
had incomes below the
poverty line, for whites,
blacks, and Hispanics,
1959–2004. (*Source:* U.S.
Bureau of the Census, 2005d)

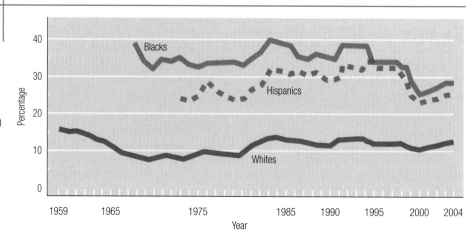

Figure 4.2 shows the percentage of families with children under 18 that fell below the poverty line each year from 1959 to 2004. Information on African American
families is available only from 1967 onward, and for Hispanic families (which may
be of any race) from 1972 onward. As can be seen, the percentage of families below the line dropped for white families from 1959 through the early 1970s, and
for African American families from 1967 through the early 1970s. (Other statistics
in the same government report suggest that African American poverty had been
declining sharply throughout the 1960s.) When the economy began to weaken in
the mid-1970s, the decline in the percentage of families in poverty stopped.
Poverty levels fell when the economy was strong during the mid-to-late 1990s
and rose when it cooled off in the 2000s. In 2004, among families with children
under 18, 12.4 percent of whites, 25.5 percent of Hispanics, and 28.6 percent of
blacks had incomes below the poverty line (U.S. Bureau of the Census, 2005d).

Poverty has also become increasingly concentrated in the growing numbers of
households headed by divorced, separated, never-married, or widowed mothers.
Whereas about one-fourth of all poor families were headed by single mothers in
1960, one-half were headed by single mothers in 2004 (U.S. Bureau of the Census,
2005g).

Earnings by Family Type   During the 1970s and 1980s, many families in
the middle of the income distribution kept up with the cost of living only because wives took jobs outside the home. Figure 4.3 shows the trends since 1973
in the median incomes of three kinds of families. (The median is the midpoint in
the distribution, the point at which as many families have higher incomes as have
lower incomes. All dollar figures are expressed in 2001 dollars, adjusted for increases over time in the cost of living.) The bottom line shows that there was little change in the median incomes of families that were headed by women
without husbands present until the mid-1990s. The middle line shows how
married-couple families without wives in the paid labor force fared. The median
income for this group showed little change—a sharp break from the increases of
the 1950s and 1960s. The largest increase in income came for married-couple
families in which the wife worked for pay, as shown by the top line. The gap
between the median incomes of single-earner married couples and dual-earner

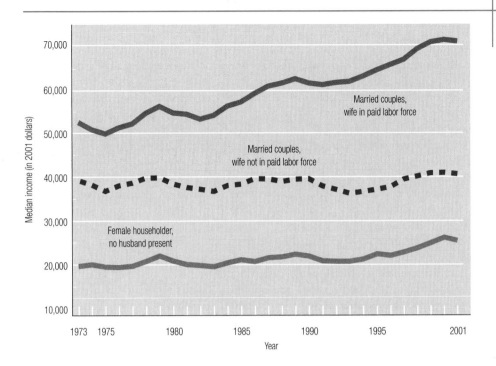

FIGURE 4.3
Median income of three types of families, 1973–2001. (*Source:* U.S. Bureau of the Census, 2003h).

married couples rose from $13,180 in 1973 to $30,052 in 2001 (U.S. Bureau of the Census, 2005b). With housing prices rising and young men's wages declining, families needed a second income to live the kind of lives they aspired to. An increasing number of them chose to have wives enter the paid labor force.

These income trends led economist Frank Levy, in his study of U.S. income distribution since the 1940s, to note how much more important family composition is now than at midcentury (Levy, 1998). In the 1940s, Levy notes, most families had two parents and one earner, whether they were rich or poor. There wasn't much variation in family structure. Yet by the end of the century, more than half of the wealthier families had two earners, while most poor families had no earners or only one earner. In the 1940s, the key economic difference between families was how much the husband earned. Today, the key differences include whether or not there is a husband in the household at all and whether the wife works for pay.

Quick Review

- The kinds of jobs that used to allow a high school–educated adult to support a family have become scarce because of economic restructuring.
- Homelessness has increased due to economic restructuring, the growth in single-parent families, and, possibly, time limits on welfare receipt.
- The distribution of family income has become more unequal since the 1970s.
- Family poverty increased from the 1970s to the mid-1990s before declining in the late 1990s; it is increasingly concentrated in single-parent families.
- Since the early 1970s, family income has been rising only for dual-earner married couples.

Defining Social Class

social class an ordering of all persons in a society according to their degrees of economic resources, prestige, and privilege

life chances the resources and opportunities that people have to provide themselves with material goods and favorable living conditions

status group a group of people who share a common style of life and often identify with each other

Another key difference is whether the family's earners have college degrees. By a college degree I mean a bachelor of arts or sciences degree, usually earned in four years. The differences in economic opportunity for people with and without college educations and the growing inequality of family incomes suggest that the concept of class may be useful in understanding family life. Sociologists write about **social class,** an ordering of all persons in a society according to their degrees of economic resources, prestige, and privilege. All agree that income and wealth are core elements of this ordering. But the German sociologist Max Weber added other concepts (Gerth & Mills, 1946). One is the broader idea of **life chances,** the resources and opportunities that people have to provide themselves with material goods and favorable living conditions. People's life chances may be augmented by the higher education they obtain or their family's contacts in the labor market. Their life chances may be limited by discrimination or racial segregation. A second concept is a more subjective category: the **status group,** a group of people who share a common style of life and often identify with each other. They are sometimes distinguished by prestige—the honor and status a person receives—such as the prestige of medical doctors or university professors. They often differ in their level of privilege—that is, their access to special advantages such as attendance at elite universities.

BRINGING IN GENDER AND FAMILY

The great theories of class were developed at a time when relatively few married women worked outside the home. Theorists focused on the kinds of jobs men typically did: physical labor, factory work, supervising, or managing. Therefore, these theories really refer to the class positions of individual men (Acker, 2000). But if you are interested in the pooling of resources and the sharing of living conditions, you might want to analyze the class location of a family. For instance, if your ultimate interest is children's living conditions, the family would be a more

A manager at a fast-food restaurant chain both supervises workers and is supervised by higher-level executives.

appropriate unit to study than the individual parent. In the days when most families had two parents and only one (almost always the husband) worked for wages, one could assign to a family the class location of the husband. One could speak of a "working-class" family and mean a family in which the husband worked in a factory and the wife did not work outside the home. (Note that wives' unpaid labor inside the home isn't counted as "work" in these theories; we will discuss this problem in Chapter 8.)

But this simple procedure doesn't work well any more. Because of the great increase in married women's work outside the home, both the husband and the wife work for pay in the majority of married-couple families: In 2004, both parents were employed in 65 percent of all married-couple families with children under 18 (U.S. Bureau of the Census, 2005k). Studies in the United States and other Western nations suggest that, depending on the definition of social class, husbands and wives may belong to different classes in up to one-third of all two-parent, two-earner families (Sørensen, 1994).

Moreover, many women work in the expanding service sector (i.e., sales, clerical, personal services) of the economy. It's harder to assign a class position to these jobs, in part because they tend to pay less than the jobs that men with comparable education obtain. Consider a woman who works as a salesclerk in a department store. She might be considered part of the "middle class" as long as she is married to a husband with a well-paying job. But if the marriage ends and she becomes a single parent, her standard of living is likely to drop. Whether she necessarily leaves the middle class is unclear—she has less income, but she retains the same level of education and many of the same friends and interests.

Yet when people are asked in surveys whether they are "working class" or "middle class," they give ready answers. How, in fact, do husbands and wives decide what social class they are in? There are three models of how they make their decisions (Davis & Robinson, 1998). The oldest is the "status-borrowing" model, in which wives are assumed to derive their class location from their husbands' income, education, and occupation. This model worked best in the 1950s and 1960s, when few wives worked for pay; and nearly all of the studies of social class prior to 1970 used it. The second is the "independence model," which assumes that each spouse thinks only of her or his own characteristics. The third model, the most widely used today, is the status-sharing model, in which both wives and husbands use a combination of their characteristics in deciding what class they are in.

Which model is accurate? Research suggests that both spouses consider the husbands' and the wives' incomes and weigh them about equally when deciding what class they are in. In terms of income, then, women and men in dual-earner couples follow the status-sharing model. (And both women and men seem to consider income as the most important determinant of class.) But women and men diverge in their thinking about education and occupational prestige: Women tend to consider theirs and their husbands' more or less equally, whereas men tend to weight their own more heavily. Overall, then, women follow the status-sharing model; but men follow a weaker sharing model that veers toward independence when they think of education or occupation (Davis and Robinson, 1988, 1998; Yamaguchi & Wang, 2002).

SOCIAL CLASSES AND STATUS GROUPS

Clearly, thinking about families in class terms is complex, but it also seems unavoidable. Let us examine the four social class categories commonly used in sociological research: upper class, middle class, working class, and lower class. But think of them as ideal types rather than concrete realities. Introduced by Weber, the **ideal type** refers to a hypothetical model that consists of the most significant characteristics, in extreme form, of a social phenomenon. It is useful for understanding social life, even though any real example of the phenomenon may not have all the characteristics of the ideal type.

ideal type a hypothetical model that consists of the most significant characteristics, in extreme form, of a social phenomenon

The Four-Class Model   Americans understand the four-category scheme, but they overwhelmingly say they are either middle class or working class. For instance in the 2002 General Social Survey (GSS), a biennial national survey of adults, 3 percent of the respondents said they were upper class, 46 percent said middle class, 45 percent said working class, and 6 percent said lower class (Davis, Smith, & Marsden, 2003). Both extremes apparently sound unpleasant to people, probably because of the stigma of being "lower class" and the embarrassment of admitting to being "upper class." By most reasonable criteria, however, the lower class is larger than 6 percent. For instance, 10.7 percent of American adults had incomes below the official poverty level in 2004 (U.S. Bureau of the Census, 2005e).

There is little consensus on the size of the upper class or on just how to define it. In general, **upper-class families** are those that have amassed wealth and privilege and that often have substantial prestige as well. They tend to own large, spacious homes, to possess expensive clothes and furnishings, to have substantial investment holdings, and to be recognized as part of the social and cultural elite of their communities. Upper-class husbands tend to be owners or senior managers of large corporations, banks, or law firms. Their wives are less likely to work for pay outside the home than women in other social classes, and they may be instrumental in maintaining ties to wealthy kin. (See *Families in Other Cultures:* Kinship Networks among the Mexican Upper Class.)

upper-class families families that have amassed wealth and privilege and that often have substantial prestige as well

Middle-class families are those whose connection to the economy provides them with a secure, comfortable income and allows them to live well above a subsistence level. Middle-class families can usually afford privileges such as a nice house, a new car, a college education for the children, fashionable clothes, a vacation at the seashore, and so forth. The jobs that middle-class men and women hold usually require some college education and are performed mainly in offices and businesses. Middle-class men tend to hold higher-paying jobs such as a lawyer, pharmacist, engineer, sales representative, or midlevel manager at a corporation. Jobs such as these usually have some prestige and include fringe benefits such as health insurance, paid vacations, paid sick leave, and retirement pensions. Women in general are underrepresented in the higher-paying professional and managerial occupations, although their numbers are growing. Women professionals still tend to be found in occupations that require a college education, such as nursing and teaching, but that don't pay as much as male-dominated professions.

middle-class families families whose connection to the economy provides them with a secure, comfortable income and allows them to live well above a subsistence level

Working-class families are those whose incomes can provide reliably for the minimum needs of what people see as a decent life: a modest house or an apartment, one or two cars, enough money to enroll children at a state or community college, and so forth. Working-class men tend to hold manual jobs in factories, automobile repair shops, construction sites, and so forth, that involve little or no authority over others. Layoffs are more common in manual occupations than in the office and business jobs middle-class men tend to have, so working-class men are more vulnerable to periods of unemployment. Moreover, working-class men and women are less likely to work a full week and have fringe benefits. Clerical jobs,

working-class families families whose income can reliably provide only for the minimum needs of what other people see as a decent life

Middle-class families have a secure, comfortable income and can afford privileges such as a lakeshore vacation.

such as secretary, or service jobs, such as cafeteria cashier or hospital orderly, are common among working-class women; a minority work in factories.

Lower-class families are those whose connection to the economy is so tenuous that they cannot provide reliably for a decent life, either because they work steadily at low-paying jobs (the so-called "working poor") or because they are frequently unemployed. They may live in deteriorated housing in neighborhoods with high crime rates. They may not be able to afford adequate clothing for winter, and they may need government-issued food stamps to purchase enough food. Lower-class men, who have little education and few occupational skills, can find jobs that pay only at or slightly above the minimum wage and that have few, if any, fringe benefits and little security.

lower-class families
families whose connection to the economy is so tenuous that they cannot reliably provide for a decent life

Three Status Groups   Although these four categories seem ingrained in both social scientific research and popular thought, the definitions are so broad that it is very difficult to draw a clear distinction between middle-class and working-class families or between working-class families and lower-class families. In the remainder of this chapter, rather than trying to precisely define the boundaries of these broad categories, I will refer primarily to three social class groupings that are more like Weber's status groups. The boundaries of these status groups are based on education. The first group comprises people with a college degree. I will draw this boundary based on two arguments: First, the restructuring of the American economy has increased the life chances of those with college degrees to a much greater extent than those without college degrees; and second, the college educated form a status group, in the Weberian sense of sharing a common style of life, because their patterns of marriage, divorce, and childbearing appear to be diverging from the patterns of people without college degrees. About one-third of all adults between the ages of 25 and 54 have a four-year college degree.

The second group comprises people who graduated from high school and may have attended college but did not obtain a four-year degree; they are the most

Homeless Families: The Tip of the Iceberg

It is one of the paradoxes of public debates about the family that the phenomenon of homeless families, which emerged in the 1980s, has received so much attention compared with the more general problems of poor families. To be sure, homelessness is worthy of public concern. Although few homeless families were visible in 1980, their numbers appear to have increased over the 1980s and 1990s (Rossi, 1994). By one recent estimate, between 900,000 and 1.4 million children experience a spell of homelessness each year in the United States (Burt, Aron, & Lee, 2001).

But these families are just a small share of the number with incomes so low that they face the same kinds of risks the homeless face. Several studies have examined why some families become homeless and others don't and why the number of homeless families has increased.

To become homeless, a family must have both a low income and weak ties to other kin. That is to say, it must have too little money to pay rent and too few relatives to call upon for shelter. Single-parent families are vulnerable on both counts; their incomes tend to be low, and they cannot rely on the resources of a second parent and his or her kin. That is why the vast majority of homeless families are single-

parent families (Jencks, 1994). Most families have one or two spells of homelessness, but a minority have repeated spells. Mothers who gave birth as teenagers or who have experienced domestic violence are at higher risk for repeated homelessness (Metraux & Culhane, 1999; Gladwell, 2006).

Yet most poor single-parent families are not homeless. Peter Rossi (1994) estimated that in the mid-1980s more than 2 million single-parent families had incomes that were less than half the poverty level. At most, about 5 percent of these families spent a night in a shelter during a given year.[1] The other 95 percent constitute what Rossi calls the "precariously housed," those who are especially vulnerable to homelessness through deep poverty and the lack of a second parent, but who manage to avoid it.

Why have a small but growing percentage of the poor appeared at the door of public shelters for the homeless since 1980? Several factors contribute. Rossi emphasizes the consequences of the restructuring of the economy, especially the worsening job opportunities for young adults without a college education. Moreover, marriage may have decreased among the poor and nonpoor alike for other reasons having to do with women's greater

economic independence or with cultural changes such as increased individualism. In any event, the growth of poor single-parent families was a key factor. According to Rossi's estimates, in the 1970s there were 1 million single-parent families with incomes less than half the poverty level, but by 1991 there were 2.5 million.

Rossi and Christopher Jencks also note that the average value of welfare payments has dropped substantially since the mid-1970s because Congress and state legislatures did not adjust them for increases in the cost of living. So families with no other sources of income have been less able to afford housing. Moreover, the supply of low-cost rental housing has declined since the 1980s, either through demolition, remodeling into high-rent properties, or neglect and abandonment by slum landlords (Koegl, Burnam, & Baumohl, 1996).

The increases in very poor single-parent families in the 1980s and 1990s were real. It must be noted, though, that the increase in serious poverty affected many more "homed" families than homeless families, and yet public attention focused on the latter. Americans seemed far more sympathetic to families living in shelters than to the larger and growing number of poor families sharing cramped quarters

difficult to categorize in terms of social class because they sometimes share the characteristics of the groups above and below them.

The third group comprises people who did not graduate from high school, whose family patterns in some respects are diverging from both groups above them. These three status groups are roughly equivalent to what people think of as the "middle class," "working class," and "lower class," respectively; but these labels are so imprecise that I will avoid them for the most part.

The number of homeless families seems to have increased during the 1980s and 1990s.

with relatives or barely avoiding eviction from their own apartments.

The public reaction suggested that most Americans think every family ought to have a home, whether or not their poverty is in any sense their own making. Homelessness grabbed the guts of many Americans whose hearts were hardened against stories of hardship among the poor. But family homelessness is just the tip of the iceberg of serious poverty among families—an iceberg that grew ominously in the 1980s and early 1990s and again in the mid-2000s. Passengers aboard the *Titanic* learned the hard way that it's dangerous to ignore the rest of an iceberg. We would be wise to heed their lesson.

Ask Yourself

1. Has anyone in your family ever been forced to move into a friend's or relative's home, or perhaps into a homeless shelter? If so, what caused the crisis?

2. What can the government do to prevent families from becoming homeless? What can families themselves do?

[1] I derived this figure by dividing 100,000 by 2 million and converting the result to a percentage.

www.mhhe.com/cherlin5

Quick Review

- Social scientists use the concept of social class to order all individuals in a society.
- Max Weber maintained that one needs to consider status groups as well as classes defined by income and wealth to understand how a society is stratified.
- Wives and husbands both consider each other's income, education, and occupation in identifying their social class, but wives do so more than husbands.
- Sociologists typically assume that four broad social classes exist: the upper class, middle class, working class, and lower class.
- Differences in life chances and styles of living suggest that three status groups defined by education may also be useful.

Social Class Differences in Family Life

Figure 4.3 showed that the median incomes of different types of families have diverged in the past few decades: dual-earner, married-couple families have seen their incomes grow while other families have seen their incomes change very little. There are several other ways in which the family lives of parents and children vary from status group to status group, including patterns of marriage, divorce, and childbearing, the kind of assistance they receive from relatives living in their household and elsewhere, and their approaches to child rearing. They are not completely different, of course; similarities run across status groups that would be apparent to someone visiting from a non-Western culture where, for instance, parents are heavily involved in helping their children choose spouses, newly married couples move in with the husband's family, and adult children care for their aged parents in their homes.

DIVERGING DEMOGRAPHICS

In the 1960s and 1970s, as noted in Chapter 2 [➡ p. 67] the typical ages at marriage rose for nearly all groups, and so did the likelihood that a marriage would end in divorce (Cherlin, 1992). But since about 1980, the family patterns of people with college degrees have moved in a different direction than those of people with less education. And in some respects, the family patterns of people who did not graduate from high school have moved in the opposite direction.

Age at Marriage   People with four-year college degrees are displaying a pattern we might call catch-up marriage: Until age 25, relatively few of them marry, which is consistent with the societywide trend toward later marriage. But in their late twenties and thirties, their rates of marriage exceed those of the less educated (Martin, 2004b). By the time they are in their forties, a higher proportion of them have married than is the case for people without college degrees (Goldstein & Kenney, 2001). In other words, if you just followed a group of young adults until their mid-twenties, you would conclude that college graduates have lower marriage rates, and you might even predict that fewer of them will ever marry. You would be missing, however, the action that occurs later on, after men and women have completed their higher education and begun to establish careers, which more than compensates.

Childbearing Outside of Marriage   Most college-educated women also wait to have children until after they are married—childbearing outside of marriage remains almost as uncommon among them as it was a half-century ago (Ellwood & Jencks, 2004). Among women without college degrees, however, and especially among women who have never attended college, far fewer wait until marriage to have children than was the case a half-century ago. I will return to this topic shortly, when I discuss reproductive strategies.

The Marriage Market   Education has become a more important factor in who marries whom over the past half-century or so. Sociologists call the tendency of people to marry others similar to themselves **assortative marriage.** In

assortative marriage the tendency of people to marry others similar to themselves

the 1930s, religion was a more important determinant of who marries whom than was education: A college-educated Protestant was more likely to marry a Protestant high school graduate than to marry a college-educated Catholic. But since the middle of the twentieth century, college graduates have become much more likely to marry each other than to marry people with the same religion but less education. Religion remains a factor, but the college educated have largely removed themselves from the rest of the marriage market (Kalmijn, 1991). And since the 1970s, people who did not complete high school have become less likely to marry people with more education; rather, they have become more isolated in the marriage market. (Schwartz & Mare, 2005). In the middle of the educational distribution, on the other hand, more marriage across educational groups exists (for example, a marriage between a high school graduate who did not attend college and someone who attended college but did not get a bachelor's degree). In sum, the marriage market today seems to be stratified by education into three submarkets of people who choose partners primarily like themselves: people with college degrees; people who graduated from high school and may have attended college but did not get a bachelor's degree; and people who did not graduate from high school.

Divorce   The trends in divorce also show a divergence. Figure 4.4 shows the percentage of first marriages that end in divorce or separation within 10 years for women in each of four education groups, according to the year they married. As you scan the figure from left to right, you move from marriages begun in the early 1970s to marriages begun in the early 1990s. In the 1970s the risk of divorce was rising for all groups, but starting in 1980 the risk for college graduates (the solid blue line) began to drop faster than among other groups; and by the early 1990s the risk was substantially lower for college graduates. Over the same period, the risk of divorce rose fastest for women who did not complete high school (the solid red line) so that by the early 1990s they had the highest risk. Another study confirms that divorce risks rose fastest for people without high school degrees

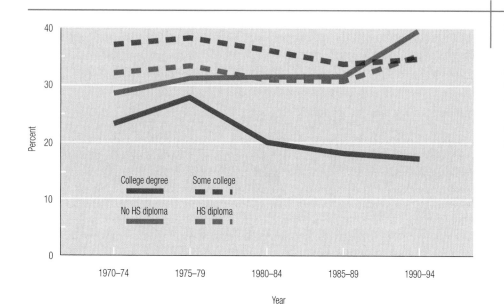

FIGURE 4.4
Percent of first marriages that end in divorce or separation within 10 years, for women, by year of marriage and education. (*Source:* Martin, 2004a)

during the 1980s and early 1990s; and the authors estimate that the percentage of marriages that end in divorce or separation over a person's lifetime is, at current rates, 60 percent for people without high school degrees; a little over 50 percent for those who graduated high school but did not graduate from college; and 36 percent for college graduates (Raley & Bumpass, 2003). So as is the case with marriage, the risk of divorce also seems to be stratified, with a college-educated group at one end, a middle group consisting of high school graduates and people with some college in the middle, and people without high school degrees at the other end.

Differences in Early Adulthood   To sum up this picture of diverging demographics, several trends in marriage, childbearing, and divorce suggest that the family patterns of individuals in the three status groups have moved in different directions in the past few decades:

- College graduates delay marriage but ultimately have a higher lifetime probability of marrying than do people without college degrees.
- People increasingly choose a spouse with a similar level of education.
- College graduates are much less likely to have a child without marrying.
- The chances of divorce have been declining for college graduates and increasing for people who did not graduate from high school.

It is likely that the restructuring of the American economy, which improved the life chances of those with the most education and reduced them for those with the least education, influenced this divergence. But it did not act alone; rather, a broad cultural shift probably played a role: Alternatives to marriage (having a child as a single parent or cohabiting) have become more acceptable, and the meaning of marriage has changed. I will return to the theme of cultural change in marriages and partnerships in Chapter 7.

In any event, people in the three status groups increasingly experience the life stage of early adulthood [➡ p. 70] in different ways. The college educated continue their schooling into their twenties, postpone both marriage and childbearing, but eventually marry and have a lower risk of divorce. Individuals who did not graduate from high school are increasingly isolated in the marriage market, and are much more likely to have a child prior to marrying. In addition, when and if they marry, their risk of divorce is high. Finally, individuals with a high school degree and perhaps some college credits are in the middle range with regard to marriage, childbearing outside of marriage, and risks of divorce.

REPRODUCTIVE STRATEGIES

One aspect of this divergence has puzzled social scientists and policymakers. People in all status groups have been postponing marriage; but people in the lowest status group (and, to some extent, the high school graduates above them) have not postponed having children as much. It is as if marriage and childbearing—so closely linked in Western culture—have become separate phenomena among the least educated, with childbearing often preceding marriage by years. One way of thinking about this difference is to view Americans as following different **reproductive strategies**—ways of fitting childbearing into the life course—according to their status group.

reproductive strategies
ways of fitting childbearing into the life course

A study of young women in low-income Philadelphia-area neighborhoods found that many of them think it unlikely that they could find suitable marriage partners (Edin & Kefalas, 2005). They see few men who are earning steady, decent incomes—still a requirement for a husband in the United States—and who are free of the problems such as substance abuse and illegal activity that often come with limited earning potential. Consequently, they think that to postpone having a child until one is married carries a high risk of never having children—a risk they are unwilling to take. And they do not think that having a child outside of marriage will hurt them subsequently in the marriage market. Moreover, they do not expect to attend college. So they often follow the strategy of having children at a relatively early age without marrying and then thinking seriously about marriage many years later. The authors, Kathryn Edin and Maria Kefalas (2005), write:

> *Unlike their wealthier sisters, who have the chance to go to college and embark on careers—attractive possibilities that provide strong motivation to put off having children—poor young women grab eagerly at the surest source of accomplishment within their reach: becoming a mother.*

Young women who are confident that they will graduate from college, on the other hand, can reasonably expect to find a suitable husband afterwards and to have children after they marry. Most of them can make the conventional strategy—finish your education, marry, and then have children—work successfully. Thus, the most- and least-educated groups tend to follow different strategies for ensuring that they will have children. The group in the middle of the educational distribution range is somewhat more likely than the college educated to have children outside of marriage, and they increasingly do so in cohabiting unions rather than marriage. I will discuss the role of cohabitation in more detail in Chapter 7.

Quick Review

- Since about 1980, the family patterns of people with different levels of education have diverged in several ways.
- People with college degrees have been delaying marriage but ultimately marrying at higher rates, waiting until they are married to have children, and experiencing declining divorce risks.
- People who have not graduated from high school are more likely to have children prior to marrying, less likely to marry, and if they marry, more likely to divorce.
- Over the past several decades, people have become increasingly likely to choose a spouse with a similar level of education.
- The less educated are increasingly following a reproductive strategy of having children before marrying, whereas the well educated tend to follow the conventional path of finishing their education, marrying, and only then having children.

ASSISTANCE FROM KIN

As the different reproductive strategies show, there is variation around the norm of the two-parent-and-children conjugal family. [➡ p. 39] Families differ not only in terms of marriage but also in terms of their ties to other kin, both the kin that a person is born to or acquires at marriage and the kin that some people construct from distant relatives, friends, partners, partners' families, and so forth. These kinship patterns differ by social class, although some of the class differences appear to be fading or overstated.

A couple plays with their child before going to work: dual-earner families have shown the greatest income gains in recent decades.

Kinship among the Poor and Near Poor   A large literature dating back to the Great Depression shows that a husband's place in the family is heavily dependent on whether he has a job.[2] In the cultures of all industrialized nations, men have been viewed as the main earners; providing a steady income has been seen as their responsibility. Rightly or wrongly, women's economic contribution has been viewed as secondary, although this perception may be changing as they increasingly work outside the home. When wives choose not to work for pay, or when they lose their jobs, they are not looked down upon. But when husbands lose their jobs, as happens frequently to husbands in poor and near-poor families, their authority in their homes decreases, their self-respect declines, and other family members treat them with less respect as well. Chapter 9 examines in more detail how a husband's unemployment affects a married couple and their children.

Chronic Poverty and Kin Networks   When a man's unemployment problems are chronic—when he is unable or unwilling to find steady employment over many years—he may be viewed, and may view himself, as having failed to fulfill a central role in his life. In a community with many chronically unemployed men, young mothers rely less on marriage and more on other kinship ties for support. Commonly, in poverty areas, young mothers, many of them unmarried, receive help from their own mothers in raising their children. They may also get money or assistance from sisters and brothers, friends, and, sometimes, the fathers of their children. The result is **women-centered kinship,** a kinship structure in which the strongest bonds of support and caregiving occur among a network of

women-centered kinship
a kinship structure in which the strongest bonds of support and caregiving occur among a network of women, most of them relatives, who may live in more than one household

[2]See, for example, Robert Cooley Angell, *The Family Encounters the Depression* (New York: Charles Scribner's Sons, 1936); Ruth Shonle Cavan and Katherine Howland Ranck, *The Family and the Depression: A Study of 100 Chicago Families* (Chicago: University of Chicago Press, 1938); and Mirra Komarovsky, *The Unemployed Man and His Family* (New York: Octagon Books, 1971).

Women-centered kinship ties are an important source of strength among many low-income families.

women, most of them relatives, who may live in more than one household. Mothers, grandmothers, sisters, and other female kin hold most of the authority over children and provide most of the supervision.

The extended kinship ties of the women-centered network help its members survive the hardships of poverty. If the members of a household have little to eat or are evicted from their homes, relatives and friends in their network will provide whatever assistance they can. Sisters or aunts who are themselves poor will nevertheless give food or money because they know that in the future they may need emergency help. In this way, the kinship networks of the poor spread the burdens of poverty, cushioning its impact on any one household and allowing its members to get by from day to day. In a widely cited study of The Flats, a low-income African-American neighborhood in the Midwest, anthropologist Carol Stack found that individuals could draw upon a complex network of relatives and friends that extended over many households (Stack, 1974).

In fact, individuals actively cultivate these networks so that they will have assistance when they need it. For example, Stack writes of Lydia, a woman in The Flats who did not need assistance from kin as long as she was married and therefore did not want to be obligated to them. Instead of sharing with kin, Lydia used the money she and her husband were earning to buy a house and furniture. She generally refused to trade clothes or lend money, and on the few occasions when she and her husband gave something to a relative, they never asked for anything in return. Then, however, Lydia's marriage broke up. During the five-month period when the marriage was ending, Lydia suddenly began to give things to relatives. She gave some of her nice clothes to her sisters and nieces, a couch to her brother, and a television set to her niece (Stack, 1974).

By giving away these things, Lydia was attempting to create a kinship network that she could rely on when she was no longer married. Her actions are typical of how poor people actively construct extended kin networks by exchanging goods and services with others who are in need. Poor people cannot afford to rely solely on *assigned kinship*—the more restricted set of kinship ties that middleclass people acquire automatically at birth and when they marry: father, mother, grand-parents, husband, wife, children. Rather, they make use of *created kinship* to recruit assistance wherever it can be found. [➥ p. 14]

The Costs of Kin Networks   Yet membership in such a kinship network is not without cost—which is why Lydia was reluctant to exchange resources with kin as long as she was married. Because an individual's meager income must be shared with many others, it is difficult for her or him to rise out of poverty. Stack described what happened when an older couple unexpectedly inherited $1,500. At first, they wished to use the money for a down payment on a house. Then other members of their network, upon learning of the windfall, asked for help. Several relatives needed train fare to attend a funeral in another state; another needed $25 so her telephone wouldn't be turned off; a sister was about to be evicted because of overdue rent. Moreover, the public assistance office cut their children off welfare temporarily. Within six weeks, the inheritance was gone. The couple acquiesced to these requests because they knew they might need assis-tance in the future. Even someone who finds a good job may not withdraw from a network unless she is confident that the job will last a long time.

Thus, these kinship-based sharing networks, admirable and necessary as a bul-wark against destitution, can nevertheless serve to perpetuate poverty across gen-erations. When another young woman in Stack's study decided to marry, the relatives and friends in her network tried to talk her out of it. Her contributions were valuable, and they did not want to lose her. Recognizing that she and her husband couldn't accumulate enough money to rise above poverty unless she left the network, the young woman married and then left the state that same night (Stack, 1974). Moreover, it's not clear how widespread these networks are today. Stack's study of The Flats is 30 years old. Newer scholarship on low-income African American families, to be reviewed in the next chapter, suggests that their kinship networks either were never as strong as The Flats showed or have deteri-orated in strength in recent decades.

Kinship among the Nonpoor   The core of kinship among the nonpoor in the United States has been the conjugal family of wife, husband, and children (Schneider & Smith, 1973). The married couple is expected to spend their in-come on their children and themselves rather than to provide financial assistance to siblings or other relatives. Any assets or savings are passed from parents to children, rather than being spread throughout a kin network. Income sharing is not as necessary, to be sure, because the standards of living of kin tend to be higher than among the poor. Yet standards of living are higher in part *because* it is expected that the conjugal family will spend its savings on a down payment for a house rather than doling it out to relatives who need train fare to attend funer-als or to pay bills and *because* it is expected that the family will move away from kin, if necessary, to pursue better job opportunities.

A clever survey of adults in the Boston area in 1984 and 1985 demonstrated peo-ple's beliefs about the restricted kinship obligations of the conjugal family (Rossi & Rossi, 1990). Alice and Peter Rossi presented 1,393 mostly white people whom they identified as "middle class" with a set of "vignettes": brief, hypothetical descrip-tions of relatives and friends who were experiencing crises that might require "some financial help" or "comfort and emotional support." For example: "Your

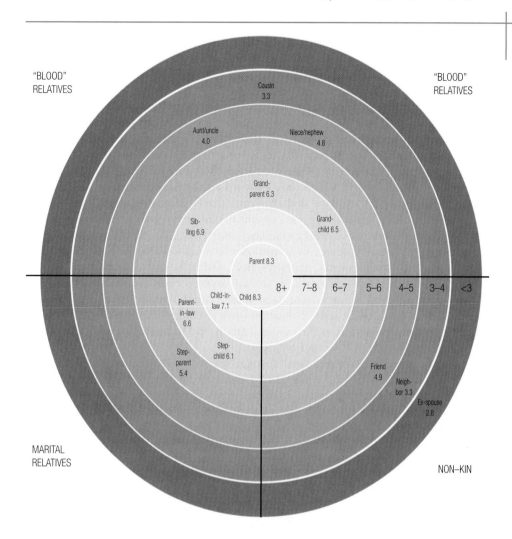

"BLOOD"
RELATIVES

"BLOOD"
RELATIVES

MARITAL
RELATIVES

NON–KIN

Cousin
3.3

Aunt/uncle
4.0

Niece/nephew
4.8

Grand-
parent 6.3

Grand-
child 6.5

Sib-
ling 6.9

Parent 8.3

Parent-
in-law
6.6

Child-in-
law 7.1

Child 8.3

8+   7–8   6–7   5–6   4–5   3–4   <3

Step-
parent
5.4

Step-
child 6.1

Friend
4.9

Neigh-
bor 3.3

Ex-spouse
2.8

FIGURE 4.5
"Wheel of obligation":
degree of obligation
felt by survey
respondents to
various relatives and
friends, for
Boston-area adults,
1984–1985.
(*Source:* Rossi &
Rossi, 1990)

unmarried sister has undergone major surgery and will be bedridden for a few weeks. This problem is straining her financial resources." From a list of relatives and friends (e.g., child, father-in-law, cousin, neighbor), eight crises (e.g., "run out of unemployment benefits and no job in sight"), and two obligations ("to offer some financial help," "to offer comfort and emotional support"), a computer program selected one relative or friend, one crisis, and one obligation at random and printed a vignette. The process was repeated until 26 crisis vignettes had been generated randomly to present to each of the survey respondents. We will focus on the vignettes for which the respondent was asked to rate "How much of an obligation would you feel to offer some financial help?" on a scale from 0 to 10, where 0 meant no obligation at all and 10 meant a very strong obligation.

The mean obligation scores for offering financial help, for 15 common relatives and friends, averaged across the various vignettes, was plotted by Rossi and Rossi on a "wheel of obligation," which is reproduced as Figure 4.5. The closer to the center of the wheel, the stronger the sense of obligation people felt: A mean score of 10 would be plotted at the hub of the wheel, whereas a mean score lower than 3 would be plotted in the outer circle. Note first that most of the mean scores are close to the hub, indicating that people felt a moderate to high level of obligation to most kin. Only neighbors and ex-spouses had mean scores lower than four. (Of course, these are hypothetical obligations; we don't know whether people actually would provide financial assistance this freely.) Since it did not make sense to ask these kinds of questions about a person's current husband or wife, there is no score for spouses. Other studies suggest that strong bonds of obligation exist between spouses (Schneider, 1980).

Note also that the highest levels of obligation were expressed toward a person's parents and children. Indeed, all the relatives in the two circles surrounding the hub are related to a person through a child, a parent, or a spouse. This pattern suggests that adults felt the most obligation to the members of the conjugal or single-parent families in which they grew up and to the conjugal or single-parent families in which they have had children. These vertical kinship ties—up and down the chain of generations from parents to children to grandchildren—engender the strongest feelings of obligation. They are created by direct descent and by marriage. Contrast the degree of obligation adults felt toward more distant relatives such as aunts, uncles, nieces, nephews, and cousins: None has an average score of five or above. Kinship ties from a person's marriage—even a second marriage—are stronger than kinship ties toward these more distant blood relatives. For instance, note that the adults felt more obligation toward a stepchild than toward a cousin or a nephew. Obligations to the conjugal family, and to one's parents, seem to take precedence over those to other relatives.

The image of middle-class kinship suggested by these findings is of a tall, solid tree trunk with skinny branches: The vertical axis is strong as one moves from parents to children to grandchildren, but the horizontal links are weaker as one moves from parents to uncles, or from children to nieces. Resources are passed from a person's parents to his or her spouse and children, and then to the grandchildren. Assistance to elderly parents is likely to be much more substantial and more common than assistance to elderly aunts and uncles.

Kinship among the Wealthy

Whereas the main economic task for families from other classes is to accumulate wealth, the main task for upper-class families is to preserve and increase their wealth. Traditionally, this has meant that wealthy parents take an active role in determining whom their children will marry. They know that their children will be highly desirable marriage partners, and they wish to obtain a good match: someone from a family that also has wealth or, at least, someone who is likely to help the children manage their wealth wisely. In England in the 1500s, rich families usually chose their child's spouse, creating what is termed an **arranged marriage.** When two wealthy families were involved, arranged marriages often seemed more like economic alliances than romantic partnerships (Coontz, 2005). Indeed, historians suggest that there was little romance in many aristocratic marriages (Stone, 1977).

arranged marriage a marriage in which the parents find a spouse for their child by negotiating with other parents

However, by the 1600s, the ideals of companionship and intimacy in marriage spread and arranged marriages became less common. (They always had been uncommon among the poorer classes, who had less to gain by an arranged marriage.) Still, many parents strongly influenced their child's choice. Records from Hingham, Massachusetts, show that prior to 1700 families tended to marry their oldest daughters first, then their next oldest, and so on, suggesting substantial parent involvement (Smith, 1973). Records from Andover, Massachusetts, indicated that in the 1600s and early 1700s, sons tended to marry only when their fathers were ready to turn over control of their land (Greven, 1970).

By the nineteenth century, parental influence over the timing of marriage and the choice of a partner had diminished substantially in the more prosperous classes. Even among the elite, it is likely that most children chose their spouse. Yet well-to-do parents retained an indirect influence on their children's marriage partners through strategies that persist to this day. First and foremost was separate schooling. Wealthy children were much more likely to attend the nation's private boarding schools, where they met children from other wealthy families. John D. Rockefeller, Jr., heir to the most famous nineteenth-century fortune in the United States, met his future wife, Abby Aldrich, while attending Brown. Rockefeller certainly chose his wife; but he did so at an elite Ivy League university where, not coincidentally, the woman he chose came from a powerful Rhode Island family (Keller, 1991).

This pattern of separate education continued into the twentieth century. A study of marriage announcements in the Sunday *New York Times* from 1962 to 1972 found that 70 percent of the men and 84 percent of the women reported attending private schools, such as St. Paul's, Exeter, Andover, and Miss Porter's (Blumberg & Paul, 1975). Children from wealthy families were also more likely to attend elite universities: 52 percent of the men in the *Times* wedding announcements had attended an Ivy League college, and 29 percent of the women had attended one of the Seven Sisters colleges. Let me caution, however, that we don't know the extent to which these patterns still hold as the twenty-first century begins. Starting in the 1960s, the elite universities enrolled more public school students and most of them became coeducational; consequently, the educational experiences of the children of the wealthy may not be as distinctive as they were. There is little current research on the wealthy, in large part because sociologists are more interested in studying disadvantaged groups.

SOCIAL CLASS AND GENDER ROLES

In the women-centered kin networks of the poor, women are obviously more active than men in maintaining kinship ties. In fact, women are more active even when a husband is living at home. On average, women spend more time than men doing the work of kinship (di Leonardo, 1987). They are more likely to send cards and flowers on birthdays and holidays, to plan family get-togethers, and to help frail elderly parents. Many men rely on their wives to keep these contacts alive and to provide assistance. "On topic after topic," wrote Rossi and Rossi at the end of their book, "we have found that ties among women were stronger, more frequent, more reciprocal [i.e., both giving and receiving], and less contingent on circumstances [i.e., not just given in a crisis] than those of men" (Rossi & Rossi, 1990). Moreover, across all social classes, men still do less of the child care and housework, as we will discuss in Chapter 8.

Otherwise, however, social class differences in gender roles have lessened. Researchers in the mid-twentieth century reported that women's and men's worlds were highly segregated in families in which the husband had a blue-collar job (Bott, 1957; Gans, 1962; Rubin, 1976). Even when the women in Lillian Rubin's well-known study worked outside the home, they defined themselves primarily as wives and mothers (Rubin, 1976). Being the sole earner was a source of pride for men, an ideal to strive for. One husband said:

She doesn't have to work. We can get by. Maybe we'll have to take it easy on spending, but that's okay with me. It's worth it to have her home where she belongs. (Rubin, 1976)

In contrast to attitudes prevalent a half-century ago, wives (and their husbands) view working for pay outside the home as a necessary and proper activity.

Many wives shared their husbands' views that, ideally, they ought to stay home. But by 1992, when Rubin published a new edition of her book, these attitudes had changed: Women viewed employment as a proper activity, necessary to maintain their families' lifestyles and also a source of satisfaction and self-esteem (Rubin, 1992). Surveys confirm that husbands and wives are both more likely to support women's work outside the home than they were a few decades ago and that high school–educated men are no longer more traditional in this regard than college-educated men. The revolution in attitudes toward wives' work has washed over both genders and all social classes.

SOCIAL CLASS AND CHILD REARING

Families still differ by social class in how they raise their children. In general, college-educated parents often act in ways that encourage autonomy and independence, whereas less-educated parents more often encourage conformity and obedience to (and distrust of) authority. Not all parents fit this pattern, of course; there is substantial variation within social classes. Moreover, as the twentieth century progressed, parents in all social classes moved toward emphasizing independence (Alwin, 1988). On average, though, intriguing class differences remain.

Social Class and Parental Values   Beginning in the 1960s, Melvin Kohn pioneered a line of research showing the connections between the conditions a person experiences on the job and his or her child rearing values (Kohn, 1969). He noted that working-class employees (by which he meant blue-collar industrial workers), for the most part, are closely supervised, work with physical objects (as would carpenters), and perform simple tasks repetitively (as on an automobile assembly line). It is important for workers in these jobs to obey their supervisors and to accept the discipline of doing repetitive tasks. In contrast, middle-class workers

Families in Other Cultures: Kinship Networks among the Mexican Upper Class

It is well established that lower-class family members frequently belong to extended kin networks that share resources and provide support to one another. These networks enable individuals to survive the economic crises of poverty by turning to their relatives for aid. Among the middle class, extended kinship ties are less important. Yet among the upper class, the importance of kinship often rises once again (Goode, 1982). Anthropologist Larissa Adler Lomnitz has demonstrated the importance of kin in two studies of the extremes of poverty and wealth in Mexico City. First, she studied poor people living in shanty towns in the city—sprawling settlements made up of one-room shacks or brick cabins without running water. The residents of these neighborhoods survived by pooling their resources among a kinship network, much as the residents of Potter Addition or The Flats did (Lomnitz, 1977).

Lomnitz next studied kinship ties at the other end of the social spectrum, the Gómez family, which traces its roots back to Don Carlos Gómez, nineteenth-century farmer and village trader (Lomnitz, 1987). In 1978, the Gómez family was a large, mostly wealthy network of business owners and their wives and children, comprising 360 people in five main branches. The businesses were privately held and family controlled, rather than being publicly held corporations. Prominent family members hired cousins, nephews, and brothers-in-law from their own branch, and sometimes from others, to work in their firms. It was expected that sons, who started to work for their fathers at an early age, would eventually take over the businesses. But as long as the father was alive, he retained control.

These economic arrangements, Lomnitz found, were supported by—or perhaps better said, made possible by—the structure of family and kinship. The basic unit was the grandfamily, a three-generation family composed of a father and mother, sons and daughters and their spouses, and grandchildren. Although married couples lived in their own households, the grandfamily members lived near one another and met often. For instance, once a week they went to their father and mother's home for a family dinner. The women of the grandfamily saw one another almost every day; moreover, the women kept in contact with women in other grandfamilies, maintaining the links of kinship. In each generation of each branch, at least one woman seemed to specialize in maintaining the links of kinship; Lomnitz called these **centralizing women**. Their conversations included not only personal news but also news about family businesses in their own branch and others. Frequent ritual events, such as christenings, first communions, marriages, and funerals, provided occasions for contact among members of different branches.

These extensive ties were useful for two reasons. First, wealthier family members were a source of employment and of money to invest in new business ventures. With so much wealth controlled by the family, individuals looked to their kin for economic opportunities. Second, kinship ties provided some protection against the risks of doing business. An individual could have trust, *confianza,* that a relative would abide by the terms of an agreement to produce, deliver, or sell goods. If a person broke a business agreement or was consistently unable to meet the terms of agreements, he would be subject to the ridicule and scorn of the other members of the family. Family ties thus enforced honesty and hard work.

Ask Yourself

1. Does your family participate in a close-knit kin network like those in Mexico? If so, for what reasons?
2. In the United States, wealthy families do not need the support of kin networks to do business. Why not?

www.mhhe.com/cherlin5

(by which he meant white-collar professional and technical workers), are less closely supervised, usually work with data (as would computer programmers) or people (as would personnel managers), and perform a variety of tasks (as would physicians). Middle-class jobs, Kohn argued, encourage more independence than working-class jobs and often reward creativity and individual initiative.

When working-class and middle-class parents are asked to select the most important characteristics that children should have, their preferences reflect their occupational positions. Working-class parents are more likely to select obedience to authority, conformity, and good manners, whereas middle-class parents are more likely to select independence, self-direction, curiosity, and responsibility (Alwin, 1990). Working-class parents emphasize the kinds of characteristics their children would need if they were to enter blue-collar jobs. To work on an assembly

centralizing women
women who maintain the links among kin in large, extended families

Middle-class parents tend to actively enhance their children's skills.

line for 40 years requires obedience and conformity; someone who is creative and independent might have a harder time tolerating the job. In contrast, to be a successful manager requires independence and initiative. Thus, each class socializes its children to fill the same positions their parents have filled. Because of his or her conformist upbringing, a child from a working-class family may be less successful as a manager than a self-directed child from the middle class. In this way, socialization by parents both is influenced by and helps to perpetuate the social class divisions in the United States.

Concerted Cultivation versus Natural Growth   More recently, sociologist Annette Lareau intensively studied 12 families with third-graders and found class differences in the way parents view the task of raising children (Lareau 2002, 2003). These differences, which are consistent with Kohn's research, applied to both African-American and European-American children in her sample; at least for these families, class, more than race, determined parents' approaches to child rearing. Lareau defined a group of families in which the parents had jobs requiring college or more advanced degrees as "middle class" and a group with jobs requiring less education as "working class" or "poor." Middle-class families tended to actively enhance children's talents, opinions, and skills, a cultural style she calls "concerted cultivation"—as if parents were cultivating a garden so its plants would grow as well as possible. Working-class (and poor) parents, on the other hand, did not focus on developing their children's special talents; rather they emphasized providing a safe environment and love and letting children grow on their own. Lareau calls this cultural pattern the "accomplishment of natural growth." In everyday life, these different styles affected children's time use, language use, and family ties. Middle-class parents filled their children's weeks with a whirlwind of formal activities such as lessons, sports, tutoring, and play dates, whereas working-class parents were often content to let their children hang out at home or in the neighborhood. Middle-class parents talked with their children more, reasoning with them rather than telling them what to do. Children from working-class and poor families had closer ties to uncles, aunts, and children than did middle-class children.

As a result, argues Lareau, middle-class children have advantages in school and, later, in the job market: They are more assertive with authority figures such as teachers and coaches, they are more verbal, and they have a more independent sense of self. Working-class and poor children (and their parents) are less likely to speak up for themselves and challenge authority; they are more deferential and less trusting of authority. Middle-class children gain a sense that they are entitled to a stimulating, rewarding daily life, whereas working-class and poor children get a sense that their opportunities are constrained. So as they grow up, middle-class children are in a better position to achieve a middle-class lifestyle themselves. The main point, for Lareau as for Kohn, is that the social class of the family you grow up in affects the way you think about school, authority figures, and work.

Quick Review

- Poor families often depend on women-centered kinship networks, in large part because men cannot consistently earn enough to support a family.
- Nonpoor families typically center on a wife, husband, and children who have obligations to their parents and their grandchildren but are otherwise independent of kin.
- Women, more than men, maintain kinship ties across all social classes.
- Working-class parents tend to emphasize conformity and obedience to authority in raising children; middle-class parents tend to emphasize independence.

■ Social Class and the Family

A half-century ago, most families with children, rich or poor, had two parents and one earner. Today, half of all poor families have one parent, who may or may not be working outside the home; and a majority of well-off families have two parents and two earners. Thus, the association between the type of family you live in and your social class position is stronger today than in the past. This great sorting-out of families by social class has occurred for both economic and cultural reasons. On the economic side, two developments stand out: the movement of married women into the workforce and the declining employment prospects of men without college educations. On the cultural side are the rise in expressive individualism [➥ p. 7] and people's higher aspirations for material goods.

In the 1960s and 1970s, social commentators debated whether it was "necessary" for married women to work. After all, standards of living had been far lower in the first half of the twentieth century, and yet few married women had worked outside the home. However, the economic slide after 1973 more or less ended that debate. Among those without college educations, objections to married women working outside the home faded as decent-paying entry-level blue-collar jobs—the kind of jobs young husbands used to take—dwindled. Whereas in the 1970s wives' employment was seen by many as a sign of a husband's failure to provide adequately for his family, now it is seen as a necessary and acceptable contribution.

Among couples with college educations, the employment situation has been better; still, only two-earner couples have been beating inflation consistently. Moreover, the price of housing has risen far faster than wages, placing the American dream of homeownership out of reach of more and more single-earner

Extended families are more important to the working class than the middle class.

couples. In the 1950s and 1960s, payments on a median-priced home required just 15 to 18 percent of the average 30-year-old man's income. That figure rose to 20 percent in 1973 and then doubled to 40 percent in 1987 (Levy & Michel, 1991). Census Bureau figures suggest that housing affordability deteriorated further through at least 1995 (U.S. Bureau of the Census, 1999d). Consequently, for college-educated couples, too, wives' employment was seen as necessary and acceptable.

Concurrently, adults in a more individualistic culture were freer to choose not to marry or to end marriages. Having children outside of marriage became more acceptable. People's expectations about what constitutes a good life also changed. Young middle-class couples could, in theory, aspire only to the standard of living of the late 1940s and early 1950s—which for many consisted of an apartment or a small, one-story home, one car, a clothesline in the backyard for drying the laundry, one telephone, no stereo system, few restaurant meals, no airplane travel, and, of course, no VCRs or computers—and still keep one parent home all day. This is not an appealing prospect in a country where people have gotten used to a higher standard of living that is promoted by advertising and reinforced by the media.

With regard to kinship and gender roles, however, class difference may have lessened over the past few decades. To be sure, the women-centered kinship networks of low-income families remain distinctive. Yet not all low-income families have functioning networks, and the number of single-mother families has increased among the nonpoor as well. The distinctive working-class gender segregation and resistance to wives' employment, presented in several widely read mid-twentieth-century studies, seems to have faded. Child rearing patterns do still seem different, with college-educated parents instilling in their children a sense of independence and of entitlement to a rewarding life, while less-educated parents tend to stress obedience, safety, and natural growth. These class differences in child rearing could affect the quality of education that children obtain and the type of occupations they will eventually get.

Until the 1980s, families at all educational levels seemed to move in parallel as rates of marriage, divorce, and childbearing rose and fell in waves. Since then, however, we see evidence that families at the top and bottom of the social ordering are moving in different directions. The college educated appear to be consolidating their gains in the restructured economy: Young adults postpone marriage while obtaining advanced educations, then they marry spouses who also have college degrees, and only then do they have children. Their marriages have become more stable in recent years, quite possibly reflecting their improved economic position. In contrast, individuals without high school degrees seem increasingly marginalized. They are isolated in the marriage market, as if shunned by those with better economic prospects. They often have children years before marrying, if they marry at all. And their marriages are increasingly brittle, with a high and rising risk of divorce. These are not encouraging trends in a nation that thinks of itself as a land of equal opportunity.

Social class is not the only way that American society classifies families. Racial and ethnic distinctions are also frequently made, and it is to these differences in family patterns that we now turn.

Looking Back

1. **How have changes in the American economy since the 1970s affected families?** The restructuring of the U.S. economy since the 1970s has caused a shortage of well-paid semiskilled and skilled jobs that do not require a college education—the kind of jobs less-educated young men used to rely on to support their wives and children. Now many of these jobs no longer exist or have been moved to other countries where wage rates are much lower. Since the early 1970s, family incomes have mainly increased among the growing number of families in which both husband and wife work for pay outside the home. Poverty has become more concentrated among single-parent families.

2. **What factors determine the social class position of families?** Sociologists agree that income and wealth are important. In addition, they examine whether the worker belongs to a status group with shared levels of prestige, privilege, and lifestyle. Since many families have more than one earner, the social class position of families can be ambiguous. Therefore, the four social classes that are usually defined—upper, middle, working, and lower—should be considered as hypothetical models (ideal types). Recent trends suggest that it may be useful to use people's educational levels to define a set of status groups.

3. **How have the family lives of people at the top and bottom of the social order diverged recently?** The typical life course of people who obtain college degrees involves completing one's education, then marrying someone else who is a college graduate, and then having children. For a person who does not graduate from high school, the life course may involve having children well before marrying, having a restricted choice of marriage partners, and having a high risk of divorce if one does marry at all. The reproductive strategy—the way of fitting in having children—is less conventional among those who do not have college educations.

4. **Are there social class differences in kinship?** Poor and near-poor families are distinctive because many of them consist of single-parent units embedded in kin networks. These networks share resources in order to ease the burdens of poverty. Nonpoor families consist mainly of two-parent households that are relatively independent of kin except for vertical ties to grandparents and grandchildren. Wealthy families attempt to preserve their assets by isolating their children in elite institutions where they will meet acceptable mates.

5. **Are there differences across classes in how parents raise children?** Poor and working-class parents tend to emphasize obedience and conformity in raising children, whereas middle-class parents are more likely to emphasize independence. As a result, sociologists suggest, poor and working-class children are not as assertive with authority figures such as teachers. They also show less self-direction and independent initiative. Middle-class children develop a sense that they are entitled to a rewarding life. These child rearing differences tend to steer poor and working-class children toward blue-collar and service work and to steer middle-class children toward professional and managerial work.

Go to the Online Learning Center at www.mhhe.com/cherlin5 to test your knowledge of the chapter concepts and key terms.

Study Questions

1. Why has the globalization of production affected workers without college educations more than the college educated?
2. Why has the entrance of wives into the paid workforce increased income inequality among all families in recent decades?
3. What is the difference between the "independence" and "status-sharing" models of how married people determine what class they are in?
4. What is a "status group" and how does it relate to the concept of social class?
5. How has the role of education in the marriage market changed over the past several decades?
6. Why might a young woman with little education choose a reproductive strategy of early childbearing?
7. What are the costs and benefits of the sharing networks commonly used by low-income families?
8. What advantages accrue to children with college-educated parents who engaged in "concerted cultivation" of them?

Key Terms

arranged marriage   132
assortative marriage   124
centralizing women   135
distribution of family
   income   114
ideal type   120

life chances   118
lower-class families   121
middle-class families   120
nonstandard employment   113
poverty line   115
reproductive strategies   126

social class   118
status group   118
upper-class families   120
women-centered
   kinship   128
working-class families   120

Thinking about Families

The Public Family	The Private Family
What obligations do you think extended kin like grandparents, uncles, and aunts have to aid parents and children?	How are the relationships between men and women different from social class to social class?

Families on the Internet   www.mhhe.com/cherlin5

Note: While all the URLs listed were current as of the printing of this book, these sites often change. Please check our Web site (http://www.mhhe.com/cherlin5) for updates.

It used to be that you had to go to the library and sort though government publications to find statistics on family income and poverty. Now most of the key statistics are available online, and you can download and print many reports. For statistics on poverty, the place to go is the U.S. Bureau of the Census home page (www.census.gov). Click on *Subjects A-Z,* then *P,* then *Poverty Data.* The Bureau's annual statistical reports on poverty, from which Figure 4.2 was tabulated, are in Portable Document Format (PDF). Historical tables are available as well. How does the Census Bureau measure poverty?

The Population Reference Bureau maintains a Web site that summarizes recent information on income, poverty, marriage, and families, in the United States and around the world. Log on to www.prb.org and click on "poverty" to see recent postings.

Race, Ethnicity, and Families

Looking Forward

1. How is immigration changing the racial and ethnic balance in the United States?

2. How has African American family life changed over the past several decades?

3. What are the family patterns of the major Hispanic ethnic groups?

4. What are the distinctive characteristics of the family patterns of Asian Americans?

5. How does the concept of "social capital" apply to immigrant families?

6. How is intermarriage affecting racial and ethnic groups?

Rowena Bautista moved from the Philippines to the United States in 1995 to work as a nanny for American families. She is part of a steady stream of immigrant women from Southeast Asia and Latin America who have come to the United States in the past two decades to be caregivers and house-cleaners. A half-century ago, the demand for domestic workers was fading away. New labor-saving devices such as the vacuum cleaner and the automatic washing machine and dryer made it easier for wives to clean their homes (husbands have never done much cleaning). In addition, African American women, who had historically done domestic work for white families, abandoned these jobs for higher-paying and less subservient work. The nanny and the maid seemed like a thing of the past.

But pull- and push-factors have since brought domestic work back. The pull-factor is the demand for domestic workers caused by the movement of middle-class married women into paid employment. They no longer have the time for all of the domestic chores; and their husbands, while they are doing somewhat more, have not picked up the slack. Consequently, harried dual-earner couples have been looking for people to care for the kids and clean the house. And here they meet the push-factor of migration. The globalization of the world economy, coming at a time when many developing nations are struggling, increased the flow of people migrating from the poorer countries to the wealthier ones. At first, the migrants were men looking for jobs as laborers. But, increasingly, women looking for jobs in domestic service have joined them. The reason is simple: The wages a nanny earns, which by American standards are low, are higher than what a well-educated professional can earn in many developing countries. Ms. Bautista's $750 monthly salary is more than the main doctor in her home village makes.

And so the great flow of Latin American and Asian women, such as Ms. Bautista, began. A *Wall Street Journal* reporter, interested in this phenomenon, interviewed her and discovered that in order to take a job caring for American children, she had left her two children in the Philippines (Frank, 2001). In fact, she was paying a woman back home to help her mother and husband care for the children. Every month, she sent her family $400, of which $50 went to pay her children's nanny. In doing this, she was not alone. It is common for immigrant Latina or Asian domestic workers to leave children at home. In doing so, they become what some sociologists are calling "transnational mothers" (Hondagneu-Sotelo and Avila, 1997). They believe that by providing for their children financially from afar they are doing what is in their children's best interests. Meanwhile, American families benefit from their caring work. Sociologist Arlie Russell

These immigrants, shown taking the oath of U.S. citizenship, are among the large number of Latin Americans and Asians who have immigrated since the law was changed in 1965.

Hochschild (2002), commenting on Ms. Bautista's story, suggests that in addition to the familiar "brain drain" of highly trained professionals who leave developing countries for greener pastures in the United States, we are now beginning to see a "care drain." Ms. Bautista's children would probably agree. (See *Families in Other Cultures:* Transnational Families, on p. 168.)

The care drain is one of the ways that a surge of immigration to the United States in recent years is altering American society. In 1965, a revision of the immigration laws allowed larger numbers of non-Europeans to enter the country. Since then, the number of Latin American and Asian immigrants to the United States has grown rapidly. The Census Bureau estimated that in 2002 Hispanics supplanted African Americans as the nation's largest minority group. Demographers predict a great increase in racial and ethnic diversity over the next few decades. According to Census Bureau estimates, if immigration rates remain at current levels, by 2030 only about half of American children will be non-Hispanic whites (U.S. Bureau of the Census, 2002g).

The surge in immigration is raising issues as new as transnational motherhood and as old as discrimination. These issues often cut across gender, class, and race ethnicity (as in the example of Asian and Latina women who work for low wages for affluent families), suggesting again the connection among them. This chapter will examine the implications for family life of the growing racial and ethnic diversity. In addition, we will study the variation in family relations across racial and ethnic groups.

■ Racial-Ethnic Groups

All this, however, begs the question of what constitutes a racial or ethnic group. We generally think of racial groups as people with a common set of physical features that distinguish them from other groups. The boundaries of racial groups, however, vary from country to country and from the past to the present. For instance, in other New World countries such as Brazil, there is no sharp division between black and white but rather a continuum of skin color distinctions. As recently as 1910, the U.S. Census included a mixed black and white ancestry category labeled "mulatto." Yet during the twentieth century, the image of two distinct groups, black and white, became fixed in American culture, despite the mixed racial ancestry of many Americans.

Other racial categories remain more flexible, in part because none carries the long history of slavery and racial discrimination faced by African Americans. Consider the individuals in the United States who are descended from the original, indigenous peoples of North America. These peoples include American Indians, the name still often used for Native Americans in the contiguous 48 states, and Alaska natives, such as the Eskimo and Aleut. The 2000 Census questionnaire presented "American Indian or Alaska native" as one of 15 "race" categories. Of the 4.1 million people who chose it, 40 percent chose a second category, most often "white" (U.S. Bureau of the Census, 2001c). Since the 1970 Census, the American Indian population has increased at a far higher rate than counts of births and deaths during the 1970s would suggest (Snipp, 1989; O'Hare, 1992). The increases in reporting were greater in California and the East than in traditional American Indian population centers. This pattern suggests that individuals residing in metropolitan areas far from tribal lands and having some Native American ancestry have become more likely to think of themselves as American Indians (Eschbach, 1993). Nagel (1995, 1996) writes of an "ethnic renewal" in which people of mixed heritage have increasingly identified themselves as American Indians due to factors such as American ethnic policies and American Indian political activism.

CONSTRUCTING RACIAL-ETHNIC GROUPS

It is even more difficult to define an ethnic group than it is a racial group. Most generally, an ethnic group consists of people who think of themselves as distinct from others by virtue of common ancestry and shared culture—but not necessarily physical characteristics. For example, the skin color and physical features of Mexican Americans range from distinctly European to distinctly Native American, with most people displaying a mixture of the two. Given the ambiguities and overlap between race and ethnicity, let me combine them and define a **racial-ethnic group** as people who share a common identity and whose members think of themselves as distinct from others by virtue of ancestry, culture, and sometimes physical characteristics. Often racial-ethnic group members' shared identity is reinforced by the way they are treated by outsiders. For instance, racial prejudice and, until the 1960s, racially discriminatory legislation have contributed to the sharp distinction between African Americans and whites.

Thus, racial-ethnic groups are social creations, reflecting cultural norms, social inequality, and political power. Consequently, people can redefine these groups or create new ones as circumstances dictate. The clearest recent example of the redefinition of a racial-ethnic group in the United States is the rise of Hispanic ethnicity. In this chapter, the term **Hispanic** refers to persons in the United States who trace their ancestry to Latin America.[1] An alternative term, Latino, is sometimes used instead. A few decades ago, the terms Hispanic or Latino were hardly

racial-ethnic group people who share a common identity and whose members think of themselves as distinct from others by virtue of ancestry, culture, and sometimes physical characteristics

Hispanic a person living in the United States who traces his or her ancestry to Latin America

[1]Strictly speaking, "Hispanic" also includes people who trace their ancestry directly to Spain.

used; rather, one referred to specific groups such as Puerto Ricans, Mexican Americans, or Cuban Americans. There was no Hispanic category, for example, in the full 1970 Census. During the 1970s and 1980s, however, political leaders of Latin American ancestry formed alliances based on their shared interest in improving the lives of their disadvantaged constituents. A Hispanic caucus was formed in Congress, the category "Hispanic" was added to the census, and Hispanics came to be seen as a coherent racial-ethnic group. In the 1980 Census, after the individual responding for the household checked boxes indicating which of the so-called races each person in the household belonged to, she or he was asked "Is this person of Spanish/ Hispanic origin or descent?" The categories were: (1) No; (2) Yes, Mexican, Mexican American, or Chicano; (3) Yes, Puerto Rican; (4) Yes, Cuban; and (5) Yes, Other Spanish/Hispanic.

A similar scheme was used in the 2000 Census, in which about 12.5 percent of the U.S. population chose one of the Hispanic categories. This question was asked separately from the racial question because Hispanics can be of any race. In 2000, 42 percent of people who listed themselves and their household members as Hispanic checked none of the specific racial categories but rather the catchall racial category "Some other race" (U.S. Bureau of the Census, 2001c). That 42 percent of Hispanics considered themselves to be neither white nor black may reflect both the Latin American tradition of intermediate racial categories and also the sentiment that Hispanics are a separate group from European whites and African blacks.

Similarly, the category **Asian American** has become an umbrella for an extremely diverse group of people who hail from nations as far apart as Japan and Pakistan—people who differ in language, religion, alphabet, and race. For instance, South Asians, such as Indians, Pakistanis, and Bengalis, are classified as Caucasian by physical anthropologists; they are mostly Hindus or Muslims; and they speak languages belonging to the same Indo-European family from which English evolved. Asian Indians alone were estimated to comprise 1.7 million U.S. residents in 2000, which is four times their population in 1980. East Asians (e.g., Chinese, Japanese) and Southeast Asians (e.g., Filipinos, Vietnamese), in contrast, are classified as Mongoloid by anthropologists, are heavily Buddhist or Confucian, and speak languages of Asian and Pacific origin. They numbered an estimated 7.3 million in 2000 (U.S. Bureau of the Census, 2005k). Unlike the category "Hispanic," there was no overall "Asian" category in the 2000 Census but rather a list of many Asian nationalities (e.g., "Chinese," "Asian Indian") in the "race" question. Census tabulations of Asian Americans sometimes include U.S. residents who are Pacific Islanders—people indigenous to Hawaii and to the Pacific islands that are territories of the United States.

Asian American a person living in the United States who comes from or is descended from people who came from an Asian country

Marriage patterns are one sign that the umbrella categories of "Asian" and "Hispanic" are beginning to take on a life of their own. In the marriage markets of many metropolitan areas in the United States, the number of marriages in which the bride and groom are both "Asian," meaning any Asian racial category at all, or are both "Hispanic," meaning any of the Hispanic groups, is substantially larger than we would expect by chance (Rosenfeld, 2001). In other words, it's not just that Japanese Americans are more likely to marry each other but also that Japanese Americans are more likely to marry anyone from the many groups that make up the Asian category—and the same holds for Mexican Americans and the Hispanic category. The author of the study suggests that we are seeing the emergence of "pannational" identities in which people identify as "Asian" or "Hispanic."

Nevertheless, for studying family life, the category "Hispanic" is not very useful, and "Asian American" is not much better. As will be discussed, there is nearly as

Multiracial families constitute a small but growing share of all families.

much variation in family patterns among the various subgroups of the Hispanic population as there is between Hispanic families and non-Hispanic families. Indeed, there is substantial variation in family patterns within each of the major racial-ethnic groups. Still, the political discourse on racial-ethnic groups in the United States is increasingly structured around five racial-ethnic groups: African Americans, Hispanics, Asian and Pacific Islanders, Native Americans, and a category we can call **non-Hispanic whites,** meaning people who identify their race as white but do not think of themselves as Hispanic. These categories are still a subject of debate and controversy. (See *Families and Public Policy:* How Should Multiracial Families Be Counted? on pp. 150–151.)

non-Hispanic white
people who identify their race as white but do not think of themselves as Hispanic

"WHITENESS" AS ETHNICITY

Do non-Hispanic whites—the majority group—have an ethnicity? In the past, most scholars wrote as if the concept of ethnicity applied only to minority groups. But of late, many academics have begun to study the social construction of "whiteness" as an ethnicity that ordinarily provides power and privilege (Rasmussen, Klinenberg, Nexica, & Wray, 2001). Whiteness is not an inherent characteristic of people; rather, those considered white can differ over time and from place to place (McDermott & Samson, 2005). For example, when European immigrants from Ireland and Italy first began arriving in the United States in the 1800s, they weren't considered white. Only as they moved out of poverty and into the middle class did they acquire "whiteness" and the privileges that go with it.

Since nearly all whites are descended from European immigrants, their family and kinship patterns derive from the European historical experience. In fact, some scholars now prefer the label "European American" to "white," in order to

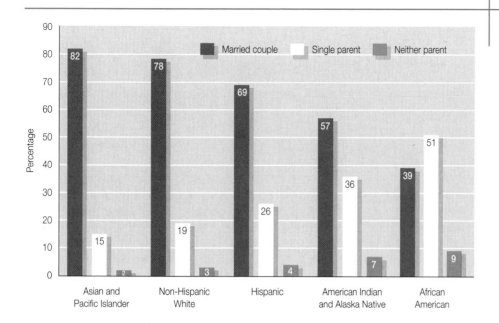

FIGURE 5.1
Percentage of children under 18 living with two parents, a single parent, or neither parent, for all children living in households in 2001, by race and ethnicity. (*Source:* U.S. Bureau of the Census, 2005f)

emphasize the origins of white culture. As noted in Chapter 2 [➡p. 39], the conjugal family of husband, wife, and children dominated the European family. Moreover, European families did not appear to rely on kin for support as much as families in other regions of the world (Goode, 1963). This heritage can still be recognized today. Figure 5.1 shows the differences in children's living arrangements among the five racial-ethnic groups. It comprises all children under 18 who were living in households at the time of the 2001 Survey of Income and Program Participation conducted by the Bureau of the Census (a small number were in juvenile institutions, group homes, or the military). As the purple columns show, 82 percent of Asian and Pacific Islander children and 78 percent of non-Hispanic white children were living with two parents. Hispanic, American Indian and Alaska Native, and African American children were less likely to be living with two parents. As the burnt orange columns show, Asian and Pacific Islander children were least likely to be living with neither parent—an arrangement that is much more common among American Indian and African American children. Many of these children were living with grandparents or other relatives. Figure 5.1 suggests, then, that the roles of marriage and of the extended family vary considerably across racial-ethnic groups—an insight we will pursue in the following sections.

Quick Review

- Racial-ethnic groups are socially created and vary from society to society and from time to time.
- Two broad racial ethnic groups that have emerged recently are "Hispanics" (sometimes called "Latinos") and "Asians."
- Some scholars are now studying the social creation of "whiteness" as an ethnicity that provides power and privilege.
- The 2000 Census allowed individuals, for the first time, to choose more than one race.

Families and Public Policy

How Should Multiracial Families Be Counted?

How can a child whose parents have different races have only one? Logically impossible, you might think; but until 1997, federal government statistical policy required that individuals check just one race for themselves or their children on official forms such as the Census of Population. And before 1997, the government recognized four races: (1) white, (2) black, (3) Asian and Pacific Islander, and (4) American Indian and Alaska Native. It also required its agencies, in a separate question, to ask about membership in one ethnic group: Spanish or Hispanic origin.

Interracial couples represent a small but growing share of all families. About 5 percent of married couples were interracial in 2000 (Lee & Edmondston, 2005). Their numbers are large enough, however, that they have become a visible presence and a reminder that the old categories may not fit much longer. In 1993, Representative Thomas Sawyer of Ohio, chair of the subcommittee of the House of Representatives that oversees the census and statistical policy, listened to the testimony of Susan Graham, an advocate for multiracial children and a mother of two of them. She told Representative Sawyer:

When I received my 1990 census form, I realized there was no race category for my children. I called the Census

Bureau. After checking with supervisors, the Bureau finally gave me their answer, the children should take the race of the mother. When I objected and asked why my children should be classified as their mother's race only, the Census Bureau representative said to me, in a very hushed voice, "Because in cases like these, we always know who the mother is and not the father." (U.S. House of Representatives, Committee on Post Office and Civil Service, Hearings, 1994)

Ms. Graham said her son had been classified as white by the census but black by the school he attended. Her solution: Add a new category, "Multiracial," to the official government list and to the 2000 Census. Yet this seemingly logical step was opposed by many of the political leaders of the minority groups that would be most affected. They opposed a multiracial category because the statistics that agencies collect are used not just to describe the population but also to determine whether federal laws have been carried out. Congress and the courts use the information on race and ethnicity from the census to determine whether congressional districts are providing fair representation to blacks and Hispanics. Agencies that oversee banks use the information to determine

whether banks are willing to loan money to members of racial-ethnic groups. Other agencies use the information from employers to determine whether employers are discriminating on the basis of race or ethnicity. Consequently, the political leaders opposed a multiracial category because they feared it would lower the number of blacks, Hispanics, or Asians counted in the census and would therefore dilute the political power that comes with greater numbers (Wright, 1994).

Faced with this dilemma, the government considered what, if anything, to do about Susan Graham's children and the many others like them when it fielded the 2000 Census of Population. In 1997, a government statistical committee decided that the 2000 Census (and all other government surveys) would allow individuals to choose more than one race; but it rejected a separate "multiracial" category. It also decided to place the question about Hispanic ethnicity before the question on race (rather than after it, which was the old policy), a change that probably increased the number of people who said they were "Hispanic." So when Americans filled out the 2000 Census, they saw the ethnic and racial questions shown in the figure. First they were asked whether they were "Spanish/Hispanic/Latino," and then they were asked their race. There

African American Families

The economic ups and downs of the last half of the twentieth century had a profound effect on African Americans. In the 1960s, as the economy boomed and the civil rights movement lowered barriers, African Americans made unprecedented gains in employment and income. But the post-1973 economic slowdown hit African Americans hard, especially the men (Levy, 1998), many of whom had moved into industrial jobs in the 1950s and 1960s. In the 1970s, as growth in manufacturing jobs slowed, African American men who did not have a college

United States Census 2000

→   **NOTE: Please answer BOTH Questions 7 and 8**

7. **Is Person 1 Spanish/Hispanic/Latino?** *Mark* ☒ *the "No" box if not Spanish/Hispanic/Latino.*

☐ **No**, not Spanish/Hispanic/Latino   ☐ Yes, Puerto Rican
☐ Yes, Mexican, Mexican Am., Chicano   ☐ Yes, Cuban
☐ Yes, other Spanish/Hispanic/Latino – *Print group.* ↗

[ ][ ][ ][ ][ ][ ][ ][ ][ ][ ][ ][ ][ ][ ][ ][ ][ ][ ]

8. **What is Persons 1's race?** *Mark* ☒ **one or more races** *to indicate what this person considers himself/herself to be.*

☐ White
☐ Black, African Am., or Negro
☐ American Indian or Alaska Native – *Print name of enrolled or principal tribe.* ↗

[ ][ ][ ][ ][ ][ ][ ][ ][ ][ ][ ][ ][ ][ ][ ][ ][ ][ ]

☐ Asian Indian   ☐ Japanese   ☐ Native Hawaiian
☐ Chinese   ☐ Korean   ☐ Guamanian or Chamorro
☐ Filipino   ☐ Vietnamese   ☐ Samoan
☐ Other Asian – *Print race.* ↗   ☐ Other Pacific Islander – *Print race.* ↗

[ ][ ][ ][ ][ ][ ][ ][ ][ ][ ][ ][ ][ ][ ][ ][ ][ ][ ]

☐ Some other race – *Print race.* ↗

[ ][ ][ ][ ][ ][ ][ ][ ][ ][ ][ ][ ][ ][ ][ ][ ][ ][ ]

were 15 choices, and for the first time, Americans were allowed to check all the categories that applied to them. Overall, only 2.4 percent of the population checked two or more race categories. But 5 percent of those who checked "Black, African American, or Negro" also checked another category, as did 14 percent of those who checked one of the Asian categories, 40 percent who checked "American Indian or Alaska Native," and 54 percent who checked "Native Hawaiian" or "Other Pacific Islander" (U.S. Bureau of the Census, 2001b). Clearly, many members of minority groups think of themselves as having more than one race.

Ask Yourself

1. Have you ever been frustrated by questionnaires that require you to select just one racial or ethnic group to describe yourself or a family member? If so, what do you think of the excerpt from the Census 2000 form shown here?

2. Relate the controversy over the wording of the census questions to the concepts of the public and the private family. What was the private family's interest in this matter? The public family's interest?

www.mhhe.com/cherlin5

education watched their economic prospects plummet. African American women had established a position in the growing service sector, so the changing economy did not affect them as much.

These great economic changes, in turn, had a significant impact on less-educated blacks. Without a stable economic base, some African American men were reluctant to marry, for fear they could not provide for their families. And some African American women were reluctant to marry them. In fact, William Julius Wilson argued in two influential books that the drop in semiskilled and skilled blue-collar jobs—their flight to the suburbs or to low-wage nations such as Mexico or Taiwan—is the major reason for the sharp decline in marriage among

Poverty and Altitude

Rarely are social class differences in America as visible as they were in the first few days after Katrina made landfall as a Category 4 hurricane in Louisiana and Mississippi on August 29, 2005. After levees in New Orleans were breached and neighborhoods flooded, television networks showed image after image of low-income families, nearly all of them African American, trapped in high water or marooned at the Louisiana Superdome. It turns out that the geography of New Orleans starkly illustrated the American social divide: Many wealthy families lived in neighborhoods that were above sea level and therefore spared the worst of the flooding. But poorer families tended to live in neighborhoods such as the Lower Ninth Ward that were below sea level and were devastated when the levees failed.

The images were so disturbing that they caused a flurry of attention in the media to the problems of poverty and race in America. In the midst of this discussion, I had a minor Katrina moment. A *Newsweek* reporter asked me to comment on the lessons of Katrina for thinking about poverty. Here is what I said: "Americans tend to think of poor people as being responsible for their own economic woes. But this was a case where the poor were clearly not at fault. It was a reminder that we have a moral obligation to provide every American with a decent life."

During the next week, I received several e-mail messages from *Newsweek* readers who disagreed with my statement. For instance, one person wrote, "I absolutely do not have a moral or legal obligation to provide every American with a decent life. I have a moral and legal obligation to provide every American with the opportunity to create a decent life for themselves. That opportunity has existed for all persons in this country for several decades."

Newsweek published a letter to the editor that said, "Sociologist Andrew Cherlin's notion that 'we have a moral obligation to provide every American with a decent life' is ridiculous. Nobody has the obligation to provide me with anything. I have a responsibility to provide for myself and my family."

So I guess I would ask you, the reader, what you think the lessons of Katrina are. Do we have an obligation to provide every American with a decent life or not? Send me an e-mail message (cherlin@jhu.edu). I'll respond.

New Orleans city council president Oliver Thomas hugs his wife Angelle and daughter Leah, 12, when he is reunited with them in Houston for the first time in the two weeks since Hurricane Katrina struck. Thomas came to Houston with Louisiana Gov. Kathleen Blanco and visited one of the refugee centers. Many families were separated during the evacuation of New Orleans.

Left

Milvertha Hendricks, 84, center, waits in the rain with other flood victims outside the convention center in New Orleans, three days after the hurricane. Officials called for a mandatory evacuation of the city, but many low-income residents did not have cars and could not leave without assistance. Some had to be rescued from flooded homes and hotels.

Below

Hurricane Katrina refugees Natasha Lewis, left, and her 5-year-old son Malik Martin from New Orleans, sit on cots at a shelter at Reunion Arena in Dallas, a few days after the storm. "We don't have nothing but what we came here with," said Lewis, a 27-year-old single mother of three. Low-income neighborhoods were the hit hardest by flooding because many were below the water level of the lake; the wealthier neighborhoods, in contrast, were mostly on higher ground.

African Americans (Wilson, 1987, 1996). Yet since the 1960s, a sizable group of more prosperous African Americans has emerged for the first time in American history.

THE DECLINE OF MARRIAGE

That there has been a sharp decline in the place of marriage in African American family life is not in doubt. To be sure, the decline of marriage has also occurred among whites, but it has not been as great. Table 5.1 presents three indicators of the decline of marriage among African Americans and whites. The first row shows that the proportion of young adults who will ever marry has fallen more for African Americans than for whites since the 1950s. At current rates, about 64 percent of African American young adults would ever marry. As will be discussed in Chapter 12, black women are less likely to marry, more likely to separate from their husbands if they do marry, and less likely to remarry than white women. The second row shows that for both groups, the percentage of children born to unmarried mothers increased sharply between 1970 and 2002. By 2002, 68 percent of all African American births were to unmarried women. And the third row shows that the percentage of family households (meaning households containing parents and children under 18) that were headed by one parent rose for both groups between 1970 and 2003. A majority of African American family households are now headed by one parent.

When we include cohabitation in the picture, the differences between blacks and whites are smaller but still substantial. Let me define **union formation** as the process of beginning to live with a partner either through cohabitation or marriage. The first unions formed by blacks are almost twice as likely to be cohabitations (rather than marriages) than is the case for whites. Therefore, studies that only examine the timing of first marriages produce greater differences between blacks and whites than do studies that examine the timing of first unions, either marital or cohabiting. In fact, racial differences in the timing of first unions are only about half the magnitude of racial differences in the timing of first marriages (Raley, 1996).[2]

> **union formation** the process of beginning to live with a partner either through cohabitation or marriage

The Impact of Economics   African American women and men seem to weigh economic considerations more heavily than white women and men in deciding when to marry—as might be expected, given their more precarious economic situation. For instance, in the 1987–1988 National Survey of Families and Households, never-married African Americans were more likely than comparable whites to rate such factors as "having one's spouse established in a job" as important in making the decision to marry (Bulcroft & Bulcroft, 1993). In a study of unmarried couples who had just had a child together, researchers found that if the fathers earned $25,000 or more during the next year, the chances of the couple marrying doubled (Carlson, McLanahan, & England, 2004). As noted earlier, job losses in the 1970s and 1980s hit African Americans especially hard. Fewer young black men work at all now than in the 1960s. Studies in the 1990s suggested that for every three black unmarried women in their twenties, there was roughly one unmarried black man with earnings above the poverty line (Lichter, McLaughlin, Kephart, & Landry, 1992). Greater benefits available to mothers through public

---

[2] Still, black cohabiting unions are less likely to lead to marriage (and more likely to lead to a breakup) than are white cohabiting unions (Manning & Smock, 1995).

Table 5.1 Indicators of the Decline of Marriage among African Americans and Whites		
INDICATORS OF THE DECLINE OF MARRIAGE	**AFRICAN AMERICANS**	**WHITES**
The percentage of young women who will ever marry has fallen more for African Americans than for whites[a]	88% in 1950s → 64% in 1990s	95% in 1950s → 93% in 1990s
The percentage of children born to unmarried mothers has risen for both African Americans and whites[b]	38% in 1970 → 68% in 2002	6% in 1970 → 29% in 2003
The percentage of family households headed by one parent has risen for both African Americans and whites[c]	36% in 1970 → 60% in 2003	10% in 1970 → 27% in 2003

[a]Rodgers & Thornton, 1985; Goldstein & Kenney, 2001.
[b]U.S. Bureau of the Census, 1991; U.S. National Center for Health Statistics, 2005a.
[c]U.S. Bureau of the Census, 2003a; 2004a.

assistance may also have increased women's independence and reduced the pressure to marry. Studies suggest that the effect of welfare on marriage behavior is modest but may have increased during the 1980s (Moffitt, 1990).

In addition to job losses—or perhaps as a result of them—there are other reasons why young black women may face a difficult time finding a suitable spouse. Consider the terrible toll that violence and drugs are taking on young black men. Homicide rates for young African Americans have risen to appalling levels over the past decade. If the rates in 2000 were to continue, about 2 of every 100 black 15-year-old boys would die violently before reaching age 44.[3] The rates of imprisonment and institutionalization of young black males are also strikingly high. The prison population grew rapidly during the 1980s and 1990s, and about half of all inmates are black. In 2004, 8 percent of black men aged 25 to 29 were in prison (U.S. Bureau of Justice Statistics, 2005). Moreover, about 1 of every 100 black men aged 18 to 44 is admitted to state and county mental hospitals each year, and others are incapacitated by drug addiction or alcoholism (Cherlin, 1992).

What if we could place African Americans in an environment where there is less unemployment and discrimination—would their marriage rates go up? To answer that question, researchers examined the marriage histories of young African Americans in the military, arguing that military life provides a natural experiment of sorts: There is no unemployment, little racial segregation, and less racial discrimination. They found no difference between the marriage rates of black and white soldiers, which suggests that greater unemployment and discrimination in the civilian world may be depressing black marriage rates (Lundquist, 2004; Lundquist & Smith, 2005). The results are not conclusive—the individuals in the survey data they analyzed were young, and there may be other, unmeasured differences between African Americans who enlist in the military and those who do not. But the findings are an intriguing suggestion that economic conditions and racial discrimination do make a difference in African Americans' propensity to marry.

---

[3]Author's calculation from homicide rates for black males 15–44 in U.S. National Center for Health Statistics (2002c).

Marriage has declined among African American young adults at all educational levels.

Is the decline in marriage, then, due to the shortage of men who are "marriage-able," as Wilson calls them, by virtue of steady employment? Overall, the research suggests two conclusions: (1) The employment problems of black men are indeed an important factor in the decline in marriage, but (2) the racial difference remains substantial even after employment problems are taken into account. Several demographic studies have measured the relative numbers of employed black men in the local areas or states where black women live. The authors find that black women are more likely to marry if they live in areas with greater relative numbers of employed black men—thus supporting Wilson's hypothesis. Yet they also find that the drop in the availability of employed men cannot account for all—or even most—of the gap in marriage rates (Mare & Winship, 1991). For instance, a study of Census Bureau data from the 1980s and 1990s reported that African American women were less likely to marry if they lived in states with lower wages and less job growth in the manufacturing sector—a finding that is consistent with the importance of economic restructuring (Lichter, McLaughlin, & Ribar, 2002). However, the study also reported that African American women had substantially lower marriage probabilities than white women even after economic conditions were taken into account. Reviewing the evidence in his more recent book, Wilson (1996, p. 97) acknowledges that "even though the joblessness among black men is a significant factor in their delayed entry into marriage . . . it can account for only a proportion of the decline in marriages in the inner city, including postpartum marriages."

A similar pattern can be seen in a comparison of Census data on the percentage of black and white family households that are headed by a married couple (as opposed to an unmarried woman or man). Figure 5.2 shows this comparison for family households at different income levels. As the reader can see, for both African Americans and non-Hispanic whites, the higher the family's income, the greater is the percentage that are headed by a married couple. Clearly, among

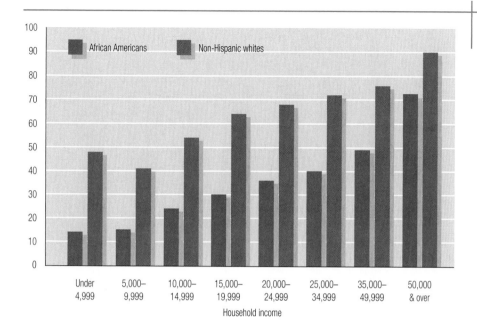

FIGURE 5.2
Percentage of family households that were headed by a married couple, by household income, for African Americans and non-Hispanic whites, 2001. (*Source:* U.S. Bureau of the Census, 2005i)

both African Americans and non-Hispanic whites, married couples are less commonly found in low-income households. Note also, however, that at each income level, non-Hispanic white family households are more likely to be headed by a married couple than black family households. Even when there are no income differences between the families being compared, a racial gap still exists, and the gap is particularly pronounced among the poor and near poor. Economics, it seems, is part of the story of racial differences in family structure; but it is not the whole story.

The Impact of Culture   To more fully understand the differences in the family patterns of African Americans and whites, we must turn from economics to culture. There has been a resistance among liberal social scientists and activists to acknowledge the role of culture in shaping African American family patterns. In part, this concern arises from the entirely negative way in which black families are often portrayed: problem-ridden, weak, overwhelmed. The strengths of black families are often overlooked. Figure 5.3 helps to show where these strengths may lie. Graphed across income levels from low to high are the percentage of family households that are "extended"; that is, the percentage that contain relatives other than parents (or stepparents) and their children (Farley & Allen, 1987). Often the additional relatives are grandparents. Note that at all income levels—even among those earning more than $200,000—black family households are much more likely than white households to include a grandparent or other relative. In fact, since about 1970, African Americans have become increasingly more likely to live in extended family household than whites (Goldscheider and Bures, 2003).

Indeed, grandparents play a stronger role in African American families, on average, than they do among white families. In 1982, just before Frank Furstenberg and I carried out a national survey of grandparents, we visited a group of black grandmothers at a senior citizens' center in Baltimore. The grandmothers told us how involved they were with their grandchildren's upbringing. Most of them had lived at

FIGURE 5.3

Percentages of family households that are extended (contain relatives other than parents and their children), by family income, for African Americans and whites, 2004. (*Source:* Tabulations by Reynolds Farley from 2004 U.S. Bureau of the Census American Community Survey data)

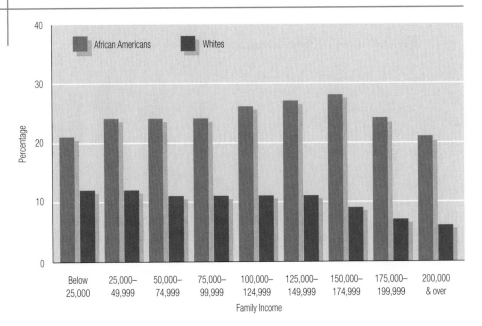

least temporarily with their grandchildren. One woman, for example, said about her grandchildren:

> *I was always named "sergeant"— "Here comes the sergeant." I loved them. I did for them, and gave to them, so that they had an education, so that they had a trade. I went to school regularly to check on them; they didn't know I was coming. (Cherlin & Furstenberg, 1992)*

Very few white grandparents had this kind of hands-on involvement and authority. Our national survey confirmed that black grandparents, on average, were more involved in parentlike activities with their grandchildren than were white grandparents. Moreover, this racial difference still remained when we compared black and white grandparents of similar incomes. Even among more prosperous families, black grandparents seem to play a stronger role than white grandparents.

More generally, in African American families, ties to a network of kin are more important, compared with marital ties, than is the case in white families. When Alice and Peter Rossi measured the strength of people's feelings of obligations toward kin [➡ p. 129], they found that African Americans felt much stronger obligations to aunts, uncles, nieces, nephews, and cousins than did whites (Rossi & Rossi, 1990). It follows, then, that when African Americans face adversity, they are probably more likely to seek help from kin than are whites. Moreover, African cultural patterns may still be influential [➡ p. 52]: In West Africa marriage is more of a process than an event, with childbearing sometimes occurring before the process is completed.

In poor black families mothers' partners are often incorporated into the kin networks, not on the basis of whether they are the biological fathers of the mothers' children, but rather whether they provide support to the children. Frank Furstenberg interviewed a group of low-income African Americans in an Eastern city who distinguished between "fathers" and "daddies." The former were biological fathers, whereas the latter were men who were providing support. A woman's current partner, for example, might become a daddy by helping with the care of a child from a previous relationship whose father provided little support. It was the daddies—the men who were providing assistance—not the fathers, who became members of the sharing networks (Furstenberg, Sherwood, & Sullivan, 1992).

The chapter on class also discussed the strengths and weaknesses of relying on kin for support. Briefly, membership in a network of kin helps people subsist because it allows them to spread the burdens of poverty by borrowing when they are in need and lending when they are able. It also, however, makes escaping from poverty more difficult because it is difficult and risky for poor people to withdraw from the network. Ever since Stack's (1974) influential account of African American kinship networks in "the Flats," many writers have assumed that black families receive more assistance from their networks than do white families. Several statistical studies, however, have cast doubt on that conclusion (Hofferth, 1984; Roschelle, 1997). It may be that the poor have fewer resources to share now than in the 1970s. We know that the share of income going to the bottom fifth of the population has been declining. [➥ p. 114] Some kin networks, therefore, may be overwhelmed by their members' needs. Or it may be that blacks and whites differ in the kind of support they provide rather than in the quantity of support. According to one study, white women were more likely to give financial support to kin and to receive it (in large part because they had more money to give) than were black women; but black women were more likely to give and receive help with child care, transportation, and housework (Sarkisian & Gerstel, 2004).

In addition, studies of kin networks also show that support from kin tends to decline over time. In a national survey of young adults, about two-thirds of the black single mothers were living with their own mothers at age 19, compared with about half of 21-year-olds and about one-third of 25-year-olds (Hogan, Hao, & Parish, 1990). This decline suggests that many single mothers move out of their mothers' homes as their children become older. Moreover, many of the grandmothers are themselves working outside the home and, therefore, are less available to their daughters. As the children enter adolescence, then, the support that kin provide to mothers may be substantially less than the support that was provided when the children were small. Several studies suggest that single mothers living without relatives provide less supervision and monitoring of their children's schoolwork and behavior than do mothers who live with a husband or other adult (Astone & McLanahan, 1991; Dornbusch et al., 1985). Despite their best efforts, many poor single mothers may have difficulty providing adequate parenting to their school-age children.

EXPLAINING THE DECLINE

How, then, can we explain the great decline of marriage among African Americans and the sharp increase in the proportion of children born to unmarried mothers? Although African Americans have had a higher proportion of single-parent households than whites since at least the beginning of the twentieth century [➥ p. 52], the difference has become more pronounced over the last few decades. There is no consensus as to why. Without doubt, changes in the economy are very important. In fact, some observers think the changes in families are entirely due to changes in the economy; others believe that culture may have played a role. I think that both were likely involved. As one sociologist has argued, culture is a sort of "tool kit" (Swidler, 2001). It provides people with a particular set of tools they know how to operate. When faced with difficulties, people tend to reach into their tool kits to fix the problem. For African Americans over the past several decades, the problem has been a very unfavorable economic environment. Not only did they battle discrimination, but as globalization and automation proceeded, they also faced a growing shortage of the kinds of jobs that can sustain families in which the parents do not have college educations. The job situation was worse for black men than for black women because the latter group had attained a foothold in the kinds of service-sector jobs (secretaries, waitresses, health care workers) that grew while blue-collar factory jobs disappeared.

Faced with this problem, African Americans increasingly reached into their tool kit and seized the kind of family support system that their history and culture provided: extended kinship networks rather than married-couple families. These networks usually relied on women—mothers, sisters, grandmothers—who were able to find jobs or were able to qualify for government assistance to single-parent families. Women-centered kinship [➡ p. 128] was part of the cultural repertoire of African American families. Had it not been, African Americans might not have retreated as much from the marriage-centered kinship patterns of European Americans. Relying on extended kin has risks, but it can allow low-income families to obtain the support they need to make it from day to day.

GENDER AND BLACK FAMILIES

intersectionality (of black women's experience) the extent to which black women's lives are affected by overlapping systems of class, racial, and gender-based disadvantage

Both black men and black women face discrimination and economic disadvantages. But black feminist writers argue that black women face an additional source of disadvantage because of their gender. For example, unlike black men they may face the earnings gap between jobs primarily held by men and jobs primarily held by women. [➡ p. 98] As women, they are more likely to be victims of domestic violence (see Chapter 11). But their situation also is unlike that of white women; they have always had to work outside the home, so the role of homemaker was rarely available to them. Social scientists with this perspective stress the **intersectionality** of black women's situation: the extent to which their lives are affected by overlapping systems of class, racial, and gender-based disadvantage (Hill, 2005). It is as if black women stand at the intersection of overlapping circles of race, class, and gender. [➡ p. 101] This perspective challenges the idea that there is a universal black experience shared by all African Americans. Instead, it emphasizes the diversity of the black experience, the extent to which it differs for women and men and also for middle-class families and low-income families.

THE RISE OF MIDDLE-CLASS FAMILIES

A small group of prosperous African Americans has long existed, often through the efforts of two-earner married couples. Landry (2000) presents evidence that in the late nineteenth and early twentieth century, more prosperous black women pioneered the ideology that women should combine marriage, careers, and community service. Because black women had been excluded from the "cult of True Womanhood" that enveloped white women in the late 1800s [➡ p. 49], they were freer to pursue careers. At all times during the twentieth century, the percentage of black women who worked for pay was higher than that of white women. Moreover, the wealthiest black women had the highest rates of paid work, suggesting that better-off black women were working for satisfaction as well as income.

Since the 1960s, the number of relatively prosperous blacks, whom observers tend to call the "black middle class," has expanded substantially. How large is this group? A national study followed American families every year from 1979 to 1991 and found that one-third of the black families were never poor (Blank, 1997). Most were not affluent, but they were consistently able to make ends meet. Many, although not all, would fit the general label of "middle class." Although these percentages are modest compared to whites in the study (three-fourths of whom were never poor), they signal an overlooked social advance. Educational statistics also show great improvement. In 2004, 81 percent of African Americans age 25 and older had graduated from high school, compared to 20 percent in 1960 (U.S. Bureau of the Census, 2005l).

In fact, the black middle class has been growing long enough that a second generation is moving into higher education. Among black freshmen entering 28 selective colleges in 1999, 60 percent had a father who graduated from college, 25 percent came from families earning over $100,000 per year, and 72 percent said that their parents owned their home (Massey, Charles, Lundy & Fischer, 2003). Still, middle-class black families tend to have less money in assets (savings, investments, homes, cars) than comparable white middle-class people. In a study of the assets of respondents to the Census Bureau's Survey of Income and Program Participation in 1987 through 1989, Oliver and Shapiro (1995) also found much larger differences, on average, in wealth (assets) between blacks and whites than in income. Comparing college-educated blacks with college-educated whites, for instance, they found that whereas the blacks earned 76 cents for each dollar earned by the whites, blacks had assets of just 23 cents for every dollar of white assets. And if homes and cars were excluded from assets (leaving savings accounts, stocks, small businesses), black college graduates had *one cent* of assets for every dollar of white assets. Oliver and Shapiro ascribe the difference to three factors: (1) whites are more likely to inherit some wealth or borrow money for a down payment on a home or car from their parents; (2) whites can more easily obtain home mortgage loans from banks; and (3) homes in predominantly black neighborhoods don't appreciate in value as much as homes in white neighborhoods.

Since the 1960s, a sizable middle class has emerged among African Americans. They are often ignored in the public focus on African American poverty.

Moreover, many members of the new black middle class were able to move upward in part through the assistance of kin, such as siblings who helped pay for college or an uncle who provided a first job. These extended kinship ties tend to remain after a person has attained middle-class status, but the flow of assistance often reverses. The sister who has attained a job as a computer programmer may have an unemployed brother who needs a short-term loan to stave off his family's eviction from their apartment or a bright cousin from a poor family who needs financial help so he can go to college. Having benefited from the assistance of her kin on her way up the economic ladder, the computer programmer has a difficult time refusing their requests. Yet her salary may be insufficient to maintain her middle-class status as well as help all the relatives who are in need. The resultant financial pressure can create what Andrew Billingsley called "the mixed blessings of upward mobility" (Billingsley, 1992). Moreover, because of residential segregation, middle-class black neighborhoods tend to be closer to poor black neighborhoods, and in fact they usually contain some poor families. Pattillo (2005) writes of the "inbetweenness" of the black middle-class residential experience. Middle-class blacks tend to live in neighborhoods that have less crime and poverty than the neighborhoods of low-income blacks, but much more crime and poverty than the neighborhoods of middle-class whites. As a result, middle-class African American parents may struggle to shield their children from the lure of street life, with its criminal behavior and drug usage. And middle-class African Americans must coexist with neighbors and relatives in the underground economy in ways most whites need not (Patillo-McCoy, 1999). Still, the growth of the African American middle class is a success story that is too often lost in the understandable focus on the African American poor.

Black churches have been a great source of social support to African Americans who have newly gained middle-class status. Throughout African American history the church and the family have been the enduring institutions through which black families could gain the strength to resist the oppression of slavery, reconstruction, segregation, and discrimination (Berry & Blassingame, 1982). The church has served as a **mediating structure,** a midlevel social institution (other examples are civic groups, neighborhoods, and families themselves) through which individuals can negotiate with government and resist governmental abuses of power (Berger & Berger, 1983). It has been the greatest source of continuity, outside of the family, in the African American experience. Today the church also

mediating structures
midlevel social institutions and groupings, such as the church, the neighborhood, the civil organization, and the family

Quick Review

- Marriage has declined among African Americans even more than among European Americans.
- The impact of economic restructuring—and the employment problems it has caused for African American men—is an important factor in the decline of marriage.
- But cultural differences between African Americans and European Americans are probably important too.
- In general, African American families rely on ties to extended kin more than European American families do.
- Over the past several decades, a substantial African American middle class has emerged for the first time.
- African American women's family lines are affected not only by their race and class but also by their gender.

serves as a link between the black middle class, many of whom have moved out of inner-city neighborhoods, and the black poor. Often by virtue of sanctuaries that are still in poor neighborhoods, churches provide a direct way for middle-class congregants to provide assistance to the poor (Gilkes, 1995). In some of the poorest black neighborhoods, which have lost both population and organizations over the past few decades (Wilson, 1996), churches are among the few non-governmental institutions left.

■ Hispanic Families

The label "Hispanic" covers groups that are so diverse with respect to family patterns that it makes little sense to combine them, yet that is the direction public discussions have taken. It lumps together recent immigrants with citizens whose families have been in the United States for generations, and white, well-educated political émigrés with darker-skinned, poorly educated laborers looking for work. Americans of Mexican origin are by far the largest group, constituting two-thirds of all Hispanics. Central and South Americans accounted for 14 percent, Puerto Ricans for 9 percent, and Cubans for 4 percent (U.S. Bureau of the Census, 2003i).

MEXICAN AMERICANS

The United States and Mexico share a long history and a long border—the longest border between a developed and a developing country in the world. Some of the 20.6 million people who identified themselves as of the Mexican origin in the 2000 U.S. Census are the descendants of the early settlers in the Southwest. [➡ p. 55] Others are second- or third-generation Americans, while still others are recent immigrants. In fact, far more immigrants arrive from Mexico than from any other country. In the 1990s alone, 2.25 million Mexicans migrated legally to the United States. An unknown number migrated illegally; the government estimates that about 5 million immigrants from Mexico do not have proper legal documents (U.S. Bureau of the Census, 2005l). In order to understand Mexican American families, one must keep the scale of this immigration in mind.

For example, immigration plays an important role in the perception of Mexican Americans as more "familistic" than non-Hispanic whites. Here are some of the facts that fuel this perception:

- *Marriage.*   Mexican Americans marry at a younger age than other Hispanics, non-Hispanic whites, or African Americans. In 2000, for instance, 48 percent of 20- to 24-year-old Mexican American women had already married, compared to 29 percent of comparable white non-Hispanics (Raley, Durden, & Wildsmith, 2004). Even though Mexican Americans are more economically disadvantaged, which should lower their likelihood of marrying, they still marry younger. Moreover, two-parent, single-earner families are more common among Mexican American families than among other Hispanic families (Lichter & Qian, 2004).
- *Number of children.*   The Mexican-origin population has a high birthrate by American standards. Figure 5.4 shows, for racial-ethnic groups, the **total fertility rate (TFR)** in 2002. The TFR is the average number of births that

total fertility rate (TFR)
the average number of children a women will bear over their lifetime if current birthrates remain the same

FIGURE 5.4
Total fertility rate for racial-
ethnic groups in 2003.
(*Source:* U.S. National Center
for Health Statistics, 2005a)

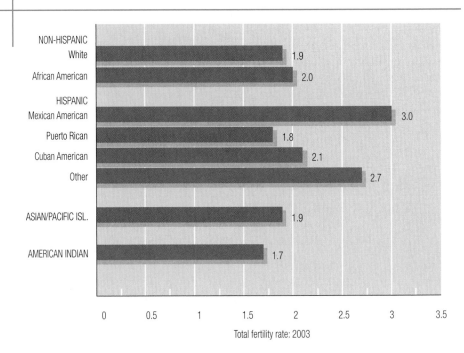

Total fertility rate: 2003

women would have over their lifetime if current birthrates were to remain the same. As can be seen, Mexican American women would average three children, a substantially higher number than the TFR for non-Hispanic whites, blacks, or other Hispanic groups.

But these patterns of marriage and fertility reflect, in part, the characteristics of immigrants. In Mexico the average age at marriage is younger than in the United States (U.S. Bureau of the Census, 2003p; Raley et al., 2004); so immigrants come from a culture where early marriage is more common. Moreover, many Mexican immigrants are already married when they get here. Because most legal immigrants receive visas under a program to reunite them with relatives already living in the United States, many spouses immigrate; in fact, a majority of Mexican women who migrated after age 15 did so after marrying. Moreover, immigrants who arrive in the United States before marrying have an incentive to marry because it will usually allow them to apply for permanent residence. In contrast, Mexican-origin individuals who were born in the United States—who are more distant from Mexican culture and who may have less incentive to marry—marry at similar ages to non-Hispanic whites (Raley et al., 2004).

Birthrates also differ between Mexico and the United States. In 2005 the Mexican TFR was 2.6 and the American TFR was 2.0 (Population Reference Bureau, 2005). Mexicans who immigrate have grown up in a society that values higher fertility, and they have more children than do non-Hispanic whites. But their children—the second generation—are more influenced by American values and their level of childbearing is not much different from non-Hispanic whites (although there are signs that birthrates are going back up a bit in the third generation; Bean, Swicegood, & Berg, 2000). Values, however, are not the whole reason for differences in the number of children (or in marrying early). Immigrants tend to have less education than American natives, and less-educated people tend to marry earlier and to have more children than people with more education.

In sum, ages at marriage are higher and birthrates are lower among U.S.-born Americans of Mexican origin than among Mexican immigrants. Yet even with the lower birthrates among those born in America, the massive scale of Mexican immigration is greatly affecting the size of the American population. Between 2000 and 2004, for instance, births to new Hispanic immigrants (a large share of them from Mexico) and births to Hispanics already in the United States accounted for half of the nation's population growth (Haub, 2006). One demographic study predicts that by 2040, Mexican immigrants since the 1980s and their descendants will have produced 36 million additional births (Johnson & Rendall, 2004). Hispanic fertility, with the Mexican-origin Americans in the lead, is an important reason why Americans are much less concerned about population decline than are European nations with less immigration and lower birthrates.

Mexican-origin households also are more likely than non-Hispanic white households to live in extended families rather than conjugal families. A family's household is said to be extended horizontally when a relative in the same generation as the household head—a brother, sister, or cousin—lives there. It is said to be extended vertically when a relative in the generation above the household head— a parent, an uncle, or an aunt—lives there. Mexican-origin households are more likely to be both horizontally and vertically extended than are non-Hispanic white

Mexican Americans constitute about two-thirds of all Hispanics in the United States.

households, in large part due to the migration of relatives (Glick, Bean, & Van Hook, 1997). An extended family can assistant newly arrived kin; or older parents can provide child care assistance to their children and grandchildren. Other immigrant groups, particularly Asians, are also more likely to live in extended family households. Aided by modern means of communication, the ties between Americans of Hispanic- and Asian-immigrant origin and their relatives in the countries of their birth are surprisingly active. (See *Families in Other Cultures:* Transnational Families.)

PUERTO RICANS

All Puerto Ricans are U.S. citizens because the island of Puerto Rico is a U.S. territory. Consequently, Puerto Ricans, unlike all other major Hispanic groups, are free to move to the mainland if they wish, and many have done so. In 2000, 3.4 million people who identified themselves as Puerto Ricans were residing on the mainland, whereas 3.8 million people lived in Puerto Rico. In other words, 47 percent of all people who claimed Puerto Rican ethnicity lived on the mainland (U.S. Bureau of the Census, 2005l). It is more difficult for individuals from other Hispanic groups to immigrate to the United States; they must either obtain visas, for which there may be a long wait, or find a way to enter and remain illegally. Demographers have long known that when the barriers to immigration are substantial, the people who manage to immigrate tend to have more education and skills than the average person in their home country. Immigration, in other words, is more selective when the barriers are high. People with greater skills are more confident that they can find decent-paying work in the United States, so they are more likely to take the trouble to immigrate. When the barriers are lower, on the other hand, immigration is less selective. We might expect, then, that Puerto Rican immigrants would tend to have less economic success, on average, than other Hispanic immigrants because Puerto Rican migration has been less selective.

Until recently, at least, that is what the data showed. Puerto Ricans have been the most economically disadvantaged of the major Hispanic groups. (From here on I will be referring only to Puerto Ricans on the mainland, unless otherwise noted.) According to one summary, "Of all the Hispanic-origin groups, Puerto Ricans have the lowest labor force participation rates, the highest unemployment levels, the highest incidence of poverty and of welfare utilization, and the lowest average levels of education" (Sandefur & Tienda, 1988). In 2004, however, fewer Puerto Rican family households had incomes below the poverty line (21 percent) than did Mexican American households (23 percent). Both groups had higher levels of poverty than Central and South American family households (16 percent) or Cuban American households (11 percent) (U.S. Bureau of the Census, 2005a). We do not know yet whether the improvement in Puerto Rican incomes relative to Mexican American incomes occurred because of gains among Puerto Ricans or because incomes of recent immigrants from Mexico have adversely affected Mexican American incomes rates.

Consistent with their lower economic standing, Puerto Ricans are second only to African Americans in the percentage of children born to unmarried mothers. Figure 5.5 shows the percentage of unmarried woman who gave birth in 2000 for racial-ethnic groups. Yet many of the formally unmarried Puerto Rican mothers are living in a partnership that they consider to be a marriage. In Puerto Rico and other Caribbean islands, a long tradition of **consensual unions** exists. These are

consensual union a cohabiting relationship in which a couple consider themselves to be married but have never had a religious or civil marriage ceremony

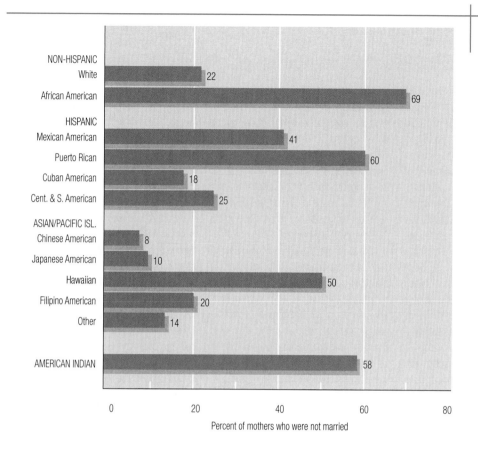

FIGURE 5.5
Percentage of women giving birth who were not married, for racial-ethnic groups in 2000. (*Source:* U.S. National Center for Health Statistics, 2002a)

cohabiting relationships in which couples consider themselves to be married but have never had religious or civil marriage ceremonies. From the viewpoint of the state and the Church, people in consensual unions are unmarried; but from the viewpoint of the couples and their peers, they are in a marriagelike relationship. Still, Puerto Rican couples who are formally married do exhibit some differences; for instance, married men are more likely to pool their incomes with their partners' incomes (rather than, say, to give their partners an allowance) than are men who are not formally married (Oropesa, Landale, & Kenkre, 2003).

Among Puerto Ricans, then, there are three kinds of socially recognized unions: cohabiting unions, in which the partners do not consider themselves married; consensual unions, in which they have not undergone a marriage ceremony but still consider themselves to be informally married; and formal marriage, in which they have had a marriage ceremony and registered with the state. In a 1985 survey of Puerto Rican women aged 15 to 49 in the New York City area, the participants were asked:

As you know, there are various ways in which a man and a woman live in a union. Some couples legally marry, that is, they obtain a license; some couples consider themselves married but without a license; and some couples just live together and do not consider themselves married, legally or informally. I would now like to ask you some questions about your marital history. (Landale & Fennelly, 1992)

Transnational Families

In 2000, Mexico conducted the most openly contested Presidential election campaign in its history, one that unseated a political party that had held power for decades. During the campaign, Mexican politicians flooded the southwestern United States with Spanish-language advertisements. Why? Because of the large number of Mexican immigrants to the United States who remain Mexican citizens, take strong interest in Mexican politics, and are eligible to vote in Mexican elections. The phenomenon of immigrants who live in one country but maintain continuing ties with another is becoming more and more common as modern technology reduces the cost of international communication and travel. Increasingly, demographers are seeing what some call **transnational families:** families that straddle a sending country, such as Mexico, and a receiving country, such as the United States, by traveling frequently between them and maintaining continual contact across the borders (Baca Zinn, Wells, & Wells, 2000).

Immigrants have long sent part of their earnings back to family members in their country of origin; indeed, that was the main reason why many people migrated. Today, families in developing nations still send members to work temporarily in a developed nation to earn higher wages and send some of their earnings back. Mexicans in the United States sent home an estimated $14.5 billion in 2003; and about one in five Mexicans regularly receives money from relatives in the United States (Thompson, 2003).

In addition, some immigrant entrepreneurs travel back home regularly to obtain products such as clothing to sell in the United States. Others work with home country partners to deliver packages to other immigrants. Still others return to their home country with their savings to start businesses based on American examples such as video stores and laundromats (Portes, Haller, & Guarnizo, 2002).

But the transnational family goes beyond such financial transfer. Family members in the country of origin may continue to involve themselves in the immigrants' personal lives. For example, a study of Koreans in Los Angeles found that one-third of those who had married in the previous five years had flown back to Korea to obtain a spouse. There they were introduced to prospective partners chosen by parents and relatives (Min, 1993).

As shown by the case of Rowena Bautista from the Philippines (see the beginning of this chapter), transnational families increasingly involve transnational motherhood. The proportion of international migrants who are women has been growing. About two-thirds of the migrant workers from the Philippines are women, and the remittances [➡ p. 57] they send home constitute one of the country's largest sources of foreign currency—over $7 billion in 1999 (Parreñas, 2002). And, like Ms. Bautista, many leave behind children whom they try to stay in touch with from afar.

Sometimes immigrants return to their country of origin for services they cannot easily afford in their new country. For instance, the 1996 welfare reform law restricted immigrants' eligibility for social welfare benefits. In a study of the effect of welfare reform on families, my colleagues and I found one immigrant mother who returned home in part to obtain dental care for her children, which she could not afford in the United States.

What caused this change in the way immigrants relate to their families? The same technological forces that are allowing American families to keep in closer touch—cheaper long-distance calls, discount airline tickets, e-mail—also allow many immigrant families to keep in touch with kin in their countries of origin. Consequently, some immigrants may have begun to think of themselves as living in two (or more) countries at once. While in the past, immigrating often meant cutting off all contact with one's family, except for financial transfers and letters, that's not necessarily true anymore. For some immigrants today, the family transcends national boundaries.

Ask Yourself

1. Do you know a transnational family? If so, what is their country of origin, and how do they keep in touch with family members there?

2. To the people who belong to a transnational family, what might be the advantages and disadvantages of living in two or more countries at once? To the sending and receiving countries?

www.mhhe.com/cherlin5

transnational families
families that maintain continual contact between members in the sending and receiving countries

Among all women who had borne a child, 32 percent said they had ever lived in an informal marriage without a license, whereas just 13 percent said they had ever cohabited. The authors of the study report that whether or not a woman has borne a child in a union is a key factor in whether she defines it as an informal marriage or as a cohabitation. The birth of a child seems to change the social meaning of a union, making it more like a marriage (Landale & Fennelly, 1992).

CUBAN AMERICANS

Most major immigrant groups today in the United States arrived in labor migrations: They came looking for higher-paying jobs. In contrast, the first waves of Cuban Americans came here in a political migration, fleeing the Communist government of Fidel Castro, who had led a successful revolution in 1959. The U.S. government allowed Cuban citizens to enter the country as political refugees. Indeed, the early migrants were drawn from the Cuban upper and middle classes, the elite that Castro's Communist party overthrew. These immigrants arrived with substantial amounts of education, skills, and capital. In addition, they were largely white in racial appearance. The U.S. government, sympathetic to their plight and wishing to isolate and embarrass Castro, welcomed them enthusiastically and provided assistance in retraining (Suarez, 1993).

Despite government efforts at resettlement, most Cuban immigrants chose to settle in the Miami metropolitan area, where 29 percent of Miami-Dade County is now of Cuban origin (U.S. Bureau of the Census, 2005j). Classic sociological theories of immigration held that immigrants would adjust better and prosper more if they assimilated into the mainstream. (**Assimilation** means the process by which immigrant groups merge their culture and behavior with that of the dominant group in the host country.)[4] In the U.S. context, assimilation implies learning English, sending children to public schools, and dispersing geographically. Many Cuban immigrants chose, instead, to remain clustered in the Cuban neighborhoods of one metropolitan area, to listen to Spanish-language radio stations, to buy their food at markets owned by Cuban Americans, to eat at Cuban restaurants, and to send their children to private Cuban schools. They limited much of their lives to a large, dense, single-ethnic-group, almost self-sufficient community of the type that Kenneth Wilson and Alejandro Portes have called an **immigrant enclave** (Wilson & Portes, 1980).

According to classic immigration theory, then, Cuban immigrants should have suffered. Instead, they prospered. By 1970 the median income of Cuban American families was higher than that of any other Hispanic group or of African Americans, at 80 percent of the median income of non-Hispanic white families; and by 1980 it had reached 88 percent of the median income for non-Hispanic white families (Bean & Tienda, 1987). Portes and other observers claim that Cuban immigrants successfully used the ethnically based connections of the enclave to obtain loans to start businesses when no Anglo bank would lend to them; they also used their connections to find jobs at Cuban enterprises. (See the section, later in this chapter, Social Capital and Immigrant Families.) He argues that the enclave strategy is a viable way for an immigrant group to achieve economic success.

Yet it must be remembered that these immigrants started out with a friendly reception from their hosts, arrived with substantial education and skills, received government assistance, and had white skin. These advantages were not shared by those who were part of a later wave of Cuban immigration that began in 1980, when Castro allowed a flotilla of small boats to depart from the port of Mariel. The Cuban government declared that many of the Mariel Cubans were criminals and undesirables; in addition, about 30 percent were nonwhite (Suarez, 1993). Unlike the first wave of Cuban immigrants, who arrived during an economic boom, the Mariel Cubans arrived at a time of stagnant wages and high unemployment.

assimilation the process by which immigrant groups merge their culture and their behavior with that of the dominant group in the host country

immigrant enclave a large, dense, single-ethnic group, almost self-sufficient community

---

[4]A fuller definition of assimilation can be found in Gordon (1964).

Like the majority of Cuban Americans, the customers at this Miami restaurant chose to settle in the Miami metropolitan area.

They were not welcomed enthusiastically or assisted, and they experienced discrimination from the earlier wave of immigrants. Later studies showed that only a small minority were criminals or otherwise socially undesirable; in fact, 14 percent of Mariel refugees interviewed in 1983 and 1984 had been managers or professionals in Cuba and another 24 percent had been skilled blue-collar workers (Portes, Stepick, & True-love, 1986). By 2001, the median income of Cuban-origin families had slipped to 61 percent of the median for non-Hispanic white families, reflecting the influx of Mariel refugees. Nevertheless, Cuban Americans remained the most prosperous of the major Hispanic groups (U.S. Bureau of the Census, 2005l).

The prosperity of Cuban Americans is derived in large part from business ownership. Cuban immigrants have become entrepreneurs, opening new businesses in far greater numbers than other Hispanic immigrants. The number of Cuban firms in the Miami area rose from about 900 in 1967 to approximately 25,000 by the mid-1980s (Portes & Jensen, 1989). The rate of business ownership among Cuban Americans in 1987 was three times higher than the rate among Mexican Americans and six times higher than among Puerto Ricans (O'Hare, 1992).

Many of the businesses were organized on a family basis. Married Cuban men were more likely to be self-employed, even after taking into account differences between married and unmarried men in education, work experience, citizenship, and English proficiency. If the men had children, they were even more likely to be self-employed (Portes & Jensen, 1989). Moreover, married men living with adults other than wives in their households were less likely to be self-employed, suggesting that the conjugal family of husband, wife, and children was most congenial to business ownership. Cuban immigrants appear to have used conjugal families as a means of pooling the labor and accumulating the capital necessary to start a business. Too many adults represented a drain on capital that could be used for the business; too few children or the absence of a spouse, on the other hand, resulted in insufficient labor or outside income (as from a wife's job) for starting a firm.

Quick Review

- Mexican Americans have high birthrates, marry at younger ages, and tend to live in extended families, in large part because of the extensive migration from Mexico.
- Mexican immigrants and their descendants are contributing greatly to the American population growth.
- Transnational families, in which members maintain ties with the home country and the United States, are becoming more common.
- Puerto Ricans are the most economically disadvantaged of the major Hispanic groups.
- Puerto Ricans have a tradition of consensual unons, in which couples consider themselves married although their unions have never been formalized.
- Cubans, many of whom settled in immigrant enclaves, are the most prosperous Hispanic group.

Asian American Families

Less has been written about Asian American families than about African American and Hispanic families because of their modest numbers prior to the 1965 immigration act. For example, the Korean population increased from an estimated 69,000 in 1970 to 350,000 in 1980 and to 980,000 in 1998 (Lee, 1998). In the 2000 Census, 11.9 million people checked one of the Asian racial categories (Asian Indian, Chinese, Filipino, Japanese, Korean, Vietnamese, or "other Asian") or wrote in entries such as Pakistani or Thai (U.S. Bureau of the Census, 2001c). The family patterns in the many sending nations are diverse, but, in general, Asian cultures emphasize interdependence among kin more, and individualism less, than Western culture (Goode, 1963). Asian families place a greater emphasis on children's loyalty and service to their parents than do Western families. In fact, Asian immigrant parents are more likely to live in households in which their adult children provide most of the income (Glick & Van Hook, 2002).

These Asian ways can conflict with American ways. Two researchers, for instance, read a series of vignettes to a sample of Chinese American immigrants from Taiwan and their parents in Chicago and Los Angeles. Here is one:

Wang Hong has to transfer three times on public transportation to get from where he lives to his office. Because of the time and inconvenience of taking public transportation, Wang Hong has tried very hard to save money to buy a car before winter. However, Wang Hong's parents have a need for money and ask Wang Hong to give them the money Wang Hong has saved.

Both the parents and their adult children were asked to react to this vignette. The authors noted that when a similar vignette had been read to a general U.S. sample of the elderly and their caregivers, about three-fourths of both groups had thought that the child should buy the car. Yet a majority of the Chinese adult children and parents said that Wang Hong should give the money to his parents—placing obligation to one's parents over convenience of transportation (Lin & Liu, 1993).

Immigrants' families frequently pool economic resources to start businesses or to buy homes. Several Asian-origin groups have very high rates of business ownership, often accomplished by borrowing funds from kin and close friends. As for

Asian immigrants, such as these Vietnamese in California, often pool their resources to start family-run small businesses.

homeownership, shared residence and income pooling often help, as one Vietnamese immigrant told an interviewer:

> *To Vietnamese culture, family is everything. There are aspects which help us read-just to this society. It is easy for us because of [the] tradition of helping in the family.*
>
> *We solve problems because [the] family institution is a bank. If I need money and my brothers and my two sisters are working I tell them I need to buy a house. I need priority in this case. They say OK, and they give money to me. After only two years, I bought a house.*
>
> *Some Americans ask me, "How come you came here with empty hands and now you have a house?" I told them, it is easy for us because my brother and sister help with the down payment. Now I help them. They live with me and have no rent. (Gold, 1993)*

This is not to say that all Asian immigrants adjust well and prosper. The first wave of Vietnamese immigration occurred in the immediate aftermath of the Vietnam War in 1975. Like the initial Cuban influx, it was a political migration of middle-class business and military personnel who were assisted on arrival. They have been successful as a group. Yet like the Mariel immigration, a later, less-educated stream of Vietnamese immigrants such as the families of Hai Nguyen and Cuong Dan, escaped in overcrowded boats to refugee camps in Southeast Asia. Those who have emigrated to the United States have fewer skills, have received less assistance, and have encountered a sluggish economy. A 1984 study of some of the later immigrants found that 61 percent had household incomes of less than $9,000 (Gold, 1993). Nevertheless, Asian Americans are a prosperous group overall. In 2004, the median family income for Asian and Pacific Islander families was $57,518, which was 17 percent higher than the median for non-Hispanic white families, an impressive achievement for a population that includes so many recent immigrants (U.S. Bureau of the Census, 2005e).

Church activities can provide immigrant communities with "social capital."

The extent to which Asian-style patterns will survive through the second and third generations of Asian Americans remains to be seen. Among Asian Americans whose families have been in the United States for a few generations, the traditional Asian patterns are less apparent. For instance, the relations between women and men are more egalitarian in third-generation Japanese American families than in the older, immigrant generation (Ishii-Kuntz, 2000). And rates of interracial inter-marriages are high among Asians, a topic to which I will turn in a few pages.

◼ Social Capital and Immigrant Families ◼

The recent literature on immigrants refers often to a concept developed by the French sociologist Pierre Bourdieu (1980) and expanded on by the American sociologist James S. Coleman (1988). **Social capital** is the resources that a person can access through his or her relationships with other people. To understand this concept, think about the social connections that might allow you to get a ticket to a sold-out concert (because your friend's cousin works in the box office), to be admitted to a competitive college (because your mother is an alumna), or to get your first job after college (because your roommate's father runs the company). In all these cases, the resources you would draw on would not be monetary (which social scientists refer to as "financial capital") or educational (which social scientists call "human capital"), but rather your social links to a network of people who can help you reach a goal you might otherwise fail to achieve.

social capital the resources that a person can access through his or her relationships with other people

That is the essence of the concept of social capital. In the literature on immigrants it is sometimes used more broadly to refer to a person's links to an entire immigrant community. The idea is that the community provides members with resources that help them to achieve goals they could not achieve alone, or even as families working together. For example, to explain why the children of Vietnamese immigrants in Versailles Village do better in school than their low social class would predict, Zhou and Bankston (1998) point to the social capital created by the close-knit Vietnamese community. They describe a Vietnamese Catholic church that offers after-school courses, and the Vietnamese Education Association, a community group that holds an annual awards ceremony to honor high achieving students. Through these institutions, the authors argue, the Vietnamese community in Versailles Village provides social capital that boosts school achievement among Vietnamese students.

As I mentioned earlier, the literature on Cuban immigrants provides another example of the use of social capital. One reason for the growth in the number of Cuban American-owned firms from the late-1960s to the 1980s was that immigrants could use their social standing in the Cuban community in Miami to obtain the initial loans needed to start a business. In the mid-1960s, according to Alejandro Portes and Julia Sensenbrenner, a few small banks owned by South Americans hired Cuban immigrant ex-bankers. The Cubans began to make loans to their fellow immigrants that other financial institutions would have thought risky. As one Cuban banker said:

> *At the start, most Cuban enterprises were gas stations; then came grocery shops and restaurants. No American bank would lend to them. By the mid-sixties we started a policy at our bank of making small loans to Cubans who wanted to start their own business, but did not have the capital. These loans of $10,000 or $15,000 were made because the person was known to us by his reputation and integrity. All of them paid back; there were zero losses. With some exceptions they have continued being clients of the bank. People who used to borrow $15,000 on a one-time basis now take $50,000 in a week. In 1973, the policy was discontinued. The reason was that the new refugees coming at that time were unknown to us. (Portes & Sensenbrenner, 1993)*

Whereas American banks would have required more proof that an applicant would be able to pay back a loan, the Cuban bankers relied solely on the applicant's "reputation and integrity." That reputation was established through a network of ties within the Cuban enclave in Miami. The banker might have known someone who had married the sister of the applicant and could vouch for the applicant's character. To enforce the terms of the loan, the banker relied on the humiliation and, perhaps, ostracism that would befall a person who defaulted. In this way, Cuban immigrants were able to use their ties to a network of relatives and friends to obtain the money they needed to buy a grocery store or restaurant.

Beside the Vietnamese, many other Asian immigrant groups also have used their social capital to obtain the support they need to start businesses. Among some Chinese and Japanese immigrants, for example, a group of relatives and friends was formed in which each person invested a modest amount of money into a single credit fund. Subsequently, one member was allowed to borrow the entire amount in the fund to start an enterprise, and he was required to pay it back with interest. Then the fund was made available to another member of the group, and then another. The members trusted that their loans would be repaid because of the loss of face a person who did not repay would suffer from the other members of the group. These "rotating credit associations" provided their members with an advantage not shared by outsiders—an advantage based on close kinship and friendship ties (Light, 1972).

■ American Indian Families

Before the twentieth century, kinship ties provided the basis for governing most American Indian tribes. A person's household was linked to a larger group of relatives who might be a branch of a matrilineal or patrilineal clan [➡ p. 43] that shared power with other clans. Thus, kinship organization was also political organization. Under these circumstances, extended kinship ties reflected power and status to a much greater extent than among other racial-ethnic groups in the United States. American Indian kinship systems allowed individuals to have more relatives, particularly distant relatives, than did Western European kinship systems (Shoemaker, 1991). Even today, extended family ties retain a significance for American Indians that goes beyond the sharing of resources that has been noted among other groups (Harjo, 1993). Kinship networks constitute tribal organization; kinship ties confer an identity.

Only one-third of the individuals in the 2000 Census who identified themselves as solely of American Indian origin and who said they were members of a tribe were living in tribal areas (U.S. Bureau of the Census, 2006b). By 2000, New York and Los Angeles were the cities with the largest American Indian populations (U.S. Bureau of the Census, 2002b). As noted earlier, a substantial share of the growth of the American Indian population in urban areas in the East and on the West Coast reflects a rise in the number of people who considered themselves to be American Indians. In addition, migration from reservations to urban areas may have accounted for some of the drop in the percentage living near tribal lands.

American Indians remain an economically disadvantaged population. Their median family income is slightly higher than that of African Americans (U.S. Bureau of the Census, 2005l). Consistent with their high levels of poverty, the percentage of American Indian families headed by an unmarried woman is substantial: As Figure 5.1 shows, 36 percent of American Indian Families with children in 2001

Despite a decline in the power of lineages, extended families remain significant for American Indians.

were headed by an unmarried woman. Only African Americans had a higher percentage. Consistent with these figures, 61 percent of American Indian mothers who gave birth in 2003 were unmarried—a percentage exceeded only by African Americans (U.S. National Center for Health Statistics, 2005a). The percentage of adults who are divorced is also higher among American Indians than among the U.S. population as a whole (Sandefur & Liebler, 1997).

It's likely that many of the unmarried mothers were enmeshed in kinship networks that provided assistance. Little research, however, has been done on contemporary American Indian family patterns—especially among American Indians outside tribal lands. Beyond these lands, intermarriage and shifting conceptions of American Indian ethnicity make the study of families more complex. It is increasingly difficult to talk of the "American Indian family": There always has been diversity in family patterns among Indian tribes and among persons residing on reservations versus persons not on reservations, and now an American Indian family is often a multiracial family, as the next section discusses.

Quick Review

- Asian family patterns traditionally have placed a greater emphasis on children's loyalty and service to parents than have Western family patterns.
- Ties to family and community can provide social capital to immigrants.
- Kinship networks traditionally provided organization and identity to American Indians.
- The high intermarriage rate and shifting conceptions of identity make American Indian family patterns diverse.

Racial and Ethnic Intermarriage

As recently as 1967, 15 states had laws forbidding marriages between whites and nonwhites. Then, in a case brought by a white man, Richard Loving, and his black wife, Mildred Jeter, against the state of Virginia, the Supreme Court declared such laws unconstitutional (*Loving v. Virginia*, 1967). In 1972, when the General Social Survey (GSS) started its annual survey of American adults, 39 percent of whites still favored laws against racial intermarriage (Davis, Smith, & Marsden, 2003); and interracial married couples comprised only about 1 percent of all American married couples (Lee & Edmonston, 2005). By the year 2000, just 12 percent of whites favored these laws, and the roughly 3,000,000 interracial married couples comprised 5 percent of all American married couples. To be sure, the other 95 percent of American couples are of the same race, but young adults are intermarrying in large enough numbers that the boundaries of American racial groups are becoming more fluid.

The rates at which people of different races marry interracially vary greatly. There are so many whites in the United States that even though millions of them marry someone of another race, the percentage who intermarry remains low. Among whites age 20 to 34 in 2000, 2.7 percent had intermarried (all statistics in this section are from Lichter & Qian, 2004, unless otherwise stated). The racial group with the next lowest percentage intermarrying is African Americans: In 2000, 7 percent of African American women and 14 percent of African American men age 20 to 34 were married to spouses of a different race. These modest percentages suggest that barriers to intermarriage are still high for African Americans. And yet the sheer number of black-white intermarriages increased nearly 600 percent between 1970 and 2000, rising from 65,000 couples to 363,000 couples. So in relative terms, the increase has been large; but it is still the case that most African Americans do not intermarry. The social distance between African Americans and other racial groups remains substantial.

At the high end are Asian Americans: In 2000, 47 percent of U.S.-born Asian men and 61 percent of U.S.-born Asian women aged 20 to 34 were married to spouses of different races. So among young Asian Americans, intermarriage is becoming the norm. The same can be said for American Indians: 57 percent of men and 58 percent of women ages 20 to 34 were interracially married. Hispanics, although technically an ethnic group rather than a race, also have substantial rates of out-marriage: 51 percent of U.S.-born Hispanic men and 46 percent of U.S.-born Hispanic women in the 20-to-34 age range in 2000 were married to non-Hispanics. Puerto Ricans are the Hispanic subgroup most likely to be intermarried, whereas Cubans are the least likely (Lee & Edmonston, 2005).

If these rates continue into the future, far more people could identify as "multiracial" when the Census Bureau comes around to ask about race a generation or two from now. Already, as noted earlier in the chapter, 40 percent of people who checked the American Indian box on the 2000 census form also checked another race. As the children of interracial marriages involving American Indians reach adulthood, the continuing high rates could result in a further decline in the number of people identifying themselves solely as American Indians and a further increase—to a clear majority—in the proportion of people who identify themselves as American Indians and another race. Similarly, a majority of U.S.-born Americans with an Asian American parent could identify themselves as multiracial in a generation. The ultimate number of such people in the United States in the mid–twenty-first century will depend on whether intermarriage increases further and also on two other factors. The first is the level of immigration: Immigrants from Latin America and Asia will replenish the Hispanic and Asian American single-race groups while the U.S. members of these groups continue to marry out. Second, the propensity of people to think of themselves as multiracial could rise. Consider the golfer Tiger Woods, who has become a symbol of twenty-first-century multiracial identity. He describes his race as "Cablinasian": His father was black, Chinese, and American Indian, and his mother is Thai, Chinese, and white. If having a multiracial identity becomes more acceptable, it could provide a further boost to the multiracial numbers that the census will count.

Still, the social distance between African Americans and Americans of other races and of Hispanic ethnicity remains substantial. African Americans are less likely to identify as multiracial and their intermarriages rates remain lower than other nonwhites and Hispanics. Until recently, the United States had a sharp color line between blacks and whites (Du Bois, 1903; Farley & Allen, 1987). The increasing rates of intermarriage have the potential to finally blur that line. Yet some sociologists note apprehensively that if intermarriages involving African Americans do not increase as fast as other types of intermarriages, then the United States could end up replacing the old color line with a new one, the "black/nonblack divide" (Lee & Bean, 2004). African Americans would be on one side of the line, and the descendants of Asians, Hispanics, American Indians, and non-Hispanic whites would be on the other side. But this result is not foretold; it is too soon to know how intermarriage will alter racial identity in the next half-century.

Quick Review

- Racial and ethnic intermarriage has increased greatly over the past few decades.
- Rates vary greatly, with intermarriages of Asians and American Indians at the high end and those of African Americans and non-Hispanic whites (due to their large population size) at the low end.
- Intermarriage has the potential to reshape individual and group identities over the next half-century.

Race, Ethnicity, and Kinship

Family ties have been central to the successes and the struggles of racial-ethnic groups in the United States. All the minority groups that have been discussed in this chapter have relied on their relatives for support—whether that support be food for dinner or money to buy a restaurant. Their reliance on extended kinship contrasts with the nuclear family ideal among non-Hispanic whites. To be sure, there are substantial differences among racial-ethnic groups in the kinds of family lives they tend to lead. Some of these differences reflect economic forces. Put another way, sometimes what we think of as ethnic or racial differences may, in large part, be class differences. For example, to compare Puerto Ricans on the mainland with Cubans on the mainland is to compare an economically disadvantaged group with a more economically privileged one.

Still in Chapter 4 and this chapter, we have seen similarities across racial-ethnic groups in the ways low-income families organize family and kinship. Among these disadvantaged groups, the strongest family tie is often between a mother and her adult daughter. In what I have called women-centered kin networks, women organize exchanges of support that extend across households, linking networks of people who share their meager resources.

Nevertheless, the precise form of kinship varies from group to group, reflecting, in my opinion, long-standing cultural differences. For example, the distinctive characteristic of Puerto Rican households is the consensual union, although there are also many households headed by women without live-in partners. Single-parent households, or grandmother-daughter-grandchild households, are the common form among African Americans, with young mothers often residing with their own mothers for several years. For all these groups, assistance from family members other than one's spouse or partner is crucial for subsisting from day to day.

Among many immigrant groups, family ties provide critical assistance to individuals who wish to start small businesses. Most banks will not lend money to new immigrants because they are not sure they will be repaid. Immigrants tend not to have homes or other assets that they can use as collateral to secure a bank loan. Sometimes, however, they can obtain start-up loans from members of their kinship and community networks. Those who loan the money rely upon kinship and community ties as a form of moral collateral: A borrower puts his reputation and standing among his peers on the line when he or she obtains a loan. If the borrower were to default, he or she would be dishonored before family and friends. Thus, kinship ties provide a form of social capital that immigrants can use to obtain the financial capital—money, equipment, storefronts—needed to start an enterprise. These same ties also become recruiting networks through which members of the group can find jobs.

The immigrant entrepreneurs utilize what we might call marriage-centered kin networks. These exchanges tend to connect households that are headed by husbands and wives. It is the married couple that starts and maintains the business, although other relatives may work in it. Ties to a wider network of kin provide financial assistance that the married couple is allowed to manage largely for its own benefit. In contrast, women-centered kin networks require that any surplus be shared. In this way, the kin networks of the poor allow the maximum number of people to get the resources they need to avoid becoming destitute. Thus, the two kinds of kinship networks discussed in this chapter and the previous one have different functions: Marriage-centered networks allow for the accumulation of resources by the husband-wife household, whereas women-centered networks allow for the maximum sharing of resources across predominantly single-parent households.

I would suggest that these two forms of kin networks have different strengths and limitations. The women-centered networks are superior for easing the hardships of persistent poverty. They have allowed many poor individuals to subsist from day to day. Yet they make it difficult for network members to accumulate the resources necessary to rise above poverty. The marriage-based networks, on the other hand, are superior for allowing people to be upwardly mobile by accumulating enough resources to start a business or move to a better neighborhood. Yet they make it difficult for network members to provide assistance to all kin who need it. The differences between the two networks suggest, therefore, a tension that many people with low incomes may face: helping all of one's kin who need assistance versus accumulating enough money to better the position of one's own household. Different racial-ethnic groups resolve this tension in different ways.

This is not to suggest that whether a household escapes from poverty is solely, or even primarily, a matter of kinship networks. For instance, education matters, and Asian Americans have a higher percentage of college graduates than non-Hispanic whites (U.S. Bureau of the Census, 2005l). As mentioned previously, most of the early Cuban immigrants were white and therefore did not face racial discrimination. A case could be made that, although there has been discrimination against Asian Americans, it has not been as institutionalized and as pervasive as has discrimination against African Americans. Moreover, the restructuring of the economy has had a major effect on the family lives of African Americans. Still, within these constraints, family and kinship patterns appear to make a difference in the life chances of the members of racial-ethnic groups, allowing many to survive and some to prosper.

Looking Back

1. **How is immigration changing the racial and ethnic balance in the United States?** Since the immigration laws were modified in 1965, the proportion of all immigrants coming from Latin American and Asian countries has increased greatly. One in five children in the United States is now an immigrant or the child of an immigrant. Within the Hispanic and Asian ethnic groups there is great diversity in family patterns. Transnational immigrants maintain ties to their home country.

2. **How has African American family life changed over the past several decades?** African Americans have been adversely affected by economic changes that have reduced the number of semiskilled and skilled blue-collar jobs available to American workers. In part as a result of this economic transformation, the importance of marriage in African American families has declined substantially relative to ties to extended kin such as grandmothers.

The link between childbearing and marriage has also weakened; about two-thirds of black children are now born to unmarried mothers. African Americans have responded to these changes by drawing on the network of kin for mutual support. During the same period, however, a substantial African American middle class has emerged.

3. **What are the family patterns of the major Hispanic ethnic groups?** The largest Hispanic group, Mexican Americans, is characterized by high birthrates and large households. Nevertheless, Mexican American women (and women in most other Hispanic groups) have entered the labor force in large numbers over the past few decades. Among Puerto Ricans, the poorest of the major Hispanic groups in the United States, a relatively high number of children are born to unmarried mothers. But some of these unmarried mothers live with partners, often in consensual unions that they consider to be like marriages. Cuban Americans are the most prosperous Hispanic group, although recent immigrants have reduced the group's economic standing. Most Cuban Americans settled in an immigrant enclave in the Miami area and many started family-based businesses.

4. **What are the distinctive characteristics of the family patterns of Asian Americans?** More than in any other group, including non-Hispanic whites, Asian American families are headed by married couples. These families also have comparatively few children born outside of marriage and low divorce rates—characteristics that probably reflect a greater emphasis on the interdependence and mutual obligations of kin. Although some Asian subgroups are poor, Asian American families as a whole have a higher median income than non-Hispanic white families. A majority of young adult Asian Americans now marry non-Asians.

5. **How does the concept of "social capital" apply to immigrant families?** Some Hispanic immigrant groups, most notably the Cubans, and many Asian immigrant groups use ties to others in their ethnic community to achieve certain goals, such as starting a business. This use of social connections to advance oneself is an example of what sociologists call social capital.

6. **How is intermarriage affecting racial and ethnic groups?** Rates of intermarriage have increased greatly in recent decades. For some groups, such as Asians and American Indians, rates are so high that a majority of each group may soon identify as multiracial. Hispanics also have high rates of intermarriage. Rates of intermarriage are lower among African Americans, although they also have increased. Whether intermarriage will alter the color line in America is still unknown.

 Go to the Online Learning Center at www.mhhe.com/cherlin5 to test your knowledge of the chapter concepts and key terms.

Study Questions

1. What are the pros and cons of the use of "umbrella" racial-ethnic group designations such as "Hispanic" and "Asian"?

2. Does it make sense to consider "whites" as a racial-ethnic group?

3. What does research suggest about economic and cultural influences on the decline of marriage among African Americans?

4. Why might middle-class African American families have more difficulty maintaining their status than middle-class white families?

5. What problems to transnational families face? What opportunities do they have?

6. Why might Mexican American and Puerto Rican family patterns be different?

7. What are the likely implications of the high rates at which Asian Americans and American Indians marry outside of their racial-ethnic groups?

8. Why might marriage-centered kin networks be advantageous to immigrant entrepreneurs?

Key Terms

Asian American 147	intersectionality 162	total fertility rate (TFR) 163
assimilation 169	mediating structures 162	transnational families 168
consensual union 166	non-Hispanic white 148	union formation 154
Hispanic 146	racial-ethnic group 146	
immigrant enclave 169	social capital 173	

Thinking about Families

The Public Family	The Private Family
Should more native-born Americans care for their aging parents the way many immigrant groups do?	Interracial and interethnic marriages are widespread among Asian Americans and American Indians, common among Hispanics, and uncommon but increasing among African Americans. How might intergroup marriage change American families in the early decades of the twenty-first century?

Families on the Internet   www.mhhe.com/cherlin5

Note: While all the URLs listed were current as of the printing of this book, these sites often change. Please check our Web site (http://www.mhhe.com/cherlin5) for updates.

The U.S. Bureau of the Census collects detailed statistics through its monthly Current Population Survey, its Decennial Census of Population, and other studies. The information in this chapter on the growth of racial and ethnic minority families, household composition, and interracial families was obtained from the treasure trove of information at the Census Bureau's home page (www.census.gov). For instance, to find out the latest information on Hispanic families, select "H" in the "Subjects A to Z" box; then, on the next screen, find "Hispanic" and select the subcategory "People." You can then select and view the latest annual report on the Hispanic population in the United States. What percentage of the Hispanic population is now of Mexican origin?

The National Academy of Sciences convenes panels of experts to address scientific issues. Many of the panels publish their reports as books through the National Academy Press. Recently, the National Academy Press put the complete text of hundreds of these reports online at its Web site (www.nap.edu). There you can read *America Becoming*, an edited volume on race in American society (Smelser, Wilson, & Mitchell, 2001). The report includes chapters on most major racial-ethnic groups as well as topics such as the changing meaning of race, immigration and race, and racial attitudes.

Part Three

Sexuality, Partnership, and Marriage

In the next three chapters, we move from a focus on the effects of gender, race-ethnicity, and class to a consideration of how intimate relationships are built from the ground up, how they are structured as partnerships and marriages, and how family members care for each other. These chapters examine the challenges that people experience as they come to love someone and to form partnerships and marriages. • **Chapter 6** discusses the emergence of the modern concept of sexuality, which is about a century old. It traces the great changes in sexual attitudes and practices over the past few decades and examines our living arrangements that these changes have produced. It also covers childbearing outside of marriage, which is a consequence of changing sexual practices. Attention then shifts in • **Chapter 7** to marriage and cohabitation. We will first study courtship, dating, and the marriage market. We will then review how marriage changed to a companionship in the early 1900s and how it recently has changed again to a more individualized kind of partnership. We will examine cohabitation and the vision of the "pure relationship." • **Chapter 8** will examine the complex connections between work and families. We will first examine the growth in dual-earner couples as married women have entered the paid labor force. We will also examine the important, largely unpaid, caring work that family members, most of them women, do for their partners, children, parents, and kin. We will also consider how differences in husbands' and wives' work arrangements can generate inequalities of power and authority. Finally, we'll look at the consequences of paid work for the daily lives of family members.

Chapter Six

Sexualities

Looking Forward

1. When did the idea of a sexual identity develop?

2. What determines people's sexual identities?

3. Is "sexual identity" a useful way to think about people's sexuality?

4. Are people's living arrangements going beyond the boundaries of the family?

5. What is the nature of the teenage pregnancy "problem"?

In April 1779, Alexander Hamilton wrote to John Laurens, with whom he had served in the American Revolution:

Cold in my professions, warm in [my] friendships, I wish, my Dear Laurens, it m[ight] be in my power, by action rather than words, [to] convince you that I love you. I shall only tell you that 'till you bade us Adieu, I hardly knew the value you had taught my heart to set upon you.

In September, after almost giving up hope of receiving a letter from Laurens, Hamilton wrote of his joy at finally receiving one:

But like a jealous lover, when I thought you slighted my caresses, my affection was alarmed and my vanity piqued. I had almost resolved to lavish no more of them upon you and to reject you as an inconstant and an ungrateful—. But you have now disarmed my resentment and by a single mark of attention made up the quarrel. (Katz, 1976)

Nor were famous American men the only ones who wrote intimate letters to other men. Karen Hansen tells the story of Brigham Nims, who lived for most of his life on his family's farm in New Hampshire, married, and had three children. In the 1830s, prior to marrying, Nims worked in a box factory in Boston for two years, where he struck up a close friendship with J. Foster Beal. They corresponded for a few years afterward. In one passage, Beal writes:

can not forget those happy hours [th]at we spent at G. Newcombs and the evening walks; but we are deprived of that privilege now we are separated for a time we cannot tell how long perhaps before our eyes behold each other in this world.

In a later letter, Beal reminds Nims of the time Beal nursed him through an illness:

I guess you have forgot all about you being at Boston last Sept. when you was so sick, and I took care of you, doctored you up, even took you in bed with myself; you will not do as much, as, to write me. (Hansen, 1989)

Upon discovering these accounts, it is the instinct of the contemporary reader to immediately consider whether the relationships were homosexual. Yet historians argue that such a question represents the myopia of a person steeped in contemporary culture peering back at another time. The categories of homosexual and heterosexual did not yet exist, and therefore eighteenth- and nineteenth-century people did not need to fit into them. Whether or not Hamilton's intimate friendship ever involved a sexual act was not its defining feature. As historian Jonathan Katz notes, even if many of the phrases in these letters were merely

Alexander Hamilton was one of many eighteenth- and nineteenth-century Americans who wrote intimate letters to other men.

rhetorical flourishes, it is striking how easy it was for men to use language that to-day would be seen as indicating a sexual relationship.

In fact, what seems so different about these relationships is the seeming ease with which two same-sex individuals could engage in intimacies, such as sharing a bed or declaring their love for each other, without these acts marking the relationship as sexual or asexual. (Indeed, Hansen tells us that sharing a bed was not uncommon among the working class in nineteenth-century Boston because of the lack of space.) A broad range of public affection and intimacy was open to same-sex friendships in a way that, for most men at least, it is not today (Adam, 2004).

The best-known study of same-sex intimacy in the late eighteenth and nineteenth centuries is Carroll Smith-Rosenberg's "The Female World of Love and Ritual" (Smith-Rosenberg, 1975). Smith-Rosenberg explored the "separate sphere" of middle-class women and found that they often formed deep emotional bonds of friendship with other women. Immersed in a network of female kin and friends, women helped one another in crises such as childbirth, helped to prepare one another for weddings, and spent long hours together talking. Some of their correspondence seems, by today's standards at least, to have a romantic and even erotic tone. Smith-Rosenberg writes of Sarah Butler Wister and Jeannie Field Musgrove, who first met as teenagers during a summer vacation, attended boarding school together for two years, and formed a lifelong intimate friendship. At age 29, Sarah, married and a mother, wrote to Jeannie, "I shall be entirely alone [this coming week]. I can give you no idea how desperately I shall want you." Jeannie ended one letter "Goodbye my dearest, dearest lover" and another "I will go to bed . . . [though] I could write all night—A thousand kisses—I love you with my whole soul."

The point of studying exchanges such as these, as Smith-Rosenberg herself argued, "is not whether these women had genital contact and can therefore be defined as heterosexual or homosexual." Rather, the point is that these women lived in a social context that allowed them the freedom to form a friendship that was quite intimate without the friendship's being labeled as anything more than that. Middle-class women's bonds could be loving and sensual without necessarily being sexual; it is likely that even if they were, the sexual acts would not be seen as the defining characteristic of the relationship. The social context allowed women more flexibility in creating intense emotional ties than is the case today, when we tend to think that close, sensual same-sex relationships must be "homosexual."

Smith-Rosenberg believes that the creation of a separate sphere for middle-class women established the conditions that allowed such close friendships to flourish. But the correspondence between Nims and Beal suggests that some men may also have established intimate friendships. How unusual Nims was we cannot know. Other than the two years he spent in Boston, he worked on the farm. Hansen argues that rural men, who did not leave home to work in a factory every day, did not experience as strict a split between the worlds of women and men. Perhaps, she suggests, they had a more fluid conception of gender that allowed them to be intimate friends with other men.

But in the late-nineteenth and twentieth centuries, these more fluid conceptions congealed into two master categories that people saw as central to their senses of themselves—two sexual identities, heterosexual and homosexual. Most people think of them as "natural," but they are modern creations. Moreover, there are intellectuals and researchers today who argue that these identities are becoming more fluid again, and some who argue against even using the concept of a sexual identity. Moreover, some of these same writers, who include sociologists, claim that people who do not follow the dominant heterosexual model are creating new modes of living that challenge the usefulness of the concept of "the family" or even of diverse "families" to describe personal life in the twenty-first century. In this chapter we will examine the rise, and perhaps the beginning of the fall, of sexual identities and the implications for studying family life. We will then turn to the topics of sexual behavior in and outside of marriage and among unmarried adolescents.

Sexual Identities

Of course, there is nothing new about sex, or about people having sexual preferences and attractions. What's new—or at least no more than 150 years old—is the way that sexual acts and preferences are currently socially organized. Other societies have organized sexuality somewhat differently: Think of the berdaches, the in-between-gender individuals found among many American Indian tribes. [➡ p. 80] What's also new is the important role this organization of sexuality has played in social life—how one's sexual preferences and behaviors have become a central way of defining who one is. They were not as central to Alexander Hamilton or Brigham Nims.

THE EMERGENCE OF SEXUAL IDENTITIES

sexual identity a set of sexual practices and attitudes that lead to the formation in a person's mind of an identity as heterosexual, homosexual, or bisexual

Although sex isn't new, sexual identities are. By a **sexual identity**, I mean a set of sexual practices and attitudes that lead to the formation in a person's mind of an identity as heterosexual, homosexual, or bisexual. Most people in our society today could give a clear and immediate answer to the question "Are you heterosexual or homosexual?" Our sexual identity, in turn, becomes an important part of our sense of who we are. Furthermore, we see this as "natural"—everyone, we assume, has a sexual identity.

Sexual Acts versus Sexual Identities

Yet the question "Are you heterosexual or homosexual?" would have stumped Americans until the late nineteenth century. Not only the terms "homosexual" and "heterosexual" but also the idea of "being" homosexual or heterosexual had not yet been invented. There were only two categories of sexual activities: the socially approved (sexual intercourse within marriage, in moderation, and undertaken mainly to have children) and the socially disapproved (all other activities, including acts between persons of the same sex, masturbation, oral sex regardless of the genders of the partners, and so forth). To perform any of the latter was sinful, but such behavior did not define a person as having a particular sexual identity. Moreover, one's sexual acts played a smaller role in defining one's sense of self. In short, sexual acts existed, but sexual identities did not. The concept of a sexual identity requires a self-consciousness and self-examination that was not prominent until the late nineteenth century.

The Emergence of "Heterosexuality" and "Homosexuality"

Americans defined the categories they use today in part by mounting a public campaign against homosexuality beginning in the late nineteenth century. At that time, an influential body of medical literature began to describe not merely homosexual acts but homosexual persons—distinctive individuals who were seen as suffering from a psychological illness that altered their sexual preferences. Their supposedly unnatural condition was labeled "homosexuality," and it was said to pervade their personalities. They were no longer just men or women who engaged in sexual acts with a same-sex partner; they were homosexuals—seriously ill people (Foucault, 1980). In contrast to them, the same writers defined a "normal" sexual preference for the opposite sex as "heterosexuality." Heterosexuals were seen as mentally healthy as opposed to sick. This was the way sexuality entered our everyday language and our consciousness: as a means of organizing people into two contrasting sexual identities, one viewed as normal and one disparaged as diseased.

The medical model remained dominant until 1973, when the American Psychiatric Association removed homosexuality from its list of mental disorders (Silverstein, 1991). The medical model stigmatized homosexual people and served as a basis for prejudice and discrimination. But the very force of the critique also created a group identity for individuals who had previously had none. Much as the ideology of separate spheres created conditions that allowed for social and political action by women's groups, so the discourse on homosexuality as an illness created conditions that ultimately provoked social and political actions by homosexual persons. "Homosexuality began to speak in its own behalf," wrote Michel Foucault, "to demand that its legitimacy or 'naturality' be acknowledged, often in the same vocabulary, using the same categories by which it was medically disqualified" (Foucault, 1980).

Quick Review

- The idea that people have a sexual identity did not arise until the late nineteenth century.
- Homosexuality was initially defined as a "psychological illness," whereas heterosexuality was seen as "normal."

THE DETERMINANTS OF SEXUAL IDENTITIES

Given this history, and given the variety of ways in which societies have organized sexual life, some sociologists and like-minded scholars take the position that sexual identities are completely determined by society. Others take the position that biological influences may also play a significant role in determining people's sexual identities. Here is the case for each of these viewpoints.

> **social constructionist perspective** (on sexuality) the belief that human sexual identities are entirely socially constructed

The Social Constructionist Perspective   What we might call the **social constructionist perspective** on human sexual identities is that sexual identities are *entirely* socially created (Seidman, 2003). Advocates of this perspective point to many kinds of evidence. They note the unclear boundaries of the two-gender, heterosexually dominant model. For instance, they might cite the between-man-and-woman genders such as the berdaches. They might remind us of the deep friendships of women such as Sarah Butler Wister and Jeannie Field Musgrove. They would note that in much of ancient Greece and Rome, men were allowed, even expected, to desire sex with other men or boys as well as with women (Aries, 1985b). The Greek biographer and historian Plutarch wrote:

> *The noble lover of beauty engages in love wherever he sees excellence and splendid natural endowment without regard for any difference in physiological detail. The lover of human beauty [will] be fairly and equably disposed toward both sexes, instead of supposing that males and females are as different in the matter of love as they are in their clothes.*[1]

Yet although the Greeks had words for specific sexual tastes, they had no general term comparable to "homosexuality" (Weinrich & Williams, 1991).

The social constructionists would also argue that even today sexual identities vary from culture to culture. For example, in Brazil and some other Latin American countries, a man who always takes the active, penetrating role in sex with other men would not necessarily be thought of as a "homosexual," whereas a man who always take the passive role would (Rebhun, 1999). In other words, a man's sexuality depends on whether he plays the "masculine" role in sex, in which case he may be considered heterosexual even if he sometimes has sex with other men. Cultural and historical variations such as these lead sociologists to argue that the sexual categories we use are defined by the society we live in.

> **Kinsey Report** a 1948 book by Alfred Kinsey detailing the results of thousands of interviews with men about their sexual behavior

No one did more to demonstrate that the boundaries between heterosexuality and homosexuality are unclear in American society than Alfred Kinsey, a zoology professor at the University of Indiana. In 1948 he published the results of thousands of interviews with men about their sexual behavior. Kinsey's dry, statistical book with 173 figures and 162 tables, often referred to as the **Kinsey Report,** became an immediate best seller. His findings on homosexuality shocked the country: Half of all men in his sample, he reported, acknowledged having had erotic feelings toward other men; one-third had had at least one sexual experience with another man; one out of eight had had sexual experiences predominantly with other men for at least three years; and 4 percent had had sexual experiences exclusively with other men (Kinsey, Pomeroy, & Martin, 1948). Kinsey concluded from his study that sexual orientation was a continuum running from exclusively heterosexual behavior to a mixture of heterosexual and homosexual behavior to

---

[1] Quoted in Boswell (1982).

Sex researcher, Alfred Kinsey sits at his desk at Indiana University surrounded by his co-authors and associates (left to right) Wardell B. Pomeroy, Paul H. Gebhard, and Dr. Clyde E. Martin.

exclusively homosexual behavior. Thus the book contained two far-reaching con-clusions. First, the proportion of men whose experiences were predominantly ho-mosexual was higher than most had imagined. Although Kinsey gave a range of figures, the one that came to dominate public discussion was that 10 percent of males were "more or less exclusively homosexual" for at least three years be-tween the ages of 16 and 55 (Kinsey et al., 1948). Second, an even larger number of men had had some homosexual experience or feelings.

Although Kinsey's general conclusions still stand, his figures are not represen-tative of the U.S. population now and probably were not then either. His study was based entirely on interviews with volunteers, the vast majority of them white, well educated, young, and from the Midwest and Northeast. In 1992, re-searchers at the University of Chicago directed the first, detailed survey of a large, random sample of the U.S. adult population on sexual activity (Laumann, Gagnon, Michael, & Michaels, 1994). More recently, a U.S. government agency repeated many of the Chicago questions in a 2002 survey of childbearing, contraceptive use, and sexual activity—the National Survey of Family Growth, or NSFG. (Al-though the researchers strongly defend their methods, some observers have ex-pressed skepticism about the possibility of doing a survey on sexual behavior. See *How Do Sociologists Know What They Know? Asking about Sensitive Behavior.*)

The NSFG measured sexual orientation in several ways, four of which are shown in Figure 6.1 (on page 194). Each person was asked whether he or she had had any same-sex sexual contact in their lifetime; the set of two bars on the left shows that 11.2 percent of women and 6.0 percent of men said yes. The second set of bars shows the percentage with same-sex contact during the previous 12 months; women also reported more contact than men. The questions were worded differently for women and men, however, so these percentages are not di-rectly comparable. Women were asked broadly about "sexual experience of any kind with a female," whereas men were asked only about specific acts of oral and anal sex. The third set of bars reports responses to a question, "People are differ-ent in their sexual attraction to other people. Which best describes your feel-ings?" Then a range of responses was presented, from "only attracted" to the opposite sex to "mostly" to "equally attracted to males and females" to "mostly" and "only" attracted to the same sex. The bars show that 14.3 percent of women

How Do Sociologists Know What They Know?   Asking about Sensitive Behavior

How do sociologists collect information on people's behaviors and attitudes? For the most part, they ask them. The most common way of doing so is through the random-sample survey. [➥ p. 18] Typically, a survey research organization will be hired to randomly select households and to ask the occupants a list of questions. In 1992, the National Opinion Research Center, one of the leading academic survey research organizations, asked a random sample of 3,432 adults detailed questions about their sexual activities and preferences. Researchers from the University of Chicago, who had written the questions, tabulated the results and published *The Social Organization of Sexuality* (Laumann et al., 1994). Some of their findings are presented in this chapter.

But can those findings be trusted? After all, the interviewers were inquiring about some of the most private and sensitive aspects of behavior. Biologist Richard Lewontin, writing in the *New York Review of Books* (Lewontin, 1995a), ridiculed the sociologists for believing the responses of their subjects. His scathing critique, and the subsequent exchange of letters between social scientists and him, addressed the limits of survey- based sociological research.

Lewontin's main objection is that sociologists can't be sure that people tell the truth when asked about their behavior, especially when the topic is as sensitive as sexuality. Some people may lie, while others may not even admit the truth to themselves. Lewontin also pointed to a discrepancy in the data: Men reported 75 percent more sexual partners in the previous five years than did women. A few complexities aside, the average number of sexual partners of men and women should be almost the same. The authors examine this discrepancy and conclude that the most likely cause is that men exaggerate or women understate the number of partners when asked. Writes Lewontin: "If one takes the authors at their word, it would seem futile to take seriously the other results of the study" (1995a, p. 29).

The authors responded that although they "readily admit that we were not always successful in securing full disclosure," they "spent a great deal of time worrying about how we could check the reliability and honesty of our respondents' answers" (Laumann et al., 1994, p. 43). They used techniques such as asking similar questions at different points in the interview to see if a person's responses were consistent. For some sensitive questions, the respondents were given a form to fill out that they could return in a sealed envelope.

Lewontin was not appeased. For him, the sex survey is an example of sociology reaching for knowledge that is beyond its grasp. When they accept self-reports of sensitive behaviors and statistically analyze them, he argues, sociologists are trying too hard to imitate the natural sciences. Without adequate ways to measure information such as sexual behavior, and above all without the possibility of performing experiments, he maintains, sociology is limited:

> [Sociologists] are asking about the most complex and difficult phenomena in the most complex and recalcitrant organisms, without that liberty to manipulate their objects of study which is enjoyed by natural scientists. In comparison, the task of the molecular biologist is trivial. . . . Like it or not, there are a lot of questions that cannot be answered, and even more that cannot be answered exactly. There is nothing shameful in that admission. (Lewontin, 1995b, p. 44)

Lewontin's argument must be taken seriously by sociologists. There are indeed limits on how much sociologists can learn about human behavior; and random-sample surveys and statistical analyses can't surmount these limits. For some problems, sociologists might be better off abandoning surveys and turning to the kind of intensive, long-term field observations that anthropologists and some sociologists

reported at least some attraction to the same sex (in other words, they did *not* choose "only attracted to males"), compared to 7.8 percent of men. The last set of bars shows responses to a question on sexual identity: "Do you think of yourself as . . . Heterosexual, Homosexual, Bisexual, or Something else?" Among both women and men, 4.1 percent chose homosexual or bisexual. Among that 4.1 percent of the sample, however, women were more likely to choose bisexual (2.8 percent) than homosexual, while men were more likely to choose homosexual (2.3 percent) than bisexual.

The NSFG survey, therefore, shows that the percentage of Americans who think of themselves as homosexual or bisexual is lower than the percentages who do—even though the findings from field studies aren't necessarily representative of the population under study.

Does it follow that we should reject all findings from the study of sexual behavior because it is likely that men exaggerated, or women understated, their number of partners? This is a matter of judgment. My answer would be no. For one thing, comparisons among different groups represented in the 1992 sample are likely to be valid even if the individual responses aren't entirely accurate.

In addition, survey researchers have developed a better technique for asking about sensitive topics—the audio computer-assisted self-interview. Interviewees are given a laptop and provided with earphones. They see and hear questions that no one else in the room can see or hear. They respond merely by pressing number keys on the laptop, as instructed by the program. Studies have shown that this technique raises substantially the reported rates of injection drug usage, violent behavior, risky sex, and abortion (Turner, Forsyth et al., 1998; Turner, Ku et al., 1998). This technique was used in the 2002 NSFG, results of which are presented in this chapter. The technique is an improvement, but its very success confirms that older surveys probably did underestimate sensitive behavior.

We should be wary of pushing survey research techniques beyond the limit of their usefulness. The sex surveys press on that limit. The more sensitive the material and the more subjective the questions, the more skeptical readers should be. Nevertheless, we needn't dismiss the contributions of survey research to understanding sensitive issues. We should seek to supplement surveys with other, more intensive forms of data gathering. And we should recognize that there may be some questions about society that are beyond the capability of sociology to answer.

Ask Yourself

1. If you were asked to participate in a study of college students' sexual behavior, would you answer all the questions truthfully? Would you participate in the study?

2. Why is knowing about people's sexual behavior and attitudes important? Give a specific example.

Survey researchers are administering sensitive questions by giving people laptops that display the questions and accept keyed-in responses privately.

www.mhhe.com/cherlin5

have ever had a same-sex sexual experience or who find same-sex activity at least somewhat appealing. Its findings confirm Kinsey's claim that homosexuality is multidimensional and that no single number can adequately represent its prevalence. (Nevertheless, all the relevant percentages in the NSFG survey are considerably lower than comparable percentages reported by Kinsey in 1948.) This conclusion suggests that there is no clear dividing line between heterosexuality and homosexuality and that the distinction is at least in part socially created. In addition, the NSFG suggests that women's sexual identities may be more fluid than men's: More women find same-sex experiences at least somewhat attractive and more describe themselves as bisexual than homosexual.

FIGURE 6.1
Prevalence of four
measures of same-sex
sexual activity, women
and men, age 15 to 44
(sexual contact) and 18 to
44 (sexual orientation and
attraction), in the United
States, 2002. (*Source:*
U.S. National Center for
Health Statistics, 2005d)

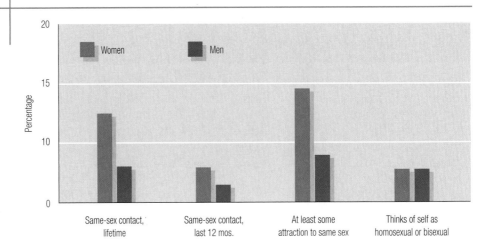

integrative perspective
(on sexuality) the belief that
human sexual identities are
determined by both social and
biological factors

The Integrative Perspective   Does biology also play a role in people's sexual identities? Almost no sociologists take the position that human sexuality is entirely driven by genes and hormones. However, some sociologists (I am one of them) take what Schwartz and Rutter (1998) call the **integrative perspective** on human sexuality: They argue that it is influenced by both social and biological factors. They would claim that while the social construction of sexual identities is very important, people may also be born with a sexual nature—a tendency to be attracted to partners of the opposite or the same gender. These sociologists reject the argument that genes and hormones have no influence on sexuality just because some societies have in-between genders and because the boundaries between the orientations are unclear. They note the evidence of biological influences on heterosexual and homosexual orientation.

Some of the evidence comes from studies of twins that suggest genetic links to sexual orientation. Several studies have recruited men and women who identified as gay or lesbian, each of whom had a same-sex sibling who was an identical twin, a fraternal twin, or an adopted sibling. The researchers then ascertained the sexual orientation of the subjects' twin or adoptive siblings. Identical twins have identical genetic material; fraternal twins share, on average, half their genetic material; and adopted siblings share no genetic material. Consequently, if homosexuality were partly biological in origin, one might expect the greatest similarity of sexual orientation among the identical-twin pairs and the least similarity among the adoptive-sibling pairs. If homosexuality were not at all biological in origin, one might expect no difference in the similarity of sexual orientation among the three groups of siblings, since both siblings in every pair had been raised in the same home by the same parents. In one such study, the authors found that, among the men, 52 percent of the identical twins, 22 percent of the fraternal twins, and 11 percent of the adoptive brothers were homosexual, which supports the biological model (Bailey & Pillard, 1991). Similarly, among the women, 48 percent of the identical twins, 16 percent of the fraternal twins, and 6 percent of the adoptive sisters were homosexual (Bailey, Pillard, Neal, & Agyei, 1993). A review of these sibling studies concluded that there are "almost certainly" genetic influences on sexual orientation for men, although it is "somewhat less certainly so" for women (Bailey & Dawood, 1998).

These studies, however, also show that sexual orientation is *not* completely genetically determined. After all, about half the identical twin pairs—who shared the

More men and women are living an openly gay or lesbian lifestyle than a half-century ago, as these marchers in New York City's Gay and Lesbian Pride Parade show.

same genetic material—had different sexual orientations in the studies cited above. Clearly, something about the twins' environments influenced them differently. As is the case with gender differences, any biological effects probably operate not by determining a person's sexual orientation but rather by creating predispositions toward one orientation or the other. Social and cultural factors then further influence sexual orientation. But unlike gender differences—where substantial evidence exists of the different treatment boys and girls receive from parents, peers, schools, and the like—there is little evidence that parents or peers treat children who will grow up to be gay or lesbian differently than they do other children. Moreover, the general failure of psychiatrists and psychologists to change the sexual orientation of gay and lesbian clients who wish to do so has undermined the credibility of the psychoanalytic explanation for homosexuality, which emphasizes unresolved issues of identification with one's parents (Haldeman, 1991). Nor is there much evidence that children and adolescents learn homosexual behavior from adults. So, although social and cultural factors clearly play a role in sexual orientation, no satisfactory theories have been advanced to explain their role.

The biological studies have been controversial, in large part because of their political implications. Some observers argue that if homosexuality is not a lifestyle choice but rather an inherent, immutable part of an individual's personality, there is little justification for restricting the legal rights of gay men and lesbians. Other gay advocates argue that the studies are less consequential because civil rights should not depend on whether a person's style of life is cultural or biological in origin. And some opponents of legal rights for homosexuals, noting that there is evidence of biological influences on behaviors such as alcoholism, argue that a person needn't give in to biological predispositions if they are undesirable or objectionable to others.[2]

[2] Examples of the positions noted in this paragraph can be found in Angier (1993).

To be sure, research into the biological origins of sexual orientation need not have political significance. Rather, its purpose could be the same as that of most of the research discussed in this book—to increase our understanding of why people behave as they do in their family and personal lives. The great variation from society to society in the ways that sexual orientation is structured—the berdache tradition, the acceptance of homosexual relations among the ancient Greeks and Romans, the mental illness model of the United States in the first half of the twentieth century, the recent emergence of an open lesbian and gay subculture—shows that social forces are an important part of the explanation for the behaviors and attitudes that emerge. But it seems likely that biological forces are also part of the story.

Points of Agreement and Disagreement   In sum, almost all sociologists agree that the type of society a person lives in influences such characteristics as whether individuals become exclusively heterosexual or homosexual, what social groups they draw their partners from, and what range of sexual acts they undertake. The main disagreement, then, between partisans of the social constructionist and integrative perspectives is whether society *completely* determines sexual identities. The former group would say that the influence of biology is minimal, whereas the latter group would say that both society and biology matter.

Quick Review

- Some sociologists believe that sexual identity is entirely socially created; they cite variations over time and from society to society.
- Surveys suggest that a substantial number of people have some homoerotic feelings but a smaller percentage are exclusively homosexual.
- Other sociologists believe that both biological and social factors determine sexual identities; they point to studies of twins, ordinary siblings, and adopted siblings.

QUESTIONING SEXUAL IDENTITIES

Over the past decade or so, a newer perspective has emerged which questions the whole idea of fixed, stable sexual identities. Whereas the older literature focused on questions such as the extent to which a person's gay or lesbian identity is socially constructed, the newer literature focuses on whether it is meaningful to speak of a gay, lesbian, or heterosexual identity at all. In reality, the newer perspective says, such identities are always shifting, unstable, and arbitrary. There are many kinds of "gay identities" the writers argue, including the resident in a "gay" neighborhood who openly lives with a partner; the business executive who restricts his social life to weekends; and the married suburbanite who occasionally and furtively has sex with men. Because of this diversity, it is argued, you cannot simply label someone as gay (or straight). To use these labels is to buy into a system in which heterosexuals regulate everyone's sexual behavior along rigid and constraining lines. Instead, sociologists are urged to examine the entire system by which we classify people's sexual lives in a way that privileges the people we call heterosexual and puts the rest at a disadvantage.

Queer Theory   The name that the advocates of this point of view, who span cultural studies, comparative literature, history, sociology, and other disciplines, have chosen for their perspective is "queer theory" (Seidman, 1996; Gamson & Moon, 2004). By deliberately choosing a term that until recently, at least, was offensive and derogatory, the writers suggest a challenge to the conventional understanding of sexuality. **Queer theory** is not a formal, scientific theory but rather a critical standpoint (Green, 2002). Its essence is the view that sexual life is artificially organized into categories that reflect the power of heterosexual norms. These norms restrict the possibilities for a more fluid, changing sexual identity in order to protect the dominance of heterosexuality as it is currently organized. Queer theorists reject a sharp split of sexual activity into either a heterosexual or homosexual way of life. Some of them even reject the subdiscipline of gay and lesbian studies, arguing that to accept these categories as the starting point is to accept what must be questioned: the restrictive organization of sexuality (Gamson, 1996).

The queer theorists suggest studying how this organization came about and how it is maintained. They reject the view that there are any biological influences on the organization of sexuality. Rather, scholars (e.g., Butler, 1990) argue that we unconsciously re-create heterosexual "masculinity" and "femininity" in everyday interactions. In other words, we "do sexuality" in a way that is similar to how the interactionists say we "do gender." [➡ p. 94] Without this daily reinforcement, it is said, our sexual categories would be less rigid and more subject to change. Just as some feminist theorists say that gender distinctions are problematic, so do queer theorists say that distinctions on the basis of sexuality are problematic.

Strengths and Limitations   One does not have to agree with all the claims of queer theory to appreciate the point that the labels we attach to people—she's a lesbian, he's straight—are complex social constructions that give social advantages to the straights and create disadvantages for the lesbians and gay men. For instance, straights can marry and receive many legal protections and rights that gays cannot obtain. Queer theorists and many other Americans believe these inequalities to be oppressive; other Americans believe they are morally justified. But what this perspective reminds us is that these inequalities, whether justifiable or not, were consciously created rather than being "natural." Americans had to create a body of family law, for example, that allows a man with the legal status of "married" to visit his dying wife in the hospital but may prevent a gay man with the legal status of "single" from visiting his dying partner.

One must also agree that the boundaries of sexual identities are more fluid than people ordinarily think. Queer theory contributes the insight that a rigid split between heterosexual and homosexual is not "natural" but rather reflects prevailing heterosexual norms in our society. Nevertheless, many observers (I am one) think that in its rejection of the concept of sexual identity, queer theory goes too far. Because the boundaries of concepts are unclear doesn't mean that the concepts are invalid. After all, the boundaries of "class," "gender," and "race" are all unclear, yet rare is the sociologist who doesn't use any of these concepts.

Moreover, in rejecting the utility of studying gays and lesbians as such, queer theory restricts our ability to understand important aspects of American society. Topics such as whether and how a gay person can be a parent, whether marriage ought to be extended to same-sex couples, how gays and lesbians create networks of friends and relatives they call family, and so forth, should be studied because they represent issues with real consequences for the lives of Americans today. Perhaps these topics reflect an unequal distribution of power, but they are no less consequential because of it. To be sure, the identities of gay and lesbian are socially

queer theory the view that sexual life is artificially organized into categories that reflect the power of heterosexual norms

constructed at least in part; but, as a critic of queer theory writes, these constructions still "may exhibit an extraordinary capacity to shape identities, sexual interactions, social movements, and political histories as a whole" (Green, 2002, p. 528).
Consequently, I will use the categories of heterosexual, gay, and lesbian in this book.

Quick Review

- Queer theorists claim that sexual identities are always unstable and arbitrary.
- They argue that we should reject the concept of sexual identities as meaningful, fixed categories.
- They urge instead that we study the ways in which conventional sexual identities are organized according to norms that privilege heterosexuals.
- Their rejection of sexual identities, however, makes it difficult to study important social issues involving gay men and lesbians.

■ Beyond the Family?

In addition to questioning the usefulness of the concept of sexual identity, some
sociologists are questioning the useful of the concept of family, even if it is used
in the plural form "families" to acknowledge diversity. They argue that emerging
forms of sexual and other close relationships stretch the boundaries of "families"
so far that the concept becomes inadequate for understanding them (Budgeon &
Roseneil, 2004; Roseneil & Budgeon, 2004). You'll recall that my definition of the
private family in Chapter 1 included the requirements that family members live in
the same household and pool their incomes and household labor. [➡ p. 13] Some
emerging types of what we might call personal communities (Pahl & Spencer,
2004) fail to meet these requirements. One type is the network of friends and relatives that gay men and lesbians sometimes construct for intimacy and care. Another is the living arrangements of couples who have the kinds of committed,
intimate relationship that cohabiting or married couples have but who choose, or
are forced, to live in different households. Let us examine them in more detail.

NETWORKS OF FRIENDS

family of choice a family
formed through voluntary
ties among individuals
who are not biologically or
legally related

Some lesbians and gay men use the term "family" to describe their close relationships,
but they mean something different from the standard, marriage-based family. Rather,
they often refer to what sociologists have called a **family of choice:** one that is
formed largely though voluntary ties among individuals who are not biologically or
legally related (Weston, 1991; Weeks et al., 2001). That is to say, lesbians and gay men,
who cannot marry in most jurisdictions and who may have little contact with parents
or siblings who do not accept their sexuality, must actively construct their families.
Networks of friends and cohabiting partnerships are central to these constructed
families. In fact, friends may be more central to your family than a partner because of
the high likelihood that you and your partner will eventually dissolve your union. The
families that Weston (1991) studied consisted fundamentally of networks of friends
and lovers who provided social and emotional support for one another. Similarly,
Weeks et al. (2001), in a study of the intimate lives of 96 lesbian and gay individuals in
Britain, noted the frequent use of the term "family" to refer to a more or less stable
group of people who served as a support network for one another.

In some respects, these families of choice are similar to the kin networks found among the poor [➡ p. 128] or to the complex families formed after divorce and re-marriage (as we will see in Chapters 12 and 13). Yet the largely friendship-based family networks may be even more important to lesbians and gay men than to heterosexuals because lesbians and gay men often cannot rely on their biological and legal relatives to the extent that heterosexuals can. What gay people must do is create a family from the relationships they can retain with biological kin, the close friends they have, and their partners. One person told Weston, "Gay people really have to work to make family" (Weston, 1991). The families woven together by lesbians and gay men are another example of created kinship—the kind of kinship that people must work to construct. [➡ p. 14] In practice, these families of choice are often complex and frequently do involve relatives as well as friends. But even the ties with relatives are in some sense created, as gays and lesbians include only those family members with whom they feel comfortable and enjoy spending time. In this way, the families of choice blur the boundaries between relatives and friends, as relatives become more like friends to the person at the center of the network, while close friends become more like relatives (Pahl & Spencer, 2004).

Most research on lesbian and gay men's personal communities is based on studies of white, prosperous individuals in major urban areas. Carrington (1999) studied both "upper-middle-class" and "lower-middle-class" gay and lesbian couples and found that extensive, friendship-based families of choice were more common among the upper-middle-class couples. The reason is that maintaining large friendship-based families takes time and money. Couples with better-paying, more flexible jobs could more easily arrange social events and spend more on entertaining, travel, long-distance calls, and presents. Carrington found, in contrast, that less affluent couples often described themselves as isolated. In addition, African American, Latino, and Asian couples had less extensive friendship networks and were more likely to rely on biological kin. This study suggests that substantial class and racial-ethnic variation exists in the ways that lesbians and gay men organize their personal communities.

LIVING APART TOGETHER

The second challenge to the household-based idea of family comes from hetero-sexual and gay couples who are carrying on cohabitation or marriagelike relation-ships, who define themselves as couples, but who live in separate households. The phenomenon was first noticed in Europe in the late 1970s and became known as "living apart together," or LAT. There is little data about LAT relation-ships in the United States. Moreover, it's not clear how to ask about it in a demo-graphic survey. But reports from national statistical agencies and Britain and Canada suggest that LAT relationships are common. In 2002 and 2003, the British agency asked the following question of people in national samples who were not married or cohabiting: "Do you currently have a regular partner?" After excluding people still living in their parents' homes and full-time students, the report's au-thor found that about 15 percent of all individuals who were not cohabiting or married responded "yes" and therefore could be considered "living apart to-gether" (Haskey, 2005). The Canadian agency used a question that is probably too broad, "Are you in an intimate relationship with someone who lives in a separate household?" and reported higher percentages (Milan & Peters, 2003).

There are two types of LAT relationships, those in which the partners live apart because of a constraint and those in which they live apart by choice (Levin, 2004).

One of the constraints is children from previous relationships; researchers have uncovered many LAT couples in which one or both is raising children from a previous relationship and prefers not to alter the household. A divorced mother who cares for her children during the week may prefer to live apart from her partner and then spend time with him when her ex-husband has the children on the weekends. In the Canadian survey, 23 percent of the women in LAT relationships were living with children (Milan & Peters, 2003). Another constraint occurs when the couple would prefer to live together but each partner has a good job which he or she does not wish to give up, even though the jobs are in different cities.

Other LAT couples may live apart by choice because they prefer to be more independent of each other. One Swedish couple with two children saw their relationship deteriorating but still loved each other. They sold their house and bought two apartments a few minutes walk from one another. The children stayed with the mother but spent time at their father's apartment, and he spent a good deal of time at the mother's apartment. They viewed this move as saving their relationship (Levin, 2004). Other individuals in LAT relationships include people who have previously divorced and are hesitant to move in with a partner for fear of experiencing a second disruption.

To some extent, an LAT relationship may be a stage in an individual's life course. In both the Canadian and British studies, LAT relationships were more common among people in their twenties than among older people. One's twenties is the period of "early adulthood," the emerging life stage in which some individuals are not fully taking on adult roles. [➡ p. 70] As people age out of that stage, the chances may increase that they will live with their partners. During their twenties, early adults may be obtaining advanced education or working long hours at entry-level positions such as an associate at a law firm—situations they may see as incompatible with a living-together relationship. About half of the Canadians in LAT relationships expected to live with their partners at a future time (Milan & Peters, 2003), suggesting that some individuals will transition out of an LAT relationship and into a living-together one.

In fact, the line between living apart and living together may be so fuzzy that the partners themselves may not be sure whether they are living together. In a study of moderate-income early adults in the Toledo, Ohio, area who had cohabited, two sociologists found that it was not always easy to determine when a cohabiting relationship began (Manning & Smock, 2005). For half the individuals, living together was not a deliberate decision but more of a "slide" into cohabitation: "Respondents say, 'it wasn't planned,' 'it just snuck up on me,' or 'it just happened'" (p. 996). People with separate residences may gradually spend more and more time together, and they may keep their residences for a while even after they are cohabiting full-time.

BLURRED BOUNDARIES

As all of these studies suggest, the personal communities being constructed today often blur the boundaries between relatives and friends, between living together and living apart, and between being part of a family and not being part of one. Moreover, these personal communities are fluid, with people moving into and out of various relationships over the life course. The flexibility of these new arrangements allows people to construct ways of obtaining intimacy and of giving and receiving care that fit their particular preferences and constraints at a particular point in their lives. These arrangements can be used by gay men and lesbians whose options for building a conventional family are limited. They can be used by heterosexuals who, due to either constraints or preferences, would like intimacy and care without coresidence.

Because these arrangements are based on voluntary participation, however, they are also less stable than institutionalized family forms such as marriage. A person can withdraw from a network of close friends or an LAT relationship at any time. To some, this easy exit may be a further advantage of the new arrangements. But instability can undermine the hard work of building a personal community or investing in a shared partnership. "There's a way of doing it gay," another person remarked to Weston about building familylike ties, "but it's a whole lot harder, and it's less secure" (Weston, 1991). Moreover, instability can be a problem for children, who, as we will see in Chapter 12, may be at higher risk for developmental problems if they live in unstable families. For that reason, flexible networks may better suit the needs of adults than the needs of children. In fact, the focus of the literature that questions the idea of family is almost entirely on adult relationships. Two such theorists, for example, criticize the sociologies of family and gender for being "overwhelmingly focused" on relationships "which have produced children, and on changes within these relationships" (Roseneil & Budgeon, 2004). But there is a reason for that focus: Children are a public good. [➡ p. 11] How they are being raised is an important public issue that queer theory avoids (but gay and lesbian studies address, as we will see when we consider gay parenthood in Chapter 9).

Do couples in LAT relationships or networks of friends constitute families? Not in terms of the definitions I provided in Chapter 1. But one lesson of these new arrangements is that the boundaries of the category "families" are becoming fluid and blurred, much as the boundaries between sexual identities are becoming blurred. And many people move across the boundaries at various points in their lives. This does not imply that family is a "zombie category"—a walking corpse—as two theorists of late modernity have alleged (Beck & Beck-Gernsheim, 2002). But it does suggest that the category has limitations and needs to be supplemented with other perspectives as new forms of sexual relationships and caring arrangements are formed.

Quick Review

- New living arrangements are challenging the conventional definitions of what constitutes a family.
- Lesbians and gay men construct families of choice from partners, friends, and some relatives.
- Some partners view themselves as a couple and yet live apart in what is called living-apart-together (LAT) relationships.
- These arrangements blur the boundaries between family living and nonfamily living.

■ Marital and Nonmarital Sexuality

Neither LAT relationships nor same-sex or opposite-sex cohabiting partnerships would be so common without the increasingly acceptability of sexual activity outside of marriage in the United States. To understand that story, we need to step back a bit. There have been three eras in the attitudes toward sexuality and love in the United States. Before about 1890, sexual attraction and romantic love were thought to be inappropriate bases for choosing a spouse. (See *Families in Other Cultures:* How Maud Almost Married Elmer.) Moreover, even within marriage,

Families in Other Cultures

How Maud Almost Married Elmer

Between 1882 and 1884, Isabella Maud Rittenhouse was courted by several suitors. Maud's diary, discussed by Steven Seidman, reveals that two stood out (Seidman, 1991). The first was Robert Witherspoon, a handsome, charming, educated, and cultivated man, to whom Maud was powerfully attracted. The other was Elmer Comings, a rather plain-looking and socially awkward man who was, nevertheless, hard-working, reliable, and responsible. Today, the choice between them would be easy: 9 out of 10 Mauds would pick Robert, the object of romantic love, over unexciting Elmer. The real Maud, however, chose Elmer. Her reasoning shows how different was the relationship among sex, love, and marriage in the Victorian era than it is now.

To Maud and to most other nineteenth-century women and men, marrying someone because of strong romantic feelings was considered risky. Passionate, romantic love was thought to be a base emotion that

faded away quickly, leaving little support for the couple. Far longer lasting was a spiritual love in which the partners joined together in a moral, uplifting marriage. The spiritual relationship rested upon a deep knowledge of each other and a sense of mutual obligation. Spiritual love was "true love," a union not only of the heart but also of the soul and the mind. Strong sexual attraction was equated with "romantic love," a dangerous emotional state that was hard to control. True love was much to be preferred.

There were practical reasons rooted in the structure of nineteenth-century society why people thought this way. The general standard of living was far lower than it is today, and most married women did not work outside the home. In order to have a comfortable life, it was crucial for a woman to marry an economically reliable, hard-working man. Correspondingly, a man needed to marry a woman who would raise children and manage a home competently.

Feelings of romantic love could tempt a person to choose passion over partnership. Indulging in passion was a luxury most nineteenth-century people could not afford.

And so Maud decided that her romantic love for Robert was immature and that she could not overlook some lapses of character. She wrote that he had "beauty of feature and charm of tongue with little regard for truth and high moral worth"; whereas Elmer, "though not graceful . . . and handsome . . . [had an] inward nobility in him." Maud was well aware that she was rejecting romance when she rejected Robert: "If I do marry [Elmer] it will be with a respectful affection and not with a passionate *lover* love."[1] Moreover, Maud knew that, unlike Robert, Elmer did not share her knowledge of and interest in the arts and literature: "All the time I am planning to bring him up to a standard where I *can* love him." Thus, she girded for the task of marrying Elmer. Fortunately for her—although not for Elmer—she

sexual expression was thought to be an activity best done in moderation. From about 1890 to about 1960, in contrast, sexual attraction and romantic love were increasingly viewed as not only appropriate but, in fact, crucial criteria. Within marriage, people increasingly valued the emotional fulfillment they could obtain through sex and romantic love. The idea of a sexual identity, based on one's attitudes and practices, passed into common usage. Still, sexual expression outside marriage continued to be seen as illicit.

Since the 1960s, the positive value given to sexual expression and gratification has continued and even increased. In addition, sexual activity has become defined even more as a private matter. In 1965, for example, the Supreme Court ruled that a state law prohibiting the use of contraceptives violated marital privacy by allowing police to search the "sacred precincts of marital bedrooms" (*Griswold* v. *Connecticut*, 1965). In 1972, the Court, using similar reasoning, overturned laws prohibiting the sale of contraceptives to unmarried persons (*Eisenstadt* v. *Baird*, 1972). The rationale for these laws had been that sexual activity was carried out in order to have children and that the state had an interest in seeing that married couples did, in fact, have children and that unmarried persons did not. In this way, the state could promote and control the reproduction of the population. By the time of these court decisions, however, sex had become primarily a means of individual fulfillment. Therefore, the rationale for state intervention had weakened.

broke off the courtship when Elmer entered into some suspicious business dealings that cast doubt on his character. But even in ending the courtship, Maud relied on practical and ethical considerations rather than on her feelings.

This separation between romantic love and sex, on the one hand, and marriage, on the other hand, was typical of the cultural tradition of the Western nation-states prior to the twentieth century. One historian studied the detailed writings on marital sexual activity by 25 medieval theologians and found that only 2 of them ever addressed the subject of love (Flandrin, 1985). Sexual relations that were too passionate were thought to be immoral and to compete with a person's worship of God. Sensual pleasures were for the love affairs a person had outside of his or her marriage—never sanctioned by theologians but tolerated, in practice, for men only. St. Jerome, quoting the Roman philosopher Seneca, wrote:

A prudent man should love his wife with discretion, and so control his desire and not be led into copulation. Nothing is more impure than to love one's wife as if she were a mistress. . . . Men should appear before their wives not as lovers but as husbands. (Aries, 1985a)

This separation between erotic love and marriage evaporated during the twentieth century. Both Seneca and Maud would be surprised to read the 1987 treatise *Super Marital Sex: Loving for Life*, the author of which states, "Super marital sex is the most erotic, intense, fulfilling experience any human being can have" (Pearsall, 1987). They would also be surprised by an article in a social science journal which reported that men and women who were married, or who expected their current relationships to last a lifetime, reported greater pleasure from their sex lives than men and women with short-term partners (Waite & Joyner, 2001). More

surprising still would be the increase in sexual activity outside the context of any kind of long-term relationship, the increase in childbearing outside of marriage, the emergence of an open homosexual subculture, and the public display of sexually oriented goods, services, performances, and advertisements. All these changes, to which we have become accustomed, were nearly unthinkable until the twentieth century.

Ask Yourself

1. Is it still risky to rely on feelings of romantic love in choosing a spouse?
2. Do you know of any married couples who have a "spiritual love" for each other?

[1] All quotations are from Seidman (1991).

This changing view of sexual activity is part of the broader growth of individualism during the twentieth century. In the post-1960 era, cultural changes were spurred, in part, by the increasing economic independence of women, which made it possible for young adult women to postpone marriage without postponing intimate sexual relationships. In turn, young men were able to initiate sexual relationships with women without making a commitment to support them. (Women's economic independence will be discussed in more detail in Chapter 8.) The changes in sexual behavior were also guided greatly by the availability of more effective means of contraception, notably the birth control pill.

Within marriage, the changes have increased the possibility of mutually and personally fulfilling sexual relations. Yet as the idea of sex for personal pleasure spread during the twentieth century, the rationale for restricting sex to married couples weakened. Through the 1950s, moralists were successful in limiting sexual intercourse to engaged or married persons, especially among middle-class women. But beginning in the late 1960s, sexual activity prior to marriage rose to unprecedented levels. Moreover, in the 1970s, unmarried, middle-class young adults began to live together openly, a previously unheard-of arrangement except among the poor. Rates of cohabitation rose so high that more than half of young adults in the 1990s were likely to live with a partner before marrying.[3]

[3] See Chapter 7 for evidence on the trends discussed in this paragraph.

FIGURE 6.2
Number of opposite-sex sexual partners in the past 12 months, for never-married, noncohabiting women and men, ages 15 to 44, in the United States, 2002. (*Source:* U.S. National Center for Health Statistics, 2005d)

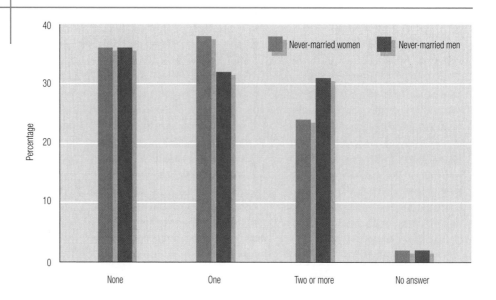

NONMARITAL SEXUAL ACTIVITY

The changes in the late 1960s and 1970s are reflected in the answers that women in the 1992 University of Chicago survey of adults' sexual activity gave to the question of how many sex partners they had had by age 30. Among women who had entered adulthood in the 1950s, two-thirds had had only one partner. Clearly, having sex just with one's husband was the norm. Only a daring few had many sex partners: 3 percent reported five or more (Laumann et al., 1994). In fact, although there are few numbers in the historical record, virtually every historical study suggests that through the 1950s, a majority of American women had their first intercourse only after they were engaged to be married (Rothman, 1984). Women's sexual needs still were thought to be less than men's, and women were still seen as the guardians of virtue—which in this case meant abstinence until marriage. Yet among women who entered adulthood in the 1960s, just 46 percent reported only one partner by age 30; and 18 percent reported five or more. The proportion reporting only one partner by age 30 fell further to 36 percent among women who entered adulthood in the 1970s, whereas the proportion reporting five or more rose to 22 percent.

The changes over time have been less dramatic for men, for whom the sexual double standard always allowed more nonmarital sexual activity than it allowed women. Still, the double standard has now disappeared. Figure 6.2 shows the number of opposite-sex sexual partners in the past 12 months reported by never-married, noncohabiting women and men in the 2002 NSFG. The proportion reporting no partner was an identical 36 percent for both women and men; under the double standard we would have expected this proportion to be higher for women. Yet, as the figure shows, women were more likely to have had just one partner, and less likely to have had two or more, than were men.

extramarital sex sexual activity by a married person with someone other than his or her spouse

MARITAL AND EXTRAMARITAL SEX

Given the increases in sexual activity outside marriage, you might expect that married persons would be increasingly likely to have **extramarital sex**. Indeed, widely read books published in the 1960s and 1970s, such as *Open Marriage* (O'Neill & O'Neill, 1972), argued that marital relationships could coexist with, and perhaps even be enriched by, openly acknowledged extramarital affairs. Yet **sexual monogamy**—having just one sex partner—is still the rule rather than the exception among married persons. Consider trends in public opinion. There is no doubt that the American public has become more tolerant of sexual activity among persons who have not yet (and may never be) married. Almost every year since 1972, the General Social Survey, or GSS, an annual or biannual national survey of American adults, has asked people their opinions about both premarital and extramarital sex. Between 1972 and 2002, the proportion who agreed that *premarital* sex was "always wrong" or "almost always wrong" declined from 48 percent to 36 percent. During the same period, however, the proportion agreeing that *extramarital* sex was "always wrong" or "almost always wrong" increased from 84 to 94 percent.[4]

Moreover, when the GSS in 1988 and 1989 asked its respondents about their sexual behavior, 98 percent of married women and 95 percent of married men said that they had had no sex partners other than their spouses during the previous 12 months (Greeley, Michael, & Smith, 1990). Clearly, most married couples adhere to the norm of monogamy almost all the time. Indeed, in the 1992 University of Chicago survey of adults' sexual activity, over 90 percent of women and over 75 percent of men said that they had never had another sex partner during the duration of their marriages, giving rise to wry newspaper headlines such as "Study Sees Marital Fidelity Rampant" (Laumann et al., 1994).

sexual monogamy the state of having just one sex partner

Sexual activity prior to marriage rose greatly in the late 1960s and the 1970s.

---

[4] The question on extramarital sex was first asked in 1973; for both questions I have excluded "Don't know" and "No answer" responses (Davis, Smith, & Marsden, 2003).

The emphasis on sexual gratification for both partners in marriage, new in the twentieth century, has provided wives and husbands with the potential for greater intimacy and emotional satisfaction. And access since the 1960s to modern methods of contraception, such as the birth control pill, has allowed individuals to separate sex-as-pleasure from sex-as-reproduction. Especially for women, whose sexual desires were often denied or ignored prior to the twentieth century, the legitimation of sexual gratification can be considered an advance. "Twenty years ago," wrote three feminist authors in 1986, "the woman dissatisfied with sex was made to believe she was lacking something; the woman who selfishly advanced her own pleasure was made to worry about being less than normal" (Ehrenreich, Hess, & Jacobs, 1986). Now it is taken for granted that both women and men should receive pleasure from sexual activity. The three authors praise the acceptance of "*pleasure*—perhaps especially sexual pleasure—as a legitimate social goal" (Ehrenreich et al., 1986). Yet observers have also noted that the emphasis on sexual satisfaction can create its own tyranny, since couples may believe that unless their sex lives are continually fulfilling there is something wrong with their marriages.

Adolescent Sexuality and Pregnancy

One consequence of the cultural changes in sexuality is the rise in childbearing outside of marriage. Starting in the mid-1960s, young adults' sexual lives changed in two ways. First, having sexual intercourse prior to marriage, often many years before, became common. Figure 6.3 displays the findings of a series of national surveys of unmarried adolescent girls, age 15 to 19, since 1971 and of boys the same ages since 1988. The percentage who had ever had sexual intercourse rose sharply during the 1970s and then peaked in the late 1980s. Second, in the half-century between the mid-1950s and the mid-2000s, the age at which half of all first marriages occurred rose by nearly five years for men and five and one-half years for women

FIGURE 6.3
Number of 15- to 19-year-olds who have ever had sexual intercourse, 1971–2002 for girls, 1988–2002 for boys, in the United States. (*Sources:* U.S. National Research Council, 1987; and U.S. National Center for Health Statistics, 2004b. For 1971–1982, percentages are for girls residing in metropolitan areas only. However, the 1982 percentage, which is available for both the U.S. and metropolitan areas, is nearly identical.)

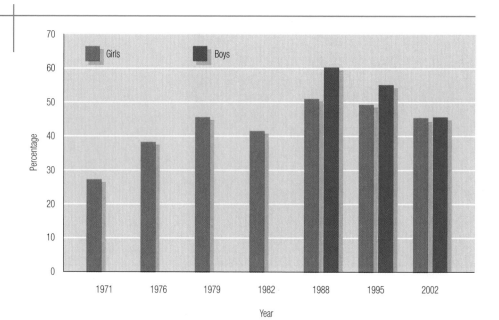

(U.S. Bureau of the Census, 2005m). Because of this enormous jump, the average age at marriage is higher today than at any time in the last 150 years (Fitch & Ruggles, 2000). The average first-time bride is now almost 26, and the average first-time groom is between 27 and 28. Consequently, far more young women and men remain single throughout late adolescence and early adulthood.

Earlier sexual activity and later marriage have lengthened the stage of life when young adults can have a child outside of marriage. In fact, making the transition to motherhood without a husband is now the predominant experience for African-American women: In 2001, 77 percent of first births to black women were to unmarried mothers. (Childbearing outside of marriage was also the majority experience among Hispanic women, at 53 percent.) But recently this has been rising more rapidly among whites: 30 percent of first births to non-Hispanic white women were to unmarried mothers in 1998. Although media stories tell of middle-class women in their thirties having a first child on their own, those kinds of first birth are still uncommon in the aggregate. Rather, unmarried first-time mothers tend to be young: In 1998 45 percent were teenagers and 37 percent were aged 20 to 24.[5]

CHANGES IN SEXUAL BEHAVIOR

Adolescent sexual activity, however, appears to have declined slightly in the 1990s. The percentage of never-married adolescent girls and boys who reported having had intercourse declined between 1988 and 2002, as shown in Figure 6.3. Recent surveys of high school students suggest that AIDS education may have been a factor: 89 percent of high school students reported being taught about AIDS in school, and there was a sharp rise in the use of condoms (which effectively prevent the spread of HIV) among sexually active adolescents (U.S. Centers for Disease Control and Prevention, 2004). The increased use of condoms is just one example of the policy response to the spread of HIV and Aids. (See *Families and Public Policy: The Policy Response to AIDS in the United States.*) Still, sexual activity among unmarried adolescents remains much more common than in 1970.

The teenage birthrate has been declining, but the proportion of teenage mothers who are unmarried has been increasing.

[5] The figures in this paragraph are from unpublished tabulations provided by the U.S. National Center for Health Statistics.

Families and Public Policy

The Policy Response to AIDS in the United States

By the end of 2004, almost one million cases of AIDS had been diagnosed in the United States since the start of the epidemic, and over a half-million people had died of the disease (U.S. Centers for Disease Control and Prevention, 2006). The number of fatalities from AIDS is equivalent to the number of Americans who died in combat in all the major wars of the twentieth century. From the beginning of the epidemic through 1995, the highest number of deaths occurred among non-Hispanic whites, reflecting the early pattern of transmission through homosexual contact among whites. But by the end of the 1990s, substantially more non-Hispanic blacks than non-Hispanic whites were dying of AIDS every year, a change that reflected the rising proportion of intravenous drug users among AIDS victims.

The public policy response to AIDS was slow in starting. Some activists believe that little was done because AIDS was perceived—inaccurately, it turned out—as a disease that affected only gay people. It wasn't until the late 1980s, by which time over 50,000 people had the disease and it had begun to infect heterosexuals, that a large-scale response began (Shilts, 1987).

Even then, there was much disagreement about how to respond. The dilemma is that AIDS places two sets of principles at odds: (1) individual freedom versus the collective interest; and (2) discouraging unpopular behavior versus trying to limit its consequences. As for the former, gay rights groups had fought for sexual freedom in the 1970s, had achieved something close to it in large cities, and were reluctant to give it up. In the 1970s, a growing number of bathhouses and sex clubs provided settings for impersonal gay sex. Moreover, an affirmative attitude toward gay sex became a centerpiece of the gay liberation political movement. Consequently, even when the link between unprotected sex and HIV transmission became apparent to public health officials, calls for the closing of the bathhouses were resisted by some gay political leaders and by the sex industry (Shilts, 1987).

Social conservatives and some public health professionals advocated widespread testing for HIV in the collective interest of identifying infected persons to prevent contact with them. Gay advocates argued, however, that mandatory testing would impose an unacceptable restriction on individual freedom because it would allow organizations such as the military or insurance companies to identify gay men and exclude them from membership or coverage. Nevertheless, Congress allowed the armed forces to institute HIV tests and exclude those who tested positive.

As for the second clash of principles, many social conservatives genuinely felt that homosexual relations—and even heterosexual relations outside marriage—were morally wrong and should not be condoned.

Their response to the AIDS epidemic was to urge chastity for the unmarried and monogamy for the married (D'Emilio & Freedman, 1988). In contrast, other interest groups argued that, even though sex outside heterosexual marriage might be objectionable to some people, the threat AIDS posed to health required accepting its existence and urging people to limit risky behavior and to use condoms. By the late 1980s, the latter view had prevailed, as exemplified by the explicit brochure Surgeon General C. Everett Koop sent to every home in the United States in 1988.

The development of effective drug therapy has produced a new policy question: Should all persons with AIDS have equal access to the new drugs—and at what cost? They are very expensive—well over $10,000 per year—and they require expensive medical supervision and blood testing. Most middle-class people belong to health insurance plans through their employers that cover the expenses of treatment. But the United States has tens of millions of people who have no health insurance coverage; in 2003, 45 million were without coverage (U.S. Bureau of the Census, 2005l). Many are in working-class families where wage earners have jobs that do not provide health insurance. The cost of the AIDS treatment is far more than they could afford. Some of the poor—including families that are receiving what

---

But differences in sexual activity between adolescent boys and girls appear to have narrowed considerably. In the middle of the twentieth century, adolescent boys were more sexually active than girls (Darling, Kallen, & VanDusen, 1984). Yet by the end of the century, the gap had disappeared, as Figure 6.3 shows, in part because in the 1970s and 1980s, the increase in premarital sex was greater for girls, and in part because in the 1990s and early 2005, the decline in premarital sex was greater for boys (Santelli, Lindberg, Abma, McNeely, & Resnick, 2000). Class and racial differences in premarital sexual activity were also smaller at the

The spread of AIDS led to frank public discussion of condom use.

used to be called Aid to Families with Dependent Children and is now called Temporary Assistance for Needy Families (see Chapter 14)—are covered by the government's Medicaid program of health insurance. But not all state Medicaid plans include sufficient funds for treating those who are infected with the new drugs. As a result the poor and near-poor have limited access to the new treatments.

The response to AIDS shows that public health issues involving sexual activity often involve more than technical and medical considerations. The social context of a sexual issue can determine what action, if any, the government takes. Prevailing moral values influence public opinion about whether the affected persons are worthy of assistance—whether they are blameless or, in some sense, to blame for their health problems. Concerns about individual freedom determine how restrictive the public response will be. These social and political conflicts influence the nature of the response.

Ask Yourself

1. Do you know anyone who has been denied treatment with expensive new AIDS drugs? If so, for what reason?
2. Should HIV testing be mandatory? What about health education that stresses limiting risky behavior?

www.mhhe.com/cherlin5

end of the century because the rise in adolescent sexual activity had been greater among the middle class than among the poor, more noticeably among whites than among blacks (Forrest & Singh, 1990).

Summing up these trends:

- Adolescent sexual activity is much more common today than it was in the middle of the twentieth century, although it declined somewhat in the 1990s and early 2000s.

- The historical difference in the sexual activity of adolescent boys and girls has nearly disappeared.
- The increases in adolescent sexual activity have been greater for the middle class and whites than for other groups, although sexual activity is still more common among the poor and African Americans.

Yet even with the declines that occurred in the 1990s, adolescent sexual activity still was much more widespread than it had been at midcentury, especially for girls. Coupled with a rising age at marriage, this increase in sexual activity among adolescents led to a greater proportion of teenage pregnancies and births outside marriage.

THE TEENAGE PREGNANCY "PROBLEM"

Most people have read or heard something about the teenage pregnancy "problem," but few people have a good understanding of exactly what the problem is. About 1 out of 12 15- to 19-year-old women in the United States becomes pregnant each year. About one-third of these pregnancies are ended by an abortion (Alan Guttmacher Institute, 2004), leaving 422,000 births in 2003 (Child Trends, 2005). Despite widespread talk about an "epidemic" of teenage childbearing, this is a lower number of births than was the case 10 or 20 years ago. In fact, the birthrate for teenage girls is at an all-time low (Child Trends, 2005). That is to say, the probability that a teenage girl will have a baby in a given year is lower than at any time since the federal government began to keep statistics in the 1940s.

Then what is the problem? Marriage, or rather the lack of it. Marriage among teenagers has decreased faster than birthrates have. A pregnant 18- or 19-year-old who got married in 1960 would have had plenty of company—31 percent of all 18- to 19-year-old women were married. But to marry at those ages today is to stand out: Just 5 percent of 18- to 19-year-old women were married in 2003. Because the age at first marriage has risen even faster for blacks than for whites, married black teenagers are even rarer: Only 2 percent of black 18- to 19-year-old women were married in 2003 (U.S. Bureau of the Census, 2004a).

As sexual activity among unmarried teenagers increased and as the proportion of teenagers of all races who were unmarried rose, the consequence was a sharp rise in the proportion who were risking a pregnancy outside marriage. Teenagers can lower that risk by using contraceptives more effectively; and, as noted, contraceptive usage has indeed increased among teenagers. But over the long run, the increased use of contraceptives has merely kept pace with the increasing numbers of unmarried teenagers who are sexually active. Consequently, the **nonmarital birth ratio**—the proportion of all births that occur to unmarried women—has increased sharply for teenagers, even though the *birthrate*—the probability that a teenager (married or not) will have a birth—has declined. For example, in 1970 the nonmarital birth ratio for 15- to 19-year-olds was less than one out of three; by 2002 it had risen to more than four out of five (U.S. National Center for Health Statistics, 2005a). The increased ratio is the source of public concern.

nonmarital birth ratio the proportion of all births that occur to unmarried women

THE CONSEQUENCES FOR TEENAGE MOTHERS

Despite support from their parents and other kin, adolescents who bear children appear worse off later in life, on average, than adolescents who wait until their twenties to begin having children. Teenage mothers complete fewer years of schooling, have jobs that pay less, are more likely to be dependent on public assistance payments, and are less likely to have stable marriages. The more difficult issue to resolve is whether these differences are due to having a child as a teenager per se or to the kinds of impoverished backgrounds common among teenage mothers. It may be that having a baby as a teenager poses few penalties for young women who are already poor, because they are likely to remain poor regardless of whether they bear children or not. This latter point is an example of a **selection effect,** the principle that whenever individuals sort, or "select," themselves into groups nonrandomly, some of the differences among the groups reflect preexisting differences among the individuals. Selection effects frequently complicate the interpretation of data that sociologists collect.

For example, suppose we want to know whether teenage mothers grow up to be poor at a higher rate because of the effects of (1) having a child as a teenager or (2) coming from low-income families. To truly settle this issue, a truth-seeking but cold-blooded social scientist would want to conduct the following experiment: Obtain a list of all families with teenage girls in the United States and then assign at random some of the girls to have children and others to remain childless until their twenties. Because of the random assignment, teenage childbearing would be about as likely to occur in middle-class families as in poor families. In this way, the social scientist could eliminate family background as a cause of any differences that emerge between teenage mothers and nonmothers.

In the real world, of course, teenage pregnancies don't occur randomly; rather, they are more likely to occur in families that were poor before the teenager gave birth. The teenage childbearers are self-selected, in a sense, from less-fortunate families. It is very difficult to separate out the selection effect of family background from the true effect of having the baby per se. Recent studies suggest that some of the apparent effect of teenage childbearing is indeed a selection effect—in other words, teenage mothers probably would grow up to have somewhat lower incomes even if they had waited until after age 19 to have children (Geronimus, 1991; Geronimus & Korenman, 1992; Hotz, McElroy, & Sanders, 1996). But some studies still suggest that the economic circumstances of teenage mothers remain worse after the selection effect is accounted for. For example, these young women are somewhat less likely to graduate from high school (Hoffman, Foster, & Furstenberg, 1993).

Moreover, the life course of teenage mothers varies substantially. Some of those who drop out of school later return to school and obtain a high school diploma or its equivalent. In 1984, Frank Furstenberg and two collaborators, Jeanne Brooks-Gunn and S. Philip Morgan, reinterviewed about 300 women who had been in Furstenberg's original Baltimore study of adolescent mothers 22 years earlier (Furstenberg, Brooks-Gunn, & Morgan, 1987). Five years after the original interview, only 51 percent had graduated from high school, and few of the dropouts were enrolled in school. But by the 22-year reinterview, 67 percent had graduated from high school or received a general equivalency diploma—still fewer than among nonmothers, but an improvement. About one-third of the mothers who had not graduated at the 5-year mark had done so by the 22-year mark (Furstenberg et al., 1987). Moreover, at the 22-year reinterview their incomes varied widely: One-fourth were on welfare, one-fourth had family earnings of less than $15,000 (equivalent in purchasing power to about $19,000 in 1990 dollars), one-fourth had family earnings between $15,000 and $25,000 (equivalent to about $32,000 in 1990 dollars), and one-fourth had family earnings of $25,000 or more (Furstenberg et al., 1987).

selection effect the principle that whenever individuals sort, or "select," themselves into groups nonrandomly, some of the differences among the groups reflect preexisting differences among the individuals

To sum up what we know about teenage mothers:

- They are disadvantaged in education, income, and employment.
- Some, although probably not all, of their disadvantages are due to other factors in their lives, such as growing up in low-income families.
- There is much variation in the way their lives turn out.

Quick Review

- Sexual activity among teenagers is much more common than it was prior to the 1970s.
- Both the birthrate and the marriage rate have been declining among teenagers.
- The proportion of teenage births that are to unmarried girls and women has increased.
- Some of the problems shown by teenage mothers reflect disadvantages they had prior to becoming pregnant.

Looking Back

1. **When did the idea of a sexual identity develop?** The idea that individuals have a coherent sexual identity involving a preference for either opposite-sex or same-sex partners did not exist until the late nineteenth century. Before then, though religious doctrine and civil law forbade numerous sexual practices, a person who broke those laws was not thought to have a different personality from people who displayed conventional sexual behavior.

2. **What determines people's sexual identities?** Social constructionists believe that sexual identities, such as "heterosexual" and "gay," are entirely created by the way society is organized—the dominant norms and values, the legal privileges and restrictions, and so forth. They note the different ways in which sexual identities have been expressed in other societies cross-culturally and historically. They cite surveys which suggest a continuum, rather than a sharp line, between heterosexuality and homosexuality. Other social scientists think that there is a biological component to sexual identities. They cite evidence from behavioral genetic studies.

3. **Is "sexual identity" a useful way to think about people's sexuality?** A group of cultural theorists questions whether stable, fixed sexual identities really exist and whether they are useful concepts for understanding social change. They point to the multiple forms that each "identity" takes. They charge that current social norms restrict sexual behavior and force people into arbitrary

categories. Those who disagree say that the categories we commonly use have important consequences for the lives of Americans and should be used to study topics such as parenthood, marriage, and other contested issues.

4. **Are people's living arrangements going beyond the boundaries of the family?** People whose sexual activity is outside of marriage and cohabitation are creating living arrangements that do not clearly fit into the conventional definition of a family. Two examples are, first, the personal networks of friends and relatives that many gay men and lesbians create as an alternative form of family and, second, the living-apart-together relationships of people in committed partnerships who choose to, or are compelled to, live apart. Personal communities such as these are blurring the boundary between family and nonfamily life. They are valuable to the individuals who use them, but are probably less stable than conventional arrangements.

5. **What is the nature of the teenage pregnancy "problem"?** Over the past few decades, the proportion of teenage births that occur outside of marriage has risen sharply because of a decline in marriage among teenagers. Bearing a child as a teenager somewhat reduces a woman's chances of leading an economically successful adult life. Yet some of the disadvantages observed in these cases occur because teenage mothers tend to come from disadvantaged families, not solely because they had a child at a young age.

Go to the Online Learning Center at www.mhhe.com/cherlin5 to test your knowledge of the chapter concepts and key terms.

Study Questions

1. What cultural features of American society influence people's senses of their sexual identity?
2. Does it make a difference whether there is a biological component to sexual identities? If so, why?
3. What is the case for discarding the concept of a sexual identity?
4. How far can the definition of a "family" be stretched before the concept loses its value?

5. Compare trends in attitudes toward premarital sex with trends in attitudes toward extramarital sex.
6. Why has concern about teenage pregnancy grown if the likelihood that a teenager will give birth has been declining?
7. Explain what a "selection effect" is.
8. What was the social significance of the Kinsey Report?

Key Terms

extramarital sex   204
family of choice   198
integrative perspective
    (on sexuality)   194

Kinsey Report   190
nonmarital birth ratio   210
queer theory   197
selection effect   211

sexual identity   188
sexual monogamy   205
social constructionist perspec-
    tive (on sexuality)   190

Thinking about Families

The Private Family	The Public Family
Has the contemporary American culture gone too far in accepting sex without romantic love?	Should the government be involved in discouraging teenage pregnancy?

Families on the Internet   www.mhhe.com/cherlin5

Note: While all the URLs listed were current as of the printing of this book, these sites often change. Please check our Web site (http://www.mhhe.com/cherlin5) for updates.

The Sexuality Information and Education Council of the United States (www.siecus.org), an organization that favors the dissemination of information about sexuality and sex education through the schools, maintains a Web site with a great deal of information about sexuality and sex education in schools. A search on the topic "homosexuality," for example, will return links to a number of fact sheets and articles. For a conservative perspective, consult the Web site of the Traditional Values Coalition (www.traditionalvalues.org), which opposes gay rights and sex education that does not stress abstinence. Click on "topics" and you are likely to find several articles. Read an article or two about gay and lesbian issues at each of these sites. Can you understand the two organizations' basic positions, and how they differ?

The Alan Guttmacher Institute, a research center devoted to family planning issues, offers much relevant information about adolescent pregnancy and childbearing, birth control, and abortion at its Web site (www.agi-usa.org). Click on "sexual behavior," and on the next page, select a report under "Latest statistics—facts in brief." What information can you find on recent trends in sexual activity, contraceptive use, or pregnancy?

Cohabitation and Marriage

Looking Forward

1. What is the history of courtship and dating?

2. How has marriage changed over the past century?

3. What is marriage like today?

4. What is the role of cohabitation in the American family system?

5. How does the marriage market work?

In June 1998, Randy Heisey, a postal worker from Harrisburg, Pennsylvania, traveled to Russia and the Ukraine along with 64 other men hoping to find a bride. A single man in his 40s, Randy had found American women to be too independent. Like most of his traveling companions, he sought a wife who would put husband, home, and children first. But the 800 women who awaited his group in Moscow and Kiev had other motivations. Well-educated, they could not earn much in Russia as professionals, and they believed Russian men don't treat their wives as well as men in other countries. So they were hoping to marry a genteel American man and move to the United States.[1]

In Moscow and Kiev, Randy and the other men, each supplied with a translator, sat in large rooms where they interviewed hundreds of women. Most of the prospective brides were in their twenties, and many had traveled long distances in hopes of finding a husband. In Kiev, Randy was intrigued by Lora Shcherbakova, a 29-year-old gymnastics coach who was divorced and had an eight year-old son. After several conversations and some evenings together, he asked her if she would come to the United States and live with him. She accepted.

A few months later Lora and her son arrived in Pennsylvania, and the couple soon married. All went well for the first several months. But in August 1999, Lora filed divorce papers in New Jersey, seeking a protection order against her husband that alleged "ongoing abuse; physical against my son, emotional, economical, constant yelling and throwing of items, threats to return child to Ukraine." Randy denied the charges and complained he had been deceived. He too wanted a divorce.

Randy and Lora's marriage was arranged by an American matchmaking company that recruits Russian women, sends catalogs with their photographs and brief biographies to American men, and arranges group trips to Russia for a fee. (Randy paid $3,100.) In 1996, 961 people, the vast majority of them women, arrived in the United States from Russia and the Ukraine on fiancé visas, under which they had 90 days to marry or return home. Other would-be brides came on tourist visas. Such brokered marriages seem odd to most Americans, but they have been common in the past. In the 1800s, "mail-order brides" traveled west to join and marry pioneers and prospectors they hadn't ever met. Those marriages, like many others of the time, were working partnerships in which each spouse contributed to a joint household. Romantic love was nice if it happened, but not expected. Today, there are still many cultures in the world in which love is not important, although mores are changing rapidly.

---

[1] The story of Randy Heisey is drawn from a series of articles in the *Philadelphia Inquirer* by Donald C. Drake that appeared from November 29 to December 26, 1998, and from an update by Drake on the newspaper's Web site, www.phillynews.com.

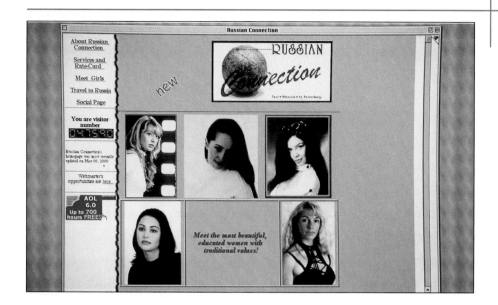

Several matchmaking companies introduce American men looking for docile wives to Russian women who think life will be better in the United States.

In the United States today, however, expectations about marriage have changed dramatically. Most people view romantic love, compatibility, and companionship as essential to a good marriage. For that reason, the failure of Randy and Lora's marriage isn't surprising. Their rushed courtship probably wasn't sufficient for either to judge their compatibility, and their high expectations must have made disappointment all the more likely. In this chapter we will examine the expectations Americans have about their marriage partners, and more generally, about the meaning of their unions. I define a **union** as a stable, intimate relationship between two people who live in the same household, but may or may not be married. Increasingly, people's expectations are played out first in a cohabiting union and then in marriage. Consequently, we need to study the growth of cohabitation over the past few decades. Then we will turn to the changing nature of marriage.

union a stable, intimate relationship between two people who live in the same household but may or may not be married

▌ Forming a Union

If brokered brides seem odd to Americans it is because most select their spouses without much direct assistance from outsiders—or even parents. Parental influence was more direct in most societies historically, and it is still more direct in some developing nations today. For instance, in rural villages throughout the developing world, parents who have land or wealth to pass on to their children are especially likely to have a voice. In many Asian nations, it is still common for parents, even prosperous city dwellers, to play an important role in the choice of their children's spouses. In the boxed essay on "Transnational Families" [➡ p. 168], I described the Korean immigrant practice of returning home to Korea to marry a spouse chosen by parents and relatives.

In general, parents took control of the matchmaking process when the choice of whom to marry was too important to them to be left to their children alone. In the past, a good marriage and many children were crucial to the survival of the

The Rise of the Love Marriage

Over the past decade or so, a surprising number of studies of marriage have reported increases in the importance of love, emotional involvement, shared partnership, and sexual fulfillment in countries as diverse as Brazil (Rebhun, 1999), Egypt (Hoodfar, 1997), Korea (Kendall, 1996), Mexico (Hirsch, 2003), and Spain (Collier, 1997). For instance, older women in the Mexican study told ethnographer Jennifer S. Hirsch (2003) that what was most important when they married was that a husband "respected you." They described how the ideal of marriage has changed over a generation from *respeto* (respect) to *confianza* (trust, intimacy). Among the older generation, Hirsch was told, if a husband showed respect to his wife, his sexual infidelity was not seen as a failing serious enough to warrant a separation or divorce. But among the younger generation, a woman expects her husband to be an intimate companion and would view his infidelity as a serious threat to a marriage.

There are a number of forces pushing marriage in this direction:

1. *Urbanization and the shift to wage labor.* Women and men, once bound to the authority of parents in the villages, can escape that authority in the cities. The anonymity of city life—in contrast to the web of kinship and friendship ties in a typical village—allows for more privacy in the development of a marital relationship. And when women and men both earn wages, they become co-partners in a way that suggests a more egalitarian relationship. Anthropologist L. A. Rebhun (1999) argues that in impoverished Northeast Brazil, migration to the cities and a shift to a cash economy have increased the salience of romantic love in marriages.

2. *Exposure to Western media.* Seeing Western movies and television programs can alter people's views of marriage. In one region of Nepal, the first movie theater was built in 1969 and television first appeared in the late 1980s. In that region, younger adults were more likely to have participated in the choice of their spouse than were older adults, most of whom had no influence in their parents' choice of whom they would marry. Researchers found that adults who had listened to radio, seen a movie, and watched television were particularly likely to have taken part in the choice of their spouses. These media outlets provided messages from the Western countries that, in the words of the authors, "include the information that those who are the very richest in today's world choose their own spouse and do not necessarily marry a person of their par-

household. A son who would inherit the farm needed a wife to help him and to have children who would provide more help. A woman needed to marry a man whose parents owned land, or whose relatives owned cattle, or who would inherit a trade. It is probable that throughout human history practical considerations have dominated the search for a spouse. I think it likely that only within the past 100 years in the Western nations—and within the past few decades in newly developed nations—has the standard of living improved so much that young adults have had the luxury of paying more attention to a partner's personality than to his or her industriousness or family worth.

Parental influence also erodes when children can find ways of making a living that don't depend on their parents' resources. In eighteenth-century Austria, the heir to the farm had no other good sources of income and couldn't marry without his father's permission. Often permission wasn't granted until the father retired. A folk song of the time expressed the frustration of the unmarried son:

Father when ya gonna gimme the farm,
Father when ya gonna sign it away?
My girl's been growin' every day,
And single no longer wants to stay. (Berkner, 1972)

ents' choosing" (Ghimire, Axinn, Yabiku, & Thornton, 2006).

3. *Migration flows.* Direct contact with the developed world also influences the nature of marriage. In Mexico, many families include women and men who have spent time in the United States as migrants. Their earnings allow families to pay for satellite television antennas that enable them to watch American movies dubbed in Spanish. When they return to Mexico they carry with them not only money and new possessions but also new values. Mexican men who had been in the United States told Hirsch that one of the reasons American women have more power than Mexican women is that in the United States, women can dial 911 if they are beaten and the police will respond. Attitudes toward domestic violence were changing in the village Hirsch studied, in part be-

cause of the circular movement of migrants to and from the United States.

These kinds of marriages, as Hirsch writes, "give women a moral language with which to define the limits of acceptable behavior rather differently than it was defined for their mothers" (2003, p.149). For example, women now have the right to travel and visit female friends and relatives without a husband's permission or to ask a husband to spend less time hanging out with his friends and more time at home. Yet love marriages are still compatible with gender inequality, as was the case in the United States, where at the height of the companionate ideal in the 1950s (see discussion in this chapter), people still cited the common adage, "a man's home is his castle." Many husbands in Mexico still used physical force, even if some made a distinction to Hirsch between a "slap," which they said may be justified, and a "blow," which is

never justified (p. 134). Spanish women who had become "housewives" in the city—not unlike their mid-twentieth-century American counterparts—sometimes felt trapped in their apartments and cut off from the assistance of other kin (Collier, 1997, p. 124).

Nevertheless, the images suggest striking change—as when the Northeast Brazilians watch Portuguese-language soap operas in which characters declare meaningfully to each other, in borrowed English, *Ai lóvi iú* ("I love you") (Rebhun, 1999, p. 184). Anthropologist Jane Fishburne Collier (1997), who studied social change in a Spanish village, aptly summed up the change in marriage as a shift "from duty to desire."

Ask Yourself

1. What messages about finding someone to marry have you received from television programs and movies?

But as wage labor spread, sons could find paying jobs away from the farm, and they gained greater independence from their parents. Sometimes the transformation in marriage practices can occur with startling speed. This has been the case in the rapidly industrializing nations of East Asia, where strong parental influence has been eroded over a generation or two. (See *Families in Other Cultures*: The Rise of the Love Marriage.)

ANGLO-AMERICAN COURTSHIP

By the 1800s most young adults in the United States at least shared with their parents the responsibility for choosing a spouse. Indeed, young adults from the lower economic classes probably had substantial autonomy because there was little property for parents to worry about. (Among the upper classes, parents undoubtedly retained a stronger role.) Young people went about finding a spouse through courtship, a process that had been developed in Europe. **Courtship** is a publicly visible process with rules and restrictions through which young men and women find a partner to marry. The words *publicly visible* emphasize the important role of the community—and, in particular, parents—in watching over, and participating in, the courting a young adult does. For instance, in early modern Britain, the first stages of courtship occurred mainly outdoors, in plain view of

courtship a publicly visible process with rules and restrictions through which young men and women find a partner to marry

peers and kin (Gillis, 1985). By and large, it was acceptable for casually acquainted young men and young women to be seen together only at public events such as festivals, games, or dances, and even then only in groups. At dances young people changed partners so frequently that no couple spent too much time together.

According to historical studies, American courtship, like British courtship, retained this basic character through the mid-1800s. (The historical studies, unfortunately, tell us little about the poor, African Americans, or immigrants, who left few diaries and letters.) The first phase of courtship still took place at out-of-home events such as picnics, sleigh rides, and church socials. In a later phase, young men called at the homes of young women. Yet there were subtle changes over time. Most notably, the role of love increased. In the 1500s and 1600s, love had been an emotion people distrusted in selecting a spouse. To be sure, it was desirable to choose a partner whom you might grow to love after you were married, but more practical considerations—inheritance of land, strength, health—were expected to guide one's choice. By the 1800s, however, young adults wanted to love their partners before they married them (Rothman, 1984). Even so, love had a different meaning than it has today, as Maud Rittenhouse's diary showed. [➡ p. 202] Young people were wary of passion, which was seen as wild and uncontrollable and therefore dangerous as a basis for a long-term relationship. Love was defined more in terms of sympathy, openness, candor, and understanding than of passion. Thus, Maud rejected her romantic love for Robert in favor of responsible Elmer.

This centuries-old system of courtship met its demise after 1900. Its decline in the United States was linked to great social and economic changes: migration from rural areas (and from overseas) to cities, the rise of industrial capitalism, higher standards of living, and the lengthening of adolescence. As more and more people moved to cities and worked in factories and offices, the number of potential partners and the places where they could meet grew. Consequently, it became harder for parents to monitor and oversee the process. And as standards of living rose, it became possible for young adults to keep some of their earnings or to receive allowances from their parents. Thus, young people began to accumulate a key resource: spending money. The city provided plenty of places to spend it, most notably the movie theater and the dance hall. Rising standards of living also allowed many families to buy an automobile. This marvel of technology let young couples wander far from home; it also gave them a private place for necking (kissing) and petting (touching below the neck). As a result, courtship, in the words of historian Beth Bailey, went from "front porch to back seat" (Bailey, 1988).

Finally, a new view of the teenage years arose: They were seen as a time during which teens needed to develop their personalities and capabilities free of the pressures of the adult world (Kett, 2003). In an influential 1904 book, psychologist G. Stanley Hall popularized the term "adolescence" for this newly recognized stage of life (Hall, 1904). Attention to adolescence emerged as child labor laws restricted how much younger teenagers could work and as more prosperous middle-class families no longer needed their children to work. Moreover, it arose as changes in the economy made it clear to parents that children needed at least a high school education in order to obtain better-paying jobs. Consequently, adolescence was embodied most clearly in the high school, which removed teenagers from the world of adults. Not until the early decades of the twentieth century did a majority of teenagers enroll in high school. College enrollments also increased early in the century and then skyrocketed after World War II. The high school and college years gave adolescents a protected time in which they could create and participate in their own subculture, relatively free of parental involvement.

THE RISE AND FALL OF DATING

What evolved, then, after the turn of the twentieth century was a new system of courtship based on dating. Although some might think that dating has been around for a long time, it was rare until 1900 or so, and the term was not even used until then. The spirit of the change was captured in a 1924 short story in *Harper's* magazine. A man comes calling at the home of a young woman, expecting to spend the evening in her parlor. But when she opens the door, she has her hat on—a clear sign that she expects to go out.[2] As the story suggests, suddenly a young man was expected to take a young woman somewhere on a date—which meant he had to spend money. A firm rule of the dating system was that the young man paid the expenses. In return, he enjoyed the company of the young woman. Dating placed courtship on an economic basis. Young men provided goods such as movie tickets or restaurant meals in exchange for companionship and, often, necking and petting. Through these rules, argues Bailey, dating shifted the balance of power in courtship from women to men (Bailey, 1988). Under the old system, women received men in their own homes, at times they chose, and usually with their parents nearby. (During a girl's first season of receiving callers, her mother might initially invite the young men.) Now the evening was initiated and controlled by males, and it depended on cash earnings, which favored men over women.

Dating also shifted power from parents to teenagers and young adults. The movement of activity away from public gatherings and the home made it much harder for parents to influence the process. Rather, adolescents became oriented toward the dating system of their peer group—the other adolescents in the local school or neighborhood. With the triumph of dating, courtship moved from a parent- and other-adult-run system to a peer-run system where the participants made the rules and punished the offenders.

By the 1920s, sexual activity was more common, although intercourse was still rare. Some parents were alarmed at the apparent spread of necking and petting, which became a central part of the youth culture of dating. Popular accounts warned of the spread of "petting parties" among high school students, and adults sought unsuccessfully to stop them (Rothman, 1984). Colleges wielded parentlike authority through residence and visiting rules. Sometimes their efforts at control verged on the comic: In 1947, the dean of Northwestern University decreed that any mixed group of more than two people listening to the Michigan-Northwestern football game on the radio must register as a "party" and have an appropriate number of approved chaperons (Bailey, 1988).

The dating system probably had its heyday in the 20-year period—1945 to 1965—after World War II. Throughout the period, college enrollments rose sharply and most young adults at least completed high school. Postwar parents had grown up in the dating system, and so there was less parent-child disagreement about it than had been the case in the 1920s and 1930s. At the same time, young people in the 1950s may have started to date earlier than their parents.[3] In a national survey of high school students conducted in 1960, about two-thirds of

---

[2] This story is cited in both Rothman (1984) and Bailey (1988). It is cited by Bailey as Black (1924).

[3] Both Bailey and Rothman suggest that adolescents began to date at younger ages in the 1950s. But when a random sample of Detroit-area women in 1984 was asked to recall when they had begun to date, there was little difference in the responses of those who had married before the war versus after the war; see Whyte (1990).

all boys and three-fourths of all girls stated that they had begun to date by grade 9; virtually all had dated by grade 12 (Modell, 1989).[4]

But as age at marriage began to rise in the 1960s and 1970s, the dating system became less closely connected to marriage. Steady dating in high school seemed more and more remote from serious attempts to find a spouse. What's more, cohabitation, perhaps a new stage of courtship, became a common event in young adults' lives prior to marriage. Also, the sharp rise in premarital intercourse for teenage boys and girls demonstrated that the dating system was increasingly ineffective in holding sexual activity to petting. Adolescents may have begun to socialize more often in larger, mixed-sex groups (Modell, 1989). To be sure, dating remained a part of youth culture, but it became less formal and less tied to marriage. And the old limitations on sexual activity were greatly weakened.

THE TREND TOWARD INDEPENDENT LIVING

The dating and courtship model assumes that most young adults will be living in their parents' homes and receiving at least some supervision from them. Historically, that was the case: At the start of the twentieth century, a lower standard of living, a shortage of housing for single people, and the predominant values of the time precluded almost all young adults from living independently of their parents until they married. Even at midcentury, many young adults did not leave home until they married. But since then, an increasingly larger percentage of single young adults have moved into apartments or homes, either by themselves or with roommates.

The trend toward independent living reflected the generally rising standard of living during the twentieth century. One hundred years ago, most single young adults helped support their families by turning over their wages to their parents; today it is common—even expected—for young adults to keep their wages. In addition, the rise in independent living was consistent with the broader growth of individualism in the twentieth century, which uncoupled sexual activity from marriage for young adults. The increase in divorce also spurred independent living: Studies have shown that adolescents whose parents divorce, and in particular those whose parents divorce and remarry, leave home sooner than adolescents whose biological parents remain married (Cherlin, Kiernan, & Chase-Lansdale, 1995).

In addition, since midcentury the average age at first marriage has risen substantially. [➡ p. 65] Consequently, it has become common for young adults to set up an independent household years before they marry. But young adults who live independently are more likely to return to their parents' homes than are young adults who marry. (Usually, married young adults will return only if their marriages dissolve.) Frances Goldscheider (1997) calculated that, since the 1950s, the odds that a young adult who left the parental home would return have increased by more than 50 percent. Parents whose children move out have learned to expect that the children may move back in if, for example, they lose their jobs. Some of the unmarried, independent young adults are, in fact, cohabitating, as will be discussed later in the chapter. But cohabiting relationships have higher rates of dissolution than do marriages, and young adults who end cohabiting relationships are more likely to return home than are young adults who end marriages (Goldscheider & Goldscheider, 1994).

---

[4] The data came from the Project Talent survey of 4,000 high school students nationwide.

Quick Review

- Parents are more involved in spouse choice when a child's marriage is important to the well-being of the entire family.
- Parental influence over spouse choice declines when their children have an independent way to make a living.
- In the 1800s, young adults found spouses through the publicly visible process of courtship.
- The rise of dating in the twentieth century shifted much of the control over meeting partners from adults to their children and their children's peer group.
- Single young adults are much more likely to live separately from parents than was the case a century ago.

■ Marriage

Even though many adults will live in cohabiting unions, about 9 out of 10 whites and 2 out of 3 African Americans are projected to marry eventually (see Table 5.1). Their expectations, the kinds of marriages they form, and the way their social and economic environment affects their chances of forming and maintaining a marriage have been the topics of much social scientific research and theory. The literature suggests two great changes in the meaning of marriage during the twentieth and early twenty-first centuries.

FROM INSTITUTION TO COMPANIONSHIP

Family life in preindustrial Western nations was guided more by law and custom than by affection and emotional stimulation. The local government in Plymouth Colony, you will recall, kept a close watch over the conduct of family members. [➡ p. 45] Parents played a greater role in selecting a spouse for their children than was the case in later centuries. In general, husbands and fathers had greater authority than they do today: Religion and law certified the father as head of the family, with broad powers over his wife (whose property he could sell) and his children (who remained with him in the event of a divorce). In addition, the marginal existence of poor farm families and the modest standard of living of most urban families made the family's subsistence a higher priority than the personal development of the parents and children.

The Institutional Marriage   We might call this pre-twentieth-century form of marriage, the **institutional marriage**. A social institution, you will remember, consists of a set of rules and roles that define a social unit of importance to society. [➡ p. 30] Marriage prior to the twentieth century fit this description. It was held together by clear rules and roles: The husband was expected to be the head of the household, the wife was to be dutiful and submissive, and the children obedient. Although the husband and wife may have been fond of each other, romantic love wasn't necessary or even desirable—which is why Maud Rittenhouse chose Elmer over Robert. [➡ p. 202] Rather, spouses were expected to work together under the husband's authority to manage the farm, raise children, and keep food on the table. The local community, the church, and the law all supported the rules and roles of the institutional marriage.

institutional marriage a marriage in which the emphasis is on male authority, duty, and conformity to social norms

But in the early twentieth century, companionship and sexual fulfillment became more important to a successful marriage. Prior to that time, as noted in the previous chapter, sexual relations in marriage (and there was relatively little sexual activity outside marriage) were seen more as a means of producing children than as a means of emotional fulfillment. But after the turn of the twentieth century, progressive writers argued that an active sex life was central to a happy marriage. In the 1920s, Robert and Helen Lynd conducted a famous study of life in Muncie, Indiana, which they selected as a typical American town and called "Middletown" (Lynd & Lynd, 1929). The Lynds reported that, compared with the 1890s, young adults were more likely to view romantic love as the only valid basis for marriage. In this new romantic climate, they wrote, women were more concerned with "youthful beauty." Throughout the country, mass production and rising incomes made fashionable clothing affordable. Advice columnist Dorothy Dix told her readers that "good looks are a girl's trump card." And she counseled, "Dress well and thereby appear fifty percent better looking than you are. . . . Make yourself charming" (May, 1980).

This emphasis on sexual allure was new: Prior to the twentieth century, a young woman needed to convince a suitor that she could be a good partner; but it was less important that she be attractive. Although a young man expected that his wife would bear children and that their sexual relations would be pleasurable, he didn't necessarily expect much emotional fulfillment from sex. However, by the 1920s or 1930s, as historian Elaine Tyler May concluded, a young man wanted "both excitement *and* domesticity in a wife" (May, 1980).

The Companionate Marriage   In a 1945 textbook, Ernest Burgess, the leading family sociologist of the first half of the twentieth century, famously described this transition in the meaning of marriage:

The single-earner families of the 1950s exemplified the companionate marriage.

The central thesis of this volume is that the family in historical times has been, and at present is, in transition from an institution to a companionship. In the past the important factors unifying the family have been external, formal, and authoritarian, as the law, the mores, public opinion, tradition, the authority of the family head, rigid discipline, and elaborate ritual. At present, in the new emerging form of the companionship family, its unity inheres less and less in community pressures and more and more in such interpersonal relations as the mutual affection, the sympathetic understanding, and the comradeship of its members. (Burgess & Locke, 1945)

Burgess meant the family-as-institution and the family-as-companionship to be seen as ideal types. [➡ p. 119] Thus, he cautioned that purely institutional or purely companionship families exist "nowhere in time or space." In the spirit of the ideal type, we can call the kind of marriage that was emerging in the 1940s the **companionate marriage.** It emphasized affection, friendship, and sexual gratification. Keep in mind, however, that the style of marriage Burgess saw emerging was the single-earner, breadwinner–homemaker marriage that flourished in the 1950s—not the dual-earner family that emerged only in the last half of the twentieth century. The husband and wife in the companionate marriage ideally adhered to a sharp division of labor (he worked outside the home, she worked inside the home). Nevertheless, they were supposed to be each other's companions—friends, lovers—to an extent not imagined by the spouses in the institutional marriages a generation or two earlier. Husbands' authority, although still substantial, was less than in the institutional marriage. Young women were increasingly seen as needing higher education, not so they could establish careers but rather so they could be stimulating conversationalists and efficient homemakers. By midcentury, large state universities enrolled hundreds of thousands of bright young women who majored in home economies or consumer science and joked that what they really hoped to get at college was an "MRS." degree.

> **companionate marriage**
> a marriage in which the emphasis is on affection, friendship, and sexual gratification

Marriage patterns were somewhat different among African Americans in the first half of the century. Because of discrimination and lack of economic opportunity, African American men often did not have the strong earnings record necessary to claim the authority and duty of a husband; consequently, the institutional marriage was never as strong. Statistics show that from the beginning of the twentieth century, blacks were more likely to end a marriage if there were serious difficulties than were whites (Preston, Lim, & Morgan, 1992). A comparison of the life histories of whites and blacks in the South in 1938 and 1939 collected by the Federal Writers' Project found that African American women were more likely to leave abusive marriages than were white women (Pagnini & Morgan, 1996). Although the higher rate of divorce may reflect cultural differences, it also may reflect the lower economic benefits for African American women of being married. Among African Americans, then, the transition from the institutional marriage to the companionship marriage was less well defined.

FROM COMPANIONSHIP TO INDIVIDUALIZATION

The companionate marriage reached its peak at midcentury. The spouses who married at young ages and in record numbers in the late 1940s and the 1950s were its exemplars. Most wives, except among the poor, did not work outside the home. Instead, they focused on creating an emotionally satisfying home life centered on affectionate relations between spouses and on child rearing—these were, after all, the parents who produced the baby boom. They found meaning in the successful performance of their social roles: the homemaker who raised children well and was a pleasant companion and friend to her husband; the man who supported his family through steady employment, enjoyed the company of his wife, and was a loving, if sometimes distant, father.

By the mid-1960s, however, the breadwinner–homemaker companionate marriage was losing ground as both a cultural ideal and a demographic reality. It was gradually overtaken by family forms that Burgess had not foreseen, particularly marriages in which both the husband and the wife worked outside the home. Although women continued to do most of the housework and child care, the roles of wives and husbands became more flexible and open to negotiation. Moreover, an even more individualistic perspective on the rewards of marriage took root. When people evaluated how satisfied they were with their marriages, they thought more in terms of individual satisfaction with how their own lives were developing than in terms of satisfaction gained through building a family.

For instance, compare the results of two national surveys of mental health, one of which was carried out in 1957 and the other in 1976 (Veroff, Douvan, & Kulka, 1981). These surveys detected a shift in the criteria people use to evaluate whether they were satisfied with their lives. When people in the 1957 survey were asked to rate their life satisfaction, their thoughts turned to the social roles they played, such as spouse or parent. For example, in the 1950s, the editors of *McCall's* magazine wrote of a "new and warmer way of life," through which people would become fulfilled "not as women alone or men alone, isolated from one another, but as a family sharing a common experience" (Friedan, 1963).[5] Men who felt they were good workers and good providers tended to be more satisfied, as did women who felt they were good mothers and supportive wives. In other words, in 1957, people often used criteria external to themselves to decide how satisfied they were with their lives.

Toward the Individualized Marriage   But by 1976, people were more likely to use internal criteria. When asked how satisfied they were, the people in the 1976 survey responded in terms of their own sense of personal fulfillment, emotional satisfaction, and self-development. It mattered less how well they were performing the roles society expected of them, such as earning money, raising children, or working hard on the job. It mattered more how much they enjoyed their jobs, how much emotional gratification they were getting from their marriages, how gratifying their sex lives were, and how pleased they were with the ways their lives were changing and developing. Being a good citizen or a responsible parent was less important; being emotionally satisfied was more important. Feeling that you were meeting your obligations to others was less central; feeling that you had opportunities to grow as a person was more central.

Francesca Cancian documented the changing beliefs about marriage by studying popular magazine articles offering marital advice in every decade between 1900 and 1979 (Cancian, 1987). She identified three themes that characterized beliefs about the post-1960-style marriage. The first was "self-development," the belief that each person should develop a fulfilling, independent self instead of merely sacrificing oneself to one's partner. Second, roles within marriage should be flexible and negotiable; and, third, communication and openness in confronting

[5] Cited in Mintz & Kellogg (1988).

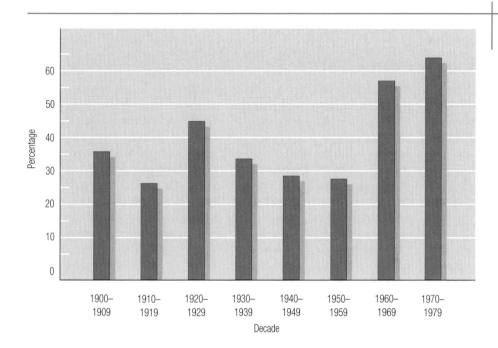

FIGURE 7.1
Percentage of magazine articles containing at least one of three themes about marriage: self development, flexible and negotiable roles, and communication and openness, 1900–1979. (*Source:* Cancian, 1987)

problems are essential. She then tallied the percentage of articles in each decade that contained one or more of these three themes. The results are presented in Figure 7.1. As the reader can see, the presence of these themes rose in the 1920s but then declined through the 1950s. After 1960, however, these themes rose to new heights. Assuming the content of these magazines reflects cultural beliefs about love and marriage, there is indeed evidence of a shift toward a more individualized conception of marriage (Cancian, 1987). (On the use of historical records by sociologists, see *How Do Sociologists Know What They Know? Archival Research.*)

This shift produced the second great change in the meaning of marriage during the twentieth century. Given its emphasis on self-development, flexible roles, and open communication, we might call the form that emerged after 1960 the **individualized marriage.** It, too, is something of an ideal type: Even people who evaluate their satisfaction in very individualistic terms may also take pride in being a good parent. But its general form represents an important break with the meaning of marriage in the past. Cancian called the change in meaning that accompanied the transition to the individualized marriage a shift in emphasis "from role to self" (Cancian, 1987).

Individualized marriage a marriage in which the emphasis is on self-development, flexible roles, and open communication

The Influence of Economic Change

In addition, both transitions—from institution to companionship and from companionship to individualization—had economic roots. First, both are related to changes in the nature of work. The transition from institution to companionship occurred as the United States was becoming increasingly industrialized and urbanized. Husbands (although not wives at first) took jobs that paid wages. Farm families needed to function as production units—as small-scale firms if you will—in order to be successful. In most agricultural societies, older men retained substantial authority to run these production units. Wage work, in contrast, provided young adults with some

How Do Sociologists Know What They Know? Archival Research

Both Francesca M. Cancian's study of the changing content of women's magazines from 1900 to 1979 (Cancian, 1987) and Deanna L. Pagnini and S. Philip Morgan's study of biographies of African Americans and whites collected in the 1930s by the Federal Writers' Project (Pagnini & Morgan, 1996) are examples of **archival research.** This term refers to research that uses printed or written documents stored in libraries or other data archives. Historians rely on archival research of necessity because the written records of events are often the only information they have. Sociologists sometimes use this method, too, especially when they want to study social change by examining the past and comparing it with the present.

For each five-year period, Cancian selected eight articles listed in *Reader's Guide to Periodical Literature* under the heading "marriage," from large-circulation magazines addressed primarily to women, such as *Ladies' Home Journal, McCall's,* and

Reader's Digest. She recorded codes for each article according to its "dominant themes," and then tallied the codes by decade to see whether the themes had changed over time (see Figure 7.1). Pagnini read all 1,170 life histories that were collected by the Federal Writers' Project in 1938 and 1939 in the South and stored at the Southern Historical Collection at the University of North Carolina at Chapel Hill. Every time she encountered material on marriage or nonmarital childbearing, she prepared an excerpt that had no identifying information except an identification number. Later, Pagnini and Morgan analyzed the content of each excerpt (e.g., whether a woman who had an abusive marriage had left it), without knowing the race of the person whose excerpt they were examining. Only after the excerpts had been examined did they use the identification numbers to assign the proper race to each excerpt. (If you are interested in the biographies that the Federal Writers' Project collected, you

can view some of them through the Web site of the Library of Congress [http://memory.loc.gov/ammem/wpaintro/wpahome.html] and search their contents through key words such as "marriage" or "divorce.")

Archival research presents many challenges. The best archival researchers know these limitations, face them squarely, and take pains to minimize them. First, it is difficult to know how representative the materials are. For instance, did the articles Cancian selected represent the views of American women at the time? Cancian forthrightly acknowledged this limitation:

The intended audience of the magazines seems to come from a higher social class in the earlier decades, and the content of the articles partly reflects the policies of editors and advertisers and the attitudes of the writers. Nonetheless, the magazines seem to provide a fairly valid measure,

archival research
research that uses printed or written documents stored in libraries or other data archives

independence from their parents: They could move away to jobs in the city. Their parents had less control over whom they married. Moreover, men's authority was reduced in urban marriages because of the demise of the family as production unit. Later, the transition from companionship to individualization occurred as married women took paid jobs in large numbers. In doing so, they gained greater independence from men and were exposed to new ideas beyond the home. Women as well as men could now think in terms of their own individual development through adulthood. These circumstances supported the emergence of a more individualistic perspective on the rewards of marriage.

Second, both transitions are related to increases in families' standards of living. When most people's living standards were so low that they had difficulty earning enough money for food and shelter, few had time for personal fulfillment. People needed to pool earnings and housework with spouses and children in order to subsist, and marriage was therefore more of an economic partnership. The rising standard of living during the twentieth century gave more people the luxury of focusing on their own feelings of satisfaction. They did so first in the context of the companionate marriage in which a higher standard of living allowed many

since my findings are consistent with the other sources of data described in this chapter.

Pagnini and Morgan frankly noted that the life histories gathered in the South overrepresented poor whites and included many blacks:

While these could be termed limitations in that they do not statistically reflect the class, marriage, and geographical distribution of the Southern population, we would label them as strengths. So often in historical work we are not able to find materials about the working class or blacks; to have both is an advantage.

Another difficulty in archival research is determining how accurate the information is. For instance, the biographies of the Southerners are told through the words of the writers, who determined what questions to ask and what words to write down. Moreover, the subjects were recalling events that took place, in some cases, decades earlier.

Pagnini and Morgan claimed that they could make a virtue out of this necessity:

Thus, we must be aware that we are dealing with subjective perceptions and selected events. . . . For those interviewed, we have memories and perceptions of what was important to these individuals and their families. We stress that for our purposes this is what we seek—there are superior sources that simply record the events themselves. Our goal here is interpretive. . . .

It is also difficult to know how to analyze the information. What categories should one use and how does one tell if a record fits in the category? For instance, how does a scholar reading women's magazines determine whether an article conveys a tone of self-sacrifice or self-fulfillment toward marriage? Cancian had pairs of people read and code each article independently. She set rules for interpreting the content of the magazines and refined the rules until both

coders in each pair agreed on 85 percent of the coding for a particular article.

Archival research does not necessarily provide a representative picture of social history. But it is one of the only tools we have. If social scientists recognize the limitations of archival research, inform their readers about them, and take care to minimize them, the written record can provide an enlightening window on the past.

Ask Yourself

1. Do popular magazines present an accurate picture of present-day attitudes toward love and marriage? A hundred years from now, what might sociologists think when reading them?
2. What other documents could sociologists examine to see how Americans' views of marriage have changed over time?

www.mhhe.com/cherlin5

wives to stay home rather than work for pay. But increasingly high standards of living meant that people could live alone if their marriages were not personally fulfilling, and this development accelerated the transition from companionate marriage to individualized marriage.

Quick Review

- In the institutional marriage, wives and husbands' behavior is governed by strong social norms, tradition, and law. Men have substantial authority.
- In the companionate marriage, the spouses expect affection, friendship, and sexual gratification and find satisfaction in being good parents and spouses.
- In the individualized marriage, each spouse expects self-fulfillment, intimacy, and continuing personal growth.
- Industrialization and urbanization hastened the transition to the companionate marriage.
- The increase in married women working for wages, as well as rising standards of living, underlay the transition to the individualized marriage.

Growing financial pressures on working-class families may have limited the focus on personal development.

THE CURRENT CONTEXT OF MARRIAGE[6]

Overall, research and writing on the changing meaning of marriage suggest that it is now situated in a very different context than in the past. This is true in at least two senses. First, individuals now have a great deal of choice in how they live their personal lives. More forms of marriage and more alternatives to marriage are socially acceptable. You may fit marriage into your life in many ways: You may first live with a partner, or sequentially with several partners, without thinking about whether the arrangement will lead to marriage. You may have children with your eventual spouse or with someone else before marrying. You may, in Massachusetts and Canada, marry someone of the same gender and build a shared marital world with few guidelines to rely on. Moreover, you can have partnerships and children without ever marrying at all. Within marriages and cohabiting unions, roles are more flexible and negotiable, although women still do more than their share of the household work and child rearing (as we will see in the next chapter).

The second difference is in the nature of the rewards that people seek through marriage and other close relationships. People want the individualistic rewards of what's often called personal growth or self-development—a sense that your inner life is changing and developing in a way that gives you great satisfaction—and deeper intimacy. People try to attain these rewards through more open communication and mutually shared disclosures about feelings with their partners. To attain personal growth, they may feel justified in insisting on changes in a relationship that no longer allows them to grow in the directions they wish. In contrast, they are less likely than in the past to focus on the rewards to be found in fulfilling socially valued roles such as the good parent or the loyal and supportive

---

[6] This section draws upon Cherlin (2004), which provides a fuller discussion of the current context of marriage.

spouse. The result of these changing contexts is that social norms about family and personal life count for less than they did during the heyday of the companionate marriage, and far less than during the period of the institutional marriage. Instead, personal choice and self-development loom large in people's construction of their marital careers.

Why Do People Still Marry? There is, however, a puzzle within the story of the changes in marriage that needs solving: Why do most people still want to marry? After all, with the many choices adults have, it's not necessary, strictly speaking, to marry anymore. To be sure, fewer Americans are marrying than during the peak years of marriage in the mid-twentieth century, but most—nearly 90 percent, according to the best estimate—will eventually marry (Goldstein & Kenney, 2001). A survey of high school seniors conducted annually since 1976 shows no decline in the importance they attach to marriage. The percentage of young women who respond that they expect to marry has stayed constant at roughly 80 percent (and has increased from 71 percent to 78 percent for young men). The percentage who respond that "having a good marriage and family life" is extremely important has also remained constant, at about 80 percent for young women and 70 percent for young men (Thornton & Young-DeMarco, 2001). Clearly, marriage remains important to many people in the United States. Consequently, I think the interesting question is not why so few people are marrying, but rather, why so many people are marrying, or planning to marry, or hoping to marry, when cohabitation and single parenthood are widely acceptable options.

The dominant theoretical perspectives on marriage in the twentieth century do not provide much guidance on the question of why marriage remains so popular. The functionalist sociologists of the mid-twentieth century, such as Talcott Parsons, argued that the breadwinner–homemaker family was functional, and implicitly superior, to other arrangements, [➡ p. 21] but tens of millions of married women have entered the workforce since then. Economist Gary Becker (1965, 1991) and others developed a similar model of the utility of "specialization" by husbands and wives, but it too seems less applicable now, as I will argue later in this chapter when we examine the marriage market.

One kind of reward still applies, although with less and less force: Marriage still makes it easier to trust that your partner will stay with you than does cohabitation. It still requires a public commitment to a long-term, possibly lifelong relationship. This commitment is usually expressed in front of relatives, friends, and religious congregants. Cohabitation, in contrast, requires only a private commitment, which is easier to break. Therefore, marriage, more so than cohabitation, lowers the risk that your partner will renege on agreements that have been made. It conveys what we might call **enforceable trust**—the ability to call on family and friends to help enforce the agreements you have made with a partner (Cherlin, 2000; Portes & Sensenbrenner, 1993). As a result, you can invest in the partnership with less fear of abandonment. For instance, it allows the partners to invest financially in joint long-term purchases such as homes and automobiles. It allows caregivers to invest in raising the couple's children—investments of time and effort that, unlike strengthening one's job skills, would not be easily portable to another intimate relationship (England & Farkas, 1986).

enforceable trust the ability to call on family and friends to help enforce the agreements you have made with a partner

Nevertheless, the difference in the amount of enforceable trust that marriage brings, compared with cohabitation, is eroding. Although relatives and friends will view a divorce with disappointment, they will accept it more readily than their counterparts would have two generations ago. In addition, cohabiting couples are increasingly gaining the rights previously reserved to married couples. It seems likely that over time, the legal differences between cohabitation and marriage will become minimal in the United States, Canada, and many European countries. The advantage of marriage in enhancing trust will then depend on the force of public commitments, both secular and religious, by the partners themselves.

Marriage as the Capstone Experience   Why, then, are so many people still marrying? What has happened, I would argue, is that although the practical importance of being married has declined, its symbolic importance has remained high. Marriage is less dominant than it was—you don't have to marry anymore. But it is also more distinctive than it was—precisely because it is optional, it causes married couples to stand out from others. It has evolved from a marker of conformity (doing what every adult was virtually required to do) to a marker of prestige (attaining a special status). Today, marriage is a status young couples build up to, often by living with a partner beforehand, by gaining steady employment or starting a career, by putting away some savings, and even by having children. A half-century ago, marriage's place in the life course used to come before those investments were made; but now it often comes afterward. It used to be the foundation of adult personal life; now it is sometimes the capstone—the last brick put in place when the structure is finally complete.

How Low-Income Individuals See Marriage   Paradoxically, it is among the lower-income groups in the United States, where marriage rates are lowest, that both the persistent preference for marriage and its changing meaning seem clearest. Although marriage is optional and often forgone, it has by no means faded away among the poor and near-poor. Instead, it is a much sought-after but elusive goal. People tell observers that they wish to marry, but will do so only when they are sure they can do it successfully: when their partner has demonstrated the ability to hold a decent job and treat them fairly and without abuse, when they have a security deposit or a down payment for a decent apartment or home, and when they have enough in the bank to pay for a nice wedding party for family and friends. Edin and Kefalas (2005), who studied childbearing and intimate relationships among mothers in low- and moderate-income Philadelphia neighborhoods, wrote,

> *In some sense, marriage is a form of social bragging about the quality of the couple's relationship, a powerfully symbolic way of elevating one's relationship above others in the community, particularly in a community where marriage is rare.*

In a study of low-income families in three United States cities that I am helping to conduct (Cherlin et al., 2004), one woman, who was already living with the man she was engaged to and had children with, told an ethnographer she was not yet ready to marry him:

> *But I'm not ready to do that yet. I told him, we're not financially ready yet. He knows that. I told him by the end of this year, maybe. I told him that last year. Plus, we both need to learn to control our tempers, you could say. He doesn't understand that bills and kids and [our relationship] come first, not [his] going out and getting new clothes or [his] doing this and that. It's the kids, then us. He gets paid good, about five hundred dollars a week. How hard is it to give me money and help with the bills?*

Note that for this woman, more is required of a man than a steady job before he is marriageable. He has to learn to turn over most of his paycheck to his family rather than spending it on his friends and himself. He must put his relationship with his partner ahead of running with his single male friends, a way of saying that a husband must place a priority on providing companionship and intimacy to his wife and on being sexually faithful. And he and his partner have to learn to control their tempers, a vague referent to the possibility that physical abuse exists in the relationship. In sum, the demands low-income women place on men include not just a reliable income, as important as that is, but also a commitment to put family first, provide companionship, be faithful, and avoid abusive behavior—similar standards to those better-off women have.

How Young Adults in General See Marriage   The changing meaning of marriage is not limited to the low-income population. It is apparent, for instance, in a study of moderate-income young adults in the Toledo, Ohio, area who typically had graduated from high school and perhaps had some college courses. Many did not want to marry until they had a financial package in place that often included homeownership, being out of debt, and having a stable, adequate income. A twenty-five-year-old woman told the authors that she and her partner were interested in getting married, but they had a lot to accomplish beforehand:

> *Um, we have certain things that we want to do before we get married, We both want very good jobs, and we both want a house, we both want reliable transportation. I'm about to start taking cake decorating classes, and so I can have me some good income, and he—he's trying his best you know? He's been looking out for jobs everywhere, and we—we're trying. We just want to have—we gotta have everything we need before we say, "Let's get married." (Smock, Manning, & Porter, 2005)*

Two generations ago, young adults got married *before* they had everything they needed. But cohabiting was not an option back then, so they faced the choice of marrying or not living together. Today, with cohabitation as an acceptable option, many young adults are postponing marriage until they pass the milestones that used to occur early in marriage.

Consider a nationally representative survey of 1,003 adults, ages 20–29, conducted in 2001 on attitudes toward marriage (Whitehead & Popenoe, 2001). A majority responded in ways suggestive of the view that marriage is a status that one builds up to. Sixty-two percent agreed with the statement, "Living together with someone before marriage is a good way to avoid an eventual divorce," and 82 percent agreed that "It is extremely important to you to be economically set before you get married." Moreover, most indicated a view of marriage as centered on intimacy and love more than on practical matters such as finances and children. Ninety-four percent of those who had never married agreed that "when you marry, you want your spouse to be your soul mate, first and foremost." In contrast, only 16 percent agreed that "the main purpose of marriage these days is to have children." And over 80 percent of the women agreed that it is more important "to have a husband who can communicate about his deepest feelings than to have a husband who makes a good living." Being a soul mate, communicating deep feelings: These are hallmarks of the individualistic marriage.

The Wedding as a Status Symbol   Even the wedding has become an individual achievement. In the distant past, a wedding was an event at which two kinship groups formed an alliance. More recently, it has been an event organized and paid for by parents, at which they display their approval and support for their child's marriage. In both cases, it has been the ritual that provides legal and social approval for having children. But in keeping with the individualized marriage, it is now becoming an event centered on and often controlled by the couple themselves, having less to do with family approval or having children than in the past.

You might think, then, that weddings would become smaller and that many couples would forgo a public wedding altogether. But that does not appear to have happened for most couples. The wedding, it seems, has become an important symbol of the partners' personal achievements and a stage to display their self-development. Studies suggest that the percentage of weddings held in a religious institution, the percentage with receptions, and the percentage followed by a honeymoon have increased (Whyte, 1990). In recent decades, then, when partners decide that their relationship has finally reached the stage where they can marry, they generally want a ritual-filled wedding to celebrate it (Boden, 2003; Bulcroft, Bradley, & Simpson, 2000; Bulcroft, Bulcroft, Smeins, & Cranage 1997; Ingraham, 1999).

Even low- and moderate-income couples who have limited funds and who may already have children and may be living together seem to view a substantial wedding as a requirement for marriage. Some of the young adults in the Toledo study said that merely going "downtown" for a civil ceremony at a courthouse or a justice of the peace's office did not constitute an acceptable wedding. A home health care aide said she was waiting for her boyfriend to change his mind about a church wedding because, "until he does, we just won't get married. I'm not going downtown. . . I say, you don't want a big wedding, we're not going to get married" (Smock, Manning, & Porter, 2005). The authors of the Philadelphia study write, "Having the wherewithal to throw a 'big' wedding is a vivid display that the couple has

Big weddings are popular as a symbol of a successful personal life.

achieved enough financial security to do more than live from paycheck to paycheck" (Edin & Kefalas, 2005). The couples in these studies wanted to make a statement through their weddings, a statement both to themselves and to their friends and family that they had passed a milestone in their personal development. Through wedding ceremonies, the purchase of a home, and the acquisition of other accoutrements of married life, individuals hoped to display their attainment of a prestigious, comfortable, stable style of life. They also expected marriage to provide some enforceable trust. But as I have argued, the enforcement value of marriage is less than it used to be. People marry now not only for the social benefits that marriage provides but also for the personal achievement—the capstone experience—it represents.

Quick Review

- People have more choices today about how to live their personal lives.
- The rewards that people seek in marriages and other close relationships center on personal growth and deeper intimacy.
- Marriage still provides partners greater trust that both will honor their commitment, although less so than in the past.
- Marriage is still important as a symbol of status and prestige.
- Increasingly, young adults are delaying marriage until they have accomplished other goals such as obtaining steady employment or buying a home.

MARRIAGE AND RELIGION

Organized religion in the United States has always supported marriage, and it has continued to do so throughout the transitions to the companionate and independent marriages. The United States is the most religious nation in the Western world, with the possible exception of Italy. A comparable set of surveys conducted in more than 60 nations between 1999 and 2001 shows that Americans go to church more often than do people in every other Western nation except Ireland and that they think of themselves as "religious persons" more than in any Western nation except Italy. Moreover, they tend to believe that what they learn from religion is relevant to their family lives. When asked, "Generally speaking, do you think that the churches in your country are giving adequate answers to . . . the problems of family life?" more Americans (61 percent) said yes than did people in any other Western country (Inglehart et al., 2004).

Among married persons, those who are active religiously describe themselves as somewhat happier with their marriages (Booth, Johnson, Branaman, & Sica, 1995); and they also tend to report better mental health (Waite & Lehrer, 2003). Couples who attend religious services frequently have a lower risk of divorce than do those who attend less often (Bramlett & Mosher, 2002). (I will have more to say about divorce risks in Chapter 12.) It is not clear, however, whether religious activity causes these differences or whether other, unmeasured factors cause both greater well-being and more religious activity.

In recent years, churches have been an expanding base for counseling, educational programs, and other attempts at "marriage strengthening." For example, churches have participated in the development of programs to teach communication skills to engaged or recently married couples so that they will be better

Studies show that married men and women tend to live longer than divorced or never-married men and women.

equipped to discuss and resolve problems that may arise (Markman et al., 2004). The main exception to the emphasis on marriage among religious groups is among African American churches. Although these churches are strong supporters of African American families, they emphasize marriage relatively less and extended family ties relatively more than do predominantly white churches (Gilkes, 1995).

IS MARRIAGE GOOD FOR YOU?

Do individuals benefit from being married? A substantial body of literature shows that married men appear advantaged compared with unmarried men in many ways and that, to a lesser extent, married women seem advantaged as well. But it is difficult to know whether marriage *causes* these differences. For example, married men and women live longer, on average, than do unmarried men and women. One study estimated that married men and women who are age 48 have a greater-than-80-percent chance of reaching age 65, whereas never-married and divorced men and women have a less-than-70-percent chance of living that long (Waite & Lillard, 1995). A number of studies have found evidence that married men and women have substantially better health then unmarried men and women, in terms of general life satisfaction, depression and anxiety, and treatment for psychiatric difficulties (Simon, 2002; Waite & Lehrer, 2003).

There are two possible reasons for these findings:

1. *Being married actually causes people to feel better and live longer.* Waite (1995) suggests two ways that marriage might be good for one's physical and mental health. First, it may deter people from undertaking risky behavior. Married men and women are less likely to drink and drive, abuse alcohol or drugs, and get into serious arguments (Umberson, 1987).

Marriage may provide people with a sense of responsibility to children and spouses that leads them to take fewer risks. In addition, marriage may provide a partner who monitors a person's health closely and urges a healthier lifestyle. Second, married people have higher incomes and more wealth (Smith, 1994), in part because of economies of scale (two people can share a home or a car). A higher standard of living eases stress and makes people less likely to abuse alcohol or drugs.

2. *Mentally and physically healthier people are more likely to get married and to stay married.* As women and men choose partners, we would expect them to favor the healthy and the happy over the troubled and the ill. So there should be *positive selection into* marriage: People with positive qualities are more likely to enter into it. Recall the discussion of the selection effect on teenage childbearing: Young women who have children as adolescents are not a random sample of all adolescents. [➡ p. 211] Similarly, people who marry are not a random sample of all adults; rather, they represent the most attractive 90 percent of the population in the marriage market. Moreover, people with poorer mental health have marriages that are more troubled and are therefore more likely to divorce. So as couples age, there is *negative selection out of* marriage: People with negative characteristics are more likely to leave it. Because of selection into and out of marriage, we would expect currently married individuals to be physically and mentally healthier even if what goes on in a marriage has nothing to do with it.

Because sociologists cannot randomly assign some people to marry and others to stay single and then study them, we cannot say definitively whether being married actually causes people's health and mood to improve or whether we are merely witnessing a selection effect. But the findings for men, at least, are so strong and consistent across a number of studies of different domains of life as to suggest that some of the advantages shown by married men are caused by the marriage relationship itself. And it is likely that there are benefits for women as well (Simon, 2002). If the effects of marriage were purely due to selection, we would expect that as people get older, the difference between the married and unmarried would increase—because the unmarried group would be composed more and more of unhealthy individuals who never married or who divorced. But data on death rates and treatment for mental illness do not show a gap between the married and the unmarried that increases with age (Gove et al., 1990).

Waite and Gallagher (2000) claim not only that the benefits of marriage are real, but that women gain about as much from marriage as men. Compared to current alternatives for women, the claim of equal benefits for each gender is probably true. For instance, women typically earn less than men, so wives tend to gain more in household income than husbands (because their husbands tend to earn more than they do). But as England (2000) argues, husbands typically gain greater bargaining power in the household than wives, because husbands can threaten to leave the marriage and take their higher incomes with them. (More will be said about earnings and bargaining power in the next chapter.) Waite and Gallagher also claim that marriage benefits women because it protects them from domestic violence. How so? Married women are less likely to be victimized than cohabiting women. But women who are neither living with a man nor married have an even lower risk, so a woman who is concerned about avoiding domestic violence might reasonably decide to avoid heterosexual unions altogether, rather than to marry. Nevertheless, even if the presumed benefits to women are inflated, Waite and Gallagher do convincingly refute an older literature which held that marriage lowers a woman's well-being (Bernard, 1972).

Marriage might benefit men more than women because unmarried men have fewer social resources to draw on. As Chapter 10 will show, women are enmeshed in support networks with other women—mothers, sisters, grandmothers—much more than men are. In contrast, men tend to rely heavily on their wives for social support; and they therefore have more to gain from marrying. In addition, marriage has played a crucial role in defining what it means to be an adult male in our society (Nock, 1998). One theory of gender suggests that men define themselves by separating from their birth family more than women do. [➡ p. 91] Marriage has been the culturally approved way for men to achieve this separation in adulthood. It leads to noticeable changes in their public behavior: Married men spend more time with relatives or at religious services and events, and less time with friends and at bars or taverns, than they did before they married (Nock, 1998). It is the way that men in American society have taken on the culturally prescribed roles of wage earner, father, and public citizen.

Quick Review

- Organized religion supports marriage and is involved in marriage-strengthening activities. Religious married couples seek to control their emotions and have faith that problems will be solved.
- The advantages married people show may be partly due to selection and partly to marriage itself.

Cohabitation

cohabitation the sharing of a household by unmarried persons who have a sexual relationship

Whether or not marriage is good for you, many adults are cohabiting before it, after it, or instead of it. By **cohabitation,** commonly called "living together," I mean a living arrangement in which two adults who are not married to each other but who have a sexual relationship share the same house or apartment. Before the 1960s, cohabitation was common mainly among the poor and near-poor. With little in the way of resources to share and little prospect of leaving money or possessions to their children, the poor had less reason to marry. For many, cohabitation had served as an acceptable substitute for legal marriage. But beginning around 1970, the proportion of all young adults who lived with someone prior to marrying increased sharply. By the early 1990s, a majority of first marriages were preceded by a period of cohabitation (Bumpass & Lu, 2000).

In 2000, the Census Bureau estimated that there were about 4.9 million households in the United States maintained by two opposite-sex persons who said they were unmarried partners. (There also were about 600,000 unmarried-partner households maintained by two same-sex persons.) In contrast, there were only about a half-million unmarried partner households in 1970 (U.S. Bureau of the Census, 1993a, 2003a). So great has been the increase in cohabitation that it has compensated in large part for the postponement of marriage. That is to say, far fewer young adults marry today by their mid-twenties, but the proportion of young adults who live in either kind of union—marital or cohabiting—has declined much less (Bumpass, Sweet, & Cherlin, 1991).

Cohabiting couples are more diverse than many people realize. Consider these facts about heterosexual cohabitation:

- Although in many people's minds the image of a cohabiting couple is one of college-educated professionals living together, cohabitation continues to be more common among the less affluent and less well-educated. In a 1995 national survey of women ages 19 to 44, 59 percent of those without a high school diploma had cohabited, compared to 37 percent of those with a college degree (Bumpass & Lu, 2000). To be sure, cohabitation has increased greatly among the well-educated, but it has also increased among the less well-educated.
- Although we read more about young people living together before a first marriage, cohabitation is more common before a remarriage than before a first marriage. Indeed, about half of remarriages are preceded by a period of cohabitation (Smock & manning, 2004).
- Although the common image is one of a childless couple, many cohabiting couples have children in their households: In 2003, two out of five opposite-sex unmarried partners had the children of one or both partners present, including 60 percent of Hispanics, 52 percent of African Americans, and 34 percent of non-Hispanic whites (U.S. Bureau of the Census, 2004a).

In fact, about 40 percent of the births listed in official statistics as occurring outside of marriage are in reality births to cohabiting couples rather than to single mothers living without partners (Bumpass & Lu, 2000). One recent study of unmarried mothers who had just given birth in urban hospitals found that about half were living with the fathers of their children (Sigle-Rushton & McLanahan, 2002). In fact, over the past decade or two, most of the rise in childbearing

A majority of first marriages are preceded by cohabitation.

Domestic Partnerships

Getting married is not only a way for couples to express their love and commitment to each other but also a way for them to obtain important practical and financial advantages not available to couples who cohabit or live apart. In most nations the law has long recognized marriage as a privileged relationship in which the spouses have special rights and responsibilities. Here is a partial list of rights and responsibilities that married couples have but cohabiting couples, in most jurisdictions in the United States, do not have:

- They can include each other as beneficiaries on pension and annuity plans offered by their employers, and they can purchase health insurance for each other through their employers.
- They can file a joint income tax return, which may reduce their tax liability.
- They can receive Social Security survivors' benefits if their spouse dies, and they can inherit from each other even when there is no will.

- They are jointly responsible for their children, and each can give legal permission to schools, doctors, and the like, for trips, operations, and so forth.
- They can adopt children together.
- In the event of a divorce, they are both normally entitled to either custody or visitation rights.

This list reflects the view, virtually unchallenged until a few decades ago, that marriage constitutes the only legitimate context for the raising of children. It also reflects the ideal, prominent in the first half of the twentieth century, that families should have one wage earner (the husband), who should be able to provide health insurance, survivors' benefits, and so on, to his wife.

Yet social changes have made the granting of rights solely to married couples debatable. For instance, about 12 percent of all births in the United States occur to women who are cohabiting with the fathers of their children.[1] Cohabitation itself is so

common that some observers question the rationale for denying cohabiting couples similar rights to those married couples have. They argue that there is little difference between a cohabiting couple raising children and a married couple raising children—and that the former ought to have the same rights and receive the same benefits as the latter. Others favor retaining the privileged place of marriage for any of several reasons: because of a moral or religious belief that heterosexual marriage is the only proper setting for having and raising children; because of a pragmatic belief that marriage provides a more stable two-parent setting than cohabitation; or because of a wish to avoid further spending by government or business that would be triggered by treating cohabitors like spouses.

In the United States, states and municipalities are moving toward granting cohabiting couples some of the rights and responsibilities that married couples have.

outside of marriage has been the result of births to cohabiting couples, not births to women living alone (Bumpass & Lu, 2000).

More often the children who live in these families are from earlier relationships. In these cases the household is a like a stepfamily: a parent (usually the mother), her child, and a resident man who is not the father (Seltzer, 2000). We might call these households quasi-stepfamilies. We will discuss this topic more fully in Chapter 13, Remarriage and Stepfamilies. They are so numerous that, using this expanded definition, more children enter a stepfamily through cohabitation than through remarriage (Bumpass, Raley, & Sweet, 1995).

Cohabitation is still evolving: Each year it becomes more common, and its role in the family system increases. States and localities have been implementing legal changes that give cohabiting couples more rights that once were reserved for married couples. (See *Families and Public Policy:* Domestic Partnerships.) Moreover, comparing cohabitation with marriage is difficult because as Smock (2000) notes in a review of articles on heterosexual cohabitation, the meaning of marriage is changing, too. Nevertheless, we can examine the major perspectives on the meaning of cohabitation.

Canada has gone further: Under the Modernization of Benefits and Obligations Act of 2000, legal distinctions between married and unmarried same-sex and opposite-sex couples were eliminated for couples who have lived together for at least a year. Still, married partners have some rights that cohabiting partners do not: The Supreme Court of Canada ruled in 2002 that when cohabiting partners dissolve their unions, they do not have to divide their assets equally, nor can one partner be compelled to pay maintenance payments to the other, even when children are involved (*Nova Scotia [Attorney General] v. Walsh*, 2002).

In France, where almost 9 out of 10 unions begin outside of marriage, opposite-sex and same-sex cohabiting couples may enter into Civil Solidarity Pacts, which give them most but not all of the rights and responsibilities of married couples after the pact has existed for three years (Martin & Théry, 2001). Some Scandinavian countries also have registered partnerships for opposite-sex couples (Lyall, 2004). Others, such as the United Kingdom have domestic partnerships exclusively for same-sex couples.

The issue of whether the state should recognize same-sex partnerships or allow same-sex marriage is contentious in the United States, as we will see in Chapter 14. But even giving opposite-sex cohabiting couples a legal status is controversial. The debate reflects the weakening role of marriage in the institution of the family. Although still dominant, heterosexual marriage is no longer the only acceptable way for couples to live together. Rather, heterosexual cohabitation is broadly tolerated. This toleration is so recent, however, that there is little consensus on the rights and responsibilities heterosexual partners should have toward each other and toward the children in their households.

Ask Yourself

1. Are any of the couples you know cohabiting? If so, have their relationships reached the point at which legal considerations would be meaningful to them?
2. Should couples who are cohabiting have the same legal rights as married couples? Why or why not?

[1]About 30 percent of all births occur outside marriage. And of these 30 percent, about 40 percent occur to women who are cohabiting with the fathers of their children (Bumpass & Lu, 2000).

www.mhhe.com/cherlin5

DIVERSE MEANINGS

The phenomenon of cohabitation covers many different kinds of couples. Two young childless adults, one or both still in college, may interpret the meaning of their relationship quite differently from two divorced individuals with children from their previous marriages. We can group cohabiting relationships into three categories.

An Alternative Way of Being Single   The first group includes couples for whom the relationship is an alternative way of being single. These couples have not thought much about marriage and would consider themselves single and not necessarily looking for a spouse. Because cohabiting partners have no legal obligations to each other and either one may end the relationship at any time, cohabitation may appeal to individuals who want an intimate relationship without binding commitments. This kind of partnership is similar to an emerging form that social theorist Anthony Giddens has called the **pure relationship:** an intimate relationship entered into for its own sake and lasting only as long as both partners are satisfied with the rewards they get from it (Giddens, 1991, 1992).

pure relationship an intimate relationship entered into for its own sake and which lasts only as long as both partners are satisfied with it

Giddens maintained that the pure relationship is becoming more common in the late modern era. It is in some ways the logical extension of the increasing individualization of unions that occurred throughout the twentieth century. "Entered into for its own sake" means that the couple form their relationship without necessarily thinking about finding a spouse or having children. "Only so long as they are satisfied" means that the relationship is entered voluntarily and either partner is free to leave whenever he or she wants to. "Rewards" refers mostly to the emotional rewards from love and intimacy—rewards that are intrinsic to the relationship itself. It is "free-floating," independent of social institutions or economic life. Giddens did not intend "pure" to mean a relationship without flaws but rather a relationship that is mainly an intimate partnership and little more. (In his view, the term could include nonsexual relationships between close friends, but I will restrict it to intimate sexual relationships.)

Some cohabiting unions may indeed be close to "pure relationships." Among college-age young adults, for example, those who are cohabiting are nearly as likely to be enrolled in college as are those who are living without a partner. In contrast, those who are married are much less likely to be enrolled (Rindfuss and Vanden-Heuvel, 1990). This pattern suggests that young cohabitors act more like their single counterparts than like married couples focused on employment, housework, and child care. The authors of the Toledo study, as noted in Chapter 6, [➡ p. 200] reported that many cohabiting young adults seemed to drift into living together without much thought as to what the relationship might become in the long run and sometimes even without a deliberate decision to cohabit. A computer consultant described the beginning of his cohabiting relationship this way:

> It began by attrition of this thing at her parents' house. In other words, she stayed at my house more and more from spending the night once to not going home to her parents' house for a week at a time and then, you know, um, so there was no official starting date. I did take note when the frilly fufu soaps showed up in my bathroom that she'd probably moved in at that point. (Manning & Smock, 2005)

Other individuals in this study told of cohabiting relationships that started on the first date or involved people who alternated between two households. In fact, none of the 115 cohabiting young adults in this study said that he or she was deciding between marriage and cohabitation at the start of the union, although about one-third had discussed marriage or had some type of plans to marry (Manning & Smock, 2005). Another study of 25 cohabiting young adults with college experience in New York City found similar patterns: About half had moved in within six months of meeting. In addition, very few had discussed their relationship goals prior to cohabiting, although the topic of marriage was commonly raised during their first year together (Sassler, 2004). The fluidity of these relationships is similar to the "free-floating" character of the pure relationship.

A Testing Ground for Marriage

A Testing Ground for Marriage   If they begin to discuss long-term options, then the couples may transform their relationship into a testing ground for marriage. Of course, it may be a testing ground even if they do not acknowledge it as such. There are certainly many couples for whom cohabitation is a stage in the marriage process, even though the partners have not made a permanent commitment to each other. In the 1996 and 1998 General Social Surveys, cohabiting individuals were asked "How likely is it that you two will get married? Would you

say that it is very likely, somewhat unlikely, or very unlikely?" In response, 51 percent said "very likely," and another 25 percent said "somewhat likely" (Davis, Smith,
& Marsden, 2003). Moreover, Americans tend to resolve their cohabiting relationships in a relatively short time by either marrying or breaking up. In fact, the median length of a cohabiting union in the United States was less than in any other
Western country in cross-national surveys conducted in the mid-1990s—just a little more than a year before either separation (for about half) or a marriage (for
about half) (Heuveline & Timberlake, 2004). If you observe young couples who
have just moved in together, you will probably find men and women who devote
little time to thoughts of marriage except when a stray sociologist wanders in and
asks about it. Nevertheless, if you pay a return visit a few years later, you are likely
to find that either they have married or they are no longer together.

Just what role does cohabitation play in the marriage process? One example is
that young women who are in a strong economic position seem to be using it to
learn whether their male partners will be good earners—and possibly whether
they will share equitably in the housework. A study that followed a national sample of high school graduates for 14 years showed that young single women with
high earnings were more likely to cohabit than they were to marry. In contrast,

Children are present in the
household of two out of five
cohabiting couples.

young single men with high earnings were more likely to marry than to cohabit (Clarkberg, 1999). It is as if women with the highest—and therefore most attractive—earning potential were using these resources to establish cohabiting relationships in which they could find out more about their partners. They may be able to determine whether men seem to be steady wage earners and whether they will share the work at home. In this way, cohabitation may aid the search process undertaken by young women with strong marriage market positions.

An Alternative to Marriage   In some Western countries, cohabitation is becoming an alternative to marriage—a way of living that is similar to marriage but does not involve a legal commitment. In France, for example, about one-fourth of all children in the mid-1990s were living with cohabiting parents in families that typically lasted 9 or 10 years (Heuveline & Timberlake, 2004). In Sweden, cohabitation is becoming indistinguishable from marriage (Kiernan, 2002); in the mid-1990s half of all children were living with cohabiting parents, many of whom eventually marry (Heuveline & Timberlake, 2004). So far, at least, this is not the case in the United States as a whole. Still, among disadvantaged racial-ethnic groups, there are some signs that cohabitation is taking on the characteristics of an alternative way of being married. Hispanic and black cohabiting couples are more likely to conceive a child together and to remain cohabiting, rather than marrying, after the child is born (Smock & Manning, 2004). Having a child with a cohabiting partner but not marrying afterward seems to be especially common among Puerto Rican couples, whose culture has a tradition of consensual unions (Manning & Landale, 1996).

Canada, which has both English-speaking and French-speaking populations, also shows the difference that culture and language can make in the role of cohabitation. About 80 percent of the residents of Quebec primarily speak French at home, while most of the residents of the other provinces speak English. Cohabitation is far more common in Quebec, where 30 percent of all couples were cohabiting in 2001, compared to 12 percent in the rest of Canada (and about 8 percent in the United States); and fewer people ever marry in Quebec than in the rest of Canada. About half of all births in Quebec in the late 1990s were to cohabiting couples, compared to 15 percent in the rest of Canada. Two Canadian demographers argue that cohabitation in Quebec is not only an acceptable alternative to marriage, as in France, but is becoming indistinguishable from marriage, as in Sweden (Le Bourdais and Lapierre-Adamcyk, 2004). Cohabitation in English-speaking Canada, on the other hand, is more similar to that in the United States.

COHABITATION AND FAMILY AMONG LESBIANS AND GAY MEN

For lesbians and gay men in the United States cohabitation has been the only form of partnership available to date. In the 1992 University of Chicago survey of sexual behavior [➡ p. 191], cohabitation was found to be common among individuals who said they had engaged only in homosexual sex the previous year: 44 percent of these women and 28 percent of these men reported that they were living in such partnerships (Black, Gates, Sanders, & Taylor, 2000). Moreover, according to the 2000 Census, 33 percent of women in same-sex partnerships and 22 percent of men in same-sex partnerships had children living with them (U.S. Bureau of the Census, 2003q).

Studies that have compared gay, lesbian, and heterosexual couples find no significant differences in love or relationship satisfaction (Savin-Williams & Esterberg, 2000). When a sample of homosexual and heterosexual couples was asked what were the "best things" and "worst things" about their relationships, a panel of raters who were given the written comments could not tell which comments came from which group of couples (Peplau, 1991). Weston (1991), who studied lesbian and gay couples in San Francisco in the 1980s, reported a concern about excessive "merging." Subsequent research suggests the issue is more relevant for lesbian partnerships than for gay male partnerships (Savin-Williams & Esterberg, 2000). The problem, Weston wrote, is to avoid becoming so united with and dependent on your partner that you lose your independence and can't develop as an individual. This language recalls the way that many married persons talk about the need to maintain a growing, independent self.

Among lesbian and gay couples, both partners tend to work for pay; and they seem to split the domestic chores more equitably and flexibly than the typical heterosexual couple (Seidman, 1991; Weeks, Heaphy, & Donovan, 2001). However, Carrington (1999) observed the daily home lives of 52 gay and lesbian couples and found that a majority of them did not divide the homework equally—even though most said they did. In homes where one partner worked longer hours and earned substantially more than did the other partner, the one with the less demanding, lower-paying job did more housework or more of the work of keeping in touch with family and friends. Carrington suggests that holding a demanding professional or managerial job may make it difficult for a person to invest fully in sharing the work at home, regardless of gender or sexuality.

COHABITATION: A SUMMING UP

Trying to characterize cohabitation is like trying to hit a moving target. It is changing so rapidly, and taking on so many forms, that a simple summary is likely to soon be outdated. But for the moment, cohabitation in the United States seems to an alternative form of singlehood for some people, especially young adults without children, and a testing ground for marriage for others. Even though Americans may not think of their cohabiting unions as a way of finding a suitable marriage partner, few will remain long in a union that they do not want to convert to a marriage. People who do not marry are likely to have a series of short-term partners rather than one or two long relationships.

Yet the link between cohabitation and marriage may be weakening. Fewer cohabiting unions end in marriage now than a few decades ago: In the 1970s, about 60 percent of cohabiting individuals married within three years, compared to about 35 percent in the early 1990s (Seltzer, 2000). The percentage could have fallen further since then, but we lack more recent data. And from the 1980s to the 1990s, the percentage of cohabiting couples who had children together but did not marry increased. Many cities are providing cohabiting couples with the some of the same legal rights and protections married couples have. Whether cohabitation becomes more of a long-term alternative to marriage, as in France and Scandinavia, remains to be seen.

There is more to say about cohabitation's relationship to other family issues such as domestic violence, divorce, and the well-being of children. Consequently, we will revisit it in later chapters.

Quick Review

- Cohabitation is a rapidly growing and diverse living arrangement.
- For some, cohabitation is an alternative way of being single and is begun without any discussion of long-term plans.
- For others, it is a stage in the process of finding a spouse.
- And for others, such as minority groups in the United States or French-speaking Canadians, cohabitation may serve as an alternative way of being married.

THE MARRIAGE MARKET

Despite the rise of cohabitation, most Americans eventually marry. When sociologists and economists study who marries whom, they often make an analogy to the labor market, in which people seeking employment look for employers who will hire them at an acceptable wage. In the **marriage market,** unmarried individuals (or their parents) search for others who will marry them (or their children). Instead of an acceptable wage, the searchers require that a partner have an acceptable set of desired characteristics, such as a college education, good looks, a pleasant disposition, and so forth.

marriage market an analogy to the labor market in which single individuals (or their parents) search for others who will marry them (or their children)

There are three components to this market model of marriage. The first component is simply a group of people who are actively looking for a spouse at the same place at the same time. They constitute the *supply* of men and women who are in the marriage market. The second component is *preferences*. Each person has an idea of his or her own preferred characteristics in a spouse. Some people may care more about good looks, others more about personality or earning potential. A person will try to find a mate who ranks as high as possible on the characteristics she or he prefers. And that same person will probably have a minimum set of characteristics that she or he will accept. The third component is *resources*. These are the characteristics a person possesses that are attractive to others. In a sense resources are the flip side of preferences: Resources are what I have that a partner might want; preferences are what I want a partner to have.

So people who are looking for spouses, who have preferences about the qualities they want, and who have resources to offer create a marriage market. To be sure, it is difficult in real life to decide just who is looking for a spouse and who isn't. The growth of cohabitation makes this problem even more difficult. Moreover, this depiction of searchers as rational, calculating individuals who tote up the pluses and minuses of prospects is at odds with the popular image of people falling in love with each other. Clearly, the market metaphor can't explain everything about who marries whom. Nevertheless, in the aggregate, the behavior of unmarried persons resembles that of job searchers enough that the metaphor is useful.[7]

Sometimes preferences and resources are so incompatible that the market can't provide acceptable spouses for all who are looking. One explanation for the drop in the African American marriage rate [➡ p. 154] is that decent-paying industrial jobs—making steel or cars or television sets—have moved to suburban plants or to firms in developing countries, so that men without college educations (and African American men are less likely to have attended college) have a harder time finding a job that can support a family. Therefore African American women, so this argument goes, can't find enough employed African American

---

[7] The job search analogy has been carried furthest by Oppenheimer (1988).

men to marry (Wilson, 1987). Recent studies have indeed found that women's marriage rates are lower in areas where more men were unemployed, although the effect has not been large enough to fully explain racial differences in marriage patterns.[8] High levels of homicide, imprisonment, and drug use also remove some black men from the marriage market. [➡ p. 155]

The Specialization Model In the predominant marriage bargain of the mid-twentieth century, men placed a greater emphasis on the homemaking skills of their wives; conversely, women placed a greater emphasis on the earning potential of their spouses. This, as I noted earlier in the chapter, is the bargain hailed in the writings of Parsons and his associates in the 1950s. It is also the bargain implied by the theory of the division of labor advanced by economist Gary Becker, whose theoretical work since the 1960s pioneered the economic approach to studying the family.[9]

Becker drew his model from the theory of international trade, under which each country is said to have a "comparative advantage" in producing particular goods relative to other countries. For example, a poor, underdeveloped country with land and farmers but few schools and factories might be able to produce grain more "efficiently" (meaning cheaply) than tractors. In contrast, a developed country such as the United States, with its assembly-line factories and skilled workers, may be able to produce tractors (and other manufactured goods) more efficiently than grain. If so, according to the theory, each country will benefit if the underdeveloped country specializes in producing grain, some of which it can trade for tractors, and the developed country specializes in producing tractors, some of which it can trade for grain. Becker's application of this model to the family is straightforward: If women are more "efficient" at housework and child care relative to earning money—either because they are better at caring for children or because they tend to be paid less than men—and men are more efficient at earning money rather than at housework and child care, both will benefit if the wife specializes in housework and child care and the husband specializes in paid work outside the home. Consequently, the model predicts that in the marriage market women will search for good providers and men will search for good homemakers. We might call this the **specialization model** of the marriage market.

The Income-Pooling Model But the specialization model no longer fits the marriage market well. Consider a set of 18 characteristics of potential marriage partners that was presented to a sample of college students in 1939 and then again to college samples in 1956, 1967, 1977, 1984/1985, and 1996 (Buss, Shackelford, Kirkpatrick, & Larsen, 2001). The students were asked to rank the characteristics in order of importance to them. Several of the most highly valued characteristics hardly changed their rankings: dependable character, emotional stability and maturity, and pleasing disposition were among the top five at all times. What's of interest are the characteristics that increased or decreased in the rankings over the decades. Table 7.1 shows, for men and women, characteristics that increased in value (defined as increasing by at least three ranks) or decreased in value (decreasing at least three ranks), along with their final, 1996 rank.

specialization model a model of the marriage market in which women specialize in housework and child care and men specialize in paid work outside the home

---

[8] See, for example, Lichter, McLaughlin & Ribar (2002).

[9] See Becker (1991).

Table 7.1 Changes in the Importance College Students Attach to Characteristics of Potential Marriage Partners, 1939–1996

CHARACTERISTICS THAT HAVE INCREASED IN VALUE (1996 RANKING IN PARENTHESES)

FOR MEN	FOR WOMEN
Love (1)	Love (1)
Education (5)	Education (5)
Sociability (7)	Sociability (8)
Good looks (8)	Good looks (13)
Similar educational background (12)	
Good financial prospects (13)	

CHARACTERISTICS THAT HAVE DECREASED IN VALUE (1996 RANKINGS IN PARENTHESES)

FOR MEN	FOR WOMEN
Desire for home and children (9)	Ambition, industriousness (7)
Refinement, neatness (11)	Good health (9)
Good cook, homemaker (14)	Refinement, neatness (7)
Chastity (16)	Chastity (17)

(*Source:* Buss, Shackelford, Kirkpatrick, & Larson, 2001)

It's clear from Table 7.1 that characteristics associated with intimacy and companionship, such as love, sociability, and good looks (the last of which is ranked higher by men than by women), have increased in value for both men and women. But notice, in addition, that good financial prospects increased in importance for men, which suggests that men increasingly value the earnings prospects of potential wives. Moreover, education, which can cannote both shared cultural values and better earnings prospects, increased for both men and women. The bottom half of the table shows that characteristics associated with domesticity, such as caring about home and children, being a good cook, and being refined and neat have declined in value for men. For women, characteristics associated with being a good provider, such as good health, ambition, and industriousness, have declined in value. For both men and women, the value of chastity declined in importance, reflecting the greater acceptance of premarital sexual activity.

Overall, the changes in the rankings are consistent with a newer marriage bargain in which, relative to earlier in the twentieth century, the following conditions hold: (1) Both men and women place more importance on companionship and intimacy, (2) men place more importance on a woman's earning power, (3) men place less importance on a woman's domestic skills, and (4) women place less importance on signs that the man is a good provider. The changes suggest that the breadwinning-for-homemaking bargain is less salient to young adults today. Of course, these studies only included college students, but other more representative surveys suggest similar conclusions (South, 1991).

In general, the specialization model of the marriage market predicted that women with less education and lower earnings would be *more* likely to marry than better-educated, higher-earning women. The former group, it was said, has more to gain by marrying a man who will earn money while they specialize in housework and child care. But the newer bargain suggests an **income-pooling model** of the marriage market, in which both spouses work for pay and pool their incomes. Under this model, a woman with greater earning potential should be more likely to marry because she is more attractive to men seeking to pool incomes. This now seems to be the case: Men with higher earning potential are more likely to marry women with higher earning potential than they were a generation or two ago—suggesting a shift from a specialization model to an income-pooling model. The change may have occurred in the 1980s. Sweeney (2002) and Sweeney and Cancian (2004) compared data for young adults in the 1970s, on the one hand, and the 1980s and early 1990s; they found that the tendency for men and women with higher earning potential to marry each other strengthened over that period. This development probably means that young men are paying more attention to young women's earning potential when they choose a wife because women tend to earn more than they used to. (But it could also mean that women are paying even more attention to men's earning potential than in the past because college-educated men now earn so much more than men without high school educations [England, 2004]).

Comparisons across countries also support this shift in the marriage market. Ono (2003) found that in Japan, where few women work and the specialization model would seem to apply, women with more income are less likely to marry, whereas in Sweden and the United States, where many women work and the income-pooling model is gaining strength, women with more income are more likely to marry. Several other studies of the United States also show that women with greater earning potential have higher rates of marriage (Lichter, McLaughlin, Kephart, & Landry, 1992; Qian & Preston, 1993; Oppenheimer, Blossfeld, & Wackerow, 1995; Oppenheimer & Lew, 1995; McLaughlin & Lichter, 1997), although one study found that women's earning potential was unrelated to the likelihood of marriage (Xie, Raymo, Goyette, & Thornton, 2003).

It appears, then, that the marriage bargain now includes the preference, for most couples, that both spouses will contribute to the family's income. Why has this change occurred? In part, it reflects the greater acceptance of married women's work outside the home. In addition, it reflects the prolonged stagnation of men's wages since the early 1970s. Valerie Oppenheimer (2003) finds that young men with a recent history of unstable employment are less likely to marry than are men with stable employment; but they are *more* likely to cohabit—as if cohabiting is a fallback position for young men whose employment situations are not adequate for marrying. Her article implies that the declining employment prospects of less-educated young men may be a factor in the increase in cohabitation and the later age at first marriage.

Income-pooling model a model of the marriage market in which both spouses work for pay and pool their incomes

Quick Review

- A specialization model of the marriage market, in which men traded earning potential for women's housework and childbearing efforts, predominated in the mid-twentieth century.
- An income-pooling model, in which women and men both offer earning potential, arose over the past few decades.
- The greater acceptance of married women's work outside the home and the declining earning power of men without college educations underlie this transition.

■ Social Change and Intimate Unions

Prior to about 1960, marriage was the only acceptable way for adults to have intimate partnerships and to raise children. So dominant was marriage that people who never married were viewed as having incomplete lives and as being perhaps defective in some way. Never-married older women were derided as "spinsters" or "old maids." A historian labeled the period from 1850 to 1960 in Britain, which had similar trends, "the age of mandatory marriage" (Gillis, 1985). During this age a strict division of labor arose, in which husbands were to work outside the home and wives were to manage the home and care for children. But great changes have occurred since the mid-twentieth century.

CHANGES IN UNION FORMATION

Table 7.2 summarizes the changes since the 1950s in the process by which adults form intimate partnerships and in the way they relate to their partners. In the 1950s, most young women and many young men did not have sex until they were engaged or married. If a premarital pregnancy occurred, the mother and father usually married quickly to avoid the stigma of an "illegitimate" birth. Cohabitation was scandalous and virtually unknown among the middle class; and even among the poor it was less common than today. Nearly everyone married, and they did so at younger ages than before or since. The birthrate rose to a twentieth-century

Table 7.2 Changes in Union Formation Since the Mid-Twentieth Century

	1950s	1990s
When do sexual relations begin?	For a majority of women and many men, sexual relations began only after engagement or marriage.	Sexual relations typically begin many years before a union is formed.
What happens when premarital pregnancies occur?	Usually led to a hasty marriage because childbearing outside of marriage was highly stigmatized.	Much less likely to lead to marriage because childbearing outside of marriage is more acceptable. Still, many cohabiting couples marry when a pregnancy occurs.
Who cohabits?	Cohabitation is common only among the poor; it is not considered respectable among the nonpoor.	About half of all young adults will cohabit before they marry. It has become an important part of the process of finding a marital partner.
Who marries and when?	About 95 percent of whites and almost 90 percent of blacks married; average age at marriage was younger than in any other decade.	90 percent or more of whites will marry, and about two-thirds of blacks will marry. Typical ages at marriage are several years older than in the 1950s.
What is the economic bargain?	Men typically exchanged their earning power for women's housework and child rearing effort. Middle-class and working-class married women rarely worked outside the home.	Men and women typically pool their earnings and achieve economies of scale (i.e., only one mortgage to pay for). Women with higher earning potential are more likely to marry.
What is the cultural expectation?	Companionship and satisfaction through playing the roles of spouse and parent.	Ongoing self-development, intimacy, and communication.

high. Women expected to stay at home after marrying, and men expected to be the family's sole earner—the so-called "good provider" (Bernard, 1981). Husbands and wives expected to be loving companions and friends and to derive great pleasure from being successful spouses and parents.

As we enter the twenty-first century, nearly all these conditions have changed. Most young adults begin to have sex many years before they marry; and better birth control technology and legalized abortion make it easier for them to do so. The typical age at marriage is much higher than at midcentury; and the proportion of people who never marry has grown. Unmarried women can give birth to children outside of marriage with little stigma, although many cohabiting couples marry before the child is born if a pregnancy occurs. About half of all young adults cohabit prior to marrying. For some, cohabitation is an alternative form of single life, a kind of twenty-first century analog to the steady dating relationships of the mid-twentieth century. For others, it is a way to see whether they and their partners are compatible enough to marry. And for a few who are disproportionately low-income minority group members, it is a form of marriage without legal recognition—a longer, informal partnership in which children are born and raised.

The marital bargain has also changed. It is based more on a pooling of joint earnings than on an exchange of men's earnings for women's housework and child care. Men are still required to be good, steady earners in order to be acceptable as husbands; but increasingly women are expected to be good earners as well. Although women still provide more of the housework and child care, the marital bargain typically calls for men to do more work at home than was the case at midcentury. Women with higher earning potential may be using their economic attractiveness to strike a bargain that results in a more equitable distribution of work in the home. On an emotional level, wives and husbands are increasingly concerned with self-development, intimacy, and communicating their feelings and desires. In addition, more lesbian and gay couples are living openly in same-sex cohabiting relationships. Like heterosexual couples, many are concerned with self-development, intimacy, and communication.

Many of the changes since the mid-twentieth century have weakened the role of marriage in personal life. In fact, given the greater acceptability of alternative living arrangements, one might ask why so many people still marry. I have argued that marriage still allows a partner to have greater trust in the commitment the other partner has to the relationship. Marriage requires a commitment to a long-term, possibly lifelong, relationship, although that advantage is weaker than it used to be.

In addition, marriage is still a marker of prestige and distinction. In fact, as fewer people marry and young adults take longer to do it, the prestige that marriage confers may be growing. Marriage is now, in part, a step people take to distinguish themselves from others. Some cohabiting couples are postponing marriage until after they have achieved job stability, have amassed enough savings to buy a home, and in some cases have had children together. Marriage used to be the foundation of adult personal life; now it is sometimes the crowning achievement. Church ceremonies and wedding parties seem to be popular, even among people who aren't particularly religious, in part because they demonstrate commitment, as noted above, but also because they show family and friends that one's personal life is a success. Nevertheless, despite these advantages, it is clear that marriage does not hold as privileged a position in our family system as it did in midcentury. The gains to marriage, relative to alternatives, are perceived to be lower on average today than they were 40 or 50 years ago.

The marital bargain is increasingly based on pooling the earnings of wives and husbands.

MARRIAGE AS AN ONGOING PROJECT

Perhaps the most fundamental change in marriage is this one: Whereas in earlier times what mattered most in a marriage was how well you and your spouse carried out your duties, now what matters most is whether the marriage helps you to achieve a more fulfilling sense of self, to grow as an individual, or to experience a greater level of personal satisfaction. Intimacy and love are now a quest for fulfillment and identity (Swidler, 2001). Unlike in the past, the quest doesn't end when you find a marriage partner; on the contrary, it involves a continuing effort to find a better personal life through an evolving relationship. It also implies a new model of adulthood. In the old model, you developed an identity in young adulthood, found a partner compatible with that identity, got married, and then further personality development stopped. Now there is a cultural imperative to keep changing and developing your identity throughout adulthood in order to maintain, or better yet, increase your personal fulfillment.

Developing a satisfying sense of self through love and sexual expression, then, becomes an ongoing project throughout adulthood. To carry out this project, a married person must be able to communicate openly and honestly with his or her spouse about thoughts and feelings. Consequently, communication and understanding become highly valued qualities. But suppose one partner isn't satisfied with his or her self-development in the relationship. Or suppose one partner feels he or she has gotten all the personal benefits out of the relationship that are possible. Then, given the new emphasis on self-development as the standards by which to judge intimate relationships, there is little reason for the unsatisfied partner to stay in the relationship. On the contrary, the emphasis on self-development encourages this partner to leave.

In this way, the emphasis on self-development devalues qualities such as commitment, trust, and permanence (Swidler, 2001). And herein lies an important reason for the sharp rise in the divorce rate in the United States and other Western nations in the 1960s and 1970s and the continued high rates since then (see Chapter 12). The cultural changes surrounding love and marriage have made it more acceptable for a person to leave a relationship if he or she feels personally dissatisfied. One is no longer expected to keep a marriage together for the sake of the children. This emphasis on self-fulfillment and development in marriage has placed high expectations on the relationship. Only in the twentieth century has marriage had to bear such a heavy responsibility for personal happiness, and the institution may not be able to match the expectations spouses now have. To be sure, there are other important causes of the post-1960 rise in divorce, foremost among them the increasing economic independence of women and the declining economic prospects for men without college degrees. (This topic will be examined in detail in Chapter 12.) Nevertheless, the cultural changes in the way people evaluate love and marriage have certainly played a significant role.

The increased emphasis on self-development in marriage has been criticized as creating shallow, potentially exploitative relationships in which each partner seeks what's best for his or her own development—but not what's best for the marriage and for their children. Yet there is also a positive side to this form of marriage. Communication and negotiation may allow couples to attain greater intimacy than if they were forced to retain their initial way of relating. Although it is easy to criticize the excesses of the search for a more fulfilling personal life, the ability of couples to increase their satisfaction through communication and openness may revitalize some marriages. The independence of the partners may also create a more democratic marriage in which husband and wives are equals. Giddens even holds out hope that the democratic style of negotiating in the "pure relationship" could spread to other arenas, improving public discussions of political issues, making government decisions open and more accountable (Giddens, 1992).

The egalitarianism of late-modern marriage has also relieved men of the obligation to be the sole supporters of their families. Its flexible roles have provided men with the opportunity to be more involved in their children's roles. In these ways, the individualized marriage holds out the possibility of a fuller life, and a more equal partnership for both spouses. Whether the emergence of the individualized marriage is favorable for children is another issue, which will be examined in Chapter 9. Moreover, even for the spouses, the possibilities are not always realized: Few fathers share the child care and housework equally, and power imbalances remain a feature of many marriages, as the next chapter will show.

Looking Back

1. **What is the history of courtship and dating?** In the United States and other Western nations, for centuries young adults went about finding a spouse through the publicly visible process of courtship. The practice declined in the United States after 1900 due to migration to large cities, growing affluence, and the emergence of adolescence as a protected time between childhood and adulthood. The rise of dating after 1900 placed courtship on an economic basis and transferred power from young women (and their parents) to young men. The heyday of dating was probably 1945 to 1965; during the 1970s and 1980s, as the average age at marriage rose and cohabitation became more common, the practice became less closely connected to marriage.

2. **How has marriage changed over the past century?** The institutional marriage was held together by community pressure and the authority of the family head. But by the mid-twentieth century, it had been eclipsed by the companionship marriage, which was held together more by mutual affection and intimacy. The ideal type of companionate marriage was the single-earner breadwinner–homemaker family that flourished in the 1950s. Beginning in the late 1960s, this model was overtaken by the individualized marriage, in which both spouses were increasingly concerned with personal growth and self-fulfillment. In the individualized marriage, the relationship between spouses tends to be seen as an ongoing project that is open to negotiation and change.

3. **What is marriage like today?** Although Americans now have more choices about their personal lives, most still marry. Marriage still provides some benefits that cohabitation does not, such as greater trust in one's partner's commitment. However, people also see marriage as a symbol of achieving a successful adult life. They build up to marriage, postponing it until they have all of the prerequisites in place. They use religious wedding ceremonies (rather than courthouse weddings) to display their personal achievements to friends and relatives.

4. **What is the role of cohabitation in the American family system?** Prior to 1970, cohabitation was found largely among the poor. Since then the practice has expanded greatly at all income levels. In the United States today, a majority of marriages are now preceded by a period of cohabitation. These unions tend to lead within a few years either to marriage or a breakup. Cohabitation is a diverse phenomenon that includes not only childless young adults, but also couples with children. A substantial share of the children who are officially born outside of marriage are actually born to two cohabiting parents. For some people, cohabitation is part of the marriage process; for others it is an alternative way of being single; and for others, particularly low-income minority group members, it is an alternative to marriage.

5. **How does the marriage market work?** The marriage market—a model that is widely used by social scientists—consists of individuals who are searching for a spouse in a particular geographic area, who have a set of preferences concerning the type of person they wish to find and a set of resources to offer in return. The predominant marriage bargain at mid-twentieth century, based on the specialization model of marriage, involved a husband who traded his earnings in return for child care and housework by his wife. This model of marriage no longer fits the present-day marriage market. In particular, evidence suggests that both men and women now prefer partners with good earnings potential.

 Go to the Online Learning Center at www.mhhe.com/cherlin5 to test your knowledge of the chapter concepts and key terms.

Study Questions

1. What are the differences between nineteenth-century courtship and twentieth-century dating?

2. What did Burgess mean when he wrote that marriage was "in transition from an institution to a companionship"?

3. What distinguishes the individualized marriage from the companionate marriage?

4. What are the symbolic rewards of being married in the United States today?

5. Why is it difficult to tell whether marriage improves the well-being of women and men?

6. The "pure relationship" is an ideal type. How close do cohabiting relationships of various kinds come to it?

7. What characteristics of women and men have become more highly valued on the marriage market in recent decades, and why?

8. Is marriage so weakened as an institution that it is likely to become just one of many possible adult lifestyles?

Key Terms

archival research   228
cohabitation   238
companionate marriage   225
courtship   219

enforceable trust   231
income-pooling model   249
individualized marriage   227
institutional marriage   223

marriage market   246
pure relationship   241
specialization model   247
union   217

Thinking about Families

The Private Family	The Public Family
Do people expect too much emotional satisfaction from a cohabiting partner or spouse?	Should the public be concerned about the rise of cohabitation and childbearing outside marriage?

Families on the Internet   www.mhhe.com/cherlin5

Note: While all the URLs listed were current as of the printing of this book, these sites often change. Please check our Web site (http://www.mhhe.com/cherlin5) for updates.

To investigate the market in Russian women who are willing to marry an American man, visit one of the many Web sites maintained by matchmaking firms like the one Randy Heisey used. When I entered "Russian brides" into a search engine, it returned the Web addresses of numerous matchmaking agencies. For information on the modern mail-order bride industry, go to www.bridesbymail.com, which includes an online resource library. It lists 75 Web sites offering introductions to Russian women, 15 Web sites for Ukrainian women, and 35 for women elsewhere in Eastern Europe.

In recent years, a loosely knit "marriage movement" has arisen to promote marriage. Visit the Web site of the Coalition for Marriage, Family, and Couples Education (www.smartmarriages.com) to obtain information. What is the case this group is making for marriage?

Chapter Eight

Work and Families

Looking Forward

1. How has married women's work changed over the past half-century?

2. How has the amount of housework and child care done by husbands and wives changed over the past half-century?

3. How does our society treat the labor of caring for others?

4. How do sociologists think about power and authority within marriage?

5. What are some of the strains working parents can experience?

6. How is the workplace responding to the needs of working parents?

"After I started earning money," a billing clerk who was married to a forklift operator told a sociologist, "my husband showed me more respect" (Hochschild, 1989). She was not alone. A woman who earned less than her husband for years noticed a sudden difference when she took a high-paying job. One evening she told her husband she was tired, and he replied, "Well, you work as hard as I do." He had never said that before, she told a reporter (Goldstein, 2000). "A little light went off in my head: 'Oh, now I make what you do, I work as hard as you do,' " she said. Unasked, her husband started to do the laundry. "I'd say, 'I need to vacuum today' and the next thing I know, he'd be doing the vacuuming."

Another woman who earned far less than her husband complained to interviewers:

Gordon still has to have the last word on everything. We get annoyed with each other over that, but when I start to push back, he reminds me just who supports me and the children. He doesn't always bring that up, but if I start to win an argument or make more sense about something we should do, I think he gets frustrated and so he gives me his big final line which is something like, "If you're so smart, why don't you earn more money?" or how dumb I am 'cause if I had to go out and support myself I'd be a big fizzle. (Blumstein & Schwartz, 1983)

As these women's comments show, many Americans still believe that paid work is important but that unpaid work—including the child care, cooking, cleaning, and emotional support that is provided, mostly by women—is less important. In fact, as we will see, unpaid work in the home isn't even counted as work in official government statistics. That's why a husband might think that his wife works as hard as he does only if she makes as much money as he does. Or why he might think that his paid work supports his children but her unpaid work does not. Or why he might think that he should have the last word on all decisions unless his wife earns a comparable amount of money.

Some people still think that it's "natural" to divide a family's work so that husbands do paid work outside the home and wives do unpaid work in the home. But that conception of the division of labor—the so-called breadwinner–homemaker family—didn't arise until the mid-nineteenth century and peaked in the mid-twentieth century. [➡ p. 66] It was based on the assumption that wives would be available to do unpaid work. Since the mid-twentieth century, tens of millions of married women have taken paying jobs outside the home. Moreover, the number of single parents, most of them women, has increased greatly. These changes have undermined the old system in which wives did almost all of the housework and child care for free. Most married couples and single parents must now pay some-one else to do part of this work or rely on kin, such as grandmothers, for unpaid help. And as they pay for child care, house cleaning, restaurant meals, and other services, they are suddenly seeing the value of the unpaid work wives used to provide. They are coming to appreciate not just how much it costs to replace wives' unpaid work but also how important this caring work is to maintaining a family. In this chapter, we will examine how families deal with the crowded schedules that often result when both parents (or the lone parent present) work outside the home. We will also examine the ways in which business and govern-ment are responding to these developments. And we will step back to consider, more generally, the meaning and importance of the work of caring for others.

The transformation from the breadwinner-homemaker model to a new, twenty-first-century model isn't finished. Even though wives commonly work out-side the home, many husbands still expect them to do more of the housework and child care. As this chapter will show, husbands are doing a larger portion of these tasks than was the case a few decades ago, but wives still do more. In part, this imbalance reflects wives' lower earnings, which are associated with having less power in their marriages (England & Farkas, 1986). That's why a woman might report that after she started earning money, her husband suddenly showed her more respect. To be sure, lower earnings aren't the only reason why wives typically have less power in their marriages. Both wives and husbands may have been socialized to expect that husbands should be the head of the household, the person who makes the final decisions. Nevertheless, earnings and employment are important determinants of the relations between wives and husbands. In this chapter, then, we will also explore differences in power and authority between wives and husbands and the consequences of those differences for daily life.

From Single-Earner to Dual-Earner Marriages

In the early twentieth century, few white wives worked outside the home; but many earned money by taking in boarders and lodgers or doing piecework. [➥ p. 51] However, by the mid-twentieth century, white wives had largely with-drawn from these informal sources of income. They had withdrawn because of increases in men's earnings and because of reduced demand for home services such as lodging. Teenage and young adult children stayed in school longer and worked fewer hours, often keeping for personal use most of what they did earn. The two-parent family usually had only one paid worker—the husband. The 1950s were probably the high point of the single-earner, two-parent family in the United States. Many commentators refer to this breadwinner-homemaker family as the "traditional" family, but the history of women's work demonstrates how atypical the single-earner family was.

MOTHERS ENTER THE LABOR FORCE

Figure 8.1 shows the low levels of married women's work outside the home at the middle of the twentieth century and the great changes since then. The two lines show the percentage of married women with children who were in the

FIGURE 8.1
Labor force participation rates of married women with children under age 18, by age of youngest child, 1948–2004. (*Sources:* U.S. Bureau of Labor Statistics [1988]; and U.S. Bureau of the Census, Statistical Abstract of the United States, various years)

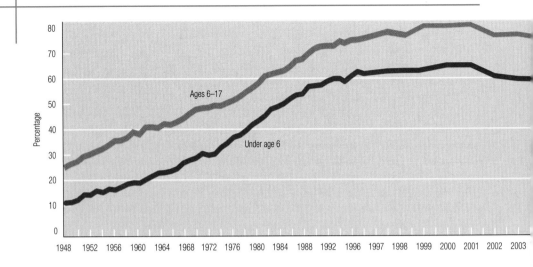

| labor force | all people who are either working outside the home or looking for work |

labor force for every year since 1948. Government statistical agencies consider the **labor force** to be all people who are either working outside the home or looking for such work. In 1948, only about one-fourth of married women whose youngest children were at least six-years-old (and therefore in school) were in the labor force, as were only about one-tenth of married women with children under age six.

At first, the rate of participation increased faster among those whose children were in school. Because women began childbearing at relatively younger ages in the 1950s and early 1960s and rarely had more than three or four children, they were still at a prime working age when all their children reached school age. With school to use as a child care center and less child rearing effort necessary at home, many women with school-aged children reentered the labor force. Starting in the 1970s, the rate increased faster among those with at least one pre-school-aged child. The rates leveled off around 2000 and have declined modestly since then. For the moment, at least, the historic rise in married women's labor force participation rates seems to have peaked. In 2004, 76 percent of all married women with school-aged children, and 59 percent of those with pre-school-aged children, were in the labor force, although a majority were working part-time (Cohen & Bianchi, 1999; U.S. Bureau of the Census, 2005l).

BEHIND THE RISE

Several factors contributed to the increase in married women's labor force participation. During the twentieth century, the service sector of the economy expanded greatly. The **service sector** consists of the workers who provide personal services such as education, health care, communication, restaurant meals, legal representation, entertainment, and so forth. Many of the jobs in the service sector had come to be stereotyped as women's work; these jobs usually required some education but paid less than men's work. Examples include secretary, nurse, and elementary school teacher. As the demand for these kinds of jobs increased, wages increased (although they remained lower than men's wages) and more married women were drawn into the labor force (Oppenheimer, 1970).

| service sector | workers who provide personal services such as education, health care, communication, restaurant meals, legal representation, entertainment, and so forth |

The movement of married women into the paid work force is one of the most important changes in family life.

In addition, as the population shifted from farms to cities, each generation (except for the parents of the baby boomers) had fewer children. There was no longer a need for lots of child labor to help on the farm; moreover, the rising wages of women in the labor force meant that women who stayed home were passing up more and more income (Butz & Ward, 1979). As a result, parents' preferred strategy was to have fewer children and to invest more resources in each—to pay for college education or job training courses, for example. This strategy reduced the number of years in which young children would be present in the home and therefore freed married women sooner from child care, the major responsibility that had kept them out of the labor force. Moreover, the decline in the wages of men without college educations since the early 1970s [➡ p. 113] has motivated many wives to take paying jobs. Finally, the high divorce rate of the past several decades made it increasingly risky for married women to leave the labor force and let their job skills deteriorate. Given the low amount of child support payments that most divorced women receive (see Chapter 12), they need to be able to rely on their earning power.

A PROFOUND CHANGE

This great movement of married women into the labor force is one of the most important changes in American family life in the past century. It has profoundly altered women's and men's lives. It has affected the balance of power between women and men, as will be discussed in this chapter. It has been instrumental in the shift from the companionship marriage to the independent marriage, as described in the previous chapter. It has provided the backdrop for debates on issues such as abortion, about which women whose identity is bound up in home and child rearing tend to disagree with women who value working outside the home (see Chapter 14). To be sure, the change has been less pronounced for women from poor or minority backgrounds, who have always had a greater need to work.

FIGURE 8.2
Labor force participation
rates for U.S. women by
age, 1970 and 2004.
(*Sources:* Bianchi & Spain
[1986], Figure 5.1; U.S.
Bureau of Labor Statistics
2005c)

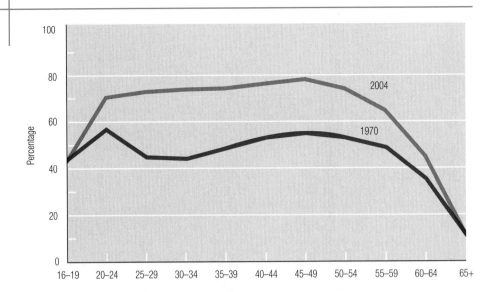

For example, census statistics show that in 1975, when only 35 percent of white married women with pre-school-aged children were in the labor force, 55 percent of comparable African American women were. Still, labor force participation has increased sharply among African American women as well: By 2003, 71 percent of married African American women with pre-school-aged children were in the labor force (compared with 60 percent of whites) (U.S. Bureau of the Census, 2004a).

THE CURRENT SITUATION

By the beginning of the twenty-first century, it was common for married women to remain at work outside the home from young adulthood to retirement. More-over, the post-1960 rise in divorce and childbearing outside marriage created a large number of unmarried mothers who needed to provide their own incomes. This increasingly continuous labor force participation can be seen more clearly in Figure 8.2. For two time points, 1970 and 2004, the figure displays the percentage of women who were participating in the labor force, according to the women's ages. In 1970, the percentage of women in the labor force was higher for women in their early twenties than for teenagers; but then it dropped among women in their mid-twenties and early thirties, which are the most common years for hav-ing small children at home. The percentage then rose again to a second peak among women in their forties, whose children tend to be older. Therefore, the second peak reflects women who returned to the labor force after their children entered school. This double-peaked pattern typifies a society in which many women enter the labor force before marriage, drop out while raising young chil-dren, and then enter again. Yet by 2004 the dip between the peaks had disap-peared; rather, the graph has a single, high plateau for women between about 25 and 50, reflecting women's higher and more-continuous levels of work outside the home throughout the prime working years of adulthood.

Despite women's increased attachment to the labor force and rising wages, it is still the case that they earn substantially less, on average, than men. From 1960 to about 1980, the average woman who worked full-time, year round, earned about

"Bring Your Daughter to Work Day" allows mothers to interest their daughters in jobs and careers.

60 cents for each dollar earned by a comparable man.[1] To be sure, women have worked outside the home less, on average, than men have during their adult lives, so they have accrued less seniority, on-the-job training, and so forth. Yet differences in job experience appear to account for only about one-fourth to onehalf of the gap (England & Farkas, 1986). A substantial proportion reflects a more complex process involving employer discrimination and the resultant way that parents socialize their daughters. (See *Families and Public Policy:* The Earnings Gap, on p. 98.)

Since 1980, however, women's median earnings have increased faster than men's, reaching 80 cents for each dollar a man earned in 2004, compared to 63 cents when the statistic was first calculated in 1979 (U.S. Bureau of Labor Statistics, 2005a). Women's wages rose during this period because some women workers were doing better economically and some men were doing worse. As for women doing better, demographers Daphne Spain and Suzanne Bianchi (1996) note that in the 1980s, women born during the baby boom were finishing school and entering the labor force. Conversely, the mothers of the baby boomers were exiting the labor force to retire. Since the mothers had married at early ages and had children soon after marrying, they had received less education than their daughters and spent less time working outside the home prior to having children. As a result, their earning potential had been limited. In contrast, their daughters had received more education, postponed marriage and childbearing, and spent more time in the labor force before having children—all of which had increased their earning potential. Well-educated women moved into professional occupations in unprecedented numbers: Women's share of law school degrees rose from 5 percent in 1970 to 48 percent in 2002, and their share of medical school degrees rose from 8 percent to 44 percent during the same period (U.S. Bureau of the Census, 2005k). So in the 1980s, 1990s, and early 2000s, as the baby boom daughters (and now their granddaughters) replaced their mothers in the labor force, the average earnings of college-educated women increased.

---

[1] This figure represents the ratio of women's median earnings to men's median earnings, for year-round, full-time workers.

Yet that is only half the story. Earnings did not rise much for baby boom daughters without college educations, most of whom were clerical and service workers such as secretaries, bank tellers, or cafeteria workers. The men they tended to marry—baby boom sons without a college education—saw their incomes decline as skilled blue-collar jobs became scarce. Therefore, the ratio of women's earnings to men's earnings rose among the less well educated not because women were earning substantially more but rather because men were earning substantially less. The rising ratio demonstrates how important wives' earnings have become in maintaining the standard of living of married couples who do not have college educations (Bianchi & Spain, 1996).

Among African Americans, the ratio of women's earnings to men's earnings has long been higher than among whites. In the first half of the twentieth century, discrimination severely limited job opportunities for both black women and men, but black women were hired as household workers for white families—jobs that may have been demeaning but were at least available and steady. In 1940, 60 percent of all black women in the labor force were private household workers. Beginning in the 1960s—a decade of civil rights legislation and economic prosperity—employment opportunities for African Americans improved. The improvement, however, was greater for black women, who took advantage of the expanding opportunities in service sector occupations, than for black men. By 1990, just 2 percent of black women were household workers (Bianchi, 1995). What is more, young black women were earning virtually as much, on average, as young white women. Because black men's economic progress (like the progress of less-well-educated white men) lagged behind, the median earnings of black women rose to 89 cents for every dollar earned by black men in 2004, compared with 80 cents for every dollar among whites (U.S. Bureau of Labor Statistics, 2005a).

Quick Review

- The percentage of married women who work outside the home increased greatly during the last half of the twentieth century.
- The expansion of the service sector of the economy was a factor in this increase in paid work outside the home.
- The drop in the number of children per family also was a factor.
- Currently, most married women are in the labor force almost continuously from their twenties through their fifties.

Care Work and Marital Power

We have seen that the role of women in the paid labor market has changed dramatically over the past half-century. Change has also occurred in housework and child care. Let us view the trends in housework over the past few decades and consider a new perspective—care work studies— that has arisen in response to the trends.

WHO DOES THE HOUSEWORK?

Figure 8.3 presents the results of studies done in 1965, 1975, and 1998 in which national samples of adults were asked to keep diaries of the amount of time they spent on various activities during a week. The figure displays the average weekly

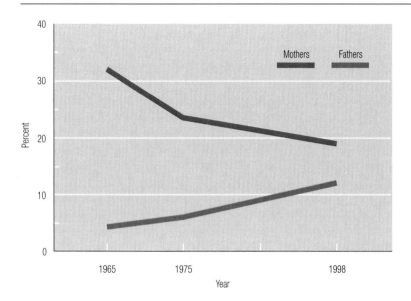

FIGURE 8.3
Mean weekly time spent doing housework for mothers and fathers, from time diary surveys of American adults, 1965 to 1998. (*Source:* Sayer, 2005)

hours spent on housework by married mothers and fathers. (Major categories included cooking, meal cleanup, cleaning, laundry, outdoor chores, repairs, and paying bills.) The blue line shows the average time spent by mothers dropped substantially, from 32 hours to 19 hours. As the burnt orange line shows, during the same period the average time spent by fathers increased from 4.4 to 12 hours. Overall, these trends suggest the following conclusions:

- The division of housework has become less unequal. In 1965, women's average hours of housework were about seven times greater than men's; by 1998, they were about one and one-half times greater. This declining ratio reflects both a large decrease in the time women spend in housework and a smaller but still substantial increase in men's time spent in housework.
- The total amount of housework done by married couples has declined, because women have reduced the time they spend doing housework more than men have increased theirs. Married couples have replaced some of the housework they used to do by purchasing services such as restaurant meals or housecleaning. They may also have become accustomed to slightly dirtier homes and more wrinkled clothing than married couples of the past.

In sum, if the question is who does the housework, the answer is that women still do more than men; but the division is much more equitable than in the past. In addition, couples increasingly pay other people to do some of the housework. Daily life depends not only on the couple's labor but also on cleaning services and McDonald's.

RETHINKING CARING WORK

It's clear that society can no longer rely on the unpaid labor of stay-at-home wives and mothers to provide the care that family members need. In this sense, the movement of women into the labor force has created a "crisis in care" (Glenn, 2000a). The crisis has also spawned a growing body of social research, theory, and advocacy on the topic of caring. In this new literature, "care work" has emerged as the central

care work face-to-face
activity in which one person
meets the needs of another
who cannot fully care for
her-or himself

concept—one might even speak of a care work movement (Stone, 2000). Some authors conceive of care work very broadly, but I will propose a narrower definition
consistent with this book's focus on families. Let us define **care work** as face-to-
face activity in which one person meets the needs of another person who cannot
fully care for her- or himself. The person who does the care work is the caregiver;
and the person who gets the care is the care-receiver. Within families, children, the
frail elderly, and the ill or disabled are the obvious care receivers. Caring for healthy
adults is a gray area: One could argue that wives and husbands perform care work
by providing emotional support to each other and that wives provide further care
by providing their husbands with household goods and services. Many writers
would include these activities, too, as care work, although I will not.

Breaking the Work/Family Boundary   The writers in the care work
movement put forth at least four principles. First, they argue that the separation between what goes on in families and what goes on in the world of work is artificial
and should be abolished. As the suffix "work" in care work suggests, these authors
maintain that what caregivers do should be thought of as work. This seems obvious
when one thinks about Rowena Bautista, hired to care for an American family's children while her remittances, in turn, paid someone to care for her own children in a
Filipino village. [➡ p. 144] It may be obvious when one thinks about the many
workers in child care centers and nursing homes (see Chapter 10). But it wasn't obvious a half-century ago, when much of the care work in families was undertaken
by wives in their own homes. Stay-at-home wives did the work of meeting the
needs of other family members for daily sustenance, clothing, a clean and healthy
home environment, and an esthetically pleasing home. Yet their contributions
were—and, to some extent, still are—hidden. For example, when the U.S. government computes the total value of the goods and services bought and sold in the nation, the gross domestic product, or GDP, it ignores unpaid care work. The care an
adult daughter provides to an elderly parent doesn't count. But if the same daughter
hires a home healthcare worker to tend to her parent, the workers' wages are
added to the GDP (Folbre, 2001).

Care Work as a Public Responsibility   Second, care work, it is argued, should be considered a public as well as a private responsibility. In the past,
caring for children and the elderly has not been recognized as a socially important
contribution. For instance, workers can accrue eligibility for Social Security retirement benefits only through paid work. Unpaid work does not apply. A full-time
housewife builds eligibility for Social Security benefits only through her husband's
paid work—suggesting that the work she does is purely a private, family matter
(see Chapter 14). But children can be considered public goods [➡ p. 11] because
when they grow up, they will do socially useful work that will benefit parents and
nonparents alike. For example, they will pay the taxes that will allow Social Security benefits to be paid (Folbre, 2001). So in rearing children, parents do work that
will benefit others. In the terms of this book, the care work movement suggests
that we view caring labor not just through the lens of the private family but also
through the lens of the public family. To be sure, care work provides private, emotional satisfaction for family members, but it also provides a publicly useful service.

Valuing Caring Labor   Third, caring labor, the writers maintain, is often
underpaid, undervalued, and even demeaned relative to other kinds of work

American society has relied on stay-at-home wives to perform much of the care of infirm elderly parents.

(Tronto, 1993). Recall the women quoted at the beginning of this chapter who received more respect from their husbands when they worked for pay than when they did care work at home. Care is often considered "women's work," a phrase that often implies unpaid or low-paid work of marginal importance. Women constitute the vast majority of paid caregivers: 95 percent of child care workers and 89 percent of health aides, for example (U.S. Bureau of the Census, 2005l). Moreover, they are disproportionately drawn from the less advantaged racial-ethnic groups—such as immigrant Hispanic and Asian women like Rowena Bautista.

People who do paid care work earn less than people who do comparable work that does not involve care. Three researchers estimated the "wage penalty" that women who are employed at child care centers or as nannies pay for doing care work: Even taking into account the skills required for the job, the education needed, and the prior work experience they tend to have, women who are employed as child care workers earn 26 percent less then women who work at comparable noncaring jobs (England, Budig, & Folbre, 2002). Other statistics tell the same story of low pay for child care work: A government earnings survey in 2004 reported that full-time child care workers had average hourly earnings of $9.42, which was two cents less than the average hourly earnings of garage and gas station workers (U.S. Bureau of Labor Statistics, 2005b).

Paula England (2005) presents three possible reasons why care work does not pay as much as noncaring work:

- As noted above, people tend to devalue and even demean labor that is thought of as "women's work," which care work historically has been. Employers either underestimate the value of the work women do or are culturally biased against paying women as much as they pay men for comparable work. For example, they may still believe it's more important to pay men well because they should be the breadwinners for their families—a common position a half-century ago.

- Labor that creates public goods, such as children who will grow up to be responsible members of society, tends to be underpaid. The reason is that it is difficult to stop people from "free-riding" [➡ p. 12], obtaining the benefits of the public goods without having to pay for them. I don't have to pay child care workers to benefit from the next generation of responsible workers because I will receive a Social Security check based on the taxes they will pay whether or not I have children.

- Many people find satisfaction in caring for others. In other words, they may find caring work intrinsically fulfilling and be willing to accept lower pay for a caring job than for a noncaring job. Child care workers may enjoy caring for children and accept low pay to enter the field, or they may get attached to the children they are caring for and not leave the job for a higher paying one. Employers of child care workers may, in a sense, take advantage of people's desire to help others by offering low wages.

The care work movement urges that caregivers such as child care workers and nursing home aides receive higher pay and greater respect.

Toward an Ethic of Care   Fourth, some writers urge the development of an "ethic of care" (Tronto, 1993) in American society. They argue that Americans overvalue individualism and autonomy and undervalue interdependence and caring. Americans are not just autonomous, they contend, but also interdependent. Therefore, everyone needs care on some level (Glenn, 2000a). As the old morality in which housewives were the guardians of caring has faded, the writers maintain, a newer morality of interdependence and mutual caring must replace it. Currently, women and economically disadvantaged individuals seem to value an ethic of care more than other Americans. For example, Michèle Lamont (2000) interviewed both white and African American working-class men. The white men, she wrote, evinced a "disciplined self," in which hard work and responsibility—showing up at work each day to earn a paycheck for one's family—are of paramount importance. In contrast, many of the African American men evinced more of a "caring self," in which solidarity with the less fortunate and generosity to those in need are central. An ethic of care would seek to balance these orientations to the world—to temper autonomy with interdependence, to augment personal responsibility with care for others. It is an attractive vision, but it isn't clear that it can successfully take root in late modern culture.

Quick Review

- Women have greatly reduced the hours of housework they do, while men have increased their housework hours by a lesser but still substantial amount.
- The movement of wives into the paid workforce limits their ability to provide unpaid caring work in the home.
- The resulting "crisis in care" has focused attention on care work, the face-to-face caregiving that used to be done in families by wives who weren't working for wages.
- From the care-work perspective, the caring that goes on in families should be considered as "work" whether or not the caregivers are paid.
- Caring labor is often undervalued; it is also done disproportionately by women and members of minority racial-ethnic groups.
- Some writers urge that American society adopt an "ethic of care."

MARITAL POWER AND AUTHORITY

The Meaning of Power   The increased labor force participation of married women and the growth of woman's incomes relative to men's might be expected to increase wives' power in marriages. A large research literature exists on marital power, in which the word "power" is used loosely in two different senses. These parallel the distinction that sociologists make between two ways in which a person or group of people can dominate others: power and authority (Gerth & Mills, 1946). **Power** is the ability to force a person to do something even against his or her will. It is the "possibility of imposing one's will upon the behavior of other persons" (Bendix, 1960), whether or not one actually exercises this power. For example, in some societies a man can take a second wife even if his first wife objects.

Sometimes widespread cultural beliefs and values lead some people to accept the domination of others. When a group of people acknowledges the right of others to supervise and control their behavior, sociologists say that those in command are in **authority.** In distinguishing between power and authority, the key words are "acknowledged" or "accepted." I have authority over an aspect of your life if you acknowledge and accept it. The great sociologist Max Weber wrote of "patriarchalism" (most people now use the term *patriarchy*) [➡ p. 96]—meaning a social system based on the domination of husbands and fathers over wives and children— in so-called traditional societies. Here, wrote Weber, the right of the husband to be dominant is supported by long-standing, widely held norms and values that both women and men accept. Therefore, Weber asserted, the patriarch rules through "traditional authority." A farm wife might accept the authority of her husband as part of the natural and correct order of society. But male authority isn't just a preindustrial phenomenon. When Adlai Stevenson told the Smith graduates in 1955 that their place in politics was to influence men through the role of housewife [➡ p. 105], he was repeating a widespread cultural belief that even many educated women themselves agreed with at the time. Many women in the audience that day must have accepted Stevenson's statement as part of the natural order of family life.

power the ability to force a person to do something even against his or her will

authority the acknowledged right of someone to supervise and control others' behavior

A wife's investment in raising her children is valuable to her husband but not to other prospective husbands, should she divorce.

In practice, however, it is often difficult to distinguish between power and authority. Your power over me may be latent—under the surface, hidden—most of the time, but it may be real nonetheless. For instance, if you have power over me, I may refrain from doing something I know you don't like—which means that you will obtain the results you want without having to flex a muscle or withhold a penny (Komter, 1989). If a wife knows her husband adamantly opposes her working outside the home and if she fears his anger, she may not even raise the issue of taking a job. An observer might not notice the wife's latent desire to work outside the home and the husband's power over her.

Moreover, persons in power may grant limited authority to their subordinates. I would argue that this often occurs in family life. During the nineteenth century, men accepted—even promoted—the authority of wives over moral and domestic matters. Yet wives' access to opportunities in the emerging world of paid work was limited. Today, wives often have substantial authority in the home because husbands—who do less domestic work—accept their wives' authority in this sphere. Still, most husbands retain substantial power, based on their greater earning power, and they still retain substantial authority, based on widely held, though changing, beliefs about what is proper behavior for women and men.

Marital Power and Wage Work

A number of writers have proposed that greater power accrues to family members who work for wages than to those who produce primarily for consumption at home. This proposition is, in fact, the core of Friedrich Engels's analysis, more than a century ago, of the source of inequality between women and men; and related propositions have been stated frequently by others since then. Whereas men are compensated with money for their work, women's valuable work of raising children, which creates the next generation of the labor force, is unpaid. Under socialism, Engels wrote, child care would be performed by public agencies and all women would work outside the home. Once this happened, Engels (and presumably his collaborator Karl Marx, who wrote nothing directly on the subject) believed, male domination would fade away: "The supremacy of the man in marriage is the simple consequence of his economic supremacy, and with the abolition of the latter will disappear of itself" (Engels, 1972). (Socialist nations have not, however, eliminated male domination.)

In nearly all societies, wives' ability to work for wages is limited because they must also carry out household and child rearing tasks. England and Farkas (1986) have argued that the investments of time and effort that a wife typically makes in the home—raising the children, providing emotional support to her husband, keeping in touch with the husband's relatives, and so forth—cannot easily be transferred to a new marriage. Rather, they are **relationship-specific investments,** efforts that are valuable only in a person's current relationship. That is to say, if a wife initiates a divorce, keeps custody of the children (as is usually the case), and wishes to remarry, she will likely find that the children—in whom she has invested much time and effort—lower her attractiveness to prospective husbands. Her efforts to nurture and support her first husband and her ties to his family also won't do her any good in the marriage market. If she doesn't wish to remarry, her income will probably be lower than before she divorced. Husbands, in contrast, tend to invest time and effort in their jobs, accruing, if they are fortunate, seniority, promotions, and wage and salary increases. These job investments can more easily be transferred to another marriage, because prospective wives will value the increased earnings (England & Farkas, 1986).

relationship-specific investment time spent on activities such as child rearing that are valuable only in a person's current relationship

Historically, African American married women have worked outside the home more than white married women; but the percentage who work has increased further in recent decades.

Even when mothers work for pay, they typically do not earn as much as women without children. In fact, the more children a woman has, the lower are her wages, on average, compared to women without children (Waldfogel, 1997; Budig & England, 2001; Avellar & Smock, 2003). Some researchers have called this gap the "motherhood penalty" or "family penalty." Part of the gap reflects the lesser work experience and education of mothers, relative to nonmothers. But a gap of about 4 percent per child still exists after differences in job experience, education, and other factors are taken into account. The reason for the so-called penalty is not clear. It is possible, some authors suggest, that mothers may be less productive on the job because of the distractions, responsibilities, and energy demands of childrearing. It is also possible that employers discriminate against mothers (possibly paying them less or promoting them less often).

Exchange Theory and Housework

Overall, husbands' investments *outside* the home make them more attractive to alternative partners, should they divorce and wish to remarry, whereas wives' investments *inside* the home do not make them attractive to alternative partners. According to social exchange theory

Families in Other Cultures — "I Also Have Some Rights"

Sometimes it is easier to recognize inequalities of power in a social setting different from one's own. Consider the relations between wives and husbands in poor Mexico City neighborhoods studied by Lourdes Benería and Martha Roldán (1987). Like nineteenth-century wives, married women in industrializing nations today often contribute to the family's income through means other than a job outside the home. Sociologists who study national development distinguish between the **formal sector** and the **informal sector** of a nation's economy. The formal sector consists of jobs that meet legal standards for minimum wages, are relatively long-lasting and secure, include fringe benefits such as contributions to Social Security or health insurance, often have possibilities for advancement, and are sometimes unionized. In contrast, the informal sector consists of temporary or casual jobs that sometimes offer illegal subminimum wages, have little security, little possibility for advancement, and no fringe benefits. In the United States

an example of a formal sector job would be a computer programmer at a large corporation; an informal sector job would be a seamstress at an illegal sweatshop in the garment district in New York City. The distinction is useful even though, in practice, it is sometimes hard to draw a line between the two sectors.

In industrializing nations, the informal sector is far larger than in the United States and, in fact, is an important part of the way production is organized. Established firms in the formal sector often let out work to subcontractors, who hire workers on a temporary basis, sometimes in violation of laws about wages and working conditions. By subcontracting, firms save money because they pay lower costs, evade labor laws regarding fringe benefits and hours, and avoid the fixed costs of directly hiring more workers (such as constructing more space at the factory). Some of the subcontracts involve labor that can be done on a piecework basis at home, and married women today do much of it.

Precisely because it can be done at home, piecework is acceptable even to husbands who would not want their wives to work outside the home. It allows husbands to feel that they are still the main earners in the family and yet to obtain the benefits of a higher family income. It allows wives to combine working for pay with the care of younger children, which is almost always seen as their responsibility. What is more, older children can help with the piecework, thus increasing the family's income even more. Thus, piecework by wives fits with the dominant ideology about what husbands and wives should do in many industrializing nations.

Doña Goya was a 33-year-old married woman interviewed by Benería and Roldán. As a teenager, she labored at times as a child care worker and domestic for several families. After she married, she stopped paid work and she and her husband—who was steadily employed as a factory worker—moved in with her parents. Like most working-class families in their neighborhood, they

formal sector the part of a nation's economy that consists of jobs that meet legal standards for minimum wages, are relatively longlasting and secure, include fringe benefits such as contributions to Social Security or health insurance, often have possibilities for advancement, and are sometimes unionized

informal sector the part of a nation's economy that consists of temporary or casual jobs that sometimes offer illegal subminimum wages and that have little security, little possibility for advancement, and no fringe benefits

[➡ p. 23], if person A needs the income partner B provides and values being married, and if person A has fewer alternative sources of partnership (because her investments of time and effort aren't as transferable), then A is said to be dependent on B. The degree of dependency is greater the more A needs the income and the fewer her alternatives are—which implies, in this case, that wives with little job experience and lower earning potential are more dependent. And the more A is dependent on B, the theory states, the greater is B's power over A (Emerson, 1972). He can use his greater power to shape his family's daily life and to control key decisions.

In some cultures, Even when wives do work for pay, they may be required to turn over their income to their husbands or fathers. But where wives have control over earnings, so the argument goes, they have more power. Their earnings give them the stature to speak their grievances. (See *Families in Other Cultures:* "I Also Have Some Rights.")

Exchange theory predicts that if wives' earnings increase relative to their husbands' earnings, they should become less dependent and their household power should increase. Unless they enjoy doing most of the housework (unlikely for most people), they should be able to use their increased power to get their husbands to do more of it. In short, exchange theory leads to the clear prediction

accepted the idea that men should be the main earners of the family and women should be the main caregivers. After having six children, Doña Goya began to take in washing and to work as a domestic in the neighborhood. After her 10th child, she began to do piecework at home, assembling toys with the help of 8 of her 10 children. She also continued to work as a laundress and domestic. Her assembly work was brought to her home by a middle person who had obtained a subcontract from a toy company. Whereas her husband worked in the formal sector, albeit for wages that were insufficient to support a family, Doña Goya and her children supplemented the family's income by working in the informal sector and by unpaid childcare and household work.

This division of labor between formal sector employment for married men and informal sector employment for married women is common in Mexico City, state the authors of the study. Because formal sector employment is more secure, pays more,

and has more benefits, this division virtually ensures that most married women will remain economically dependent on their husbands. Benería and Roldán found that husbands exercised control at a number of points in the process of spending income. Many husbands, first of all, gave their wives allowances without telling them how much their wages were. Second, husbands often kept back some money for personal spending. The wives were expected to meet all of the family's expenses without asking for further contributions. And in all cases, the wives contributed their entire earnings to the family pot.

Still, in those cases in which women contributed a substantial proportion of the household's income, they did report more power over family decision making. Thus, a Mexico City woman said that, because of her relatively large earnings, "I obey and respect him [her husband], but I feel I also have some rights." Most women like her, Benería and Roldán found, had won the right to answer back when their husbands

demanded that they do something and to make their views known to their husbands, as long as they did not embarrass their husbands publicly. These may seem like minor victories, but for the women involved, they were significant changes that bolstered their self-esteem and offered some protection from abuses of power by their husbands.

Ask Yourself
1. When you first went to work, did you notice a change in your relationship with your parents or spouse? Did you gain more respect?
2. Are the money and increased power married women gain by performing part-time or temporary work worthwhile, given the benefits and job security they are denied? Are married women who work part-time exploited?

www.mhhe.com/cherlin5

that as the proportion of household income earned by wives increases, the proportion of housework done by wives should decrease. Does this happen? Several researchers have studied data on wives' and husbands' earnings and housework, and for the most part the relationship is as exchange theory would predict.

Wives with no earnings, these studies show, do the vast majority of the housework, as exchange theory would lead us to expect. As their earnings increase, the share of housework they do decreases, all the way up to the point where their earnings equal their husbands' earnings (Brines, 1994; Greenstein, 2000; Bittman, England, Sayer, Folbre, & Matheson, 2003). When wives increase their paid work hours, surveys in the United States, the United Kingdom (Britain), and Germany show, they tend to reduce their household work hours quickly. Their husbands adjust their hours upward but not enough to fully compensate and more slowly, over a period of months or years (Gershuny, Bittman, & Brice, 2005). Still, the exchange theory prediction holds up.

"Doing Gender" and Housework   But in the modest number of households where wives are the main earners, the laws of exchange theory appear to give way to gendered norms about how women and men are supposed to behave. You will recall the interactionist perspective on gender differences [➡ p. 94], the idea that people produce and reproduce gender differences in social interactions.

Consistent with that perspective, some sociologists argue that husband and wives accept the common expectations about what women and men are supposed to do in the home and the labor market and they want to present themselves as following these gendered expectations. When their marriages deviate sharply from these expectations, they take steps to bring their behaviors back in line. In particular, in families where women's earnings substantially exceed their husbands' earnings, women and men sometimes act in ways that are just the opposite of what exchange theory would predict. An Australian survey shows that women may increase the amount of housework they do when they are the primary earners (Bittman et al., 2003); and American surveys show that men may decrease their housework when they are far out-earned by their wives (Brines, 1994; Greenstein, 2000). They are "doing gender" in the sense of trying through their behaviors to counterbalance their atypical gender roles and to show that they are still doing what people expect women and men in a marriage to do (Greenstein, 2000; Bittman et al., 2003).

In sum, for most married couples the principles of exchange theory seem to hold: When wives earn more, they do less housework and their husbands do somewhat more. But in the rarified atmosphere of couples in which wives are the principal earners, gender norms sometimes take precedence. Rather than appear radically different from people's expectations, wives who earn more may start doing more at home or their dependent husbands may start doing less. In 2001, wives were the sole or primary earners in 12 percent of married-couple households (Raley, Mattingly, & Bianchi, 2006). In the division of labor in some of these households, as one team of researchers put it, "gender trumps money," much as a hand in spades trumps the same hand in another suit (Bittman et al., 2003).

Quantity or Quality?   In a widely read book, Arlie Russell Hochschild (1989) wrote of a "stalled revolution," in which wives have moved into the labor force but husbands have not yet adjusted. The result, she asserted, is that employed wives work a "second shift" of household tasks and child care. The most recent time use studies, conducted between 1998 and 2000, suggest that the situation is no longer this simple. As noted earlier, women still do more of the housework, but the gap has narrowed. Moreover, men still work longer hours for pay than women. The result is that if you add up the total number of hours of work—paid and unpaid—that married parents with children do, you find very little difference between mothers and fathers: 65 and 64 hours, respectively (Bianchi, Robinson, & Milkie, 2006). It may be that some wives would like to work for pay more hours but do not because their husbands are unwilling to work more at home. Still, the difference is less than the second-shift thesis would lead us to expect.

Yet the kind of free time that men and women get when they are not working may differ. Australian and American time-use studies suggests that men may enjoy higher "quality" leisure time (Bittman & Wajcman, 2000; Mattingly & Bianchi, 2003). Compared to women, their free time is less likely to combine leisure with child care. For instance, when they are watching television, they may not also have to keep an eye on their children. Fathers also spend more of their leisure time with just adults than do mothers. Among parents with children under age two in Australia, for instance, fathers have five hours per week more adult-only leisure, which suggests that mothers are more likely to have the infant with them during their "free" time than are fathers. In addition, Australian fathers' spells of free time are longer, which suggests that their leisure is less likely to be interrupted by the needs of other family members. And marriage reduces American women's leisure time more than it reduces men's leisure time. Overall, these differences imply that women and men may experience their free time differently—mothers may experience less relaxation, more vigilance, more responsibility for the children and the household during their leisure time. In fact, women report feeling rushed more than do men who have the same amount of free time (Sayer & Mattingly, 2006). In short, the quality, rather than the quantity, of leisure may be what distinguishes mothers' and fathers' so-called free time.

Quick Review

- Over the past few decades, the share of housework done by women has decreased, although they still do more than men.
- Scholars of "care work" urge us to think of caring for others as valuable work that should be rewarded and respected.
- Sociologists distinguish between two ways a person or group can dominate others: power and authority.
- Wives have less power in marriage in part because they invest in activities such as raising children that are valuable to their current husband, not to other potential spouses.
- The division of housework follows the principles of exchange theory except in the modest number of families where wives are the primary or sole earners.

Overload and Spillover between Paid Work and Family Life

The growth of dual-earner families and employed single parents has raised concerns that parents may be performing too many roles with conflicting demands—a condition that is sometimes called **role overload.** The roles these adults play can include worker, spouse, parent, and sometimes caregiver to other relatives. A 1997 survey of employed women and men found that 85 percent lived with family members and had daily responsibilities at home. Forty-six percent had children under age 18 at home, and 13 percent were providing care to an elderly or other adult relative (Bond, Galinsky, & Swanberg, 1998). Clearly, most employed adults have to juggle the demands of home and work.

role overload the state of having too many roles with conflicting demands

However, research has *not* found a clear relationship between the number of roles a person must manage and the degree of distress she or he experiences (Thoits, 1992). In fact, there is some evidence that people with multiple roles (including nonfamily roles such as being involved in the activities of a religious organization) may in some cases have better mental health than people with fewer roles (Thoits, 1986; Barnett & Hyde, 2001). People with multiple roles may be able to compensate for stress in one by success in another. Multiple roles may also increase one's social network and therefore provide more opportunities for social support (Barnett & Hyde, 2001). It may be that multiple roles increase a person's sense of meaning and purpose in life and therefore improve mental health. Or it may be that mentally healthier people join more organizations, are more likely to marry, and have busier lives. In any case, paid work and family roles may sometimes enhance each other rather than conflict (Galinsky, 2001).

OVERWORKED AND UNDERWORKED AMERICANS

Some observers have suggested that balancing work and family has become more difficult for Americans because they are working longer hours. This was the thesis of the best-selling book *The Overworked American* (Schor, 1992). Yet a closer look reveals that while some Americans are overworked, others are underworked. Jerry A. Jacobs and Kathleen Gerson (2004) compared Census data from 1970 and 2000 and found two very different trends. People with professional and managerial jobs were indeed working longer hours in 2000 than in 1970. Most of these people received weekly salaries that remained the same no matter how many hours they worked. Consequently, employers had an incentive to pressure them to work longer hours, especially given the downsizing of the workforce in many firms. In contrast, people in other occupations were working fewer hours in 2000 than in 1970. These workers tended to receive hourly wages, which meant their employers had to pay them more for every extra hour worked. Instead of encouraging these sales and these service workers to work longer hours, employers have tended to hire more part-time workers. Often part-time workers are not eligible for fringe benefits such as health insurance, which provides further savings to employers. In sum, the labor market seems to be moving in opposite directions at the top and bottom, toward longer hours among the college educated and shorter hours among the less well educated.

Still, workers can *feel* overloaded, even if they are not working longer hours than they used to. Today, fewer families include a wife who devotes all her time to housework and child care. More families now feel the faster pace of combining paid employment with raising children. But again, people's feelings about this trend may differ according to their education and occupation. More than half the college graduates in a 1992 survey of employed women and men said they would prefer to work fewer hours than they currently worked. Yet less than one-third of those without a high school degree said they would prefer to work fewer hours (Jacobs and Gerson, 2004). At the top of the labor market, workers are feeling overloaded but economically secure; at the lower end, they are feeling underemployed and economically insecure.

SPILLOVER

spillover the fact that stressful events in one part of a person's daily life often spill over into other parts of her or his life

Another motif in the research literature is that stressful events in one part of a person's daily life often spill over into other parts of her or his life. **Spillover** can occur whether or not the person experiences role overload. In other words, a bad day at even an enjoyable job can cause a parent to come home and behave angrily toward his or her children. In the 1997 survey of employed women and men, 26 percent of employees said they had not been in a good mood at home because of their work over the past three months; and 28 percent said they did not have enough energy for their families and other important people (Bond, Galinsky, & Swanberg 1998). In an influential article in the late 1970s, Joseph Pleck argued that spillover involving work and family operates in opposite directions for employed men and employed women. The demands of family life—a school vacation, an ill child—are permitted to intrude into women's jobs more than into men's jobs, he wrote, because supervisors and co-workers expect that when a family emergency arises, mothers rather than fathers will be called upon to deal with it. In contrast, according to Pleck, the stresses of work are permitted

The stresses of work can spill over to the home lives of married couples.

to intrude on family life more for men than for women. Because men's jobs are often seen as more demanding and more central to the family's well-being than are women's jobs, it is more acceptable, for example, for husbands to miss school concerts because of business trips than it is for employed wives to do so (Pleck, 1977).

It may also be more acceptable for husbands to come home from work irritable or preoccupied than it is for wives. Wives are often cast in a more supportive role, even though their daily lives may be stressful. One woman talked about her husband to two researchers:

> He takes a lot of crap [at his job]. He gets very few rewards for what he does, and people are not very facilitating there. So it's up to me when he comes home to try and fill that need and make him feel good about himself. And yet, I am not getting any reverse back. (Pearlin & McCall, 1990)

Wives may serve to buffer husbands from further stress at home more than husbands do for them. One woman in the same study said that when she sees her husband come home troubled, she tells her children, "Dad has a lot on his mind. If you want to ask him for something, wait until later" (Pearlin & McCall, 1990).

Psychologists Nicole A. Roberts and Robert W. Levenson (2001) studied the effects of stress on the marriages of 19 male police officers who, at the end of each workday for a month, completed questionnaires about their level of job stress. Once per week the officers and their wives came to a university laboratory, where they were wired to machines that monitored their physiological responses. They were then told to discuss the day's activities. On days when the police officers reported more job stress, they showed heightened arousal in their autonomic nervous system—the "fight or flight" response that people may feel if surprised by something unpleasant. They also displayed less positive emotion and more negative emotion in their conversations with their wives. These reactions—the arousal, the greater negative emotion in conversations—have been shown to be correlated with marital distress and divorce in other studies conducted by the authors and their collaborators.

Men also appear more likely to withdraw from their families in reaction to a stressful day at work. One author suggests that the male professionals he studied view displays of stress at home as signs of failure in meeting work responsibilities. Men may instead act weary, which is more acceptable because it can be seen as a sign of hard work, or they may tune out their wives and children. But worries are hard to hide, and withdrawal can lead to irritability and anger, as in this case:

> *A situation that is perfectly normal and next to nothing—something happens with a kid—I may go into a tailspin over it. I might boil up or boil over. Norma will then fly up and say, "You are not treating them fairly." And then it will come out that at that particular point I was up to my eyebrows with the damned business and I just wasn't relaying that. In fact, I was keeping it in. (Weiss, 1990)*

For many blue-collar workers, other causes of stress may be low pay, dirty or dangerous work, or dehumanizing treatment by supervisors. Blue-collar men, some studies show, bring their troubles home in ways similar to professionals who have had a bad day at the office. Tired and irritable, blue-collar men sometimes withdraw from their wives and children in the evenings (Mortimer & London, 1984).

Among the better-educated, work weeks are indeed long. Overall, the percentage of Americans who work very long weeks (50 hours or more) is higher than in Canada and eight European countries, including the United Kingdom, France, and Germany (Jacobs & Gerson, 2004). And dual-earner couples in the United States work a higher number of total hours than do couples in these countries. Yet despite the number of parents working long hours, fewer preschool children are in publicly financed child care in the United States than in most of these countries. So although more parents work long hours in the United States, public support for child care is relatively low.

SHIFT WORK AND CHILD CARE

One surprisingly common way in which dual-earner couples manage child care is to work different shifts. In one study, one-third of all dual-earner couples with preschool-aged children had at least one spouse working an evening, night, or rotating shift (Presser, 1999). Husbands who were home when their wives were working did more cooking, cleaning, and washing than husbands who were never home when their wives were working (Presser, 1994). The increase in nonday-shift and weekend work isn't due solely to couples' child care needs. The growth of the service sector of the economy is also responsible. Nevertheless, when asked why they were working evening or night shifts, a majority of married women in a Census Bureau survey said the main reason was that their hours made it easier to care for their children or other relatives (Presser, 1989).

In fact, it appears that wives and husbands in many of these split-shift couples are sharing the child care (Presser, 1989). How best to care for the children of employed parents is a topic that will be discussed in later chapters. Some observers view staggered-shift parent care as a good solution to the child care problem. Other things being equal, parents arguably provide better care in most instances than nonrelatives. But split-shift child care sharing is not without its difficulties. Employed wives, who still tend to accommodate their working hours to their spouse's needs more than their husbands do, may be forced to turn down better jobs or work fewer hours so that they can be available when their husbands aren't home. Couples working different shifts may have little time for each other, and their marriages may suffer. In a national sample of recently married couples with children who were followed for five years, divorce was six times more likely among husbands who worked a night schedule rather than a day schedule (Presser, 2000). One repair worker told Lillian Rubin:

> *I usually get home about forty-five minutes or so before my wife has to leave for work, so we try to take a few minutes just to make contact. But it's hard with the kids and all. Most days the whole time gets spent with taking care of business— you know, who did what, what the kids need, what's for supper, what bill collector was hassling her while I was gone—all the damn garbage of living. It makes me nuts. (Rubin, 1994)*

Single parents, of course, do not have the luxury of relying on a spouse to provide care, regardless of when they work. Yet never-married, separated, or divorced mothers are even more likely to work nonday, weekend, or rotating shifts than married mothers, perhaps because of their more limited education or work experience (Presser, 1989). With few commercial child care providers offering evening, night, or weekend care, single mothers must often rely on their own mothers or other relatives (Presser, 2004). Here again, one could argue that, as caregivers, grandmothers are superior to nonrelatives. Many of the grandmothers, however, are themselves working or are caring for their own aging parents (see Chapter 10); providing care may be a strain on them. Some single mothers, with no one to rely on, attempt to care for their children themselves while working. Nationally, 8 percent of all preschool-aged children with employed mothers were cared for by the mothers themselves. For example, a mother might earn money by caring for the children of several other employed mothers as well as her own children. Employed single parents are sometimes successful in constructing new support networks made up of kin and friends. Still, it seems likely that overload and spillover are a greater problem for employed single parents than for employed married parents.

UNEMPLOYMENT

Most of the studies of spillover between work and family assume that adults in the family who want to work outside the home can find and keep a job. Yet unemployment also creates stress. Research dating back to the Great Depression suggests that unemployment is more likely to cause marital problems among couples whose marriages were already shaky before the husband or wife lost a job (Komarovsky, 1971). More recently, a Boston area study of 82 families in which the husband had recently lost his job found that spouses who rated their marriages as satisfactory prior to the job loss were less anxious and depressed afterward (Liem & Liem, 1990). The Boston study, an Iowa study of 76 rural families, and a few others like them provide some insight into the process by which job loss leads to family problems. At the first interview, the unemployed husbands in the Boston study were more depressed and anxious than a matching group of employed husbands, but their wives were not more depressed or anxious than the wives of employed husbands. Four months later, however, the wives were experiencing more depression and anxiety. The authors speculate that many husbands become upset soon after the job loss and begin to act irritably and angrily toward their wives and children. Most wives are not as upset initially, but as their financial concerns grow and their husbands' behavior worsens, they often develop psychological symptoms. The Iowa study showed similarly that economic strain leads husbands to behave in a hostile way toward their wives—as well as to reduce their warm, supportive behavior. The husbands' hostility and lack of warmth, in turn, lead wives to feel less positively about their marriages. If the wives then respond with hostile behavior, their husbands' satisfaction with the marriage also declines (Conger et al., 1990).

On the whole, the available studies suggest that it is not as much the absence of supportive behavior as the presence of angry, irritable, hostile behavior that triggers these declines in the quality of the marriage. The results are consistent with laboratory observations that cycles of negative behavior from husband to wife and back are central to escalating marital conflict (Gottman, 1979). The studies also suggest that spouses with fewer prior psychological problems and more social support from kin and friends are more likely to weather the storm of unemployment. Finally, moderate-income and higher-income families show similar distress when a parent loses his or her job, despite their differing economic circumstances. Moderate-income families, who typically have few financial reserves, experience the more immediate economic consequences, but they report receiving more support from kin and friends than do higher-income families. Among the latter group, losing a job, as has happened to executives during the recent waves of corporate "downsizing," means losing status and social identity (Liem & Liem, 1990).

TOWARD A RESPONSIVE WORKPLACE?

To judge by the concerns of workers and, increasingly, of corporate managers, the strict separation of paid work and family life is indeed breaking down. When employed women and men in the 1992 survey who had been at their current jobs for less than five years were asked how important various factors were in their original decisions to take their jobs, 60 percent said that the job's effect on personal and family life was very important and 46 percent said that family-supportive policies at the job were important. In contrast, only 35 percent said that wages and salary were important. Moreover, one-quarter to one-third of those without access to flexible working hours said they would switch jobs or sacrifice advancement in their companies to obtain flexible hours. About half without access to time off to care for sick relatives said they would trade salary or other benefits to obtain it (Galinsky, Bond, & Friedman, 1993). Clearly, family responsibilities are on the minds of many workers. Congress has been paying more attention, too. (See *Families and Public Policy:* Putting Work–Family Issues on the Agenda, on pp. 282–283.)

During the 1980s and 1990s, corporations began to address these concerns. They did so largely out of self-interest. The Census Bureau estimates that 58 percent of the new entrants to the labor force between 2004 and 2012 will be women, many of whom will have family responsibilities (U.S. Bureau of the Census, 2005l). Employers who wish to recruit and retain good workers realize that they must make their jobs attractive to people who are caring for children—and to the growing number who are caring for elderly parents. Most large firms now have some personnel policies to help employees with family responsibilities (Glass & Estes, 1997). Small firms are much less likely to offer family-friendly policies for several reasons:

- They typically do not invest as much time and money training new workers, so they don't have as much to lose if employees quit because of family-related problems.
- They don't have the volume of workers necessary to make services such as on-site child care cost-effective.
- Because of their lower sales revenues, they cannot pass along the costs of the policies to consumers as easily as large firms can.

Consequently, a two-tiered class system is developing: Larger firms, which tend to have better-paying, steadier jobs and better-educated workforces, offer better policies to help workers achieve balance between the demands of work and family; smaller firms, which tend to have lower-paying, less-steady jobs and less-well-educated workforces, provide less help. So well-paid, well-educated managers and professionals and better-paid blue-collar factory workers are much more likely to be offered assistance with family demands than are less-advantaged workers (Deitch & Huffman, 2001).

Even among large firms, much of the assistance is limited, such as establishing information and referral offices to match parents with child care openings. Cash benefits are usually limited to salary reduction plans that allow workers not to pay taxes on the part of their earnings (up to a limit) they spend on child care. Yet these plans are of more value to higher-paid employees—who can afford to have the extra earnings withheld from their paychecks by their employers and who pay a greater percentage of their incomes in taxes—than to working-class employees.

One of the most common, and most widely used, employee benefits is **flextime**, a policy that allows employees to choose, within limits, when they will begin and end their working hours. For example, a company might allow its employees to begin work anytime between 7:00 and 9:00 A.M. and to leave anytime from 3:00 to 5:00 P.M., as long as they work eight hours. Studies suggest that this is the family-friendly policy workers use the most (Galinsky, 1992; Hochschild, 1997). In 2004, 28 percent of full-time workers had flexible work schedules, allowing them to choose, within a range of hours, when they began and ended their workdays (U.S. Bureau of Labor Statistics, 2005e). Again, college-educated employees benefit more than high-school educated employees: The more prestigious the occupational category, the more likely workers are to have flextime. Employed parents use flextime to match their work schedules to the school or day care schedules of their children. Flextime doesn't necessarily increase the amount of time parents can spend with their children, but it does allow them to avoid stressful conflicts between childcare and job responsibilities.

flextime a policy that allows employees to choose, within limits, when they will begin and end their working hours

To be able to spend more time with their children, especially when they are infants or when they are sick, employed parents need other options. One of these is **parental leave,** time off from work to care for a child, with a guarantee that the employee can have her or his job back when she or he returns. Many employers have been reluctant to grant parental leave automatically because they have feared it would hurt their productivity and cost too much. Most Western European nations require corporations to provide parental leave; yet in this regard, as in many family policies, the United States lags behind. Many European countries, as well as Canada, have policies that provide a minimum of several months of leave with partial replacement of pay (Clearinghouse on International Developments in Child, Youth, and Family Policies, 2004). A modest parental leave bill was enacted in 1993. It required companies with 50 or more employees to offer unpaid leaves of up to 12 weeks to employees with newborn babies or seriously ill children or other relatives. Employers must allow employees to return to their jobs at the end of the leave. In 2002, California became the first state to require employees to provide parental leave with partial pay (Broder, 2002).

parental leave time off from work to care for a child

Other innovations are as yet less common. These include part-time work with fringe benefits and job sharing. Whether significant numbers of part-time jobs with fringe benefits will be created remains to be seen. In job sharing, two people split the time and duties of a full-time position usually held by one person. Unlike

Families and Public Policy

Putting Work–Family Issues on the Agenda

Half a century ago, the breadwinner–homemaker family was at its peak. Few married women with young children worked outside the home, and few members of Congress favored assistance for employed mothers. But today several laws provide benefits for working parents, and Congress may pass more legislation. When and how did this change?

Sociologist Paul Burstein and his colleagues examined this question by counting the number of members of Congress who sponsored (officially supported) various kinds of work–family bills between 1945 and 1990 (Burstein & Bricher, 1997; Burstein, Bricher, & Einwohner, 1995; and Burstein & Wierzbicki, 2000).

The results are presented in the figure, which shows the number of sponsors for three different types of legislation over the 45-year period. Though most of the bills did not become law, their content is informative. The first type, "separate spheres" bills, contained proposals that would support families in which the husband worked outside the

home and the wife did not. An example was legislation that would have limited the number of hours women could work, to protect their ability to be good mothers. Unthinkable today, such bills were commonplace in the first half of the twentieth century. The black line in the chart shows a modest but steady number of sponsors for these bills throughout the 1945–1990 period.

The second type of legislation, "Equal opportunity" bills, was based on the premise that working women were entitled to the same opportunities as working men. For instance, they might require employers to pay equal wages to women and men doing the same job. Such an idea might seem obvious, but before the 1960s many employers paid women less than men, on the theory that men were the main earners for their families and so deserved more than women. The green line in the figure shows a modest number of sponsors for equal-opportunity bills until the mid-1960s, after which sponsorships rose sharply. Not coincidentally, the mid-1960s was the era of

the civil rights movement and the birth of the modern feminist movement.

Most recently, legislators have supported "work–family accommodation," including an income tax credit for child care expenses. These bills attempt to help parents combine paid work with child rearing. The red line in the figure shows that sponsorship of this type of bill was rare through most of the period, but rose dramatically during the 1970s and 1980s. Had the study continued into the 1990s, it undoubtedly would have shown further growth. In 1993, for example, Congress passed the Family and Medical Leave Act, which allows workers to take time off to care for newborns and seriously ill children or to handle other family medical emergencies.

Why have work–family accommodation bills been proposed only recently? Not until the 1980s did a majority of married mothers of young children take jobs outside the home (see Figure 8.1). In other words, not until that time did members of Congress face a large constituency of working

part-time positions, which are often in low-status occupations, shared jobs presumably can be on a higher level—and therefore more appealing. The small number of existing shared jobs tend to be in such professions as teaching, psychology, and social work. Few have been created in for-profit corporations (Kamerman & Kahn, 1987).

Overall, there has been progress in making the workplace more responsive to workers' family needs. The least progress, however, has occurred in occupations that don't pay well. Yet workers in low-paying jobs need assistance *more* than those who are better paid. For instance, a 1990 survey showed that, among mothers who were paying for care and had a child under age 5, those earning less than $15,000 spend 23 percent of their incomes for child care, whereas mothers earning more than $35,000 spent just 7 percent of their incomes for child care (Hofferth, 1992). Another study showed that the cost of child care keeps some low-income women from taking jobs (Baum, 2002). Future changes in the nature of work could widen the gap between poor and nonpoor. Visionaries write that as the economy turns to information processing rather than manufacturing, computer-assisted communication could allow large numbers of workers to do their jobs from home. Such a shift, it is proposed, could make it

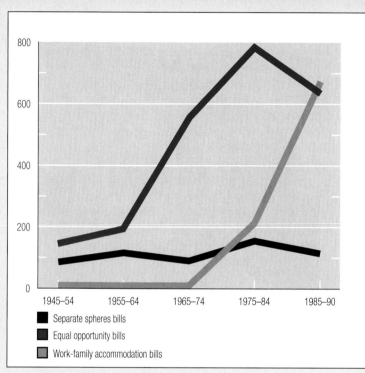

Sponsorship of Work-Family Legislation, 1945–1970.
(*Source:* Burstein, Bricher, & Einwohner, 1995)

parents clamoring for help in accommodating their children as well as their jobs.

Ask Yourself

1. Do you know any couples who are trying to raise a family while both of them work full time? If so, what is their major problem? Could a change in public policy help to solve it?

2. Should American workers receive paid parental leaves, like workers in some European countries?

www.mhhe.com/cherlin5

easier for family care takers to mesh the demands of family and job. In 2004, about 15 percent of people with nonagricultural jobs said they worked at home at least one day per week (U.S. Bureau of Labor Statistics, 2005d). Yet changes such as these are easier to imagine in professional and clerical jobs than in lower-paying part-time service jobs such as janitors and waiters. In fact, nearly two-thirds of those who said they worked at home at least one day per week in 2004 were managers and professionals. It may be more of a challenge, therefore, to provide a responsive workplace for workers at the low end of the occupational distribution than at the high end.

Corporate efforts, although increasing and important, are unlikely to meet the demands of employees for assistance in caring for children and the elderly. To the extent that they do, they will benefit college-educated employees and those in large firms more than high-school-educated employees or those in small firms. These conclusions led advocates of the so-called **responsive workplace**—meaning a work setting in which job conditions are designed to allow employees to meet their family responsibilities more easily—to urge that corporate initiatives be supplemented by government assistance targeted at low-income workers. In the 1990s, pressure from working parents prompted Congress to enact legislation

responsive workplace a work setting in which job conditions are designed to allow employees to meet their family responsibilities more easily

Most Western European governments provide parental leave with partial pay to care for newborn or seriously ill children. In all U.S. states except California, only unpaid leave is offered.

providing child care assistance, beginning with a 1990 bill. The 1996 welfare reform law (see Chapter 14) also included child care assistance funds for parents who left the welfare rolls to take jobs. But in the 2000s, little further assistance has been forthcoming (Center for Law and Social Policy, 2006a).

Quick Review

- In spite of some concerns, having multiple roles (parent, spouse, paid employee) does not seem to reduce mental health.
- A greater percentage of American workers, and American dual-earner couples, put in very long work weeks than do workers in most other developed nations.
- The stress of one's paid job can spill over into one's family life and cause family conflict.
- Workers in large firms receive more benefits to help them balance their family and paid work lives.

Looking Back

1. **How has married women's work changed over the past half-century?** In the second half of the twentieth century, married women entered the labor force in large numbers. A majority of married women with young children are now employed outside the home. The rise of the service sector and the long-term decline in fertility are two important reasons for women's increase in labor force participation. Women still earn less money than men, in part because they have less labor market experience, but also because employers tend to pay women less than they pay men for comparable work. Women's earnings rose relative to men's in the 1980s, 1990s, and early 2000s, because well-educated women workers were faring better and less-well-educated men were faring worse than they had in the past.

2. **How has the amount of housework and child care done by husbands and wives changed over the past half-century?** Wives have greatly reduced the amount of housework they do, while husbands have increased theirs. As a result, the relative amount of housework done by husbands and wives has become less unequal. Overall, the total amount of housework being done has declined; couples are buying more services, such as restaurant meals, than they used to.

3. **How does our society treat the labor of caring for others?** Much of the caring labor in families was provided by wives in the home. It was not considered "work" because it was unpaid and consisted of caring for people. As women have moved into the paid labor force, the value of the caring they provided has become evident and has proven difficult to replace. Some authors suggest that we must place a higher value on caring labor—paid and unpaid.

4. **How do sociologists think about power and authority within marriage?** By power, sociologists mean the ability to force someone to take an action against her or his will; by authority, they mean the acknowledged right to supervise other people or to act on their behalf. In general, working for pay outside the home increases a person's power in the family; therefore, wives who work outside the home tend to have relatively more family power and, consequently, do a smaller share of the housework.

5. **What are some of the strains working parents can experience?** Working parents may suffer from overload due to their multiple roles as workers, parents, caregivers, and spouses. Difficulties at work can spill over into their home lives, leading to their emotional withdrawal from the family or to irritable, angry exchanges. One increasingly common way for dual-earner couples to manage child care is to work split shifts, a practice that provides children with parental care but can strain a marriage to the point of divorce.

6. **How is the workplace responding to the needs of working parents?** Workers are concerned about meshing their jobs with their family responsibilities, and corporations and government are responding. Large corporations are increasingly providing limited assistance such as child care information and referral offices and flexible hours. So far, these and other reforms have benefited college-educated workers and employees of large corporations more than high-school-educated workers and employees of small corporations.

Go to the Online Learning Center at www.mhhe.com/cherlin5 to test your knowledge of the chapter concepts and key terms.

Study Questions

1. How has the life of the typical married woman changed since the middle of the twentieth century?
2. Why have the earnings of women risen relative to the earnings of men since 1980?
3. Why has caring labor been undervalued relative to other kinds of work?
4. What does an "ethic of care" mean?
5. What are the bases of men's power and authority over women in marriage?

6. Why do women seemingly pay a "motherhood penalty" in lost wages relative to childless women?
7. Why do some Americans feel overworked while others feel underworked?
8. Why do well-paid workers typically receive more family-related benefits than workers who earn less?

Key Terms

authority   269
care work   266
flextime   281
formal sector   272
informal sector   272

labor force   260
parental leave   281
power   269
relationship-specific
   investment   270

responsive workplace   283
role overload   275
service sector   260
spillover   226

Thinking about Families

The Public Family	The Private Family
Are benefits such as family leave or tax credits for child care unfair to workers without children?	Might couples' feelings toward each other be different if they shared the housework and child care equally?

Families on the Internet   www.mhhe.com/cherlin5

Note: While all the URLs listed were current as of the printing of this book, these sites often change. Please check our Web site (http://www.mbhe.com/cherlin5) for updates.

Blogs (Web logs) by parents who are combining caregiving with work are popping up on the Internet. For instance, go to www.businessweek.com, click the pull-down menu "careers," and select "working parents blog." The site will display blogs by *BusinessWeek* staff members who are themselves dealing with work/family issues such as working part-time, working from home, caring for a young child, and being a single-parent.

Shift work (evening, night, weekend, or rotating work schedules) has become such a common strategy for handling work and child care that at least one Web site is devoted to it: www.shiftworker.com. What are the particular challenges this site focuses on?

Dealing with the family issues of employees has become a speciality for some managers. A clearinghouse for information on work–family issues and problems is www.workfamily.com. Read the tip of the month, scan the list of important studies, and explore other features of this site. If you were an employer using this site, what would you learn about managing workers with work–family conflicts?

An advocacy group on care work, www.takecarenet.org, seeks to link academic researchers and practitioners of care with policymakers and the media. It provides links to a number of useful sites on issues such as paid family leave and early education and child care.

Part Four

Links across the Generations

In this part, we shift from same-generational relations of spouses and partners to intergenerational relations between parents and children. How adequately parents are meeting their overall responsibilities for raising children is a topic of much discussion and concern. In addition, working-age adults bear most of the responsibility for supporting and taking care of the elderly. The increasing number of elderly persons raises the question of whether family care will continue to be adequate. In the terms of this book, the issue is whether the public family is meeting its caretaking responsibilities for children and the elderly. • **Chapter 9** examines the care of children by their parents. No public issue involving the family has received more attention in recent years than the well-being of children. The chapter begins by asking two questions: What are parents supposed to do for children? And what might prevent parents from doing what they are supposed to do? It then evaluates the complex question of whether children's well-being has declined. In • **Chapter 10** the focus shifts from the young to the old. The chapter first reviews the substantial changes that have occurred in the lives of the elderly during the twentieth century. It subsequently examines the assistance provided to, and provided by, the elderly, as well as levels of contact and affection between the elderly and their adult children and grandchildren.

Children and Parents

Looking Forward

1. What are the main goals in socializing children, and how do parents differ in the way they fulfill their role?

2. How does the socialization of children vary by ethnicity, class, and gender?

3. What barriers must parents overcome in socializing their children?

4. How much time do parents and children spend together?

5. How has the well-being of American children changed over time?

On her midyear report card, Crystal Rossi, then a seventh-grader in Brooklyn, New York, got a 65 in social studies and failing grades in English, math, science, foreign language, and physical education. She was 12 years old, white, and lived with her mother and stepfather. Her father lived a few blocks away. "The classes are boring," she told a *New York Times* reporter (Manegold, 1993). "Kids who study are all nerds. Who'd want to be like that? Everybody makes fun of them." An assistant principal told the reporter, "We have already sent the family an 'at risk' letter. She's on a decline."

Crystal said she wanted to be a lawyer because "you get to talk back to people" and "you make a lot of money." But she had never met one. In fact, if Crystal were to graduate from high school, she would be the first person in her family to do so. Her mother told her to do her homework but conceded to the reporter that she rarely checked to see if it was done. Threatening to send Crystal to her room didn't do much good: She and her sister shared a television, VCR, radio, Nintendo system, and their own telephone line.

On the streets—and even in the school's halls—Crystal faced crime, violence, and drugs. She had tried alcohol and cigarettes but not, she said, marijuana, LSD, or crack. Still, she knew kids who had tried them all: "Everybody drinks," she said. "They drink and do acid in the park." She had friends who had joined one of the two girls' gangs, Bitches on a Mission and Five Million Hoodlums. "They can protect you," she told the reporter. "They can keep you safe."

Crystal talked tough but was vulnerable underneath. "I'm always nervous," she confided. "I get nervous over nothing. And then I'll get a really big headache. . . . Sometimes I can't even sleep. I stay up all night and then I'm too tired to get up in the morning."

Lafayette Rivers was 10, and his brother Pharoah 7, when a reporter first met them in a largely black public housing project in Chicago (Kotlowitz, 1991). Their high-rise building sat in a neighborhood vacated by middle-class whites and blacks alike. Their parents had separated, and their father—steadily employed but addicted to drugs—rarely showed up. Shootings were an almost daily occurrence; sometimes children were killed in the crossfire. When the reporter asked Lafayette what he wanted to be, he replied, "If I grow up, I'd like to be a bus driver." *If* I grow up—Lafayette wasn't sure he would.

Given the horrible violence in his neighborhood, his fear was perfectly understandable. His mother certainly thought so—she had recently begun paying $80 per month out of her public assistance check for burial insurance for Lafayette, Pharoah, and her younger triplets. Her three eldest children had already been in drug-related trouble with the law. A 20-year-old daughter worked occasionally as a prostitute to support her drug habit. A 19-year-old son had been imprisoned for burglary. A 17-year-old son had been selling drugs since he was 11.

When they heard gunfire outside their first-floor apartment, Lafayette and Pharoah knew to run into the hallway and dive onto the floor. During the summer of his ninth year, Pharoah developed a stammer that worsened as the shooting wore on. He listened to classical music on the radio, he said, because it relaxed him. During one incident, as bullets whizzed by the apartment, a stuttering Pharoah asked his mother to make them stop. Then he fainted. In his quest for safety and peace, he would sit on the lawn of a calm condominium three blocks from the project until someone shooed him away.

Rachel, 14, lives a life of privilege that Crystal, Lafayette, and Pharoah see only on television. She resides in an exclusive neighborhood of an Eastern city and attends an expensive private school. It is taken for granted that she will attend college. Yet she is drifting toward trouble. Some nights, she sneaks out of the house where she lives with her mother, a lawyer, and her stepfather, a pharmacist, to rendezvous with boys. She and her girlfriends smoke marijuana and drink together, occasionally stealing liquor bottles from their parents' cabinets. She has a difficult relationship with her biological father, whom she visits once a month. Her grades aren't good, and her teachers are worried about her.

The Crystals, Lafayettes, Pharoahs, and Rachels are all too common in the United States. One in six children lives in poverty (U.S. Bureau of the Census, 2005e). One in 12 15- to 19-year-old girls becomes pregnant every year (Alan Guttmacher Institute, 2004). Homicide is the leading cause of death for black teenage males (U.S. National Center for Health Statistics, 2005b). About 4 in 10 children will witness the breakup of their parents' marriage before they reach 18, and perhaps 1 in 10 will witness a divorce, a remarriage, and a second divorce (Bumpass, 1984). Grim statistics such as these have led to a growing sense of concern about the well-being of American children. Is their quality of life deteriorating? Is our society failing to meet their needs?

Much of that concern centers on the family. Some critics charge that the institution of the family is not providing children with the care, supervision, and discipline they need to become well-adjusted, productive adults—that it is failing in perhaps the central responsibility of the public family. If one agrees with that charge (and not everyone does), it leads to another important question: To what extent are larger social forces such as the restructuring of the economy, racial discrimination, and the cultural drift toward individual autonomy and self-fulfillment undermining the ability of the family to raise children well? These are difficult questions, about which observers have strong, conflicting opinions. Although this chapter can't provide definitive answers, it can introduce you to the extensive social scientific evidence that scholars and policymakers have produced in recent years.

What Are Parents Supposed to Do for Children?

First, however, we need to ask what it is that parents are supposed to do for their children. For the first several years of life, at least, families provide the main setting in which children's fundamental needs are met. In the United States, parents are given broad powers to shape their children's lives. (See *Families and Public Policy:* Elián, the Troxels, and Parents' Rights.) What are the lessons children need to learn from their families, and how are those lessons shaped by social forces such as ethnicity, class, and gender? What behaviors by parents provide the best foundation for children's development?

First and foremost, parents, and sometimes other adult relatives, supply most of the love, nurturing, and care that children need in order to develop a basic sense of trust in other human beings. They also train young children in the skills they need to become more autonomous, such as dressing and feeding themselves. Later they provide the guidance, support, and discipline children need in order to become competent members of their society. In other words, family members socialize their children. [➡ p. 88] Indeed, families are the major source of primary socialization—the settings for the first lessons children learn about their society.

SOCIALIZATION AS SUPPORT AND CONTROL

As parents socialize their children, they act in two broad ways. First, they provide emotional support—love, affection, warmth, nurturing, or acceptance. Emotional support shows children that parents care about their actions. It makes children feel more positively about themselves. Because children want to continue receiving such support, they try to act in ways they think will please their parents. Second, parents exercise control—they seek to limit or change children's behavior. Sometimes parental control is coercive, consisting of the use or threat of punishment or force. But control also may be inductive—that is, based on setting consistent limits, explaining the reasons for these limits to the child, requesting that the child comply, and praising her or his compliance. Parents may also exercise control by threatening to withdraw their love if the child does not behave well.

authoritative style (of parenting) a parenting style in which parents combine high levels of emotional support with consistent, moderate control of their children

permissive style (of parenting) a parenting style in which parents provide emotional support but exercise little control over their children

authoritarian style (of parenting) a parenting style in which parents combine low levels of emotional support with coercive attempts at control of their children

Numerous studies have examined the ways in which parents combine various aspects of support and control. In what is probably the most influential analysis, psychologist Diana Baumrind distinguished among three styles of parental behavior (Baumrind, 1971). In the **authoritative style,** parents combine high levels of emotional support with consistent, moderate control. Children are provided with warmth and affection and with firm, consistent discipline. But the discipline is moderate and is based on requests and explanations rather than on the use of force or punishment. Baumrind and others claim that authoritative parenting produces children who are more socially competent—meaning that they have higher self-esteem, cooperate better with others, develop a better moral sense, and are more independent. The two other styles of behavior, it is claimed, produce children who are less competent and who may show more behavior problems, anxiety, or depression. In the **permissive style,** parents provide support but exercise little control over their children by any means. And in the **authoritarian style,** parents combine low support with coercive attempts at control. The implication of this research tradition is that children are socialized best when parents set

Families and Public Policy

Elián, the Troxels, and Parents' Rights

In November 1999, the U.S. Coast Guard rescued a six-year-old boy floating on an inner tube off the coast of Florida. Like many Cubans before them, Elián González and his mother had attempted to reach the United States by crossing the sea in a small boat. When the boat capsized, Elián's mother drowned.

After his rescue, Elián's relatives in Florida attempted to take custody of him, arguing that he should be granted political asylum in the United States rather than be sent back to communist Cuba. But Elián's father, still in Cuba, asked that the boy be returned; he had not given permission for Elián to leave the country. The United States Department of Justice agreed, ruling that parents have a fundamental right to custody of their children that supersedes the claims of other relatives, even when political considerations might dictate otherwise. The decision infuriated anti-communist Cuban immigrants, who mounted a fierce campaign to prevent the boy's return. When Elián's Florida relatives refused to relinquish the boy, Federal agents raided the house where he was staying and returned him to his father.

Cuban President Fidel Castro helped Elián González, right, celebrate his twelfth birthday on December 6, 2005, by giving a two-hour speech.

Elián has since become a celebrity in Cuba. He gave his first political speech in 2005, at age 11 at a rally in Havana. He lives with his father, who was elected to the Cuban National Assembly in 2003, in the city of Cárdenas. A small museum holds mementos of his voyage, the protests it led to, and his return (Bauza, 2005).

At about the same time, another struggle over parents' rights, this one in the state of Washington, made the headlines. The state legislature had recently passed a law allowing anyone to petition the court for visiting rights on the grounds that they would be in a child's best interest. Grandparents Jennifer and Gary Troxel had asked the court for overnight visiting rights to the children of their late son and Tommie Granville Wynne. The children's mother, whose fitness as a parent was not in question, had offered more limited visits. When the family court ruled in favor of the Troxels, Wynne appealed.

On appeal, the Washington State Supreme Court declared the law unconstitutional, ruling in favor of Wynne. The Troxels appealed to the U.S. Supreme Court, but in June 2000 the Court sided with the Washington State Supreme Court by a six to three margin, agreeing that the law was unconstitutional.[1] Those justices in the majority reasoned that Wynne was, by all accounts, a fit parent, and that fit parents are presumed to act in their children's best interest. The state, they reasoned, should not interfere with parents' ability to make decisions for their children.

Since the Troxel ruling, however, state courts have upheld more narrowly drawn grandparent visitation statutes. For instance, the Ohio Supreme Court upheld a law that allows parents of a deceased parent to petition for visitation rights to their grandchild. In the case in question, a single mother who had been living with her parents while raising her daughter Brittany died of cancer. The grandparents, Gary and Carol Harrold, were then granted temporary custody of Brittany, but a court awarded custody to her father, who removed her from the Harrolds' home and denied them access to her. The Harrolds asked for, and were granted, visiting rights under Ohio's law (Dao, 2005).

In both the González case and the Troxel case, the winning argument was that parents have close to a fundamental right to direct their children's upbringing— at least as long as their decisions do not greatly harm the children. In cultures that place a greater value on extended family ties, grandparents and other kin might be granted more extensive custody and visitation rights. But in the American legal system—and probably in American public opinion as well—parents' rights prevail.

Ask Yourself

1. Has anyone in your family been involved in a child custody dispute? If so, were parents' rights, as opposed to other relatives' rights, an issue?
2. Besides the issues of custody and visitation, what other ways can you think of that the government limits parents' rights in order to ensure the well-being of their children?

[1] *Troxel v. Granville*, No. 99–138, 2000.

www.mhhe.com/cherlin5

clear standards, enforce them consistently but without harsh punishment, and provide substantial emotional support. One can spare the rod without spoiling the child, it seems, but setting no limits on children's behavior is virtually as bad as relying solely on the stick.

SOCIALIZATION AND ETHNICITY

The three-category classification of parenting styles is still widely cited, and the authoritative style is generally seen as more effective than the authoritarian style. Yet recently, some scholars have questioned whether the model can be applied to racial and ethnic minority families. African American parents, for instance, are somewhat more likely than white parents to use physical punishment; and Asian American parents are more likely than white parents to insist on discipline and obedience (McLoyd, Cauce, Takeuchi, & Wilson, 2000). Within African American or Asian American culture, according to critics, these actions may not have the negative meaning that whites, especially middle-class whites, attach to them (Chao, 1994). In fact, one study found that parent's physical discipline—mostly spanking or slapping—in the first five years of a child's life and during early adolescence was associated with more behavior problems among eleventh-grade European American children but fewer behavior problems among eleventh-grade African American children (Lansford, Deater-Deckard, Dodge, Bates, & Pettit, 2004). However, another study found that among non-Hispanic whites, African Americans, and Hispanics alike, young children whose parents spanked them more showed increased problem behavior, particularly when mothers provided low levels of emotional support (McLoyd & Smith, 2002). The contradictory results of these studies suggest that it is premature to discard Baumrind's classification but that researchers must be careful in extending it to racial and ethnic minority parents (Cancian, 2002).

One of the primary tasks in socialization, in fact, is to familiarize children with the culture in which they are growing up. Consider the acquisition of language. Learning to talk not only allows children to communicate with others, but also carries important lessons about their society. A French child learns two words for *you:* Siblings and friends are called *tu,* and parents and other adults are called *vous.* Thus the child learns which relationships are characterized by equality and intimacy and which are characterized by respect and social distance. A Japanese girl learns to show deference to men by addressing them differently than she does women. At a conference I attended in Tokyo, a female Japanese professor was criticized by a male colleague—in Japanese. She replied to him in English. When asked later why she responded in English, she said that, had she chosen Japanese, she would have had to use the "respect language" a polite woman must employ when addressing a man. In English, she could respond as a linguistic equal.

norm a widely accepted rule about how people should behave

value a goal or principle that is held in high esteem by a society

Socialization also involves teaching children norms and values. **Norms** are widely accepted rules about how people should behave. **Values** are goals and principles that are held in high esteem by a society. The norms and values may be those of the dominant culture in the society, of a subculture, or of both. Families begin this process; schools, churches, peer groups, and even the media carry it on. For example, Japanese children learn to place a higher value on loyalty to the group in situations where an American child would learn to value independent action. Their greater dependence on others begins in the first few years of life. Japanese mothers tend to wean their children from breast-feeding later than American mothers. They also carry their children on their backs when they go

Japanese children are taught to be loyal to the group, whereas American children are taught to be more independent.

shopping and often sleep with them (Preston & Kono, 1988). Child rearing manuals in Japan urge parents to emphasize the child's dependence on the family. A leading manual discounts the importance of teaching a baby to eat vegetables or any particular kind of food; rather, its author stresses the importance of teaching the baby to eat with the family and to share the same food (Boocock, 1991). Japanese preschool teachers seem to be more lenient than American teachers in allowing rough play and noise, but the Japanese teachers treat a child's reluctance to participate in group activities as a more serious problem. A reluctant child will experience more pressure to join the group in a Japanese setting than in an American preschool (Boocock, 1991).

SOCIALIZATION AND SOCIAL CLASS

In Chapter 4 we reviewed studies showing that middle-class parents tend to socialize their children somewhat differently from working-class and low-income parents. (➡ p. 134) These differences can be overstated—there are many commonalities— but they seem important. To review, middle-class parents tend to emphasize autonomy and self-direction. They seek actively to enhance their children's talents and opinions, in a style that Lareau (2002, 2003) called "concerted cultivation." Others have called it "intensive mothering" (Hays, 1996). Working-class and lower-income parents, on the other hand, are more likely to emphasize obedience and conformity. They seek to provide a safe, loving environment in which children can grow on their own—in Lareau's terms, they aim for "the accomplishment of natural growth." Kohn (1969; Kohn & Schooler, 1978) claims that the differing parenting styles derive from the occupational conditions of the parents. Middle-class parents whose jobs provide autonomy and self-direction are more likely to emphasize those values with their children. Thus, middle-class parents socialize their children, in effect, to grow up and take middle-class jobs. Working-class parents, with their emphasis on obedience and conformity, socialize their children for the kinds of blue- and pink-collar jobs the parents have held.

SOCIALIZATION AND GENDER

Chapter 3 presented evidence that parents socialize their daughters differently than their sons [➡ p. 88]; here that discussion will be briefly summarized. Researchers now think of socialization as a two-way process in which children and parents influence each other. Because of their predispositions or because of other factors that may make them behave differently, children can influence how parents treat them. Parents then make decisions that reinforce these differences, such as buying stereotypically female toys for girls and stereotypically male toys for boys. The distinctions parents make may reflect, in part, biologically based differences between girls and boys (Rossi, 1984); yet parents' actions also tend to magnify and exaggerate gender differences. The emphasis in sociological studies of this process has been on the conscious social learning children do as they are rewarded for some behaviors and punished for others—and as they watch and imitate adults of the same gender. In addition, girls and boys may also develop different senses of self because of unconscious, psychoanalytic processes of merging and separating from those who were their primary caretakers as infants, who are nearly always women (Chodorow, 1978). Schools, peer groups, and the media further exaggerate gender differences, so that adult gender roles are far more distinctive than any inherent differences might warrant.

RELIGION AND SOCIALIZATION

Do religious denominations differ in what they say parents are supposed to do for their children? Are some religious beliefs more consistent with authoritarian than authoritative parenting? Some social scientists have suggested that conservative Protestantism leads fathers to be more authoritarian with their children. The argument is that conservative Protestantism—the denominations and independent churches sometimes called evangelical or fundamentalist, such as the Southern Baptist Convention, the United Pentecostal Church, and the Assemblies of God—teaches that men are the head of the family and therefore encourages a strict, discipline-oriented, distant style of fathering (Gottman, 1998). But national surveys that ask parents about their religious activities and their relationships with their children suggest that the story is not that simple (Wilcox, 2004). Yes, conservative Protestant men are more likely to believe in traditional gender roles: It's better if the husband is the earner and the wife stays home to raise the family, the wife should do more of the housework, and so forth. But they are also more likely to combine discipline with what sociologists call "emotion work" (Hochschild, 1979), the act of influencing and managing the emotions of others—in this case their wives and children.

W. Bradford Wilcox (1998, 2004) reports that conservative Protestant fathers who frequently attend church spank their children more often, which fits the authoritarian style, but in other ways they are quite authoritative: They hug and praise their children more than other fathers, yell at them less, and spend more time in leisure activities like playing together or having private talks. Wilcox argues that conservative Protestant churches teach that being the household head means, in part, being an involved father. The churches urge fathers not just to be disciplinarians but also to be emotionally expressive toward their children and to spend time with them. As a result, Wilcox argues, fathers become "soft patriarchs" who combine strict discipline with warmth and involvement in a style that blends the authoritarian with the authoritative. Religious fathers from "mainline" Protestant groups, such as the Episcopal, Lutheran, Presbyterian, Lutheran, and Methodist churches, are less authoritarian—they spank their children less—but they are aren't as involved in activities with them (and are less likely to set rules for television viewing or to know where their children are when they're not at home).

WHAT'S IMPORTANT?

Social class and gender differences do exist, then, in how children are socialized. Nevertheless, it is possible to make some general statements about what parents are supposed to do. First, they should provide support to their children. This includes material support such as food, clothes, and shelter, as well as emotional support such as love and nurturing. The need for the former is obvious: Without material support, the child is in physical danger. Yet without emotional support, she or he is likely to grow up without a sense of security or a capability for trusting and loving other people. Second, parents should provide control. They must supervise and monitor their children's behavior not only to help them avoid physical harm but also to teach children the limits of acceptable behavior.

One could supplement this basic list according to one's values. Some might stress the importance of religious and ethical training—an upbringing that teaches children about the spiritual and moral side of life. Those who believe that people of both genders should undertake a wide range of behaviors that are now stereotyped as masculine or feminine—who believe, for example, that men should provide more care for children and women should have better opportunities for careers—might add that parents should encourage more **androgynous behavior** (i.e., behavior that has the characteristics of both genders) in their children. From this perspective, boys should be encouraged to be more nurturing and girls more aggressive. Similarly, those who believe that the values passed along to working-class children limit their occupational achievements might add that parents of all classes ought to encourage autonomous behavior in their children.

androgynous behavior
behavior that has the characteristics of both genders

Quick Review

- Parents socialize their children by providing emotional support and control and by teaching them about norms and values.
- Authoritative parenting—combining warmth with consistent, moderate discipline—is thought to be most beneficial, but this conclusion may not apply to racial-ethnic minority groups.
- Middle-class parents tend to emphasize autonomy and self-direction, while working-class and lower-income parents tend to emphasize obedience and conformity.
- Parents tend to socialize their daughters differently than their sons, creating or magnifying gender differences.

WHAT DIFFERENCE DO FATHERS MAKE?

Most of the literature on parenting focuses on mothers rather than fathers—an understandable emphasis, since mothers do more child rearing than fathers in nearly all societies. But during the 1980s and even more so in the 1990s and early 2000s, scholars conducted a great deal of research on the role of fathers in child rearing. Most studies were conducted in the context of families with two heterosexual parents and in which the mother is the primary caregiver. This is the most typical

The amount of time fathers spend with their children is less important than how actively engaged they are.

scenario, but others do exist—such as single heterosexual fathers or single or coupled gay men. Although the quality of these studies is uneven, the best of them suggests that fathers do make a difference in their children's lives (Marsiglio, Amato, Day, & Lamb, 2000). For example, Mosley and Thomson (1995) examined information on two-parent families from the 1987–1988 National Survey of Families and Households. They found that in both white and African American families, when fathers were more involved with their children (reading to them, helping them with homework, or restricting their television viewing), the children had fewer behavior problems, got along better with others, and were more responsible. This relationship held even if researchers controlled for the mother's involvement with the children and the family's racial and class background. Other research suggests the following conclusions:

Fathers Relate to Young Children Differently Than Mothers

Fathers relate to young children more through playing with them than do mothers (Lamb, 2002). They employ a vigorous style of play that is often labeled "rough and tumble" in the literature. Picture a father throwing his toddler up in the air and catching her, or rolling on the floor with her, and you have the idea. Psychological studies suggest that these active play sessions help children learn to regulate their emotions (Parke, 1996). Children learn the limits of excitable behavior (e.g., no biting or kicking) and how to bring their emotions back down when it is over. These lessons, it is thought, lead them to be better playmates, to have more friends, and, in adolescence and adulthood, to have more self-control in highly charged situations.

Fathers' Influence Is Often Indirect

Fathers' influence often works through mothers rather than directly to the children (Lamb, 2002). Fathers exercise this indirect influence in part through providing emotional support to mothers or backing up the mothers' authority. The better the quality of the father and mother's relationship, the better is the child's behavior and school achievement, on average (Amato, 1998). Fathers also provide income to the family—in fact, that has often been seen as their major contribution—although studies suggest that income by itself doesn't help children as much as does parental input (Mayer, 1997). Frank Furstenberg and I have speculated that one reason why some divorced fathers have difficulty relating to their children is that they are not used to interacting directly with them in a context where mothers are absent (Furstenberg & Cherlin, 1991).

Fathers' Influence on Children Is Long Term as Well as Short Term

Because mothers tend to be the more hands-on parent in everyday life, fathers' influence is likely to be more subtle and long-term. Consider a study of over 200 Boston-area men, who were first interviewed as schoolboys in the late 1940s and reinterviewed periodically for about 40 years. In the 1980s, John Snarey (1993) reinterviewed the men and their adult children to study the long-term effects of fathers' **generativity**—a term coined by psychologist Erik Erikson (1950) to mean concern about guiding and shaping the next generation. Using information from past interviews, Snarey rated each father's parental generativity—caring activities with children that developed or shaped their capacities, such as rocking to sleep or reading to younger children, or taking an older child to an art gallery or teaching him or her how to fish. He then asked the (now grown-up) children about their education and occupation. He found that in families where fathers had been more generative, the children had had greater educational and occupational success, even when he took into account other important characteristics of the parents and children.

> **generativity** a feeling of concern about, or interest in, guiding and shaping the next generation

How Fathers Act toward Their Children, Not How Much Time They Spend with Them, Makes a Difference

A large proportion of children experience their parents' divorce or are born to single mothers (see Chapter 12). Most of these children live with their mothers. One might think that the more time these children spend with their fathers, the better their development would be, but a majority of studies on this topic do not show a strong link between the frequency of a father's visits and child development (Marsiglio et al., 2000). What studies do show is that children whose nonresident fathers have an authoritative parenting style (for example, who encourage their children and discuss their problems) tend to develop better than children whose visits with their fathers are purely recreational (Amato & Gilbreth, 1999). Within limits, then, the way nonresidential fathers behave as parents seems to make more of a difference than how often they see their children. (A father who rarely sees his children has little influence on them.) Even among fathers who live with their children, the simple amount of time they spend together is less important than how actively engaged they are and how much responsibility they take for the children's care (Palkovitz, 2002).

An Appraisal

This list is far from exhaustive; many other studies report effects of fathers on children. However, there are also many studies that have failed to find effects of fathers. For example, studies that also control for mothers' influences and that interview both generations yield weaker evidence of the effects of fathers (Amato, 1998). This newly emerging research literature leaves the reader with two impressions: (1) fathers do have significant effects on children's development, but (2) fathers' effects are, in general, weaker than mothers' effects—especially in terms of the day-to-day behavior of children. As for the latter impression, it is hard to see how it could be otherwise: Mothers do far more of the childcare in the typical two-parent family than do fathers. One might predict that fathers' influence would be stronger in families where both parents shared the childcare responsibilities equally, but that topic remains to be studied.

Another unresolved question is whether any second adult in the household—a grandmother, a lesbian lover—can provide the same benefits to children or whether a father is needed. Some observers argue that men and women have evolved differing approaches to childrearing—as evidenced, for example, by fathers' rough and tumble play and mothers' greater nurturing—and, therefore, that a mother and father are needed (Popenoe, 1996). Many other sociologists would disagree and claim instead that fathers' behaviors aren't programmed by evolution but rather are learned from parents and peers; they would argue that the benefits of having a father rather than a different second caregiver are not proven. Unfortunately, the research evidence isn't sufficient to provide a clear answer; it may be that both evolutionary psychology and socialization contribute to shaping fathers' caregiving behaviors (Parke, 1996).

ADOPTION

The 2000 Census included, for the first time, a separate question about adoption. Although it had limitations, it provides the first good national statistics; the tabulations show that about 2.5 percent of all children under age 18 in the United States were adopted (U.S. Bureau of the Census, 2003a). The nature of adoption has been changing over the past few decades. The typical adoption used to involve an unmarried, white mother placing an infant for adoption with an unrelated married couple. But after the introduction of the birth control pill in the 1960s and the legalization of abortion in the 1970s, the number of unplanned births declined sharply. Moreover, the stigma of raising children outside of marriage decreased. As a result, the proportion of white, unmarried mothers who gave up their newborns for adoption declined from almost 20 percent in the early 1970s to 2 percent in the first half of the 1990s (U.S. National Center for Health Statistics, 1999). (The proportion of African American mothers who give up their newborns for adoption has always been lower and is estimated at about 2 percent.) But other forms of adoption appear to have become more common, although statistics are incomplete.

Adoptions increasingly occur in the following settings. Adoptive children who have been placed in foster care and whose parents' rights to them have been terminated due to neglect or abuse are sometimes adopted by foster parents or by kin such as aunts or grandparents. (See Chapter 11, *Families and Public Policy: Foster Care.*) Stepparents do "second-parent" adoptions of stepchildren so that both parents in the home will have legal rights and responsibilities (see Chapter 13). Parents in developing countries who are unable economically to provide care place young children with an agency that finds adoptive parents in developed countries such as the United States. Lesbian and gay couples adopt children, sometimes by doing a second-parent adoption of the biological child of one partner, sometimes by adopting children from birth mothers unrelated to the couple.

The census statistics reflect the changing nature of adoption. Thirteen percent of adopted children were born in other countries compared to 4 percent of biological children. Half of the foreign-born adopted children were from Asian

Americans are adopting children from developing countries whose parents are too poor to care for them.

countries, with China and Korea supplying the largest numbers. Adopted children also were about twice as likely to have a disability as were biological children. The most common disability was "difficulty learning, remembering, or concentrating." This relatively high prevalence of learning disabilities probably reflects the origins of many adoptions in the foster care system, as well as the quality of care that some children born in other countries may have received prior to being adopted. In addition, adopted children were less likely to live in poor families than were biological children, suggesting that adoptive parents tend to be better off financially than biological parents (U.S. Bureau of the Census, 2003a).

The forms of adoption are clearly diverse, but all have in common the voluntary nature of their actions. They constitute another example of constructing families of choice. [➡ p. 198] An adoptive parent who is also a law professor wrote:

> *Adoption involves choice on a scale most of us don't generally experience. You can't fall accidentally into adoption as you can into pregnancy. You exercise choice down to the wire. (Bartholet, 1993)*

Yet we know very little about how adoptive parents and children form and maintain these families of choice (Fisher, 2003).

Adoptive families are usually successful, and most adopted children exhibit normal emotional development. A minority of adopted children, however, do show elevated levels of emotional or behavioral difficulties (Brodzinsky, Schechter, & Marantz, 1992). These difficulties may stem from events prior to the adoption, such as maternal substance abuse during pregnancy, time spent in multiple foster homes, or neglect in an overseas orphanage. But despite the successes of the majority, adoption may still be, in the words of one recent observer, "a devalued status" (Fisher, 2003). Most people may admire it in the abstract, but many seemingly good candidates for adoptive parenthood, such as middle-class couples who are unsuccessful in efforts to conceive a child, avoid it in practice, either out of a strong preference for biological children or a fear that an adoption will not work out.

Quick Review

- Conservative Protestant men tend to combine strict discipline with an involved style of fatherhood.
- Fathers tend to relate to young children differently than mothers do and their influence is often indirect.
- Adopted children are more likely than biological children to be foreign born and to come from the foster care system but less likely to live in low-income families.
- In diverse ways, adoptive parents and children construct families of choice.

What Might Prevent Parents from Doing What They Are Supposed to Do?

Yet even parents with the best intentions sometimes cannot care for their children and socialize them as well as they would like to. The larger society sometimes interferes, as when a parent loses a job or a family cannot climb out of poverty. The transformation of the U.S. economy over the past few decades [➡ p. 113] has hurt many parents and made child rearing more difficult. Social change also may interfere: Some observers have argued that recent changes in the organization of families make successful parenting more difficult. Among the changes causing these alleged difficulties are the great increase in the proportion of children who are cared for by someone other than a parent because their parents work for pay, the doubling of the divorce rate since the 1960s, and the increasing proportion of children born outside marriage. Newer arrangements, such as children who live with lesbian or gay parents, have also generated interest and concern. In this section, the effects of these developments on the quality of parenting will be examined.

UNEMPLOYMENT AND POVERTY

On the most basic level, low income means fewer clothes and less food. It can mean being evicted from your apartment. It can mean that your children's bedroom has peeling, lead-filled paint. The effects of poverty on children can start before they are born. Pregnant, poor women are more likely to receive inadequate prenatal care and to engage in behaviors harmful to the fetus—such as smoking (which reduces birth weight), using drugs, and eating an unhealthy diet (Halpern, 1993).

In addition, the consequences of unemployment and poverty can be more subtle. They can change the ways parents act toward each other. [➡ p. 279] They can also change the way parents and children interact. Consider the declining fortunes of agricultural communities in the American Midwest. In 1987, sociologist Glen Elder, psychologist Rand Conger, and several collaborators studied 76 families in a rural Iowa county (Elder, Conger, Foster, & Ardelt, 1992). All were white, a majority were middle class, and each consisted of a married couple and at least two children, one of whom was in seventh grade. After obtaining background information from the family members, the research team set up a video camera. While the tape rolled, they asked the parents to spend 30 minutes reviewing the history and present status of their marriage. Then they taped a 15-minute discussion in which the parents attempted to solve a problem in their marriage. They

Unemployed fathers, like this out-of-work carpenter, can become depressed and act irritably toward their partners and children.

then taped one of the parents and the seventh-grader in two discussions: talking about a family activity and talking about a family problem such as doing chores or getting along with a younger sibling. Finally, they taped the other parent and the seventh-grader in the same two discussions. Over the next several months, trained raters viewed and reviewed the videotapes, coding the kinds of behaviors each person displayed, such as warmth, affection, or anger.

Unemployment   Nineteen of the fathers had lost their jobs, had had their hours cut back, or had been demoted in the preceding year. Other families had experienced a drop in income or very little growth. The researchers combined these events into a measure of how much "economic pressure" each family was facing. (Even though most of the mothers were employed outside the home, the researchers focused on fathers, who were still the main earners in nearly all the families.) Studies of families during the Great Depression had shown that men who had lost their jobs were tense and irritable in their relations with wives and explosive and punishing in their relations with their children (Liker & Elder, 1983). The tapes showed similar behavior: Fathers in families under economic pressure were more irritable and hostile toward their wives and children. Their wives often replied in kind. One daughter said that at dinnertime "we are kinda cautious, like walking on hot ground or something" (Elder et al., 1992). The interviews revealed that fathers under economic pressure tended to be depressed, lacking energy and interest—more so than their wives. One father said, "There would be some good days, but there would be more bad ones than good ones. Kind of lethargic. Oh, I know it's gotta be done, but I'll do it tomorrow. We kind of floated." Moreover, during the taped discussions, children whose fathers were more hostile and irritable were themselves more sullen, angry, and abrasive. In their interviews, these children admitted to more symptoms of depression (e.g., feeling lonely, hopeless, no interest) and aggressiveness (e.g., I am tempted to break a rule if I don't like it; I do the opposite of what a bossy person says; I yell back if I'm yelled at).

The study suggests a chain of events running from economic difficulties to children's behavior problems. The loss of a job or a drop in income causes psychological distress for the husband, who is still expected to be the family's main earner. The distress in turn leads to depression and to angry, explosive exchanges with his wife and children. And the children then become more depressed, hostile, and aggressive. It is possible, however, that causation could run the opposite way: Men who are depressed and hostile may be more likely to lose their jobs and to have children with similar characteristics. Still, the sequence proposed by the Iowa researchers is plausible and is supported by other studies (Kessler, House, & Turner, 1987).

Poverty   Studies of poor urban families show similar dynamics (Seccombe, 2000). A parent in poverty may be depressed about job prospects, anxious about paying the bills, or angry about crime and drugs in the neighborhood. One mother receiving public assistance payments in New York City said, "Every month I have to decide which bill to pay, which doesn't give you a clear mind. You're always depressed" (Halpern, 1993). Such a parent has few psychological resources left to devote to her or his children. Instead of reasoning with the child or explaining why a certain behavior is good or bad, a depressed and anxious parent may respond to perceived misbehavior simply by threatening harsh punishment—but may then give in if the child refuses to obey. Thus, the child obtains little emotional support and receives discipline that is inconsistent, harsh, and punitive. As noted earlier, this style of parenting has been associated with diminished social competence among children, although some scholars question its application to racial-ethnic minority groups. One set of studies suggests that low income has more of an effect on children's school achievement than it does on their behavior; moreover, low income seems to be more detrimental to younger children than to adolescents (Duncan & Brooks-Gunn, 1997).

Since such a large proportion of African American children live in persistently poor, single-parent households, the distress their mothers often experience is particularly consequential for their development. One research review suggests that poor black single mothers may be more vulnerable to psychological distress than white single mothers with comparable incomes because of the former's chronic economic difficulties (McLoyd, 1990). A higher proportion of black single mothers have never married, whereas a higher proportion of white single mothers are divorced. The divorced mothers are more likely to have avoided economic problems prior to the breakup of their marriages; the never-married mothers are more likely to have lived persistently in poverty.

In addition, it is more common among poor black children than among poor white children to be raised by a grandmother—particularly among children whose mothers (and often grandmothers) were teenagers when they gave birth. In these families, teenage childbearing compresses the generations, producing grandmothers who are in their thirties and forties rather than their fifties and sixties (Burton, 1990). To be sure, many young grandmothers provide crucial support and child care. Moreover, the role of the grandmother in African American families is stronger, in general, than in European American families. [➥ p. 157] Nevertheless, some grandmothers may not be at a life stage at which they expect to be caring for grandchildren, and they may be holding jobs themselves. Psychologist P. Lindsay Chase-Lansdale and her colleagues videotaped interactions between young African American mothers and their children, and between grandmothers and the same children, in two kinds of families: those in which the three generations lived in the same household and those in which the grandmother lived in a separate household (Chase-Lansdale, Brooks-Gunn, & Zamsky, 1994). To the research group's surprise, the quality of parenting—by both the mother and the grandmother—was *lower* when the three generations lived in the same household. The only exception occurred when the mother had given birth in her early teens. It seems likely that a selection effect [➡ p. 211] is at work: Young mothers who have the financial and psychological resources to live on their own probably are more competent, on average, at raising a child. Mothers who have fewer resources are more likely to live with grandmothers. Joint residence is an arrangement often born of necessity. It has mixed effects on adolescent mothers and their children in poor families (McLoyd et al., 2000).

DIVORCE AND REMARRIAGE

The most common way in which children come to live with a single parent is when their parents divorce. Chapters 12 and 13 will examine the effects of divorce and remarriage on children, so I will only summarize the findings here. In the first two years or so after the separation, most children are distressed. The custodial parent, usually the mother, often sees her income go down as the father withdraws much of his support; she may be forced to sell the family home and move to a new neighborhood. She may be so depressed and angry that she cannot provide the consistent support and supervision her children need. The children may be caught in the middle of continuing contact between the former spouses. This "crisis period" is typically a difficult time for both children and parents. Yet some of the problems that children display after a separation were present before the parents split up—suggesting that they might have occurred even had the parents stayed together.

Moreover, over the long term, as Chapter 12 will note, most children do not seem to suffer substantial harm because of their parents' divorce. To be sure, their risk of experiencing outcomes such as dropping out of school, having a child as a teenager, or receiving public assistance increases. The remarriage of a custodial parent, as Chapter 13 will note, does not appear to lower these risks—the well-being of children in stepfamilies is similar to that of children living with unmarried, divorced parents. These increased risks should be troubling to those who are concerned with children's well-being. Still, most children do not experience these undesirable outcomes; rather, most appear to enter adulthood without serious divorce-related problems. It is likely, then, that the increase in divorce has produced short-term trauma for most children and has, on average, reduced their long-term well-being moderately. I think the most prudent conclusion is that divorce is neither a benign event nor an automatic disaster for children. Over the years, most children appear to cope adequately with it and do not suffer serious harm. Yet it deserves to be a source of public concern because it adversely affects most children in the short run and a minority of children in the long run (Cherlin, 1999a).

SINGLE PARENTHOOD

What are the effects of single parenthood itself, apart from any effects of poverty or of divorce? What if, say, an unmarried middle-class woman decides to have a child? Some critics have claimed that, regardless of their income levels, single parents are hindered by the absence of a second parent. These claims are controversial because defenders of single parents counter that, given the appropriate resources, they can provide care that equals the quality of care by two-parent families. There is little doubt that many of the problems single parents face can be traced to low incomes or to continuing conflicts with former spouses—and therefore could be eased by greater income support from ex-spouses or the government and a lessening of postmarital tensions. In this sense, single parents per se are capable of adequate parenting much more than critics contend.

Even so, the presence of only one parent is sometimes a handicap, even after lower income is taken into account. An analysis of four national surveys found that low income, and declines in income, could account for about half the disadvantages of living in a single-parent family, such as the higher risk of dropping out of school or having a birth prior to marriage; yet half of the higher risks remained (McLanahan & Sandefur, 1994). Several studies show that single parents do not monitor and supervise their children as well as married or cohabiting parents. For instance, in a national survey of high school students, those in single-parent families were less likely to report that their parents kept close track of how they were doing in school than students from two-parent families. They were also less likely to report that their parents almost always knew where they were and what they were doing. These differences remained even after controls for the socioeconomic status of the families (Astone & McLanahan, 1991). Other studies of adolescents have found that single parents engaged in less consistent parenting and more arguments (Hetherington & Clingempeel, 1992; Dornbusch et al., 1985). Overall, I would draw two conclusions: First, single parents, if they have adequate incomes, usually provide good care for children. Second, it is nevertheless the case that, other things being equal, it is better for children to be raised by two parents than by one. We do not know, however, whether these parents must be of opposite sexes. It is quite possible that two same-sex parents could provide care that is just as good.

Quick Review

- Unemployment and poverty can change the way parents act toward each other and the way they interact with their children.
- Among low-income African American families, it is more common for children to be raised by grandmothers.
- Divorce creates a short-term crisis period that is difficult for parents and children, but most children do not have serious problems in the long run.
- Single parents typically provide good care for children, but raising children is a more difficult task when only one parent is present.

LESBIAN AND GAY PARENTHOOD

It is only since the 1960s that circumstances have allowed children to live with an openly lesbian or gay parent and, often, that parent's partner. Those circumstances, which are discussed elsewhere in this book, include the following: the sharp, post-1960 rise in divorce, which encouraged more homosexual men and women who were in heterosexual marriages (often with children) to end their marriages; the emergence of an openly gay subculture in large cities, which provided a supportive environment for lesbian and gay couples; the greater tolerance of childbearing outside marriage and single parenting in general; and the development of reproductive technologies that make conception possible without heterosexual intercourse.

There are three main types of gay and lesbian families with children (Patterson, 2000). In the first type, the children were born to a married parent who later came out as lesbian or gay, obtained a divorce, and retained custody of the children. Because women retain custody of children much more often than men after a divorce, most of these families include a lesbian mother, her children, and often her new partner. Children in this type of family have experienced the transitions and difficulties associated with a parental divorce (see Chapter 12). The second type of gay and lesbian family consists of existing lesbian or gay couples who have either adopted a child or conceived one through **donor insemination**—the insertion of donated semen into the uterus of an ovulating woman. The third type is the emerging number of gay male fathers who have children through arrangements such as hiring a surrogate mother to carry fetuses inseminated with their (or their partner's) sperm or through adoption, often of children from the foster care system (Stacey, 2006). In the 2000 Census, children were present in 168,000 same-sex partner households; an unknown number of children were being raised by single lesbian or gay male parents (U.S. Bureau of the Census, 2003h).

donor insemination a procedure in which semen is inserted into the uterus of an ovulating woman

Studies of Children in Gay and Lesbian Families   Many studies have attempted to compare children living with lesbian parents and children living with heterosexual single or married parents (Tasker, 2005). Most of the early studies were of lesbian or gay families of the first type: children born to mothers who were married and who subsequently divorced and began living openly lesbian lives. More recently, several studies have been published of lesbian families of the second type, those with planned births, usually by donor insemination. There have been far fewer studies of children living with gay male parents, all of them of the first type; so too little information exists to draw any conclusions. As for the lesbian mothers, virtually all have been white and well-educated, typically with managerial or professional occupations. Moreover, almost all the studies have been based on modest-sized, nonrandom samples, which means that the subjects either volunteered to be studied or were recruited through acquaintances or organizations known to the authors. They may not, therefore, be representative of lesbian mothers in general.

The results of these studies consistently show that children raised by lesbian parents are very similar to children raised by heterosexual parents (Patterson, 2000; Stacey & Biblarz, 2001; Tasker, 2005). They have similar levels of behavior problems and perform similarly in school. They seem to be as well-adjusted emotionally. Consider a British study that followed 25 lesbian families that had planned the birth of their child, along with 38 single heterosexual mothers and 38 two-parent heterosexual families, from the birth of their children until the children were twelve years old (MacCallum & Golombok, 2004). The three groups of children did not differ significantly in school adjustment, peer relationships, and self-esteem. When asked a set of questions about characteristics typically associated with masculinity and femininity, boys in lesbian homes and heterosexual single-mother homes showed higher scores on "femininity" (being loyal, affectionate, and sympathetic), but their scores on "masculinity" (being self-reliant, ambitious, assertive) were just as high as boys living with two heterosexual parents. These results suggest that boys living without fathers, regardless of their mothers' sexual orientation, may display a more androgenous character; but they do not suggest that boys from lesbian homes are any different from boys from the homes of heterosexual single mothers.

The 2000 Census counted over 168,000 same-sex partner households with children.

Researchers have also attempted to study the sexual orientation of adults who were raised in lesbian mother households with those raised in heterosexual households. If sexual orientation is at least partially socially constructed, we might expect differences between children raised in lesbian and heterosexual households (Bailey & Dawood, 1998). If lesbian parents provide children with fewer opportunities to interact with a heterosexual father, it is possible that the children's sexual orientation as adults could be affected. One research group followed 46 children until they were 23.5 years old, on average (Tasker & Golombok, 1995). They found that the children who had grown up in lesbian families were more open to the possibility of same-gender sexual relationships. The greater openness was observable in two ways: First, 6 of 25 children from lesbian families reported at least one same-gender relationship, ranging from a kiss to cohabitation; but none of the 21 children from heterosexual families reported a same gender relationship. Second, 14 children from lesbian families said they had considered the possibility of a same-gender relationship, compared with 3 of the children from heterosexual families. Nevertheless, only two of the children from lesbian families were currently in a same-gender relationship and identified as lesbian (both were women). In other words, growing up in a lesbian family seems to have made the children more open to same-gender sexual relationships, but most still identified as heterosexual.

Tentative Conclusions   It is hard to know how much confidence to place in these and other similar studies. What we have is a growing body of consistent findings, almost all of which, unfortunately, are limited by their nonrandom, well-educated samples. Yet it's not clear how social scientists *could* obtain a good random sample because the number of same-sex families is still small. For instance, three researchers mined the data from a large nationally representative, random-sample survey of adolescents but could only identify 44 adolescents who appeared to live with cohabiting same-sex parents. For what it is worth, these adolescents did not appear to differ in their personal, family, and school adjustment from a matched set of adolescents who were living in heterosexual two-parent families (Wainright, Russell, & Patterson, 2004). Keeping in mind the limitations of this research literature, one might draw the tentative conclusion that children raised by lesbian parents are as well-adjusted as children raised by heterosexual parents and that most appear to develop a heterosexual orientation, although they may display more openness to same-gender relationships.

TIME APART

Because of the great increase in the proportion of mothers who work outside the home, more children face daily periods of separation from their parents. Neither parent may be available to care for a preschool child or to be home when an older child returns from school. The issue is usually framed in terms of "working mothers" even though fathers are working outside the home and could provide care when they are home. This development raises two questions: How much less time do children spend with their parents? and What are the consequences of spending more time apart?

How Parents Compensate for Time Apart   You would think children must be spending much less time with their parents now than in the past. But recent studies suggest that the increase in time apart has been smaller than one would expect. Bianchi, Robinson, and Milkie (2006) report on several national surveys between 1965 and 1970 that collected information on parents' use of time during a day. Figure 9.1 displays the average weekly hours of child care of all mothers and fathers living with children under age 18. As you can see, time spent in child care declined for mothers between 1965 and 1985 but then increased; by 2000 it was higher than at any previous survey. For fathers, the time spent also increased between 1985 and 2000 to its highest point. Two-parent

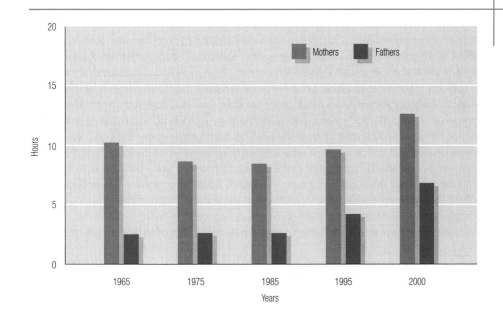

FIGURE 9.1
Average Weekly Hours of Child Care of Mothers and Fathers, 1965–2000. (*Source:* Bianchi, Robinson, & Milkie, 2006)

families drove this increase; the time that single mothers spend with children actually decreased between 1975 and 2000. This trend toward more, rather than less, time with children despite the increase in mothers' work outside the home also occurred in two-parent families in other nations, as a comparative study of time-use data on families with young children in 16 industrialized countries showed (Gauthier, Smeeding, & Furstenberg, 2004).

Employed parents seem to be compensating during nonemployed hours for some of the time they spend away from their children. Booth, Clarke-Stewart, Vandell, McCartney, and Owen (2002) compared the time spent with parents by two groups of infants in a national study: those who were in child care 30 hours or more per week and those who were not in child care at all. ("Child care" is the term commonly used for nonparental care provided to children while their parents work.) Although the mothers of the first group could potentially have spent 30 fewer hours with their infants, they only spent 12 fewer hours with them, on average. Thus, they had compensated for more than half the hours their children were in child care settings.

How are they doing it? First, they are cutting back on housework. Women have reduced their hours of housework substantially, while husbands have increased theirs to a lesser extent. The typical household today, as noted previously, is either a little less clean or is cleaned by someone the parents pay. [➡ p. 265] Second, they have less leisure time. Married women, for instance, spend less time reading, visiting people, and participating in clubs or other organizations. All parents are spending less time eating, suggesting quicker meals. Third, they are combining activities much more—working or trying to relax while taking care of their children at the same time, for example (Bianchi et al., 2006). Fourth, in the time that they have with their children, parents are making a priority of intensive activities with children, such as playing or reading to them, rather than just monitoring them (Bittman, Craig, & Folbre, 2004). Overall, family life would seem to be a bit more hectic for parents, with less time for leisure and household tasks. But as a result, children's time apart from parents has not increased as much as labor force trends would lead one to expect.

The Consequences of Nonparental Care
Still, an increasing number of children are experiencing daily separations from employed parents. Sixty-three percent of all preschool children today spend some time each week in child care (U.S. Bureau of the Census, 2005o). Some observers worry that nonparental child-care is inferior to the care parents can provide. During the 1990s and early 2000s, several studies suggested that, in general, children are not harmed by child care (Perry-Jenkins, Repetti, & Crouter, 2000). But it appears that children whose mothers work full-time in the first year of life tend to have lower cognitive (i.e., reading skills) achievement test scores, at least through ages seven and eight (Waldfogel, 2006). Mothers' employment after the first year, however, does not seem to have detrimental effects on cognitive skills. We don't know much about the effect of paternal employment because researchers have assumed that fathers don't provide much care. Yet fathers provide substantially more child care than in the past; [➡ p. 265] therefore, it may be time to study paternal caregiving and employment more closely.

Moreover, a large and intensive study suggests that more child care may be linked to more aggressive and disobedient behavior in kindergarten, although the size of the effect is modest. The study was conducted by a research network

More than half of all preschool children now spend some time each week in nonparental care.

organized by the National Institute of Child Health and Human Development (NICHD). Researchers studied over 1,000 infants in eight states, visiting the children's families and child care settings repeatedly from birth through age five. When the children reached kindergarten, teachers and parents were asked a battery of questions about them. The more time that children had spent in care provided by anyone but their mothers from birth through age five, the more likely they were to engage in behavior such as talking back to teachers, having temper tantrums, and getting in many fights (NICHD Early Child Care Research Network, 2003).

Three caveats are in order: First, very few of the children showed levels of aggression and disobedience that were serious enough to warrant the intervention of a mental health professional, regardless of how much nonmaternal care they had experienced. Rather, the typical pattern was a modest rise in problem behaviors. Second, the study did not include children who were living in neighborhoods the researchers judged too unsafe for interviewers to enter, nor did it include children whose mothers didn't speak English, which means that children from the poorest neighborhoods and children of immigrants were underrepresented. Other recent studies suggest that poor children may benefit from out-of-home care, presumably because their home environment is not as enriching (Love et al., 2003). Third, not all children were equally at risk. Children whose temperaments are more difficult are likely to be affected; and boys were generally more affected than girls (Waldfogel, 2006).

Nevertheless, the findings suggest some caution in assessing the effects of nonparental care on young children. We cannot confidently say that child care has no negative effects on young children. The NICHD research network is continuing to follow its children, and their future reports will be of great interest. On this important topic, an old sociological cliché may apply: More research is needed.

Quick Review

- Lesbian and gay male parents are becoming more common, sometimes after a divorce, through donor insemination, through adoption, or through surrogate pregnancy.
- The development of children in lesbian families is similar to that of children in heterosexual families, although the former may be more open to the possibility of same-gender relationships.
- Employed parents appear to compensate for time away from children by spending time with them when not at work.
- Nonparental child care, in certain circumstances, may have modest negative effects on children's development.

The Well-Being of American Children

Now that we have studied what parents should do for their children and how social changes may have aided or hindered parents' tasks, we are ready to confront what is probably the most critical question to be asked about the public family: Has the well-being of children declined? This is a question that, in recent years, has often been posed and answered affirmatively by national commissions, politicians, and editorial writers. Yet the American public believes that children's well-being is worse than it actually is. Half or more of participants in national surveys in 2002 and 2003 estimated that at least 30 percent of children live in poverty (almost twice the true figure), that about 20 percent have no health insurance (the true figure is about 12 percent), and that the number of children on welfare has increased or stayed the same since the welfare laws were changed in 1996 (the true number has dropped sharply) (Guzman, Lippman, Moore, & O'Hare, 2003). (We should also examine how children's well-being is studied by sociologists and other participants in this debate: See *How Do Sociologists Know What They Know?:* Measuring the Well-Being of Children.) The answer to the question of how children are doing depends on two further questions: (1) Compared with when? and (2) Which children?

COMPARED WITH WHEN?

The reality of children's lives in the past was harsher than the nostalgic picture that is sometimes drawn. In the early 1930s, my Aunt Rose gave birth to a son, William, who caught strep throat as an infant. Half a century later, when the pediatrician told me that *my* son had strep throat, I trudged to the drugstore, bought an antibiotic, and nonchalantly spooned it into him. Within two days, he was fine. But antibiotics such as penicillin had not yet been isolated when William took ill, and sulfa drugs, their precursors, were not yet in general use. William died, a victim of an illness that today is hardly more serious than the common cold. The death of an infant, though tragic, was not an unusual event in 1935; 1 in 18 babies died before their first birthday. Nearly 1 in 10 died before reaching age 15 (U.S. Bureau of the Census, 1975).

We tend to forget how much lower the typical standard of living was in the first half of the twentieth century than it is today. One-third of all homes in the 1940s had no running water, two-fifths had no flush toilets, half had no refrigerators, and three-fifths had no central heating. The average person ate half as much beef and one-third as much chicken as has been the case in recent years.[2]

---

[2] These statistics are cited in Levy (1987).

<table>
<tr><td>How Do Sociologists
Know What They Know?</td><td>Measuring the Well-Being
of Children</td></tr>
</table>

Concern about the well-being of American children has created a demand by policymakers, journalists, and other observers for better information about the well-being of children. Until the 1980s, the federal government collected relatively little information about children. Family sociologists were focused on the conjugal family of husband, wife, and children—but paid little attention to the children themselves. The rise in divorce and in childbearing outside of marriage in the 1960s and 1970s increased the demand for better knowledge about the consequences for children, and academic researchers and government agencies began to respond.

The first questions they had to consider were the following: How do you measure children's well-being in the large-scale surveys that the federal government tends to fund and that sociologists study? And what aspects of children's lives are important for well-being? The most obvious areas are basic needs such as a child's standard of living and health. The Bureau of the Census gathers information annually about income levels and poverty of households with children. In 1981, the government fielded the first child health supplement to the National Health Interview Survey, a large, ongoing survey of Americans' health. The data from these and other government surveys are made available (with names and addresses deleted to ensure confidentiality) to sociologists who wish to analyze them.

But these indicators tell only part of the story. Sociologists and psychologists are interested in two other important domains: *cognitive* indicators of what children are learning and *socioemotional* indicators of

how they are feeling and behaving. Cognitive indicators are relatively straightforward; sociologists studying random samples of children and their families can ask permission to talk to children's teachers and to obtain test scores from their schools. For pre-school-aged children, of course, there are no test scores to obtain. As a result, survey researchers interested in young children sometimes administer short tests directly to them. For example, a child might be shown a progressively more difficult series of pictures and asked to identify each one.

More difficult to measure are the socioemotional aspects of well-being. For younger children, the best strategy for survey researchers is to ask parents questions about their children's behavior. Older children can be asked directly about problematic behavior.

For instance, since 1991 a federally funded national study, Monitoring the Future, has annually asked nationwide samples of 8th-, 10th-, and 12th-graders about drug use. To be sure, we cannot determine whether students are being fully truthful in their responses. (See *How Do Sociologists Know What They Know?* Asking about Sensitive Behavior.) [➡ p. 192] But even so, changes in their responses from year to year are likely to represent real increases or decreases. For example, the surveys showed that between 1991 and 2002, the percentage of college students who reported ever using the drug "ecstasy" rose from 2.0 to 12.7 (Johnston, O'Malley, & Bachman, 2003).

Demographer Kenneth Land and his colleagues have developed an "index of child well-being," a number they have

calculated for each year from 1975 to the present. They combine 28 statistical indicators in domains such as health, economic well-being, safety/behavioral concerns, and emotional/spiritual well-being. They state that their index declined through 1993 but has increased every year since then and as of 2005, was 4.5 percent higher than in 1975 (Land, 2005). But not everyone agrees that it's possible to derive a single number that adequately reflects a condition as complex as child well-being.

Overall, far more information on children's well-being is available from survey research today, compared with two decades ago. In recent years, interest in indicators of children's well-being has been so high that federal government agencies have coordinated their data gathering. The U.S. Department of Health and Human Services publishes an annual volume entitled *Trends in the Well-Being of America's Children and Youth,* filled with graphs and tables. It provides very useful information for sociologists and for students writing papers on the well-being of children and is available on the Internet. (See "Families on the Internet" at the end of this chapter.)

Ask Yourself

1. Have you ever responded to a survey of children's well-being? If so, were you truthful in your responses?

2. Which measures of children's well-being—income and health, cognitive achievement, or socioemotional status—do you think are most critical? Explain your viewpoint.

www.mhhe.com/cherlin5

Thousands of children contracted polio each year. The infant mortality rate—the proportion of children who die in their first year of life—was three times higher than it is today (U.S. Bureau of the Census, 1975; U.S. Bureau of the Census, 2005l). Just 53 percent of persons in their twenties had graduated from high school, compared with 86 percent today (U.S. Bureau of the Census, 2004b). I could go on; the point is that a nostalgic picture of a carefree childhood in the "good old days" is inaccurate. Even as late as the 1940s, life was far tougher for children in many respects than is the case now.

Consider, for instance, trends in the income of families with children. Whether the economic situation of children has become worse or better over time depends on when you start looking. Figure 9.2 shows the percentage of children living in families with incomes below the official government poverty line from 1949 to 2004. By this standard, as the figure shows, nearly half of all children in the country were poor in 1949—a far higher percentage than is the case now. But the great economic boom of the 1950s and 1960s changed all that. [➡ p. 64] By 1969, as Figure 9.2 shows, just 15.6 percent of children were living in families below the poverty line. Childhood poverty had declined for whites, blacks, and Hispanics—a rising tide of prosperity had lifted all boats. Then the post-1973 economic decline, which particularly affected the kinds of entry-level jobs for which young parents tend to be qualified, reversed the trend. By 1993, the poverty rate had risen to 22 percent—higher than in 25 years—before dropping to 17.8 percent in 2004. It was far higher among children of Hispanic origin—28.9 percent in 2004—and black children—33.6 percent in 2004 (U.S. Bureau of the Census, 2005e).

This evidence suggests that, to answer the question about the declining well-being of children, we must ask, compared with when? The well-being of American children during the first half of the twentieth century cannot be judged to be better overall than their well-being today. But in some ways, children's well-being may have been better during the 1950s and 1960s than it is today. That was the era when the baby boom generation was born and raised. It was also a time of economic prosperity. In this period, as Figure 9.2 shows, rates of childhood poverty

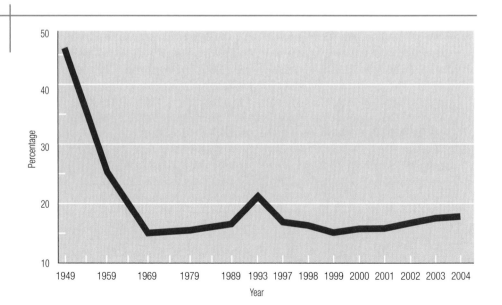

FIGURE 9.2
Poverty rates for children in the United States, 1949 to 2004. (*Sources:* for 1949–1969, Smolensky, Danziger, & Gottschalk, 1988; for 1979 to 2004, U.S. Bureau of the Census, various years)

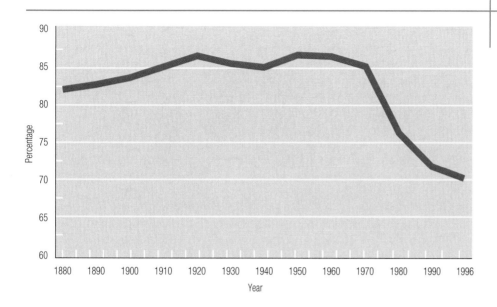

FIGURE 9.3
Percentage of children living with two parents, 1880–1996. (*Sources:* U.S. Bureau of the Census, 2001b)

declined to lower levels than before or since (although recent declines are close to the all-time low). Moreover, more children were living with two parents than before or since. To be sure, single parents can raise children effectively, as I have noted; but most researchers would agree that, other things being equal, it's better to live with two parents than with one. At the beginning of the twentieth century, almost one-fourth of children saw one of their parents die by the time they were age 15 (Uhlenberg, 1980); but parental death rates declined substantially by midcentury. Divorce rates, however, did not spike upward until the mid-1960s. In the 1950s, with death rates down and divorce rates still modest, the percentage of children living with two parents peaked, as Figure 9.3 shows. By the 1970s and 1980s, the continuing decline in parental deaths had been overwhelmed by the sharp rises in divorce and childbearing outside of marriage, and the percentage living with two parents plunged to its lowest level since at least 1880.

WHICH CHILDREN?

Over the past few decades, the fortunes of children have diverged, with some doing better while some are doing worse. In other words, we need to ask, which children? Since the 1970s, the distribution of income in the United States became more unequal. [➡ p. 114] Figure 9.4 shows what growing income inequality has meant for children. Demographer Donald Hernandez divided all children into four groups according to their family's income:

Relative poverty: A family income less than one-half the median family income. (The median is the point in the income distribution at which as many families have higher incomes as have lower incomes.)

Frugality: A family income above the relative poverty level but less than three-fourths of the median family income.

Comfort: A family income above the frugality level but less than 50 percent above the median family income.

Luxury: A family income at least 50 percent above the median family income.

FIGURE 9.4
Percentage of U. S. children who were living in "poverty," "frugality," "comfort," and "luxury," 1939–1988.
(*Source:* Hernandez, 1993)

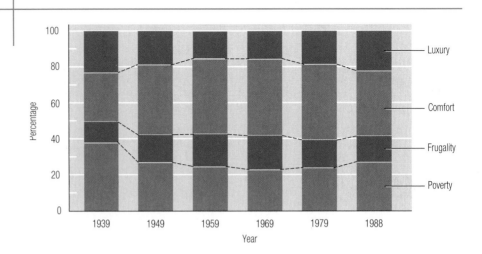

Children by Socioeconomic Status   Although these divisions and their labels are arbitrary, they can be used to follow trends over time. Using census data, Hernandez calculated the percentage of children in each group in 1939, 1949, 1959, 1969, 1979, and 1988. Each bar in the figure shows the distribution in one of these years. For example, the leftmost bar shows that nearly 40 percent of children were in the "poverty" group in 1939, at the end of the Great Depression. Yet, moving down from the top of the same bar, we can see that more than 20 percent of all children were in the "luxury" category. Not all children suffered during the Depression; some were in families that weathered the storm well. It was the middle categories that were squeezed. During the next 30 years, the percentage in both the "poverty" and "luxury" groups declined, as the middle expanded, suggesting widespread "comfort" among children. Yet since 1969, the middle has once again been squeezed: The proportion of children in *both* the "poverty" group and the "luxury" group increased between 1969 and 1988. Children at the top of the income distribution in 1988 were doing better than they were in 1969, whereas children at the bottom were doing worse. It is likely that these trends have continued since 1988.

Another recent study reached a similar conclusion. Two economists studied data on American children in the years 1976 and 1996, and divided the children into three rough categories (Sawhill & Chadwick, 1999):

1.   Children were classified as having poor prospects for adulthood if they had three of the following four characteristics: an unmarried mother, a teen mother, a mother without a high school degree, and a family income below the poverty line.

2.   Children were classified as having good prospects for adulthood if they had three of the following four characteristics: a married mother, a mother who was 26 or older when they were born, a mother who had completed college, and a family income at least four times the poverty level.

3.   Children who fell between these two groups were classified as having average prospects.

Like Hernandez, the authors reported a good news, bad news story. Over the 20-year period, the percentage of children with good prospects rose from 9 to 26

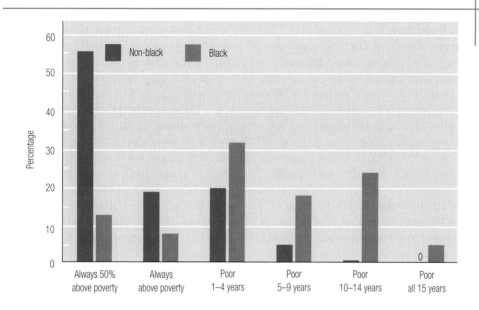

FIGURE 9.5
Fifteen-year poverty experiences of children who were under the age of four in 1968, by race. (*Source:* Duncan, 1991)

percent—a substantial increase. However, the percentage with poor prospects rose from 8 to 12 percent. Both groups grew in size, and the average group shrank from 83 to 62 percent. In sum, the size of the group of children who have been doing better has increased, as has the size of the group of children who have been doing worse. The size of the middle-income group has been shrinking.

Children by Race and Ethnicity   The bars in Figure 9.4 are like photographs: They present a snapshot of all children in the United States at six different points in time. Whether those same children will be poor or comfortable or wealthy the next year cannot be determined from the snapshots. In fact, a national study that has followed thousands of children and their families for more than 30 years shows that the snapshots conceal great movements of children and their families in and out of poverty over the course of childhood. Many children experience poverty for a short period. Among whites, relatively few experience it throughout their childhood; but among blacks, persistent childhood poverty is common.

Figure 9.5 shows the experiences of children in the Panel Study of Income Dynamics (PSID), who were under the age of four in 1968 and whose families were reinterviewed in each of the next 15 years—a period when poverty rates were similar to those of the late 1990s (Duncan, 1991). The first set of bars on the left shows the percentage of nonblack children (whom I will call "white" for the sake of simplicity since most were, indeed, white) and black children whose families had incomes that were always at least 50 percent above the poverty line in each of the 15 years. A majority (56 percent) of white children fell into this category, compared with 13 percent of black children. The next set of bars represents children whose families were always above the poverty line but were close to the line in at least one year. Combining these two categories, we see that 75 percent of white children and 21 percent of black children never experienced poverty. The racial difference is great. Still, the figure demonstrates that a substantial number of black children were never poor. These children are often overlooked in articles about the economic situation of African Americans.

The next set of bars represents what we might call "temporary poverty": those who were poor 1 to 4 years out of 15. About one-fifth of white children—a substantial number—experienced temporary poverty. It was common to be poor for a few years. Among black children, it was even more common. But the racial differences are most dramatic in the final three sets of bars, which represent what we might call "persistent poverty," that is, being poor at least 5 of the 15 years. By this measure, only about 6 percent of white children experienced persistent poverty. The modest amount of persistent poverty among whites was a great social accomplishment of the post–World War II era; before then, persistent poverty was much more likely. Yet any pleasure at that accomplishment is matched by displeasure at the situation among black children, 47 percent of whom were poor for at least five years. There are other ways of defining persistent poverty, but they all show that the percentage of white children who were affected was less than 10 percent, and often less than 5 percent (Duncan & Rodgers, 1991). Moreover, Hispanic children were included in the "white" category of the PSID analyses, which means that the rates for non-Hispanic whites were probably even smaller. Alternative definitions all show that the percentage of persistently poor black children was 30 percent or higher. Although many white children experience poverty at some point, then, persistent childhood poverty is far more common among African Americans.

The PSID further indicated that children who were persistently poor were much more likely to live in single-parent families. According to the PSID study, the average black child who lived with one parent spent more than seven years in poverty—nearly half of her or his childhood (Duncan, 1991). This is not to say that family structure is the only cause of the high rates of persistent poverty among children. Many poor single mothers were poor *before* they gave birth to their children. In addition, black single parents tend to live in racially segregated neighborhoods with high concentrations of poverty. These neighborhoods often have high levels of crime and drug abuse, few social services, and few jobs. One study found that the absence of affluent neighbors was associated with higher rates of childbearing and school dropout among teenagers, even after attempts to control for family structure and race (Brooks-Gunn, Duncan, Klebanov, & Sealand, 1993).

Information on poverty trends for Hispanic children is sketchier because government statistics were very limited until the 1970s. Even today, most tabulations display data on all Hispanic children combined; yet, there is great diversity within the Hispanic category. [➡ p. 163] With this caveat, one can examine recent trends in the annual poverty rate. Between 1976 and 1994, the rate for Hispanic children increased from 30 to 42 percent, a larger increase than among either African Americans or non-Hispanic whites. It is likely that the sharp increase reflected, in part, the continuing immigration of individuals and families from low-income backgrounds. But by 2004, the rate had fallen to 29 percent (U.S. Bureau of the Census, 2005c).

DIVERGING DESTINIES

Like the diverging demographics of families in different status groups, [➡ p. 124] the trends in well-being we have reviewed suggest what one observer recently called "diverging destinies" for America's children (McLanahan, 2004). In the first half of the twentieth century, most children, rich or poor, white or black, lived in two-parent families (Tolnay, 2004). But since then, as divorce and childbearing outside of marriage increased, the living arrangements of children have diverged by income. Most of the decline in two-parent families took place among people with less education and lower incomes. In 1960 about one-fourth of all poor families were headed by single mothers; but by 2004 about half were headed by single mothers.

Children who are persistently poor are especially likely to be living in single-parent families (Duncan & Rogers, 1991). And by most reasonable definitions, close to a majority of all persistently poor children today are African Americans. The U.S. government provides less assistance to children in low-income families than almost any other Western nation. It may be that the racial polarization between the heavily black population in deep poverty and the white majority prevents Americans from reaching out to the poor. (See *Families in Other Cultures: U.S. Children in International Perspective.*)

Poor and Wealthy Children   As a result of these trends, you can tell more about a child's standard of living by the type of family he or she is living in than was the case a half-century ago. Children whose families are prosperous usually live with two parents, both of whom work outside the home—in fact, these have been the only kinds of families whose incomes have grown in the last few decades. [➡ p. 117] Children who are poor are more likely to live with one parent. To the extent that living in a single-parent family makes it more difficult to escape from poverty, poor children may be experiencing hardships for a longer period of their lives. To the extent that single parents have more difficulty supervising and monitoring teenagers, children may be receiving less supervision than they need. Yet it's simplistic to blame single parents for persistent poverty. As noted earlier, many poor single mothers were poor before they became mothers. Becoming a single parent didn't make them poor—they already were. In addition, the past few decades have seen a great deterioration in the labor market prospects of young adults without college educations, which made it more difficult to start and maintain a two-parent family. One study estimated that, even if there had been no increase in single-parent families since 1960, about 80 percent of poor children would still be poor; moreover, the gap between white and black child poverty rates would still be large (Hernandez, 1993). The growth of single-parent families hasn't helped matters for poor children, but it is probably not the major cause—and certainly not the sole cause—of the problems of poor children.

Among children from families that are not poor, I submit, the decline in well-being since the 1960s has not been as great. A fortunate, growing minority of children live in relatively wealthy families. Although they too face an increased risk of parental divorce or teenage pregnancy, the risks are lower than among the less fortunate. It's not at all clear that their well-being has declined; in fact, it may have improved.

Children in the Middle   It is among children from families in the narrowing middle, neither poor nor affluent, many of which have been hard-pressed to maintain their standard of living, that a judgment about trends in well-being is most difficult. My own sense is that, on average, the children in the middle have experienced a moderate downward drift in well-being since the 1960s. They are less likely to live with two parents, due mainly to increases in divorce. They have grown up during a period of economic belt tightening by the working and middle classes.

U.S. Children in International Perspective

The decline in children's well-being raises the question of how well U.S. children are doing compared with children in other developed countries. The answer is not very well. U.S. children learn less about mathematics and science. They must cope with the highest rate of divorce of any Western nation (although if the breakup of cohabiting parents is included, Sweden's overall rate of family dissolution might be higher). Rates of adolescent homicide (and also adult homicide) are far higher than anywhere else. The percentage of teenage girls who give birth is higher, even among white Americans, than anywhere else. And so forth. No nation presents as pale a statistical portrait of children as the United States.

Consider information about child poverty collected from 25 countries between 1987 and 1995. For each country, the figure on page 323 shows the percentage of children who lived in low-income families, defined as families with incomes less than half of the median (or middle) family income. Russia, its postsocialist economy in shambles, barely exceeded the United States' high percentage of poor children. No other country came close. Why do so many U.S. children live in low-income families? One possibility is the high rate of poverty among racial-ethnic groups in the United States. Yet even when childhood poverty among U.S. whites is compared with that of whites in other Western countries, Americans still show higher rates. Another possibility is the large number of single-parent families in the United States. But even when the comparisons are restricted to children living in single-parent families in other countries, U.S. children are poorer than those almost anywhere else.

What really accounts for the difference are the more generous social welfare programs in most other countries. The governments of most other countries provide more benefits to all families, regardless of income. For example, most have a child allowance that is paid to parents solely on the basis of how many children they have. Most have unemployment benefits that are more generous and are paid for a longer period of time than in the United States. Most provide payments to parents who take a short-term leave from their jobs following childbirth. These universal benefits are popular with citizens of other countries because they are seen as aiding everyone, not just the poor.

In contrast, the United States relies more on so-called means-tested benefits, which are given only to families that fall below an income threshold. These benefits are not as generous as in the other countries. For example, the main cash benefit available to families with children is Temporary Assistance for Needy Families (TANF), which was known as Aid to Families with Dependent Children before the 1996 welfare legislation, and which is provided primarily to single-parent families in poverty. AFDC was so unpopular that most states did not increase it to keep up with inflation; consequently, its real value declined after the mid-1970s.

Because means-tested benefits are usually less popular with voters, they tend to be less generous than universal benefits. For example, Social Security is a universal benefit in the United States because it is available to all elderly persons regardless of income. In contrast to TANF, Social Security benefits have risen dramatically over the last few decades. The lack of universal benefits for parents of young children in the United States seems to reflect the strong individualistic ethos in this country. In the American myth, each person is supposed to make it on his or her own. The poor are often viewed as "undeserving" of help—of having failed at the task of providing for themselves and their children.

When I travel in Western Europe, I find that people have a greater sense that their fellow countrymen are deserving of assistance purely because they are citizens. The French, for example, seem to believe that every French person has a right to a minimally adequate standard of living. I find a greater sense of "we-ness," a feeling that we are all French (or British or German) and must assist the less fortunate—especially children. In the United States, I see a greater split between "us"—the middle class—and "them" the undeserving poor. This split may well be aggravated by the ethnic and racial differences in the United States between the poor and the better off.

Lingering prejudice and discrimination encourage some middle-class whites to see black or Hispanic poor people as

Children in Scandinavian families, such as this one in Norway, are less likely to be poor than children in most other countries because of generous social welfare programs.

different from them and therefore less worthy of their support. The split between us and them and the strong belief in individual initiative result in less support to poor children than in any other developed country.

Ask Yourself

1. Do the statistics shown in the graph surprise you? In your opinion, is a 26.3 percent child poverty rate acceptable in the richest nation in the world?

2. What are the long-term implications for American society when more than a quarter of all children grow up in poverty?

www.mhhe.com/cherlin5

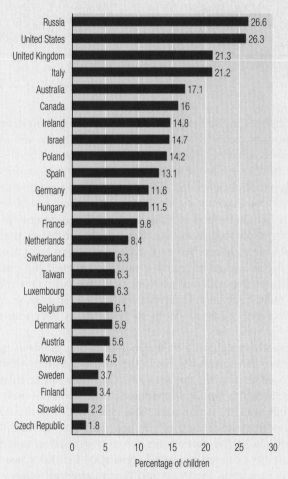

Percentage of children living in families with incomes less than half of the median income for all families, 1987–1995.
(*Source:* Bradbury & Jäntti, 2000.)

Single parents who work outside the home may have difficulty monitoring children during the after-school hours.

Probably the two greatest changes in the family among this middle group have been the increases in the number of mothers who work outside the home and in divorce rates. Little was said about divorce in this chapter because it will be discussed in Chapter 12. Nearly all children are intensely upset when their parents separate, and their risk of dropping out of school, having a child as a teenager, or experiencing other undesirable consequences rises. These effects are troubling and worthy of serious concern. It appears, however, that most children do not suffer long-term harmful effects from divorce. Moreover, some of the problems that we blame on divorce are visible in children before their parents even separate, which suggests that some of the problems might have occurred even if the parents had stayed together. As for having both parents (or one's only parent) work outside the home, spending more time in nonparental child care settings may have a modestly negative effect on children's problem behavior as they enter school, as noted earlier.

Nevertheless, even a moderate deterioration in well-being among children in the middle is cause for concern to those who believe in the idea of progress—the idea that our society ought to be improving the lives of its citizens rather than backsliding. I think that changes in the family contributed to this deterioration, but I'm not convinced the family was the major actor. The family itself was acted upon by larger forces such as the restructuring of the economy and a cultural shift toward ever-greater individualism. Yet parents are not merely passively acted on by social forces; they must be assigned some responsibility for the consequences of their actions, such as getting divorced and having children outside marriage.

And although I am skeptical of those who claim that there is a pervasive crisis in the well-being of American children, I do think that a real crisis is occurring among children at the bottom of the income distribution. Behind the dismal statistics lie the lives of children like Lafayette and Pharoah Rivers, diving for cover during the daily gunfights and wondering if they will get to grow up. When the reporter proposed to their mother that he write a book about Lafayette, Pharoah, and other children in the neighborhood, she thought that was a great idea. Still, she warned, "But you know, there are no children here. They've seen too much to be children" (Kotlowitz, 1991).

Quick Review

- Children's well-being is probably better than it was a century ago, when parental death rates were higher and standards of living lower.
- Children's well-being may have peaked in the mid-twentieth century, after parental death rates had declined but before a large increase in divorce rates occurred.
- Over the past few decades, the well-being of children in wealthier families probably has improved, whereas the well-being of children in low-income families probably has worsened.
- Trends in the well-being of children in the middle are harder to assess; they may have experienced a moderate decline in well-being.

Looking Back

1. **What are the main goals in socializing children and how do parents differ in the way they fulfill their role?** By socializing their children, parents equip them to function well in society. Among other things, parents teach children norms (widely accepted rules about how to behave) and values (goals and principles that are held in high esteem in a society). Parents provide both material and emotional support to their children and exercise control over them. A combination of high levels of emotional support and consistent, moderate discipline, called an authoritative parenting style, seems to produce children who are most socially competent, at least among white families.

2. **How does the socialization of children vary by ethnicity, class, and gender?** In racial and ethnic groups such as African Americans and Asian Americans, parents rely more on strong discipline than white parents. Working-class parents stress obedience and conformity more than middle-class parents; conversely, middle-class parents stress autonomy and self-direction more than working-class parents. Members of each social class emphasize values that are consistent with the kinds of jobs they perform. Parents also socialize boys and girls differently, so that any preexisting differences are exaggerated in childhood and adult behavior.

3. **What barriers must parents overcome in socializing their children?** Unemployment and poverty can affect the way parents act toward each other and toward their children. Job loss or low earnings can cause a parent to become depressed and angry; fathers in these situations are likely to have angry, explosive exchanges with their wives and children. Single parenthood also raises the risk of some adverse consequences, such as a child dropping out of school. Evidence on children who grow up with lesbian parents suggests that they do not differ much from children with heterosexual parents, although they may be more open to the possibility of same-sex relationships. There is evidence of modest, negative effects of nonparental child care.

4. **How much time do parents and children spend together?** While it seems as though parents should be spending less time with their children because so many mothers have entered the paid workforce over the past half century, parents are spending as much time with children as they did several decades ago. They accomplish this feat in several ways. They have fewer children today. They cut back on leisure time. They do less housework, either leaving their houses less clean or paying someone to clean them. And they combine other activities with child care.

5. **How has the well-being of American children changed over time?** Comparisons between the "average" child today and the "average" child a few decades ago can be misleading. Economic inequality has increased since the early 1970s: The percentage of children at both the bottom and the top of the income ladder has risen, whereas the middle group has decreased in size. The growing proportion of children who live in relatively wealthy settings tends to be doing well. At the other extreme, persistently poor children appear to have suffered greatly. Children in the shrinking middle group may have suffered a moderate reduction in well-being over the past few decades, a trend that eroded some of the gains of the 1950s and 1960s.

 Go to the Online Learning Center at www.mhhe.com/cherlin5 to test your knowledge of the chapter concepts and key terms.

Study Questions

1. Why might authoritative parenting be more effective in some social settings than others?
2. In what ways is the typical parenting done by fathers different from the parenting done by mothers?
3. What do adoptive families, stepfamilies, and gay and lesbian families have in common?
4. Why might adoption be a "devalued status"?
5. How does a father's unemployment change the relations among parents and children in a household?
6. What are some factors that could make single parents less effective than parents in two-parent families?
7. In what ways might we expect children in lesbian families to be similar to children in heterosexual families? In what ways might we expect them to be different?
8. Why is it too simplistic to conclude, as some observers have, that children's well-being has declined among all social classes and races–ethnicities in recent decades?

Key Terms

androgynous behavior   299
authoritarian style
  (of parenting)   294
authoritative style
  (of parenting)   294
donor insemination   309
generativity   301
norm   296
permissive style
  (of parenting)   294
value   296

Thinking about Families

The Public Family	The Private Family
What are the crucial duties society expects of parents in raising their children?	What kind of satisfaction do parents get from raising children?

Families on the Internet   www.mhhe.com/cherlin5

Note: While all the URLs listed were current as of the printing of this book, these sites often change. Please check our Web site (http://www.mhhe.com/cherlin5) for updates.

A great deal of information on children is available on the Internet. Several federal statistical agencies jointly maintain the site www.childstats.gov. From there, click on "America's Children Monitoring Report" to access the latest edition of "America's Children: Key National Indicators of Well-Being," an annual compendium of statistical trends. It includes graphs and charts on topics such as family composition, poverty, health, education, and substance abuse. Click on "International" to compare the well-being of American children with that of children in other countries. Other resources include the National Center for Children in Poverty (www.nccp.org), which maintains a Web site with several well-done reports about child poverty. For example, click on "Fact Sheets" to obtain summaries on various topics.

Monitoring the Future (www.monitoringthefuture.org) is an annual survey of 8th-, 10th-, and 12th-grade students, undertaken by the University of Michigan's Institute for Social Research. The survey includes information about drug and alcohol usage and cigarette smoking (click on "Data Tables and Figures") as well as many publications that can be downloaded.

Chapter Ten

The Elderly and Their Families

Looking Forward

1. How has grandparenthood changed over the past century?

2. How much support do the elderly provide to, and receive from, their kin?

3. Who cares for the frail elderly?

4. Are the elderly isolated from their kin?

5. What sources of tension exist in intergenerational relations?

In early 2005 a reporter for the *New York Times* called me to say that she was working on a story about grandparents and grandchildren in an age of high divorce and remarriage rates. Some grandchildren, she said, had more than four grandparents because one or more grandparents had divorced and remarried, bringing a stepgrandparent into the family. Did I know anything about this? Yes, I replied, not only because I study families, but also because I was one of eight grandparents of two young children. All four of their biological grandparents had divorced and remarried before they were born. Their maternal grandmother had married me. I was technically one of their stepgrandparents, but that sociological distinction was lost on them. They eagerly accepted the attention and affection of all eight: Grandma Peach, Grandma Linda, Oma (German for granny) Gerda, Nanny, Papa Andy (me), Papa Jay, Papa David, and Papa Dude. "The upside of all this is that children can have more grandparents who love them," the reporter quoted me as saying. "What message it will give them about marriage, I'm not quite sure" (Harmon, 2005).

In fact, the more-than-four grandparents phenomenon is so new that no one is sure what influence it may have on family life. For one thing, the divorce rate reached its current peak in 1980, so that the adults who drove its rise are only now aging into later life. (We will discuss divorce and remarriage in Chapters 12 and 13.) For another, people are living longer than they used to, making it possible for so many grandchildren to have so many grandparents. Until the last few generations, it was far less common for children to have four (let alone eight) living grandparents (Uhlenberg, 2004). Now grandparents are a dime a dozen, it seems, and many are active and independent.

This is not to say that all elderly persons are healthy and active. As the elderly population has expanded, so has the number of frail persons in need of care. The cost of the technology-driven health care provided to the increasing numbers of frail elderly has risen dramatically in recent years and has become a major problem for the nation. In addition, a disproportionately large part of the elderly population sits precariously just above the poverty line—not poor, but not by much.[1] The incidence of poverty is greater for elderly women than for men, as we shall see.

This chapter will focus on the family lives of the elderly—their interactions with spouses, children, grandchildren, and other relatives. As birthrates and death rates both decline, there are relatively more older people and relatively fewer younger people in the population. Whether society will be able to adequately meet the needs of the elderly is an issue of great importance from the perspective

---

[1] Figures will be given later in this chapter.

Adults live much longer, healthier lives than a century ago.

of the public family. Spouses and relatives, as will be demonstrated, provide most of the assistance to the elderly. Providing adequate assistance is likely to be more difficult when the huge baby boom generation begins to retire. Other changes in family life, such as the increase in women's work outside the home and the rise in divorce, may also affect the task of caring for the elderly.

But it would be a mistake to think of the elderly only as *recipients* of assistance because they are also important *providers* of assistance to children and grandchildren. Much of that assistance is provided on an as-needed basis: help with a down payment for a house, help when employed parents need child care, help when a daughter separates from her husband. In fact, over the past few decades, the percentage of grandchildren who are living in their grandparents' homes—sometimes without either parent present—has been increasing. We will examine more closely the assistance that the elderly give to their families.

Although recent trends in the well-being of children are mixed, as noted in the previous chapter, recent trends in the well-being of the elderly deserve at least two cheers. Programs for the elderly have been the one indisputable success of U.S. social welfare policy since the Great Depression. In fact, so successful have the programs been, and so far have both death rates and birthrates fallen, that most people fail to realize how new is the kind of life most elderly Americans are leading today—a longer, healthier life in which the elderly provide substantial assistance to their family members. In order to understand what has happened, we need to begin by looking back in history.

■ The Modernization of Old Age

We tend to associate grandparents with old-fashioned families—the large, rural, three-generation kind that can be seen on reruns of *The Waltons*. We have a nostalgic image of Grandma, Grandpa, Aunt Bess, Mom, Dad, and the kids sitting around the hearth, baking bread and telling stories. Correspondingly, many observers think that the role of older people in families has become less important since the farm gave way to the factory. According to this view, industrialization meant that older people could no longer teach their children and grandchildren the skills needed to make a living. Moreover, older people no longer controlled the resources—such as farmland—that gave them influence over the lives of the young. There is some truth to this perspective. But the historical facts suggest that grandparenthood—as a distinct and nearly universal stage of life—is a post-World War II phenomenon. To be sure, there have always been grandparents around, but never this many and never with so few of their own children left to raise.

MORTALITY DECLINE

mortality the number of deaths in a population

The Statistics   First of all, a century ago—even 50 years ago—far fewer people lived long enough to become grandparents. Much of the decline in adult **mortality** (the demographers' term for deaths in a population) from preindustrial levels occurred in the twentieth century. Only about 37 percent of all women born in 1870 survived to age 65; in contrast, about 77 percent of women born in 1930 reached age 65 (Uhlenberg, 1979; Uhlenberg, 1980). The greatest declines occurred in midcentury, especially for women. The number of years that the average 40-year-old white woman could expect to live increased by four between 1900 and 1940, by seven between 1940 and 1980, and by one since then. For white men the increases have been smaller: a gain of two years between 1900 and 1940, four between 1940 and 1980, and 2.5 since then (U.S. Bureau of the Census, 2003i). The trends for nonwhites are similar, but in every decade the life expectancy of nonwhites has been lower than that of whites. In 2003, white babies had a life expectancy of 78 years, compared with 73 years for black babies (U.S. Bureau of the Census, 2005l).

active life expectancy the number of years a person can expect to live without a disability

A more difficult question is whether the gains in life expectancy that have been occurring recently have added healthy years or infirm years at the end of life. Have modern medicine and improved standards of living allowed the elderly more years of activity or merely more years in which they are ill or disabled? **Active life expectancy** is the term for the number of years a person can expect to live without a disability. A series of national surveys shows that rates of chronic disability among the elderly declined from 1982 to 1999, with the rate of decline increasing in the more recent years (Manton and Gu, 2001). Moreover, the time that the elderly spend with health problems that require hospital or nursing home care has increased very little in recent decades (Crimmins, Saito, & Ingegneri, 1997). The elderly seem to be gaining not just longer lives but also healthier years of life.

The Social Consequences   The decline in mortality during the twentieth century has had two consequences. First, both women and men can expect to live much longer lives than was the case several decades ago. Second, women tend to outlive men. In 2003, the average female baby could expect to live 81 years, the average male baby 75 years (U.S. Bureau of the Census, 2005l). A century ago the sex difference was much smaller because many more women died in childbirth. So it is the case today that (1) there are many more older people in the population than there used to be, and (2) 6 out of 10 older people are women. Figure 10.1 shows the growth of the U.S. population aged 65 and over since 1900 and projections to

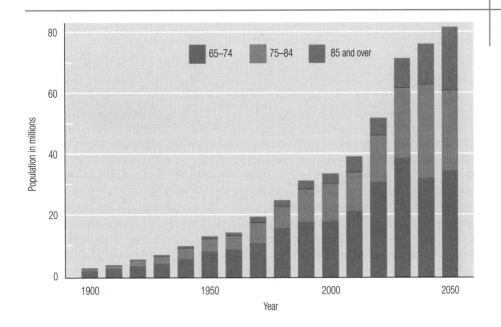

FIGURE 10.1
Actual and estimated population 65 years old and over in the United States: 1900–2050. (*Source:* U.S. Bureau of the Census, 1983, 2002g)

the year 2050. Under the usual convention, which I will follow, the **elderly population** is defined as all persons aged 65 and over. This is an arbitrary cutoff point that is used because 65 has been the age at which a person could retire and receive full Social Security benefits. Most 65-year-old persons are healthy and active, however, and a recent law will gradually raise the retirement age to 67. As can be seen, there were relatively few elderly people in 1900—about 3 million. In contrast, there were 35 million in 2000, and there will be an estimated 67 million in 2050 (although projections that far into the future should be seen only as educated guesses). By 2030, when today's college students will be middle-aged, about one in five Americans will be elderly (Himes, 2002).

Moreover, as recently as 1950, according to Figure 10.1, most of the elderly were aged 65 to 74. Then, in midcentury, the proportion of the elderly who were aged 75 to 84 began to grow more rapidly, and more recently the proportion who are aged 85 or older has risen. In other words, since 1900 not only has the elderly population increased greatly but the elderly population itself has become older and older, increasingly top-heavy with those in their seventies and eighties. As the older elderly population expanded, **gerontologists** (social and biological scientists who specialize in the study of aging) invented the following terms to differentiate among the aged: **young-old** for those 65 to 74, **old-old** for those 75 to 84, and **oldest-old** for those 85 and over. Now they are talking about **centenarians**—people who are at least 100 years old. In 2000, the census counted 50,000 centenarians, 80 percent of them women (U.S. Bureau of the Census, 2005).

The sharp decline in mortality has caused a profound change in the relationship between older persons and their children and grandchildren. For the first time in history, as I noted at the beginning of this chapter, most adults live long enough to get to know most of their grandchildren, and most children have the opportunity to know most of their grandparents. The chances were only 50–50 that a child born at the beginning of the twentieth century would still have two living grandparents when he or she reached the age of 15. In contrast, the comparable chances rose to 9 in 10 for a 15-year-old in the 1970s (Uhlenberg,

elderly population the group of people aged 65 years and over

gerontologist a social/biological scientist who specializes in the study of aging

young-old the group of elderly people 65 to 74 years of age

old-old the group of elderly people 75 to 84 years of age

oldest-old the group of elderly people 85 years of age and over

centenarian a person who is 100-years-old or older

1980). Currently, then, nearly all children have the opportunity to get to know at least two of their grandparents—and many get to know three or four (or even eight). But children born at the beginning of the century were not nearly as fortunate.

FERTILITY DECLINE

fertility the number of births in a population

The decline in **fertility** (the demographers' term for births in a population) is the second reason why grandparenthood on a large scale is a recent phenomenon. As recently as the late 1800s, American women gave birth to more than four children, on average (Ryder, 1980). Many parents still were raising their younger children after their older children left home and married. Under these conditions, being a grandparent took a backseat to the day-to-day tasks of raising the children who were still at home. Today, in contrast, the birthrate is much lower, and parents are much more likely to be finished raising their children before any of their grandchildren are born. When a person becomes a grandparent now, there are fewer family roles competing for her or his time and attention. Grandparenthood is more of a separate stage of family life, unfettered by child care obligations—one that carries its own distinct identity. It was not always so.

The combination of falling mortality and fertility rates has also altered the bonds of kinship that people have. Because birthrates have fallen, younger people tend to have fewer brothers and sisters than their parents and grandparents. So the horizontal bonds of kinship—those to relatives in the same generation as you—have tended to shrink. In contrast, lower mortality means that you have a much greater chance of having living parents well into your middle years than your parents or grandparents. Vertical kinship ties—those to relatives in preceding or following generations—have tended to grow. The result is a kinship structure with growing links up and down the generations and withering links across them sometimes referred to as the "beanpole family" (Bengtson, 2001). A number of gerontologists have argued that lowered mortality rates are making the four- and five-generation family (e.g., my grandparents, my parents, me, my children, and my grandchildren) common. Yet although there are more of these linkages than there used to be, they are still the exception rather than the rule. A survey in the Boston area showed that at no stage of the adult life course up through age 70 did more than 20 percent of the respondents belong to more than a three-generation linkage of kin. And the number in five-generation linkages never topped 2 percent. At all ages, the most common generational depth was three. In young adulthood, the three generations were typically my grandparents, my parents, and me; in middle age the three were my parents, me, and my children; and at older ages they were me, my children, and my grandchildren.

The authors of the Boston study, Alice and Peter Rossi, conclude:

> *The truly remarkable demographic change over the twentieth century is the impact of increased longevity on the number of years when the majority of the population may still have at least one living parent. (Rossi & Rossi, 1990)*

The watershed age, they argue, is 50. Prior to age 50, there is little drop-off in the percentage of adults who have at least one living parent; at about age 50 the percentage declines sharply. (And at about the same age, the percentage who have grandchildren increases sharply.) Thus, the lives of most parents and children now overlap by about 50 years. These long, potentially rich cobiographies are the product of lower mortality.

RISING STANDARD OF LIVING

Older people also have more money, on average, than they did a few decades ago. As recently as 1960, older Americans were an economically deprived group: 35 percent had incomes below the poverty line, compared with 22 percent of the total population. Now they have caught up: Their poverty rate of 9.8 percent in 2004 was lower than the rate for nonelderly adults (U.S. Bureau of the Census, 2005e). The main reason they are no longer disadvantaged is Social Security, the federal government program that provides retirement benefits to persons aged 62 and over. Beginning in the 1950s and 1960s, Congress expanded Social Security coverage, so that nearly all workers, except some who are employed by government, are now covered. And since the 1960s, Congress has increased Social Security benefits far faster than the increase in the cost of living. As a result, the average monthly benefit has doubled in purchasing power since 1960, even after taking inflation into account (U.S. Congressional Budget Office, 2003). Today's elderly benefited from the societywide rise in economic welfare in the 1950s and 1960s, when they were working; then, as they reached retirement, they benefited from the increase in Social Security benefits.

Variations by Age, Race, and Gender Still, there are sharp variations by age, race, and gender in the proportion of the elderly who are poor. Overall, older elderly persons are more likely to be poor than younger elderly persons, elderly women are more likely to be poor than elderly men, and African American and Hispanic elderly persons are more likely to be poor than white elderly persons. For example, in 2004, 9.4 percent of persons aged 65 to 74 were poor, compared with 10.3 percent of those aged 75 and over. Only 7.0 percent of elderly men were poor, compared with 12 percent of women. And 7.5 percent of the non-Hispanic white elderly were poor, compared with 23.9 percent of the black elderly and 18.7 percent of the Hispanic elderly (U.S. Bureau of the Census, 2005e).

Moreover, as I said earlier, a larger percentage of the elderly than of the nonelderly have incomes that place them just above the poverty level. In 2004, 14 percent of the elderly had incomes between 100 and 150 percent of the poverty level, compared with 7 percent of all adults under the age of 65 (U.S. Bureau of the Census, 2005e). This nearly poor group is in some ways more vulnerable to economic and health crises than the poor elderly. Economist Timothy Smeeding has named them the **'tweeners** because they fall between the poor, who can qualify for additional public assistance, and the middle class, who can supplement their Social Security checks with savings and pensions (Smeeding, 1990).[2] Although nearly all elderly persons are covered by **Medicare,** the government program of health insurance for the elderly, Medicare pays for less than half of the health expenditures of the elderly. Moreover, it pays nothing for nursing home care. Persons with incomes below the poverty line are also eligible for **Medicaid,** the government health insurance program for the poor of all ages, which does pay for nursing home costs. Middle-class elderly persons can afford to purchase private health insurance to pay the bills Medicare doesn't cover. But the 'tweeners typically have too much income for Medicaid and too little to buy private insurance.

'tweeners the group of elderly people who have incomes that place them between the poor, who can qualify for public assistance over and above Social Security, and the middle class, who can supplement their Social Security checks with savings and pensions

Medicare the government program of health insurance for all elderly people

Medicaid the government program of health insurance for people with incomes below the poverty line

---

[2] Smeeding defines the 'tweeners as elderly persons with incomes between 100 and 200 percent of the poverty line, but the precise cutoff is not important. By his definition, the 'tweeners constitute 20 percent of all elderly persons and 40 percent of all elderly persons living alone.

It is also uncertain whether the Social Security and Medicare systems will provide the elderly of the future with the same level of benefits that today's elderly receive. Low birthrates today mean that there will be fewer workers in a decade or two to pay Social Security taxes for the growing number of elderly. In 2000 there were five people of working age (20 to 64) for every elderly person; by 2030, according to current estimates, there will be only three people of working age for every elderly person. In addition, the increases in the number of old-old and oldest-old may strain the already costly Medicare system. (See *Families and Public Policy:* Financing Social Security and Medicare, on pp. 338–339.)

Social Consequences   Nevertheless, because of the general rise in their standard of living, older parents and their adult children are less dependent on one another economically. Family life in the early decades of the twentieth century was precarious; lower wages, the absence of social welfare programs, and crises of unemployment, illness, and death forced people to rely on their kin for support to a much greater extent than is true today. There were no such things as unemployment compensation, welfare checks, food stamps, Medicare, Social Security benefits, or government loans to students. Often there was only your family. Some older people provided assistance to their kin, such as finding a job for a relative, caring for the sick, or minding the grandchildren while the parents worked. Sometimes grandparents, their children, and their grandchildren pooled their resources into a common family fund so that all could subsist. Exactly how common these three-generational economic units were, we do not know; it would be a mistake to assume that all older adults cooperated with their children and grandchildren at all times. Still, historical accounts suggest that intensive intergenerational cooperation was more common than it is today because it was needed more.[3]

Although Social Security income helps the elderly greatly, a substantial number have incomes just above the poverty line.

---

[3] See, for example, Anderson (1971); Hareven (1982).

SEPARATE LIVING ARRANGEMENTS

The increased independence of the elderly is clearly shown in the great changes in their living arrangements over the past half century. Figure 10.2 on page 340 displays trends in living arrangements between 1940 and 1980 for persons aged 60 and over, and it also displays living arrangements in 2003 for persons aged 65 and over.[4] Living arrangements are grouped into four categories: (1) living alone, (2) living with their spouse, (3) living without a spouse but with other relatives, or (4) living with nonrelatives only. The upper panel is for women, the lower for men. Among women, there was a sharp increase in the percentage who were living alone—as you can see from the increasing size of the uppermost section of each bar, moving from left to right. Conversely, there was a sharp fall in the percentage who were living without a spouse but with other relatives (such as a daughter or son). By 2003 it was nearly as common for an elderly woman to live alone as to live with a husband.

This shift toward elderly women's living alone has occurred for two reasons. First, women have been outliving men by a greater and greater margin each decade, so that the number of elderly widows has grown much larger. About 7 in 10 wives survive their husbands (Treas & Bengtson, 1987), and few widows remarry because of the imbalance between the sexes. Second, an elderly widow today is much more likely to live alone than an elderly widow 40 or 50 years ago. In a Los Angeles survey, elderly persons were asked, "Would you prefer to live with your own children or in a separate residence?" Ninety-eight percent of the non-Hispanic whites, 83 percent of the blacks, and 72 percent of the Mexican Americans replied that they would prefer to live on their own.[5] The increases in the income of the elderly have allowed more of them to attain this desire. Overall, 1 of every 11 households in the United States in 2000 was maintained by an elderly person living alone (U.S. Bureau of the Census, 2004a). This represents an enormous change from midcentury, when such households were rare.

Gender Differences in Living Arrangements   Nevertheless, Figure 10.2 shows a very different pattern for elderly men than for elderly women. To be sure, the percentage living alone has increased, as indicated by the top section of the bars, but the increase has been modest. At all times since 1940, the vast majority of elderly men have been married and sharing a household with their wives. Moreover, the proportion who were married *increased* between 1940 and 2000—as you can see by the increasing size of the next-to-the-top section of each bar. This marriage bonanza for elderly men was the flip side of the spouse drought for elderly women. Men had a higher risk of dying than women, but if they managed to live longer than their wives, their remarriage prospects were better than were elderly women's. The current generation of elderly men has been cared for by women throughout their lives—by their mothers when they were growing up and by their wives (many of whom did not work outside the home after marriage) in middle age. They continue to be cared for by women in old age. Most elderly widows, on the other hand, must continue to care for themselves or to rely on relatives living mostly in other households. And so the older

---

[4] Figure 10.2 excludes elderly people who were living in nursing homes. Data for 2000 are taken from a published report from the Census Bureau's Current Population Survey, which presented information for people aged 65 and over.

[5] The study was carried out by Vern Bengtson and collaborators and is cited in Treas and Bengtson (1987).

Families and Public Policy

Financing Social Security and Medicare

Families and Public Policy

Until the recent debates about how to finance Social Security, many people believed in a myth: The government saved the Social Security taxes they paid—as if the money were put in a drawer with their name on it—and paid it back to them when they retired. In fact, Social Security is a pay-as-you-go system in which the taxes workers pay today are mostly given to today's elderly recipients. But as the proportion of the population that is elderly rises, the tax burden on the nonelderly, working-age population becomes greater. The problem could become severe after 2010, when the large baby boom generation begins to retire.

Even today, the expenditures are huge: Social Security benefits accounted for 22 percent of the federal budget in 2004— $40 billion more than all expenditures on national defense. Benefits under Medicare, the government health insurance program for the aged, constituted another 12 percent (U.S. Bureau of the Census, 2005k). In other words one-third of the federal budget was spent on benefits for the elderly.

In 2005, President Bush proposed to partially replace Social Security with a new system based on investing some of people's Social Security taxes in the stock and bond markets (Kosterlitz, 2005). Under this plan, part of the taxes workers pay would indeed be saved under their names, just as the myth suggested, only instead of keeping the money in a drawer the government would invest it. Partial privatization, as the plan is called, would eventually save federal money, since the government would reduce the benefits it pays to retired workers and substitute the proceeds of their personal accounts. Supporters of the plan have touted it as a way to reduce the growth of Social Security spending while relying on private investments. Critics of the plan, however, opposed investing people's tax dollars in the markets because the returns are not guaranteed. Although in the past the returns from stocks and bonds have been substantial, no one can be certain what future returns will be. Moreover, the transition to private accounts would

involve large transitional costs to the government, as it maintained benefits for today's elderly while phasing in the new system. So far, the opposition to partial privatization has been so strong that no action has been taken on it in Congress. Although the public pays more attention to the cost of Social Security than to the costs of Medicare, Social Security is actually in better shape. In 1983, Congress passed legislation that greatly strengthened the long-term financial status of the system. Among other things, the legislation increased the payroll taxes that workers and their employers pay into the government's Social Security trust fund. The legislation also raised the age at which people can retire and receive full benefits from 65 to 67 in 2027. (Although a two-year increase may seem modest, it will save money because 3 to 4 percent of 65-year-olds die within two years, and others will keep working and paying taxes.) Due to the increased payroll taxes, the Social Security trust fund is collecting large surpluses that

years have taken on an increasingly different character for women than for men—women more likely to be living apart from kin, men more likely to be living with their wives. (The rise in divorce in early and mid-adulthood has also separated the worlds of men and women; more on that in a few pages.)

Cultural Underpinnings   The notion that older parents should retain their independence is deeply rooted in the culture of the Western nations. Historical studies suggest that the preference for heading one's household until as late in life as possible has long been entrenched in Western Europe (Laslett & Wall, 1972). In many areas, the households were formed and maintained under the stem family system: The father eventually gave ownership of the farm to the one son who remained home (and thus formed the "stem"); he then brought in a wife. Ordinarily, the son was not allowed to marry until he was given control of the property. But older parents were often in no hurry to turn over their house and land to their son and heir, as demonstrated by the eighteenth-century Austrian folk song [➡ p. 218]: "Father, when ya gonna gimme the farm?" A U.S. historian has documented the reluctance of first-generation settlers in Andover, Massachusetts, to turn over control of their property to their sons. As in the

theoretically should be saved to pay for future costs. Unfortunately, politicians are finding it difficult to resist the temptation to use the surpluses to balance the federal budget today rather than to save it for the future. Consequently, the surpluses may not provide as much help as they should.

Elderly Americans, their numbers expanding, have become an important political interest group.

Little has been done, however, to control the spiraling growth of Medicare payments. Three factors are contributing to the growth: the increase in the elderly population, the growing share of the elderly population that is in the old-old and oldest-old categories (and therefore at greatest risk of serious illness and disability), and the increasing cost of health care. According to one projection, Medicare expenditures are expected to grow by almost 7 percent per year between 2004 and 2013 (Kaiser Family Foundation, 2003). There are several options that could help contain the costs of health care. The government could raise the payroll tax that pays for Medicare, as has been done with the Social Security payroll tax. Workers see one combined deduction on their paychecks for Social Security and Medicare; given the recent increases in this deduction, there could be substantial opposition to further hikes. The government could also raise the age of eligibility for Medicare and instead cover the youngest elderly through a national health insurance program. In addition, elderly people who are better off economically could be charged larger deductibles (the amount an individual must pay for a service before Medicare pays anything) or larger co-payments (the percentage of the cost of a service that the individual, not Medicare, must pay after the deductible is met). But it is very difficult to make major changes in popular programs for the elderly.

Ask Yourself

1. Do you have elderly relatives who receive Medicare benefits? If so, how important is government health insurance to them? If the government did not offer Medicare benefits, would your relatives, or their children, be able to afford their medical care?

2. Should Medicare beneficiaries be charged according to their ability to pay? Explain your reasoning.

www.mhhe.com/cherlin5

Austrian case, the young men in Andover needed their own farmland in order to marry. The reluctance of fathers to part with their land sometimes meant that sons were forced to postpone marrying until relatively late ages (Greven, 1970).

Today, of course, most children do not wait to inherit their parents' land but rather leave home to work for wages. Consequently, older parents' households are usually devoid of adult children. Still, the preference for retaining an independent household is strong. Most elderly persons in the United States, Canada, and Western Europe want to see their children and grandchildren often but do not want to live with them. What they want, according to a famous phrase, is "intimacy at a distance" (Rosenmayr & Kockeis, 1965). This trade-off between intimacy and independence has probably reduced the amount of contact the elderly have with their kin. For example, three of five elderly persons in the United States in 1900 were living with at least one (usually unmarried) child (Smith, 1979), and until recently few were living alone. But the preference that today's elderly express for living alone is genuine, and it is consistent with deeply held values of individualism in Western culture. It is not merely a rationale that the modern elderly have invented to mask disappointment at living apart from kin.

FIGURE 10.2

Living arrangements of women and men 60 years old and over in the United States, 1940 to 1980, and for women and men 65 years old and over, 2003. (*Sources:* Sweet & Bumpass, 1987; U.S. Bureau of the Census 2004a)

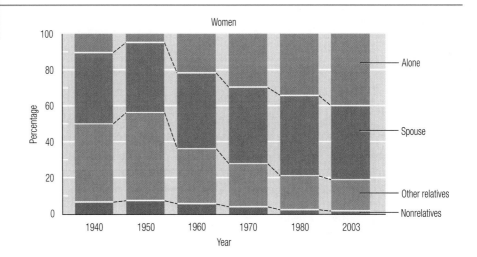

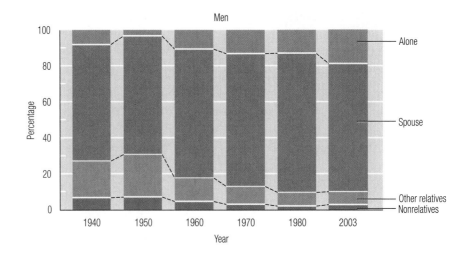

DYING AND DEATH

Changes in life expectancy and living arrangements have altered the ways in which families experience dying and death. The death of a child or a mother during childbirth is no longer common. Rather, grandparents usually die before their children and grandchildren. Although the death of a spouse is difficult for either partner, studies suggest that elderly men may have more difficulty adjusting to being widowed than elderly women (Quadagno, 2005). Today's elderly men, many of whom entered breadwinner–homemaker marriages in the 1950s and 1960s, typically have not done much cooking, cleaning, or other household tasks. One study found that on average, widowers were more depressed than widows following the loss of their spouses (Umberson, Wortman, & Kessler, 1992). Other studies have reported that men are more likely than women to die in the first few years after widowhood (Quadagno, 2005).

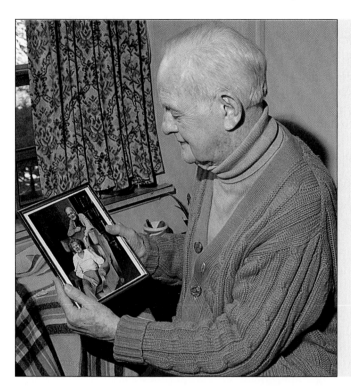

Elderly widowers often find it difficult to manage the daily household tasks their wives did.

As we have noted, most adult children are in their fifties when they first experience the death of a parent. Even if their parents were no longer providing much assistance, losing them can still be emotionally difficult. In general, middle-aged adults who have lost a parent show greater psychological distress and poorer physical health than other adults in their age group. But not always: If the parent had mental health, alcohol, or other problems, their children's functioning may improve after their death (Umberson & Chen, 1994). An adult child's experience in losing a parent varies according to the parent–child relationship.

Quick Review

- Because of dramatic declines in mortality, grandparents' and grandchildren's lives overlap much more than in the past. Also, women tend to live longer than men.
- Because of declines in fertility, most grandparents are no longer raising children, which makes grandparenthood a more distinct stage of life.
- A rising standard of living, due in large part to Social Security, has made the elderly less dependent on their children.
- Elderly women are much more likely to be living alone than in the past, and elderly men are more likely to be married than in the past.

Giving and Getting

In middle and old age, as in childhood, most people in need of assistance turn to their kin. The majority of help that the elderly and their adult children receive comes from one another. And because of lengthening life expectancy, this stage of mutual assistance lasts longer than ever before. At current rates of fertility and mortality, according to one demographic estimate, the average person can expect his or her life to overlap slightly longer with a parent over the age of 65 than with children under the age of 18 (Watkins, Menken, & Bongaarts, 1987). But although adult children will provide assistance during the years when they have aging parents, most of them also will *receive* substantial help from their aging parents as well. Until their last years, most aging parents are relatively healthy and economically independent.

MUTUAL ASSISTANCE

In fact, until they are very old or very ill, the elderly typically give more assistance to their adult children than the children provide them (Soldo & Hill, 1993). Assistance is episodic rather than continual: Parents or children help out or give money when there is a particular need. For instance, grandparents spend much more time providing assistance to their adult children when their grandchildren are in their preschool years than when they are adolescents. Indeed, in 1999, grandparents were the primary source of child care for 22 percent of preschool children whose mothers worked outside the home (U.S. Bureau of the Census, 2003t). As will be mentioned in Chapter 12, it is common for a divorced daughter to move back in with her parents temporarily after her marriage breaks up. Financial assistance also tends to occur in lump transfers rather than continual flows. Older parents might provide a child with a few thousand dollars toward the down payment on a home, or they might help a child pay for a grandchild's college tuition.

These patterns of giving assistance only when there are specific needs imply that, at any given time, most older parents and adult children are not providing much assistance to each other. In a national survey of adults with living parents, only 17 percent of the adults reported getting $200 or more from their parents, and only 4 percent reported giving $200 or more, within the previous five years—excluding help with mortgage payments. Child care is more common: About 13 percent had received baby-sitting or child care assistance from their parents in the previous month. Giving and getting advice and support are more common still: 27 percent had received, and 25 percent had given, advice or emotional support in the previous month (Eggebeen & Hogan, 1990).

The kind of assistance the two generations provide to each other is complementary. According to the Boston study, adult children tend to provide more personal support, such as comfort or care during an illness, whereas older parents tend to provide more material help: a loan, part of a down payment on a house, or help with finding a job (Rossi & Rossi, 1990). This pattern allows the older generation to maintain a sense of independence, so central to American values. In fact, as I was finishing the revisions for this chapter, another *New York Times* reporter called me. She was doing a story about the assistance that grandparents provide to their adult children and grandchildren. She had met the previous day with several middle-class grandparents who told her they provided financial help with such expenses as tuition payments for a private school. The next day, almost everyone called her to ask that their names not be printed in the newspaper. They were all worried that they and their children would be embarrassed if their financial assistance became public. Their discomfort shows the power of the middle-class norm that adult children and their older parents should be "independent" of each other. That's the way Americans like to think of themselves. But behind the scenes, grandparents help out when there's a specific need.

And in reality, adult children also provide substantial financial support to their parents—but in such a way that no one need notice. The hidden subsidy is Social Security, the role of which in raising the living standard of the elderly was discussed earlier. I pay thousands of dollars a year in Social Security taxes, and the program sent thousands of dollars a year to my elderly parents while they were alive. Yet the genius of the system is that my parents and I didn't have to acknowledge this connection; we could both maintain that, as good American parents and children should be, we were economically independent of each other.

MOVING IN WITH GRANDPARENTS

Over the past few decades, a modest but growing percentage of grandchildren have been living with grandparents. In all, 5.6 million children lived with their grandparents in 2002 (U.S. Bureau of the Census, 2003c). Observers have particularly noted the growing percentage who are living in their grandparents' homes (as opposed to living in their parents' homes with grandparents present). Figure 10.3 shows that between 1970 and the early 2000s, the percentage of children who lived in their grandparents' homes rose from about 3 to about 5 percent. Figure 10.3 also shows that the growth occurred primarily in homes where one parent was present (the orange segment of the bars) or where neither parent was present (the green segment of the bars) rather than in families where both parents were present.

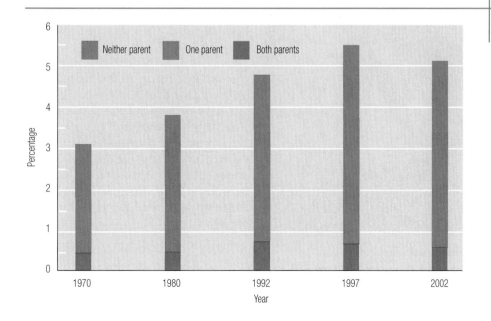

FIGURE 10.3
Percentage of all children under 18 who are living in grandparents' homes, by presence of parents, 1970–2002. (*Source:* U.S. Bureau of the Census, 1999a, 2003w)

Grandparents as Parents

In the 2000 Census, about 2.4 million grandparents said that they were "currently responsible for most of the basic needs" of a grandchild whom they were living with. In about one-third of these households, no one in the middle generation was present.

A grandmother who raises her grandchildren in a cramped public housing apartment in Detroit cooks dinner with her ten-year-old grandson.

These are the so-called "skipped-generation households" in which grandparents are raising grandchildren alone. We are used to thinking of grandparents as a source of support in reserve—as kin who will step in and help parents whenever needed. But in skipped-generation households, the grandparents, in a sense, are the parents.

This is not necessarily a social problem. Other things being equal, it's beneficial for grandchildren to have close ties to their grandchildren. Nevertheless, many of these skipped-generation households are formed when the parents in the middle generation are unable to care for their children. The parents may be ill, deceased, in prison, or incapacitated by substance abuse. Under these circumstances, grandparents step in to provide the childrearing. While they love their grandchildren and want to help out, they may find full-time care difficult to carry out. They may be living on fixed incomes from pensions or social security and may not be able to easily afford having their grandchildren join the household. Others may find that just when they thought they had launched their children and grandchildren successfully, the needs of their grandchildren suddenly force them to curtail plans they had made for their own lives.

We don't know whether the number of grandparents caring for grandchildren in skipped-generation households has increased because the questions were not asked in prior censuses. But the overall percentage of children living with grandparents, whether or not the parents are present, has been increasing and stood at 8 percent in 2002. Grandparents are still an important source of support for American children.

Left

In so-called "skipped-generation households," grandparents are raising their grand-children without the presence of the parents.

Below

Grandparents, such as this grandfather fishing with his grandson in Austin, Texas, enjoy being with their grandchildren; but raising them may cause a financial or physical strain.

Multigenerational Households   Households in which grandparents, grandchildren, and one parent are present usually are formed after either of two events: The parent gives birth to a child while neither married nor cohabiting, or the parent separates from a spouse or partner after the birth of the children. The former event tends to involve young mothers in low-income families, and the latter tends to involve working-class and middle-class parents in the midst of a divorce. In these **multigenerational households,** as we will call households in which at least three generations of family members reside, grandparents can provide important child-rearing assistance. For instance, in one national survey it was found that teenagers who lived with at least one grandparent in a multigenerational household were just as likely to graduate from high school and no more likely to smoke or drink than were children who lived with two married parents (DeLeire and Kalil, 2002). On the other hand, studies of low-income adolescent mothers who live with their parents show a mixed pattern of positive and negative effects. [➡ p. 306]. Grandparents in the household, it seems, sometimes can help children being raised by single parents, but not necessarily in all settings. When they do help, they can contribute in several ways: They can provide more income if they are employed. They can provide child care that allows mothers to work outside the home. They can also help by being directly involved in raising a child, even to the point of being the child's primary caregiver. Living with a grandparent can sometimes provide advantages that a second parent would provide.

Skipped-Generation Households   Researchers sometimes refer to households with grandparents and grandchildren but neither parent present as **skipped-generation households** (Fuller-Thomson, Minkler, & Driver, 1997). One-third of all the grandparents in the 2000 Census who said they were responsible for most of the basic needs of a grandchild were in skipped-generation households—meaning that neither of the grandchild's parents were in the home (U.S. Bureau of the Census, 2003g). Skipped-generation households tend to form when parents are unable to care for their children. The parents may have had their children removed from them and placed with a grandparent due to child abuse or neglect; the parents may have been incapacitated by drug abuse or illness; or they may have been incarcerated. Skipped-generation households are the most disadvantaged of all the kinds of grandparent–grandchild households: They have higher poverty rates, greater usage of public assistance, and less health insurance coverage (U.S. Bureau of the Census, 1999a).

As one might expect given the greater emphasis on extended family ties in African American kinship, African American children are more likely to be living in a grandparent's household (9 percent of all African American children in 2002) than are Hispanic children (6 percent), non-Hispanic white children (4 percent), or Asian American children (3 percent) (U.S. Bureau of the Census, 2003c). And when they do, they live with just a grandmother three-fourths of the time, rather than with two grandparents. These caregiving grandmothers tend to have more health limitations than other African American grandmothers and to show more signs of depression (Fuller-Thomson & Minkler, 2000).

Rewards and Costs   Overall, the movement of more grandchildren into their grandparents' homes seems to represent a response to family crises rather than a greater preference for intergenerational living. Although some middle-class mothers have moved in with their parents after a separation or divorce, most of the families involved in this trend tend to be poor or near-poor. So while the typical middle-class

multigenerational households households in which at least three generations of family members reside

skipped-generation households households containing grandparents and grandchildren without either parent present

grandparent attains "intimacy at a distance," a growing share of poor and near-poor grandparents are directly involved in raising their grandchildren. This is particularly true among African American grandparents, 30 percent of whom, in one national survey, reported having the primary responsibility for raising a grandchild for at least six months at some point in their lives (Fuller Thomson & Minkler, 2000). Grandparents tend to find caring for their grandchildren rewarding, but it can also be hard on their health and finances and can occur at times in their lives when they would prefer not to be caring for children anymore (Burton, 1992). It is a situation that can produce ambivalent feelings—a point to which I will return shortly.

CARE OF THE DISABLED

You might think that most seriously impaired elderly persons are cared for in nursing homes, but that is not so. More are living in the community (that is, in private homes or apartments, not institutions) than in nursing homes. In order to measure physical impairment, gerontologists have developed standard questions about the activities a person needs help with. The most common set, **activities of daily living,** or ADLs, refers to personal care, including bathing, dressing, eating, getting into and out of bed, walking indoors, and using the toilet. Among all elderly persons with limitations in one or more ADLs in 1994, two-thirds were living in the community. Even among those with limitations in three or more ADLs, nearly half were living in the community (Liu, Manton, and Aragon, 2000).

activities of daily living (ADLs) personal care activities, including bathing, dressing, getting into or out of bed, walking indoors, and using the toilet

Much of the care of the disabled elderly who live in the community is provided by relatives. According to a 1999 national survey of dependent elderly persons, 58 percent of their caregivers were spouses and children and an additional 10 percent or so were other family members (Wolf, 2004). Moreover, women do more of the care of the elderly than do men. Two-thirds of the caregivers identified in the survey of the dependent elderly were women (Wolf, 2004). And there is a rough hierarchy of caregivers. If the elderly person's spouse is alive and reasonably healthy, she or he will normally become the primary caregiver; if the spouse is not alive, an adult daughter is usually next in line; and if there is no daughter who can manage the care, another relative, such as a son or a sister, may be called upon (Gatz, Bengtson, & Blum, 1990). Since a majority of elderly women survive their husbands, this hierarchy means, in practice, that elderly women are likely to be cared for eventually by their daughters. For an unmarried elderly person, having a daughter is the key to receiving support. In a 1984 national health survey, elderly respondents were asked if they needed help with any of 13 activities of daily living and home management. If they answered affirmatively, they were asked whether or not they received help from one of their children. Among those who were unmarried and not living with a child, persons who had at least one daughter were more likely to receive help than those who had just a son or even two sons (Spitze & Logan, 1990).

These mostly female caregivers not only assist their relatives but also perform a critical public service. Without the care that they provide, our already expensive government health care programs would be much more costly. Since Medicare does not pay for nursing home care, individuals must pay nursing home costs by spending their own money first. Only when individuals have spent most of their savings—and therefore meet the government requirements for being poor—are they eligible for Medicaid, which will then step in and pay the bills. Typically, persons of modest means who enter nursing homes—the costs of which average more than $40,000 per year— "spend down" their assets in several months and then turn to Medicaid. Public spending for nursing home care totaled about $67 billion in 2003. Individuals in care spent another $44 billion out of their own pockets (U.S. Bureau of the Census, 2005l).

Four and one-half percent of the elderly in the United States resided in nursing homes in 2000 (U.S. Bureau of the Census, 2005l). As was noted in the discussion of Figure 10.1, the oldest-old, those aged 85 and over, are the fastest-growing segment. Their numbers virtually doubled from 2.2 million in 1980 to 4.3 million in 2000, and are still increasing rapidly. Perhaps 60 percent of them, at current rates, will reside in a nursing home at some point during their last years. From the public standpoint, it is crucial to hold down the number of persons who will need institutionalized care.

THE REWARDS AND COSTS OF CAREGIVING

Holding down the number of persons who need institutionalized care is precisely what family members do now. If family caregivers went on strike tomorrow, nursing homes would be flooded with new patients and Medicaid would pay out billions of dollars more. According to one estimate, the economic value of the unpaid caregiving that family members and friends give to ill and disabled adults was $196 billion in 1997—about twice the cost that government and private citizens are currently paying for nursing home care (Arno, Levine, and Memmott, 1999). Of course, it is absurd to imagine that so many caretakers would quit because most are relatives who love the persons they care for and feel a sense of obligation to help. There is reason, nonetheless, to be concerned about the future availability of caregivers. The informal care system has depended on the availability and goodwill of middle-aged women. A few decades ago, most married women were not employed outside the home; presumably, they had more time to devote to caring for an aging parent. But a majority of married women now work outside the home, and the proportion will likely increase further in the next decade or two. Sons and daughters who are employed full-time give less help to, and receive less help from, their parents (Rossi & Rossi, 1990). In addition, the fall in birthrates since the 1950s means that there are proportionally fewer adult daughters per elderly parent.

As a result, an increasing number of disabled elderly rely on paid health care aides to supplement unpaid family care. Between 1982 and 1994, the percentage who received help from paid caregivers increased from one-quarter to more than one-third (Liu, Manton, & Aragon, 2000). Families paid about 60 percent of the costs of these workers, and government programs and private insurance paid the rest. Employed, middle-aged adults are increasingly hiring someone else to help care for elderly parents, just as they are increasingly hiring others to do the housecleaning and to provide child care. Care for dependents up and down the family tree is becoming more of a commodity that you purchase rather than a service you provide. Consequently, the role of paid home health care aides is likely to grow further in the years ahead.

FAMILY STRESS

As family caregivers increasingly combine working outside the home with caregiving for an elderly spouse or parent, one might imagine that their levels of stress would increase. Yet having other roles to play (employee, wife) may lower the stress that caregivers of the elderly feel. Having a job you like, for instance, may take your mind off your caregiving responsibilities, making it easier to pro-

vide care. Some studies have noted this "buffering" effect: Success or social support in one role may compensate for the stress provoked by another. [➡ p. 275]
From this perspective, the stress caregivers feel largely derives from the care they
give, not from an overload of responsibilities.

Moreover, adult children with disabled parents may find the situation stressful
even if they are not the main caregivers. According to one national survey of
adults in their fifties, those who had a parent who needed extensive care were, in
some circumstances, more depressed if they were *not* the main caregiver than if
they were (Amirkhanyan and Wolf, 2003). The authors suggest that caregivers
feel the stress of having a disabled parent but also reap the rewards of providing
care, whereas their husbands, wives, or siblings feel the stress but get none of the
rewards. And the rewards can be substantial: becoming closer to a parent, making
a difference in his or her daily life, gaining a greater sense of the meaning of life.
Caregiving to the elderly is not simply a burden, as difficult as it may be. It can
also give people a sense of connectedness and satisfaction.

When an adult cares for a disabled parent, her caregiving affects her spouse,
children, and siblings, who do not receive the psychological benefits of providing
care, but whose daily lives are nevertheless likely to be altered. The caregiver may
be less emotionally available to her husband; or the time she spends may upset
her family's routines; or her caregiving may provoke conflicts with a sister who
wants the caregiving done another way. Among adults who are caring for parents
with Alzheimer's disease, the progressive dementia that typically requires years of
care, caregiving may affect a person's marriage, parenting, job, and social life
(Pearlin, Pioli, and McLaughlin, 2001). The point is that caregiving for the elderly
affects entire families, not just the caregivers.

Quick Review

- Until they are very old or ill, the elderly provide more assistance to their children and grandchildren than they receive.
- A modest but growing number of grandparents are caring for their grandchildren, sometimes in skipped-generation households in which no parent is present.
- Family members provide more of the care of the frail elderly than do nursing homes.
- Caring for the elderly can be both rewarding and stressful, and the entire family system may feel the stress.

■ The Quality of Intergenerational Ties ■

Beyond giving and receiving care when needed, what can be said about the quality of the relationships between older people and their kin today? What does it
mean that so many elderly women live alone and so few elderly persons of either
sex live with their children? Are they lonely and isolated? Are they a part of their
children's and grandchildren's lives? Sociologists studying these issues often define the subject as "intergenerational solidarity." The concept is a broad one, and,
fittingly, *solidarity* is a word with many connotations. When asked, a word
processor pops up the following synonyms: cooperation, fellowship, harmony,
unity, stability, and reliability. An unabridged dictionary defines solidarity as "an

entire union of interests and responsibilities in a group," and it quotes a phrase from Joseph Conrad: "Solidarity that knits together innumerable hearts" (*Webster's Third New International Dictionary*, electronic version). We might say, after Conrad, that **intergenerational solidarity** refers to the characteristics of family relationships that knit the generations together.

intergenerational solidarity the characteristics of family relationships that knit the generations together

With respect to the older parents and their adult children, three broad characteristics of intergenerational solidarity have received the most attention from social scientists. They have been given slightly different names and definitions (Rossi & Rossi, 1990; Roberts, Richards, & Bengtson, 1991; Silverstein & Bengtson, 1997). Here are the names and definitions I will use:

- *Contact:* How frequently parents and children see each other and are in touch electronically through telephone calls or e-mail messages.
- *Affinity:* How emotionally close parents and children feel and how much they agree on values, attitudes, and beliefs.
- *Assistance:* The amount of assistance, in either time, goods, or money, that parents and children provide to each other.

We have already discussed assistance. Let us focus on the first two: contact and affinity. They are relevant for judging whether the elderly obtain the closeness and emotional support they wish—and whether they provide closeness and emotional support to their children and grandchildren. These are the kinds of questions included under the umbrella of the private family.

CONTACT

It might seem logical to infer that, in a society in which 1 in 11 households contains an elderly person living alone and in which few elderly persons live with their children, the elderly must be isolated from their children and grandchildren. "Isolated" is a value-laden term, however, and what might seem like isolation to a Japanese grandparent might seem like a surfeit of contact to an American grandparent. (See *Families in Other Cultures:* The Elderly and Their Families in Japan, on pp. 358–359.) Statistics cannot settle a matter such as this, but they can describe the patterns of contact.

In a 1992–1993 national survey, 39 percent of grandparents reported that at least one set of grandchildren lived less than 10 miles from them; and a majority reported that they saw at least one grandchild every week (Uhlenberg & Hammill, 1998). In the mid-1980s, Frank Furstenberg and I interviewed the grandparents of a national sample of children and asked them "When was the last time you saw any grandchild?" About half of the grandparents had seen at least one grandchild that day or the day before, and 70 percent had seen a grandchild within the last week. Just one in six had not seen a grandchild within the previous month (Cherlin & Furstenberg, 1992). Elderly persons living alone who don't have children (about 3 in 10), of course, have much less frequent contact with relatives. But overall, the amount of contact that the elderly have with their children and grandchildren is surprisingly high.

Geographical Distance between Generations Many studies have shown that the strongest predictor of how often grandparents see their grandchildren is how far apart they live (Cherlin & Furstenberg, 1992; Uhlenberg & Hammill, 1998). The dominance of distance illustrates both the strength and the vulnerability of the grandparent-parent-grandchild relationship. As for its strength: When grandchildren live close by, grandparents see them regularly, except under unusual circumstances. Parents and children, with few exceptions, make sure they visit the grandparents. The pull grandparents exert when they live nearby shows how strong is the sense of obligation among adult children to keep in touch with their parents and their in-laws. This sense of obligation is usually overlaid with love, concern, and assistance, but even when it is unsupported by these props, it is often still honored. The uniformly high frequency of visiting among nearby kin suggests that the bond among grandparents, their adult children, and their grandchildren is still strong.

On the other hand, when adult children move away, grandparents' access to their grandchildren drops dramatically. To be sure, adult children who have weaker ties to their parents may be the ones who tend to move from their hometowns. Job possibilities, marriage, and many other events also enter into the decision to move. Still, from the grandparents' point of view, whether or not adult children live close by involves a large element of luck. When a son takes a job in another state or a daughter-in-law moves away after a divorce, the grandparent is rarely able to overcome this impediment to regular contact.

Mother–Daughter Relationships   In addition to living close by, grandparents see their grandchildren more frequently if they have a close relationship with the mother of the grandchild—their daughter or daughter-in-law. Middle-aged women do the work of "kin keeping" more often than middle-aged men, and studies show that their ties with older and younger generations are stronger and more consistent, on average, than men's (Rossi & Rossi, 1990). In general, grandmothers see their grandchildren more than grandfathers do, and grandmothers on the mother's side see even more of them than grandmothers on the father's side (Uhlenberg & Hammill, 1998).

AFFINITY

Hand in hand with the demographic and economic changes in the lives of the elderly have come great changes in the emotional content of their relationships with their children and grandchildren. During the twentieth century, there appears to have been an increasing emphasis on bonds of sentiment: love, affection, and companionship. There is no evidence that the emotional ties between parents and children have grown weaker. Before Furstenberg and I conducted our national survey, we talked with many grandparents at senior citizens' centers. When we asked grandparents whether grandparenthood had changed since they were grandchildren, we heard stories of their childhood that differed from our idyllic image of the past. Their grandparents, we were told, were respected, admired figures who often assisted other family members. But again and again, we heard them talk about the emotional distance between themselves and their grandparents:

> *The only grandmother I remember is my father's mother, and she lived with us.*
>
> *INTERVIEWER: What was it like, having your grandmother live with you?*
>
> *Terrible [laughter]! She was old, she was strict.... We weren't allowed to sass her, I guess that was the whole trouble. No matter what she did to you, you had to take it.... She was good, though.... She used to do all the patching of the pants, and she was helpful. But, oh, she was strict. You weren't allowed to do anything, she'd tell on you right away.*

INTERVIEWER: So what difference do you think there is between being a grand-parent when you were a grandchild and being a grandparent now?

It's different. My grandma never gave us any love.

INTERVIEWER: No?

Nooo. My goodness, no, no. No, never took us anyplace, just sat there and yelled at you all the time.

INTERVIEWER: Did you have a lot of respect for your grandmother?

Oh, we had to whether we wanted to or not, we had to.

Grandma may have helped out, and she certainly was respected, even loved; but she was often an emotionally distant figure. This is not to say that affection was absent from the relations between young and old. But there has been a shift in the balance between respect and affection. For example, we asked grandparents who knew at least one of their own grandparents "Are you and [your grandchild] more friendly, less friendly, or about the same as your grandparents were with you?" Forty-eight percent said "more friendly"; only 9 percent said "less friendly." Similarly, 55 percent said their relationship with grandchildren was "closer" than their relationship had been with their grandparents; just 10 percent said "not as close."

Demographic and Economic Change   Granted, it is hard to judge the accuracy of these recollections of two generations ago. But the story that the grandparents consistently told us fits with the demographic and economic developments that have been discussed. It is easier for today's grandparents to have a pleasurable, emotion-laden relationship with their grandchildren because they are more likely to live long enough to develop the relationship, because they are not still busy raising their own children, because they can travel long distances more easily and communicate over the telephone, and because they have fewer grandchildren and more economic resources to devote to them. Earlier in the nation's history, the generations were often bound up in economic cooperation that took

The ties between grandparents and grandchildren are increasingly based on love and affection, rather than authority and discipline.

precedence over affection and companionship. In fact, there may be a trade-off between bonds of obligation and authority, on the one hand, and bonds of sentiment. Historian David Hackett Fischer, in his book on the history of aging in America, noted the following differences between the nation's early and later years:

> *Even as most (though not all) elderly people were apt to hold more power than they would possess in a later period, they were also apt to receive less affection, less love, less sympathy from those younger than themselves. The elderly were kept at an emotional distance by the young. (Fischer, 1978)*

Conversely, in modern America:

> *As elders lost their authority within the society, they gained something in return. Within the sphere of an individual family, ties of affection may have grown stronger as ties of family obligation grew weak. (Fischer, 1978)*

This increasing emphasis on affection appears to be continuing among the elderly and their children and grandchildren today. Nearly all studies report a high level of warmth and emotional closeness among the different generations in a family (Silverstein & Bengtson, 1997; Bengtson, 2001). Nevertheless, the degree of emotional closeness between parents and children varies over the life cycle. It will come as no surprise to parents that closeness and intimacy decline as children move into adolescence. That is the life stage when children must establish their autonomy. As the children reach adulthood, closeness improves again, and it improves further as the parents enter old age and their children enter middle age (Rossi & Rossi, 1990). Moreover, there appear to be substantial gender differences in closeness. The Boston study found that in mid- and later life, mother–daughter relationships are the closest, mother–son relationships are second, father–daughter third, and father–son fourth. In a 1990 national survey, individuals with living parents were asked how close their relationships were with their parents. Seventy-two percent said that they had a "very close" relationship with their mothers, but only 57 percent said that they had a very close relationship with their fathers (Silverstein & Bengtson, 1997). These differences suggest once again that it is women who invest more in family ties.

Shared Values   The second component of affinity is agreement between the generations on values, attitudes, and beliefs. Most studies show substantial agreement between older parents and their adult children. In the 1990 survey, individuals were also asked how similar their opinions were to those of their mothers and fathers. Sixty-nine percent said that their opinions were "very similar" or "somewhat similar" to their mothers' opinions. Agreement with fathers was not quite as high: 60 percent said their opinions were "very similar" or "somewhat similar" (Silverstein & Bengtson, 1997). Substantial agreement between parents and children is to be expected for two reasons (Roberts et al., 1991). First, parents socialize their children in their own values while raising them—both at home and at the family's place of religious worship. Second, parents and children often share the same social class position and therefore have similar kinds of jobs and leisure activities. As noted in the previous chapter, a person's social class position can influence her or his opinions about independence, conformity, and other values.

Nevertheless, the experiences of parents and children do diverge in ways that can cause differences of opinions. Studies suggest that individuals' beliefs are affected by the social context during their adolescence and young adulthood and

cohort replacement model a model of changing public opinion in which each successive birth cohort experiences a different social environment and retains distinctive opinions throughout his or her adult life

that these beliefs, once formed, tend to remain throughout adulthood. For example, growing up during an economic depression may make a person frugal for a lifetime. Consequently, if the social context in which children grow up differs from the context when their parents grew up, some differences in beliefs are likely. This process is called the **cohort replacement model** of public opinion because it presumes that each successive *birth cohort* [➡ p. 65] experiences a different social environment and retains distinctive opinions throughout adult life (Alwin, 1996). Your values in childhood are shaped both by how your parents raised you and by the social climate in which your birth cohort grew up.

Quick Review

- Intergenerational solidarity depends on frequent contact, emotional closeness, and mutual support.
- Although most grandparents live apart from their grandchildren, they tend to see at least some of them often.
- Living geographically close, having a good relationship with the mother, and having a strong family culture predict how often grandparents see their children.
- Sentiment and affection have become increasingly central to intergenerational relations, whereas the authority of the elderly may have declined.

■ Sources of Tension

Not all families, of course, have strong intergenerational ties. When Silverstein and Bengtson (1997) examined the variation in solidarity reported by adult children in a 1990 national survey, they found that adult daughters and their mothers were more likely to have high levels of all indicators of solidarity—contact, affinity, and assistance—than were daughters and fathers or than were sons and either fathers or mothers. This finding confirms once again the central role of the mother-daughter bond in intergenerational relations. At the other extreme, adult children in the study reported low levels of all indicators of solidarity when their parents were divorced. The lack of solidarity was particularly strong between adult children and their divorced older fathers.

INTERGENERATIONAL AMBIVALENCE

What is more, even warm relationships can have tensions embedded in them. For instance, adult children may have conflicting feelings about caring for ailing parents. On the one hand, they may find caring for parents deeply fulfilling and meaningful. On the other hand, they may feel resentful of the demands that caring makes on their time and energy. Even in the mind of a dedicated, loving caregiver, these contradictory feelings may coexist. In one national study, women who began to care for an elderly parent reported both an increase in depression and a greater sense of purpose in life (Marks, Lambert, and Choi, 2002). The elderly parent may also feel ambivalent toward the adult child—at once understanding that children have independent lives to lead and yet desiring care from them. In fact, ambivalence may be more common now than in the past: More middle-aged children have living parents because of increases in life expectancy during the twentieth century; yet women, who provide the bulk of care, have greater opportunities to work outside the home than fifty years ago. Greater responsibilities for providing care and greater opportunities for self-advancement are a recipe for increasing ambivalence. In addition, as noted earlier, more grandparents are being called upon to care for their grandchildren in circumstances that can lead to ambivalent feelings.

Ambivalence is a broad concept, applicable to many situations in which a person can have conflicting feelings. Sociologists focus on situations in which ambivalence is socially structured, meaning that it reflects hierarchies of authority, power, or income. Let us define **intergenerational ambivalence** as socially structured contradictory emotions in an intergenerational relationship (Lüscher and Pillemer, 1998; Curran, 2002; Pillemer & Lüscher, 2003; Pillemer & Lüscher, 2004). Consider gender differences in intergenerational relationships. Sociologists would predict that people with fewer resources available to them would have a more difficult time managing intergenerational ambivalence and that they would be more likely to resolve it by accepting the contradictions rather than confronting them (Connidis and McMullin, 2002). Women, for instance, typically earn lower wages than men, and they are expected to do more of the work of caring than men. A son who is ambivalent about caring for an elderly parent would be more likely to hire a caregiver—because of his higher income and because sons are not expected to be caregivers—than would a daughter. She would be more likely to provide care herself, even if she had mixed feelings about it. And the parent she is caring for would be more likely to have ambivalent feelings about her than about a son who is not providing as much care.

The results of two studies confirm the prediction that women feel more ambivalence than men in their relations with elderly parents: In one study, elderly women reported more ambivalent feelings toward their daughters than toward their sons, as indicated by their greater agreement with statements such as

intergenerational ambivalence socially structured contradictory emotions in an intergenerational relationship

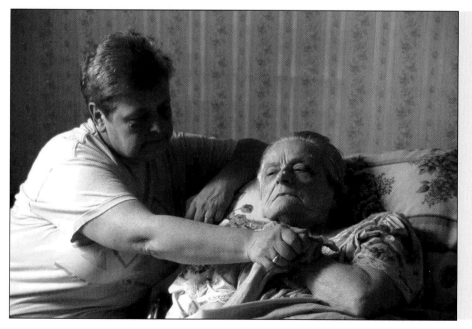

Adult children may have conflicting feelings about caring for elderly parents.

mother and daughter "get on each other's nerves but nevertheless we feel very close" (Pillemer and Suiter, 2002). Another study of rural Iowa families found that women who were caring for parents reported more ambivalence than men who were caring for parents: The women were more likely to agree with both positive statements (e.g., feeling appreciated and loved) and negative statements (feelings of conflict, tension, or disagreement) about their relationship to their parent (Willson, Shuey, & Elder, 2003). These ambivalent feelings do not necessarily prevent caregiving, but they suggest that caregiving often creates simultaneous positive and negative feelings for the provider and recipient of care.

THE EFFECTS OF DIVORCE AND REMARRIAGE

Other studies also show that older divorced fathers and their children, on average, have relationships that are far less close than the relationships of fathers and children from families with no divorce. In the study of rural Iowa families previously mentioned, grandfathers who were divorced reported less contact and closeness with their grandchildren, in part because they lived farther away and in part because they were less close to the middle generation—their adult children (King, 2003). A 1992–1993 national survey showed that grandfathers who were separated, divorced, or remarried were very unlikely to see their grandchildren from their previous marriage frequently (Uhlenberg & Hammill, 1998). In the National Survey of Families and Households, conducted in 1987 and 1988, adults were asked who, among persons not living with them, they would turn to for assistance in three situations: an emergency in the middle of the night, the need to borrow $200 for a few weeks, and the need to talk to someone about a problem. Two researchers tabulated the answers given by men aged 50 to 79 who had living adult children. About half of all the men who had been divorced did not even mention a child as someone they would turn to in any of the three situations. In contrast, less than one-fourth of never-divorced men failed to mention a child. Moreover, only 50 percent of the divorced fathers had weekly contact with their children, compared with 90 percent of never-divorced men (Cooney & Uhlenberg, 1990). Another study using the same survey found that adult children from divorced families rated the quality of their relationship with noncustodial fathers no more positively than adult children who had never lived with their fathers since birth (Aquilino, 1994). Yet another study found that if the custodial parent had remarried, thus providing the children with a stepparent, relations between adult children and the noncustodial parents were weakened further (Lye & Klepinger, 1995).

The same survey indicated that adult stepchildren saw their stepfathers less often than adult biological children saw their fathers and that adult stepchildren rated the quality of their relationship with their stepfathers lower. Moreover, if the marriage between the natural parent and the stepparent had ended, either because of a divorce or because the natural parent had died, the ties between an adult stepchild and stepparent often ended as well: 57 percent of the adult stepchildren in stepfamilies ended by divorce never saw their stepparent, and 46 percent of adult stepchildren in stepfamilies ended by death never saw their stepparent (White, 1994). Thus, the relationship between adult stepchildren and stepparents, which in any case seems less close than between adult biological children and parents, may not even survive a divorce or death. Consequently, some elderly stepparents may not receive as much support from their stepchildren as they may need.

It seems doubtful, then, that the daughters and sons who provide so much of the care for the frail elderly will provide as much care for noncustodial fathers, never-married fathers, or stepfathers as for biological fathers they lived with continuously while growing up. As Chapter 12 will note, the divorce rate doubled in the 1960s and 1970s, and the proportion of children born outside marriage rose during (and after) those decades as well. The men who reach the age of 65 after the year 2000 will be part of the first generation to have lived most of their adult lives after the great increases in divorce and childbearing outside marriage. Many fathers have little contact with their children after a divorce or a separation from the children's mother.

How will these men find care when they need it? Anthropologist Katherine Newman (2003) noticed two strategies in her study of middle-aged and elderly adults in a low-income community in New York, where childbearing outside of marriage is common. First, men sometimes reappeared unexpectedly at the homes of their former partners and their adult children. After long periods of separation, they attempted to reenter the family systems they had largely abandoned, with varying success. The second strategy was to marry a woman their age. As greater mortality among men reduced their supply, the surviving men found that the demography of the elderly cohabitation and marriage market favored them.

It is possible, however, that the strategy of finding a wife to care for you doesn't work as well as it used to. Some of the low- and moderate-income single mothers in Newman's study told her that they had no intention of having a serious romantic partner again. Moreover, the women now reaching old age will belong to the first generation to have extensive employment histories throughout adulthood. They may have more financial resources when they retire, and some may keep working at least part-time after reaching age 65. Frances Goldscheider speculates that fewer widowed and divorced women may find it attractive to remarry an elderly man: They will have less need for financial support, and they may prefer other activities to caregiving. If divorced men aren't remarried in old age, and if they can't rely on their children, they may have no one to help them in their last, frail years. In fact, the percentage of elderly men who live with their wives, after increasing from 1940 to 1980 (see Figure 10.2), has now leveled off. Research on divorce, Goldscheider writes, "has focused on women and children as the 'victims'" because of the loss of the father's income. Yet in old age, when kinship ties matter, "it is males who are at risk" (Goldscheider, 1990).

Elderly gay men and lesbians may also face challenges in obtaining support in old age. Their ability to call on others for assistance will depend on how well they have been able to construct a network of friends, partners, and biological relatives. The effectiveness of these networks is likely to vary widely. In addition, many of their ties are likely to be with people in the same generation; consequently, their access to younger adults who could provide help may be limited.

The Family National Guard

In all, how important a part of the American family system are intergenerational relations? Gerontologist Vern L. Bengtson is the leading advocate of the view that intergenerational relations are very important. In fact, Bengtson (2001, see also Bengtson, Biblarz, & Roberts, 2002) suggests that with the decline of the two-parent nuclear family, intergenerational relations are becoming more important than nuclear family ties to many Americans—and will continue to be important in the twenty-first century. Bengtson argues that the increasing longevity and better

**Families in
Other Cultures**

The Elderly and Their Families in Japan

In North America and Western Europe, people are used to a family system in which most of the elderly live apart from kin. The family system in Japan, until recently at least, could hardly have been more different. In the traditional Japanese household, all children except the eldest son left home when they reached adulthood. Until their deaths, the parents lived with the eldest son and his wife in the household. Japanese culture emphasized the importance of filial piety—obeying and serving one's parents throughout one's life. As recently as 1970, 77 percent of the elderly in Japan lived with their children.

But this system is being tested by the most rapid aging of any population in the world and by Japan's continuing economic development. By world demographic standards, the Japanese birthrate plummeted overnight. As recently as 1947, the average Japanese woman bore 4.5 children; 10 years later, the average was down to 2.0. And since World War II, life expectancy in Japan has risen to the highest level in the world (Ogawa & Retherford, 1997). This sharp fall in births and sharp increase in longevity has quickly given Japan one of the highest proportions of elderly persons of any country. And, as is well known, the Japanese economy has grown by leaps and bounds over the past few decades.

Under these changed circumstances, the proportion of the elderly who live with their children has declined. Between 1972 and 1995, for example, the proportion living in a three-generation family declined

from 56 to 33 percent (Ogawa & Retherford, 1997). Although a majority of Japanese still tell pollsters that they believe it is good, in the abstract, for children to take care of their elderly parents, fewer are counting on it. For example, the proportion of women under the age of 50 who say they plan to depend on their children in old age dropped from 65 percent in 1950 to just 11 percent in 2000 (Retherford, Sakamoto, & Ogawa, 1999; Population Problems Research Council, 2000). Japanese demographers are now predicting that by 2010 a majority of the widowed elderly will be living alone (Hirosima, 1997).

And many three-generation households are now formed because of a specific condition rather than because of a general commitment to filial piety. Japanese sociologists are reporting an emerging pattern of "eventual coresidence," in which the older parents live separately as long as their health allows them to; only after frailty or illness sets in do they coreside with a child (Oda, 1991). Moreover, some urban young adults are finding that coresidence with parents is economically advantageous given the very high cost of housing in metropolitan areas. Grandmothers can also provide child care for the growing (although still modest) number of mothers employed outside the home. So the old family forms are being retained for some new reasons.

In fact, the commitment to filial piety appears to be eroding rapidly. The figure shows the responses, in surveys from 1963 to 2000, of married women under age 50 to

the question "What is your opinion about children caring for their elderly parents?" As can be seen, the percentage responding that it is either "unavoidable" or "not a good custom" increased from 12 percent in 1963 to 37 percent in 2000, whereas over the same period the percentage responding that it is either "a good custom" or "a natural duty" declined from 80 percent to 46 percent. Most of the change occurred in the 1980s. Japanese women have moved toward the view, which predominates in the Western nations, that assistance to the elderly is something to be given for specific needs rather than out of a general sense of obligation.

Moreover, the proportion of Japanese elderly who are being cared for in institutions is not as different from that in the United States as one might expect. As noted earlier in the chapter, about 4 percent of the elderly in the United States reside in nursing homes. In Japan, the figure is about 2 percent. But the average length of a hospital stay for elderly Japanese is much higher than in the United States; these long stays have been labeled "social hospitalization." On any given day, 2.6 percent of elderly Japanese are in a hospital, compared with just 0.8 percent in the United States; some of the long stays in Japan may be a culturally acceptable alternative to nursing home care.[1]

The family lives of the Japanese elderly, then, are a mixture of persistence and change. Many—although no longer a majority—live with their children, sometimes with a younger son or even a daughter.

health of the elderly mean that adult children are fortunate enough to have parents available to them well into midlife. He would note how commonly parents take in daughters and grandchildren after a divorce or care for grandchildren when parents are unable to do so. He contrasts the durability and longevity of parent- child–grandchild bonds with the increasing fragility of marriage bonds.

General support for the cultural ideal of coresidence is still widespread. Nevertheless, the proportion of the Japanese elderly living apart from their children has been growing, and younger parents' confidence that their children eventually will support them has been slipping. To an increasing degree, coresidence is a response to an expensive housing market, a lack of available child care services, or an illness, rather than to the norm that parents ought to live with their children whatever the circumstances. If the housing market improves or child care becomes more widely available, coresidence could decrease further. I think it likely that the family lives of the elderly in Japan will continue to evolve toward greater independence from their children, although older parents will probably remain more dependent on their children than in the West.

Ask Yourself

1. Do any of your elderly relatives live with their children? If so, do they do so by choice or necessity?

2. Compare and contrast relations between parents and children in Japan and the United States. Which are more significant, the similarities or the differences in intergenerational relations?

[1] The figures for Japan are from Martin (1989). I calculated the 0.8 percent figure for the United States from Census Bureau data.

www.mhhe.com/cherlin5

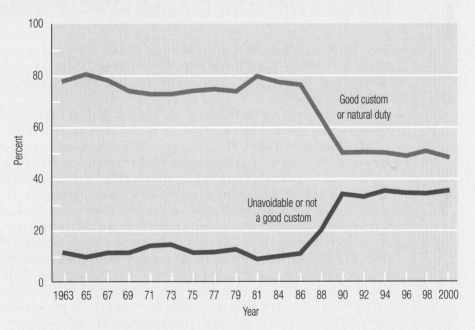

Responses of married women under 50 in Japan to the question, "What is your opinion about children caring for their elderly parents?" Orange line: percent responding either "a good custom" or a "natural duty." Green line: percent responding either "unavoidable" or "not a good custom." (Source: Retherford, Sakamoto, & Ogawa, 1999; Population Problems Research Council, 2000)

There is much to be said for this argument, but it does have limitations. Among the nonpoor, grandparents tend to leave the child rearing to parents, live independently, and seek "intimacy at a distance." Relations between many divorced older men and their adult children are strained, and it's not clear how much mutual support stepparents and stepchildren will provide to each other over the life course.

Intergenerational ties remain important to many Americans.

Some skeptics believe that there has been a loss of family feeling since the time when most elderly were living with their children. They charge that modern grandparents, in their rush to retire in the Sun Belt, have abandoned their bonds to their grandchildren.

Perhaps the best way to balance these views is to think of grandparents as the family national guard (Hagestad, 1985). In the middle classes, at least, the guard is usually on inactive reserve—keeping in contact with children and grandchildren, having pleasant relations, but providing (and receiving) little assistance. When a crisis occurs in an adult child's or a grandchild's life—a divorce, a birth outside of marriage, a sudden illness—the family national guard is called up. The key questions are how often the guard shows up for duty when called and how long they stay active. Because the elderly lead longer, healthier lives than in the past, more are available. Because most feel emotionally close to their children and grandchildren, they are motivated to help. So in most circumstances, grandparents willingly provide substantial assistance. But active duty has its costs, and, like the national guard, most grandparents prefer to return to inactive duty—to resume their independent lives. And not many may show up to help a divorced relative who has wandered away from the kin, only to show up later, hat in hand.

When Furstenberg and I were writing our book, we visited a senior citizens' center in a Jewish neighborhood in Baltimore. There we talked with a group of grandparents who told us that the new development in the neighborhood was the immigration of many families from Russia. With some envy, they described to us the relationships the Russian grandparents had with their grandchildren: "The grandparents live with their children and grandchildren." "They go on vacation together." "They go out to eat together." "They are very involved in the care of their grandchildren." After listening to these remarks, one of us asked whether anyone in the group would trade places with the immigrant grandparents in order to have their type of relationship. The question was met with immediate cries of "No way!" "No" and "I'm satisfied." The questioner pursued the point further: "Why wouldn't you trade places? There are all these strong family ties?" A woman replied, "I don't think I could live with my children," and a chorus of "No" and "No way" followed.

One grandmother said, simply, "It's too late." What she meant was that, given the opportunity for independence, most American grandparents had already seized it and couldn't give it up. To live with their children, they would have to adjust their daily schedules to fit their children's busy lives. It's easy to look at current living arrangements and criticize the elderly for emphasizing autonomy and personal satisfaction in their daily lives. But they are merely engulfed in the same flood of self-fulfillment that has washed over their children and grandchildren. To ask grandparents to lead a retreat to a family system that emphasizes cooperation over companionship, obligations over independence, duty over love, is perhaps unfair. This is the first generation in which most older Americans have had a choice in these matters; should they be criticized for making the same choices as everyone else?

Quick Review

- The elderly and their children may have ambivalent feelings toward each other that are socially structured.
- Caregivers and receivers, particularly women, may feel more ambivalence about their relationships.
- Men who have separated from the mothers of their children may not be able to rely on kin for support in old age. Stepparents may not receive support from stepchildren.
- Some observers argue that social change is making intergenerational relations a more important part of family life.

Looking Back

1. **How has grandparenthood changed over the past century?** Today most adults live long enough to get to know their grandchildren because adult life expectancy has lengthened substantially, particularly for women. And because birthrates are lower, and most adults have finished raising their children by the time they become grandparents, grandparenthood is now a more distinct stage of life. Declining births mean that the average person has fewer links to kin in the same generation; but because of declining mortality the average person has more links to kin in preceding or succeeding generations. Moreover, over the past half-century the incomes of the elderly have risen dramatically, thanks to the expansion of the Social Security rolls, increases in Social Security benefits, and the growth of private pension programs.

2. **How much support do the elderly provide to, and receive from, their kin?** Most of the help that the elderly and their adult children receive is mutual. Except when they are ill, the elderly provide more help than they receive. Among those who need care, most elderly men get it from their wives, while most elderly women must rely on daughters and other relatives. A modest but increasing percentage of grandparents are caring for the grandchildren in their own homes. These grandparents tend to have lower incomes and poorer health, and their caregiving is usually in response to a crisis in their adult children's lives.

3. **Who cares for the frail elderly?** The majority of seriously disabled elderly persons are cared for in their homes by family members, rather than in a hospital or nursing home. The most common family caregiver other than a

spouse is an adult daughter. In the future, fewer adult daughters will be available as caregivers, both because more of them will be employed and because the elderly will have fewer adult children. Caring for an elderly family member can be both rewarding and stressful.

4. **Are the elderly isolated from their kin?** The elderly value both their independence and contact with their kin. Most have frequent contact with at least one child, especially with those who live nearby. There is a greater emphasis on affection and companionship, and a lesser emphasis on economic cooperation, in intergenerational relations now. Some observers suggest that the quality of intergenerational relations has declined, but others

counter that older people and their children have chosen a style of relating to one another—that is, separate residences and fairly frequent contact—that suits them both.

5. **What sources of tension exist in intergenerational relations?** Despite the generally positive feelings the elderly and their children have for each other, ambivalent feelings do exist. Those who are giving or receiving substantial care may find it both rewarding and tension-producing. Women experience ambivalence more than men because they are expected to provide care. In addition, older men who have separated from the mothers of their children may be unable, later in life, to rely on their adult children for support.

Go to the Online Learning Center at www.mhhe.com/cherlin5 to test your knowledge of the chapter concepts and key terms.

Study Questions

1. How have the great declines in adult mortality and fertility altered old age?
2. Should the trend toward the elderly living apart from their children be viewed as a positive or negative development for family relations?
3. How do the lives of elderly women differ from the lives of elderly men?
4. How do the lives of elderly non-Hispanic whites differ from the lives of elderly African Americans and Hispanics?

5. In what ways are women the family caregivers and kin-keepers?
6. Under what kinds of circumstances would intergenerational ambivalence be high in a family?
7. What is the evidence that intergenerational relations, as some suggest, are becoming a more important part of American family life?
8. How do childbearing outside of marriage, divorce, and remarriage affect the likelihood that men will receive the support they need late in life?

Key Terms

active life expectancy   332
activities of daily living
    (ADLs)   347
centerarian   333
cohort replacement
    model   354
elderly population   333
fertility   334

gerontologist   333
intergenerational ambivalence
    355
intergenerational solidarity   350
Medicaid   335
Medicare   335
mortality   332

multigenerational households
    346
old-old   333
oldest-old   333
skipped-generation households
    346
'tweeners   335
young-old   333

Thinking about Families

The Private Family	The Public Family
Should we be surprised that American grandparents want to live near their grandchildren but not with them?	Together, the federal and state governments spend twice as much money on Social Security and Medicare as the federal government spends on the entire defense budget. Is government spending too much money on the elderly?

Families on the Internet   www.mhhe.com/cherlin5

Note: While all the URLs listed were current as of the printing of this book, these sites often change. Please check our Web site (http://www.mhhe.com/cherlin5) for updates.

The Ameristat Web site (www.ameristat.org) offers a number of interesting charts and graphs about the elderly population in the United States. Most of the data can be downloaded in tabular form. Click on "older population" to answer the following questions: What happens to the marriage gap between elderly women and men as they age? What percentage of the elderly population has health insurance coverage? Which states have the largest percentage of older people? How will the aging of the population alter American Society in the future?

The Population Reference Bureau (www.prb.org) has several good reports on aging, including "Global Aging: The Challenge of Success," on the difficulties that aging populations are bringing to nations around the world; "American Grandparents Respon-

sibilities on the Rise"; and "The Future of Social Security." Under "topics," click on "aging."

The U.S. Bureau of the Census (ww.census.gov) maintains many data-oriented publications about the elderly. In 2005 they released a report commissioned by the National Institute of Aging, a unit of the National Institutes of Health, entitled "65+ in the United States: 2005," which provides a comprehensive picture of trends in population growth, longevity, economic well-being, geographical distribution, social circumstances and more. Go to the census Web site and search on aging or find it directly at: http://www.census.gov/prod/1/pop/p23-190/p23-190.html. I have drawn upon information from that report several times in this chapter.

Part Five

Conflict, Disruption, and Reconstitution

Conflict between women and men has a public significance beyond the immediate family context. It spans both the private family, where it affects the quality of emotional support, intimacy, and cooperation, and the public family, where its social consequences are played out on a larger scale. Conflict between adults can also lead to separation, divorce, and remarriage.

• **Chapter 11** considers violence and abuse between spouses and partners and by parents against children. After a brief review of the history of domestic violence, the chapter summarizes current knowledge. The most important theories of domestic violence are presented, followed by an examination of sexual aggression and violence in dating relationships and a discussion of public policies. Marital conflict, these days, often leads to divorce. About one in every two marriages in the United States at current rates would end in divorce.

• **Chapter 12** probes the causes and consequences of this high level of marital dissolution. It examines the process that divorcing couples experience and the consequences for both children and adults. A majority of divorced persons remarry. Yet remarriage, as • **Chapter 13** shows, can bring difficulties for adults and children. The chapter describes the new kinds of family relationships and kinship networks that form after remarriages. Then it discusses why children whose parents are remarried seem to fare no better than children in single-parent families.

Domestic Violence

Looking Forward

1. When did domestic violence become a social issue?

2. What do we know about violence between intimate partners?

3. What is the extent of child abuse?

4. What do we know about sexual aggression by dates or acquaintances?

5. Why does domestic violence occur?

6. What are the public policy debates concerning domestic violence?

In October 2003, a churchgoing New Jersey couple was arrested after a neighbor saw one of their children looking for food at 2:30 A.M. in the neighbor's garbage cans. Although the boy rummaging through the trash was 19-years-old, he stood 4 feet tall and weighed 45 pounds. The parents had adopted him from the New Jersey foster care system. The authorities charged that, along with three other boys they had also adopted, he had been locked out of the kitchen and fed a diet of pancake batter, peanut butter, and breakfast cereal. The boys were so chronically hungry, it was said, that they ate wallboard and insulation. Meanwhile, five other children in the household—biological, foster, and adopted—were well fed. The parents denied the charges. The public uproar about the case grew when it was reported that a caseworker from the state Division of Child and Family Services had visited the home 38 times in the previous two years without noticing that anything was wrong. Nine child welfare service workers were fired as a result of the arrest. The family was receiving about $30,000 in stipends from the state for caring for the adopted and foster children (Peterson, 2003; Polgreen & Worth, 2003).

Cases such as this one—and the death in 1995 of six-year-old Elizabeth Izquierdo, who was beaten to death by her mother after several visits by caseworkers—often lead to demands that child welfare service workers be more aggressive in removing children from potentially abusive parents. Yet removing children from their homes has its own risks, as when children separated from their families drift through the foster care system.

The problem is that the public hears about child abuse or marital violence mainly through sensational cases, such as the New Jersey boys' malnourishment, Elizabeth's death, or O.J. Simpson's trial for the murder of his former wife. A few decades ago, even social scientists ignored **domestic violence,** which will be defined in this chapter as violent acts between family members or between women and men in intimate or dating relationships. Not a single article on the topic appeared in *Journal of Marriage and the Family*, the major scholarly journal in the field, between its founding in 1939 and 1969 (O'Brien, 1971). Now, however, hardly an issue appears without one. In fact, the increase in research has been so sudden and so massive that it requires an explanation. It wasn't spurred by an increase in domestic violence, because there isn't convincing evidence of an increase, as will be noted later. Rather, its rise reflects the increased political power of the feminist movement, which views domestic violence as an important barrier to women's equality, and the increasing cultural emphasis on individualism in marriage and family life. To appreciate what has occurred, it is necessary first to examine the history of domestic violence as a social problem.

domestic violence violent acts between family members or between women and men in intimate or dating relationships

Domestic Violence in Historical Perspective

The recent attention to highly publicized cases of child abuse and wife battering is not the first outpouring of public concern about domestic violence. Rather, the history of domestic violence in the United States shows short periods of public attention separated by longer periods of neglect. The periods of attention have had less to do with the prevalence of violence than with the power of various political and social groups (Pleck, 1987).

EARLY HISTORY

In the New England colonies, the Puritans believed that it was the responsibility of the government to enforce moral behavior, even if that meant intervening in the affairs of the family. And moral behavior excluded violent acts by husbands against their wives. The well-known minister Cotton Mather told his congregants that for "a man to Beat his Wife was as bad as any Sacriledge" and that "any such a Rascal were better buried alive, than show his Head among his Neighbours any more" (Pleck, 1987). Friends, neighbors, and fellow churchgoers watched over a family's conduct in ways we would view today as nosy, if not meddlesome. In 1641, the Massachusetts Bay Colony enacted the first law against wife beating in the Western world, according to historian Elizabeth Pleck; it also prohibited parents from exercising "any unnatural severitie" with their children (Pleck, 1987).

How strictly this law was enforced, however, is unclear because the number of persons actually charged with wife beating was small. The Puritans must have felt the tension between respecting the integrity of the family and intervening to protect women and children from abuse. After the Puritans, government officials in most eras were even more reluctant to intervene. Indeed, the history of the issue of domestic violence is, in large part, a story of conflict between the goals of preserving the family unit and of protecting women and children. When intervention was seen as shoring up the family (as among the Puritans), it received broader support; when it was perceived as undermining men's authority and contributing to divorce, it received less.[1]

A peak of concern occurred in the late 1800s, when the child protection movement arose. In 1874 the first society for the prevention of cruelty to children was founded; 40 years later there were 494 of them. Pleck argues that the growth of these societies, usually started by leaders of the local social elite, reflected a desire to control the behavior of the unruly, growing immigrant and working-class populations. In addition, I think, the growth came at a time when attitudes toward children were evolving from seeing them as economic assets to seeing them as emotionally rewarding beings to be nurtured (Zelizer, 1985). Still, leaders of the movement were careful to reassure parents that their authority to discipline their children, even by occasional physical punishment, was not in question. The founder of the New York Society for the Prevention of Cruelty to Children assured nervous supporters that he favored "a good wholesome flogging for disobedient children," although he wished to protect children from "undue parental severity" (Pleck, 1987). And the few organizations that sought to

---

[1] This paragraph, and the next several, draw heavily from Pleck (1987).

Ichabod Crane flogs a disobedient student in a late-nineteenth-century edition of *The Legend of Sleepy Hollow*. Corporal punishment in schools was acceptable until the twentieth century.

" *Spare the rod and spoil the child.* —P. 121.

help battered wives had to fight suspicion that they were encouraging the breakup of the family.

THE TWENTIETH CENTURY

The Political Model of Domestic Violence

During the twentieth century, two ways of thinking about domestic violence have emerged. The first is what might be called the *political model* of domestic violence—political not in the sense of Democrats and Republicans but rather in the sense of the relations of power and authority between men and women. Historian Linda Gordon has argued that domestic violence has been a politically constructed problem in two senses:

> *First, the very definition of what constitutes unacceptable domestic violence, and appropriate responses to it, developed and then varied according to political moods and the force of certain political movements. Second, violence among family members ... usually arises out of power struggles in which individuals are contesting real resources and benefits. These contests arise not only from personal aspirations but also from changing social norms and conditions. (Gordon, 1988)*

The struggles are usually about men's power to control the behavior of women. Resorting to force is a way for a husband to compel his wife to behave as the husband wishes. Traditionally, social structure has supported men's control over women through law and social custom. Laws that allowed husbands to use

Little attention was paid to domestic violence until the feminist movement succeeded in making it a political issue.

physical force against their wives are an example: The term "rule of thumb," for instance, comes from a rule in old English law that a husband was allowed to hit his wife with a stick no thicker than his thumb (Gelles & Cornell, 1990). The political model implies that domestic violence is deeply rooted in laws and customs that reinforce male dominance and is unlikely to be ended without political action by women's groups and their allies.

The Medical Model of Domestic Violence   The second way of thinking is the *medical model*, under which domestic violence is seen as an illness and a source of injuries. In contrast to the political model, the main concern is not with relations of power but rather with illness and well-being. Health and social welfare professionals who have campaigned against child abuse, for example, have focused attention on the physical and mental harm that children suffer from physical and sexual violence. Some have argued that both the victims and the perpetrators of violence suffer from various "syndromes," illnesslike complexes of symptoms, injuries, and attitudes, that need to be treated. The professionals point to links between being violent and such personal problems as a history of abuse as a child, alcoholism, or mental illness. The medical model therefore conceives of the problem as though it can be solved by the intervention of health and social welfare professionals, much as they might attack schizophrenia or tuberculosis.

The first two decades of the twentieth century were a time when domestic relations courts, which treated family disputes more as social welfare cases than as criminal cases, were established throughout the states. But the issue of domestic violence was relatively quiescent until 1962, when pediatrician C. Henry Kempe and his colleagues, troubled by X-ray pictures of broken bones in children and reports of maltreatment, published an article entitled "The Battered Child Syndrome" (Kempe, Silverman, Steele, Droegemuller, & Silver, 1962). Kempe and his colleagues brought the medical model of domestic violence to the public's attention. In their view, child abuse was centered on a "syndrome" of repeated violence and inadequate parenting. This perspective created sympathetic concern not only for the blameless victims but also for the abusers, who seemed to be fighting a mental illness that needed treatment. In these ways the "syndrome" attracted broad public interest; within five years, every state had enacted laws that required medical personnel to report suspected cases of child abuse.

Still, there was little attention paid to wife beating until the mid-1970s, when feminist groups succeeded in making violence against women into a political problem. A decade earlier, the feminist movement had undergone a major revival, boosted by the parallel growth of the civil rights movement. Some feminist groups focused on combating rape. Part of their strategy was the formation of services for rape victims, such as hot lines, crisis centers, and legal support. The issue of rape led organizers to the issue of sexual and physical violence directed toward married women. The movement's fundamental goal was not to treat the injuries of the victims or ease the personal problems of the perpetrators—valuable as those steps might be—but rather to remove the social supports for male violence, such as a reluctance to prosecute alleged offenders. Consequently, activists worked for changes in the law, funds for crisis centers and shelters for battered women, and the rejection of social norms that tolerated violence directed at women. With feminist influence at a high point in the 1970s, political pressure for action grew. By the end of the 1970s, nearly every state had enacted laws to protect women from violence through a mixture of support services, requirements that physicians report suspected cases, and tougher criminal procedures.

Quick Review

- The New England colonies passed the first laws against wife beating in the Western world.
- The issue of domestic violence historically has reflected a conflict between the goals of preserving the family unit and protecting women and children.
- A political model of domestic violence, reflecting relations of power and authority, arose in the twentieth century.
- A medical model of domestic violence, which views it as an illness and a source of injury, also developed in the twentieth century.

■ Intimate Partner Violence ■

The beatings that many women in shelters have endured from husbands and live-in boyfriends would fit anyone's definition of family violence. But how far in the other direction should the concept of domestic violence go? Is a slap in the face domestic violence, or should the term be reserved for more serious acts of aggression? There is disagreement among the public and academic researchers about exactly what constitutes domestic violence. It's not even clear how to define the term "domestic." Most early studies of adult domestic violence focused on married and cohabiting couples, but many recent studies have focused on the broader concept of "intimate partners," or boyfriends and girlfriends.

TWO KINDS OF VIOLENCE?

Some researchers recommend that we distinguish between two types of violent behavior among intimate partners. This view emerged after sociologists began to study the extent of violent acts among intimate partners in random-sample surveys of the general population. They asked people whether, and how often, in the previous year they had engaged in behaviors against their spouses or cohabiting partners that ranged from the less serious (e.g., grabbing, pushing, or slapping) to the more serious (e.g., hitting with a fist) to the very serious (e.g., threatening or using a knife or gun) (Straus, 1979; Straus et al., 1996). Surprisingly, men and women in 1975 and 1985 national surveys were about equally likely to report engaging in these acts in the previous year, although most acts were of the less serious kind (Straus & Gelles, 1986). This pattern has been confirmed in more recent surveys (Fergusson, Horwood, & Ridder, 2005a). In other words, surveys suggest that both women and men at times initiate violence against their intimate partners. In contrast to the picture of battered women and violent men that the shelter and social services studies show, surveys paint pictures of violent couples in which both partners engage in aggression.

To reconcile this seeming contradiction, some researchers argue that there are two distinct types of intimate partner violence. Michael Johnson and his colleagues call the first kind **situational couple violence** (Johnson, 1995; Johnson & Ferraro, 2000; Leone, Johnson, Cohan, & Lloyd, 2004). It is the more common kind of conflict; and it usually involves the less serious kinds of aggression. It typically occurs, the authors say, when a specific dispute leads one partner to get angry and to lash out at the other; and it rarely escalates into serious violence or injury. That is, it arises from a particular situation rather than from a larger, long-term pattern of violence. Moreover, men and women are about equally likely to initiate it. Most of the violent acts reported in surveys are of this type.

> **situational couple violence** violence that arises from a specific situation in which one or both partners act aggressively in anger

Johnson claims that a second, more serious kind of violence exists, which he labels **intimate terrorism** (Johnson, 1995). I think the use of the word "terrorism," with its connotation of suicide bombers and September 11, is unfortunate. Two psychologists (Emery & Laumann-Billings, 1998) suggest instead that we distinguish between "maltreatment" (less serious) and "family violence" (more serious); but the label "intimate terrorism" seems to be sticking in the literature. This is the type of violence, Johnson argues, that researchers who study shelters or the legal system see. While it affects a much smaller share of the national population than does situational couple violence, its consequences are more dire. It involves a pattern of violence such as repeatedly beating one's partner; it is therefore more likely to cause injuries; and unlike situational violence, it is almost entirely perpetrated by men. Johnson argues that the heart of the distinction between these two types is that the men who engage in intimate terrorism are trying to control women's behavior: whom they see, whom they talk to, when they leave the house, where they go, and so forth. These men may also seek to dominate their wives or girlfriends by keeping them economically dependent and by instilling fear of the consequences of disobeying them. The key difference is motivation: control rather than mere anger. Table 11.1 compares these two hypothetical kinds of domestic violence.

> **intimate terrorism** a pattern in which a man seeks to control the behavior of his partner through repeated, serious, violent acts

Table 11.1 Characteristics of Situational Couple Violence and Intimate Terrorism		
	SITUATIONAL COUPLE VIOLENCE	**INTIMATE TERRORISM**
Prevalence	Common	Less common
Type of aggression	Less serious (e.g., slapping)	More serious (e.g., beating up)
Gender of perpetrators	Both men and women	Almost entirely men
Motivation	Anger	Control

Without doubt, far more seriously injured and abused women than men show up at shelters or hospital emergency rooms or testify at the trials of abusive partners who have been arrested. Even among studies of the general population, women are more likely to be reported engaging in the less serious acts such as slapping or kicking, whereas men are more likely to be reported engaging in serious acts such as beating up or choking; and women are more likely to report being injured than are men (Archer, 2000; Archer, 2002). So while a majority of violent incidents involving couples may involve minor acts of aggression by both spouses, it seems clear that a minority of incidents do involve serious aggressions by men which cause injuries in women.

What's still controversial is whether the serious incidents with male perpetrators and female victims are a distinct kind of violence or are just one end of a continuum running from mild to extreme domestic violence. We do not know yet why some couples progress from situational violence to intimate terrorism (Holtzworth-Monroe, 2005). And we do not know how many of the serious incidents involve men who are engaged in a pattern of controlling women through violence and how many are merely expressing anger violently. I do not mean for these conclusions to minimize the physical and psychological harm men can inflict on women even if they are not trying to control them. Rather, I am trying to understand whether we are seeing two distinct phenomena (Johnson, 2005) or rather a situation in which men are overrepresented among people with tendencies toward severe violence toward partners (Fergusson, Horwood, & Ridder, 2005b). Perhaps it is best to see Johnson's two kinds of violence as ideal types [➡ p. 119] while in reality most violent couples are arrayed somewhere on a line stretching from one kind to the other.

The research and debate about distinguishing types of intimate partner aggression can be seen as an extension into the twenty-first century of the tensions between the political and medical models of domestic violence. The idea of situational couple violence fits the medical model; however, in this case the doctor is not a pediatrician like C. Henry Kempe but rather a clinical psychologist or a psychiatrist. The problem is framed as a dysfunctional couple who cannot resolve conflicts peacefully. This framing suggests remedies such as family psychotherapy or marital counseling. In contrast, the idea of intimate terrorism fits the political model. Here the problem is framed as a controlling male who dominates his wife or girlfriend in part by inflicting serious and even life-threatening violence. The remedy is to remove the violent man from the household and prevent him from having contact with the woman. This remedy suggests not psychotherapy but rather legal action: an arrest, a restraining order, or incarceration. Researchers and advocates for battered women were incensed by the findings from sociological surveys that women seemed to engage in partner violence as often as men because they saw no battered men at their shelters, only women who had been the victims of severe violence at the hands of controlling men. Johnson (1995) proposed his distinction in order to show that both models of intimate partner violence had their place. In a sense, he and his colleagues are arguing that the medical model may be more appropriate for the majority of incidents, but that the political model may still be valid for the minority of incidents that cause serious injury and trauma.

THE PREVALENCE OF INTIMATE PARTNER VIOLENCE

In this mixture of concern and debate, one important question often gets lost: How much intimate partner violence is there? We know little about how much violence there was in the past. The official records of court proceedings can tell us only about the rare instances when abuse came to the attention of the legal system. Consequently, it's impossible to know whether domestic violence has increased, decreased, fluctuated, or stayed the same over the past few 100 years—or even over the past 50 years. Most likely, what has changed the most over time is not the prevalence of intimate partner violence but the amount of attention we have paid to it. (See *How Do Sociologists Know What They Know?*: Advocates and Estimates: How Large [or Small] Are Social Problems?, on p. 377.)

Lifetime Prevalence   The best estimate of how many people ever experience intimate partner violence in their lifetimes comes from the National Violence Against Women Survey, a government study of 8,000 women and 8,000 men conducted between November 1995 and May 1996. Individuals were asked whether they had ever experienced violent acts or stalking by "intimate partners," defined as current or former spouses, cohabiting partners, and boyfriends or girlfriends. As in most surveys of domestic violence, the questions referred to acts that ranged from less serious to very serious. Figure 11.1 displays women's responses. The top bar shows that 22 percent of the women reported having experienced at least one type of act. The other bars show that the most common types were the less serious ones. (Individuals could

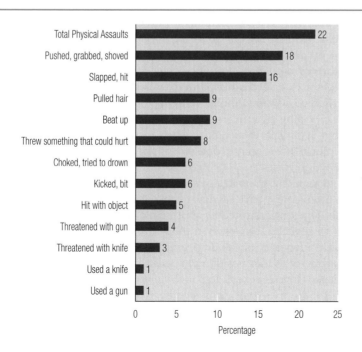

FIGURE 11.1
Percentage of women who reported having been physically assaulted by an intimate partner, by type of assault. (*Source:* U.S. National Institute of Justice, 1998)

answer positively to more than one type.) Smaller but still disturbing numbers of women reported more serious assaults. For example, 9 percent of female respondents had been beaten up, and 4 percent had been threatened with a gun.

Overall, women reported substantially higher rates of intimate partner violence over their lifetimes than men. Only about 8 percent of men reported experiencing a violent act of any kind by an intimate partner (compared to 22 percent for women). The gender difference even carried over into same-sex couples. Men who had lived with male partners were more likely to have experienced violence than men who had lived only with women, while women who had lived with female partners were less likely to have experienced violence than were women who had lived only with men (U.S. National Institute of Justice, 2000). All in all, the survey suggested that women are much more likely than men to experience violent acts by intimate partners.

Responses to the National Crime Victimization Survey of 1999 similarly suggest that women are victimized by criminal intimate violence far more often than men (U.S. Bureau of Justice Statistics, 2000a). The survey asked a national sample of adults whether they had been the victims of rape, robbery, or assault and, further, whether the perpetrator had been an intimate partner (spouse, ex-spouse, boyfriend, girlfriend). Women reported that 20 percent of the rapes, robberies, and assaults they had experienced were committed by an intimate partner, whereas among men, intimates had committed just 3 percent. Moreover, women who had been victimized by intimates were more likely to have been injured than were men who were victimized. For instance, 10 percent of women who had been victimized by intimate partners reported receiving medical or hospital care, compared with 5 percent of men (U.S. Bureau of Justice Statistics, 2000b). The statistics paint a picture in which women face a higher risk of being injured by someone they know well than men. Nevertheless, between 1993 and 2001, the rate of intimate partner violence against women dropped by 49 percent and the rate against men dropped by 42 percent (U.S. Bureau of Justice Statistics, 2003).

Intimate Partner Rape   Almost 8 percent of women in the National Violence Against Women Survey reported being raped or experiencing an attempted rape by an intimate partner (U.S. National Institute of Justice, 2006). The typical partner rape does not take place in a happy home, in which an otherwise nonviolent man forces his partner to have sex. Rather, it appears to take place in a troubled, violent home. Thirty-six percent of the women who reported being raped by an intimate in the 1995–1996 National Violence Against Women Survey also reported being injured in the most recent rape. Although most of the injuries were minor, one out of six injured women reported lacerations or knife wounds.

Attention to rape by intimates—especially by husbands—is fairly new. Until recently, laws against rape have specifically excluded sexual relations between husband and wife. The long-accepted legal principle was that by marrying, wives give their consent to sexual intercourse, so their husbands may demand it, by force if necessary. Some advocates of family privacy and the traditional authority of the husband still agree with that position. But as attitudes toward physical violence in marriage changed, forced sexual acts among married couples increasingly came into question. By the mid-1990s, almost every state had fully or partially repealed the exemption of spouses from rape statutes (Bennice & Resick, 2003).

Advocates and Estimates: How Large (or Small) Are Social Problems?

In February of 1997, the U.S. Department of Justice released studies showing that (1) the number of rapes reported to police had dropped in 1995 to the lowest rate per person in a decade; and (2) the number of people who said they were raped or sexually assaulted in the annual National Crime Victimization Survey had dropped by 44 percent from 1993 to 1995 (Butterfield, 1997). This was good news—except to some advocates for victims of rape and sexual abuse. Professor Mary Koss told the *New York Times* that reports showing a decrease in rape "upset me because it lessens the sympathy for rape victims" and makes them even less likely to come forward (Butterfield, 1997, p. A1). She disputed the new figures: "The Justice Department looks at the incidence of rape year by year, but many mental health experts believe it is common sense to look at prevalence, over a lifetime," as if this criticism somehow meant that a sharp decrease in the annual rate was meaningless.

Professor Koss was acting no differently than many advocates for (and against) social causes when they describe the scope of the problem they care about. As a general rule, advocates for social causes tend to use the broadest definition of the problem, whereas opponents tend to use the narrowest. Consider homelessness. [➡ p. 122] In the 1980s, advocates for the homeless repeated an estimate by activist Mitch Snyder that two to three million people were homeless. When government officials or academic researchers produced far lower estimates, they were sharply criticized. Then Snyder was asked about the basis of his

estimate in a television interview, and he replied:

> Everybody demanded it. Everybody said we want a number . . . . We got on the phone, we made a lot of calls, we talked to a lot of people, and we said, "Okay, here are some numbers." They have no meaning, no value (Jencks, 1994, p. 2).

Nor is the tendency to define the magnitude of a problem in a way that's consistent with one's view of the problem limited to liberals and feminists. In 1995, three conservatives published an analysis of welfare benefits in every state. Welfare benefits, they argued, were so generous that they destroyed the incentive to work; therefore, welfare benefits should be sharply limited (Tanner, Moore, & Hartman, 1995). The benefit levels they reported were startlingly high. For example, in Maryland, the "full package" of welfare benefits was equivalent to $22,000 per year—so high that a worker would have to earn $11.00 per hour to match them. But the "full package" included $5,864 of housing assistance, even though only one-fourth of welfare recipients in Maryland received such assistance; $1,028 for the value of the food given to pregnant and nursing mothers and their young children under another program that most recipients don't receive; and other such benefits. When the package was restricted to Aid to Families with Dependent Children, food stamps, and Medicaid, it was reduced to $12,124.

This is not to say that any of the advocates described here are distorting the data or lying. There is more than one way of defining most

social problems. It is probably true, for example, that rape and sexual assaults are still underreported in government surveys, as advocates would claim. So the problem is larger than official statistics show. It is difficult to find all of the homeless, who hide themselves in the abandoned buildings and alleyways of low-income neighborhoods. And housing assistance is worth money to those welfare recipients fortunate enough to receive it. So just focusing on cash benefits to the poor is too restrictive.

My point is only that, as a consumer of social statistics, you should always ask yourself what the biases are of the people who are presenting you with the numbers. If they have a strong stake in convincing you that the problem is large in scope, they will probably choose an expansive definition of it. If they want to convince you the problem is not serious, they'll usually choose a much narrower definition. Evaluate not only their numbers but also their social and political arguments with this tendency in mind.

Ask Yourself

1. In doing student research or observing local politics, have you noticed dramatic differences in the statistics people quote to support their positions? If so, give an example. Did you understand the reason for the discrepancy?

2. What other reasons besides bias might help to explain conflicting statistics on social problems?

www.mhhe.com/cherlin5

WHICH PARTNERSHIPS ARE AT RISK?

Some intimate partnerships are more likely to lead to violence than others. Whether the couple is married seems to matter, as does their social class and race.

Marital Status   A few older studies suggested that married couples had lower rates of domestic violence than cohabiting couples (Stets & Straus, 1989). The 1995–1996 survey confirmed that difference: Married women had a 57 percent lower risk of experiencing violence than women who were cohabiting (U.S. National Institute of Justice, 2000). There are several possible explanations for the lower risk for married women and little evidence on which explanations are important (Brownridge and Halli, 2002). The lower risk for married women could be a selection effect [➡ p. 211]: Women may refuse to marry men who seem violent, or their partners may be men whose past marriages have failed due to violence (Repetti, 2001; Kenney & McLanahan, 2006). It is also possible that cohabiting women are more likely to have been abused as children, which is associated with greater subsequent abuse as an adult. The difference in risk could also reflect aspects of cohabitation that differ from marriage: The lesser commitment in cohabiting unions could lead to one partner having a sexual relationship with someone else, initiating a jealous reaction from the other partner; or the greater differences in age and education in cohabiting unions, compared to marriages, could lead to more disagreement and conflict (Wilson & Daly, 2001).

Social Class and Race   Although domestic violence affects all social classes, several studies report substantially higher rates of domestic violence among low-income than among middle-income couples (U.S. Bureau of Justice Statistics, 1995; Sorenson, Upchurch, & Shen, 1996). Part of this difference may reflect a greater reluctance of middle-income individuals to admit to violence or a greater vigilance toward poor families by social welfare agencies. Still it appears that there is at least a modest association between lower social class and violence against spouses and partners. Sorenson, Upchurch, and Shen (1996) analyzed the responses of married couples in the 1987–1988 National Survey of Families and Households to questions about physical violence in the past year. Controlling statistically for many standard socioeconomic and demographic characteristics, they found that persons with household incomes under $25,000 were more likely to report incidents than were persons with incomes of $25,000 to $40,000. The same studies also suggest that African Americans have somewhat higher rates of domestic violence than do white families (U.S. Bureau of Justice Statistics, 1995; Sorenson, Upchurch, & Shen, 1996).

These findings do not necessarily mean that low-income or African American couples are inherently more violent; rather, they may be responding to factors such as frustration over lack of resources, social isolation, or racism (Hampton, Jenkins, & Vandergriff-Avery 1993; Ptacek, 1999). In fact, there are theoretical reasons to expect these associations: Several decades ago, William Goode suggested that men with more income and education have additional resources besides force that they can use to control the behavior of their wives (Goode, 1971). This relationship between social class and violence against wives also holds in developing countries: A Bangkok, Thailand, survey found that men with more income, education, and prestigious occupations were less likely to have hit, slapped, or kicked their wives (Hoffman, Demo, & Edwards, 1994). In addition, the frustrations of poverty and

Women report substantially higher rates of intimate partner violence than do men.

unemployment create stress that may lead some men to beat their wives. Studies show that unemployed men have rates of assault on their wives that are nearly double the rates for men who are employed (Gelles & Cornell, 1990; Ptacek, 1999; U.S. National Institute of Justice, 2004).

Quick Review

- Most incidents of intimate partner violence involve minor acts of aggression that usually do not lead to injuries and that are initiated by both men and women.
- A minority of incidents involve serious acts of aggression that more often lead to injuries and are initiated by men in order to control their partners.
- Married couples have lower rates of violence than cohabiting couples.
- Violence against spouses and romantic partners occurs in all social classes but is more common in lower-income families.

CHILD ABUSE

Hitting children is the most tolerated form of family violence. Indeed, nearly all parents spank or slap their children at some point (Straus & Stewart, 1999). Although it is difficult to make historical comparisons, the use of physical force against children may have been more prevalent in colonial times than ever since. The Puritans believed children were born tainted with sin, and expressed their diabolical nature through stubbornness, willfulness, and disobedience. Consequently, good parents had a moral duty to defeat such expressions of sin. When two- and three-year-olds first began to act contrary, the task of the father was to "break the child's will" and instill obedience through stern discipline. Even a

Although there is widespread support for parents' right to spank or slap children, most people probably view beating or punching as child abuse.

century ago, physical force was probably more common than it is now. No one to-day could imagine the head of a children's welfare organization announcing his support for flogging.

Even if we grant parents the right to spank or slap, at some point physical force shades into physical abuse. As with violence between spouses and partners, there is no single definition of exactly what constitutes **child abuse.** The definition that earns the greatest consensus among child welfare professionals is serious physical harm (trauma, sexual abuse with injury, or willful malnutrition) with intent to injure—although it is difficult to determine whether there has been intent to injure (Starr, 1988). There is less consensus about other possible forms of abuse, many of which adults would find disturbing, such as sexual abuse without injury or various forms of neglect (e.g., leaving young children home by themselves all day). The 1985 national survey of married or cohabiting adults with children found that 2 percent had kicked, bitten, punched, or beaten up their children during the previous year. (This percentage excludes parents who had hit their children with an object such as a stick or a belt.) I think that most people would view repeated kicking, punching, and beating as child abuse (Straus & Gelles, 1986).

Prevalence   Further information comes from several national surveys of child welfare professionals. In 1980, 1986, and 1993, the National Incidence Study of Child Abuse and Neglect (NIS) interviewed a broad range of professionals who serve children; they were asked whether they had seen children who appeared to

child abuse serious physical harm (trauma, sexual abuse with injury, or willful malnutrition) of a child by an adult, with intent to injure

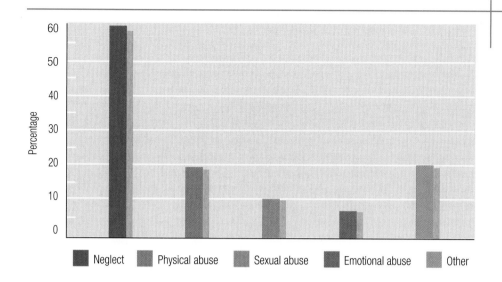

FIGURE 11.2
Substantiated cases of child abuse and neglect, 2001. (Percentages add to more than 100 because some children experienced more than one type of abuse or neglect.) (*Source:* U.S. Department of Health and Human Services, 2003)

be abused or neglected (Westat, Inc., 1981; Sedlak, 1991; Sedlak & Broadhurst, 1996). In addition, the government collects annual reports of cases of child abuse seen by state child protective agencies. Although all of these reports miss children who were not seen by professionals or reported to state agencies, they still provide some of the best recent information. Figure 11.2 shows the percentage of substantiated cases (i.e., verified as accurate by state or local agencies) in 2001 by type of abuse or neglect, based on the government statistics. The percentages represented by the bars add to more than 100 percent because some children experienced more than one type of abuse or neglect.

More than half the reports were of parental neglect rather than abuse. The NIS surveys of professionals found that more than half of the neglect cases referred to educational neglect, which typically means that the children weren't attending school regularly and that their parents were not making much effort to have them attend. The remainder of the cases of neglect referred to physical neglect, which usually means that children were left unattended or poorly supervised by their parents. Figure 11.2 also shows that less than one-third of all cases referred to physical or sexual abuse, the kinds of child-related domestic violence that are of greatest public concern.

The surveys also suggest that child abuse was not equally likely in all families. Rather, it was more likely to occur in low-income families, in single-parent families, and in families in which the husband did not have a full-time job (Sedlak & Broadhurst, 1996; Steinmetz, 1987). The 1993 NIS found that, compared with children in families with incomes of $30,000 or more per year, children in families with incomes below $15,000 were 22 times as likely to experience some form of maltreatment (Sedlack & Broadhurst, 1996). To be sure, some of this social class difference could merely reflect a greater tendency of doctors, nurses, social workers, and neighbors to report poor families for suspicion of neglect or abuse (Hampton & Newberger, 1985). Even so, a review article concludes, "Child abuse *is* class related" (Starr, 1988).

As was the case with spouse abuse, there is good theoretical reason to think that the hardships of poverty might lead distressed parents to have less patience with their children or at least to be more neglectful. In fact, neglect appears to be more closely associated with poverty than does abuse: Low-income families were nine times more likely to have been involved in educational or physical neglect than other families, according to the professionals' reports, compared with three to five times more likely to have been involved in physical or sexual abuse (Besharov & Laumann, 2001). It is poor families that are more often forced to leave a child unattended while adults work or who have little faith in the present system of education and therefore don't make sure their children attend school.

Sexual Abuse and Its Consequences

The state child protection officials' reports indicate a low prevalence of child sexual abuse, but social surveys find a higher rate. In the 1992 survey of sexual activity, the adult subjects were asked, "Before you [reached puberty] did anyone touch you sexually?" (Laumann et al., 1994). Seventeen percent of the women and 12 percent of the men said yes. Among the women, nearly all the touching had been done by men (63 percent) or adolescent boys (28 percent) rather than by women. Men, however, were most likely to report touching by adolescent girls (45 percent), followed by men (23 percent) and adolescent boys (15 percent). Nearly all the incidents for both sexes had involved touching genitals, with a minority reporting vaginal, oral, or anal sex.

The interviewers also asked who did the touching (Laumann et al., 1994). Among women, the most common responses were an older relative (29 percent) or a family friend (29 percent); even more men named a family friend (40 percent). As for cases of sexual abuse that would fit the usual legal definition of **incest**—sexual relations between a child and her or his parent, brother, or sister—16 percent of women who had been touched named a father or brother. Thus, our best estimate is that, overall, about 3 percent of adult American women (that is, 16 percent of the 17 percent who reported touching by anyone) had experienced incest as children. As for abuse at preschools or schools, only 3 percent of the women who were touched and 4 percent of the men reported that a teacher had done the touching. Despite attention in the media to alleged incidents of sexual abuse of children in day care centers, less than 1 percent of all substantiated cases of child abuse in 1992 occurred in day care or foster care settings (McCurdy & Daro, 1994).

A large research literature suggests that having been sexually abused as a child can have profound long-term consequences for an adult's sexual behavior and intimate relationships (Loeb et al., 2002). The seriousness of the consequences is associated with factors such as the number of incidents, the severity and duration of the incidents, and the age of the child during the incidents. Traumatic sexual experiences can produce inappropriate sexual behavior and feelings of betrayal, lack of trust, and powerlessness (Kendall-Tackett, Williams, & Finkelhor, 1993). They can produce later-life consequences such as poor self-image, depression, and lack of a clear sense of boundaries between oneself and others (Briere & Elliott 1994). In adolescence and adulthood, these conditions can lead to early onset of sexual activity, riskier sexual activity, and multiple partners (Fergusson, Horwood, & Lynskey 1997; Thompson, Potter, Sanderson, & Maibach, 1997). As adults, women who were sexually abused as children may have more frequent sexual encounters and relationships from which they derive less pleasure than other women. The 1992 national survey of sexual activity found that women who said they had been touched sexually as children by older persons were, as adults, more likely to experience forced sex, to have multiple sex partners, to engage in riskier sexual behavior, and to experience difficulties such as greater anxiety about sex and less pleasurable sex (Laumann et al., 1994). One-fourth of about 2,000 low-income women in Boston, Chicago, and San Antonio reported that they had been sexually abused as children; and these women were more likely to have had a series of

incest sexual relations with one's child, brother, or sister

short-term intimate relationships, many of them violent, in adulthood (Cherlin, Burton, Hurt, & Purvin, 2004).

Physical Abuse and Its Consequences   Physical abuse can lead to some of the same consequences as sexual abuse, such as lower self-esteem, lack of trust, and depression. In addition, physical abuse can lead to brain injuries and growth retardation (English, 1998). Young children are at the greatest risk of dying from physical abuse: Of the roughly 1,100 fatalities in 1999 from child abuse, 86 percent involved children under six and almost half involved children under one (Chalk, Gibbons, & Scarupa, 2002). Physical abuse is also associated with behavior problems such as aggression and increased risk of arrest for violence (English, 1998; English, Widom, & Brandford, 2001). Some children, however, do not show lasting consequences of physical abuse; these children tend to have been abused fewer times and to have had a supportive adult available to them.

Rising Abuse or Rising Reports?   In 2001, according to the state child protection officials, three million reports of suspected cases of child abuse and neglect were made to state or local government officials (U.S. Department of Health and Human Services, 2003). This compares with slightly over one million reports in 1980 and about 150,000 reports in 1963 (Besharov & Laumann, 2001). No one, however, believes that there is 18 times as much child abuse and neglect now as in 1963. In fact, it's not clear whether there has been any increase. The state laws passed after the Kempe article was published clearly increased the number of cases of suspected abuse that doctors and nurses reported to government authorities. In the 1980s, the expansion of reporting requirements to include other professionals such as teachers, as well as a general rise in public consciousness about child abuse, resulted in further increases in the number of reported cases. People seem to be increasingly likely to report a family to the authorities if they suspect maltreatment. Of the three million cases that were reported in 2001, enough evidence existed to substantiate or indicate

Physical or sexual abuse of children can lead to emotional problems such as depression.

abuse in about 900,000 cases (U.S. Department of Health and Human Services, 2003). (States now investigate each reported case to see whether there is evidence of maltreatment.) Moreover, in the mid-to-late 1990s the number of substantiated cases of child abuse actually declined by 30 percent for physical abuse and 40 percent for sexual abuse. A thorough review of the decline in sexual abuse cases concluded that it likely reflects a true decline rather than just administrative or reporting changes (U.S. Office of Juvenile Justice and Delinquency Prevention, 2004).

Poverty or Abuse?   Not surprisingly, studies show that children who are physically or sexually abused often experience greater emotional problems, including depression, aggression, low self-esteem, troubled relationships with peers, and many others. Not all abused children, of course, show all—or even any—of these problems. Furthermore, it is unclear what proportion of the problems these children display are the result of their abuse, as opposed to other difficulties (Emery, 1989). Many abused children, for example, grow up in families that are troubled by poverty and unemployment. Consequently, some of the problems that abused children show would probably have occurred even if they hadn't been abused. In fact, Douglas Besharov, the first director of the National Center on Child Abuse and Neglect, argues that child protective workers sometimes overreact to families in which the real problem is poverty, not maltreatment. When they remove a child from his or her parents in cases of neglect without physical or sexual abuse, Besharov maintains, workers often make his or her problems worse. Such children are usually sent into the foster-care system, which has its own problems and is not a clear improvement over living at home. (See *Families and Public Policy:* The Swinging Pendulum of Foster Care Policy, on pp. 386–387.) Besharov and Lisa Laumann advocate, instead, that more social services be focused on assisting the parents of these children (Besharov & Laumann, 2001).

Is there a "cycle of abuse," in which adults who were abused as children are more likely to abuse their own children? One review of the literature estimated that about 30 percent of persons who were abused as children become abusers when they reach adulthood, compared with about 5 percent among persons who were not abused. Those who were abused as children but managed to avoid repeating the behavior were more openly angry about the abuse, were more likely to have been abused by just one parent, and were more likely to have had a supportive relationship with the nonabusing parent (Kaufman & Zigler, 1987). If this estimate is accurate, two conclusions can be drawn: (1) Adults who were abused as children are indeed more likely to become abusers; but (2) most adults who were abused as children do not become abusers. The effect of abuse on children is to raise the risk of undesirable consequences, including becoming an abuser, yet many children do not experience these consequences.

ELDER ABUSE

elder abuse physical abuse or neglect of an elderly person by a caregiver

Another kind of domestic violence that has drawn public attention is **elder abuse,** which we might define as physical abuse or neglect of an elderly person by a caregiver. Yet relatively few elderly are abused in this sense: A National Academy of Sciences report estimates that perhaps one to two million elderly Americans have been "injured, exploited, or otherwise mistreated" by a caregiver (Bonnie & Wallace, 2002). That would be 3 to 6 percent of all elderly persons;

Much of the abuse of the elderly is neglect or financial exploitation, such as these victims of a scam experienced.

and if we restricted the definition to just physical abuse the percentages would be even lower. In the only large, random-sample American survey on the topic—a study of about 2,000 elderly persons in the Boston area—2 percent reported that they had been the victims of physical abuse at least once and a total of 3 percent reported having had any type of abuse or neglect (Pillemer & Finkelhor, 1988). Four percent of a random sample of Canadian elderly reported abuse or neglect (Podnieks, 1992). When elder abuse first became a public issue, commentators focused on abuse of the elderly by their adult children, but more than half of the abusers in the Boston area survey had been the elderly person's spouse. Still, maltreatment of even a few percent of the elderly is troubling. Researchers think that elderly persons have a higher risk of maltreatment if they and their caregivers are isolated from family and friends, if the caregiver has mental health problems, and if the caregiver is financially dependent on the abused (Lachs & Pillemer, 2004).

Quick Review

- Definitions of child abuse range from a narrow focus on serious physical harm to an inclusion of sexual abuse without injury and various forms of neglect.
- More than half of official reports of child abuse are for neglect.
- Like adult domestic violence, child abuse occurs in all social classes but is more common in lower-income families.
- Childhood sexual abuse can have long-term negative consequences for sexual behavior and intimate relationships in adulthood.

Families and Public Policy

The Swinging Pendulum of Foster Care Policy

Foster care—the removal of children from their parental home and their placement in another home—is a program with few admirers and many critics. Like abortion policy, foster care policy involves a difficult choice between two worthy goals, in this case protecting the integrity of the family unit and protecting children from physical and mental harm. In most circumstances, the children are removed without their parents' permission after a child protective worker investigates a report of abuse or neglect. Consequently, foster care embodies the most severe form of state interference between parents and children—seizing the children against the parents' will. Because child protective workers tend to be middle-class and the affected children tend to be poor, it is sometimes criticized as a class-based intrusion into family life (Liss, 1987). Because it substitutes state-directed care for parental care, it is sometimes criticized as antifamily (Berger, 1986). Because it fails to return many children to their families in a timely manner, it is criticized for warehousing children from problem families, rather than helping the parents provide better care (Steiner, 1981). Yet few would disagree that children should be protected from some parents—the drug-addicted, the physically or sexually abusive, for instance—who are not fit to raise them.

In the late 1970s, when about 500,000 children were living in foster care, a policy consensus formed: Alarmed by the numbers of children in care, both conservatives and liberals agreed that child protective workers should place a higher priority on helping troubled parents keep their children and care better for them. If a foster care placement was needed, greater efforts should be made to return the children to a permanent home—either by sending them back to their parents or, if absolutely necessary, by putting them up for adoption. Congress codified this consensus in the Adoption Assistance and Child Welfare Act of 1980.[1]

The new consensus worked as intended for several years. As the pendulum swung toward keeping children with their parents, the number of children in foster care declined to about 275,000 in 1983 through 1985. Then, suddenly, it rose sharply to 340,000 in 1988 and to 442,000 in 1992 (Toshio, 1993).[2] By 1999, it was back over the 500,000 mark and reached 523,000 by 2003 (U.S. Administration for Children and Families, 2005). The new law, it appears, was overwhelmed by a huge, unexpected wave of children at risk of harm. The wave was greatest in large cities such as New York and Chicago, and the largest percentage increases in foster care occurred among newborns and infants, many of

whom were low-birth-weight or otherwise impaired babies born to mothers who had had little or no prenatal care (Wulczyn & Goerge, 1992).

Many observers speculated that at least some of this rise was the result of the rapid spread of crack cocaine usage during the same period (U.S. House of Representatives, 1993). Women in poor neighborhoods used crack more than they had used earlier addictive drugs such as heroin. An increase in mothers who were incarcerated or who died due to AIDS may also have contributed (Chipungu & Bent-Goodley, 2004). A rise in homelessness among families also occurred during the late 1980s and early 1990s. Consequently, some parents were not able to provide basic shelter and security to their children, and child protective workers are more likely to remove a child from a homeless family than from one in a home (Rossi, 1994; Jencks, 1994).

Coupled with the rise in reported cases of child abuse, the surge in abandoned and drug-impaired infants led some experts to call for seizing more at-risk children from parents (Ingrassia & McCormick, 1994). More important, highly publicized cases such as the starving boys in New Jersey, described at the beginning of the chapter, caused a public outcry against child protective workers who were seen as too slow

Sexual Aggression and Violence in Dating Relationships

foster care the removal of children from their parental home and their placement in another home

Partner, child, and elder abuse are not the only aspects of violence between men and women that have received attention of late. As courtship and dating have changed, so have attitudes toward the use of coercion to obtain sexual intercourse. Since the 1980s, researchers and clinicians have been studying sexual aggression by men against women whom they were dating and against acquaintances, as well as physical assaults by acquaintances.

to remove children from potentially abusive families (Sexton, 1996). Thus, the pendulum of professional and public opinion has swung back to the 1970s, before the movement toward keeping families intact reached its peak.

Yet neither option—vigilance and early removal of children perceived to be in danger, or increased efforts to help troubled parents so that they can keep their children—has worked well. The foster care system was designed on the basis of assumptions about families that no longer hold. It assumed that the family problems leading to foster care were temporary—as when a mother became ill with a disease such as tuberculosis and needed six months or a year to recuperate. It assumed that large numbers of mothers who did not work outside the home could be found to care temporarily for children whose parents couldn't care for them. It didn't anticipate the shortages, now occurring, of suitable and willing foster parents (Cameron, 2003). It didn't foresee families sleeping in homeless shelters and drug-addicted newborns abandoned in nurseries. In addition, it probably ignored levels of child abuse that today would be unacceptable.

The heart of the problem is that there still are no good alternatives to parental care for children. Long-term foster care,

with children frequently shuttled from family to family, is problematic. Yet abusive or neglectful parents also harm children. One recent innovation is to place children in the homes of relatives and pay them. In 2001, 24 percent of foster children were placed in relatives foster homes (National Clearinghouse on Child Abuse and Neglect Information, 2003). This so-called kinship care option preserves some of the child's family bonds and seems preferable to care by nonrelatives, but it is not without problems. Relatives may have more difficulty than strangers in restricting visits by abusive parents. Moreover, they tend to keep children for a longer period of time than other foster parents; yet they are sometimes reluctant to adopt the children for fear of angering the parents (Wulczyn & Goerge, 1992). Thus, kinship care can conflict with the goal of finding a permanent home for foster children. Moreover, foster parents typically receive substantially more money per child than parents do under Temporary Assistance to Needy Families (the cash welfare program), creating a possible incentive for families receiving TANF to place the children in kinship foster care.

In 1997, Congress embraced another strategy by enacting the Adoption and Safe Families Act. Its goal was to move children out of foster-home placements into adoptive

homes more quickly (Woodhouse, 2002). It encourages states to terminate parental rights and place children in adoptive families after the children have spent 15 to 22 months in foster care. Most of the adoptive parents are eligible to receive government subsidies after adopting children from foster care. Perhaps as a result of the 1997 Act, the percentage of foster children who are returned to their parents has declined while the proportion who are adopted has increased (Bass, Shields, & Behrman, 2004).

The only real, long-term hope is to prevent more children from being abused and neglected. That would require an assault on poverty, unemployment, and family breakups. Meanwhile, the quandary of what to do about abusive and neglectful parents and their children continues.

Ask Yourself
1. Do you know anyone with experience as a foster parent? If so, what was that person's opinion of the foster care system?
2. Which do you think is more important, protecting a family's integrity or protecting children from abuse?

[1] Public Law 96–272.
[2] The APWA's estimate for 1993 is 464,000.

www.mhhe.com/cherlin5

SEXUAL AGGRESSION

There are at least two reasons for the lack of attention to this problem before 1980. First, the rates of sexual activity among unmarried young persons were substantially lower prior to the 1970s; consequently, the incidence of acquaintance rape was probably lower also (although there are no satisfactory data). Second, young women tended to be blamed for their dates' improper sexual advances. As the practice of blaming the victim began to weaken and as rates of sexual activity increased, researchers brought forth study after study showing significant amounts of sexual coercion, including forcible rapes that were rarely reported to the police.

Prevalence   Yet adequate national data on the prevalence of sexual aggression among acquaintances still does not exist. Twenty-two percent of all adult women in the 1992 survey of sexual activity said they had been forced to have sex by a man at least once in their lives (Laumann et al., 1994). Acquaintances (defined as "someone you knew but not well" or "someone you had just met") were named in 19 percent of the incidents of forced sex reported by these women. Overall, then, we can estimate that 4 percent of all adult American women (that is, 19 percent of the 22 percent who reported forced sex by anyone) have experienced forced sex by an acquaintance. Most other studies of sexual aggression by acquaintances have focused on college students. For example, in the spring semester of 1997, interviewers contacted by telephone a random sample of 4,446 women in two- and four-year colleges (U.S. National Institute of Justice, 2000). They asked detailed screening questions about types of sexual victimization the women might have experienced in the seven months, on average, "since school began in fall, 1996." As Figure 11.3 shows, 1.7 percent reported a "completed rape," which the study defined as sexual penetration of various kinds (e.g., penile-vaginal, oral-genital, digital-vaginal) by force or the threat of force; and 1.1 percent reported, by this definition, an attempted rape. The authors calculated that, using their definition and projecting these rates to an entire four-year college career (which assumes these rates would not change over time), one-fifth of college women might be victimized by an attempted or completed rape.

Only about half of the women categorized as experiencing a completed rape answered "yes" when asked, "Do you consider this incident to be rape?" Does this mean the study, with its graphic questions, overestimates the prevalence of rape? Not necessarily. Some women may be reluctant to define an incident as rape because of embarrassment or because they don't want to define themselves as victimized. Some may not know that the legal definition of rape in most jurisdictions includes not only vaginal intercourse but also forced sexual penetration of other kinds.

In addition, as Figure 11.3 shows, 1.7 percent reported a completed incident, and 1.3 percent an attempted incident, of "sexual coercion," defined as unwanted sexual penetration with the threat of nonphysical punishment, promise of reward, or pestering or verbal pressure. So about as many women experience sexual coercion as experience rape under these definitions. Slightly higher percentages reported unwanted "sexual contact" such as touching or fondling of breasts or kissing by force or the threat of force. Overall, women who reported

FIGURE 11.3
Percentage of college women reporting completed or attempted rape or sexual coercion in seven months, on average, "since school began in fall, 1996." (*Source:* U.S. National Institute of Justice, 2000)

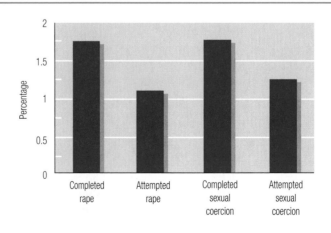

Awareness of sexual aggression in dating relationships is much greater on college campuses than a generation ago.

frequently drinking enough to get drunk, who were unmarried, and who had been a victim of sexual assault before the current school year were more likely to have been victimized.

Perpetrators   College men are far less likely to report initiating a rape or an attempted rape. The lower figures probably represent a mixture of underreporting, multiple rapes by some, and rapes committed by nonstudents. In one study of students in 32 colleges, most (88 percent) of the men who answered affirmatively to questions about forced intercourse that seemed to indicate a rape responded that it "definitely was not a rape"; moreover, these men perceived the woman's refusal as less clear than the women in the sample perceived it. Seventy-four percent said they had been drinking alcohol or using drugs, and 75 percent said the woman had been. Forty-seven percent said they expected to engage in similar behavior again (Koss, 1988).

Nationally, 57 percent of all the rapes and sexual assaults reported in the 2002 National Crime Victimization Survey were committed by a friend or acquaintance of the victim (U.S. Department of Justice, 2003). The younger the rape victim (and the victim is under age 18 in more than half of all rapes), the more likely the rapist is to be a family member. One Justice Department study of rapes that were reported to the police in several states found that 16 percent of the rapes had occurred to girls under age 12, and virtually all these rapes had been committed by family members or acquaintances ("Report Cites Heavy Toll," 1994).

Other studies suggest that young men who commit sexual aggression against acquaintances are more likely to show hostility toward women and to believe that men are supposed to be more dominant and women more subordinate (Abbey & McAuslan, 2004). The men also show greater physiological arousal when presented with rape scenarios in psychology experiments, are more likely to consider violence against women acceptable, and are more sexually active than men who don't commit sexual aggression. In contrast, there are relatively few differences between women who have been victims of sexual aggression and those who haven't (Cate & Lloyd, 1992).

The circle of friends a person has also makes a difference. At one large university, researchers found three distinct peer groups. In the first, neither the women nor the men had initiated or been victimized by sexual aggression; in the second, some of the women had been victimized but the men in the group had not been the aggressors; and in the third, women had been victimized and men had been aggressors. The peer groups in this latter category included students who used alcohol and drugs more often; tended to live in dormitories, fraternities, and sororities (as opposed to at home); and placed a higher value on the social aspects of going to college (Gwartney-Gibbs & Stockard, 1989). What can't be determined from these studies is whether belonging to an aggressive group changes a young man's behavior or whether young men who are already aggressive for other reasons join such groups.

PHYSICAL ASSAULT

Physical assault, whether or not sexual aggression occurs, also appears to be common among dating couples. A national sample of 250 never-married persons who had dated someone six or more times in the past year was asked about the incidence of physical violence in that dating relationship. The interviewer read a list of nine types of violence, ranging from less serious to very serious. Thirty percent chose answers showing that they had inflicted minor aggression on their dating partners at least once in the previous 12 months, and 11 percent reported inflicting severe aggression. Violence was more likely to be inflicted, the survey demonstrated, by persons who reported trying to control their partners' actions ("I make him/her do what I want," "If I don't like what s/he is doing I make him/her stop"). Moreover, the survey suggested that people who were better at what sociologists have called "taking the role of the other" experienced reduced levels of violence. Specifically, persons who said they could imagine the other person's point of view and put themselves mentally in the other person's place ("When something affects him/her, I feel it too," "I understand his/her feelings quite well") were less likely to inflict violence or to have violence inflicted on them (Stets, 1992).[2]

Another study compared rates of physical assault in a college student sample to national figures for cohabiting and married couples. The authors reported that dating couples had rates of physical assault (15 percent in the previous year) that were a bit lower than for married couples (20 percent), but that cohabiting couples had noticeably higher rates (35 percent) than either dating or married couples. The authors speculate that disagreements about controlling the other partner's behavior may be important. In dating relationships, they argue, the partners expect to have less control, so they may not become as angry about a lack of control. On the other hand, married couples may agree to a high level of control. In the middle, say the authors, are cohabiting relationships, where there may be more disagreement about the amount of control a partner can expect (Stets & Straus, 1989). Their argument is intriguing, but it may also be that people who choose to cohabit have personalities and backgrounds that predispose them to violence more than those who don't cohabit.

[2] The subjects were between the ages of 18 and 30.

Quick Review

- Sexual aggression and violence in dating relationships have received considerable attention since about 1980.
- In several surveys, women have reported the prevalence of forced and coercive sex with intimate partners.
- Young men who commit sexual aggression against acquaintances are more likely to show hostility to women and to believe that men should be dominant.
- Physical assaults also occur in dating relationships.

■ Explanations

Why do people abuse their spouses, partners, or children? According to the political model of domestic violence, assaults against spouses and partners arise, in part, from power struggles between men and women. Men have an advantage in these struggles because of their greater physical strength, on average, and because of a social system that often reinforces male dominance. During the many thousands of years humans spent as hunter-gatherers, male strength was central to the life of bands. Men defended the band's territory against intrusions by other bands, and men armed with spears hunted animals. It is likely that men used their strength to compete for women and to dominate them. Later, in larger social groups, men were often able to shape laws and norms—such as the belief that the husband should be the head of the household—to their advantage so that they didn't need to use force to achieve their ends. The system of male dominance that still appears to some extent in virtually every society today is based in part upon the use of, or the threat of the use of, force against women.

But most men, despite their advantage in strength and despite cultural beliefs, don't hit their wives. In addition, both men and women sometimes abuse their children. Consequently, the general notion of male dominance isn't useful in explaining why some husbands are violent and others are not or why parents abuse their children. Many other explanations have been proposed, most of which have some plausibility. These explanations are often referred to as "theories" of domestic violence, although most of them are just collections of related propositions. Some of these perspectives emphasize psychological factors, whereas others emphasize social structural factors. At the present time, we don't know enough to tie them together into a single, coherent explanation. When Richard Gelles and Murray Straus, two leaders in the field, were asked to write an essay integrating theories of domestic violence, they presented propositions and outcomes from 13 so-called theories (Gelles & Straus, 1979). Instead of mechanically discussing all 13, let me focus on the ones I think are the most important.

SOCIAL LEARNING PERSPECTIVE

The explanation that is probably cited the most draws upon the **social learning perspective** developed by social psychologists. According to this perspective, individuals learn behavior they will later exhibit by observing what others do and seeing the consequences of these actions. Thus, children from violent homes are said to learn by observation and personal experience that aggressive or violent behavior is an acceptable and often successful way of controlling others and getting what you want (Bandura, 1973). In fact, a number of studies do show that

social learning perspective the theory that individuals learn behavior they will later exhibit by observing what others do and seeing the consequences of these actions

children who grow up in homes characterized by domestic violence are more likely, as adults, to act violently toward their spouses and children. (All children may, to some extent, learn that violent behavior is acceptable through watching the pervasive violence in television programs and films.)

For example, respondents in the 1975 national survey were asked whether, as children, (1) they had ever observed either of their parents hitting the other and (2) whether their parents had hit them as teenagers. Among men who had neither seen hitting nor been hit, 1 percent committed acts of severe violence against their wives. Among men who had been hit by their parents, the corresponding figure was 3 percent. It was 6 percent among men who had observed their parents hitting each other, and it rose to 12 percent among men who had both observed their parents hitting each other and had been hit themselves (Kalmuss, 1984).

This pattern of findings can be interpreted in two ways. The glass-half-empty interpretation is that men are far more likely to beat their wives if they have witnessed hitting or been hit by their parents. This interpretation shows why the social learning perspective does help us to understand why some men are violent. The glass-half-full interpretation is that the vast majority of men who have witnessed hitting or been hit by their parents do *not* beat their wives. This second interpretation shows the limitations of the social learning perspective as an explanation for violent behavior: It doesn't explain why most people who have been exposed to violence are not themselves violent.

FRUSTRATION–AGGRESSION PERSPECTIVE

frustration-aggression perspective the theory that aggressive behavior occurs when a person is blocked from achieving a goal

An alternative explanation is derived from the **frustration–aggression perspective.** Here the central idea is that aggressive behavior occurs when a person is blocked from achieving a goal, such as when economic inequalities cause men and women to work for low wages, high unemployment rates make it hard to find a job, or racial discrimination limits the opportunities of people from racial-ethnic groups. When these conditions occur, it is said, the person may displace his or her frustration and anger onto a safer target—such as his or her spouse or children. These targets are safer than employers or strangers because there is less chance of being arrested, being hit hard in return, or losing one's job. In contrast to the social learning approach, violent behavior is not viewed as directed toward a specific end, such as dominating a wife. Rather, violence is seen as an emotional outburst of displaced anger, usually by a man. So this perspective suggests that, regardless of what people have learned about violence as children, they will be more likely to act violently if they are frustrated by forces they feel are blocking their ability to get a job, move out of a dangerous neighborhood, or attain other important goals. Consequently, the frustration–aggression approach helps us to understand why domestic violence is somewhat more common among the lower social classes, whose members are more likely to be blocked from attaining their goals (but who may also be more likely to have grown up in violent homes).

The frustration-aggression approach raises the question of where a person's basic tendency to act violently (when blocked or frustrated) comes from, other than social learning. Some evidence suggests that men's greater aggressiveness, compared with women's aggressiveness, may be partly of biological origin. [➡ p. 86] Gelles and Straus argue, however, that aggression is learned behavior; in fact, they reject the idea that there is any biological influence on domestic violence.[3] Yet a

---

[3] See Gelles & Straus (1979), footnotes 7 and 8.

| Families in Other Cultures | Wife Beating in the Developing World |

Domestic violence is not limited to developed nations such as the United States. In 1998, a man in India justified wife beating as a way of correcting improper behavior: "If [she makes] a great mistake, then the husband is justified in beating his wife. Why not? A cow will not be obedient without beatings." A survey in two Indian States found that 41 percent of the women reported ever having been beaten by their husbands (Jejeebhoy & Cook, 1997). Across the developing world, violence toward wives is justified for many reasons, including disobeying one's husband, talking back to him, or failing to care adequately for one's children or home (Heise, Ellsberg, & Gottemoeller, 2002).

What determines whether domestic violence is common in a society? Anthropologist David Levinson studied field reports from 90 preliterate and peasant societies. He found that the extent of economic inequality between the husband and the wife made a difference. Wife beating was more likely to occur in societies in which men controlled the allocation of food or cash to the members of the household; it was more likely where women could not amass or control wealth, as by earning an independent income or owning a dwelling; and it

was more likely where men had the final say in household decision making. Where men's economic power over women was greater, they had little to lose by alienating a wife or her kin through excessive violence because the wife controlled fewer resources. Therefore, husbands had less incentive to restrain their violent impulses (Levinson, 1988). In addition, wife beating was less common where female work groups, which could provide support to abused wives, existed.

Consistent with these conclusions, Yount (2005) found that women in an Egyptian village who had ever worked for cash were less likely to think that a husband is ever justified in beating his wife. And women with considerably less education than their husbands were more likely to have been beaten in the prior year. Several authors have suggested that urbanization and development might increase levels of domestic violence initially, as traditional social controls break down, but would eventually lower the level. Consider a study of domestic violence in two areas in Bangladesh. One area, close to the Indian border, was more economically developed, whereas the other, far from the border, was less developed and had more traditional norms about women's status. In

the less developed area, women who were more autonomous (e.g., freer to speak with men not in the family, directly possessing cash) were *more* likely to report being beaten. The authors suggest that in this traditional area, women's autonomy was seen as provocative and threatening to the social order. But in the more developed area, where social norms had changed and education was more common, women who were more autonomous were less likely to report being beaten. The authors suggest that only after women's autonomy is accepted and becomes commonplace in a society does it begin to reduce the risks of domestic violence (Koenig, Ahmed, Hossain, & Mozumder, 2003).

Ask Yourself

1. Are you familiar with a developing country or with immigrants to the United States from a developing country? If so, have you noticed differences in the treatment of women in that country?
2. Why might wife beating be considered a more serious social problem in cities than in rural villages?

www.mhhe.com/cherlin5

national study of armed services veterans found that husbands who had higher levels of testosterone—the male sex hormone—were more likely to have hit or thrown things at their wives (Booth & Dabbs, 1993). The possibility of biological influences is not presented here to excuse the behavior of violent men. Most people can (and do) control their urges and predispositions. Even in the testosterone study, 71 percent of men in the group that had the highest levels of the hormone did *not* hit or throw things at their wives—just as most men who come from violent homes do not beat their wives. Still, men with a greater biological predisposition toward aggression might be more likely than others to beat their wives and their children if they are frustrated and angry about events occurring outside the home.

SOCIAL EXCHANGE PERSPECTIVE

A third explanation draws upon the **social exchange perspective.** This explanation proposes that people calculate whether to engage in a particular behavior

social exchange perspective the theory that people calculate whether to engage in a particular behavior by considering the rewards and costs of that behavior and the rewards of alternatives to it

by considering the rewards and costs of that behavior and the rewards of alternatives to it. The model here is that of the rational actor. It suggests that a man may decide whether to beat his wife by considering the rewards (he can control her; he can let out his anger and frustration at the rest of the world) against the costs of violence (she might seek a divorce) and the rewards of not being violent (she will continue to do much of the child care and contribute the paycheck from her job). This approach helps to explain why wives are more likely to be the victims of violence if they don't work for wages; in that case, the costs of violence to the husband (she might seek a divorce) are lower and the rewards of not being violent (she will contribute earnings) are lower because the wife is not employed. The social exchange perspective is also consistent with cross-cultural evidence that severe violence against women is less common in societies in which women have more economic independence. (See *Families in Other Cultures:* Wife Beating in the Developing World.) Moreover, it also helps to explain the greater violence against women among the lower social classes. Men with more income can influence their wives' actions by exchanging money for the desired behavior. With money they can get the same rewards poorer men must use force to obtain, but without incurring the high costs of force—such as the possibility that the wife will seek a divorce.

Quick Review

- The social learning perspective emphasizes that people learn through observation and experience that violent behavior against intimates is acceptable.
- The frustration–aggression perspective emphasizes that violent behavior results when a person is blocked from achieving a goal.
- The social exchange perspective suggests that people engage in violent behavior against intimates when the rewards exceed the costs.

■ Domestic Violence and Public Policy ■

In the epilogue to her book on U.S. social policy against domestic violence since the Puritans, Pleck wrote:

> *The history of social policy against domestic violence has been one of persistent, even inherent conflict between protecting the victim and preserving the family, and the gradual development of alternatives within and outside the family for victims of abuse. (Pleck, 1987)*

Since the mid-1970s this often dormant conflict has surfaced again. Yet there is a subtext to the protect-the-victim versus preserve-the-family discourse. Public policies that protect the victim restrict men's use of their superior physical force and therefore decrease the power of men over women. That is why feminist groups have worked so hard to bring the problems of battered women to the public's attention, to create crisis centers, shelters, and support services, and to modify the law in nearly all states. Wrote Gordon, "Defining wife-beating as a social problem . . . was one of the great achievements of feminism" (Gordon, 1988).

THE POLICY DEBATE

Because liberals tend to favor equality between men and women more than conservatives, more liberals than conservatives favor policies such as the following: state intervention in marriages in which husbands use severe physical or sexual violence against their wives; continued growth of support services for victims in crisis; and more assistance for battered women who wish to leave their marriages (such as child care, job training, and tougher child support enforcement). But although the liberal, protect-the-victim activists have been succeeding recently, a conservative, preserve-the-family movement has also emerged since the mid-1970s. Conservatives are more likely than liberals to support male-headed two-parent families. Since this family form has traditionally been dominant (although it is becoming less so), conservatives have an interest in preserving the family status quo. That is one reason why many conservatives disapprove of state intervention in families, except in the most extreme cases, and why, in part, they believe that what occurs in a family is the private business of its members. Conservatives have not had much success on these issues recently; their most notable triumph was delaying and reducing federal funds in the early 1980s. They did not have much success in the 1990s in part because of legislation that was passed in the wake of the O. J. Simpson case. For example, within days of Simpson's arrest in 1994 on charges of murdering his former wife, the New York State Legislature passed a bill that required the police to arrest suspected perpetrators of domestic violence whether or not the victim is willing to press charges. Within two months, the U.S. House of Representatives had approved nearly all the provisions of the Violence Against Women Act, which had first been introduced, without success, six years earlier.

SOCIAL PROGRAMS

Other recent developments, mentioned earlier, also seem to have assisted the liberals. For instance, the cultural emphasis on independence and self-fulfillment implies that an unhappy spouse should be able to leave her or his marriage. These values are inconsistent with the notion that a woman should stay in an abusive marriage. Moreover, the increasing economic independence of women provides them with earning power that they can use to gain more authority in marriage or to live independently of men. In addition, the deteriorating earnings of young men, especially those without a college education, reduce their attractiveness to women and therefore make it less likely that women they abuse will remain with them. Unless there is a reversal of these trends, liberal policy positions seem likely to continue to prevail.

Still, it can be challenging to translate the protect-the-victim policy into effective programs. Consider the spread since the early 1980s of mandatory arrest policies in domestic violence complaints. This approach was influenced by an experiment conducted by the Minneapolis police force in 1981 and 1982. When responding to domestic violence complaints, the police randomly assigned the offender to one of three treatments: arresting him, ordering him to leave the home for eight hours, or trying to mediate the dispute. The results, based on subsequent arrest records and interviews with the victims, showed that arresting the suspect resulted in the lowest level of repeat violence (Sherman & Berk, 1984).

Intrigued officials at the Department of Justice decided to support replications of the experiment in other cities. But many state governments—eager to take action against the problem—legislated mandatory arrest policies without waiting

Many jurisdictions make an arrest mandatory when police are called to a domestic violence dispute.

for the results of the replications. The results of the experiments in other localities suggest, in the words of one review article, a "modest preventative effect" of mandatory arrest policies (Maxwell, Garner, & Fagan, 2002). The authors suggested that while these policies may be helpful in reducing intimate partner violence, they are far from a cure-all. Moreover, they note that prosecuting offenders rather than merely arresting them does not further reduce the chances of subsequent violence. In order to make greater progress in reducing intimate partner violence, organizations will need to identify men at higher risk of repeat offenses—due to factors such as alcohol abuse, prior arrest records, and unemployment—and treat them or restrict their actions. But our knowledge of how to go about this larger task is incomplete.

Altogether, these results illustrate the difficulty of designing programs to address spouse abuse. Still, in the current period of high divorce rates, greater gender equality, and rising individualism, the image of the bruised and battered woman has led most Americans to approve of government efforts to help her escape her husband. It is hard to imagine returning to a time when men could hit their wives with impunity or parents could boast of giving their children a good wholesome flogging.

Quick Review

- Public policy discussions about domestic violence often have a preserve-the-family versus protect-the-victim theme.
- The growing emphasis on independence and self-fulfillment in relationships undercuts the belief that women should stay in an abusive relationship.
- Still, it is difficult to design programs that effectively protect victims of domestic violence.

Looking Back

1. **When did domestic violence become a social issue?** Domestic violence has been a social issue at various points throughout U.S. history. The Puritans, who took a strong stand against wife beating, passed the first laws against it. A period of renewed interest occurred in the late 1800s, and another in the 1960s. Two theoretical models, a medical model and a political model, have been applied to this social problem. The current interest and activity are largely a result of political and social action by feminist groups and by health and social welfare professionals.

2. **What do we know about violence between intimate partners?** The more common kind is situational incidents in which spouses become angry and engage in minor violent acts. Women seem as likely to initiate these incidents as men. The less common but more serious kind is a pattern of serious violent acts carried out by a man against a woman. In many of these cases, the man is seeking to control his partner's behavior. Women are more likely to be the victims of aggressive acts over their lifetimes than are men. Domestic violence is more common among cohabiting couples than among married couples, and more common among low-income families than higher-income families. Cross-cultural studies show that wife beating occurs in most societies.

3. **What is the extent of child abuse?** Though the physical abuse of children has probably decreased over the long term, surveys continue to show disturbing levels of child abuse by parents. More than half the reported cases refer to educational or physical neglect; less than one-third, to physical or sexual abuse. Child neglect and, to a lesser extent, physical abuse are somewhat more common among low-income families than others. Some cases of neglect may reflect the constraints of poverty more than abuse by parents. Childhood sexual and physical abuse can have long-term undesirable consequences. Though reports of child neglect and abuse have risen greatly in recent decades, the increase may reflect more complete reporting rather than an actual increase in the rates of neglect and abuse. Severely neglected or abused children are sometimes placed in foster care. In the late 1980s and 1990s, the number of children in foster care rose dramatically. There is a continuing debate about whether government social programs should emphasize the preservation of families or the protection of children.

4. **What do we know about sexual aggression by dates or acquaintances?** Although adequate data does not exist, studies suggest that men commit substantial amounts of sexual aggression and violence against women they are dating and other female acquaintances. According to one national survey, about 4 percent of adult women in the United States have been forced into sex by an acquaintance. In one national study, 11 percent of dating couples reported severe physical aggression. Men who commit sexual aggression are more likely than others to show hostility to women, to be easily aroused by rape scenarios, to be sexually active, and to belong to sexually aggressive peer groups. People who try to control the other partner's behavior or are less able than others to imagine another person's point of view are more likely than others to be physically abusive. Physical assault may be more common among cohabiting partners than among couples who are dating or married.

5. **Why does domestic violence occur?** Assaults against spouses and partners arise in part from power struggles between men and women. Men have an advantage in these struggles because of their greater physical strength, and because of a social system that often reinforces male dominance. But most men do not hit their wives, so other explanations are needed for domestic violence. According to the social learning approach, children from violent homes will learn that violent behavior is an acceptable and often successful means of controlling others; consequently, they will be more likely as adults to use violence against spouse and children. The frustration–aggression approach emphasizes that individuals who are blocked from attaining a goal may displace their frustration and anger onto their spouses and children. The social exchange approach suggests that people calculate the rewards and costs of violent behavior and the alternatives to it. According to this approach, women who have some economic resources are less likely than others to be victimized, as cross-cultural studies show.

6. **What are the public policy debates concerning domestic violence?** Liberals and conservatives disagree about the desirability of early and extensive state intervention in cases of domestic violence. The fundamental issue is the conflict between preserving the family and helping the victims. Liberals, who tend to emphasize helping the victims, generally favor more equality between men and women. Conservatives, who tend to emphasize preserving the family, generally favor the continued dominance of the male-headed two-parent family. Recently, liberal activists have been more successful than conservatives in pushing their agenda.

 Go to the Online Learning Center at www.mhhe.com/cherlin5 to test your knowledge of the chapter concepts and key terms.

Study Questions

1. How would the political and medical models of domestic violence differ in the way that the perpetrators of violence are viewed?
2. How narrowly or broadly should domestic violence be defined?
3. What are some likely explanations for why domestic violence against women appears to be more common among lower-income families?
4. Most of the data on the number of new cases of child abuse come from reports by state child welfare agencies. What are the likely biases of this way of collecting information?
5. What are some of the long-term consequences of childhood sexual and physical abuse?
6. How does the trade-off between family reunification and child protection affect the foster care system?
7. Why are college-age men less likely to report sexually aggressive behavior than college-age women are to report being affected by it?
8. What patterns of domestic violence does the social-learning perspective explain well? What patterns doesn't it explain well?

Key Terms

child abuse   380
domestic violence   368
elder abuse   384
foster care   386
frustration–aggression
   perspective   392
incest   382
intimate terrorism   373
situational couple
   violence   373
social exchange
   perspective   393
social learning
   perspective   391

Thinking about Families

The Public Family	The Private Family
Should child protective workers leave children with parents who have not been violent, but who seem likely to be violent in the future, or should they take children away from potentially violent parents?	Is rape a concept that should be applied to married couples?

Families on the Internet   www.mhhe.com/cherlin5

Note: While all the URLs listed were current as of the printing of this book, these sites often change. Please check our Web site (http://www.mhhe.com/cherlin5) for updates.

Several sites offer information and links on the topic of child abuse. The National Clearinghouse on Child Abuse and Neglect Information (http://nccanch. acf.hhs.gov) provides statistics, reports, and answers to frequently asked questions. The National Committee to Prevent Child Abuse (www.childabuse.org) offers information on steps people can take to prevent child abuse. Several fact sheets are available under "publications."

The Family Violence Prevention Fund (www. fvpf.org) maintains a Web site with news briefs on recent developments. Click on "resources," then "personal stories" to read stories about people who have "triumphed over violence in their lives." The Minnesota Center Against Violence and Abuse (www.mincava.umn.edu) maintains a site that has links to thousands of documents and hundreds of organizations and research centers.

Chapter Twelve

Divorce

Looking Forward

1. What is the history of divorce in the United States and other Western nations?

2. What accounts for the trends in divorce over the past half-century?

3. What happens to parents during the divorce process?

4. What are the short-term effects of divorce on children?

5. What are the long-term effects of divorce on children?

What if you and your spouse-to-be had to sign a pledge, enforceable in court, to undergo marriage counseling before you wed and to undergo more counseling if you ever wanted a divorce? And what if you waived the right to divorce without your spouse's consent, except after a 24-month waiting period? Would that lower the chances that you would ever divorce? The Louisiana legislature hoped that it might. In 1997, legislators passed a bill creating a new, optional form of marriage called "covenant marriage." When applying for a marriage license, couples who chose covenant marriage would sign a document in which they pledged to follow these restrictive rules. Arizona and Arkansas have since enacted similar legislation.

Covenant marriage hasn't been the success its supporters hoped it would be. Less than 5 percent of couples who have married in Louisiana since 1997 have adopted it (Hawkins, Nock, Wilson, Sanchez & Wright, 2002). One study suggests that the court clerks who issue marriage licenses sometimes fail to tell couples about the option, which requires more work on their part than a standard marriage license. But even when couples do learn about covenant marriage most opt for a standard marriage license. The few couples who have chosen it tend to be much more religious and a bit more politically conservative than others (Nock, Wright, & Sanchez, 1999).

Still, covenant marriage stands as a symbol of public concern about the high levels of divorce in the United States. It represents a reaction to the introduction in every state of "no fault" divorce laws, which allow one partner to obtain a divorce after a short period, even if the other partner doesn't want one. But, as will be noted below, it's not clear whether the liberalized divorce laws helped cause the high level of divorce or whether the laws were a reaction to it. What is clear is that the United States has the highest rate of divorce of any developed country. The probability of a marriage ending in divorce doubled between the early 1960s and late 1970s. At current rates, about half of all American marriages begun since the late 1970s will end in divorce (Cherlin, 1992). (See *How Do Sociologists Know What They Know?* Measuring the Divorce Rate.)

The young adults who entered college in the 1990s and 2000s are members of the first cohort to grow up after this latest great surge of divorce. (About 40 percent of American children who grew up in the 1980s and 1990s experienced the breakup of their parents' marriages [Furstenberg & Cherlin, 1991].) When two childless adults divorce, the breakup, although emotionally painful, is straightforward. Having concluded their legal business, the ex-spouses need not, and often do not, see each other again. When children are involved, however, a clean break is not

How Do Sociologists Know What They Know? Measuring the Divorce Rate

A newspaper reporter calls a sociologist who does research on divorce and asks, "What's the most recent statistic for the divorce rate in the United States?" "In 2002," the sociologist replies, "about 18 out of every 1,000 married women divorced." "Eighteen out of a thousand," she responds, "No way! That's tiny. The divorce rate has got to be much higher than that."

"Well," says the sociologist, "another way of saying it is that about half of all marriages would end in divorce at current rates." "Great," the reporter replies, "and what year is that for?" "It's not for a year," the sociologist tries to explain, "it's a projection based on this year's rates . . ." But he can tell that the reporter is losing patience fast. She wants a figure and a year, not a lecture in demography, and she's writing a story on a deadline.

In fact, it's hard to answer the question, "what's the current divorce rate?" in a way that is both precise and meaningful. The difficulty is that the most meaningful statistic describes the proportion of all current marriages that will end in divorce, but it's impossible to know that proportion until everyone who is now married has grown old and died. So sociologists try to estimate this lifetime figure, but their estimates are just educated guesses. The precise statistic is based on the number of divorces in the most recent year for which data are available, but it doesn't tell us much about people's experience with divorce.

The 18-out-of-1,000 rate is the precise statistic; it represents the number of divorces in the United States divided by the number of married women. It includes women who have been married for many years as well as those who married only recently. It gives the probability that a married woman would have become divorced in 2002: 18/1,000, or about 2 percent. So in 2002, 2 percent of married women obtained divorces.

This does indeed sound like a very low figure, given all of the public concern about divorce. No wonder reporters are unhappy with it. It is a *cross-sectional rate,* meaning a rate at one point in time. It provides a snapshot of the experiences of married American women during a single year. In 2003, the 982 of every 1,000 married women who didn't divorce in 2002 were still at risk of divorcing, and another 18 or so did. In 2004, yet another 18 would obtain divorces, and so on, year after year, into the future. So although the average woman married in 2002 had a 2 percent chance of becoming divorced *in 2002,* she had a far higher chance of becoming divorced *over the rest of her married life.*

Just how high her lifetime chances are, we cannot know with certainty. But let us conduct the following thought experiment: Suppose the risks of divorce were to stay the same, for every age group, for the next few decades. That is to say, suppose that a woman in her thirties 10 years from now would have the same risk of divorce as do women in their thirties today and that a woman in her forties 20 years from now would have the same risk as do women in their forties today, and so on. Now think of a hypothetical young woman in her mid-twenties who married this year. We could fast-forward her through time and calculate her risk of divorce at every age throughout her lifetime—because we are assuming that these risks will remain the same as those observed this year. Then we could sum these risks. The result would be a measure of her lifetime probability of divorce.

When sociologists do this calculation, based on current rates, they find that the lifetime probability of divorce for a young woman marrying today is about 50 percent (Bramlett & Mosher, 2002). I write "about" because the exact answer depends on some of the technical assumptions in the calculations, and different sociologists make different assumptions. It's important to recognize that this figure is just a projection of current risks into the future. In fact, it is unlikely that divorce risks will stay the same for the next few decades. It is true, as Figure 12.1 (on p. 406) suggests, that the risks of divorce have not changed much since 1980. But as the figure shows, the 1950s, 1980s, and 1990s are the only decades since the Civil War in which divorce risks have remained more or less stable. They could start changing again tomorrow.

The utility of the lifetime estimate, then, is not that it will prove accurate 40 years from now—it may not—but rather that it indicates the underlying force of divorce that is implied by the behavior of married people today. The lifetime estimate, in other words, answers an important *what if* question: What if the risks of divorce at each age stayed the same as they are now; what lifetime level of divorce would these current risks imply? This is the question most newspaper readers want an answer to, even if the answer is necessarily uncertain.

Ask Yourself

1. How many couples in your family have divorced in the past year? In the past 10 years? The past 20? Is your family's divorce rate similar to the divorce rate for the country as a whole?

2. In general, do news reporters do a good enough job of explaining the significance of social statistics such as the divorce rate? What are the dangers of misreporting such statistics?

Henry VIII (1491–1547), King of England, broke with the Catholic Church so he could annul his marriage to Katherine of Aragon and marry Anne Boleyn.

in their interest. Even though divorce severs the family ties between the husband and wife, it does not sever the ties between each parent and the children. In the majority of cases, the mother keeps custody of the children, forming a single-parent family that may endure for years. The father's relationship—typically reduced to regular visits, or less—is problematic. Indeed, many divorced fathers fade from their children's lives. Nevertheless, a modest but growing number of fathers are obtaining custody of their children, either by themselves or jointly with their wives.

Moreover, for many adults and children, a divorce does not signal the end of the changes in their family lives. A substantial proportion of parents will remarry, often after a period of cohabiting with their spouse-to-be. Remarriage after divorce further complicates adults' and children's lives. It introduces a stepparent into the child's family but doesn't subtract a biological parent—unlike remarriage after a parental death. It can bring a bewildering network of quasi-relatives that extends over several households. In short, it necessitates another major adjustment for adults and children who may have struggled to adjust to postdivorce, single-parent life. In addition, almost half of all children whose custodial parents remarry will witness a *second* divorce before they reach the age of 18 (Bumpass, 1984).

These developments have greatly altered American family life. They have also been a source of concern. What do we know about the causes and consequences of the recent rise in divorce? About the effects of remarriage on stepparents and stepchildren? How are divorce and remarriage altering the nature of the family? These are the questions to be pursued in this chapter on divorce, and in the next chapter on remarriage and stepfamilies.

Three Eras of Divorce

We know the name of the first person to obtain a divorce in England: John Manners, also known as Lord Roos. We know it because the only way for someone to obtain a divorce in England prior to 1858 was to ask Parliament to pass an act granting him one. (Few women were granted divorces.) Lord Roos, whose wife had given birth to a child fathered by another man, introduced a bill in the House of Lords in 1669 that dissolved his marriage and left him free to marry again. From that time until 1858, a grand total of 325 divorces were granted by Parliament (Phillips, 1991). All were granted to wealthy persons, because a common person could not hope to get his or her case taken up by Parliament. Today, far from requiring an act of Parliament or permission from a state legislature, divorce is now easy to obtain in most Western nations. It was not always so. The law and public opinion have changed dramatically over the past two centuries, greatly altering the way in which marriage is viewed. It is useful to think of three historical eras of divorce.

THE ERA OF RESTRICTED DIVORCE

England's law before 1858 was one approach to divorce taken during what I will call the **era of restricted divorce,** which characterized the Western nations until the middle of the nineteenth century. In nearly all the countries, according to historian Roderick Phillips (1991), it was very difficult to obtain a divorce.[1] Still, the European countries differed from one another in how restrictive their divorce laws were according to what religion was most prominent in each country. Catholic countries, such as France, followed the Catholic Church's position that divorce was forbidden. Only if Church officials granted an **annulment**—a ruling that a marriage had never been properly formed in the first place—could a couple dissolve their marriage. Annulments could be granted only in situations such as a marriage between relatives of too close a degree or one in which the spouses had never had sexual intercourse. Protestant countries (except for England) were more liberal, typically granting divorces in cases of adultery or desertion. Several of the American colonies were more liberal still. Most of the colonies recognized the grounds of adultery and desertion; some also allowed divorces on the ground of extreme violence by a husband.

Nevertheless, divorce remained rare everywhere. Its rarity, in large part, reflected the strong male dominance in marriage. Most divorces were granted on grounds of the wife's adultery, but very few wives were granted divorces on grounds of the husband's adultery. In fact, as mentioned earlier, few divorces were granted to women at all. Adultery was the main ground used by men for divorce not just because of sexual jealousy but also because of men's concern about who would farm their land and inherit their property. If, for example, a farmer's wife gave birth to a child fathered by another man, the child might have a claim on the farmer's land—especially if the farmer was unaware that he was not the father. Thus, divorce in this era was very difficult to obtain and, when obtained, was usually invoked because a man wished to ensure that his wife would not bear a child by another man. Marriage, for both men and women, was primarily an economic partnership—a means of pooling labor in order to grow enough food, or to make enough money, to subsist. Its romantic aspects were decidedly secondary, if only because making a living took so much effort. One reason why wives were valuable to husbands was that they could bear children, who were a major source of labor. In fact, fathers took custody of children after divorces in colonial America.

It is inconceivable, however, that marital breakups in this era were as rare as the low frequency of divorce implies. Although divorce was usually unavailable to

era of restricted divorce the time of a restrictive approach toward divorce, until about the middle of the nineteenth century; divorces were usually granted only on the grounds of adultery or desertion, and generally only to men

annulment a ruling that a marriage was never properly formed

[1] The historical material in the next few paragraphs draws upon Phillips (1991). The eras and their titles are mine.

the landless and the poor, separation without divorce must have been commonplace. Contemporary studies of families around the world demonstrate that the legalities of coupling and uncoupling—obtaining a legal marriage or a legal divorce—are less important in the poorer classes, where little money or property is involved (Therborn, 2004). Cohabitation without marriage and separation without divorce are much more common. Moreover, the African slaves in the American colonies, as noted in previous chapters, were denied access to legal marriage or divorce. Thus, a considerable amount of separation and desertion must lie hidden beneath the history of formal divorce in the era of restricted divorce as well.

THE ERA OF DIVORCE TOLERANCE

era of divorce tolerance
the time of a tolerant approach toward divorce, from the middle of the nineteenth century until, in the United States, 1970; the grounds for divorce were widened, and divorce was made more accessible to women

The middle of the nineteenth century marked the beginning of the **era of divorce tolerance,** which lasted in the United States until 1970. During this period, it gradually became easier to obtain a divorce. As the doctrine of separate spheres, with its emphasis on domesticity for women, became more widespread, legislatures and courts grew more sympathetic to cases in which husbands' conduct toward their wives was reprehensible. Most jurisdictions in the United States added as grounds for divorce behaviors such as habitual drunkenness or failure to provide for one's wife. In the twentieth century, legislatures added less specific offenses such as "mental cruelty." These new grounds made divorce more accessible to mistreated wives.

Just as the doctrine of separate spheres was important to changes in divorce laws, so too was the shift in how marriage was viewed. Marriage in the nineteenth and twentieth centuries underwent a gradual change from an economic partnership first and foremost to an emotional partnership based on love and companionship—from an institution to a companionship, in Burgess's memorable phrase. [➡ p. 225] As this transition was made, the failure of a marriage to involve love and companionship came to be seen as a valid reason for divorce. Figure 12.1 shows the annual divorce rate for the United States from 1860 (the earliest year for which statistics exist) until 2002. It shows, for example, that about 2 of every 1,000 married couples in 1880 obtained a divorce that year, whereas about 18 of 1,000 couples obtained a divorce in each of the most recent years.

FIGURE 12.1
Annual divorce rate, United States, 1860–2002. For 1860–1920: divorces per 1,000 existing marriages. For 1920–2002: divorces per 1,000 married women age 15 and over. (*Sources:* for 1860–1988, Cherlin, 1992; for 1989–1996, U.S. National Center for Health Statistics [1993, 1995, 1997a]; for 1997 through 2002, author's calculations)

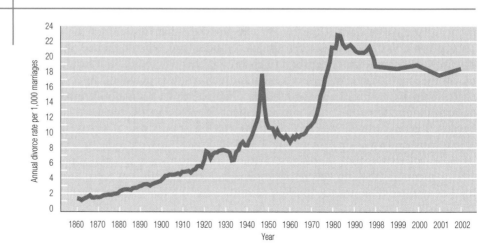

Families in
Other Cultures

Divorce among the Kanuri

What if a society had a divorce rate that made ours look low? What if every marriage ended in divorce and some individuals divorced many times? What would such a society look like, and how would it function? It turns out that there have been many societies in which divorce was more common than it is in the United States and other Western countries today. Some of the recent ones were Islamic societies, for, under traditional Islamic law, divorce was easy for a man to obtain. He needed only to say "I divorce thee" three times and he and his wife were thereby divorced. Now, a wise man did not abuse this power, and social pressure may have existed to settle disputes short of divorce. It was much more difficult for a woman to obtain a divorce, but if she was really unhappy, she could often provoke her husband into giving her one.

The Kanuri of northeastern Nigeria were a high-divorce-rate Islamic society until the 1960s (Cohen, 1971). When anthropologist Ronald Cohen studied six different sites, he found that 68 to 99 percent of all marriages had ended in divorce. Men would say "I divorce thee" only once to establish a divorce because they believed it possible for a man to remarry a woman whom he had divorced, and that could not happen if the declaration had been repeated three times.

Men were allowed to have up to four wives, although only the wealthier half had more than one and few had more than two.

Although frequent, male-initiated divorce among the Kanuri was part of a system of strong male dominance, divorce also served the interests of women at times. Girls' first marriages were arranged by relatives shortly after puberty. A young girl was frequently sent to be the wife of an older, prosperous man, whom she was expected to obey. A divorce allowed her to escape this marriage. Moreover, divorced women had much more independence than married women. The latter were often secluded in the household, whereas divorced women could move about freely. Cohen writes of the divorced woman, "she can entertain lovers, visit with relatives, and no man has a right to order her about."

In this patriarchal system, children remained with the husband after a divorce. Consequently, most children experienced being separated from their mothers. The Kanuri dealt with this problem in part by enlarging the role of the father's sister. Because Kanuri kinship is patrilineal (descent is reckoned along the male line only), the father's sister is part of his kinship group. It was believed, therefore, that she might treat the man's children better than a new wife brought into the household to replace the departed one. As a result, many children were raised for a time by their paternal aunts. In cases of frequent, rapid divorce, the paternal aunt might be the only stable female figure in the lives of the children of the household.

It was no accident, then, that the sister of the emir, the ruler of the society, was one of three female relatives who had a noble title (the others were his mother and his senior wife). She had a warm, maternal image. For example, she was the head of an organization that provided hospitality to strangers who came to town. Her membership in the royal family served to institutionalize the role of the paternal aunt as mother surrogate. In this way, the Kanuri managed the problem of mother loss that was inherent in their high-divorce-rate society.

Ask Yourself

1. What aspect of divorce among the Kanuri most resembles divorce in contemporary American society?
2. If you were a sociologist doing a follow-up study on divorce among the Kanuri, what long-term effects of divorce would you particularly want to examine? Why?

www.mhhe.com/cherlin5

The divorce rate rose substantially in the late 1800s and early 1900s. According to demographic estimates of lifetime divorce experience, 8 percent of all marriages begun in 1880 eventually ended in a divorce, compared with 12 percent of marriages begun in 1900 and 18 percent of marriages begun in 1920 (Preston & McDonald, 1979). Divorce was transformed from a rare privilege granted mainly to wealthy men in the previous era, to a common, if still frowned upon, occurrence increasingly available to women. In fact, Phillips reports that more than two-thirds of divorces in the United States between 1880 and World War I were granted to women. During the same period, divorce caused great concern among social reformers in the United States—not unlike the concern expressed today (O'Neill, 1967). Organizations such as the National Divorce Reform League encouraged legislatures to make divorce laws more restrictive. [➡ p. 60]

The doubling of divorce during the 1960s and 1970s has made scenes such as this one—a father saying goodbye to his daughter at an airport—commonplace.

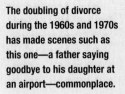

Still, the annual rate of divorce kept rising, as can be seen in Figure 12.1. The steady rise through the first half of the twentieth century was broken only by two spikes in the years after World Wars I and II and a dip during the Great Depression years. The spikes were caused by the disruption and pent-up demand for divorce that had built up during each war. The dip occurred not because marriages were happier during the depths of the Depression but rather because many unhappy couples couldn't afford to get divorced. After World War II the annual rate of divorce fell somewhat, reflecting the home- and family-oriented ethos of the 1950s baby boom years. Then, in the early 1960s, a sharp rise began. By the late 1970s, about 21 or 22 of every 1,000 married couples were getting divorced each year—a rate that has declined slightly since then (Cherlin, 1992, Goldstein, 1999). (There have long been some non-Western societies with even higher divorce rates than ours. See *Families in Other Cultures:* Divorce among the Kanuri.)

As recently as the 1960s, in order to obtain a divorce, a person had to prove that her or his spouse had done something wrong—and not just anything wrong, but rather one of a short list of specific wrongs: adultery, desertion, nonsupport, mental cruelty, and so forth. In truth, however, an increasing number of people were seeking divorces not because the other spouse had committed a terrible act but rather because the divorce seeker was unfulfilled by the marriage, unsatisfied emotionally, and trapped in a relationship that no longer seemed worth maintaining. Often, the other partner, feeling angry and alienated, consented to the divorce. Self-fulfillment, as has been discussed in earlier chapters, has become a dominant, perhaps *the* dominant, criterion for evaluating marriages. As a result, a divorce hearing was often a sham, in which one partner would "prove," with the tacit cooperation of his or her spouse, that some nonexistent or overblown wrong had occurred. In reaction to this situation, sentiment grew for eliminating altogether the idea that one spouse had to be at fault for a divorce to be granted.

THE ERA OF UNRESTRICTED DIVORCE

The first major laws to eliminate fault were implemented in the United States in 1970, ushering in the **era of unrestricted divorce,** in which a divorce has been available virtually without restriction, except for a waiting period, to any married person who wants one. In that year California became the first jurisdiction anywhere in the Western world to eliminate fault grounds for divorce and to replace them with **no-fault divorce,** the granting of divorce simply for marriage breakdown due to "irreconcilable differences" (Glendon, 1987). Coming several years after rising divorce rates had begun to clog the courts, no-fault divorce was hailed as the way to bring the law into line with changes in societal attitudes toward divorce. It reflected the belief that a person should not be forced to continue in a marriage that she or he found to be personally unacceptable. Such an individualistic view of the marriage bond would have outraged the American colonists and their Western European contemporaries; yet in 1970 it carried the day. It was consistent with the shift from the companionship marriage to the individualized marriage. [➡ p. 227] England, where a century earlier only Parliament could authorize the end of a marriage, also added no-fault grounds to its divorce law in 1969. By the end of the 1980s, virtually every Western nation and every state in the American union had adopted some form of no-fault legislation. England, France, Germany, and other countries required that if only one partner wanted the divorce, and children were involved, he or she had to wait several years before it was granted. In contrast, the typical U.S. state required a waiting period of one year or less (American Bar Association, 2003). Divorce had changed from a way for wealthy men to protect their property from heirs fathered by other men to a way for the average person to improve her or his own sense of well-being. In the most liberal no-fault states and nations, it had become something close to an individual right.

era of unrestricted divorce the time of a virtually unrestricted access to divorce, from, in the United States, 1970 to the present; divorces are usually granted without restriction to any married person who wants one

no-fault divorce the granting of a divorce simply on the basis of marriage breakdown due to "irreconcilable differences"

Quick Review

- In the era of restricted divorce, divorces were usually granted only on grounds of adultery or desertion, and generally only to men.
- In the era of divorce tolerance, grounds for divorce were widened, and divorce was made more accessible to women.
- In the era of unrestricted divorce, divorces are usually granted without restriction, except for a waiting period, to anyone who wants one.

■ Factors Associated with Divorce

As Figure 12.1 shows, the divorce rate began to rise sharply in the 1960s and continued its sharp rise in the 1970s. Since then the divorce rate has leveled off: the overall rate showed a slight decline in the 1980s and little change thereafter (Goldstein, 1999). But evidence is mounting that this recent, overall stability masks contrasting trends among people with different levels of education. As Figure 4.4 showed [➡ p. 125] the risk of divorce appears to be dropping for college graduates but rising for people who did not finish high school (Raley & Bumpass, 2003; Martin, 2004a). According to one estimate, about 60 percent of marriages of people without college degrees will eventually end in divorce, compared to 36 percent of the marriages of people with college degrees (Raley & Bumpass, 2003). I presented Figure 4.4 as part of a larger discussion of an emerging demographic divide according to social class, which also involves differences in the timing of marriage and childbearing and a growing tendency for people to marry partners who have a similar level of education.

In sum, the past half-century shows two periods: an earlier period encompassing the 1960s and 1970s in which the chances of becoming divorced increased greatly among all segments of society, and a more recent period in which divorce seems to be increasing for the least well educated and decreasing for the best educated. How can we explain these trends? Let us examine the social factors that may influence the risk of divorce on both a societal and an individual level. Table 12.1 provides a summary of these factors.

SOCIETAL RISK FACTORS

There have been some broad changes in American society that are likely to have influenced levels of divorce, most of which I have discussed in previous chapters. Here is a brief discussion of each:

No-Fault Divorce Legislation   The introduction of a no-fault divorce law seems to have caused a surge of divorces in the first few years after a state enacted it, perhaps reflecting a "backlog effect" of couples in unhappy marriages who were quick to take advantage of it (Nakonezny, Shull, & Rodgers, 1995; Rodgers, Nakonezny, & Shull, 1997). Several studies also suggest that the availability of no-fault divorce probably has increased the divorce rate somewhat in the decades after its enactment in the United States (Friedberg, 1998; Rodgers, Nakonezny, & Shull, 1999) and Britain (Binner & Dnes, 2001), although at least one suggests it has not (Wolfers, 2003). It's also likely that the enactment of no-fault legislation itself reflected widespread changes in behavior and values, such as those discussed in the next few subsections.

Cultural Change   Previous chapters have examined the growing place of individualism and personal fulfillment in marriage, and an extensive discussion will not be presented here. Cultural critics claim that this emphasis erodes bonds of obligation and trust. As a framework for thinking about relationships, it is alleged, the emphasis on personal fulfillment results in a vocabulary that is rich in ways of thinking about individual well-being but impoverished in ways of thinking about commitment (Bellah, Madsen, Sullivan, Swidler, & Tipton, 1985). For instance, numerous books, articles, lecture series, courses, and support groups exist

Table 12.1 Factors Associated with Divorce	
SOCIETYWIDE FACTORS	
No-fault divorce legislation	State no-fault divorce laws produced an initial surge of divorce in the 1970s, but it is unclear whether no-fault laws have had a lasting effect.
Cultural change	A greater emphasis on personal fulfillment made divorce a more acceptable option for people who felt unfulfilled by their marriages.
Women's employment opportunities	Women's growing employment opportunities led to a rise in the number of wives working outside the home. Employment gave wives greater economic independence, which made divorce a more attractive alternative to an unhappy marriage.
Men's employment opportunities	As young men's economic opportunities decreased since the early 1970s, their reduced earning potential may have caused stress in marriages.
INDIVIDUAL FACTORS	
Low income and unemployment	Divorce is more common among people with lower incomes. Lack of money can cause strain and tensions in a marriage.
Age at marriage	People who marry as teenagers have a higher rate of divorce. They may not choose partners as well as those who marry later.
Race and ethnicity	African Americans have higher rates of separation and divorce than most other groups. Low income and unemployment, as well as a lesser emphasis on marriage in African American kinship, may contribute.
Cohabitation	People who cohabit prior to their marriage have a higher rate of divorce. They may have a weaker commitment to marriage than do people who marry without cohabiting first.
Parental divorce	People whose parents divorced are more likely to end their own marriages in divorce. They may model their behavior on their parents' marriages, or they may have a genetic tendency toward having problems in intimate relationships.
Spouse's similarity	People who marry people who are similar to them in characteristics such as religion have a lower rate of divorce. Such couples may be more compatible in their values and interests.

on self-actualization or self-development or human potential, but much less intellectual activity is centered on maintaining personal responsibilities and obligations to others. Put another way, a focus on personal fulfillment represents a shift toward the concerns of the private family as against the concerns of the public family. Under these circumstances, divorce becomes a more acceptable option for people who feel personally unfulfilled; indeed, *not* divorcing in the face of personal dissatisfaction comes to need justifying.

The growing emphasis on personal fulfillment probably was a major contributor to the rise in divorce prior to 1980; but it does not help us explain the diverging trends since then. For example, college-educated women, who had the most permissive attitudes toward divorce laws in the 1970s, now favor restrictions on the availability of divorce more than do non-college-educated women (Martin & Parashar, 2006). This change is inconsistent with rising individualism, so there must be other reasons for it, such as an increasing attraction to marriage.

Women's Employment   In most cases, women do not earn as much as men nor do they typically earn enough to fully support themselves and their children. Nevertheless, the average wages earned by women rose substantially between 1950 and 1980; this rise, in turn, spurred the great increase in married women's movement into the paid labor force (Smith & Ward, 1985). Wives' employment theoretically could have contrasting effects on divorce.

- *Income effect.* Women's employment could lower the likelihood of divorce because the increase in the family's income could relieve financial pressures and thereby reduce tension in the marriage. Moreover, the job could increase the wife's self-esteem and make her more satisfied with her life in general.
- *Economic opportunity effect.* On the other hand, employment could raise the likelihood of divorce by providing an opportunity for the wife to support herself independently of her husband. This opportunity would make divorce a more attractive alternative for women who were unhappy with their marriages. The economic opportunity effect would even operate for wives who were not themselves working outside the home. They might be more likely to divorce if they lived in areas in which the employment prospects for women were good.

The research findings are inconsistent: Some suggest that women's employment seems to increase the risk of divorce, whereas others find no effect or, less frequently, find that women's employment decreases the risk (see White & Rogers, 2000, for a review). An analysis of the National Survey of Families and Households found that wives' employment did not raise the likelihood of divorce if both partners said they were happy with their marriage but did raise the likelihood if one or both spouses said they were not happy (Schoen, Astone, Rothert, Standish, & Kim, 2002).

Nevertheless, women by no means initiate all divorces; a wife's income might also make a husband feel less guilty about asking for a divorce. A woman's independent income facilitates divorce; equally unhappy couples in which the wife is not employed might not be able to divorce as easily. It is also possible that the chain of cause and effect works the opposite way; at least one study suggests that a woman who thinks her marriage is in trouble may be more likely to take a job outside the home in case the marriage fails (Johnson & Skinner, 1986). Moreover, the cultural change toward self-fulfillment could be the driving force behind both the greater number of women working outside the home *and* the greater number of divorces.

Men's Employment

Divorce is more likely if the husband is unemployed. In fact, it is more likely among families with low incomes, regardless of employment, than among families with higher incomes. Some middle-class observers, aware of the sharp rise in divorce among middle-class families, are surprised to learn this. During the 1960s and 1970s, the divorce rate rose sharply among families in all social classes, but at all times the rate has been greater among families with lower incomes (Cherlin, 1992). The simple reason is that lack of money can cause problems and tensions in any marriage. Also, recall evidence from Chapter 8 [➡ p. 279] on the strain that unemployment places on a marriage: It can lead to depression and then to hostile and irritable behavior by the husband, who is failing to fulfill his traditional responsibility as a provider. His behavior, in turn, can provoke anger and depression in his wife and children. Since the early 1970s, the employment opportunities for men without college educations have been declining. [➡ p. 113] Oppenheimer (1994) argues that divorce has risen not just because women's economic opportunities have *increased* but rather because young men's economic opportunities have *decreased*, leading to greater stress in marriages and more divorces. When husbands do not earn a steady income, Oppenheimer argues, their marriages are subject to greater stress and a higher risk of divorce. Oppenheimer's view cannot explain the long-term rise in divorce rates prior to the early 1970s because men's economic opportunities were improving during most of the late nineteenth and early twentieth centuries (Ruggles, 1997); but it does help explain the divergence in divorce rates by education since then.

Summing Up   The great 1960s and 1970s rise in divorce probably had multiple causes: The culture was becoming more individualistic, the laws became more permissive, and women gained more economic independence through working outside the home. We can't really determine which of these factors was most important—most likely it was a combination of all of them. As for the post-1980s divergence, we don't yet know enough about it to say with confidence what has caused it. It's tempting to ascribe it to differing employment opportunities in the globalized, twenty-first-century economy. The young men who have fared the worst economically are those without high school degrees, and they are the ones whose risks of divorcing have increased. In contrast, college-educated workers have fared the best, and their risks of divorce have decreased. We will need more research on this topic, however, to be sure.

INDIVIDUAL RISK FACTORS

In addition, there are many other social and economic factors that seem to increase or decrease an *individual's* likelihood of ever experiencing a divorce but have not contributed to the recent, *societywide* increase. Consider teenage marriage: As will be noted below, people who marry as teenagers have a greater likelihood of divorce than those who postpone marriage. Yet the societywide average age at marriage has been increasing since the 1960s. Consequently, we can rule out teenage marriage as a cause of the societywide rise in divorce. The list of individual risk factors includes the following.

Age at Marriage   Teenagers probably cannot choose partners as well as older persons can. In part, they are not mature enough. Compared with people in their twenties, teenagers may not know as well what kinds of persons they will be as adults and what their needs in a partner will be. Even if they do have a good sense of their emerging selves, they will have a more difficult time picking an appropriate partner because it is hard to know what kind of spouse an 18-year-old will prove to be over the long run. Moreover, teenage marriages are sometimes precipitated by an accidental pregnancy, and it is known that a premarital birth raises the likelihood of divorce. It does so partly because it brings together a couple who might not otherwise have chosen to marry each other. It also may be more difficult, on a practical level, for a couple to make a marriage work if a young child is present from day one. About half of all marriages of teenagers end in divorce within 15 years, compared to about one-third of marriages of people who marry in their mid-to-late twenties and about one-fourth of marriages of people who are age 30 or older (Raley & Bumpass, 2003). Still, earlier marriage cannot be an explanation for the post-1960 rise in divorce because age at marriage increased after 1960.

Race and Ethnicity   African Americans have substantially higher rates of marital separation than most other racial-ethnic groups; about one-half of the marriages of black women end within 15 years compared to about one-third of white women's marriages (Raley & Bumpass, 2003). Although lower income, unemployment, and lower educational level are important sources of this racial difference, these factors alone cannot account for it. For example, among college graduates in 1980, 44 percent of black women who had married 10 to 14 years earlier had already separated or divorced, compared with 23 percent of comparable non-Hispanic white women (Sweet & Bumpass, 1987). Indeed, at every level of education, black women are more likely to have separated. It is likely that the lesser emphasis in African American culture on marriage, relative to extended kinship ties, also plays a role. [➡ p. 157] African Americans, who can rely more heavily on mothers, grandmothers, and other kin, have less need to stay married; they also have an alternative source of support if a marriage ends (Orbuch, Veroff, & Hunter, 1999).

In addition, black women who separate from their husbands are considerably less likely to obtain a legal divorce, and again the differences are not due solely to economics or education. Within three years of separating, 55 percent of black women had obtained a divorce, according to the 1980 Census, compared with 77 percent of Mexican American women and 91 percent of non-Hispanic white women. What these statistics imply is that black women have a higher likelihood of separating from husbands, but they turn these separations into divorces at a much slower pace. Perhaps their lower expectations of remarrying, which will be discussed in the next chapter, provide less motivation to obtain a legal divorce.

Figure 12.2 compares the prevalence of divorce among 13 racial-ethnic groups in the United States, according to the 1980 Census. Comparisons this fine-grained can be made only by using the computer files from the large, decennial census, and no one has yet constructed a similar chart from the 1990 or 2000 data. For women who had married for the first time 10 to 14 years prior to 1980, the bars show the percentages that had separated or divorced by the 1980 Census. As can be seen, Native Americans have the second-highest percentage of couples who had separated or divorced. To what extent this reflects their high levels of poverty versus other factors is not clear. The figure also demonstrates the great diversity of the ethnic groups often lumped together as Hispanic. Puerto Ricans

FIGURE 12.2
Percentage of women who had separated or divorced by 1980, among all women who had married for the first time 10 to 14 years earlier, by racial-ethnic group. (*Source:* Sweet & Bumpass, 1987)

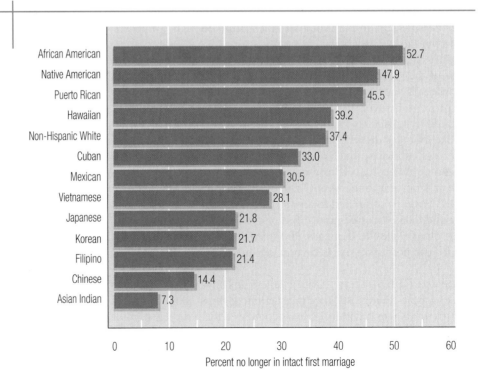

have the third-highest percentage of separated or divorced couples. Yet Cubans have a lower percentage than non-Hispanic whites, and Mexicans have a lower percentage than any other major racial-ethnic group except Asians. The Asian groups are still made up heavily of recent immigrants from countries with low divorce rates; whether they will retain their distinctively low rates of dissolution in subsequent generations remains to be seen.

Personal and Family Background The personal and family histories people bring to a marriage also matter. Since married couples who live together prior to marriage have already had, in a sense, a trial run at marriage, we might expect that they would have a lower divorce rate than couples who did not live together before marrying. Just the opposite, however, is true: Couples who cohabit have higher divorce rates (Smock & Gupta, 2002). Researchers have found that people who will not cohabit before marriage often have a stronger commitment to marriage and family life than those who will. Consider a study in which a national sample of high school seniors in 1972 was asked a series of questions about personal and family values and then was followed through 1986. Those who responded in 1972 that "finding the right person to marry and having a happy family life" was "very important" were substantially less likely to cohabit prior to marrying than

People who marry others similar to them are less likely to divorce.

those who responded that it was "not important." So were those who responded that "living close to parents and relatives" was important. Individuals who participated actively in church-related activities were also substantially less likely to cohabit prior to marrying (Waite & Gallagher, 2000). As more and more people cohabit before marriage, however, the differences in divorce between those who did and those who did not cohabit before marrying may begin to fade. Already, in the province of Quebec, where cohabitation is more common than anywhere else in North America, the divorce differential shows signs of narrowing (Le Bourdais & Juby, 2002).

A number of studies show that persons whose parents divorced while they were growing up are more likely than others to become divorced themselves (Amato, 1996; White, 1990). Yet persons who lost a parent through death while they were growing up are *not* more likely than others to become divorced (Diekmann & Engelhardt, 1999).[2] These contrasting findings suggest that more than a parent's absence must be involved, because otherwise the effect of a parental death would be the same as the effect of a parental divorce. Rather, something about growing up in a divorced family must be associated with a higher risk of divorce as an adult. One possibility is that living through a parental divorce somehow diminishes a person's ability to sustain a successful marriage. For example, children of divorce may witness more parental conflict than other children and may adopt a conflict-laden style of relating in their own marriages. A second possibility is that children in divorced families may share characteristics inherited from their parents (such as a tendency to become seriously depressed) that make a lasting marriage difficult for both generations (McGue & Lykken, 1992). But even if there were a genetic mechanism, it could not account for the nineteenth- and twentieth-century increases in the nation's divorce rate because, as noted in earlier chapters, evolutionary genetic changes occur far more slowly.

Finally, people who marry people who are similar to them are, in general, less likely to divorce, probably because the couples are more compatible in their values and interests. For example, Catholics married to Catholics and Protestants married to Protestants are both less likely to divorce than Catholics married to Protestants (Lehrer & Chiswick, 1993). People who are far apart in age also have higher divorce probabilities than people who are closer in age, particularly if it is the wife who is much older (Hall & Zhao, 1995). We don't know exactly why; it may be that a large age difference, especially if the wife is much older (which goes against the social norm), indicates that one or both of the partners had personal characteristics that made them less desirable on the marriage market.

The Process of Divorce

The unmaking of a marriage occurs in many stages over a period of time that often begins well before the couple separates and that extends well after they are granted a divorce. A number of observers of the process of divorce have attempted to describe its different aspects.[3] Here are the four major aspects.

---

[2] The association between growing up in a divorced family and being at higher risk of divorce as an adult may be weakening because growing up in a divorced family is less stigmatizing and less difficult now that divorce has become common (Wolfinger, 1999).

[3] See, for example, Bohannan (1971b). Bohannan also writes of the "community divorce" involving changes in friends and community and the "psychic divorce" involving regaining autonomy; these aspects are included elsewhere in the discussion.

THE EMOTIONAL DIVORCE

Separating from a spouse is a difficult process for nearly all the people who go through it, notwithstanding the fact that at least one spouse initiated the process and is presumably better off because of it. In instances of clear fault, such as wife battering, drunkenness, or desertion, the cause is obvious and both spouses are usually aware of it. In the many more instances in which one or both spouses are unhappy and unfulfilled, the causes are murkier, and neither spouse, at first, may be aware of the true situation. Typically, though, one person becomes dissatisfied first and begins the process of ending the marriage. Diane Vaughan, who interviewed people about the process, calls this person the **initiator** (Vaughan, 1990). The initiator has the advantages of being the first person to know that there is a chance of separation, of preparing emotionally for it, and of using the threat of leaving in order to demand change. The threat is similar to what Willard Waller, writing in the 1930s about courtship, defined as the "principal of least interest": The party that is less interested in maintaining the relationship has the advantage in bargaining (Waller, 1938).

initiator (of a divorce) the person in a marriage who first becomes dissatisfied and begins the process of ending the marriage

Early Warning Signs   The initiator begins to express discontent, but without clearly and directly stating that he or she is unhappy with the marriage. Instead, the initiator may try to change the other partner's behavior or the relationship—as by having a baby or urging the partner to change jobs or take up a new interest. One person told Vaughan:

> *Somehow I had misjudged her—who she was and what she was capable of. Maybe I thought she was someone she was not.... She needed something of her own, some friends of her own.... I encouraged her to get out in the world and get involved. (Vaughan, 1990)*

If these efforts are unsuccessful, the initiator begins to invest more energy and emotion outside the relationship. At some point, the initiator declares his or her dissatisfaction with the relationship to the partner. Only then, in many cases, does the partner realize the seriousness of the situation. The confrontation can bring about efforts by the spouses to reconcile their differences or to alter the relationship to their joint satisfaction.

> *I was very upset, hurt, crying, but at the back of my mind I thought well, maybe this too will pass if I continue to play—play, that's an interesting choice of words—play this open, warm, loving type of person, that maybe I'll get her back, still, and not be too angry or hostile at her. (Vaughan, 1990)*

Sometimes these efforts, perhaps aided by marital counseling, succeed and the separation is averted. If they fail, it is likely that the couple will separate, sometimes with the thought that it is temporary.

Separation   Often, however, the initiator has decided by that time that he or she doesn't want the marriage to continue.

> *Even at that point, at initial separation, I wasn't being honest. I knew fairly certainly that when we separated, it was for good. I let her believe that it was a means for us first finding out what's happening, and then eventually possibly getting back together. (Vaughan, 1990)*

The "temporary" separation announces the breakup to the couple's world. There may be an attempt to reconcile, but by this time the initiator's heart is usually not in it. Even if the initiator is making a good-faith effort, it may not be possible for the partner to regain a sense of trust in the initiator (Weiss, 1975). A final separation then occurs.

attachment a bonding to another person that produces feelings of security, comfort, and ease when the other person is nearby

In his studies of newly separated persons, Robert Weiss noticed the persistence of their feelings of attachment to their partners, even among initiators. **Attachment,** a concept Weiss borrows from the literature on infants, is a bonding to another person that produces feelings of security, comfort, and ease when the other person is present or nearby. Weiss found that feelings of attachment persisted for months—sometimes years after a person separated, long after feelings of anger had replaced feelings of love. The persistence of attachment caused "separation distress": The person focused his or her attention on the estranged spouse and experienced discomfort that the spouse was no longer accessible (Weiss, 1975).

Weiss estimated that it took his subjects two to four years to recover fully from the separation. The first phase of recovery—after the old pattern of life had been destroyed but before the separated person had successfully integrated a new pattern—was a time of stress, often accompanied by disorganization and depression. According to Weiss, it lasts about a year, after which time there is a longer period in which the person has put together a new pattern of life but is still vulnerable to setbacks. One man who had been the initiator of his separation told Weiss:

> *I had quite a bit of guilt over the whole thing happening, and as a result of that I was really bogged down with it. . . . I can remember the first four months of separation were just horrendous. . . . It was four months of bouncing off the walls. I couldn't eat. I couldn't sleep. I could not work. . . . And a friend of mine said, "Hey, get hold of yourself. Get some sleep." I saw a doctor who prescribed some antidepressants or something. I started to eat again, started sleeping. And then once I started eating and sleeping I started to rebuild. The first thing was my job. And then all the other things just fell into place. (Weiss, 1975)*

Eventually, most people adjust emotionally to the separation. As life moves on, people become less preoccupied with their former spouses. In fact, one study of divorced persons found that their adjustment was significantly higher when they were less preoccupied with their ex-spouses. Those who were more likely to disagree with statements such as "I can't stop thinking about my ex-spouse," "I am curious about what my ex is doing," and things "trigger thoughts about my ex-spouse" answered positively to questions about emotional well-being (Masheter, 1997).

THE LEGAL DIVORCE

Property and Assets   In addition to ending their emotional relationship, the couple must end their legal relationship. If there are no children, the separation agreement mainly specifies any continuing payments that one agrees to make to the other and divides up their property and assets. In the past, the important property, if any, has consisted of savings, homes, automobiles, and so forth. Increasingly, though, the most valuable property a person owns is intangible. This "new property," as it is sometimes called, consists of personal intangible assets, created during the marriage, from which one spouse will continue to benefit. It may include a professional license or educational credential, such as a medical school degree that allows a person to practice as a physician. Or it may include retirement benefits that one spouse has accrued for old age. As long as the couple remain married, they will share the rewards of these assets, but if they separate, only one spouse will benefit from them.

Consider a 1979 case in Kentucky, *Inman* v. *Inman.* The couple met when they were both undergraduates planning to attend medical school. After their graduations, Ms. Inman took a job as a biologist to pay for Mr. Inman's medical school expenses, with the understanding that after he received his medical degree she too would attend medical school. Instead, the couple separated a year after Mr. Inman graduated. Ms. Inman asked the court to award her compensation for her husband's medical degree, arguing that she had financed it in the expectation of joint benefits but that now the benefits would accrue only to him. The court ordered Mr. Inman to reimburse her for the costs of medical school plus inflation and interest (Weitzman, 1985). Still, there is no consensus in legal rulings about what exactly constitutes marital property, how to value it, and how to distribute it.

Although wives may request maintenance payments—known as **alimony**— from their ex-husbands, few couples now agree to it and few judges order it. As women have moved into the paid labor force, the legal system has come to assume that they can be self-supporting following a divorce, perhaps after some temporary financial assistance from the ex-husband. This assumption, however, may not hold for wives who have been out of the labor force for many years—a point I will return to shortly.

> **alimony** maintenance payments from an ex-husband to an ex-wife

Child Custody   When children are present, the legal situation is more complex. There is first the matter of custody: Who will have responsibility for the children, and where will they live? **Legal custody** refers to having the right to make important decisions about the children and to having legal responsibility for them. **Physical custody** refers to where they actually live. In the United States in the past, the two kinds of custody were usually merged; the father typically had custody in both senses prior to the mid-nineteenth century, the mother, after that. Family law throughout much of the twentieth century was based on a presumption that maternal custody was better for young children; indeed, custody was

> **legal custody (of children after a divorce)** the right to make important decisions about the children and the obligation to have legal responsibility for them

> **physical custody (of children after a divorce)** the right of a divorced spouse to have one's children live with one

After divorce, mothers typically retain custody of the children. Some noncustodial fathers take them for regularly scheduled overnight visits.

awarded to the mother in about 85 percent of the cases (Weitzman, 1985). In most states, however, that presumption has been replaced with the rule that the court should decide according to the "best interests of the child"—a standard that formally favors neither parent. Nevertheless, it is still the case today that in the majority of divorces, mothers have both legal and physical custody. (It is also the case that in a majority of divorces, fathers do not want physical custody.)

joint legal custody (of children after a divorce) the retaining by both parents of an equal right to make important decisions concerning their children

Some states are moving toward a presumption in favor of **joint legal custody,** which means that both parents retain an equal right to make important decisions concerning the children (as opposed to sole legal custody, in which one spouse can make the decisions without consulting the other) (Bartlett, 1999). A decree of joint legal custody is essentially a decree that the parents' responsibilities toward their children have not changed; despite the divorce, they both remain responsible. In California, which has led the move toward this kind of custody, two-thirds of a sample of more than 1,000 divorce cases in the mid-1980s resulted in joint legal custody. In practice, however, joint legal custody didn't mean much in this sample; legal scholar Robert Mnookin and psychologist Eleanor Maccoby found that fathers who had joint legal custody didn't see their children more often than fathers whose ex-wives had sole legal custody, nor were the fathers more involved in decisions about their children. The researchers concluded that joint legal custody is valuable mainly as a symbol of the father's continuing responsibility for his children (Maccoby & Mnookin, 1992).

joint physical custody (of children after a divorce) an arrangement whereby the children of divorced parents spend substantial time in the household of each parent

In a growing but still small number of cases, divorcing couples are agreeing to **joint physical custody,** under which the children spend substantial time in each household—perhaps alternating on a weekly basis. Joint physical custody, however, requires a great deal of cooperation between the ex-spouses, who must transport children back and forth, share clothing, coordinate schedules, and so forth. Many—perhaps most—divorcing couples cannot manage this much cooperation. To jump ahead briefly to the effects on children, the California study shows that joint physical custody can work very well for the children when the parents voluntarily choose it and can cooperate. But if the parents are still angry and warring with each other, the children tend to feel caught in the middle. For example, a parent may attempt to extract information about the private life of the ex-spouse from the children, which often causes stress and anxiety. The researchers urge judges not to impose joint physical custody on parents who don't want to undertake it (Buchanan, Maccoby, & Dornbusch, 1996).

THE COPARENTAL DIVORCE

Regardless of state laws, the reality is still that most children remain in the care of their mothers most of the time. This imbalance persists because it carries forward the typical child care situation in two-parent families—namely, the wife does most of the care. It is difficult to get fathers involved in care after the divorce because most of them were not intensively involved before. In fact, the level of contact between fathers and their children after divorce is very low. Figure 12.3 shows the amount of contact between children and their fathers, for children who were living with their mothers and whose fathers were living elsewhere. The pie charts are based on responses of the mothers of these children in the 1987–88 National Survey of Families and Households (Seltzer, 1991). More recent data are not available, and it is possible that contact with fathers has increased since then. But the basic pattern is not likely to have changed. There are separate pie charts for children

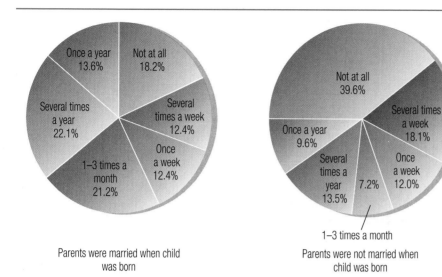

Parents were married when child was born

Parents were not married when child was born

FIGURE 12.3
Amount of contact between children and fathers, for children who were living with their mothers and whose fathers were living elsewhere, according to the National Survey of Families and Households, 1987–1988. (*Source:* Seltzer, 1991)

whose parents were married when they were born—the group of main concern in this chapter—and children whose parents were not married when they were born. About one-third of the children of previously married parents had seen their father either once in the past year or not at all. Among the children of never-married parents, the comparable figure climbed to about half. Only about one-fourth of the children of previously married parents had seen their fathers once a week or more often during the past year.

Why do so many fathers fade from their children's lives after a divorce? For some, visits to the children may be a painful reminder of the life they left behind, triggering feelings of guilt or sadness. Others may be investing their emotional energy in new families formed by remarriage. In addition, Frank Furstenberg and I have speculated that many fathers, when they were married, may have related to their children only indirectly, through their wives. They tend to see parenting and marriage as a package deal; when the wife is removed, they have difficulty connecting directly to their children (Furstenberg & Cherlin, 1991).

Even when fathers do remain involved, conflict between the parents tends to diminish over time. Still, the parents don't necessarily cooperate in rearing the children. Advocates of joint legal custody had hoped it would encourage more ex-spouses to practice **coparenting,** in which the divorced parents coordinate their activities and cooperate with each other in raising the children. Coparenting does occur, but more commonly the parents gravitate toward a more detached style: They talk as little as possible, avoid meeting each other, send messages through their children, rendezvous at restaurant parking lots to exchange them, and go about their parenting business separately. Rather than coparenting, this dominant style might be called **parallel parenting,** in recognition of the separate tracks the two parents follow in their dealings with the children (Furstenberg & Cherlin, 1991). One and a half years after they had filed for divorce, the California couples' most common style of parenting was conflicted: lots of arguments, threats, and distress (although there were many cooperative parents, too). When the parents were reinterviewed two years later, the most common style was "disengaged": little conflict and little cooperation; in short, parallel parenting (Maccoby & Mnookin, 1992).

coparenting an arrangement whereby divorced parents coordinate their activities and cooperate with each other in raising their children

parallel parenting an arrangement whereby divorced parents gravitate toward a more detached style, going about their parenting business separately

THE ECONOMIC DIVORCE

Many fathers seem to fade from their children's lives in part because they will not or cannot contribute to their children's support. Figure 12.4 displays the sad story of the child support pyramid. The figures are from a Bureau of the Census study of the 7.8 million separated, divorced, or remarried mothers who in 1999 had children under the age of 21 who were living with them and whose fathers were absent from the household. The base of the pyramid represents all these women. Moving up the pyramid, we can see that less than two-thirds had been awarded child support payments and were supposed to receive them in 1999. (Most of the rest had not been awarded child support payments for various reasons, such as inability to find the father.) Less than half had actually received any child support money in 1999. Among those who had received anything at all in 1999, the average amount was about $357 per month (U.S. Bureau of the Census, 2002d). (The situation was grimmer for the 3.7 million mothers who had never married the fathers of their children; just 27 percent had received any child support payments in 1999, and the average amount they received was about $223 per month.)

Many mothers, therefore, are hit with a financial double whammy when they divorce. First, they lose their husbands' income, which typically exceeds theirs by a substantial margin. Second, less than half receive any money in child support payments. As a result, the average mother's standard of living is reduced by about one-third in the first year after she separates from her husband. In contrast, the average father's standard of living increases somewhat, particularly if he earned most of the family income before the separation (Bianchi, Subaiya, & Kahn, 1999; McManus & DiPrete, 2001). One woman told Terry Arendell:

> *My husband really liked good food and always bought lots and the best. So when he left, it was really hard to cut the kids back.... Now there's often no food in the house, and everybody gets really grouchy when there's no food around.... We've lost $150 a month now because my husband reduced the support. It gets cut from activities—we've stopped doing everything that costs, and there's nowhere else to cut. My phone is shut off. I pay all the bills first and then see what there is for food.... I grew up playing the violin, and I'd wanted my kids to have music lessons—piano would be wonderful for them.... But lessons are out of the question. (Arendell, 1986)*

Because of situations such as these, there have been several attempts to increase the amount of child support fathers pay. (See *Families and Public Policy:* Enforcing Child Support Obligations.)

FIGURE 12.4
The child support pyramid: award and receipt of child support payments to women with children under the age of 21 living in their households who have fathers living elsewhere, 1999. (*Source:* U.S. Bureau of the Census, 2002d)

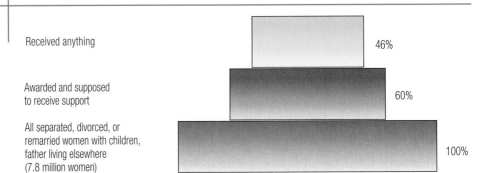

Received anything — 46%

Awarded and supposed to receive support — 60%

All separated, divorced, or remarried women with children, father living elsewhere (7.8 million women) — 100%

Enforcing Child Support Obligations

Families and Public Policy

Children in single-parent families would benefit if every absent parent knew he or she would have to pay child support. This has been the goal of several new laws that were enacted in the 1980s and 1990s. Since 1994, for example, all parents who have been ordered by the courts to pay child support have had their payments deducted automatically from their paychecks. Moreover, states are now required to adopt guidelines for the amount of child support a parent should pay, according to income and number of children; judges must follow these guidelines or state in writing why they didn't.

The 1996 welfare reform act contained a number of additional measures to strengthen the system. For instance, it provided more support for programs to establish paternity in hospitals at the birth of the children, and it penalized welfare recipients who failed to cooperate. It required employers to send the names of newly hired employees to state and federal agencies that will match the names against lists of parents who have not paid child support obligations. It allowed states to deny occupational and driver's license renewals to parents who fail to pay (U.S. Administration for Children and Families, 1996). In fact, toughening child support enforcement has been one of the most popular family policies among both conservatives and liberals. Conservatives favor tougher enforcement

because making fathers pay is consistent with their belief that parents should take responsibility for the well-being of their children. (Although the law applies equally to absent mothers who owe child support payments, in practice the vast majority of payments are collected from fathers and distributed to mothers.) The new measures send a message to fathers that they can leave their marriages, but they can't leave their children. Conservatives hope that the measures will deter men from fathering children they can't, or don't intend to, support. Liberals favor tougher measures because increased collection of child support payments will provide more economic support to children in low-income single-parent families.

There is evidence that these measures are producing results. Between 1993 and 2001, the proportion of custodial mothers who reported receiving the full amount of child support they were supposed to receive increased from 37 to 45 percent (U.S. Bureau of the Census, 2003d). However, most of the measures help middle-class single parents more than poor single parents and their children. Most middle-class fathers are employed and can make some child support payments.

Many poor fathers are not working steadily and may not be able to make the child support payments a court has or-

dered. As they fall behind, they build up an "arrearage" of back payments they owe the mothers of their children. The arrearage may get so high that a father will never be able to pay it off. In addition, child support orders and arrearages may encourage fathers to work in the underground economy—in off-the-books jobs, "hustling"—to avoid the child support system (Rich, 2001). Consequently, some experts warn that child support programs that stress enforcement of divorce decrees will not work for poor families. Rather, these experts advocate programs to increase the earnings capacity of single fathers, so that they can afford to pay child support (Meyer, 1999).

Ask Yourself

1. Do you know anyone who has had difficulty collecting court-ordered child support payments? If so, was the problem caused by the absent parent's inability to pay or simply an unwillingness to pay?

2. Besides the measures described here, what other steps could government take to improve the economic well-being of children in single-parent families?

www.mhhe.com/cherlin5

Single-Father Families   Although most single-parent families are headed by mothers, the number of single-father families has been growing rapidly. Between 1980 and 2000, the number of single fathers living with their own children under 18 more than tripled from 616,000 to 2.0 million. These families now constitute 18 percent of all single-parent families with children (U.S. Bureau of the Census, 2004a). In addition, there are hundreds of thousands of custodial fathers who have remarried and therefore are not counted in the single-father total. Single fathers tend to have higher incomes than single mothers because men's wages are typically higher than women's. However, single fathers tend to have lower incomes and less education than married fathers. A 2003 Census Bureau survey of single fathers found that 15 percent had incomes below the government poverty line (U.S. Bureau of the Census, 2003d). Yet few single fathers are granted child support awards, since most have higher incomes than their ex-wives. Nevertheless, some single fathers with low incomes may need assistance from their former wives.

About 5 percent of all children in 2003 lived in single-father families (U.S. Bureau of the Census, 2004a). Our mental image of the single-father family is the divorced dad living alone with his children. However, only one-fourth of single-father families consist of divorced men living alone with their children. Of the rest, most are sharing their households with mothers, sisters, or new girlfriends, who may be doing much of the childcare (Eggebeen, Snyder, & Manning, 1996). Yet the census counts them as "single-father families" as long as the mother of the child is not in the household.

Quick Review

- In the emotional divorce, an initiator starts the process; but even after the separation, both partners may feel separation distress.
- In the legal divorce, marital property must be divided and both legal and physical custody of children must be decided.
- Most children remain in the care of their mothers, and father involvement is highly variable.
- Mothers and the children in their custody tend to experience a decline in their standard of living after a divorce, whereas men's living standards increase somewhat.

Divorce and Children

At least one partner chooses to divorce in every case of marital disruption. Presumably, then, at least one partner's well-being is enhanced by the divorce. But children do not choose that their parents divorce. It isn't necessarily true that their well-being is enhanced by their parents' divorce. In fact, there are good reasons to think that their well-being should be, in many cases, diminished. They lose the benefit of having both of their parents living in the same household with them. They must go through an emotionally difficult process of adjusting to the breakup. Frequently, they must cope with continuing, bitter conflict between their parents. They often feel the consequences of a sharp fall in family income. Here is a description of their experiences.

THE CRISIS PERIOD

crisis period a period during the first year or two after parents separate when both the custodial parent and the children experience difficulties in dealing with the situation

Psychologists P. Lindsay Chase-Lansdale and E. Mavis Hetherington have written that the first year or two after the parents separate is a **crisis period,** a time of dramatic change during which both the custodial parent and the children—nearly all of whom are intensely upset when they learn of the separation—often experience difficulties (Chase-Lansdale & Hetherington, 1990; Hetherington & Kelly, 2002). After the breakup, the custodial parent (typically the mother) is often angry, upset, and depressed. One consequence, according to observers, is the "diminished parenting" that often occurs during the crisis period (Wallerstein & Kelly, 1980; Wallerstein, Lewis, & Blakeslee, 2000). Distracted, distressed parents may have difficulties providing

The number of single-father families has been growing.

the daily mixture of emotional support and moderate, consistent discipline that psychologists called "authoritative parenting." [➡ p. 294] Instead, parents seem to be emotionally distant and preoccupied, prone to ignore misbehavior or to lash out with harsh discipline. For example, a child misbehaves, prompting the harried, depressed parent to respond angrily. Her response can set off more negative behavior: A toy is thrown on the floor or a bowl of cereal is knocked off the table. The parent responds even more angrily, further provoking the child.

In this way, the parent and child are drawn into what Hetherington and others call "coercive cycles," in which the parent's and child's responses aggravate the situation. Hetherington found that acting-out behavior and coercive cycles are more common among boys than girls (girls show fewer outward problems, although they may be holding in feelings that will erupt years later). After a year or two, however, many custodial parents have reorganized their lives and begun to manage their anger and depression enough to provide a more supportive and structured routine for their children (Hetherington, Cox, & Cox, 1978; Hetherington & Kelly, 2002).

Moreover, as discussed earlier, the frequent decline in the family's standard of living, brought about by the withdrawal of the father's income and partial or nonexistent support payments, creates an additional source of distress for the recently separated parent and her children. In a study of families with young children, interviewed before a separation and about one year afterward, boys were showing more behavior problems in families whose incomes had dropped below the poverty line (Morrison & Cherlin, 1995). A number of studies do show that children's distress is greater during the crisis period than afterward, as parents begin to adjust to the divorce.

Several other factors are at work in making life difficult for children after the breakup, increasing the chances that they will be upset and misbehave (Amato, 2000). The situation of each child usually involves some combination of the following factors.

Loss of a Parent   Most of the early articles on the impact of divorce on children addressed the consequences of having the father leave home. Following a Freudian model, the writers theorized that a boy would have difficulty adopting the adult male role if he could not see how his father behaved and if he was not subject to his father's authority. However, there is little evidence to support this viewpoint. For example, it doesn't explain why many girls whose fathers leave home have adjustment problems. Moreover, adjustment problems are greater for children who lose a parent in the home through divorce than for those who lose a parent through death—a difference which suggests that it isn't the loss of a parent but rather the circumstances of a loss due to marital discord and disruption that affects children (Diekmann & Engelhardt, 1999; Biblarz & Gottainer, 2000). Nevertheless, many observers believe that the loss of a parent of either gender will make the tasks of the remaining parent more difficult for other reasons. For instance, if a teenager protests when a parent tells him he can't go to a party Friday night, it helps if a second parent is around to back up the first one. In other words, the tasks of monitoring and supervising the behavior of children may be more difficult if only one parent is present.

Parental Conflict   Continuing conflict between the parents harms their children's well-being, especially if the parents use the children as pawns in their battles. When parents fight, children tend to become fearful and distressed—whether the parents are married or divorced. In fact, studies show that children in two-parent families wracked by intense conflict are more depressed and show more behavior problems than children in divorced families (Amato & Booth, 1997). After the breakup, children have fewer problems if their parents can cooperate or at least engage in parallel parenting (Buchanan, Maccoby, & Dombusch, 1996; Hetherington & Kelly, 2002). For example, a study found evidence that if parents are still fighting after a divorce or separation, their sons show *more* behavior problems if they see the nonresident parent regularly than if they see him or her less often. Conversely, if there is little conflict between the parents, the sons show *fewer* behavior problems if they see the noncustodial parent regularly. (No differences were found for daughters [Amato & Rezac, 1994].)

It's important to recognize that the conflict that harms children can begin before the breakup. Divorce is not just an event that happens the day a parent moves out; rather, it is a process that typically begins much earlier. In a research project that I carried out with several collaborators, we examined the records of thousands of British and American children who had been followed from age 7 to age 11 (Cherlin et al., 1991). We focused on children whose parents had been married at the beginning of the study and watched as they split over time into two groups: those whose parents divorced and those whose parents stayed together. Not surprisingly, the children whose parents divorced were showing more behavior problems and were doing worse in school. But then we looked back to the start of the study, before anyone's parents had been divorced. We discovered that children whose parents would later divorce were *already* showing more behavior problems and doing worse in school than children whose parents would remain together. This finding suggests that some of the trauma of divorce begins before the separation, as unhappy parents begin to move apart. In addition, it suggests that the problems that children exhibit after a divorce might have occurred to some extent even if their conflicted parents had remained together.

Multiple Transitions   Apart from exposure to the parents' distress and conflict, the breakup forces children to adjust to jarring transitions. The first, of course, is the departure of a parent from the home. This is not necessarily the last transition, however. The financial settlement between the parents frequently requires that the family's house be sold. As a result, children must often move to a new neighborhood, begin classes at a new school, and make new friends. One study found that two-fifths of divorced mothers move during the first year after the divorce—a majority of them because they are forced to do so by a falling income (McLanahan, 1983). Many divorced mothers move in with their parents temporarily while they make the transition to single parenting (Goldscheider & Goldscheider, 1994).

Other adults will probably move in and out of the child's household. A majority of single parents remarry, and, as will be discussed in Chapter 13, many remarriages are preceded by a period of cohabitation. Moreover, as noted earlier, half of all children whose parents remarry will witness a second divorce before they reach age 18. More will be said about remarriage shortly; for now I will suggest that the cumulative stress of these multiple transitions may cause difficulties. A number of studies now suggest that the sheer number of transitions in family living arrangements that a child makes—how many times parents or parent-figures move in and out of the household—may cause more adjustment problems than living in any particular kind of family (Capaldi & Patterson, 1991; Wu & Martinson, 1993; Pryor & Rodgers, 2001). For instance, a large study in New Zealand found that both children whose married mothers had stayed married *and* children whose single mothers had stayed single had fewer behavioral problems than children whose mothers had changed partners (Najman et al., 1997).

Being exposed to continual conflict between their parents can harm children, whether the parents are married or divorced.

AFTER THE CRISIS PERIOD

After the crisis period, the majority of children resume normal development (Emery, 1999). Still, a study by Hetherington and W. Glenn Clingempeel found that, six years after the disruption, 20 to 25 percent of young adolescents were displaying serious behavior problems, as opposed to 10 percent of young adolescents who were still living with both parents (Hetherington & Clingempeel, 1992; Hetherington & Kelly, 2002).[4] The researchers found that the problems of some boys in the crisis period had persisted; in addition, girls were now displaying as many problems as boys. Early adolescence is a time when tension between parents and children can increase as the children try to become more independent. It is possible that this task is more difficult for children whose parents have divorced. According to the Hetherington and Clingempeel study, single mothers monitored their children's behavior less closely and engaged in more arguments with them than did married mothers. Moreover, the researchers speculated that children who are just coming to terms with their own burgeoning sexuality may have a more difficult adjustment when they must confront intimate relationships between a parent and that parent's new boy- or girlfriend or spouse.

Children can also take an active role in adjusting to their postdivorce family lives. A British study of 117 children whose parents had ended their marriages or partnerships uncovered ways in which children devised strategies to maintain relationships and to deal with physical separations from parents (Smart, Neale, & Wade, 2001.) One 10-year-old boy began an e-mail correspondence with a father who rarely visited. An 8-year-old girl described how, when on vacation with one parent, she managed feelings of missing the other parent by bringing along a photograph and sending postcards. Several children told the researchers that the divorce had increased their appreciation for their custodial parent. Through their actions, many of the children became more independent and autonomous than they otherwise would have been—"growing up a little faster," as one early observer of children and divorce put it (Weiss, 1979).

BEHAVIORAL GENETIC STUDIES

It is possible that divorce itself is just a marker for other, less observable factors that are the real causes of the seeming effects of divorce on children. One alternative explanation is that parents and children in divorced families share genetic tendencies that make it more likely that the parents will divorce *and* that the children will show behavior problems. If so, then the naïve social scientist, seeing a correlation between parental divorce and children's problems, mistakenly assumes that divorce causes the problems when in fact, both the divorce and the children's problems are the result of a genetic tendency toward, say, antisocial behavior or depression. If that's the case, we ought to see differences in the responses to divorce between people who share inherited genes and those who do not.

Researchers in the field of behavioral genetics study people of varying degrees of genetic relatedness to see whether evidence exists of possible genetic causes of behavior. One study, for example, compared the academic achievement and behavior problems of children after a divorce in two types of families (O'Connor, Caspi, DeFries, & Plomin, 2000). In the first type, the children were adopted and

---

[4] By "serious" behavior problems, I mean scores on a checklist of behavior problems that were high enough to indicate that some clinical help might be needed. See the commentary by Maccoby (1992).

therefore they shared no genes with their parents. In the second type, the children were the biological offspring of the parents. If the apparent "effects" of divorce are really the effects of common genetically based tendencies, the researchers reasoned, then the adopted children should show fewer difficulties after the divorce because they have not inherited any problematic tendencies from their adoptive parents, whereas the biological children may have. That is what they found for academic achievement: The children of adoptive parents did not show lower levels of achievement on average after divorce; but the children of biological parents did. The researchers concluded that the apparent decline in academic achievement after divorce was a selection effect [➡ p. 211] reflecting genetic relatedness rather than an effect of the divorce.

For behavior problems and substance abuse, however, the adopted children showed as many problems as the biological children. This finding, the researchers agued, suggests that divorce may truly have effects on children's behavior since the difficulties the adopted children showed cannot be due to genetic inheritance. Another behavioral genetic study with a different design also suggests that divorce may truly have effects on substance abuse and behavior problems (D'Onofrio, Turkheimer, Emery, Slutske, Health, Madden, & Matin, 2005). These researchers located pairs of twins in Australia in which one of the twins had divorced and one had not. They then compared the behavior problems of the children of the divorced twin with the problems of their cousins, the children of the nondivorced twin. If problems are driven by genes rather than divorce, they would have expected to find similarities among the cousins because they had genes in common, even though some of them had experienced a divorce and some had not. But they found that divorce made about as much difference in behavior problems among these cousins as it did among unrelated children in the same sample. So the differences among the cousins seem to have been due to something about the divorce rather than to their relatedness. Both of these studies suggest that the greater level of behavior problems shown by children after a parental divorce do not merely reflect inherited genetic tendencies.

LONG-TERM ADJUSTMENT

The Sleeper Effect   How do children of divorced parents fare over the long term? The psychologist Judith Wallerstein followed a group of such children for 25 years. Her books about their well-being after 10 years (Wallerstein & Blakeslee, 1989) and 25 years (Wallerstein, Lewis, & Blakeslee, 2000) report widespread, lasting difficulties in personal relationships. At the 25-year mark, a minority had managed to establish successful personal lives, but only with great effort. The legacy of divorce, Wallerstein claims, doesn't fade away:

> *Contrary to what we have long thought, the major impact of divorce does not occur during childhood or adolescence. Rather, it rises in adulthood as serious romantic relationships move center stage. When it comes time to choose a life mate and build a family, the effects of divorce crescendo.*

Because these young adults didn't have the chance to observe successful marriages, Wallerstein maintains, they didn't learn how to create one. Faced with the choice of a partner or a spouse, their anxiety rises; they fear repeating their parents' mistakes. Lacking a good model to follow they are more likely to make bad choices. Overall, Wallerstein states, only about half the women and one-third of the men in the group were able to establish successful personal lives by the 25-year mark.

Yet Wallerstein's study is based on just 60 families who voluntarily came to her clinic for counseling and therapy soon after a divorce. Although she screened out children who had seen a mental health professional, many of the parents had extensive psychiatric histories.[5] Troubled families can produce troubled children, whether or not the parents divorce, so blaming the divorce and its aftermath for nearly all the problems Wallerstein saw among the children over 25 years may be an overstatement.

In contrast, consider a long-term study of the effects of parental divorce on the mental health of over 10,000 British children born in 1958 (Cherlin, Chase-Lansdale, & McRae, 1998). At age 33, the mental health of persons whose parents had divorced was somewhat worse, on average, than that of persons whose parents had stayed together. However, the majority of persons from divorced families were not showing signs of serious mental health problems. In addition, some of the differences in mental health between the two groups had been visible in childhood behavior problems at age seven, before any of the parents divorced. Some of the seeming effect of divorce at age 33, then, probably reflected long-term difficulties that would have occurred even without a divorce.

In light of this British study, what can we draw from Wallerstein's research? I suggest that it is a valuable description of the lives of children from *troubled* divorced families, one that reveals what can happen to children when conflict or mental health problems accompany a divorce. And many divorcing parents do face the kinds of difficulties Wallerstein saw in her study. Moreover, her basic point that the effects of divorce can sometimes last into adulthood, or even peak in adulthood, is valid (Amato, 2000). Wallerstein was the first person to write about children who seemed fine in the short term, but experienced emotional difficulties later, in adolescence or young adulthood. In her book on the 10-year follow-up (Wallerstein & Blakeslee, 1989), she called this delayed reaction the "sleeper effect."

But the negative effects of divorce probably are not as widespread as Wallerstein claims. Some portion of what she labels as the effects of divorce on children probably weren't connected to the divorce. And the typical family that experiences divorce won't have as tough a time as Wallerstein's families did. Parents with better mental health than those in her sample can more easily avoid the worst of the anger, anxiety, and depression that comes with divorce. They are better able to maintain the children's daily routines at home or in school. And their children can more easily avoid the extremes of anxiety and self-doubt that plagued the children in Wallerstein's study.

Glass Half-Empty/Half-Full   Rather than Wallerstein's gloomy picture, the long-term view seems to encompass both a glass-half-full and a glass-half-empty perspective. When parents divorce, or when single parents raise children outside marriage, their children run a higher risk of experiencing undesirable events (such as dropping out of school) in young adulthood and beyond. Nevertheless, most children from single-parent families will not, as a consequence, experience such problems. Hetherington reported that in her 20-year study, 80 percent of the children were eventually able to adapt and become "reasonably well

---

[5] See the appendix to Wallerstein and Kelly (1980).

adjusted" (Hetherington & Kelly, 2002). This is not to say that parental divorce has no lasting effect whatsoever on most children. Even young adults who are happy and successful—college graduates with good jobs and good marriages—may nevertheless feel a sense of loss over or painful memories of childhoods spent coping with parents' divorces (Marquardt, 2005). In the terms of two psychologists they may show "distress" but not "disorder" (Laumann-Billings & Emery, 2000).

Consider studies based on national surveys by Sara McLanahan which show that, even after adjusting for parents' education, race, number of siblings, and place of residence, children who live in a single-parent family (whether with a divorced parent or a never-married parent) are more likely to drop out of high school, to have a child as a teenager, and to be "idle"—out of school and out of work (McLanahan, 1994). Her estimates imply, for instance, that 29 percent of those who grow up in single-parent families may drop out of high school compared with 13 percent of those who grow up in two-parent families. How large is this difference? On the one hand, it implies that the chance of dropping out of high school more than doubles for children from single-parent families—a substantial effect that seems worthy of concern. That's the glass-half-empty perspective. On the other hand, 7 in 10 children from single-parent families *do not* drop out of high school. That's the glass-half-full perspective.

It is possible that some of these long-term difficulties are due to the poor quality of the parents' marriages, rather than to the divorce itself. A study by Paul R. Amato and Alan Booth (1997) attempted to disentangle these two possibilities. The study began as telephone interviews with a nationally representative sample of married couples in 1980. The interviewers asked their respondents multiple questions on marital quality, including marital happiness, marital interaction (e.g., "How often do you eat your main meals together?"), marital conflict ("How many serious quarrels have you had in the past two months?"), and divorce proneness (e.g., "Has the thought of getting a divorce or separation crossed your mind in the last three years?"). The researchers divided all of the families into two groups, low conflict and high conflict, using all of the information. Then in 1992 all of the children who had lived with their parents in 1980 and who were now age 19 or older were interviewed.

The investigators report that offspring who experienced high marital conflict in 1980 were doing *better* in 1992 if their parents had divorced than if they had stayed together; on the other hand, offspring from low-conflict families were doing worse if their parents had divorced. This finding confirms the oft-stated but rarely substantiated belief that if family conflict is severe, children may benefit from a divorce. But the researchers caution that only a minority of the divorces that occurred were in high-conflict marriages (such as marriages with physical abuse or frequent serious quarrels). For that minority, the consequences of experiencing continuing conflict between their parents probably would have been worse than the consequences of the divorce. But the majority of offspring who experienced parental divorce probably would have been better off if their parents had stayed together.

Marital Happiness   Do the effects of a parental divorce carry over to an individual's own marriage? Information from the National Survey of Families and Households suggested the following picture: People whose parents divorced seemed just as happy with their marriages, on average, as did people whose parents did not divorce. However, people whose parents divorced were more likely to think that their marriages were in trouble, as if they were more sensitive to signs of marital strain. And among all people who reported their marriages as less than very happy, persons from divorced families were more likely to argue frequently and to shout or hit while arguing, as if repeating the conflictual style they may have learned or inherited from their parents (Webster, Orbuch, & House, 1995).

In Sum   Overall, the research literature on the effects of divorce on children suggests the following conclusions:

- Almost all children experience an initial period of intense emotional upset after their parents separate.
- Most resume normal development without serious problems within about two years after the separation.
- A minority of children experience some long-term problems as a result of the breakup that may persist into adulthood.

From the glass-half-empty perspective, we can conclude that divorce may cause a substantial percentage increase in the number of individuals who may need the help of a mental health professional or who may not obtain as much education as they should or who may be unemployed more often than they should. As a society, we should be troubled by this development. From the glass-half-full perspective, however, it seems that most individuals do not suffer serious long-term harm as a result of their parents' divorce. We need to keep both perspectives in mind when considering the effects of divorce.

As noted, a divorce is not the end of the changes faced by many single parents and their children. A majority of the parents will either live with another partner, marry one, or do both. The next chapter explores the determinants and consequences of remarriage. I will postpone an overall discussion of the effects of divorce until the end of that chapter.

Quick Review

- Nearly all children and parents are upset and distressed during the first year or two after the separation, sometimes called the "crisis period."
- The loss of a parent from the home, continuing parental conflict, and multiple transitions are factors that often cause difficulties for children during the crisis period.
- After the crisis period, a majority of children resume normal development, but a minority do experience continuing difficulties.
- For some children, the effects of divorce may last into or even peak in adulthood.

Looking Back

1. **What is the history of divorce in the United States and other Western nations?** There have been three eras in the history of divorce in modern Western nations. During the first era, which lasted until the middle of the nineteenth century, divorce was very difficult to obtain. It was granted mainly to wealthy men who owned land, usually to ensure that an adulterous wife would not bear a child who would have a claim on the man's property. During the second era, divorce became increasingly available in cases of reprehensible conduct, but was still frowned upon. The third era began in 1970, when the state of California eliminated the need to prove a spouse was at fault to obtain a divorce. Divorce became available on demand, with few restrictions other than a waiting period.

2. **What accounts for the trends in divorce over the past half-century?** Divorce rates rose sharply in the 1960s and 1970s. Since then the overall rate has been stable but it appears to be increasing for the least educated and decreasing for the best educated. Factors contributing to the rise in the 1960s and 1970s include: changes in divorce laws, the increased emphasis on self-fulfillment as the central criterion for judging marriages, and the growing economic independence of women. The diverging trends since then may reflect the labor market advantage of college graduates and disadvantage of those without college educations.

3. **What happens to parents during the divorce process?** A divorce begins when one spouse initiates the separation. When it occurs, both spouses typically experience great distress. Legally, couples must divide up their tangible and intangible property, and agree on custody arrangements for their children, if any. States have been moving toward joint legal custody of children; in a small but growing number of cases, parents also share physical custody. Nevertheless, many fathers see their children in-frequently after a divorce. In families in which the father does remain involved, the dominant style of parenting is a detached, low-conflict, low-cooperation mode that can be described as parallel parenting. Economically, the income of mother and children usually falls after a divorce, both because of the mother's lower wages and because many men pay little in child support.

4. **What are the short-term effects of divorce on children?** Divorce has several effects on children. First, one parent, usually the father, leaves the household, depriving the remaining parent of a source of support and help in monitoring and supervising the children's behavior. Second, during the crisis period following the separation, the custodial parent is often upset and angry; consequently, maintaining the children's daily routine and providing emotional support and consistent, moderate discipline can be difficult. In addition, the custodial parent must often cope with a substantial drop in family income. Third, the child may suffer if he or she is caught up in continuing conflict between the two parents, though the conflict and its negative effects may have preceded the separation. Finally, the sheer number of transitions involved, each requiring adjustment on the children's part, may overwhelm their ability to cope.

5. **What are the long-term effects of divorce on children?** Long-term studies suggest that parental divorce raises the risk of undesirable outcomes in their children, such as dropping out of high school, bearing a child before marrying, or suffering from mental health problems as an adult. But some of the problems that children from divorced families show probably preceded the divorce, and might have occurred even if the parents had not separated. Studies suggest that a majority of children whose parents divorce will not experience serious long-term problems.

Go to the Online Learning Center at www.mhhe.com/cherlin5 to test your knowledge of the chapter concepts and key terms.

Study Questions

1. In the era of restricted divorce, how did the rules for granting divorce reinforce male dominance?
2. How is the current era of unrestricted divorce consistent with our more individualistic approach to marriage?
3. What societywide factors were influential in the great rise in divorce rates in the 1960s and 1970s?
4. Why might wives' paid employment outside the home have two—offsetting—effects on the likelihood of divorce?
5. Why might it be difficult for divorced parents to maintain a "coparenting" style?
6. Explain the various aspects of the process of divorce for adults.
7. Why do fathers' standards of living tend to increase somewhat after a divorce?
8. Why might the "glass-half-empty/half-full" metaphor fit the effects of divorce on children?

Key Terms

alimony   419
annulment   405
attachment   418
coparenting   421
crisis period   424
era of divorce tolerance   406
era of restricted divorce   405
era of unrestricted divorce   409
initiator (of a divorce)   417
joint legal custody   420
joint physical custody   420
legal custody   419
no-fault divorce   409
parallel parenting   421
physical custody   419

Thinking about Families

The Public Family	The Private Family
Should parents in unhappy marriages stay together for the sake of their children?	Why is a divorce so emotionally difficult, even for the person who initiated it?

Families on the Internet   www.mhhe.com/cherlin5

Note: While all the URLs listed were current as of the printing of this book, these sites often change. Please check our Web site (http://www.mhhe.com/cherlin5) for updates.

There are numerous Web sites about divorce, most devoted to practical information for people who are about to divorce, in the process of obtaining a divorce, or dealing with postdivorce issues, such as modifying the legal agreement. Balanced overviews are hard to find. In addition to dispensing practical advice, www.divorceonline.com reprints many articles on divorce-related topics. See also www.divorce info.com for a sense of the issues of greatest concern to people going through a divorce.

Over the past several years, a "marriage movement" has developed among professionals and academics who believe that the benefits of marriage are underappreciated, and that too many marriages end in divorce. A key Web site is www.smartmarriages.com, which offers information about upcoming conferences, recent books and articles, and news reports. How might the resources available at this Web site help to strengthen marriages?

Remarriage and Stepfamilies

Looking Forward

1. What are the basic characteristics of remarriages and stepfamilies?

2. How can we define "family" and "kinship" in the case of stepfamilies?

3. How do stepparents, parents, and children go about building a stepfamily?

4. How does the well-being of children in stepfamilies compare to the well-being of children in other kinds of families?

5. How have increases in divorce, remarriage, and related trends altered family life?

In 1979, when Danny Henrikson was a year old, his parents divorced. Danny's mother, Nancy, was awarded custody of his eight-year-old brother, Jay; his three-year-old sister, Joie; and him. Nancy soon married James Gable, and then in 1982 she died. The children's father, Gene Henrikson, agreed that Gable would retain custody of the children. Henrikson moved from Michigan to New York and rarely visited or called his children. Gable, on the other hand, was a devoted stepfather who worked continually with Danny to overcome a learning disorder. In 1983, Jay, who was then 12, visited his father in New York. Upon his return, Jay told Gable that he wanted to live with his father. Gable consented and transferred custody of Jay to Henrikson in New York. Then, at the end of 1985, Henrikson filed a court action seeking custody of Danny and Joie.

At this point, Danny was seven and had lived in Michigan with Gable since he was one. Gable fought the transfer, arguing that it was in Danny and Joie's best interests to remain in the home where they had been, by all accounts, raised well. The trial judge ruled in Gable's favor, writing, "the length of time the children have lived in a stable, satisfactory environment and [the] desirability of maintaining continuity . . . is weighed very strongly on behalf of the Gables." Henrikson, however, appealed to a higher court. In 1987, the Michigan Court of Appeals reversed the decision and awarded custody to Henrikson. Yes, the appeals court judges wrote, an established custody arrangement shouldn't be changed unless doing so is in the best interests of the child. However, another presumption also applied:

> When the dispute is between the parent or parents and . . . a third person, it is presumed that the best interests of the child are served by awarding custody to the parent or parents. (Henrikson v. Gable, 1987)

After seven years of being Danny's dad, James Gable was not a parent, in the eyes of the court; rather, he was a "third person." Gene Henrikson, who had moved to New York and had hardly stayed in contact with Danny, was the parent. The appeals court clearly felt that the biological parents remain the legal parents, even if they have little to do with their children; whereas stepparents, even if they have raised the children since infancy, are still the legal outsiders.

■ The Incomplete Institution

Today, stepparents are still third parties—their rights and responsibilities continue to be limited (Ganong & Coleman, 2004). David Chambers, the legal scholar who unearthed the Henrikson case, notes how little standing the law gives to the relationship between stepparents and stepchildren. In most states, the stepparent has no legal obligation to contribute to the support of the stepchildren, even if he has lived with them for years and the nonresident biological parent has paid nothing. And if the stepparent and the custodial parent get divorced, the stepparent has no further obligation to support the stepchildren, even if he had been supporting them informally for years. When judges must choose between stepparents and biological parents, observes Chambers, their decisions vary widely from case to case and jurisdiction to jurisdiction:

> *The incoherent pattern of outcomes and the murky and inconsistent discussions of the governing rules almost certainly reflect our society's conflicting and unresolved attitudes about stepparents. (Chambers, 1990)*

(See *Families and Public Policy:* The Rights and Responsibilities of Stepparents, on page 440.)

The conflict and lack of resolution are even broader. A quarter of a century ago, I published an article entitled "Remarriage as an Incomplete Institution" (Cherlin, 1978). Curious about the complex families formed when divorced people remarry, I had reviewed the research literature and interviewed a number of remarried couples in Maryland. In all of them, at least one spouse had children from a previous marriage living in the household. Sometimes both did, but more often the father's children, if any, lived with his former wife. Some of the families also had a mutual child from the new marriage. What I found were people who were working hard to create a coherent family life. Every day they faced issues and problems that people in first marriages never dream of, such as, Does a stepfather have the authority to discipline his stepchild if the child does something wrong? What should a child call the woman his father married after he divorced the child's mother? Where is the "home" of a child who spends four days a week living with his father and three days living with his mother?

These daily problems often cut to the heart of more fundamental questions: What is a family, and what are its boundaries? Who is a relative and who is not? What obligations do adults and children sharing the same household owe to one another? People in first marriages rarely think about these questions because our culture provides us with a set of social roles (patterns of behavior associated with positions in society—in this case, parent, spouse, and child) and social norms (widely accepted rules about how people should behave) that address them. These roles are so ingrained that we take them for granted—we know, for example, who our relatives are; we know what a parent is. The widely accepted, taken-for-granted character of the roles and rules of family life is what makes the family a social institution. Recall that a social institution is a set of roles and rules that define a social unit of importance to society. [➡ p. 30]

But stepfamilies create situations in which the taken-for-granted rules and the well-established roles don't apply. Consequently, stepfamilies must create their own rules, their own shared meanings, through a long and sometimes difficult process of discussion, negotiation, and trial and error. In other words, as I argued in my article, life in stepfamilies is incompletely institutionalized in our society.

Families and Public Policy	The Rights and Responsibilities of Stepparents

Until recently, the legal rights and responsibilities of stepparents with regard to their stepchildren in American and English law could be summed up easily: There weren't any. Even if stepparents had resided with their stepchildren for many years, they had no obligation to support them or to care for them in any way. And even if a stepparent had provided most of the care of the stepchildren for years, the biological parent would still retain custody of the children if the marriage ended. The lowly status of the stepparent extends back hundreds of years in English common law. Under common law, a remarriage did not create any legal link between the stepchildren and their stepparent. "It was as if," British legal scholar Stephen Cretney writes, "the remarriage had never happened" (Cretney, 1993).

As noted elsewhere in this chapter, 9 in 10 remarriages are formed as a result of divorce rather than widowhood. Children typically reside with a custodial parent, usually their mother, and a stepparent, while a second biological parent resides elsewhere. Consequently, the traditional body of law gives the biological parent who resides outside the home legal priority over the stepparent who lives with the children. So sweeping is this priority that the judge in the Henrikson case was only following standard legal precedent when he gave Danny's biological father in New York custody over the objections of a stepfather who had lived with him for years.

The judge's decision stems from a time in which the custody of children was treated fundamentally as a matter of the ownership of property. For children were indeed seen as property a few centuries ago—not because they were unloved but rather because they were valuable sources of labor for a family. A man who remarried after his wife died wanted to protect his children from the claims of his new wife's family. His children were an important asset. Today, however, our conception of children has changed, and we view them primarily in terms of the emotional and financial investments parents make in them and the emotional gratification parents receive. When courts consider custody and support cases, they usually base their decisions on the standard of what is in the best interests of the child. And it is not clearly in the best interests of children to be removed from homes in which they have been given good care, even if the caregiver was not a biological parent. This is why many people find judges' decisions in cases such as *Henrikson v. Gable* troubling.

Slowly, the law concerning stepparents is changing. In England, the Children's Act of 1989 allows stepparents to assume some responsibilities and gives them the right to petition the court under a number of circumstances (Cretney, 1993). Although the stepparent does not have legal responsibility for the child, if he or she is caring for the child, he or she may do what is reasonable to promote the child's well-being. If the marriage between the parent and the stepparent ends, the stepparent may request that the children live with him or her. (The judge, of course, need not grant this request.) Should the biological parent die, the surviving biological parent has the right to take the children, as happened in the Henrikson case, but the stepparent may ask the court to let the children remain with him or her. Still, the stepparent has no recognized legal status.

In the United States, the practices of the courts seem to be evolving slowly in the direction of recognizing some rights and responsibilities for stepparents. With respect to custody, all states give biological parents priority, but about 60 percent of the states give stepparents the right to ask the court for custody (Hans, 2002). In one Ohio case, the children had been living with their biological father and their stepmother. After the father died, the court awarded custody to the stepmother, over the objections of the biological mother, ruling that the children viewed their stepmother as their mother figure and that relocating them would have "devastating" and "detrimental" effects on them (*In re Dunn*, 1992). But in general, biological parents are given custody unless there are unusual circumstances. The Montana Supreme Court, in fact, overturned a decision giving custody to a stepparent because, it said, the lower court did not have the "authority to deprive a natural parent of his or her constitutionally protected rights absent a finding of abuse and neglect or dependency" (*In re A.R.A.*, 1996).

I think it is likely that this slow evolution will continue, as parenthood comes to be defined partly in terms of what parents actually do for children, not just whether they are biologically related. This is not to say that the claims of resident stepparents should always win over the claims of biological parents living elsewhere. Yet, given the number of stepparents who are caring for children, it seems time to recognize the importance of their contribution and to provide them with some of the rights and responsibilities that until now have been reserved for biological mothers and fathers.

Ask Yourself

1. Do you know anyone who has been involved in a child custody dispute between a biological parent and a stepparent? If so, in whose favor was the dispute resolved, and on what grounds?

2. Should stepparents be given more rights and responsibilities? What might be the consequences of such a change for stepchildren? For biological parents? For society as a whole?

www.mhhe.com/cherlin5

This situation still seems to hold today. Stepparents still have few rights and obligations involving stepchildren. In many states, they still cannot sign a stepchild's field trip permission form. Should the remarriage end in divorce, the stepparent still has no responsibility to provide child support (Mason, Harrison-Jay, Svare, & Wolfinger, 2002). In a recent book about stepfathers, Marsiglio (2004) writes, "considerable confusion still exists about what norms should guide stepfamily life." The lack of shared meanings can create problems for parents, stepparents, and children. Negotiation and bargaining take time and effort and can cause bruised feelings. To be sure, stepfamilies offer the possibility of creating useful new roles that have no counterparts in first marriages (such as the trusted "intimate-outsider" roles some stepparents play—see page 453). Still, institution building is difficult work and takes its toll on stepfamilies.

There are other reasons why we might expect the tasks of family life to be more difficult for stepfamilies than for families formed by first marriages (White, 1994). In terms of social networks, individuals in stepfamilies have ties to different sets of individuals, such as biological parents living elsewhere or children living with another parent (see below). The pull that these networks exert can undermine attempts to strengthen the unity of the stepfamily. In addition, stepparents who join families well after the stepchildren were born do not have the investment of time and effort that the parent already has made; therefore, the role of stepparent may be less central to their identities. Finally, evolutionary psychologists would note that parents pass on their genes to children, whereas stepparents do not pass on genes to stepchildren (Popenoe, 1994). Therefore, they would predict that stepparents would express less warmth and support toward stepchildren, on average, than biological parents, as research on stepfamilies confirms (Hetherington & Jodl, 1994). Despite these limitations, many stepfamilies are successful. How parents and stepparents put their families together, what these families look like, and how they are changing the very nature of family and kinship are the subject of this chapter.

The Demography of Remarriage and Stepfamilies

There's nothing new about remarriage per se, but until recently most remarriages followed the death of one of the spouses. The decline in adult death rates in the twentieth century and the increase in divorce, however, have changed the balance: In the United States, 9 in 10 of all remarriages follow a divorce rather than a death (U.S. National Center for Health Statistics, 1991). Widows and widowers tend to be older persons, not parents caring for young children, and the probability of remarrying is lower for widows and widowers than it is for divorced persons. For the balance of this chapter, the term "remarriage" refers to remarriage after divorce. Because of the increase in divorce, more than 4 in 10 weddings in the United States involve a remarriage for the bride, the groom, or both (U.S. National Center for Health Statistics, 1991).

DECLINING REMARRIAGE RATES

Eighteenth-century poet and critic Samuel Johnson once said that remarriage is the triumph of hope over experience. Recently, the triumph has been occurring less often. Until the 1960s, the remarriage rate and the divorce rate went up and down in parallel—when the divorce rate increased, so did the rate of remarriage.

It seemed that divorced people weren't rejecting the ideal of being married, but were just rejecting their own first marriages and trying again. Starting in the 1960s, however, the annual rate of remarriage (the number of remarriages in a given year divided by the number of previously married persons aged 15 and older in the population) fell even though the divorce rate began to rise. The fall has continued ever since. And at current rates, about two-thirds of all divorced women will ever remarry (Bramlett & Mosher, 2002).

WHO REMARRIES?

Some divorced persons are more likely to remarry than others. Some have a greater desire to remarry. For example, one study found that women who married in their teens or early twenties are more likely to remarry than women who married later. The authors speculate that women who married young may have less experience in, and less of a preference for, living independently (Bumpass, Sweet, & Martin, 1990). Other women may be less attractive to potential spouses. Given the norm that wives should be younger than their husbands, older women face a shrinking marriage market. They are expected to marry from the diminishing pool of older single men, whereas men can choose from the expanding pool of younger women. Consequently, women who divorce at a younger age are more likely to remarry than those who divorce at an older age (Bramlett & Mosher, 2002). What is more, the greater financial independence of some older divorced women, who may be more established in their jobs, may make them less interested in remarrying.

In addition, remarriage is far more likely among non-Hispanic whites than among Hispanics or African Americans. According to one estimate, 58 percent of all divorced non-Hispanic white women will remarry within five years of their separation, compared with 44 percent of Hispanic women and 32 percent of African American women (Bramlett & Mosher, 2002). These differences occur, in part, because remarriage rates are lower for the poor than for the nonpoor. With few assets or little property to pass on to children, people with low incomes have less need for the legal protection marriage brings. Yet lower incomes don't account for the entire difference. The low remarriage rates for African Americans are also consistent with the lesser place of marriage in the African American family. Recall that fewer African Americans ever enter a first marriage and that they take longer to do so than whites. This explanation doesn't apply to Hispanics, whose rates of first marriage are more similar to those of non-Hispanic whites. It is likely that the Catholic Church's opposition to remarriage influences the behavior of this heavily Catholic group.

DIVORCE RATES AMONG THE REMARRIED

Remarriages are somewhat more likely to end in divorce than first marriages. Among women, about 39 percent of remarriages dissolve within 10 years, compared to 33 percent of first marriages (Bramlett & Mosher, 2002). Studies suggest that remarried people tend to express more criticism of spouses and to have more disagreements (Coleman, Ganong, & Fine, 2000). It may be that remarried people, all of whom have already divorced once, are more willing to resort to divorce when their marriages are unsatisfactory than are people in first marriages (Furstenberg & Spanier, 1984); or it may be that remarried people, on average, are less skilled in choosing a compatible partner or holding a marriage together (Martin & Bumpass, 1989). These explanations are another example of a selection

Remarriage rates are higher among non-Hispanic whites than among African Americans and Hispanics.

effect, [➡ p. 211] the idea that two groups differ because certain kinds of people select (or are selected into) one group more than the other. Alternatively, the greater complexity of remarriages may contribute to the higher risk of divorce. Consistent with this argument, remarriages in which stepchildren are present appear to have a higher probability of ending in divorce (Booth & Edwards, 1992).

INCREASING COHABITATION

The overall decline in remarriage, however, is deceptive. As remarriage rates have declined, cohabitation among the formerly married has increased. Consequently, the number of cohabiting couples in which at least one partner was formerly married has increased. Figure 13.1 illustrates the change. The bars on the left-hand side represent the situation around 1970. Forty-nine percent of persons had remarried within five years after they separated from their spouses. In addition, some had cohabited with a partner without marrying. When those who cohabited without remarrying are added to those who remarried, the sum is the number who were ever in a union—marital or cohabiting—within five years of separating. As can be seen, 58 percent had ever been in a union in 1970. By 1984, the pattern had changed. Only 42 percent had remarried within five years of separating, reflecting

FIGURE 13.1
Percentage who remarried within five years, and percentage who were ever in a union within five years, for persons separating around 1970 and around 1984, according to the National Survey of Families and Households. (*Source:* Bumpass, Sweet, & Cherlin, 1991)

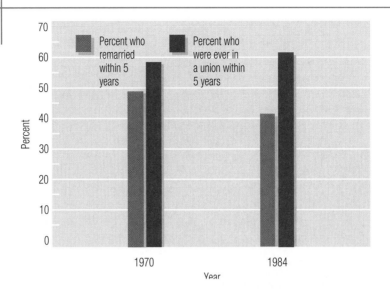

the drop in the remarriage rate. But the percentage who had ever been in a union had *increased* from its 1970 level to 62 percent in 1984. In the interim, cohabitation had become so widespread among the previously married that its increase had more than compensated for the decrease in remarriage (Bumpass, Sweet, & Cherlin, 1991). Divorced persons, in other words, are not less inclined to live with someone; rather, they have substituted cohabitation for remarriage. At least 60 percent of remarried people live with a partner—usually, but not always, their future spouse—before they remarry (Bumpass & Sweet, 1989).

In some postdivorce cohabiting relationships, children from previous marriages are present. In the past, households such as these have not been counted as stepfamilies because the potential stepparent is not married to the biological parent of the would-be stepchild. From the child's perspective, however, it may not matter whether his or her parent and live-in partner are married. In both cases, the child's relationship with his or her parent's partner is similar to that of a stepchild and stepparent. Nor may it make a difference to the child whether his or her parent was ever married previously. Suppose that a never-married woman gives birth to a child and several years later cohabits with a man other than the father. Suddenly her child must live in the same household as a man who is like a stepfather.

REDEFINING STEPFAMILIES

The rise of cohabitation among parents with children from previous relationships has led some sociologists to suggest that the definition of stepfamilies be enlarged to include cohabitation as well as remarriage. Let us, then, define a **stepfamily** as a household in which:

stepfamily a household in which two adults are married or cohabiting and at least one of the adults has a child present from a previous marriage or relationship

1. Two adults are married or cohabiting, and
2. At least one adult has a child present from a previous marriage or relationship.

This definition does not require that the adults be married. Data from the 1987–1988 National Survey of Families and Households show that under this broad definition, one-fourth of stepfamilies involved cohabiting couples rather than remarried couples. In fact, almost two-thirds of children first entered stepfamily life through cohabitation rather than marriage; in many instances, the cohabiting parent subsequently married the live-in partner (Bumpass, Raley, & Sweet, 1995).

This definition also does not require that the child's parents ever have married. It allows for the increasingly common case in which a woman gives birth to a child outside of marriage and later lives with or marries someone other than the father. This path is particularly common among African Americans: About two-thirds of African American stepfamilies, under this definition, were preceded by a nonmarital birth rather than a divorce (Bumpass et al., 1995). So this definition encompasses the kind of stepfamily, formed with little connection to marriage, that has become widespread among low-income and minority populations.

This way of conceptualizing stepfamilies is still new. Most of the research on stepfamilies has been conducted within a framework based on divorce and remarriage. In part, that is because most of the research has been conducted on middle-class families. We know little about stepfamily life among the poor and near-poor. Throughout most of this chapter, then, the discussion will pertain more to stepfamilies formed by divorce and remarriage than to stepfamilies formed by nonmarital childbearing and cohabitation.

Quick Review

- Adults and children in stepfamilies often lack established norms about how to act toward each other.
- Remarriage rates have declined in recent decades, but cohabitation among separated and divorced individuals has increased.
- Remarriage rates vary by age and by race-ethnicity.
- Remarriages are somewhat more likely to end in divorce than are first marriages.
- Stepfamilies are formed by both cohabitation and marriage.

■ The New Extended Family

Mother, father, children: These are the building blocks of the conjugal family—the family unit based on first marriage. One of the taken-for-granted aspects of family life in the Western nations is that children are born into conjugal families and that the parents and children in the conjugal family live in the same household until the children grow up. Until the last few decades, that assumption was justified. More recently, the increases in divorce, childbearing outside marriage, and remarriage have rendered it problematic. Divorce splits the conjugal family into two households—one that typically contains a custodial parent (usually the mother) and the children and a second that contains the noncustodial parent (usually the father). In the case of a nonmarital birth, the conjugal family is never even formed.

Remarriage can bring a multitude of ties across households. Consider one set of family ties studied by Anne Bernstein (1988) and diagrammed in Figure 13.2. It is centered on the marriage of Carin and Josh, who reside in household 2. They have a mutual child, Alice. Josh used to be married to Peggy, with whom he had two children, Janet and Tim, who live with Peggy in household 3. Carin used to be married to Don, with whom she had two children, Scott and Bruce, who still

FIGURE 13.2
Bruce's stepfamily.
(*Source:* Bernstein, 1988)

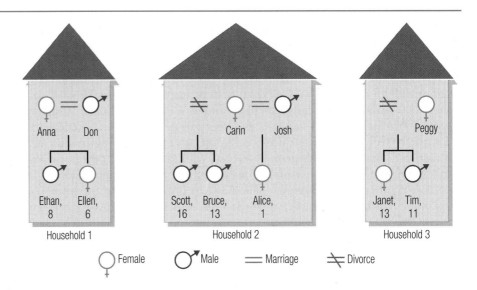

live with her. Her former husband, Don, then remarried Anna and had two more children, Ethan and Ellen, who live with Anna and him in household 1. Here is how 13-year-old Bruce described his family (you are allowed to look at the chart while reading this):

> *Tim and Janet are my stepbrother and sister. Josh is my stepdad. Carin and Don are my real parents, who are divorced. And Don married Anna and together they had Ethan and Ellen, my half-sister and -brother. And Carin married Josh and had little Alice, my half-sister. (Bernstein, 1988)*

SOME DEFINITIONS

How are we to make sense of this admixture? How many families are involved? What are their boundaries? The relationships spill over the sides of households, with children providing the links from one to the next. Let me suggest that there are two ways to define families in this context. The first is to focus on a household, even though ties extend beyond it. The advantage of this strategy is that we are used to thinking of families as being synonymous with households because we are used to thinking about first-marriage families.

Households   I have previously defined a stepfamily as a *household* that contains a parent with children from a previous union and that parent's current partner. The children from the previous union are the stepchildren, and the current partner is a stepparent. The household can be even more complex: Both partners may have children from previous unions, and they also may have a new, mutual child from the current union. But the defining criterion is that they all reside in the same household. Although there are three households in Figure 13.2, only household 2 contains a stepfamily according to our definition. Household 1 has no children from previous unions living there, and household 3 has children from a previous union and their biological parent but no current spouse or partner.

Remarriage Chains   The second way to define families is to ignore household boundaries and to focus instead on the human chains that extend from one

A stepfamily is a household in which two adults are married or are cohabiting and at least one has a child present from a previous marriage or relationship.

household to another like intertwined strands of DNA. The bonds of the chains, the forces that hold the strands together, are children from previous unions. They link a divorced woman and her new partner with her ex-husband and his new wife. Anthropologist Paul Bohannan called these pathways "divorce chains" (Bohannan, 1971a). But if our interest is the links to quasi relatives that stepfamilies bring, it is probably more accurate to refer to them as **remarriage chains,** paths that link individuals across households through the ties of disrupted unions and new unions. Bruce was describing his remarriage chain. On one end, it begins with Anna, his father's current wife, and their children, Ethan and Ellen. Bruce sees them when he goes to Anna's house to visit his father, Don. Through Don and then Bruce, the chain continues into household 2, where it comprises Bruce's brother, Scott, his mother, Carin, his stepfather, Josh, and their mutual child, Alice. In addition, Josh's children from his first marriage, Janet and Tim, are included because they come to Bruce's house to visit their father. So Bruce's chain extends from Anna to Tim. Note, however, that Bruce doesn't mention Peggy, whom he rarely sees because he has no parents to visit in Peggy's household. In contrast, if Tim were asked about his family, he would obviously include Peggy. On the other hand, he probably doesn't see anyone in household 1 very often and wouldn't include them.

In fact, if you asked the people in the figure who was in their family, you likely would get a different answer from almost every one of them. To be sure, Bruce and Scott would probably name the same chain, as would Janet and Tim, and Ethan and Ellen. Otherwise, each person has his or her own distinctive chain. Consequently, the only way to specify the members of a remarriage chain is to define it in reference to a particular person—not a household. The stepfamily household becomes a node, a switching point, that routes the chains to their various destinations.

Remarriage chains can serve as support and exchange networks, as ex-spouses and new spouses give and request favors. Family therapist Jamie Keshet describes the chain of a single mother named Marge, whose mother needed surgery. Marge

remarriage chain a path that links individuals across households through the ties of disrupted unions and new unions

wanted to spend two weeks with her mother, who lived in another state, after the surgery (all parenthetical material is in Keshet's account):

> *She called her former husband, Peter, to see if he could take the children for that time (Peter is a resource for her). Peter talked with his second wife, Jessica, and they agreed.... Jessica had two children from her first marriage. She called her ex-husband, Ron, to see if he could switch his visitation weekend so it would come after Peter's kids had gone, rather than in the middle of their stay. (Ron is a potential resource for Jessica and Peter in helping them have time alone together.) Ron agreed but found himself thinking, "I am expected to change my plans because my ex-wife's second husband's ex-wife's mother is ill." (Keshet, 1988)*

This system depends on the cooperation of all involved and can easily be disrupted. In extended-kin networks centered on conjugal families or "blood" relatives (see below), people might extend favors based on goodwill and a sense of shared purpose. In remarriage chains that sense of goodwill is limited, and decisions are more likely to be made using the calculus of self-interest. Ron is annoyed, but he will agree this time because he may need to ask Jessica for a similar favor in the future.

DOING THE WORK OF KINSHIP

Some links in the chains are weaker than others, and some fail entirely to form. When Americans think about kinship, they think about people related either through "blood" or through marriage. **Blood relatives** are people who share common ancestors: parents and children, uncles and aunts, nephews and nieces, grandparents and grandchildren. In theory, this network of blood relatives spreads out to an almost limitless number of people: second cousins (two people whose parents were first cousins), third cousins, and so forth. It spreads out on both the maternal and paternal sides, which is why anthropologists classify the Western countries as having **bilateral kinship,** a system in which descent is reckoned through both the mother's and father's lines (as opposed to kinship systems in which relatives are counted only on the mother's side or only on the father's side). Yet if I were to draw my family tree, I would include very few second cousins and no third or higher-order cousins because I don't know them. A friend of mine whose mother was estranged from her family never saw many of her maternal kin; her family tree includes many more relatives on her father's side than on her mother's side.

As these examples suggest, the mere existence of a blood tie does not make a relative. In American kinship, people must establish a relationship to consider each other kin. Having a relationship means seeing each other regularly, corresponding, and/or giving or receiving help—somehow making repeated connections. If there is no relationship, even a blood relative may not be counted as kin. Now, it's true that almost everyone considers their parents and their children to be relatives even if they haven't seen them in a long time. But you would understand what someone meant if she said, "My father left home when I was three and I never saw him again; I don't consider him part of my family." And you might not consider a cousin whom you last met when you were a child to be a relative.

To be a relative, then, you must do the work of creating and maintaining kinship. Among parents and children, this happens almost automatically—so much so that we rarely think about it. But among stepparents, it does not happen automatically. For one thing, a stepparent in a remarriage or cohabiting union that has followed a divorce or a nonmarital birth does not replace the stepchild's nonresident parent, as was the case when most remarriages followed a death. Rather, the stepparent adds to

blood relatives people who share common ancestors: parents and children, uncles and aunts, nephews and nieces, grandparents and grandchildren

bilateral kinship a system in which descent is reckoned through both the mother's and father's lines

the stepchild's stock of potential kin. If both biological parents are still involved in the stepchild's life, it's not clear what role the stepparent is supposed to play.

People think stepparents and stepchildren are more obligated to help each other the longer the relationship has lasted and the closer they feel emotionally (Ganong & Coleman, 1999). So if stepfamilies break up quickly while children are still young, an ex-stepfather isn't expected to provide support to the stepchildren. (And when the ex-stepfather is elderly, the now adult stepchildren aren't expected to provide support to him.) Where a stepfamily has existed for a long time—let's say long enough for the stepchildren to grow into young adulthood, and where the stepfather has had a close relationship with them, both are expected to continue to support each other.

There is even greater variability in how more distant stepkin relate to the stepchildren. When Frank Furstenberg and I carried out a national study of grandparents, we asked them about relationships with stepgrandchildren. The younger the children had been when the grandparents had acquired them by virtue of an adult child's remarriage, the more the grandparents reported feeling that the children were like biological grandchildren. One stepgrandmother, who had not acquired her stepgrandchildren until they were teenagers, was asked what they called her:

> *Harriett. I insisted on that. They started by calling me Mrs. Scott. . . . But from the beginning, you realize, these children were in their teens, and it was hard to accept somebody from an entirely different family, and they didn't know me from Adam. . . . Now if they were smaller—you know, younger—it would have made a difference. (Cherlin & Furstenberg, 1992)*

It also made a big difference whether the stepgrandchildren were living with the grandparents' adult children (as when a son married a woman who had custody of children from a previous marriage) or were living most of the time in another household (as when a daughter married a man whose children lived with his former wife except for every other weekend and a month in the summer). Within these constraints, the closeness of the relationship depended on how much effort the stepgrandparents and their adult children put into creating the relationship. Being a steprelative depends on doing the work of kinship.

Quick Review

- Remarriage chains link individuals—who are related by the ties of disrupted unions and new unions—across households.
- In American kinship, people must do the work of establishing and maintaining a relationship to be considered kin.

Building Stepfamilies

After a divorce, single parents and their children establish, often with some difficulty, agreed-upon rules and new daily schedules. They work out ways of relating to each other that may differ from those of earlier days. A daughter may become a special confidante to her mother; a son may assume new responsibilities, such as taking out the garbage, washing the car, and performing other tasks his father used to do. Put another way, single parents and children create a new family system.

American kinship ties spread out to a potentially large number of people through both one's mother's and one's father's sides.

Table 13.1	Relations between Stepparents and Stepchildren	
	STEPPARENT	**STEPCHILDREN**
Transitional period (first 2 to 4 years)	Goes from "affinity-seeker" or "polite outsider" to "warm friend"	Young children: Accepting of stepparent Early adolescents: May be distancing and resistant
Stabilization period (subsequent years)	Continued warmth Supportive of biological parent Avoids discipline	Accepting of stepparent (but some long-term problems with late adolescents)

Then, into that system, with its shared history, intensive relationships, and agreed-upon roles, walks a stepparent. No wonder members of the stepfamily may have difficulty adjusting to his or her presence.

There is great variation in the types of stepfamilies that are formed today. Both partners may or may not have children from previous marriages. Those children, if they exist, may be young or adolescent, and their noncustodial parent may or may not see them regularly. Finally, the couple may have biological children after they remarry—or they may not. Even within each of these categories, there is great flexibility in how family members define their roles.

Nevertheless, research is beginning to suggest some general ways in which stepparents and stepchildren tend to interact during the life course of a typical stepfamily. Table 13.1 summarizes these findings. I have labeled the first two to four years as the "transitional period," during which stepfamily members must adjust to the new family system (Bray, 1999). This is a time when parents are trying to build the stepfamily. I have labeled the subsequent years as the "stabilization period," when the new family system is firmly in place in most stepfamilies. These periods are approximate; a given stepfamily might have a shorter or longer transitional period, and some stepfamilies never stabilize.

THE TRANSITIONAL PERIOD

At the start, the stepparent is an outsider, almost an intruder into the system. At first, in what Papernow (1998) calls the "fantasy stage," the stepparent may view himself or herself naively as a healer who will nurse the wounded family back to health. But these initial efforts to help out may backfire. A stepdaughter may resent the intimacy and support a new stepfather provides to her mother; a son may not wish to relinquish certain responsibilities, such as washing the car, to a well-meaning stepfather who thinks fathers are supposed to do those chores. As Furstenberg and I wrote, "Stepparents quickly discover that they have been issued only a limited license to parent." The wiser ones among them accept the limits of their job description and bide their time (Furstenberg & Cherlin, 1991, p. 85). Stepparents who first have this fantasy soon discover that they cannot quickly become full parents to their stepchildren.

The Stepparent as Affinity-Seeker   Instead, most stepparents try to establish a more limited role. Many avoid disciplining their stepchildren and focus on being warm and friendly so that they can induce their stepchildren to begin to like them. In doing so, they become what some observers of stepfamily-building call "affinity-seekers" (Ganong & Coleman, 2004). This strategy—seeking warm, congenial relations with stepchildren—may be the best way for stepparents to establish themselves in the stepfamily. They pay attention to their stepchildren's needs and interests, endeavor to be helpful, and try to do joint activities together. At this early stage, assuming the role of disciplinarian seems to get in the way of establishing warm relationships.

The Stepparent as Polite Outsider   Other stepparents may take on the role of "polite outsider" during the early months of the stepfamily's existence (Hetherington & Stanley-Hagan, 2000). Not only do they avoid discipline but they also make fewer efforts to be friends. Rather, they adopt a more disengaged style and interact with the child less than the biological parent does (Coleman, Ganong, & Fine, 2000). They may even tone down displays of affection and support to the children. But as the family begins to adjust, the stepparent may display more warmth and support, and more actively back up the biological parent in efforts to supervise and discipline the children.

Until recently, there was no agreed-upon word by which a stepchild could call his or her stepparent. But in recent years, the use of the stepparent's first name has become increasingly common. If this usage becomes widespread, it will institutionalize the stepparent's role as neither parent nor stranger, but someone in between. That is, a child doesn't (usually) call a parent by his or her first name, nor use the first name of a stranger. Rather, the first-name usage suggests a role that is akin to that of a kindly uncle or aunt—a relative whom the child likes and can turn to for support, but not someone who has the authority to discipline the child.

Adjustment of the Stepchildren   As for the stepchildren, some show increased behavior problems in the early stage of a stepfamily (Bray, 1999). Some stepchildren also display resistance or hostility toward the stepparent, who may be surprised that his or her overtures are rejected. A key factor in how stepchildren respond is their age when the stepparent joins the household (Coleman, Ganong, & Fine, 2000.) Very young children are much more likely to consider a new stepparent a "real" parent (Marsiglio, 1992). While the evidence isn't precise enough to establish an age cutoff, I would speculate that if the stepparent arrives during the preschool years, a parentlike relationship is possible; but if the stepparent arrives in later years, that kind of relationship is much harder to establish. Still, if the stepparent arrives during the stepchild's elementary school years, the

Children making the transition to adolescence sometimes have a difficult time adjusting to a remarriage.

stepchild will probably accept the stepparent after an initial adjustment period. The outlook is especially favorable if the stepparent is a man (which is usually the case) and the stepchild a boy (Hetherington & Stanley-Hagan, 2000), because young boys seem to accept stepfathers more easily than young girls.

Research suggests that the most difficult time to start a stepfamily is when the children are in early adolescence (about ages 11 to 14). For both girls and boys, the transition to adolescence is a difficult time in which to adjust to a remarriage (Hetherington & Jodl, 1994). This is a time when children must come to terms with their own burgeoning sexuality. Having a parent's adult sexual partner move into the house—especially one for whom the traditional incest taboos do not hold—may be disconcerting.

Boundary Ambiguity   Beyond establishing stepparent-stepchild relationships, the task of the remarried couple is to create a shared conception of who is in their family and how their family is to go about its daily business. They cannot rely on generally accepted norms, as adults in first marriages do, because few norms exist. Yet it is difficult for the couple to draw a boundary around their family because of continuing ties through remarriage chains to people in other households. Their problem is a form of **boundary ambiguity**—a situation in which people are uncertain about who is in their family and what roles these people play (Boss, 1980; Ganong & Coleman, 2004). The concept extends well beyond stepfamily life—it applies, for instance, to families with a son or daughter who is missing in action during a war or to adopted children who know their birthmothers. But it is particularly apt in stepfamilies, where continuing relationships between

boundary ambiguity a situation in which people are uncertain about who is in their family and what roles these people play

stepchildren and the biological parents they don't live with can create ambiguity. Is a stepchild who lives with you every other weekend part of your family? In fact, the remarried couple may not even agree on who lives in their household and who lives elsewhere: In one national survey in which both spouses were asked about children of theirs or their partners living in their homes or elsewhere, one-fourth of the couples with stepchildren gave different answers (Stewart, 2005).

THE STABILIZATION PERIOD

Most stepfamilies come through the transition period successfully and form lasting bonds. As children emerge from early adolescence, relations with their stepparents generally improve. Even in stable stepfamilies, however, few stepparents take on a fully parentlike role. Instead, they perform a stepparent role that includes: (1) warmth toward, and support of, the stepchildren; (2) little disciplining of the stepchildren; and (3) support for the biological parent's child rearing style (Hetherington & Stanley-Hagan, 2000).

In sum, those stepparents who manage to integrate into the stepfamily successfully often play a valued role that is somewhere between that of parent and trusted friend—what one family therapist calls an **intimate outsider** role (Papernow, 1998). Teenage stepchildren, for example, may feel close enough to their stepparents to discuss with them issues that are too highly charged to discuss with their biological parents, such as sex, drugs, or their feelings about their parents' divorces. As one stepmother told Papernow:

intimate outsider a person, such as a stepparent, who plays a role in a family that is somewhere between that of a parent and that of a trusted friend

> *Mary calls me her "motherly friend." Sometimes I think of myself as her mentor. I'm the one who helped her decide she could be an architect.*
> *She confides deeply in me, and it is such an honor and a pleasure to be so intimately involved in guiding her life, and yet to be seen as someone with enough distance that she can trust me not to take what she says personally. It is worth all the struggle to have this relationship with her. (Papernow, 1988)*

Stepparents can also influence their children indirectly. In a study of 36 actively involved stepfathers in Florida, Marsiglio (2004) focuses on what he calls overlooked aspects of stepfathering. He argues that stepfathers help to build up stepchildren's "social capital"—their connections to the outside world and the resources they can draw upon. A stepfather, for example, may take the lead in talking with teachers and guidance counselors about a child's problem in school. Marsiglio also found that stepfathers sometimes become allies of the biological father in ways that help stepchildren, such as by discouraging the mother from saying negative things about the biological father in front of the children, encouraging the children to communicate with their father, and even suggesting directly to the father that he ought to keep in touch more often. Active stepfathers such as these often find that their involvement with stepchildren alters their sense of themselves, such as by deepening their sense of purpose and responsibility. They are, however, a minority. Stepfathers in general tend to invest less time and effort in their stepchildren's lives than do biological fathers. They may be focused on their marital or cohabiting relationship; they may find it difficult to find a place in the mother-child family system; or they may feel less interest in stepchildren than biological children because they are not genetically related to them (Coleman, Ganong, & Fine, 2000).

One leading researcher cautions, however, that a minority of stepchildren may be well-behaved until late adolescence or young adulthood, when they begin to

Families in Other Cultures — The Origins of the Wicked Stepmother

"It is, perhaps, too much to expect that the second wife of a working man should have the same affection toward her husband's children by a former wife as towards her own," wrote Dr. Barnardo, a nineteenth-century English philanthropist and child welfare advocate. "But case after case has come before us in which the jealousy of a stepmother has led to the most cruel treatment of the little folks committed to her charge."[1] The good doctor was repeating a charge against stepmothers that is hundreds, if not thousands, of years old. For further confirmation, just ask Cinderella or Snow White. Where did this view of stepmothers come from, and how does it relate to stepmothers today?

The prefix "step" in Old English signified a family relationship caused by death. In fact, "stepchild" originally meant "orphan," and "stepmother" can be rendered as "one who becomes a mother to an orphan." The common meaning of stepmother, however, was a woman who married a man whose wife had died. The term has long had the connotations of cruelty, neglect, and jealousy. Pliny the Elder wrote in the first century A.D., "It is far from easy to determine whether she [Nature] has proved to man a kind parent or a merciless stepmother." Leonardo da Vinci, perhaps cribbing from Pliny, asked of Nature, "wherefore art thou thus partial, becoming to some of thy children a tender and benignant mother, to others a most cruel and ruthless stepmother?" Shakespeare had the Queen say in *Cymbeline* that "you shall not find me, daughter, after the slander of most stepmothers, evil-eyed unto you."[2] Numerous fairy tales contrast the wicked, jealous stepmother to the kindly but unfortunately deceased mother.

These connotations are rooted in the reality of stepfamilies in preindustrial societies. Because of the amount of labor it took to provide food, clothes, and shelter and to raise children, a family needed two parents in order to subsist. Yet it was common for a parent to die before her or his children reached adulthood. In particular, women faced a substantial risk of dying in childbirth. If a mother of small children died, her husband had no choice but to remarry quickly. Alone, he simply could not farm the land, perform household tasks, and care for his children. If he attempted to do so, he might be risking his children's lives. Moreover, the strong patriarchal norms of preindustrial Western society discouraged him from even trying. Rather, economic necessity and social norms led him to remarry after a short period of mourning—often within several months (Mitterauer & Sieder, 1982).

Under these circumstances, the husband's remarriage choices were often limited. It was common for a second or third wife to be considerably younger than the husband; indeed, sometimes decades younger. These large age differences and the patriarchal norms sometimes led the husband to treat his second wife as if she were a child rather than a spouse (Mitterauer & Sieder, 1982). The young stepmother was relatively powerless before the older husband. In addition, she had little authority over the older children in the household, who could be roughly her age.

The stepmother's best strategy for gaining some power within the household was to bear and raise her own children. They would at least be bound to her by the

show more stress and behavior problems (Bray, 1999). This phenomenon is similar to the "sleeper effect" Wallerstein (Wallerstein, Lewis, & Blakeslee, 2000) and others have noted. It occurs at a time when children begin to establish their own identity and independence, which may require some distancing from their parents. Bray (1999) speculates that older adolescents may once again be coming to terms with their parents' divorces. Unfortunately, stepparents may react with dismay and disengage even more from their stepchildren.

DIFFERENCES BETWEEN THE ROLES OF STEPMOTHER AND STEPFATHER

During this process, being a stepmother can be harder than being a stepfather. Prior to the twentieth century, most stepmothers moved into a household in which the children's mother had died—an event for which they were sometimes blamed. (See

typical emotional bonds between mother and child. As her biological children grew, she would be able to influence their actions; and in her old age, they would be more likely to provide for her.

One could therefore imagine a stepmother's desire to advance her biological children's interests within the household and her jealousy over the advancement of her stepchildren. One could also imagine that her stepchildren would be angry at her and

The wicked stepmother is a staple of fairy tales such as Hansel and Gretel.

resent her biological children. And one could imagine the appeal of a story in which the stepmother wants her biological daughters, not her stepdaughter, to meet the prince at the ball. From household dynamics such as these, the malevolent image of the stepmother may have been formed.

Today, as noted earlier, the vast majority of remarriages are formed as a result of divorce rather than widowhood. If there are stepchildren, they probably live for most of the week with their biological mother, who, unlike the situation in the past, is still alive. The age difference between spouses in remarriages, although greater, on average, than in first marriages, is probably smaller than in the preindustrial past. Husbands and wives relate to each other as emotional equals more than in the past. The most direct route for wives to gain power in the household is not to raise loyal children but rather to work for pay outside the home. [➡ p. 270] In all these ways, stepmothers today face a situation so different from the past that perhaps we shouldn't even use the same term. In fact, the French have dropped the old, pejorative

term for stepmother, *maråre*, and replaced it with *belle-mére*, literally "fine" or "beautiful" mother, a term which also means "mother-in-law." French scholars of the family lament the absence of a prefix, such as "step," with which to precisely label relationships brought about by remarriage. But the *belles-méres* of France may be fortunate that, unlike their Anglo American counterparts, they no longer have to bear the stigma of an outmoded, archaic term.

Ask Yourself

1. Do you know anyone who fits the description of a wicked stepmother? Do you know anyone who might be described as a *belle-mére*?

2. If folktales like *Cinderella* and *Snow White* were based on real problems of the past, what kind of conflict would a modern-day children's tale describe?

[1] *Day and Night*, May 1885, p. 74. Cited in Cretney (1993).
[2] The quotations from Pliny the Elder and da Vinci are cited in Bartlett (1980). The quotation from Shakespeare is cited in Cretney (1993).

www.mhhe.com/cherlin5

Families in Other Cultures: The Origins of the Wicked Stepmother). In the typical remarriage chain today, the children live with their biological mother and a stepfather; they visit their biological father and his new wife, their stepmother. Consequently, the typical stepmother does not live with her stepchildren; rather, she must establish a relationship during the visits. She is usually dealing with children whose primary tie is to their biological mother, with whom she must compete. In contrast, stepfathers compete with noncustodial fathers, many of whom, as has been discussed, see little of their children. Moreover, in the minority of cases in which the children live with the stepmother and the biological father, other difficulties can arise. In these atypical cases, the children may have been subject to a custody battle or they may have been sent to live with the father because the mother couldn't control their behavior (Ihinger-Tallman & Pasley, 1987). And mothers who are noncustodial parents visit their children and telephone them more often than noncustodial fathers, creating competition with the stepmother (Furstenberg & Nord, 1985).

Stepfathers, in other words, can often fill a vacuum left by the departed biological father. Stepmothers must crowd into the space already occupied by the biological mother. Studies suggest that many children are able to accept two father-figures (e.g., a biological father and a stepfather) (White & Gilbreth, 2001); but it may be more difficult for them to accept two mother-figures. Moreover, stepmothers may judge themselves according to the culturally dominant view that a mother should play the major role in rearing children; if so, they may fall short of these high standards. Stepfathers, in contrast, may hold themselves to the lower standard that a father is supposed to provide support to the mother but let her do most of the hands-on child rearing. If so, they may feel satisfied with their role performance, even if they are doing less than many dissatisfied stepmothers (Keshet, 1988; Ganong & Coleman, 2004).

INCOME AND RACIAL-ETHNIC DIFFERENCES

Low-income and racial-ethnic families sometimes face a different set of issues. David Mills describes the dynamic he has seen among stepfamilies that began when an unmarried teenager bore a child. The child was often raised partly by the mother and partly by the grandmother, who may herself have given birth to the mother as a teenager. Although the families Mills studied were white, this intergenerational family system has also been noted among poor African American families (Burton, 1990). Mills found that there were frequent conflicts between the mother and the grandmother over how to raise the child. Sometime later, a stepfamily is formed when a man who is not the father of the child moves into the household as the mother's partner, or when the mother and child move in with him. In either case, this new stepfather soon faces situations in which he is urged to side with either the mother or the grandmother in their disputes about the child. If he criticizes the mother, he directly jeopardizes his relationship with her. But if he criticizes the grandmother too harshly, Mills observes, the mother may defend her and begin to reject him. Mills argues that this kind of tension makes it difficult for a stepfather to remain in an intergenerational family system for very long (Mills, 1988).

I don't want to leave the impression that stepfamily life is an interminable struggle. Most stepparents report that they are happy with their roles and their new families. After a period of adjustment, most stepchildren come to view their stepparents positively, although not quite as positively as children view their biological parents (Amato, 1999). Moreover, there is a wide variation in the roles stepparents play. For example, in the National Survey of Families and Households, stepfathers were asked to agree or disagree with the statement "A stepparent is more like a friend than a parent to stepchildren." One-third agreed, half disagreed, and the rest were neutral (Marsiglio, 1992). Stepfamilies have worked out a variety of successful ways to develop a new family life.

Quick Review

- Parents and children build a stepfamily during a transitional period of two to four years.
- Relationships solidify during a stabilization period.
- Stepmothers often face different tasks than stepfathers do.
- Stepfathers who enter low-income intergenerational families face special challenges.

The Effects of Remarriage on Children

You might think that remarriage would improve the overall well-being of children whose parents had divorced. For one thing, when a single mother remarries, her household income usually rises dramatically because men's wages are so much higher, on average, than women's wages. Consequently, if a decline in the standard of living hurts the well-being of children in single-parent families, an increase after the mother remarries should improve it. In addition, the stepparent adds a second adult to the home. He or she can provide support to the custodial parent and back up the custodial parent's monitoring and control of the children's behavior. A stepparent can also provide an adult role model for a child of the same gender.

Despite these advantages, many studies now show that the well-being of children in stepfamilies is no better, on average, than the well-being of children in divorced, single-parent households (Ganong & Coleman, 2004). To be sure, most children in stepfamilies do not demonstrate serious problems (Amato, 1994; Hetherington & Jodl, 1994). Still, both groups of children show lower levels of well-being than children in two-biological-parent families. For example, psychologists Mavis Hetherington, Glenn Clingempeel, and several collaborators studied about 200 white households, divided into three groups: nondivorced, two-parent households; divorced, single-mother households in which the mothers had been divorced for about four years, on average; and stepfamilies that had just formed (four months' average duration) and in which the wife was the biological parent and the husband the stepparent. The sample was not selected randomly but rather recruited by such means as advertisements, examining marriage records, and sending notices to community organizations. All households had at least one child between 9 and 13 years of age; these early adolescents were the main focus of the study. Households were evaluated using multiple methods, including personal interviews with the parents and children, standardized tests given to the children, and videotaped family problem-solving sessions. Evaluations were conducted three times: at the start of the study, again about a year later, and yet again another nine months later (Hetherington & Clingempeel, 1992).

BEHAVIOR PROBLEMS

At all three evaluations, the children from both the single-mother and stepfamily households were not doing as well as the children in the nondivorced households. For example, all the mothers were asked which items on a list of behavior problems applied to their early-adolescent child. Scores above a certain level on this widely used behavior problems checklist are said to indicate serious difficulties that might warrant referral to mental health professionals. Even at the last assessment, about 25 to 30 percent of the children in the single-mother and stepfamily households were above this cutoff level, as opposed to 10 percent or less of the children in nondivorced households; there was little difference between the former two groups (Maccoby, 1992).

In another research project, psychologists studied 100 stepfamilies and 100 first-marriage families, then followed most of them for three to four years (Bray, 1999). The project included extensive interviews, psychological assessments, and videotapes of family interactions. The authors reported that 20 percent of the

A parent's remarriage means a new period of adjustment for a child such as this young ring bearer, whose siblings and would-be stepmother tried to convince him to march down the aisle.

children in stepfamilies had clinically significant behavior problems, compared to 10 percent of the children in first-marriage families—results similar to those of the Hetherington and Clingempeel study.

In addition, the sheer number of family transitions might impair the adjustment of children in stepfamilies (Coleman, Ganong, & Fine, 2000). Having coped with a divorce, and possibly with the introduction of a live-in partner, these children must now cope with another major change in their family system. Some studies, as noted previously, have found a relationship between the number of family transitions a child has experienced, on the one hand, and behavior problems and subsequently bearing a child before marrying.[1] [➡ p. 427] Finally, children and parents with certain unknown personal characteristics that impair family cohesion could be self-selecting into the population of divorced and remarried families.

AGE AT LEAVING HOME

One finding about the long-term effects on children of having lived in a stepfamily is well established. Children in stepfamilies—particularly girls—leave their households at an earlier age than children in single-parent households or two-parent households (Coleman, Ganong, & Fine, 2000). They leave earlier either to marry or to establish independent households prior to marrying. An analysis of a large, six-year national study of high school students showed this pattern for girls (Goldscheider & Goldscheider, 1993). In a British study, 23-year-olds who had left their parental homes were asked the main reason why they had left. Demographer Kathleen Kiernan reported that those who had lived in stepfamilies were substantially more likely to have said that they had left due to "friction at home" than those who had not lived in stepfamilies (Kiernan, 1992). Again, the differences were greater for girls. An analysis of the National Survey of Families and Households found that girls who had lived in a stepfamily were more likely to have left home by age 19 to marry or to live independently than girls who had lived with a single parent or with two parents; the differences were much weaker for boys. If a girl had also lived with stepsiblings, her likelihood of leaving home by age 19 was even higher (Aquilino, 1991).

[1] See also Capaldi and Patterson (1991).

That tensions between stepchildren and their parents and stepparents lie behind the early home leaving is suggested by interviews in 1980 and 1983 with a national sample of currently married people. Those who had stepchildren in their households reported more family problems involving children. The authors hypothesize that one way these problems are resolved is by encouraging, or arranging for, the stepchildren to leave the household. During the three years between interviews, 51 percent of all the teenage stepchildren had left the households, compared with 35 percent of all the teenage biological children. Some may have chosen to move in with their other parent, some may have been forced to do so, and some may have left to go to school, establish their own residence, cohabit, or marry (White & Booth 1985). If this effect is indeed more pronounced for girls, it suggests that the "friction" in the household may be due to the disruption of the mother–daughter bond or to the presence of the mother's male sexual partner, whose relationship to the daughter is ambiguous.

Quick Review

- The well-being of children in stepfamilies is equivalent to that of children in divorced, single-parent households.
- The number of transitions children have experienced may impair their adjustment to stepfamilies.
- Children in stepfamilies leave home at an earlier age than children in two-biological-parent or single-parent households.

Divorce and Remarriage: Some Lessons

What can be learned from these two chapters on divorce and remarriage? The evidence we have reviewed suggests three themes. First, the emphasis on personal fulfillment, the growth of women's economic independence, and the worsening economic prospects for young men since 1973 have made marriage more fragile. There is simply less glue holding couples together than there was a half century ago. Second, divorce, remarriage, nonmarital childbearing, and cohabitation are increasing the frequency with which people create their own kinship ties out of the many possibilities available to them—rather than accepting the set of relatives that automatically come with first marriages. These efforts, like the efforts of poor people in creating sharing networks and of gay men and lesbians in constructing families of choice, are changing the nature of kinship. Third, the increases in single-parent families and stepfamilies have altered many children's lives, causing short-term distress, increasing the risk of long-term harm, but leaving the majority relatively unscathed. Let us consider the implications of the developments.

THE PRIMACY OF THE PRIVATE FAMILY

The first theme, it seems to me, is this: The transformation of divorce from a highly restricted device used by wealthy men to protect against unwanted heirs, to a frowned-upon but tolerated option for disastrous marriages, and finally to an individual right for anyone whose marriage isn't personally fulfilling, represents a triumph of the private family. The changes in divorce law mirror changes in the way marriage has been viewed. Once it was an economic partnership in which sentiment was secondary and men were the masters of their homes. The public functions of marriage were dominant: reproducing the population (which wasn't an easy task given widespread disease and poverty), educating children, preparing them for their adult roles, and caring for the ill and the elderly. This is not to say that people didn't find their marriages satisfying, but satisfaction was likely to come primarily from keeping a family alive and fed, from passing one's craft on to one's children, or from marrying a daughter into a good family.

Those days are gone. With the rise of the private family in the twentieth century, marriage is now primarily an instrument of individual fulfillment, a means of personal growth, an expression of romantic love. As such, it is much more fragile, more vulnerable to crises, than ever before (Coontz, 2005). When men and women each specialized in certain tasks and pooled their labor, their economic partnership tied them together. Now that the division of labor is less pronounced and men and women are more economically independent of each other, marriage is held together mainly by the bonds of sentiment.

It is easy to criticize the narcissistic excesses of the search for personal fulfillment in marriage. But the expansion of private life has been a great social advance. It is an advance that the standard of living of most people in our society is high enough that they need not concern themselves daily with sustenance. It is an advance that they no longer need to labor 12 hours a day on the farm or in the factory. It is an advance that they have the time to pursue gratifying intimate relationships and that they have the luxury of marrying purely for love.

The changing nature of marriage has also been an advance for women. Once unable to sever a marriage unless they were subject to terrible cruelty, women (and men) now have the ability to divorce unilaterally. This option must provide them with greater leverage against the worst excesses of husband dominance. Nor do they need to marry as much as their ancestors did. Yet the gains for women have come at a price. A half century ago, when divorce was more difficult to obtain and stigmatizing to live with, wives who specialized in rearing children could be reasonably sure that their husbands would not abandon them. It was safe for them to withdraw from the labor market and let their earning power atrophy because their husbands, according to the bargain, would have to provide for them. Today they no longer have that protection. Choosing to be a homemaker is far riskier than it was in the 1950s. Just ask any of the older, divorced women who lived up to their part of the breadwinner–homemaker bargain only to see their husbands leave them.

A central contradiction of the current era of divorce, then, is that the law assumes that husbands and wives are economic equals, when in fact they still are not. To be sure, women's wages have increased enough that life as a single parent is much more feasible than it was a few decades ago. Still, if a woman chooses to end her marriage, she must often accept a steep drop in her standard of living, like a nun taking a vow of poverty before entering an order. And if a woman chooses to stay home and raise children, she cannot count on the lifetime support of her husband.

Men, however, are not the winners in every divorce. They, too, pay a cost under the new regime. The men who have gained the most are those who care the least about their children. Divorce law allows these men to walk away from their wives and children for a modest monthly fee; sadly, many do. The men who pay the highest price are those who care the most about being a daily part of their children's lives—for they no longer have the guarantee that if they fulfill their husbandly responsibilities, their wives will remain with them. On the contrary, if their wives initiate a divorce, they know they are likely to lose custody of their children, or at best to share it.

What, then, would we expect prudent women and men to do to protect themselves in the current system of unilateral divorce? A woman would be wise to develop good labor market skills in young adulthood and to maintain a connection to the labor market throughout her child rearing years. In fact, the trends in married women's employment are consistent with this strategy. A man who cares about living with his children would be wise to spend a substantial amount of time on child rearing throughout his marriage. That way his claims to his children will be far stronger in a custody dispute, should one arise. And men are indeed doing more child rearing than their fathers did. Given the rewards and costs of the new system, we are likely to see continued investment by married women in developing job skills and careers and increased investment by men in caring for their children.

NEW KINSHIP TIES

Divorce, nonmarital childbearing, cohabitation, and remarriage are altering kinship in two fundamental ways that aren't yet fully appreciated. First, they are breaking the correspondence between family and household. Until recently, the unchallenged family unit in Western nations was the conjugal family of husband, wife, and children residing in the same household. At some points in the life cycle of the family they might have welcomed elderly parents, or young servants and apprentices, into their household. To be sure, the conjugal family members had many relatives living in other households. There was, however, a clear demarcation between the members of one's own household, who were the core of the family system, and those beyond the household's boundaries, who were the periphery. The correspondence between family and household is so deeply ingrained that we take it for granted. For example, our entire government apparatus for collecting statistics on "families" actually surveys households. The official Bureau of the Census definition of a family is two or more people living in the same household and related by blood, marriage, or adoption. It is not clear how long this definition will survive. Statistically, we may have to give up the idea that we can count families simply by knocking on doors. We may have to accept that a family can be defined only in reference to a person, not a household.

Second, the rise in divorce, nonmarital childbearing, cohabitation, and remarriage is increasing the importance of what I have called created kinship, the ties that people have to actively construct, as opposed to assigned kinship, the ties that people automatically acquire at birth or through first marriage. [➥ p. 14] In this regard, kinship after divorce and remarriage is similar to the extended kin networks among low-income and racial-ethnic populations and to the efforts of gay men and lesbians to form alternative families. In all these situations, individuals find it in their interest to build their own family ties and to create families of choice. [➥ p. 198] Being a father or a mother was once a status assigned to a person automatically at the birth of his or her child. To be sure, people have children through their own efforts; nevertheless, one does not have to do anything else to be a parent, nor can one easily resign from the post. Being a grandparent was ascribed similarly. All that is still the case when children are born to, and raised by, two married parents.

The creation of stepfamilies, though, adds a number of other potential kinship positions. Whether these positions are filled depends on the actions of the individuals

Stepfamilies are increasing the importance of created kinship-ties that people such as these stepsiblings have to actively construct.

involved. The most obvious positions are stepfather and stepmother. This chapter has described the wide variation in the roles stepparents play. Some are parent-like figures who are intensely involved with their stepchildren. Many others are more like friends or uncles and aunts. Others, particularly stepparents who don't live with their stepchildren every day, are more distant. In all cases, how much like a family member a stepparent becomes depends in large part on the effort he or she puts into developing a close relationship with stepchildren and also on the stepchild's actions. Intergenerational ties to stepgrandparents are even more dependent on individual action; they range from no contact to a kinlike role, depending in large part on the investment the stepgrandparents make.

Yet the challenge of created kinship is as follows: Kinship ties that can be created by people's actions can also be ended by lack of action. In contrast, it is much harder to end assigned kinship ties. Therefore, created kinship ties are more likely to change over the course of one's life than assigned kinship ties. Created ties may even change from year to year, as a stepparent moves into or out of the household or as contact diminishes with a stepgranddaughter who moves out of state. Just as containment within one household made families easy to spot, so, too, assignment at birth and first marriage made kinship easy to track. Now, family and kinship require new mental maps that can change from year to year. We are just beginning to draw them.

THE IMPACT ON CHILDREN

There is, finally, the important question of the effects of divorce and stepfamily life on children. I would argue that the effects are neither minor nor massive. On the one hand, the evidence suggests that most children who experience these events do not have serious, long-lasting problems because of them. Still, it must be said that we have not studied this topic long enough and intensively enough to reach a definitive conclusion. Evidence might come in over the next decade or so that changes this picture. Right now, however, the evidence suggests that divorce and stepfamily life do not inevitably scar children. On the other hand, it is clear that a minority of children do experience lasting problems that appear to be caused by divorce and remarriage. Some of these problems might have occurred even if the children's families had remained intact. Other problems, though, seem clearly linked to the disruption and its aftermath.

Let us suppose, for the sake of argument, that 10 percent of children from two-parent homes will grow up to have serious mental health problems as adults. Further, let us suppose that the prevalence of serious mental health problems is twice as high—20 percent—among children from maritally disrupted homes. A little algebra will show that if 4 in 10 children experience marital disruption (as current levels imply), the overall rate of serious mental health problems in the population would rise to 14 percent when this generation reaches adulthood.[2] An overall rise from an expected 10 percent (if there were no divorce in the population) to 14 percent may not seem like much. But it would require a 40 percent expansion of mental health facilities around the country and the training of 40 percent more mental health professionals. At current population levels, it would alter the lives of an additional three million people in each generation. It would mean that about 1 in 7, rather than 1 in 10, adults might need clinical help. In sum, it would mean a significant decline in mental health.

Consequently, even if only a minority of children will experience long-term problems, we should be troubled by this possibility. Some people might wish to work toward reducing the divorce rate, and it does appear to have declined. But we might also wish to assist divorcing parents and children. We might promote conflict-resolution strategies for divorcing couples, urge that children be kept out of conflict, and provide guidelines on how to minimize the impact of divorce. We might wish to enforce child support obligations and guarantee custodial parents a minimum benefit. We might wish to encourage support groups and services in schools. In sum, we might take whatever steps we can to reduce the negative effects of divorce and remarriage on children.

Quick Review

- The growing emphasis on personal fulfillment has made marriage more fragile.
- Newer living arrangements are increasing the frequency with which people are creating their own kinship ties.
- The changes in single-parent families have altered children's lives.

---

[2] $(.40 \times .20) + (.60 \times .10) = .14$, or 14 percent.

Looking Back

1. **What are the basic characteristics of remarriages and stepfamilies?** Remarriages that involve children from a previous marriage create situations in which well-established rules about everyday family life don't apply. Today, most remarriages occur following a divorce rather than a death. Among divorced persons, the rate of remarriage has fallen since the 1960s, but the rate of cohabitation has risen. Remarriages are somewhat more likely to end in divorce than first marriages. Though stepfamilies have traditionally been defined in terms of remarriage following a divorce, the growth of nonmarital childbearing and cohabitation suggests an expanded definition that includes households in which two adults are married or cohabiting, and at least one child from a previous marriage or relationship is present.

2. **How can we define "family" and "kinship" in the case of stepfamilies?** One way to define a family in the case of stepfamilies is to focus on a household that contains a parent, that parent's current partner, and children from a previous union. A second way is to identify remarriage chains—relationships that link individuals across households, through the ties of a disrupted union and new unions. Remarriage chains can serve as support and exchange networks, although cooperation is less assured in these chains than in other kin networks. In first marriages, the bonds of kinship among parents and children are recognized almost automatically. Stepparents and other steprelatives, in contrast, must consciously create and maintain relationships in order to be recognized as kin. There is great variation in the degree to which they succeed at becoming like kin.

3. **How do stepparents, parents, and children go about building a stepfamily?** During the transitional period, which can last two to four years or even longer, stepparents and stepchildren adjust to each other's presence.

Successful stepparents often play the roles of "affinity-seekers" or "polite outsiders." With time they often become a "warm friend" to stepchildren, a trusted and liked figure who does not discipline them or wield authority. Stepchildren need time to adjust to a remarriage and sometimes show increased behavior problems. Young children are more likely to accept a stepparent quickly; children in early adolescence, who are dealing with the changes of puberty, can be resistant to a new stepparent. In the long run, most stepchildren do adapt successfully to the addition of a stepparent to the family.

4. **How does the well-being of children in stepfamilies compare to the well-being of children in other kinds of families?** Many studies show that the well-being of children in stepfamilies is no better, on average, than the well-being of children in divorced, single-parent households. Both groups show lower levels of well-being than children in biological two-parent families. Several studies show that children in stepfamilies, especially girls, leave home earlier than children in other families.

5. **How have increases in divorce, remarriage, and related trends altered family life?** Divorce, nonmarital childbearing, cohabitation after divorce, and remarriage have altered family life in important ways. Because of the emphasis on personal fulfillment and the economic independence of women and men, marriages are now more fragile and vulnerable to crises. The nature of kinship has been altered, and the correspondence between household and family is breaking down. People are constructing new kinship ties to fit the new stepfamilies they have formed. While these new family forms cause short-term distress for many children and increase the risk of long-term harm to them, the majority of stepchildren grow up without serious long-term problems.

Go to the Online Learning Center at www.mhhe.com/cherlin5 to test your knowledge of the chapter concepts and key terms.

Study Questions

1. In what sense is remarriage an "incomplete institution"?
2. How have trends in remarriage and cohabitation rates over the past few decades reshaped the nature of stepfamilies?
3. In what ways can a stepfamily be defined?
4. How do stepparents and stepchildren decide who is related to them and who isn't?
5. What challenges do stepparents and stepchildren face in the first few years as they attempt to build a stepfamily?
6. What kind of role do stepparents settle into after the stepfamily has existed for several years?
7. What is the origin of the myth of the wicked stepmother?
8. Why isn't the well-being of children in stepfamilies better than that of children in single-parent families?
9. How concerned should we, as a society, be about the effects of divorce and remarriage on children?

Key Terms

bilateral kinship 448	boundary ambiguity 452	remarriage chain 447
blood relatives 448	intimate outsider 453	stepfamily 444

Thinking about Families

The Public Family	The Private Family
By and large, do stepfamilies do a good enough job of raising the next generation?	What are the sources of the tension that sometimes exists between stepparents and stepchildren?

Families on the Internet   www.mhhe.com/cherlin5

Note: While all the URLs listed were current as of the printing of this book, these sites often change. Please check our Web site (http://www.mhhe.com/cherlin5) for updates.

The Stepfamily Association of American is one of the oldest and most-respected stepfamily organizations. On their home page, www.saafamilies.org, you will find a link to "facts and FAQs." Keep in mind that there is more than one way to answer some of the frequently asked questions about stepfamilies. The facts and FAQs page also has links to several summaries of research findings.

The 2000 Census included, for the first time, a "stepson/stepdaughter" category. The Bureau has tabulated the information (along with information on the "adopted son/daughter" category) and released a report, available at www.census.gov/prod/2003pubs/censr-6.pdf. Because of the complexities of how the questions are answered (e.g., biological parents in stepfamilies who filled out the forms wouldn't have identified their own children as stepchildren), the numbers have limitations; but they do provide a statistical portrait of the characteristics of American stepchildren that's worth looking at.

Part Six

Family and Society

Where do all the great social changes of the twentieth century leave the institution of the family? • **Chapter 14** examines government policy toward families. We begin by studying the relationship in the past and present between the family and the state. An understanding of conservative and liberal interpretations of this relationship helps one better comprehend current political debates. We then turn to some important recent issues affecting families, such as "welfare reform." Next, we turn to two contemporary family issues. First, work–family balance: how to help employed parents manage the demands of their work and family lives. Second, marriage: whether to promote marriage and how to respond to court decisions favorable to same-sex marriage. • **Chapter 15** begins by discussing the most fundamental changes in the family in the twentieth century, the lessened economic dependence of women and the weakening of marriage. The chapter then examines changes in the nature of personal life in late modern societies. Any attempt to assess the state of the family necessarily involves the author's own interpretations. Consequently, my opinions are more prominent in Chapter 15 than in previous ones. I have tried to clearly label my opinions as such. There is no single right answer to the difficult questions posed in this chapter, and readers are encouraged to consider what they have learned from this book and to draw their own conclusions.

Chapter Fourteen

The Family, the State, and Social Policy

Looking Forward

1.   What is the "welfare state"?

2.   What are the themes that conservatives and liberals stress in debating family policies?

3.   Why was the 1996 welfare reform law a sharp break from earlier government policies toward low-income families?

4.   Should the government promote heterosexual marriage?

5.   Should same-sex marriage be allowed?

Consider two hypothetical families. In family A, a poor single mother struggles to raise two children. She receives cash assistance and food stamps from the government. When she or her children are sick, they visit the emergency room at the local hospital, where their care is paid for through Medicaid, the federal program of health insurance for the poor. She lives on the 15th floor of a publicly owned housing project that charges less for rent than she would pay if she rented an apartment privately. Her four-year-old goes to government-funded Head Start classes to learn skills that will be useful for school. It is obvious that family A receives a great deal of assistance from the government.

In family B, two employed, college-educated parents are raising two children. They are not receiving welfare, and they own their own home. It may seem as though they receive no assistance from the government, but they do. Their elderly parents in Miami Beach and Sun City receive Social Security checks, relieving family B of having to support them. Moreover, the couple deduct the interest payments for their home mortgage from their taxable income, which makes it easier for them to own a home. They receive an income tax credit for having children. They take an additional income tax credit for part of the cost of the day care center their four-year-old attends, which makes it easier for both of them to hold jobs outside the home. In addition, when Mr. B was laid off from his job as a computer programmer for three months this past year, he collected federally funded unemployment compensation.

In truth, most American families, including most middle-class families, receive substantial government assistance. It has not always been the case that most families receive assistance. In the colonial era, almost no economic assistance was provided; rather, the family was viewed as an independent entity that ought not to be interfered with—a "little commonwealth" in Demos's phrase (Demos, 1970). In fact, there was relatively little government financial assistance to families throughout the nineteenth century. In the early decades of the twentieth century, however, labor unions gained enough strength to demand higher pay, shorter hours, old-age pensions, and unemployment compensation. Moreover, civic groups led by middle-class women pressed for programs, such as pensions for widows, to assist mothers and children in poverty (Skocpol, 1992).

Then, in 1929 came the economic collapse of the Great Depression. The masses of unemployed workers looked to the government for assistance. Herbert Hoover, a Republican president who opposed most government involvement in the economy, was defeated in the 1932 election by Franklin Delano Roosevelt. Under Roosevelt, the federal government developed a number of programs to assist unemployed workers and their families. Among them was the **Social Security Act of 1935,**

Social Security Act of 1935 the federal act that created, among other provisions, Social Security, unemployment compensation, and aid to mothers with dependent children (later renamed Aid to Families with Dependent Children)

which created, among other provisions, Social Security (the system of pensions for the elderly), unemployment compensation (payments to workers who lose their jobs), and aid to mothers with dependent children. The latter program was subsequently renamed **Aid to Families with Dependent Children (AFDC).** It was the program of financial assistance to low-income, single-parent families that became commonly known as "welfare." For 61 years, AFDC was the heart of government assistance to poor mothers and children. Then in 1996 Congress passed, and President Bill Clinton signed, a bill that drastically changed the face of cash assistance to poor families. It is the ungainly named **Personal Responsibility and Work Opportunity Reconciliation Act of 1996,** which policy analysts refer to by its acronym, PRWORA.

Between the Social Security Act and PRWORA, government assistance to poor families, and programs to compensate for families' alleged limitations, expanded greatly as the following examples reveal:

- In 2002, 5.1 million people received cash assistance through Temporary Assistance for Needy Families, the program that replaced AFDC in 1996.
- In 2002, 20.2 million people received food stamps, introduced in the 1960s to reduce hunger and malnutrition.
- In 2002, 532,000 children were living in foster care, most having been removed from their homes by government caseworkers.
- In 2002, 912,000 three- to five-year-old poor children were enrolled in Head Start, a program begun in the 1960s that attempted to provide early readiness for school.

As the example of family B showed, government assistance is not limited to the poor. Consider as well the following data:

- In 2002, 29.2 million retired workers received Social Security payments, which eased their children's burden of support.
- In 2002, 8.4 million workers received unemployment compensation, enabling them to provide income to their families while looking for other jobs.
- In 2001, 6.3 million parents at all income levels deducted part of the cost of out-of-home child care from their income taxes, a subsidy that made it easier for them to work outside the home and that cost the federal government 2.7 billion dollars in lost tax revenue.
- In 2002, 37.2 million federal income tax returns deducted the interest payments on home mortgages, a subsidy to homeowners that cost the federal government $63.6 billion in lost tax revenue.[1]

This list, which could be expanded, demonstrates that the government is far more involved in supporting families economically than was the case in earlier times. Extensive federal economic support began in the twentieth century. Most government involvement is based on a concern about the well-being of children (as in the cash assistance or foster home programs) or of the elderly (as in Social Security). In other words, most government programs that affect families do so out of concern about the proper caretaking and support of dependents—people

Aid to Families with Dependent Children (AFDC) a federal program of financial assistance to low-income families, commonly known as "welfare" until it was replaced by Temporary Assistance for Needy Families (TANF) in 1996

Personal Responsibility and Work Opportunity Reconciliation Act of 1996 (PRWORA) the federal welfare legislation that requires most recipients to work within two years and that limits the amount of time a family can receive welfare

---

[1] The figures were taken from the following sources. For TANF, food stamps, Head Start, Social Security payments, and unemployment compensation: U.S. Bureau of the Census (2005l). For foster care: U.S. Administration for Children and Families (2004a). For the child care tax credit: Tax Policy Center (2006b). For mortgage interest deductions: Tax Policy Center (2006c, 2006d).

The Head Start Program, which helps young children from low-income families develop the skills they will need in school, is politically popular.

too young or too old or too ill to care for themselves. Most, therefore, reflect the perspective of the public family. [→p. 12] The great attention government pays to these issues of caretaking and dependency shows that the family is still viewed as an important source of care.

Yet many of these measures were conceived at a time when the family was different than it is today—a time when there were far fewer divorces, births outside marriage, married women working outside the home, and unmarried couples living together; a time before birth control pills allowed better control of pregnancy, before medical technology allowed fertilized eggs to be implanted in a woman's uterus, and before large numbers of gay and lesbian couples, some with children, were living openly. For example, the Social Security Act's program of aid to mothers with dependent children (the forerunner of AFDC) was originally designed to help widowed women support their children. Its designers never dreamed that, a few decades later, most of its recipients would be never-married or divorced parents.

family policy political beliefs about how the government should assist families in caring for dependents

In the wake of these changes, public support rose in the 1980s and 1990s for new laws and government policies that would assist families. **Family policy,** which I will define as political beliefs about how the government should assist families in caring for dependents, had become a major political issue. Much of the debate centered on two sets of issues: (1) how to respond to the growth of single-parent families and childhood poverty, such as by reforming welfare or by enforcing the child support obligations of absent fathers; and (2) whether, and how, to assist parents employed outside the home, such as by providing child care subsidies or work leave to care for infants or seriously ill relatives. In the presidential campaigns of the 1980s and early 1990s, "family values" was a prevalent theme. In the 1992 campaign, Bill Clinton promised to "end welfare as we know it" if he were elected. In the 2000 campaign, both candidates talked about tax cuts and other assistance to "working families," meaning working-class and middle-class families with children.

In the run-up to the 2004 campaign, the issue of marriage gained prominence after court decisions that were favorable toward same-sex marriage.

This chapter will probe these policy debates for what they reveal about the underlying themes in public discussions on the family. It will focus on the increasing public concern during the twentieth century about the family's ability to care for dependents—and on the public laws and programs that have been enacted to assist it. In order to do so, however, it is necessary first to examine more generally the often thorny relationship between the family and the state. The current debates are rooted in long-standing questions about how involved in people's family lives the government should be. More specifically, how actively should the government, through law and social policy, regulate and support the family in its care and nurturing of children, the frail elderly, and the chronically ill? And how is the government to decide what kinds of interventions are best to provide? Issues of gender roles have nearly always been central to these debates; often issues of class and race have also been important. The answers to these questions depend, in part, on ethics and morality—subjects beyond the bounds of sociology. Yet the answers also depend on social structure and social change, subjects to which a sociological inquiry can contribute.

Quick Review

- Both low-income and middle-income families receive substantial assistance from the government.
- Federal government programs of income assistance began with the Social Security Act of 1935.
- Family policy became a major political topic in the 1980s and 1990s.

The Development of the Welfare State

I will use the term **state** to mean a government that claims the right to rule a given territory and its population and to have a monopoly of force in that territory. I will use the term **nation** to refer above all to a people with shared economic and cultural interests—people who have a sense of belonging, a common bond. The countries of the world today are most accurately described by the term **nation–state,** which combines the governmental and cultural connotations of the two words it comprises. Yet most people use the simpler term "nation" rather than "nation–state" to refer to countries, and I will sometimes follow this simpler usage. The emergence of nation–states has been the central political development in the world since the late 1400s, when monarchs consolidated territories in England, France, and Spain, breaking the power of medieval lords over their lands. Today, the nation–state system, as embodied in the United Nations, is firmly entrenched throughout most of the world.

state a government that claims the right to rule a given territory and its population and to have a monopoly on force in that territory

nation a people with shared economic and cultural interests

nation–state a term that combines the governmental and cultural connotations of the two words it comprises

THE WELFARE STATE

The economic system in the Western nation–states and in most others is capitalism. [➡p. 98] It is an economic system in which goods and services are privately produced and sold on a market for profit. Workers offer their labor to the owners of the means of production, such as factories, and accept the highest offer of wages they receive. The owners then try to sell their products at a price high enough to yield a profit after they subtract the wages, rents, and other expenses they have paid. In its purest form, the ideology of capitalism argues that there should be no interference by government in the labor market or in the market for products. Beginning with Adam Smith, capitalist economic theorists have argued that the forces of the market—the interplay of the demand for and supply of goods—produce a socially optimal distribution of wages and prices. The market, in Smith's famous phrase, acts as an "invisible hand" that guides the economy toward an outcome that is the best for all (Smith, 1776).

It is but a short extension to argue that, according to capitalist economic theory, the government should not intervene in family affairs. To intervene is to disturb the workings of the invisible hand and therefore to risk doing more harm than good. For example, some critics of cash assistance to poor families argue that it discourages them from taking jobs, thereby reducing their standard of living in the long run. Yet not to intervene is to do nothing to help people in need or assist groups that might be unjustly disadvantaged in the labor market.

As noted earlier, the view that the government should not intervene in family affairs prevailed in the United States until the hardships of the Depression. Since then, the U.S. Congress has passed substantial legislation to protect workers and their families from the most harmful consequences of the labor market. In the social scientific literature on these laws and programs, authors refer to them as "social welfare" measures, and they write of the **welfare state,** by which they mean a capitalist government that has enacted numerous measures—such as Social Security, unemployment compensation, and a minimum wage—to protect workers and their families from the harshness of the capitalist system and to raise their standard of living above what wages paid in the labor market alone would do. Here the term "welfare" is used not in its common meaning of cash assistance to the poor but rather in the broader sense of the well-being of members of society. These social welfare measures expanded greatly in the 1950s and 1960s, as labor and minority groups pushed for them and as growing affluence allowed the government to raise taxes to support them.

welfare state a capitalist government that has enacted numerous measures, such as Social Security, unemployment compensation, and a minimum wage, to protect workers and their families from the harshness of the capitalist system

THE RISE AND FALL OF THE FAMILY WAGE SYSTEM

The welfare state has treated husbands and fathers differently from wives and mothers. In the terms of feminist theory, the development of the welfare state has been "gendered" (Orloff, 1993; Borchost, 2000). Beginning around the turn of the twentieth century, reformers campaigned, without much success initially, for laws that would require employers to pay male workers enough so they could support their families without wives (and children) having to work for wages. During the same period, women's organizations and labor unions campaigned, with more success, for protective legislation: laws to limit the number of hours women could work for wages to "protect" them from having to work too long and hard outside the home (Skocpol, 1992). Together, these different objectives for women and men supported the **family wage system,** a division of labor in which the husband earns enough money to support his family and the wife remains home to do housework and child care. This system is now in decline, but an examination of its development is useful for understanding the family policy debates occurring today.

The moral vision behind campaigns for the family wage system specified that the family works best when men and women inhabit separate spheres [➥p. 49]:

family wage system a division of labor in which the husband earns enough money to support his family and the wife remains home to do housework and child care

Franklin D. Roosevelt signed the landmark Social Security Act of 1935, which created the Social Security System, unemployment compensation, and aid to mothers with dependent children.

his, paid work outside the home; hers, unpaid homemaking and child rearing inside the home. This view, as has been discussed, gained in popularity in the nineteenth-century United States as industrialization moved the workplace out of the home. The family wage system was never a reality for many working-class and minority families, whose men could not earn enough to support a family. Nevertheless, it remained the dominant cultural view of the family throughout the first half of the twentieth century.

The Social Security Act of 1935 followed the division of labor implicit in the family wage system. It provided old-age pensions only to persons who "earned" them by working a certain number of years in the paid labor force; originally only industrial and commercial workers were covered. The clear expectation was that these covered workers would overwhelmingly be men. The act therefore ignored the value of the care work [➡p. 266] done by women at home. In 1939, Congress passed an extension of the act that allowed widows of Social Security recipients to receive continued benefits after their husbands died. Women whose husbands were absent for other reasons, and who were still raising children, were eligible for the Aid to Dependent Children program—but only if their income was below a certain level. Congress did not anticipate that large numbers of women raising children might need assistance because they were divorced from their husbands or had never had a husband. It did not anticipate that large numbers of women would qualify for Social Security benefits themselves by working outside the home. The system presumed that, until the death of one spouse, families would consist of a husband who would *provide* for the family and a wife who would *care* for the family.

Throughout the 1950s, the prosperous decade in which the breadwinner–homemaker family was much celebrated, the family wage system remained the cultural ideal. Beginning in the 1960s, however, it began to weaken; and by the end of the twentieth century, it had faded away. To be sure, husbands still worked for wages and wives still did the housework and child care in a minority of marriages, but the prestige and popularity of this type of marriage had greatly declined. The factor most responsible for its downfall was the enormous increase in wives working outside the home. [➡p. 260] Women worked before having children and withdrew only temporarily from the workforce when their children were young. Women who gave up paid work also risked financial hardship if their marriages ended in divorce, as more and more were doing. The rise of cohabitation and childbearing outside of marriage further challenged the dominance of the family wage system. By the 1990s, as the system lay in tatters, the family policies of both conservatives—who had strongly supported it—and of liberals had evolved beyond it. That evolution and the legislation and controversy it has engendered are the story of the rest of this chapter.

Family Policy Debates

In the aftermath of the family wage system, no dominant vision of the family has emerged. Instead family policy remains a highly contentious topic. In the mid-2000s, the most contentious issue was marriage: whether the government should promote heterosexual marriage and whether it should allow homosexual marriage—issues to which we will turn shortly. In order to understand what these issues symbolize, it helps to study the kinds of positions that conservative and liberal policymakers have taken in the recent past.

THE CONSERVATIVE VIEWPOINT

In the past, conservatives have often suggested that the family should be left alone by the government. Yet, as the earlier discussion of the Social Security Act has shown, the U.S. welfare state was constructed to support the breadwinner-homemaker family. To a large extent, its programs encouraged women to marry and men to be the main providers. For example, programs such as Social Security and unemployment compensation were designed with male recipients in mind. Full-time homemakers can accrue eligibility for Social Security only through marriage, and they cannot receive unemployment benefits. The income tax system also encourages the formation of breadwinner-homemaker marriages and discourages the formation of two-earner marriages. If a man earns $50,000 and a woman earns nothing, they will pay less in taxes if they marry than if they stay single. On the other hand, if a man and a woman each earns $25,000, they will pay more in taxes if they marry than if they stay single.

Support by conservatives for the programs and tax provisions described above demonstrates that they were not opposed to all government interventions into family life. Rather, conservatives were defending a particular set of interventions that were consistent with their vision of the family: the family wage system. The Depression-era and 1950s roots of these programs lie so far in the past that government's role can seem almost invisible. It's understandable, then, that a politician might mistakenly believe that the government has had no role in shaping the contemporary family.

In fact, conservative groups have long advocated government intervention when court rulings and legislation have undermined their vision of the family. After *Roe v. Wade*, the 1973 Supreme Court decision legalizing abortion, grass-roots conservative organizations joined with religious groups to campaign for restrictive state laws and for a constitutional amendment banning abortion. The anti-abortion forces succeeded in passing legislation that prohibited the use of federal funds for performing abortions, thus restricting poor women's ability to obtain them (Tribe, 1990). In 2003, conservatives were able to win passage of a law banning a late-term procedure opponents called a "partial-birth abortion" (Stevenson, 2003), although the law was immediately challenged in court. Abortion remains one of the most divisive issues pertaining to families. (See *Families and Public Policy:* The Abortion Dilemma.)

THE LIBERAL VIEWPOINT

Liberals, on the other hand, have often expressed a desire both to use government to assist families and to help all families equally. Actually, the kinds of measures advanced by liberals tend to help married couples in which wives are employed outside the home and single parents more than they help breadwinner-homemaker couples. This also is no coincidence. By and large, liberals, a political category in which there is a large overlap with feminists, believe that the breadwinner-homemaker family is at best no better than other family forms or at worst a form that unjustifiably restricts the autonomy of women.

In the 1980s, for example, liberals worked for the enactment of government programs that would provide employed parents with assistance in finding and paying for out-of-home care for their children. Many liberal advocates of child care legislation recommended that the government make available vouchers that low- and moderate-income parents could give to their child care providers, who in turn could exchange them for money. Also recommended were subsidies to child care providers to improve the quality of care. Women who stay home full-time to take care of their own children would receive no benefits from these vouchers or subsidies. Only in the mid-1990s, when welfare reform (see below) mandated that low-income single mothers find employment, did liberals defend the right of parents to stay home to care for their children.

In the family policy debates, liberals charged that conservatives, having set up the rules in their favor, were now saying that it's not fair to change them. Conservatives, in turn, accused liberals of feigning support for all families while pushing measures that were unfair to breadwinner-homemaker families. Conservatives asked what the justification was for new spending programs that favor one kind of family over another. Liberals replied that the current set of programs already favored one form, and they were merely trying to restore a balance. At first, these divisions led to a policy stalemate. For example in 1971, a Democratic-controlled Congress passed a comprehensive child development bill that would have established a national system of preschools for children ages three to five. But President Nixon vetoed the legislation on the grounds that it "would commit the vast moral authority of the national government to the side of communal approaches to child rearing over against the family-centered approach"—in other words, government support for child care would undermine the independent, breadwinner-homemaker family.[2]

---

[2] *Congressional Record,* December 10, 1971, pp. 46057–59. (Text of President Nixon's veto message of the Child Development Act of 1971.)

Families and Public Policy   ## The Abortion Dilemma

Abortion has been one of the most bitterly contested and divisive of issues in our society. It starkly contrasts two visions of women's roles: one that emphasizes childbearing and mothering versus one that emphasizes autonomy and employment.

From the late 1800s to the early 1970s, access to abortion was restricted in the United States, generally available only when physicians certified that it was necessary to save the life of the mother. In the 1960s, feminist groups began to demand access to abortion as a woman's right—thereby making abortion a political issue. With the fertility rate falling to about two births per woman, on average, and with life expectancy lengthening, childbearing no longer lasted most of a woman's adult life. Pro-abortion-rights activists, who prefer to be called "prochoice," sought to control the timing and numbers of the children they bore. They did so, in part, on behalf of poor women who simply wanted to limit how many children they would have. Yet the pro-choice advocates, as Kristin Luker (1984) has written, also shared a "worldview" in which women and men are equal and deserve equal opportunity to work outside the home. Legal abortions, by helping women to plan when to have children, would help them obtain equal opportunity.

Their cause was aided immensely by a 1973 Supreme Court decision, *Roe v. Wade* (1973). In this case, the Court ruled that women had the constitutional right to terminate a pregnancy by abortion during the first trimester and that in the second trimester the state may regulate access to abortion only for reasons reasonably related to the mother's health. *Roe* made abortions legal, but it also spurred the formation of a strong, national movement against abortion. The "pro-life" forces, as

Americans continue to be divided on the topic of abortion.

the anti-abortion movement came to be known, view human life as beginning at conception and therefore oppose abortion except to save the life of the mother. According to Luker (1984), they share a worldview in which women and men are fundamentally different and women's primary role is to raise children.

Abortion rights also vary by class, because the biggest victory for the pro-life forces was the passage of legislation in 1976 that prohibited the use of government funds to pay for abortions. Since most poor women receive medical care through the government program Medicaid, the law makes it difficult for them to obtain an abortion. Supporters argue that the ban on the use of public funds is morally justified because abortion is repugnant to many taxpayers. Nevertheless, the ban made abortion a class-related issue because middle-class women have an easier time finding the funds to pay for an abortion than do poor women. In a 1989 case, *Webster v. Reproductive*

Health Services (1989), a divided Court upheld some restrictions on abortion in a Missouri law. More important, the Court nearly overturned *Roe*, with four members clearly leaning in that direction. In 2002, it narrowly ruled (five to four) that states could not ban so-called partial-birth abortions (Greenhouse, 2000). However, in 2003 Congress passed a law banning this type of abortion, although the law was immediately challenged in court (Stevenson, 2003).

Public opinion remains divided. In 2004, 31 years after *Roe v. Wade*, a national sample of adults was asked, "Please tell me whether or not you think it should be possible for a pregnant woman to obtain a legal abortion if she is married and does not want any more children." Fifty-eight percent said no, and 42 percent responded yes (Davis, Smith, & Marsden, 2004). In the early years of the twenty-first century, abortion is still an issue that deeply divides Americans in ways that reflect different views of women's lives.

Quick Review

- The welfare state emerged in the twentieth century.
- At first, the welfare state supported a family wage system in which fathers were treated differently from mothers.
- The main conservative theme in family policy debates has been that the government should not intrude into family life.
- The main liberal theme is that the government should assist families.

■ Practical Compromises

Yet beginning in the late 1980s and continuing into the 1990s and early 2000s, a pragmatic consensus was often reached between conservatives and liberals that resulted in the enactment of significant legislation. In fact, Congress passed 18 pieces of legislation in the 1990s on issues as diverse as child abuse and neglect, child care, children's health insurance, child support, domestic violence, education, family and medical leave, family preservation, same-sex marriage, telecommunications, and welfare reform—evidence of both increasing concern about family issues and a greater ability to reach political agreements (Bogenschneider, 2000). The consensus is far from complete: Important differences still exist, as I will note below. But much more family-related legislation is being enacted than in the past.

THE EARNED INCOME TAX CREDIT

Perhaps the foremost example of the consensus is the expansion of the **Earned Income Tax Credit (EITC).** Introduced in 1975 but still little known except among low-income families, it cost about $42 billion in 2005, which is more that the cost of the main "welfare" program (Tax Policy Center, 2006a). The EITC provides a refundable tax credit to low-income families with children in which at least one parent is employed. Even if the family earns so little that its members owe no taxes, they still receive a check for the value of the credit from the government if they file their tax returns. Essentially, the EITC is an income subsidy for parents who earn low wages. Conservatives like it for two reasons. First, it goes only to families in which a parent is employed; in the policy jargon, it targets the "working poor," those who earn barely enough (or not enough) to stay above the poverty line. (For a family of four, benefits begin to phase out at incomes in the low $20,000s.) An unemployed single parent is not eligible. Therefore, the EITC reinforces the obligation to work. Second, it applies not only to dual-earner, two-parent families but also to breadwinner–homemaker families because a family qualifies even if only one parent works outside the home. It therefore appears neutral toward wives working outside the home.

Liberals, on their part, like the EITC because it provides income assistance to many low-income families. Liberals also realize that there are relatively few breadwinner–homemaker families among the working poor (who can't afford a stay-at-home parent), so that, in reality, most of the money goes to two-earner families and to employed single parents. Finally, liberal members of Congress in this era realized that a program of tax credits for the working poor went as far as they could convince conservatives to move with regard to income assistance. The EITC was increased several times and provides a maximum benefit of almost $4,000 to a family with two children and an income of $10,000 to $13,000.

Earned Income Tax Credit (EITC) a refundable tax credit to low-income families with children in which at least one parent is employed

Government assistance with child care costs increased in the 1990s and early 2000s.

Other programs also were enacted with bipartisan support. An important child care bill succeeded in 1990 only because a number of conservative members of Congress adopted a more pragmatic attitude than they had in the past toward women working outside the home. For instance, Republican Senator Orrin Hatch of Utah braved criticism from within his party to become a cosponsor of the child care legislation. He told his supporters that, although he might wish otherwise, women were in the labor force to stay and their children needed assistance.

THE 1996 WELFARE REFORM LAW

One piece of legislation enacted in 1996, which has become known as "welfare reform," is particularly important for the evolution of conservative and liberal views of family policy. As discussed earlier, AFDC was originally designed to support widows and their children, as part of the Social Security Act of 1935. Both AFDC and Social Security were created as entitlement programs by Congress. If a government program is an **entitlement,** the government is obligated to provide benefits to anyone who qualifies, regardless of the total cost of the program. For example, if I reach the official retirement age, walk into my local Social Security office, and ask to be signed up for benefits, they cannot say to me, "We're sorry,

entitlement a program in which the government is obligated to provide benefits to anyone who qualifies, regardless of the total cost of the program but we don't have any more money left this year. Come back next year." They *must* pay me the benefits I am entitled to. Not all government programs for low-income families are entitlements; housing subsidies, for instance, are limited: Only 19 percent of families receiving welfare benefits also received housing subsidies (or lived in publicly owned housing) in 2002 (U.S. Administration for Children and Families, 2004b). But starting in 1935, the government pledged to provide assistance through the AFDC program to any family that qualified (usually by having a low income, just one parent, and children under 18).

In 1950, Congress increased the AFDC benefit level in the hope that poor mothers would be able to stay home and care for their children. Starting about 1970, however, Congress passed a series of laws that encouraged, and later required, mothers receiving AFDC to take jobs and leave their children in the care of others. Yet "welfare" remained unpopular with the public. In a 1990 national survey, 70 percent of adults favored "reducing welfare benefits to make working for a living more attractive" (Davis, Smith, & Marsden, 2003). Bill Clinton, running against President George Bush in the 1992 election campaign, seized upon this unpopularity by promising to "end welfare as we know it." Four years later, after negotiations between President Clinton and the Republican-controlled Congress, the President signed a bill that in many ways did end welfare as we knew it. (See Table 14.1.) PRWORA, the Personal Responsibility and Work Opportunity Reconciliation Act of 1996, was a stunning rollback of policies toward poor families that had stood since 1935. First, it ended the entitlement to welfare benefits. States would be given a fixed amount of money each year—a so-called **block grant**—which they would have to match with state funds. If a state exhausted its block grant and matching funds, it could choose to turn away new applicants until the next year. (No state has yet turned anyone away.) No longer would the government guarantee to assist every poor single-parent family in need.

Second, the bill set a five-year time limit on cash assistance. People still on the rolls after five years would be cut off. States were free to set an even shorter time limit (and about 20 subsequently did). Recipients also had to accept work within two years of being on the rolls or their families would lose their benefits.

No longer could poor mothers stay home full-time to care for their children. The emphasis was on temporary assistance and on getting a job, any job. The legislation scrapped the title AFDC and renamed the time-limited cash assistance program **Temporary Assistance for Needy Families,** or **TANF.**

block grant a fixed amount of money that the federal government gives each state to spend on a set of programs

Temporary Assistance for Needy Families (TANF) a federal program of financial assistance to low-income families that began in 1996, following passage of new welfare legislation see Aid to Families with Dependent Children)

Reasons for the Policy Reversal

Reasons for the Policy Reversal   What caused such a sweeping reversal of six decades of social policy toward poor families? Three differences between the 1930s and the 1990s stand out:

1. *Attitudes toward women's roles* First, attitudes toward women's roles had changed greatly. The goal of the legislation that created AFDC was consistent with the prevailing value of the era, namely, that women's place was in the home. The legislation was an attempt to extend to poor, single mothers the same role that nonpoor mothers were supposed to play. By the 1990s, however, a majority of mothers were working outside the home. It seemed less punitive to require that poor, single mothers attempt to find jobs when the majority of middle-class mothers were employed as well. Encouraging self-reliance and independence among poor mothers seemed consistent with emerging values for nonpoor women.

2. *Characteristics of the recipients* Second, the characteristics of welfare recipients had also changed. No longer are most widowed; rather, the vast majority are separated, divorced, or never married. About 200 years ago, a distinction emerged in both American and British society between the "deserving" and "undeserving" poor (Katz, 1989). There was, and there remains, substantial public sympathy for the deserving poor, those whose poverty is seen as beyond their control. There has been much less sympathy for the undeserving poor, those whose poverty is perceived, whether fairly or not, as somehow their "fault" because they have failed to behave as society expects. Historically, the main category of "undeserving" poor had been unemployed, able-bodied men. Strong sentiment has always existed that they should be able to find jobs and be self-reliant. In contrast, as victims of their husbands' deaths, widows clearly fall among the deserving poor—their poverty is not their "fault." The situation of separated, divorced, and never-married mothers is less clear. Some observers wish to provide them with support as graciously as it is provided to widows, whereas many others do not. The latter group view the mothers—and perhaps even more so, the fathers of their children—as having chosen, in some sense, an irresponsible path to parenthood. Whether fairly or not, many Americans believe that people should refrain from having children until they can provide for them and are not willing to exempt the poor.

Moreover, there is another troubling subtext to the discourse about "deservingness." Not only the marital status but also the racial composition of the AFDC population had changed since the early days of the program. African American single-parent families are heavily overrepresented among the persistently poor [➡p. 115] and, therefore, among TANF recipients. In 2002 African Americans, who constituted 38 percent of the TANF rolls, were overrepresented compared with their percentage of the total U.S. population in 2002 (13 percent) and even compared with their percentage of the total population with incomes below the poverty line (25 percent) (U.S. Bureau of the Census, 2005l). Observers of the welfare debate have suggested that racial animosity may underlie some of the public opposition to welfare spending (Grubb & Lazerson, 1988; Quadagno, 1994). Both Heclo and Katz argue that whites in the 1960s came to identify antipoverty policy with African Americans because of the civil rights movement, the activities of welfare rights organizations, the black urban riots in Watts and northern cities, and the largely black bureaucracy that arose to administer the antipoverty programs (Heclo, 1986).

3. *Concern about "dependency"* The third reason for the policy reversal is the spread of the idea that the welfare-receiving poor had become too dependent upon public assistance. According to this line of reasoning, usually advanced by conservatives, people who receive public assistance for years and years often lose their initiative to find jobs. It is rational, they argue, for welfare recipients to stay on the rolls: If they were to take a job, they would not only lose their benefits but also incur child care, transportation, and clothing costs. Their new jobs probably wouldn't pay well and might not include health insurance (whereas AFDC/TANF recipients are covered by Medicaid). We have built a system, so this argument goes, that discourages people from moving from welfare to work (Kaus, 1992; Mead, 1992).

	AFDC	TANF
Table 14.1 Main Differences between AFDC and TANF		
Limit on government expenditures	Government expenditures are unlimited because AFDC was an *entitlement:* The government had to provide benefits to all who qualified, regardless of the cost. The federal government and the state governments each provided about half the funds.	Federal government expenses are limited because each state receives a fixed amount of funds, called a *block grant.* States may add more of their own funds to the program, but the federal government will not provide more.
Time limit on families' receipt of assistance	Families can receive benefits for an unlimited time, as long as they continue to qualify for the program.	States can use federal funds to pay for only five years of benefits for a family. States may enforce a shorter time limit if they wish. If states want to pay for more than five years of benefits, they may do so if they use only their own state funds.
Work requirements	Twenty percent of recipients were supposed to be working (usually part-time) by 1995.	Adults are required to work within 24 months after they receive assistance.

Some liberal defenders of time-unlimited welfare contested the dependency perspective. Yes, it is true, they acknowledged, that children who grow up in families that receive welfare are more likely, as adults, to receive welfare themselves (although most adults on welfare did not receive it as children [Rank & Cheng, 1995]). But this association shows only that children who grow up in poverty are more likely to be poor as adults. What's being transmitted from generation to generation, according to this line of thought, is not a "culture of poverty" (Lewis, 1965) but rather social disadvantage: Children whose parents have less education and less income are themselves less likely to graduate from high school and obtain a good job (Rank & Cheng, 1995). In other words, poverty is the illness that public policy should treat, and welfare is only the symptom. Adults on welfare don't lack initiative, it is said; rather, they lack the opportunity to find steady jobs paying wages that can sustain a family (Handler, 1995). Ending cash assistance after five years, it is argued, is a cruel step that will further impoverish many poor children and their parents.

Despite these different points of view, a Democratic president and many Democratic members of Congress joined with Republicans to enact the welfare reform law. Why did so many liberals and moderates support PRWORA? By the end of the 1980s, many liberal members of Congress had joined a new consensus that endorsed work outside the home with social support, rather than continued dependence on cash assistance, as the preferable goal for poor mothers. For one thing, they did so because so many nonpoor mothers were working outside the home. To some liberals, a program to help mothers receiving welfare obtain jobs seemed likely to increase their autonomy. In addition, many accepted the idea that persistent poverty was not just a problem of income but also of prolonged dependence on cash assistance. Finally, welfare remained deeply unpopular, and even liberal politicians were reluctant to oppose the 1996 bill, especially after it became clear that President Clinton would sign it.

With regard to gender and public policy, PRWORA also has moved conservatives and liberals close together. Although PRWORA was certainly a public policy victory for conservatives, it has undermined their claim that government should

Many former welfare recipients have taken low- and moderate-wage jobs since the welfare system was changed in 1996.

not support mothers who work outside the home. In requiring work and providing child care subsidies for TANF recipients, the Republican majority tacitly conceded that it is acceptable for the government to assist mothers who are employed. To be sure, the assistance is limited to poor, single mothers on welfare, but it will be hard for conservatives to hold the line. A number of states use PRWORA funds to subsidize child care expenses for all low- and moderate-income employed parents, whether they are on welfare or not. In discussions in the mid-2000s about renewing the welfare reform legislation, the differences between conservatives and liberals were about how much money to spend subsidizing child care for low-income women, not whether to subsidize child care.

The Effects of Welfare Reform   Welfare reform has coincided with dramatic declines in the TANF caseload and substantial increases in the employment of low-income single mothers. Between 1996 and 2004, the number of families receiving TANF declined by more than 50 percent (U.S. Bureau of the Census, 2005l). Most of the decline, however, occurred between 1996 and 2001, a period of economic prosperity. Indeed, welfare reform had the good fortune to be launched during the strongest economic boom in decades. The proportion of single mothers in the paid workforce also increased during the boom. The drop in the TANF caseload appears to have been caused by a combination of the new rules of welfare reform, the strong economy, and wage supports such as the EITC (Schoeni & Blank, 2000).

As for the impact on children in low-income families, neither the dire consequences that critics of the legislation have warned of nor the substantial benefits that some supporters hoped for have yet occurred. Instead, studies that have followed survey samples of low-income families have found that young children's well-being does not seem to change much when their mothers begin paid work or stop receiving TANF (Chase-Lansdale et al., 2003; Dunifon, Kalil, & Danziger, 2003). However, experimental studies of changes in welfare policy suggest that welfare reform could cause some declines in teenagers' well-being (Gennetian et al., 2002).

Nearly all of the research on the effects of welfare reform use information that was collected before the economic boom ended in late 2001. It is therefore difficult to disentangle the effects of welfare reform from the effects of a strong economy. Moreover, few TANF-receiving families had reached their time limits by 2001. The economic climate has been less favorable since then. It is possible that the consequences of welfare reform will be different during a time of higher unemployment and weaker economic growth. Moreover, moving off TANF or into employment could produce changes in children's behavior and cognitive development that can be seen only after several years. For these reasons, we must await the next wave of research now being conducted to confidently assess the consequences of welfare reform for parents and children.

Quick Review

- Beginning in the 1980s, conservatives and liberals were often able to reach practical compromises that led to new legislation.
- The Earned Income Tax Credit is a program that is popular with liberals and conservatives.
- PRWORA, the 1996 "welfare reform" bill, which ended entitlements and established time limits and work requirements, marked a major change in welfare policy.
- Changes in women's roles, the characteristics of recipients, and policymakers' view of "dependency" underlaid the passage of PRWORA.

▮ Current Debates

The practical consensus on family policy is far from complete. Sharp divisions still exist on a number of issues. For example, conservatives and liberals continue to disagree on the amount of help that government should provide employed parents. They also disagree on marriage. Conservatives and some moderates have supported a 2006 law that provides funds to the states for activities that promote heterosexual marriage. Liberals have questioned whether such programs are appropriate and effective. In addition, conservatives have also supported laws and constitutional amendments that would ban same-sex marriage, which is now legal in Massachusetts. Many liberals support the legalization of same-sex marriages. Let me briefly discuss the continuing debates on work-family issues and on marriage.

How much to increase government support for employed parents is a current political issue.

WORK–FAMILY ISSUES

Chapter 8 presented information about the potential conflicts employed parents feel between their work and family responsibilities: overload, spillover, and the difficulty some parents face in finding adequate child care. It discussed the movement to create a "responsive workplace" that allows workers to fulfill their family responsibilities more easily. [➡p. 280] Although most conservatives agree that government should provide support to employed parents, liberals want a much broader and more costly set of supports than conservatives. Consider parental leave. In 1993, as noted in Chapter 8 [➡p. 281], Congress enacted a law a bill requiring large employers to provide their employees with 12 weeks of unpaid leave to care for newborns or deal with other family medical emergencies. Opponents claimed it would place an unfair burden on employers, who would be required to hold open employees' jobs until they returned from parental and medical leaves. Advocates of parental leave, on the other hand, were disappointed that the leave would be unpaid. They argued that low- and moderate-income workers would not be able to afford to take an unpaid leave. The advocates noted that many European countries provide a longer leave with at least partial pay. In fact, European nations provide substantially more support to employed parents than does the United States. (See *Families in Other Cultures:* Public Opinion toward Government Assistance for Employed Parents, on pp. 488–489.)

More generally, liberal advocates maintain that the rise of the dual-earner couple has created a harried lifestyle that should be eased for the sake of parents and children. One book laid out an ambitious agenda that includes paid parental leave, responsive workplaces, a higher minimum wage, increased tax relief for parents, higher quality and more affordable child care, after-school programs, and more (Hewlett & West, 1998). Conservatives counter that the past decade or so has seen large increases in government support for working parents, such as the expansion of the EITC, and significant increases in child care funds, much of it targeted to mothers receiving TANF, who must make a transition from welfare to paid employment (Haskins, 2001). It is a debate that is likely to remain at the forefront of the family policy agenda in the near future.

MARRIAGE PROMOTION AND ITS ALTERNATIVES

Chapter 1 presented the debates between the "marriage movement" and the "diversity defenders" concerning the place of marriage in the American family system. [➡p. 5] As noted, the marriage movement favors government policies that promote marriage because it believes that marriages are the best settings in which to raise children. The diversity defenders, in contrast, urge policies that adjust to the changes in family life by providing assistance to nontraditional families as well as to married-couple families. The diversity defenders would also be more likely to support legal recognition of same-sex marriage.

Marriage Promotion   In 2006, Congress passed and President Bush signed a bill extending the welfare reform legislation. This bill included a much debated program that will provide the states with up to $150 million per year from 2006 to 2010 to promote heterosexual marriage. Many activities can receive funds, including relationship and parenting skills training for young unmarried couples; public advertising campaigns on the value of marriage; and education in high schools on the value of marriage, relationship skills, and budgeting (Center for Law and Social Policy, 2006b). Supporters, who were mainly conservative, had argued that the government should encourage low-income women and men to marry in order to ease the hardships of poverty for their children and themselves. Opponents, who were mainly liberal, argued that the government should not be promoting one kind of family over another and that, furthermore, the funds could be better spent on other needs such as providing more child care assistance or discouraging teenage pregnancy.

The debate is not just about research questions—Is it better for children to be raised with two married parents? Can single parents do as good a job if they receive more support?—but also about political and moral issues. These include the autonomy of women, the authority of men, and the wisdom of imposing a particular moral view of family life on those who choose other lifestyles. As we have seen, until the mid–twentieth century, marriage was so central to family life that its dominance was taken for granted. It was an institution in which men held considerable power, in part because of their typically greater earnings and in part because of social norms. Since midcentury, a number of options have made it possible for women to live full lives outside of marriage. Gains in the labor market provide the opportunity for an independent income, and the availability of welfare provides an income floor (although welfare reform now limits reliance on that floor to five years). The birth control pill allows for sexual activity without unwanted pregnancies, and the greater acceptability of raising a child outside of marriage allows single women to have the children they want. At the same time, the economic fortunes of men without college educations have diminished, reducing the economic benefits of marriage to women. All told, paths to parenthood and childrearing other than long-term marriage are now more feasible and more attractive.

Feminists fought for the gains in autonomy that women have achieved, and many of them see the pro-marriage movement as an attempt to reassert men's control over women's lives. Being a single parent may not be easy, but it's a more

**Families in
Other Cultures**

Public Opinion toward Government Assistance for Employed Parents

Over the past 20 years, government benefits to working parents have increased in the United States. Parents with child care expenses can now receive a partial reduction of their income tax. Low-income working parents can receive a substantial cash transfer through the Earned Income Tax Credit. And parents may take up to 12 weeks of unpaid leave from their jobs to care for a new baby or an ill child. Still, the United States provides less generous benefits to working parents than other developed nations.

The accompanying chart shows public opinion toward government assistance for working parents in the United States and four other nations. It is based on the results of surveys conducted in 1994 in 31 countries, as part of the International Social Survey Program (Smith, 1999). Random samples of adults in each country were asked two questions on this topic:

Do you agree or disagree . . .

a. Working families should receive paid maternity leave when they have a baby.
b. Families should receive benefits for child care when both parents work.

As the charts indicate, Americans show substantially less agreement with these statements than people in the other four countries. They also show less agreement than people in nearly all the other countries in the study.

What accounts for this difference in public opinion? One key factor is that in many nations, family policy toward parents is driven by a national concern with keeping up the birthrate. The belief that government should encourage people to have more children is called **pronatalism.**

"Working women should receive paid maternity leave when they have a baby."
(percent agreeing)

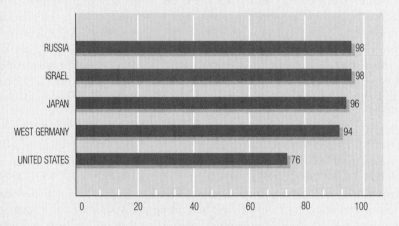

"Families should receive financial benefits for child care when both parents work."
(percent agreeing)

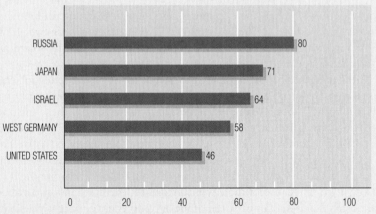

Attitudes towards government assistance for working parents in five nations, 1994.
(*Source:* Smith, 1999)

pronatalism the belief that public policies should encourage people to have children

In the United States, parents may take up to 12 weeks of unpaid leave from their jobs to care for a new baby or an ill child. In contrast, many countries in Europe and elsewhere offer several months of leave with partial pay.

Leaders in many nations have long worried that their populations will not grow as fast as the populations of neighboring and competing countries. The Germans historically have been concerned about the size of the French population (and vice versa); the Japanese have been concerned about China; the Russians hoped to make up the large losses they incurred in the twentieth century world wars; the Israelis, to replace the Jews killed in the Holocaust.

What keeps the United States immune to pronatalist pressure is its receptiveness to immigration. Unlike most other nations, the United States has a long history of letting its population increase, in part, by accepting large numbers of immigrants. Japan, in contrast, has resisted immigration. So did West Germany[1] until it admitted "guest workers" in the latter part of the twentieth century to alleviate a labor shortage. Israel accepts Jewish immigrants but few others. So there is less pressure in the United States to maintain the size of the population by encouraging births.

There are other factors, of course. For example, the American political system has never supported government social programs as much as the Russian socialist (and post-socialist) system. In addition, attitudes seem to be changing in the United States. More Americans are accepting the idea of mothers working outside the home, and some political leaders have been promoting policies that assist working parents. Whether in the future U.S. public opinion will remain distinctively unfavorable toward assistance to working parents is an open question.

Ask Yourself

1. Have you or a friend or relative ever had to go back to work sooner than desired after giving birth to a baby? If so, would a paid maternity leave have helped? In what ways?

2. The graph on the bottom shows significant differences in public opinion toward child care benefits for working parents. What might account for these variations in public opinion from one country to the next?

[1] This survey was conducted before the Federal Republic of Germany, informally known as West Germany, expanded to include the former East Germany.

www.mhhe.com/cherlin5

viable alternative than it used to be. Many feminists wish to defend women's freedom to follow this path. Feminists and liberals argue for public policies that, rather than promoting marriage, would provide more income support, childcare options, and flexible work arrangements for single-parent families so that any remaining disadvantages would be minimized.

Consequently, despite the attention paid to social scientific research, the debate over marriage promotion is, at heart, a debate over symbolism more than statistics: Does our government make the symbolic statement that marriage is to be preferred over other family forms, as the marriage movement urges, or does it make the symbolic statement that individuals should be free to choose the form they wish, as the diversity defenders desire? The marriage-promotion provision in the welfare continuation bill may be more important as a statement of how our nation thinks family life should be lived than as a source of funds for particular programs. Such statements may influence the way people view marriage and family life, even if they never participate in a federally funded marriage-enrichment course. Groups with an interest in how marriage is viewed fought hard to have their symbolic perspective prevail. The inclusion of marriage-promotion funds in the final bill signaled the renewed strength of the pro-marriage viewpoint.

Alternatives for Assisting Children

For many policymakers and advocates, marriage policy is just a means to an end: providing a better environment for children in low-income families. The supporters of the marriage movement contend that marriage provides a superior setting for raising children. They acknowledge that many single mothers and fathers are good parents, but they read the evidence as showing that for the most part, one parent can't provide care and supervision as well as two. Moreover, pro-marriage observers see the difficulty as being more than a matter of low income. At heart, they say, children need both fathers and mothers. Popenoe (1996), for instance, maintains that because of "incontestable biological differences," fathers tend to be firm and encourage autonomy, whereas mothers tend to be nurturing and provide emotional security. Children, he argues, need both, but they only get both in a two-parent family. From this point of view, the key objective of family policy should be to promote marriage in order to reduce the number of children born to unmarried women and their partners.

Yet it is not clear that we know how to promote marriage effectively. All of the existing, relationship-skills training courses have been focused on middle-class couples. They may not work well with couples who have less-developed reading skills and who come from different cultural backgrounds. Three states now allow couples to establish a marriage contract that restricts the rights of spouses to obtain unilateral divorces, but few couples have so far chosen this option. [➡p. 402] Moreover, programs that encourage single mothers to marry men other than the fathers of their children will create stepfamilies, which seem to be no better for children than single-parent families. For these reasons, we cannot be confident that marriage-promotion programs for the low-income population will be effective.

The objective of reducing nonmarital childbearing is less controversial. Teenage childbearing in particular, produces a consensus: Most people agree that it ought to be discouraged, although they don't agree on how. Some religious, community, and school groups are attempting to discourage adolescent sex by urging abstinence. Other groups accept the current level of sexual activity and urge teenagers to use contraceptives. In fact, adolescent sexuality did decline in the 1990s, especially among boys, while contraceptive usage went up—pleasing both the abstinence and contraception camps. [➡p. 206] Moreover, teenage birthrates declined before once again moving upward in the 2000s (Kane & Lichter, 2006). Still, some research suggests that teenage childbearing may be more a reflection of a young woman's disadvantaged background than a cause of future problems. [➡p. 211] If so, then discouraging teenage childbearing without addressing the underlying disadvantages might not make much difference to a young woman's life chances.

An alternative is to provide greater support for single-parent families. Many advocates of this approach believe that increases in the number of single-parent families result from broad economic and cultural trends that are not easily reversed by government programs. The pertinent economic trends are the movement of women into the workforce and the decline in the earning potential of noncollege-educated young men. Women's labor force participation increases their economic independence, reducing the necessity of their being married. Few people today would favor policies that restrict women's economic opportunities. The decline in poorly educated young men's job prospects has made them less attractive as marriage partners and may thus have increased the likelihood that teenagers and young adults would bear children outside of marriage. The cultural trend behind the increase in single-parent families is increasing individualism, which has been rising in the United States at least since de Tocqueville noticed it in the 1830s but which appeared to take another quantum leap in the latter half of the twentieth century. During the 1960s and 1970s, in particular, a turbulent time of political and social protest, the divorce rate doubled, cohabitation emerged among the middle class, and sexual activity outside marriage became more acceptable.

This analysis of social trends leads to a pragmatic argument for assisting low-income single-parent families. Like it or not, its advocates say, they are here to stay in large numbers, and withholding aid from them would hurt their children (McLanahan & Sandefur, 1994). Some writers offer a more positive view: They maintain that two-parent families are not necessarily better for children, and that the diversity of family forms may be beneficial (Stacey, 1990). Either position translates into advocacy for increased support to single parents.

A third alternative is to assist families through benefits that are universal rather than means-tested (i.e., available only to parents with incomes below a certain level). In other words, provide the same benefit to *all* families with children. Many European countries, for example, provide universal child allowances—a fixed

There is widespread support for campaigns to discourage teenage childbearing and to encourage responsible fatherhood.

annual payment per child that the government pays to all parents, regardless of their incomes. The argument is that universal benefits acquire broad political support among families of all incomes. Some students of public policy have argued that only universal social programs, such as Social Security, gather enough political strength to retain adequate funding over the long run (Skocpol, 1991). The Achilles heel of universal programs, however, is that because of their universal coverage they are very expensive. Programs targeted on the poor are cheaper but command less political support.

One universal program that was nearly established in 1994 was a national health insurance system. The failure of Congress to enact it was particularly unfortunate from the standpoint of family policy because universal health insurance would be a major antipoverty measure for children. The most obvious reason is that so many children, an estimated 8.3 million in 2004, are not covered (U.S. Bureau of the Census, 2005e). In addition, the lack of health insurance benefits in many part-time and low-wage jobs creates a perverse incentive for parents to apply for, or remain on, the public assistance rolls. This is because parents and children receiving public assistance also receive health insurance through the Medicaid program for the poor. When a parent gives up public assistance to take a job, she may find that she loses all her medical coverage, and she may decide that having protection from large medical bills dictates that she quit her job. The problem has been eased by recent expansions of Medicaid to some children in nonwelfare, low-income families, but the parents of these children are still at high risk of not having health insurance.

In sum, social observers who believe that marriage is the superior setting for children favor policies that encourage two-parent families and discourage child bearing outside of marriage. In contrast, those who believe that the growth of alternative family forms is irreversible, and perhaps beneficial, favor policies that provide direct assistance to low- and moderate-income single parents and their children. Others urge universal programs that help all parents and children equally on the theory that these programs are more popular politically. These positions are not mutually exclusive. One could favor elements of all three. But there are important trade-offs: Measures that provide assistance to unmarried parents may weaken the incentive to marry. Programs that are restricted to two-parent families risk excluding some of the neediest families. And universal programs help all parents and children but are costly. In a world of limited government budgets, expenditures on programs that support one of these positions sometimes preclude expenditures on others. How best to support children in low-income families and their parents remains a contentious issue.

SAME-SEX MARRIAGE

But while conservatives have urged support for heterosexual marriage, they have by and large opposed efforts to extend marriage, or domestic partnerships legally similar to marriage, to same-sex couples. In 2000 in Vermont, the legislature, under pressure from the state courts, enacted a law establishing "civil unions," a type of domestic partnership that gives the partners most of the legal rights the state gives to married couples. Then in 2003, the Massachusetts Supreme Court ruled that the state law restricting marriage to opposite-sex couples was unconstitutional because it denied same-sex couples a status that is "specially recognized in society and has significant social and other advantages" (Goodrich v. Department of Public Health, 2003). In 2004 same-sex marriage became legal in Massachu-setts. In 2005 Connecticut became the first state to legalize same-sex civil unions without pressure from the courts. And in 2005 same-sex marriage became legal throughout Canada.

These developments spurred strong opposition. During the 2004 presidential election campaign, President Bush stated that he would support a federal constitu-tional amendment to protect the "sanctity of marriage" by restricting it to oppo-site-sex couples. Eleven states had initiatives on the November 2004 ballot to amend their constitutions to bar same-sex marriage, and all eleven passed. Since then the drive to amend the federal constitution has been unsuccessful but several more states have amended their state constitutions. About 60 percent of Ameri-cans stated that they opposed same-sex marriage in 2004 surveys, although that percentage had fallen to about 50 percent by 2006 (Pew Research Center, 2006).

Some opponents of gay marriage state that it violates their religious teaching about marriage, and other express discomfort about homosexual sexual activity. Nevertheless, same-sex marriage is a logical consequence of the increasingly indi-vidualized meaning of marriage. [➡p. 227] In the past, most people viewed mar-riage primarily as an arrangement for having children. Since same-sex partners cannot have biological children together, same-sex marriage was not considered. But by the end of the twentieth century, this view had faded. In 1994 the General Social Survey asked a national sample of adults whether they agreed or disagreed with the statement, "The main purpose of marriage these days is to have chil-dren." Only 13 percent agreed (Davis, Smith, & Marsden, 2003). Instead, marriage is viewed by most people now as primarily a setting for love and intimacy. Given this changed meaning, the rationale for excluding same-sex partnerships is much weaker. Moreover, many lesbian and gay couples are raising children together, through adoption or donor insemination. [➡p. 309] When courts examine the is-sue, they look at the meaning heterosexuals give to marriage, and they often can find no compelling reason to uphold laws that restrict marriage to opposite-sex partners. Those who view marriage more traditionally oppose this stance.

Quick Review

- Liberals propose an expanded role in helping parents manage work and family responsibilities.
- Conservatives are supporting government programs to promote marriage in order to increase children's well-being,
- Liberals who favor accepting family diversity support policies that would aid single parents and their children.
- Some observers argue that only programs with universal parent and child benefits will gain the political support necessary for long-term existence and expansion.
- Court decisions have made same-sex marriage a public issue.

■ Family Policy in the Mid-2000s

In the mid-2000s, important debates about family policy are continuing: How much assistance should the government provide to working parents? Should the government promote marriage? Should marriage be restricted to opposite-sex cou-ples? Nevertheless, conservatives and liberals have moved closer to each other than they were twenty years ago. Most conservatives accept the principle that the

The Boundaries of Marriage

Just a few family issues—most notably abortion—have generated opposition so strong and activism so aggressive as same-sex marriages and civil unions. The strength of people's feelings about this issue reflects, I think, the strength of marriage in the United States. Even though marriage has declined as an institution, it remains a more potent symbol in the United States than elsewhere. People care more about being married in this country than in most other developed countries. When the Massachusetts Supreme Court struck down the law restricting marriage to opposite sex couples, it would not even accept civil unions as a remedy. Only legalizing same-sex marriage would suffice because anything else, the Court wrote, would create "second-class citizens." In England and France, however, civil unions aren't necessarily seen as second-class citizenship. Both countries have passed domestic partnership laws but neither has had much of a debate about same-sex marriage, in large part because fewer gay and lesbian activists view marriage as a status worth achieving. Only in the United States has right to control the boundaries of marriage produced so much controversy.

The problem for opponents of same-sex marriage is that they are defending a definition of marriage that is rooted in our past, when marriage was centered on forming a practical partnership to raise children and put food on the table. In contrast, most people–including most heterosexuals—now see marriage primarily as a relationship in which to experience love and companionship. They view it in much more individualistic terms than did their ancestors a few generations ago. In the short run, the opponents of same-sex marriage have gained victories in many states by appealing to voters who still resonate to the more traditional view of marriage. But one wonders whether, in the long run, they will be able to hold back the spread of the more individualistic definition of marriage. Under the latter definition, the rationale for denying marriage to same-sex couples is not nearly as strong.

Episcopal Bishop Gene Robinson, right, cooks dinner with his partner Mark Andrew. His election as Bishop of the Diocese of New Hampshire in 2003 caused controversy and dissension within the world-wide Episcopal/Anglican Church.

Julie Goodridge, left, and her spouse Hillary Goodridge cross the street after being married Monday, May 17, 2004, the day that same-sex marriage became legal in Massachusetts. The Goodridges were the lead plantiffs in the Massachusetts gay marriage lawsuit.

Gay marriage supporters hold up signs above an anti-gay marriage slogan during an anti-gay marriage rally at the Statehouse in Providence, Rhode Island, in 2004. In response to the legalization of gay marriage in Massachusetts, many states have passed laws or constitutional amendments restricting marriage to opposite-sex couples.

government should assist working parents, although in ways that promote individual responsibility and preserve marriage. Many liberals are willing to support limits on families' dependence on government, as exemplified by the time limits on TANF receipt, but they argue for greater income assistance and work supports for single parents and dual-earner couples.

Moreover, when I listen for the old leitmotifs in the current debates, I sometimes hear each side singing the other's tune. After decades of defending families in which wives do not work outside the home, conservatives now argue that low-income women *should* work outside the home rather than receive government benefits for staying home. That, at least, is one of the principles of welfare reform. Conservatives are now willing to provide wage supplements such as the EITC and some child care subsidies to help low-income mothers maintain paid employment. And after decades of defending the right of mothers to work outside the home and fighting for more resources for employed parents, liberals have now discovered the value of the care that mothers perform at home. That value is now praised in the new care work movement [⇒p. 266], which argues that we undervalue unpaid, caring work. Some care work–oriented liberals maintain that low-income mothers should be given the resources they need to raise children full-time if they wish. These reversals reflect the groups' fundamental stances toward the poor: conservatives urging self-reliance and liberals urging greater assistance. These differing orientations toward low-income families still underlie many of the issues in the family policy debates.

Looking Back

1. **What is the "welfare state"?** In the twentieth century, the United States and other Western nation–states enacted numerous social programs to provide support to workers and their families. These "welfare state" measures softened the hardships of the labor market. In the United States, the programs were initially designed under the assumption that husbands would work full-time for wages, and wives would do full-time domestic work in the household. Congress did not anticipate that large numbers of wives would work outside the home or that divorce and childbearing outside of marriage would become more common.

2. **What are the themes that conservatives and liberals stress in debating family policies?** In debates over family policy, conservatives often claim that they want to keep government from intruding into family life. But the government has already intervened in family life; social welfare legislation from the 1930s through the 1950s was de-signed to support the breadwinner–homemaker family. Liberals, on the other hand, tend to propose measures that would benefit single parents and those married couples in which wives work outside the home more than they would benefit breadwinner–homemaker families. Conservative legislators tend to resist such proposals.

3. **Why was the 1996 welfare reform law a sharp break from earlier government policies toward low-income families?** The 1996 welfare reform law authorized states to set a time limit of five years or less on the receipt of cash assistance in the new TANF program. The law also strengthened work requirements and ended the entitlement to cash assistance for low-income single-parent families. Supporters of the bill argued that dependence on public benefits was detrimental to low-income families; liberals countered that dependence was a symptom of the deeper problem of poverty.

4. **Should the government promote heterosexual marriage?** Some experts and advocates believe that marriage is the superior family form and that children would be helped most by efforts to promote it. In a similar vein, many people support efforts to discourage teenage childbearing through either abstinence or contraception. Others urge that Americans accept the diversity of family forms as irreversible and perhaps even beneficial. This last position argues for direct assistance to both single- and two-parent low-income families.

5. **Should same-sex marriage be allowed?** Several court decisions have made same-sex marriage, which is now legal in Massachusetts and in Canada, a much-debated topic. Some conservatives support a federal constitutional amendment to ban it, and several states have enacted constitutional amendments against it. The rise of same-sex marriage as an issue reflects the changing meaning of marriage. The most important aspects of marriage today, in the views of a majority of Americans, are love, intimacy, and companionship, rather than child rearing. Same-sex marriage, its proponents argue, is consistent with this view of marriage.

 Go to the Online Learning Center at www.mhhe.com/cherlin5 to test your knowledge of the chapter concepts and key terms.

Study Questions

1. What kinds of assistance does the government provide to middle-class families?
2. Describe the rise and fall of the family wage system.
3. Why is abortion such a contentious political issue?
4. How does the EITC exemplify the practical consensus on policy that sometimes emerged in the last decades of the twentieth century?
5. Describe the differing perspectives of liberals and conservatives on the issue of the "dependency" of the poor on government assistance.
6. What are the arguments for and against greater government support for parents who are employed?
7. What issues underlie the debate about whether the government should support marriage-promotion programs?
8. How have changes in the meaning of marriage affected the issue of whether same-sex couples should have the right to marry?

Key Terms

Aid to Families with Dependent Children (AFDC)   471
block grant   481
Earned Income Tax Credit (EITC)   479
entitlement   480
family policy   472
family wage system   474

nation   473
nation-state   473
Personal Responsibility and Work Opportunity Reconciliation Act of 1996 (PRWORA)   471
pronatalism   488

Social Security Act of 1935   470
state   473
Temporary Assistance to Needy Families (TANF)   481
welfare state   474

Thinking about Families

The Public Family	The Private Family
Many states now withhold part of a recipient's TANF benefits if she doesn't get her children inoculated against childhood diseases or if her children don't attend school regularly. Do you think this is a good policy?	Is the government inappropriately invading private life if it tries to encourage people to form one kind of family—say, a married-couple family—rather than another?

Families on the Internet   www.mhhe.com/cherlin5

Note: While all the URLs listed were current as of the printing of this book, these sites often change. Please check our Web site (http://www.mhhe.com/cherlin5) for updates.

The Families and Work Institute (www.familiesandwork.org) combines research and advocacy on the topic of combining work and family responsibilities. Its Web site has summaries of recent reports and surveys.

The Center on Law and Social Policy (www.clasp.org) offers some balanced policy briefs on the issue of government support for marriage. Click on "Couples and Marriage Policy" to see several relevant reports on marriage promotion.

Many advocacy organizations have sites that argue for or against same-sex marriage. Balanced, moderate commentary, however, is in short supply, so examine these sites critically. On the side favoring same-sex marriage, see www.freedomtomarry.org. On the other side, see www.formarriage.org, which urges individual action to defend traditional marriage.

Social Change and Families

Looking Forward

1. What are some fundamental changes in the American family over the past half century?

2. How has the role of personal choice expanded in family life?

3. How has the private side of family life changed?

When Americans are asked about the state of the family, their responses are puzzling but instructive. In a 1999 national telephone survey by the *New York Times,* far more people mentioned family and children than any other response when asked, "What aspect of your life is most fulfilling and satisfying?"[1] Without doubt, then, people find deep meaning in their family lives. The survey also included a question about the great changes that have occurred in American family life over the past several decades: "In general, do you think that because of such things as divorce, more working mothers, or single parents, etc., family ties in the U.S. are breaking down—or don't you think so?" Seventy-seven percent responded that, yes, they thought family ties were breaking down—a very negative assessment. All the more surprising, then, were the answers to the next question: "What about in your own family? Are family ties breaking down, or not?" Eighty-two percent responded that their family ties were not breaking down. In other words, most people think that the family in general is in decline, but not their own families.

These seemingly contradictory responses reflect widespread ambivalence about the changes in American family life. People are concerned about the effects of day care on children, but they approve of decisions by women in their own families to work outside the home. They are worried about the consequences of divorce, but they don't expect their relatives to remain in unhappy marriages. They believe that ideally, children should be born to married couples, but they accept the occurrence of nonmarital births in their families.

In other words, many people share both the concern about family decline voiced by conservative commentators and the defense of newer family forms voiced by liberals. Although they may endorse traditional values, such as the superiority of the stable, two-parent family, they reserve the right to deviate from those values in their own lives. And they are loath to tell others how to live their family lives. They may value the traditional family, but they accept family diversity as inevitable, and perhaps beneficial.

Many people, then, accept the fact that for better or worse, we live in an era with a variety of family forms, including cohabiting unions, dual-earner married couples, breadwinner–homemaker couples, single-parent families, stepfamilies, and same-sex marriages and domestic partnerships. Let me say what I think these developments mean for family life today.

[1] All data that I cite from the survey come from unpublished tabulations. For an overview, see Cherlin (1999b).

■ Two Fundamental Changes

First, however, it is worth reviewing the fundamental ways in which the family as a social institution has changed over the past half century. Two changes stand out: the lessened economic dependence of women on men and the weakening of marriage. Both have implications for American kinship.

THE LESSENED ECONOMIC DEPENDENCE OF WOMEN

The decline of the homemaker role and the movement of women into the paid labor force is probably the most significant shift in the family in the past half century. It has been discussed so often in this book that there's little need to say more. Here let me emphasize one point: To some extent, the movement toward greater economic independence is a movement back toward the situation of women a century or two ago. That is to say, married women probably had less economic independence in the 1950s than they had had 50 years earlier. In the nineteenth century, rural women were an important part of the family's farm labor. To be sure, as cities expanded, most urban white married women (and many urban black married women) did not work outside the home. Yet urban wives earned income by taking in boarders and lodgers or by doing other families' laundry or performing other services in their homes. By the 1950s, the greater affluence of the nation had nearly eliminated boarding and lodging, and rising wages placed the washing machine and dryer within the reach of many more families. As a result, opportunities to earn money while remaining at home declined. Still, the nineteenth-century economic activity of married women kept them at home, whereas the late-twentieth-century economic activity allows them (albeit with lower earnings than men) to live apart.

THE WEAKENING OF MARRIAGE

The greatest recent challenge to the institution of the family has been the weakening of marriage. In most societies at most times, marriage has been the central organizing principle for sexual activity and childbearing. Marriage, childbearing, and sexual activity overlapped in the 1950s to a great extent, possibly greater than in prior times. [➡p. 64] Sexual intercourse, for the majority of women at least, was restricted to marriage (or to the men they were engaged to); consequently, few children were born outside marriage. Cohabitation was rare except among the poor. Marriage was more nearly universal than at any other time in the twentieth century. The probability that a marriage would end in divorce, although substantially higher than in the nineteenth century, was much less than it is today. To be respectable, it was necessary to be married before living with a partner or having a child; to stay respectable, it was necessary to avoid divorce if at all possible.

Today, even though nearly 90 percent of whites and about two-thirds of African Americans eventually marry, the power of marriage to regulate people's personal lives is much weaker. Cohabitation both before and after marriage has become common and acceptable to most people. Although childbearing outside marriage is still frowned upon by many, it is tolerated by most. Divorce is considered to be unfortunate but acceptable if a partner wishes to end a marriage. Lifelong singlehood, although still uncommon, is also acceptable. In general, there is a greater acceptance of nonmarried adults.

The reasons for the weakening of marriage were discussed in previous chapters. Marriage is less economically necessary than it was when most people needed to pool their labor and earnings in order to subsist. Moreover, the aforementioned lessening of women's economic dependence on men has had an important effect. Even though women's wages remain, on average, lower than men's, it is less difficult now for a woman to support herself and her children. Also, the job prospects for young men without college educations have worsened since 1973, discouraging young adults from marrying. In the realm of values, marriage is increasingly viewed as a means of personal fulfillment, with the result that many married persons believe they are justified in obtaining a divorce if they feel unfulfilled. The quest for self-fulfillment may also prolong young adults' search for a spouse or lead them to try a cohabiting relationship first. Among those who do marry, relationships are more fragile and vulnerable to crises because there is less holding them together than when marriage was more of a necessity and the gendered division of labor was more strict.

Among African Americans, marriage has long been less central to family life, compared with ties to other kin, than it has been among whites; but over the past few decades, marriage has declined in importance even more. Among poor African Americans, the connection between marriage and childbearing is especially weak. Although marriage still remains an ideal, it is far from universal, and the great majority of children, especially first children, are born outside of marriage. Even when a woman does get married, it is not necessarily to the father of her first child. The decline of marriage among African Americans is linked both to the worsening labor market position of black men and to a cultural heritage of relying on extended kin in difficult times. [➥ p. 157] Hispanic groups vary greatly in the place of marriage in their family systems. Among the major groups, Puerto Ricans have the highest proportion of children living in single-parent families and Cubans the lowest. Mexican Americans display more three-generational households, suggesting the importance of extended family ties. Marriage is strongest

As marriage has weakened as an institution, lifelong singlehood has become more acceptable.

among Asian Americans, many of them recent immigrants from societies in which marriage is nearly universal.

Still, marriage is not in danger of disappearing among Americans, and it remains the preferred form of union. Most people choose to marry at some time in their lives, but the point is that they now have a choice. They don't have to be married in the sense that adults at midcentury did. Predictably, people spend less of their lives married and fewer children are raised by two married parents. Moreover, people tend to marry at a later point in their lives than they did a half-century ago. Individuals used to get married prior to living together, having children, and establishing careers. Today, before marrying you may live with your future spouse or with someone else, you may spend several years establishing yourself in the labor market, and you may even have children. It is not a status to enter into lightly; rather, you wait until you're sure it's going to work. Marriage is a status you work toward, a personal achievement, a mark of distinction. In some ways, then, marriage's symbolic value has increased even as its practical significance has decreased.

Quick Review

- The movement of married women into the paid labor force was one of the most significant changes in family life in the last half of the twentieth century.
- The weakening of marriage is another significant change in family life that occurred in the same period.
- Still, marriage remains an important part of the family system.

■ The Do-It-Yourself Family?

The decline of lifelong marriage as the organizing principle for sexual intimacy and family life has led to an important change, aspects of which have been discussed in several chapters: Today, people are more likely to choose their own family lifestyle than to unthinkingly follow social norms or the wishes of their parents. One's family lifestyle has become a central aspect of **self-identity,** by which I mean a person's sense of who he or she is and of where he or she fits in the social structure. In societies such as ours, individuals must construct their self-identities; they cannot rely on tradition or custom to order their daily lives. "We are not what we are," wrote social theorist Anthony Giddens (1991), "but what we make of ourselves." Developing one's self-identity becomes an important project—a task individuals must work on. Family life, according to two social theorists, becomes a permanent do-it-yourself project (Beck & Beck-Gernsheim, 2002).

self-identity a person's sense of who he or she is and of where he or she fits in the social structure

PERSONAL LIFE IN THE LATE MODERN ERA

Much of the development of one's self-identity occurs reflexively. As noted earlier [➡p. 27], reflexivity is a kind of feedback loop in which people reflect on information and alter their behavior as a result. Reflexive change has increased in importance because so many aspects of personal life are now subject to personal choice. The modernity theorists, discussed in Chapter 1 [➡p. 26], believe that the rise of reflexive change is a key characteristic of what they call the late modern era: the last few decades of the twentieth century and the beginning of the twenty-first. Table 15.1 compares the current era with the modern era that began with industrialization and ended in the mid-twentieth century (although, in a broader sense, modernization can be traced back to the Enlightenment in eighteenth-century Europe). These two periods are ideal types[➡p. 119]; in reality, the periods are not as distinct, and the differences are not as sharp, as the table suggests.

Behavior, according to the modernity theorists, was *rule-directed* in the earlier era, meaning that (1) rules such as social norms, laws, and customs strongly influenced personal life, and (2) the actions of individuals did not change those rules. Marriage was the only acceptable context for having children. Divorce was frowned upon and harder to obtain. Despite occasional movements to liberalize divorce laws, the norms and customs did not change much. In the current era, behavior is *rule-altering* to a much greater extent because the lifestyle choices individuals make can alter the laws and customs pertaining to families. For instance, as more gay and lesbian couples have openly lived together, many municipalities in reaction, have enacted domestic-partnership laws that give same-sex couples privileges similar to those of married couples (such as requiring that employers who offer health insurance benefits that cover the spouses of their employees also cover their same-sex partners). These new laws altered the rules about what constituted a legally valid partnership. And as privileges and acceptability increased, gay men and lesbians found it even easier to live together in marriage-like partnership, leading to further changes, such as recent court decisions favorable to gay marriage.

Lifestyle choices, as Table 15.1 suggests, were *restricted* in the earlier era. For example, people were much less likely to choose a spouse of a different religion or racial-ethnic group. In the current era, choices are not only greater but also *mandatory:* You must make choices in nearly all aspects of personal life. Having to make so many decisions has its good and bad points. It opens the possibility of developing a self-identity that is deeply fulfilling; and it allows people to seize the opportunities that may be before them. On the other hand, choices can bring insecurity and doubt. The risk of making the wrong ones can weigh on you, creating a burden as well as a boon.

Finally, kinship ties tend to shift from being *acquired* to being *created.* [➡p. 141] In the past, you acquired your relatives at birth; then, when you married, you acquired a spouse and in-laws. There was little choice in the matter. Today, people in a variety of settings are more likely to choose their own kin and create their own kinship networks. What all these settings have in common is that they are defined outside the boundaries of lifelong heterosexual marriage.

Table 15.1 Aspects of Personal Life in the Late Modern Era		
	MODERN ERA	**LATE MODERN ERA**
Time period	Industrialization to mid-twentieth century	Since mid-twentieth century
Behavior	Rule-directed	Rule-altering
Lifestyle choices	Restricted	Mandatory
Kinship ties	Acquired	Created

Note: The table is the author's, but it is based on Giddens (1991, 1992), Beck & Beck-Gernsheim (1995, 2002), and Beck, Giddens, & Lash (1994).

People who cannot rely on, or choose not to rely on, lifelong marriage must construe kinship differently. They must do the hard work of constructing a group of kin, a broader family, that they can rely on. They create these links by what they do for one another. Recall the lesbian who told Kath Weston, "Gay people really have to work to make a family." [➡ p. 199]

Created kinship is particularly valuable to people who can't find adequate support among blood-based or first-marriage-based kin. Lesbians and gay men, for example, are sometimes rejected by their parents. Poor African American mothers who cannot find suitable spouses exchange help not only with their mothers and grandmothers but also with close friends, creating kinship-like relationships. A divorced mother whose ex-husband provides little support can receive assistance from a live-in partner or second husband. Yet created kinship also presents a challenge: It requires continual attention to maintain. In contrast, relations of blood and first marriage are supported by strong social norms and the law. Lacking this support, people must actively keep up created kinship ties. If they are allowed to lapse, there is no guarantee that they can be revived.

What underlies all the changes in Table 15.1—what has propelled the transition to late modernity—is an increase in individualism. Self-identity has increasingly been defined in terms of individual goals rather than social roles. People are less concerned with playing the role of spouse or parent than with developing their sense of self—their emotional fulfillment, their self-reliance, their capacity to grow and change. They are more attuned to the project of developing the self than to externally imposed norms. In the 1950s, half of the people in a national survey said they would consider someone who did not want to get married to be sick, selfish, or immoral (Veroff, Douvan, & Kulka, 1981). In contrast, in the late 1990s, a survey suggested that Americans rated the importance of being married lower than being self-reliant or self-expressive or even than being a good neighbor. [➡ p. 8]

People are increasingly likely to choose their own kin and create their own kinship networks.

THE FEMINIZATION OF KINSHIP

Because created kinship ties require continual maintenance, the system favors those who are willing to work at keeping kinship ties and penalizes those who aren't. A great deal of evidence, reviewed in earlier chapters, shows that women, on average, do much more kinship work than men. They are the ones, by and large, who run and maintain the sharing networks in poor African American communities. They are the ones who retain the children after divorce and call upon relatives for help. Men, in contrast, seem to drift away from kinship except when they are married. Many divorced fathers, as was noted, have little to do with their children after a divorce. Many men in low-income communities have little to do with children they have fathered outside marriage. Divorced men receive comfort and support by remarrying, which they do more often than divorced women. It is unclear who provides comfort and support to the unmarried fathers in low-income communities. It seems likely that they find new partners and also rely on mothers, sisters, and grandmothers.

As marriage becomes less stable, and as kinship networks remain the work of women, more men will be left without adequate support from kin. The difference is most apparent in later life. For instance, stepfathers are less likely to receive assistance from their adult stepchildren than biological fathers are from their children. [➡p. 358] Moreover, once a man's remarriage ends, his relationship with his stepchildren, as befits created kinship, often ends as well. What, then, will happen to a man who divorces his first wife, sees little of his children afterward, remarries, and then divorces again? Who will care for him in his old age? The evidence suggests that he is unlikely to receive assistance from anyone—unless he marries again.

Kinship, then, is becoming even more feminized than it previously was. Men's classic strategy for support is to marry and to let their wives keep up ties with relatives. This strategy worked well for men as long as most were married for life. Yet with the rises in divorce and childbearing outside marriage, men often become disconnected from kin. At first, many men gain economically because they don't share their higher incomes equitably with the mothers of their children. Yet men who become divorced may be the long-run losers in the decline of lifelong marriage and the rise of created kinship. They may be isolated (unless they are remarried), distant from their adult children, and unable to forge links with other kin.

EXCESSIVE INDIVIDUALISM?

The increasingly private, self-fulfillment emphasis in marriage and cohabitation has been criticized and lamented by some. The issue is whether people's attention to their own personal satisfaction, to the growth and development of their self-identity, has reached such extreme proportions that their capacity to make commitments to others has atrophied.[2] These "others" include not only family members but also neighborhoods, church groups, and communities—the groupings that give meaning and cohesion to society. In the twenty-first-century United States, individualism is what economists call a "normal" good, meaning that the more income people have, the more of it they purchase. The elderly constitute the clearest example: They have used their higher incomes to purchase, or to remain in, separate homes and apartments. Similarly, young adults

---

[2] See, for example, Bellah, Madsen, Sullivan, Swidler, & Tipton (1985).

The elderly have used the income support of Social Security and private pensions to remain independent.

have used higher living standards to move out of their parents' homes (at least until the recent decline in their labor market prospects). Husbands and wives in unhappy marriages have used their greater economic independence to divorce.

Yet what seems excessive to the observer may seem justified and liberating to the actor. We are fortunate to live in a time and place where the standard of living is sufficiently high that a majority of the population can focus on their personal well-being. This luxury was not nearly as widespread 100, or even 50, years ago. As easy as it is to criticize excesses in others, few of us volunteer to rein in our own pursuit of happiness. Moreover, women's greater independence, some authors argue, has given them more control over their own sexual expression than previous generations had (Ehrenreich, Hess, & Jacobs, 1987). There is a case to be made, in other words, that the emphasis on individualism is an important advance that has improved societal levels of happiness. And although the case is rarely stated in words, many of us make it with actions in our own lives.

Individualism, it seems to me, can be judged a problem only if it interferes with important social functions. Yet that indeed is the charge, and in the realm of the family the specific charge is that adults have been too preoccupied with their own individual satisfaction to meet their obligations to children. In other words, it is alleged that the rise of the private family, focused on individual emotional satisfaction, has undercut the ability of the public family to carry out its responsibilities to children. There is some truth to this charge. For example, the pursuit of individual fulfillment is one factor in the greater instability of marriages and partnerships, and this instability in living arrangements, in turn, appears to be detrimental to children's well-being. It is a mistake, however, to hold individualism responsible for all of the increase in divorce, single-parent families, and the problems of children: Individualism did not cause the movement of manufacturing jobs from the United States to the Third World and the resulting deterioration in young people's labor market prospects. It did not cause the growth of the service sector of the economy during the twentieth century and the resulting expansion of opportunities in occupations that had been stereotyped as women's work. Culture and commitment have played a role in the case of children, but so has economic change. On the relative importance of each, reasonable people can, and do, disagree.

Quick Review

- In the late modern era, people must make more choices about their family lives than in the past.
- Personal behavior becomes more rule altering than in the past.
- Kinship ties tend to shift from being acquired to being created.
- The emphasis on individual satisfaction and self-development has been widely criticized.

■ A Summing Up

Through hundreds of articles and books, the debates about the state of the family have bounced between those who argue that it is in deep decline and those who counter that it is in fine shape. Neither assertion is true. The social institution of the family is experiencing a period of great change, handling some of it well and limping through the rest. It is possible that some of the current changes will stretch its adaptability so thin that it will crack, but that judgment is premature. History has shown the family to be a resilient institution, able to alter its form to fit changing circumstances. Yet it is not infinitely adaptable. In examining the state of the family, one must be able to confront its problems without losing sight of its strengths.

One problem is that the family is an institution that was designed for scarcity and is now being asked to perform in an era of greater (although not uniform) prosperity. Throughout most of human history, people have been too preoccupied with subsisting from day to day and season to season to be concerned about personal fulfillment. Marriage and family provided an efficient way to pool the labor of women and men that was necessary to grow food (or earn enough money to buy it), to make or buy clothes and other goods, and to raise future sources of labor, namely children. Today, most people take these basic tasks for granted. Families are now being asked to carry the heavy responsibility of providing not merely sustenance but also emotional satisfaction. It is a relatively new demand, and the institution has not fully adjusted to it.

Another problem is that the family, in most places at most times, has been dominated by men; now it must adapt to a society in which women have substantial (although not yet full) independence. Male dominance was probably enforced first by greater physical strength, but then male dominance became so entrenched in Western law and social norms that the use of physical force usually wasn't necessary. For example, traditional English law held that wives had few legal rights because, upon marriage, the husband and wife became one legal person—effectively, the husband. A contemporary challenge is to modify the institution so that women and men share the benefits and burdens equitably.

The institution was also designed to raise many children in order that some would survive to adulthood; it now is being asked to raise one or two who will almost certainly survive to adulthood. Prior to the twentieth century, most couples did not experience sustained periods without children around because they began to have them soon after they were married and because one or both parents often died before all the children had grown up. Before the twentieth century, then, prolonged childless periods rarely existed by choice. Now an extended period without children in the household is common at the beginning of marriage and almost universal during the latter half. During these times, family relations necessarily focus on the relationship between the spouses. A consensus on what they should offer each other and expect from each other is still emerging.

The strengths of the family include the continuing desires of most adults to experience lasting bonds of intimacy and affection and to have children. Some sociologists think these desires are solely the result of the powerful socialization children receive. But there are theories that suggest they may also have a psychoanalytic component derived from early experiences with parents or an evolutionary component derived from the need to reproduce. In addition, the institution of the family has demonstrated an ability to assume a great diversity of forms in different cultures and different eras. Countless anthropological studies show that non-Western societies have had family systems that are much less centered on the conjugal unit of husband, wife, and children. A final, and probably related, strength, which should humble those who predict its imminent demise, is its ability to outlast its critics. As with Mark Twain, its death has been greatly exaggerated. For instance, a concerned observer wrote in the *Boston Quarterly Review* of 1859: "The family, in its old sense, is disappearing from our land, and not only our free institutions are threatened but the very existence of our society is endangered" (Lantz, Schultz, & O'Hara, 1977, quoted at p. 413). Similar words can still be heard today—along with the words of those who celebrate its greater diversity.

The strengths of the family include the desires of most people for lasting intimacy and raising children.

To be sure, the breadwinner–homemaker family is in decline. But although that type of family is the point of reference for many Americans, in historical perspective it is but a blip on the radar screen. The family is not disappearing, but exactly where it is heading we cannot yet be sure.

Looking Back

1. **What are some fundamental changes in the American family over the past half century?** One fundamental change is the lessened economic dependence of women on men. To some extent, this is a return to the situation of women a century or two ago. Another fundamental change is the weakening of marriage, which is less economically necessary and less consistent with cultural values. Still, marriage remains a goal for most people.

2. **How has the role of personal choice expanded in family life?** Personal choice plays a much greater role in family life now than in the past. Through a reflexive process, people's innovative behavior alters the rule of family life. Moreover, choice plays a greater role in kinship. People used to have little choice in who was related to them, and the relationships lasted a lifetime. Now, people increasingly have to create and maintain kinship ties.

3. **How has the private side of family life changed?** During the past century, the state has become less involved in regulating intimate adult relationships. Marriage has become fundamentally a private matter, a way of achieving a personally satisfying life. This private, self-fulfilling emphasis has been criticized as excessive, yet the emphasis on individual satisfaction may also be viewed as a social advance. Traditionally, marriage has been stabilized in part by restricting women's lives more than men's. The challenge is to enhance the stability and security of marriage and intimate relationships without forcing women to pay this price.

Go to the Online Learning Center at www.mhhe.com/cherlin5 to test your knowledge of the chapter concepts and key terms.

Study Questions

1. How has the increased economic independence of women affected family life?
2. What did Giddens mean by writing, "We are not what we are, we are what we make of ourselves"?
3. How has personal life changed in the late modern era?
4. Is the institution of the family in danger of fading away?

Key Terms

self-identity   505

Thinking about Families

The Public Family	The Private Family
Are adults too preoccupied with their own relationships to meet the needs of children?	How well are American families meeting the need for intimacy and emotional support?

Families on the Internet www.mhhe.com/cherlin5

Note: While all the URLs listed were current as of the printing of this book, these sites often change. Please check our Web site (http://www.mhhe.com/cherlin5) for updates.

The debates about the state of the family and its future can be monitored on the Internet. On the liberal side, the Council on Contemporary Families (www.contemporaryfamilies.org) defends the diversity of American families and argues that the institution is not in decline. On the center-right is the Institute for American Values (www.americanvalues.org), which promotes the idea that the decline of

marriage and the increase in single-parent families have harmed children and weakened society. On the right is the Family Research Council (www.frc.org), which supports the "traditional family" in which women stay home to raise children, is strongly pro-life, and opposes gay rights.

Glossary

1965 Immigration Act   Act passed by the U.S. Congress which ended restrictions that had blocked most Asian immigration and substituted an annual quota.

action life expectancy   The number of years a person can expect to live without a disability.

activities of daily living (ADLs)   Personal care activities, including bathing, dressing, getting into and out of bed, walking indoors, and using the toilet.

ADLs   See **activities of daily living.**

AFDC   See **Aid to Families with Dependent Children.**

Aid to Families with Dependent Children (AFDC) A federal program of financial assistance to low-income families, commonly known as "welfare" until it was replaced by Temporary Assistance to Needy Families (TANF) in 1996.

alimony   Maintenance payments from an ex-husband to an ex-wife.

American Indian   The name used for a subset of all Native Americans, namely, those who were living in the territory that later became the 48 contiguous United States.

androgynous behavior   Behavior that has the characteristics of both genders.

annulment   A ruling that a marriage was never properly formed.

archival research   Research that uses printed or written documents stored in libraries or other data archives.

arranged marriage   A marriage in which the parents find a spouse for their child by negotiating with other parents.

Asian American   A person living in the United States who comes from or is descended from people who came from an Asian country.

assigned kinship   Kinship ties that people more or less automatically acquire when they are born or when they marry.

assimilation   The process by which immigrant groups merge their culture and behavior with that of the dominant group in the host country.

assortative marriage   The tendency of people to marry others similar to themselves.

attachment   A bonding to another person that produces feelings of security, comfort, and ease when the other person is nearby.

authoritarian style (of parenting)   A parenting style in which parents combine low levels of emotional support with coercive attempts at control of their children.

authoritative style (of parenting)   A parenting style in which parents combine high levels of emotional support with consient, moderate control of their children.

authority   The acknowledged right of someone to supervise and control others' behavior.

baby boom   The large number of people born during the late 1940s and 1950s.

barrio   A segregated Mexican-American neighborhood in a U.S. city.

berdache   In Native American societies, a man or woman who dressed like, performed the duties of, and behaved like a member of the opposite sex.

bilateral kinship   A system in which descent is reckoned through both the mother's and father's lines.

biosocial approach (to gender differences) The theory that gender identification and behavior are based in part on people's innate biological differences.

birth cohort   All people born during a given year or period of years.

block grant   A fixed amount of money that the federal government gives each state to spend on a set of programs.

blood relatives   People who share common ancestors: parents and children, uncles and aunts, nephews and nieces, grandparents and grandchildren.

boundary ambiguity   A situation in which people are uncertain about who is in their family and what roles these people play.

breadwinner–homemaker family   A married couple with children in which the father works for pay and the mother does not.

capitalism   An economic system in which goods and services are privately produced and sold on a market for profit.

care work   Face-to-face activity in which one person meets the needs of another who cannot fully care for her- or himself.

centenarian   A person who is 100-years-old or older.

centralizing women   Women who specialize in maintaining the links of kinship.

child abuse   Serious physical harm (trauma, sexual abuse with injury, or willful malnutrition) of a child by an adult, with intent to injure.

cohabitation   The sharing of a household by unmarried persons who have a sexual relationship.

cohort replacement model   A model of changing public opinion in which each successive birth cohort experiences a different social environment and retains distinctive opinions throughout their adult life.

compadrazgo   In Mexico, a godparent relationship in which a wealthy or influential person outside the kinship group is asked to become the *compadre,* or godparent, of a newborn child, particularly at its baptism.

companionate marriage   A marriage in which the emphasis is on affection, friendship, and sexual gratification.

comparable-worth discrimination   A situation in which women and men do different jobs of equivalent value in the same company but the women are paid less.

conflict theory   A sociological theory that focuses on inequality, power, and social change.

conjugal family   A kinship group comprising husband, wife, and children.

consensual union   A cohabiting relationship in which a couple consider themselves to be married but have never had a religious or civil marriage ceremony.

coparenting   An arrangement whereby divorced parents coordinate their activities and cooperate with each other in raising their children.

courtship   A publicly visible process with rules and restrictions through which young men and women find a partner to marry.

created kinship   Kinship ties that people have to construct actively.

crisis period   A period during the first year or two after parents separate when both the custodial parent and the children experience difficulties in dealing with the situation.

distribution of family income   The proportion of the total income of all families in the nation that each family receives.

domestic violence   Violent acts between family members or between women and men in intimate or dating relationships.

donor insemination   A procedure in which semen is inserted into the uterus of an ovulating woman.

early adulthood   Period between mid-teens and about 30 when individuals finish their education, enter the labor force, and begin their own families.

Earned Income Tax Credit (EITC)   A refundable tax credit to low-income families with a child or children in which at least one parent is employed.

EITC   See **Earned Income Tax Credit.**

elder abuse   Physical abuse of an elderly person by a nonelderly person.

elderly population   The group of people aged 65 years and over.

enforceable trust   The ability to call on family and friends to enforce the agreements one has made with a partner.

entitlement   A program in which the government is obligated to provide benefits to anyone who qualifies, regardless of the total cost of the program.

era of divorce tolerance   The time of a tolerant approach toward divorce, from the middle of the nineteenth century until, in the United States, 1970; the grounds for divorce were widened, and divorce was made more accessible to women.

era of restricted divorce   The time of a restrictive approach toward divorce, until about the middle of the nineteenth century; divorces were usually granted only on the grounds of adultery or desertion, and generally only to men.

era of unrestricted divorce   The time of a virtually unrestricted access to divorce, from, in the United States, 1970 to the present; divorces are usually granted without restriction to any married person who wants one.

evolutionary psychology   The view that human behavior can be explained in terms of evolutionary pressure to behave in ways that maximize the chances of reproduction.

exchange theory   A sociological theory that views people as rational beings who decide whether to exchange goods or services by considering the benefits they will receive, the costs they will incur, and the benefits they might receive if they were to choose an alternative course of action.

expressive individualism   A style of life that emphasizes developing one's feelings and emotional satisfaction.

extended family   A kinship group comprising the conjugal family plus any other relatives present in the household, such as a grandparent or uncle.

externalities   Benefits or costs that accrue to others when an individual or business produces something.

extramarital sex   Sexual activity by a married person with someone other than his or her spouse.

familial mode of production   A means of production in which the family produces nearly all its own food, makes most of its own clothes, and with the help of others, builds its own dwelling.

family of choice   A family formed through voluntary ties among individuals who are not biologically or legally related.

family policy   Political beliefs about how the government should assist families in caring for dependents.

family wage system   A division of labor in which the husband earns enough money to support his family and the wife remains home to do housework and child care.

feminist theory   A sociological theory that focuses on the domination of women by men.

fertility   The number of births in a population.

flextime   A policy that allows employees to choose, within limits, when they will begin and end their working hours.

formal sector   The part of a nation's economy that consists of jobs that meet legal standards for minimum wages, are relatively long-lasting and secure, include fringe benefits such as contributions to Social Security or health insurance, often have possibilities for advancement, and are sometimes unionized.

foster care   The removal of children from their parental home and their placement in another home.

free-rider problem   The tendency for people to obtain public goods by letting others do the work of producing them—metaphorically, the temptation to ride free on the backs of others.

frustration–aggression perspective   The theory that aggressive behavior occurs when a person is blocked from achieving a goal.

functionalist theory   A sociological theory that attempts to determine the functions, or uses, of the main ways in which a society is organized.

gender   The social and cultural characteristics that distinguish women and men in a society.

gender role   The different sets of behaviors that are commonly exhibited by women and men.

generativity   A feeling of concern about, or interest in, guiding and shaping the next generation.

gerontologist   A social/biological scientist who specializes in the study of aging.

gestation   Nine-month development of the fetus inside the mother's uterus.

Hispanic   A person living in the United States who traces his or her ancestry to Latin America.

hunter-gatherers   People who wander through forests or over plains in small bands, hunting animals and gathering edible plants.

hypothesis   A speculative statement about the relationship between two or more factors.

ideal type   A hypothetical model that consists of the most significant characteristics, in extreme form, of a social phenomenon.

immigrant enclave   A large, dense, single-ethnic-group, almost self-sufficient community.

incest   Sexual relations with one's child, brother, or sister.

income-pooling model   A model of the marriage market in which both spouses work for pay and pool their income.

individualism   A style of life in which individuals pursue their own interests and place great importance on developing a personally rewarding life.

individualized marriage   A marriage in which the emphasis is on self-development, flexible roles, and open communication.

informal sector   The part of a nation's economy that consists of temporary or casual jobs that sometimes offer illegal subminimum wages and that have little security, little possibility for advancement, and no fringe benefits.

initiator (of a divorce)   The person in a marriage who first becomes dissatisfied and begins the process of ending the marriage.

institutional marriage   A marriage in which the emphasis is on male authority, duty, and conformity to social norms.

integrative perspective (on sexuality)   The belief that human sexuality is determined by both social and biological factors.

interactionist approach (to gender differences)   The theory that gender identification and behavior are based on the day-to-day behavior that reinforces gender distinctions.

intergenerational ambivalence   Socially structured contradictory emotions in an intergenerational relationship.

intergenerational solidarity   The characteristics of family relationships that knit the generations together.

internal economy   The way in which income is allocated to meet the needs of each member of a household, and whose preferences shape how income is spent.

intersectionality (of black women's experience)   The extent to which black women's lives are affected by overlapping systems of class, race, and gender-based disadvantage.

intersexual   A person who is born with ambiguous sexual organs.

intimate outsider   A person, such as a stepparent, who plays a role in a family that is somewhere between that of a parent and that of a trusted friend.

intimate terrorism   A pattern in which a man seeks to control the behavior of his partner through repeated, serious, violent acts.

joint legal custody (of children after a divorce)   The retaining by both parents of an equal right to make important decisions concerning their children.

joint physical custody (of children after a divorce)
An arrangement whereby the children of divorced parents spend substantial time in the household of each parent.

Kinsey Report A 1948 book by zoology professor Alfred Kinsey detailing the results of thousands of interviews with men about their sexual behavior.

labor force All people who are either working outside the home or looking for work.

labor market mode of production A means of production in which people work for pay and thus produce less for their own use at home and buy and sell more on the market.

late modern era The period between the last few decades of the twentieth century and the present day.

legal custody (of children after a divorce) The right to make important decisions about the children and the obligation to have legal responsibility for them.

life chances The resources and opportunities that people have to provide themselves with material goods and favorable living conditions.

life-course perspective The study of changes in individuals' lives over time, and how those changes are related to historical events.

lineage A form of kinship group in which descent is traced through either the father's or the mother's line.

longitudinal survey A survey in which interviews are conducted several times at regular intervals.

lower-class families Families whose connection to the economy is so tenuous that they cannot reliably provide for a decent life.

marriage market An analogy to the labor market in which single individuals (or their parents) search for others who will marry them (or their children).

masculinity The set of personal characteristics that society defines as being typical of men.

matrilineage A kinship group in which descent is through the mother's line.

mediating structures Midlevel social institutions and groupings, such as the church, the neighborhood, the civic organization, and the family.

Medicaid The government program of health insurance for people with incomes below the poverty line.

Medicare The government program of health insurance for all elderly people.

mestizo A person whose ancestors include both Spanish settlers and Native Americans.

middle-class families Families whose connection to the economy provides them with a secure,

comfortable income and allows them to live well above a subsistence level.

monogamy A marriage system in which people are allowed only one spouse.

mortality The number of deaths in a population.

multigenerational households Households in which at least three generations of family members reside.

nation A people with shared economic and cultural interests.

nation-state A term that combines the governmental and cultural connotations of the two words it comprises.

negative externalities The costs imposed on other individuals or businesses when an individual or business produces something of value to itself.

no-fault divorce The granting of a divorce simply on the basis of marriage breakdown due to "irreconcilable differences."

non-Hispanic whites People who identify their race as white but do not think of themselves as Hispanic.

nonmarital birth ratio The proportion of all births that occur to unmarried women.

nonstandard employment Jobs that do not provide full-time, indefinite work directly for the firm that is paying for it.

norm A widely accepted rule about how people should behave.

objectivity The ability to draw conclusions about a social situation that are unaffected by one's own beliefs.

observational study (also known as field research) A study in which the researcher spends time directly observing each participant.

oldest-old The group of elderly people 85 years of age and over.

old-old The group of elderly people 75 to 84 years of age.

parallel parenting An arrangement whereby divorced parents gravitate toward a more detached style, going about their parenting business separately.

parental leave Time off from work to care for a child.

patriarchy A social order based on the domination of women by men, especially in agricultural societies.

patrilineage A kinship group in which descent is through the father's line.

patrilocal A marriage residence rule in which the wife goes to live in her husband's parents' home.

peer group A group of people who have roughly the same age and status as one another.

permissive style (of parenting) A parenting style in which parents provide emotional support but exercise little control over their children.

Personal Responsibility and Work Opportunity Reconciliation Act of 1996 (PRWORA) The federal welfare legislation that requires most recipients to work within two years and that limits the amount of time a family can receive welfare.

physical custody (of children after a divorce) The right of a divorced spouse to have one's children live with one.

polyandry A form of polygamy in which a woman is allowed to have more than one husband.

polygamy A marriage system in which men or women (or both) are allowed to have more than one spouse.

polygyny A form of polygamy in which a man is allowed to have more than one wife.

positive externalities Benefits received by others when an individual or business produces something, but for which the producer is not fully compensated.

poverty line A federally defined income limit defined as the cost of an "economy" diet for a family of four, multiplied by three.

power The ability to force a person to do something even against his or her will.

primary analysis Analysis of survey data by the people who collected the information.

private family Two or more individuals who maintain an intimate relationship that they expect will last in-definitely—or in the case of a parent and child, until the child reaches adulthood—and who live in the same household and pool their income and house-hold labor.

pronatalism The belief that public policies should en-courage people to have children.

psychoanalytic approach (to gender differences) The theory that gender identification and behavior are based on children's unconscious internalization of the qualities of their same-sex parent.

public family One adult, or two adults who are related by marriage, partnership, or shared parenthood, who is/are taking care of dependents, and the dependents themselves.

public goods Things that may be enjoyed by people who do not themselves produce them.

pure relationship An intimate relationship entered into for its own sake and which lasts only as long as both partners are satisfied with it.

queer theory The view that sexual life is artificially organized into categories that reflect the power of heterosexual norms.

racial-ethnic group People who share a common identity and whose members think of themselves as distinct from others by virtue of ancestry, culture, and sometimes physical characteristics.

reflexivity The process through which individuals take in knowledge, reflect on it, and alter their behavior as a result.

relationship-specific investment Time spent on activities such as child rearing that are valuable only in a person's current relationship.

remarriage chain A path that links individuals across households through the ties of disrupted unions and new unions.

remittances Cash payments sent by immigrants to family members in their country of origin.

reproductive strategies Ways of fitting childbearing into the life course.

responsive workplace A work setting in which job conditions are designed to allow employees to meet their family responsibilities more easily.

role overload The state of having too many roles with conflicting demands.

scientific method A systematic, organized series of steps that ensures maximum objectivity and consistency in researching a problem.

secondary analysis Analysis of survey data by people other than those who collected it.

selection effect The principle that whenever individuals sort, or "select," themselves into groups nonrandomly, some of the differences among the groups reflect preexisting differences among the individuals.

self-identity A person's sense of who he or she is and of where he or she fits in the social structure.

service sector Workers who provide personal services such as education, health care, communication, restau-rant meals, legal representation, entertainment, and so forth.

sex The biological characteristics that distinguish men and women.

sex-gender system The transformation of the biological differences between women and men into a social order that supports male domination.

sexual identity A set of sexual practices and attitudes that lead to the formation in a person's mind of an identity as heterosexual, homosexual, or bisexual.

sexual monogamy The state of having just one sex partner.

situational couple violence Violence that arises from a specific situation in which one or both partners act aggressively in anger.

skipped-generation households Households containing grandparents and grandchildren without either parent present.

social capital The resources that a person can access through his or her relationships with other people.

social class   An ordering of all persons in a society according to their degrees of economic resources, prestige, and privilege.

social constructionist perspective (on sexuality)   The belief that human sexuality is entirely socially constructed.

social exchange perspective   The theory that people calculate whether to engage in a particular behavior by considering the rewards and costs of that behavior and the rewards of alternatives to it.

social institution   A set of roles and rules that define a social unit of importance to society.

social learning perspective   The theory that individuals learn behavior they will later exhibit by observing what others do and seeing the consequences of these actions.

social role   A pattern of behaviors associated with a position in society.

Social Security Act of 1935   The federal act that created, among other provisions, Social Security, unemployment compensation, and aid to mothers with dependent children (later renamed Aid to Families with Dependent Children).

socialism   An economic system in which the number and types of goods produced, and who they are distributed to, are decided by the government rather than by the actions of a market.

socialization   The way in which one learns the ways of a given society or social group so that one can function within it.

socialization approach (to gender differences)   The theory that gender identification and behavior are based on children's learning that they will be rewarded for the set of behaviors considered appropriate to their sex but not for those appropriate to the other sex.

specialization model   A model of the marriage market in which women specialize in housework and child care and men specialize in paid work outside the home.

spillover   The fact that stressful events in one part of a person's daily life often spill over into other parts of her or his life.

state   A government that claims the right to rule a given territory and its population and to have a monopoly on force in that territory.

status group   A group of people who share a common style of life and often identify with each other.

stepfamily   A household in which two adults are married or cohabiting and at least one of the adults has a child present from a previous marriage or relationship.

survey   A study in which individuals from a geographic area are selected, usually at random, and asked a fixed set of questions.

symbolic interaction theory   A sociological theory that focuses on people's interpretations of symbolic behavior.

Temporary Assistance to Needy Families (TANF)   A federal program of financial assistance to low-income families that began in 1996, following passage of new welfare legislation. (See **Aid to Families with Dependent Children.**)

total fertility rate (TFR)   The average number of children a woman will bear over her lifetime if current birthrates remain the same.

transnational familes   Families that maintain continual contact between members in the sending and receiving countries.

'tweeners   The group of elderly people who have incomes that place them between the poor, who can qualify for public assistance over and above Social Security, and the middle class, who can supplement their Social Security checks with savings and pensions.

union   A stable, intimate relationship between two people who live in the same household but may or may not be married.

upper-class families   Families that have amassed wealth and privilege and that often have substantial prestige as well.

utilitarian individualism   A style of life that emphasizes self-reliance and personal achievement, especially in one's work life.

value   A goal or principle that is held in high esteem by a society.

welfare state   A capitalist government that has enacted numerous measures, such as social security, unemployment compensation, and a minimum wage, to protect workers and their families from the harshness of the capitalist system.

Western nations   The countries of Western Europe and the overseas English-speaking countries of the United States, Canada, Australia, and New Zealand.

women-centered kinship   A kinship structure in which the strongest bonds of support and caregiving occur among a network of women, most of them relatives, who may live in more than one household.

working-class families   Families whose income can reliably provide only for the minimum needs of what other people see as a decent life.

young-old   The group of elderly people 65 to 74 years of age.

References

Abbey, A., & McAuslan, P. (2004). A longitudinal examination of male college students' perpetration of sexual assault. *Journal of Consulting and Clinical Psychology, 72,* 747-756.

Acker, J. (1973). Women and social stratification: A case of intellectual sexism. *American Journal of Sociology, 78,* 936-945.

Acker, J. (2000). Rewriting class, race, and gender: Problems in feminist rethinking. In M. M. Ferree, J. Lorber, & B. B. Hess (Eds.), *Revisioning gender* (pp. 44-69). Walnut Creek, CA: AltaMira Press.

Adam, B. D. (2004). Care, intimacy, and same-sex partnerships in the 21st century. *Current Sociology, 52,* 265-279.

Alan Guttmacher Institute. (2004). *U.S. teenage pregnancy statistics.* Retrieved March 1, 2006, from http://www.agi-usa.org/pubs/state_pregnancy_trends.pdf.

Alwin, D. F. (1988). From obedience to autonomy: Changes in traits desired in children, 1924-1978. *Public Opinion Quarterly, 52,* 33-52.

Alwin, D. F. (1990). Historical changes in parental orientations to children. In N. Mandell (Ed.), *Sociological studies of child development* (pp. 65-86). Greenwich, CT.: JAI Press.

Alwin, D. F. (1996). Coresidence beliefs in American society, 1973 to 1991. *Journal of Marriage and Family, 55,* 393-403.

Amato, P. R. (1994). The implications of research findings on children in stepfamilies. In A. Booth & J. Dunn (Eds.), *Stepfamilies: Who benefits? Who does not?* (pp. 81-87). Hillsdale, NJ: Lawrence Erlbaum.

Amato, P. R. (1996). Explaining the intergenerational transmission of divorce. *Journal of Marriage and Family, 58,* 628-640.

Amato, P. R. (1998). More than money? Men's contribution to their children's lives. In A. Booth & A. C. Crouter (Eds.), *Men in families: When do they get involved? What difference does it make?* (pp. 241-278). Mahwah, NJ: Lawrence Erlbaum Associates.

Amato, P. R. (1999). Children of divorced parents as young adults. In E. M. Hetherington (Ed.), *Coping with divorce, single-parenting, and remarriage* (pp. 147-163). Mahwah, NJ: Lawrence Erlbaum Associates.

Amato, P. R. (2000). The consequences of divorce for adults and children. *Journal of Marriage and Family, 62,* 1269-1287.

Amato, P. R., & Booth, A. (1997). *A generation at risk: Growing up in an era of family upheaval.* Cambridge, MA: Harvard University Press.

Amato, P. R., & Gilbreth, J. G. (1999). Nonresistant fathers and children's well-being. *Journal of Marriage and the Family, 61,* 557-573.

Amato, P. R., & Rezac, S. L. (1994). Contact with nonresistant parents, interparental conflict, and children's behavior. *Journal of Family Issues, 15,* 191-207.

American Bar Association. (2003). *Grounds for divorce and residency requirements.* Retrieved November 10, 2003, from http://www.abanet.org/family/familylaw/table4.html.

Amirkhanyan, A. A., & Wolf, D. A. (2003). Caregiver stress and noncaregiver stress: Exploring the pathways of psychiatric morbidity. *The Gerontologist, 43,* 817-827.

Ammerman, N. T. (2005). *Pillars of faith: American congregations and their partners.* Berkeley: University of California Press.

Anderson, M. (1971). *Family structure in nineteenth-century Lancashire.* Cambridge, England: University Press.

Angell, R. C. (1936). *The family encounters the depression.* New York: Charles Scribner's Sons.

Angier, N. (1993, July 18). Study of sex orientation doesn't neatly fit mold. *The New York Times,* p. 24.

Aquilino, W. S. (1991). Family structure and home-leaving: A further specification of the relationship. *Journal of Marriage and Family, 53,* 999-1010.

Aquilino, W. S. (1994). Impact of childhood family disruption on young adults' relationships with parents. *Journal of Marriage and Family, 56,* 295-313.

Archer, J. (2000). Sex differences in aggression between heterosexual partners: A meta-analytic review. *Psychological Bulletin, 126,* 651-680.

Archer, J. (2002). Sex differences in physically aggressive acts between heterosexual partners: A meta-analytic review. *Aggression & Violent Behavior, 7,* 313-351.

Arendell, T. (1986). *Mothers and divorce: Legal, economic, and social dilemmas.* Berkeley: University of California Press.

Ariès, P. (1960). *L'enfant et la vie familiale sous l'ancien regine.* Paris: Librairie Plon.

Ariès, P. (1985a). Love in married life. In P. Ariès & A. Benjin (Eds.), *Western sexuality* (pp. 130-139). Oxford: Basil Blackwell.

Ariès, P. (1985b). Thoughts on the history of homosexuality. In P. Ariès & A. Benjin (Eds.), *Western sexuality* (pp. 62–75). Oxford: Basil Blackwell.

Arno, P. S., Levine, C., & Memmott, M. M. (1999). The economic value of informal caregiving. *Health Affairs, 18,* 182–188.

Astone, N. M., & McLanahan, S. S. (1991). Family structure, parental practices, and high school completion. *American Sociological Review, 56,* 309–320.

Avellar, Sarah, & Smock, P. J. (2003). Has the price of motherhood declined over time? A cross-cohort comparison of the motherhood wage penalty. *Journal of Marriage and Family, 65,* 597–607.

Baca Zinn, M., Wells, M., & Wells, B. (2000). Diversity within Latino families: New lessons for family social science. In D. H. Demo, K. R. Allen, & M. A. Fine (Eds.), *Handbook of family diversity* (pp. 252–273). New York: Oxford University Press.

Bailey, B. L. (1988). *From front porch to back seat: Courtship in twentieth-century America.* Baltimore: Johns Hopkins University Press.

Bailey, M., & Pillard, R. C. (1991). A genetic study of male sexual orientation. *Archives of General Psychiatry, 48,* 1089–1096.

Bailey, M., Pillard, R. C., Neale, M. C., & Agyei, Y. (1993). Heritable factors influence sexual orientation in women. *Archives of General Psychiatry, 50,* 217–223.

Bailey, M. J., & Dawood, K. (1998). Behavioral genetics, sexual orientation, and the family. In C. J. Patterson & A. R. D. Augelli (Eds.), *Lesbian, gay, and bisexual identities in families: Psychological perspectives* (pp. 3–18). New York: Oxford University Press.

Bandura, A. (1973). *Aggression: A social learning analysis.* Englewood Cliffs, NJ: Prentice Hall.

Banister, J. (2003). *Shortage of girls in China: Causes, consequences, international comparisons, and solutions.* Retrieved July 16, 2003, from http://www.prb.org/.

Barcus, F. E. (1983). *Images of life on children's television: Sex roles, minorities, and families.* New York: Praeger.

Barlett, J. (Eds.). (1980). *Familiar quotations.* Boston: Little, Brown.

Barnett, R., & Hyde, J. S. (2001). Women, men, work, and family: An expansionist theory. *American Psychologist, 556,* 781–796.

Bartholet, E. (1993, September 21). Blood knots: Adoption, reproduction, and the politics of family. *The American Prospect, 4,* 48–57.

Bartlett, J. (1980). *Familiar quotations* (Ed. E. M. Beck). Boston: Little, Brown.

Bartlett, K. T. (1999). Improving the law relating to postdivorce arrangements for children. In E. M. Hetherington (Ed.), *Coping with divorce, single parenting, and remarriage* (pp. 71–102). Mahwah, NJ: Lawrence Erlbaum Associates.

Bass, S., Shields, M. K., & Behrman, R. E. (2004). Children, families, and foster care: Analysis and recommendations. *Future of Children, 14* (Winter), 5–29.

Baum, C. L. (2002). A dynamic analysis of the effect of child care costs on the work decisions of low-income mothers with infants. *Demography, 39,* 139–164.

Bauman, Z. (1992). *Intimations of postmodernity.* London: Taylor and Francis Books.

Bauman, Z. (2002). Individually, together. In U. Beck & E. Beck (Eds.), *Individualization* (pp. xiv–xix). London: Sage Publications.

Baumrind, D. (1971). Current patterns of parental authority, *Developmental Psychology Monographs,* Vol. 4, no. 1, pt. 2.

Bauza, V. (2005, April 17). Elian adjusts to his fame, life in Cuba 5 years after the uproar, expectations high for 11-year-old. *South Florida Sun-Sentinel,* p. 1A.

Bawin-Legros, B. (2004). Intimacy and the new sentimental order. *Current Sociology, 52,* 241–250.

Bean, F. D., Swicegood, C. G., & Berg, R. (2000). Mexican-origin fertility: New patterns and interpretations. *Social Science Quarterly, 81,* 404–420.

Bean, F. D., & Tienda, M. (1987). *The Hispanic population of the United States.* New York: Russell Sage Foundation.

Beck, U., & Beck-Gernsheim, E. (1995). *The normal chaos of love.* Cambridge: Polity Press.

Beck, U., & Beck-Gernsheim, E. (2002). *Individualization: Institutionalized individualism and its social and political consequences.* London: Sage Publications.

Beck, U., Giddens, A., & Lash, S. (1994). *Reflexive modernization: Politics, tradition and aesthetics in the modern social order.* Cambridge: Polity Press.

Becker, G. S. (1965). A theory of the allocation of time. *Economic Journal, 75,* 493–517.

Becker, G. S. (1991). *A treatise on the family (enlarged edition).* Cambridge, MA: Harvard University Press.

Belenky, M. F., Clinchy, B. M., Goldberger, N. R., & Tarule, J. M. (1997). *Women's ways of knowing* (Tenth anniversary ed.). New York: Basic Books.

Bellah, R., Marsden, R., Sullivan, W. M., Swidler, A., & Tipton, S. M. (1985). *Habits of the heart: Individualism and commitment in America.* Berkeley: University of California Press.

Bem, S. L. (1981). Gender schema theory: A cognitive account of sex-typing. *Psychological Review, 88,* 354–364.

Bem, S. L. (1993). *The lenses of gender: Transforming the debate on sexual inequality.* New Haven, CT: Yale University Press.

Bendix, R. (1960). *Max Weber: An intellectual portrait*. New York: Doubleday.

Benería, L., & Roldàn, M. (1987). *The crossroads of class and gender: Industrial homework, subcontracting, and household dynamics in Mexico City*. Chicago: University of Chicago Press.

Bengtson, V. L. (2001). Beyond the nuclear family: The increasing importance of multigenerational bonds. *Journal of Marriage and Family, 63*, 1–16.

Bengtson, V. L., Biblarz, T. J., & Roberts, R. E. L. (2002). *How families still matter: A longitudinal study of youths in two generations*. Cambridge: Cambridge University Press.

Bennice, J. A., & Resick, P. A. (2003). Marital rape: History, research, and practice. *Trauma, Violence, & Abuse, 4*, 228–246.

Berger, B. (1986). On the limits of the welfare state: The case of foster care. In F. R. Penden & F. R. Glahe (Eds.), *American family and the state* (pp. 365–379). San Francisco: Pacific Research Institute for Public Policy.

Berger, B., & Berger, P. L. (1983). *The war over the family: Capturing the middle ground*. Garden City, NY: Anchor/Doubleday.

Berk, S. F. (1985). *The gender factory: The apportionment of work in American households*. New York: Plenum Press.

Berkner, L. K. (1972). The stem family and the developmental cycle of the peasant household: An eighteenth-century Austrian example. *American Historical Review, 77*, 398–418.

Bernard, J. (1972). *The future of marriage*. New York: Bantam.

Bernard, J. (1981). The good provider role: Its rise and fall. *American Psychologist, 36*.

Bernhardt, A., Morris, M., & Handcock, M. S. (1995). Women's gains or men's losses? A closer look at the shrinking gender gap in earnings. *American Journal of Sociology, 101*, 302–328.

Bernstein, A. C. (1988). Unraveling the tangles: Children's understanding of stepfamily kinship. In W. R. Beer (Ed.), *Relative strangers: Studies of stepfamily processes* (pp. 83–111). Totowa, NJ: Rowan and Littlefield.

Berry, M. F., & Blassingame, J. W. (1982). *Long memory: The black experience in America*. New York: Oxford University Press.

Besharov, D. J., & Laumann, L. A. (2001). Don't call it child abuse if it's really poverty. In A. J. Cherlin (Ed.), *Public and private families: A reader*, 2nd ed. (pp. 274–289). New York: McGraw-Hill.

Bianchi, S. M. (1995). The changing economic roles of women and men. In R. Farley (Ed.), *Social diversity in the United States*. New York: Russell Sage Foundation.

Bianchi, S. M., Robinson, J. P., & Milkie, M. A. (2006). *Changing rhythms of American family life*. New York: Russell Sage Foundation.

Bianchi, S. M., & Spain, D. (1986). *American women in transition*. New York: Russell Sage Foundation.

Bianchi, S. M., & Spain, D. (1996). Women, work, and family in America. *Population Bulletin, 51* (3).

Bianchi, S. M., Subaiya, L., & Kahn, J. R. (1999). The gender gap in economic well-being of nonresident fathers and custodial mothers. *Demography, 36*, 195–203.

Biblarz, T. J., & Gottdainer, G. (2000). Family structure and children's success: A comparison of widowed and divorced single-mother families. *Journal of Marriage and Family, 62*, 533–548.

Billingsley, A. (1992). *Climbing Jacob's ladder: The enduring legacy of African American families*. New York: Simon and Schuster.

Binner, J. M., & Dnes, A. W. (2001). Marriage, divorce, and legal change: New evidence from England and Wales. *Economic Inquiry, 39*, 298–306.

Bittman, M. (2004). Parenting and employment: What time-use surveys show. In N. Folbre & M. Bittman (Eds.), *Family time: The social organization of care* (pp. 152–170). London: Routledge.

Bittman, M., Craig, L., & Folbre, N. (2004). Packaging care: What happens when children receive nonparental care? In N. Folbre & M. Bittman (Eds.), *Family time: The social organization of care* (pp. 134–151). London: Routledge.

Bittman, M., England, P., Sayer, L., Folbre, N., & Matheson, G. (2003). When does gender trump money? Bargaining and time in household work. *American Journal of Sociology, 109*, 186–214.

Bittman, M., & Wajcman, J. (2000). The rush hour: The character of leisure time and gender equity. *Social Forces, 79*, 165–189.

Bittman, M., & Wajcman, J. (2004). The rush hour: The quality of leisure time and gender equity. In N. Folbre & M. Bittman (Eds.), *Family time: The social organization of care* (pp. 171–193). London: Routledge.

Black, A. (1924). Is the young person coming back. *Harper's* (August), 340.

Black, D., Gates, G., Sanders, S., & Taylor, L. (2000). Demographics of the gay and lesbian population in the United States: Evidence from available systematic data. *Demography, 37*, 139–154.

Blackwood, E. (1984). Sexuality and gender in certain native American tribes: The case of cross-gender females. *Signs, 10*, 27–42.

Blank, R. M. (1997). *It takes a nation: A new agenda for fighting poverty*. Princeton: Princeton University Press.

Blumberg, P. M., & Paul, P. W. (1975). Continuities and discontinuities in upper-class marriages. *Journal of Marriage and Family, 37*, 63-77.

Blumer, H. (1962). Society as symbolic interaction. In A. M. Rose (Ed.), *Human behavior and social processes* (pp. 179-192). Boston, MA: Houghton Mifflin.

Blumstein, P., & Schwartz, P. (1983). *American couples: Money, work, sex.* New York: William Morrow Company.

Bly, R. (1990). *Iron John: A book about men.* Reading, MA: Addison-Wesley.

Boden, S. (2003). *Consumerism, romance, and the wedding experience.* Hampshire: Palgrave Macmillan.

Bogenschneider, K. (2000). Has family policy come of age? A decade review of the state of U.S. family policy in the 1990s. *Journal of Marriage and Family, 62*, 1136-1159.

Bohannan, P. (1971a). Divorce chains, households of remarriage, and multiple divorcers. In P. Bohannan (Ed.), *Divorce and after* (pp. 128-139). Garden City, NY: Anchor Books.

Bohannan, P. (1971b). The six stations of divorce. In P. Bohannan (Ed.), *Divorce and after* (pp. 33-62). New York: Anchor Books.

Bond, J. T., Galinsky, E., & Swanberg, J. E. (1998). *The 1997 national study of the changing work force, executive summary.* Retrieved March 14, 2006, from http://familiesandwork.org/summary/nscw.pdf.

Bonnie, R. J., & Wallace, R. B. (Eds.). (2002). *Elder mistreatment: Abuse, neglect, and exploitation in aging America.* Washington, DC: National Academies Press.

Boocock, S. S. (1991). Childhood and child care in Japan: A comparative analysis. In S. E. Cahill (Ed.), *Sociological studies of child development* (Vol. 4, pp. 51-88). Greenwich, CT: JAI Press.

Booth, A., & Dabbs, J. J., Jr. (1993). Testosterone and men's marriages. *Social Forces, 72*, 463-477.

Booth, A., & Edwards, J. N. (1992). Starting over: Why remarriages are unstable. *Journal of Family Issues, 13*, 179-194.

Booth, A., Johnson, D. R., Branaman, A., & Sica, A. (1995). Belief and behavior: Does religion matter in today's marriage? *Journal of Marriage and Family, 57*, 661-671.

Booth, C. L., Clarke-Stewart, A., Vandell, D. L., McCartney, K., & Owen, M. T. (2002). Child care usage and mother-infant quality time. *Journal of Marriage and Family, 64*, 16-26.

Borchorst, Anette. (2000). Feminist thinking about the welfare state. In M. M. Ferree, J. Lorber & B. B. Hess (Eds.), *Revisioning gender* (pp. 99-127). Walnut Creek, CA: AltaMira Press.

Boss, P. G. (1980). Normative family stress: Family boundary changes across the life-span. *Family Relations, 29*, 445-450.

Boswell, J. (1982). Revolutions, universals, and sexual categories. *Salmagundi, 58-59*, 89-113.

Bott, E. (1957). *Family and social network.* London: Tavistock.

Bourdieu, P. (1980). Le capital social: Notes provisaire. *Actes de la recherchè en sciences sociales, 3*, 2-3.

Bowers v. Hardwick, 47 186 (U.S. 1986).

Bradbury, B., & Jäntti, M. (1999). *Child poverty across industrialized nations* (Innocenti Occasional Papers, Economic and Social Policy Series No. 71). Florence: UNICEF International Child Development Center.

Bradbury, B., & Jäntti, M. (2000). Child-poverty across the industrialized world: Evidence from the Luxembourg income study. In K. Vleminckx & T. M. Smeeding (Eds.), *Child well-being, child poverty and child policy in modern nations: What do we know?* (pp. 11-32). Bristol: Policy Press.

Bramlett, M. D., & Mosher, W. D. (2002). *Cohabitation, marriage, divorce, and remarriage in the United States.* Retrieved June, 2003, from www.cdc.gov/nchs/data/series/sr_23/sr23_022.pdf.

Bray, J. H. (1999). From marriage to remarriage and beyond. In E. M. Hetherington (Ed.), *Coping with divorce, single parenting, and remarriage* (pp. 253-271). Mahwah, NJ: Lawrence Erlbaum Associates.

Briere, J., & Elliot, D. M. (1994). Immediate and long-term impacts of child sexual abuse. *The Future of Children, 4*, 54-59.

Brines, J. (1994). Economic dependency, gender, and the division of labor at home. *American Journal of Sociology, 100*, 652-688.

Brines, J., & Joyner, K. (1999). The ties that bind: Commitment and stability in the modern union. *American Sociological Review, 64*, 333-356.

Brod, H., & Kaufman, M. (1994). *Theorizing masculinities.* Thousand Oaks, CA: Sage Publications.

Broder, J. M. (2002, September 24). Family leave in California now includes pay benefit. *The New York Times*, p. A20.

Brody, E. M., Kleban, M. H., Johnson, P. T., Hoffman, C., & Schoonover, C. B. (1987). Work status and parent care: A comparison of four groups of women. *The Gerontologist, 21*, 471-480.

Brodzinsky, D. M., Schechter, M. D., & Marantz, R. (1992). *Being adopted: The lifelong search for self.* New York: Doubleday.

Brooks-Gunn, J., Duncan, G. J., Klebanov, P. K., & Sealand, N. (1993). Do neighborhoods influence child and adolescent development? *American Journal of Sociology, 99*, 353-395.

Brownridge, D. A., & Halli, S. S. (2002). Understanding male partner violence against cohabiting and married women: An empirical investigation with a synthesized model. *Journal of Family Violence, 17*, 341-361.

Brugeilles, C., Cromer, I., & Cromer, S. (2002). Male and female characters in illustrated children's books or how children's literature contributes to the construction of gender. *Population: English Selection, 57*, 237-268.

Buchanan, C. M., Maccoby, E. E., & Dornbusch, S. F. (1996). *Adolescents after divorce*. Cambridge, MA: Harvard University Press.

Budgeon, S., & Roseneil, S. (2004). Editors' introduction: Beyond the conventional family. *Current Sociology, 52*, 127-134.

Budig, M., & England, P. (2001). The wage penalty for motherhood. *American Sociological Review, 66*, 204-225.

Bulcroft, K., Bulcroft, R., Smeins, L., & Cranage, H. (1997). The social construction of the North American honeymoon, 1880-1995. *Journal of Family History, 22*, 462-490.

Bulcroft, R. A., Bulcroft, K., Bradley, K., & Simpson, C. (2000). The management and production of risk in romantic relationships: A postmodern paradox. *Journal of Family History, 25*, 63-92.

Bulcroft, R. A., & Bulcroft, K. A. (1993). Race differences in attitudinal and motivational factors in the decision to marry. *Journal of Marriage and Family, 55*, 338-355.

Bumpass, L. L. (1984). Children and marital disruption: A replication and update. *Demography, 21*, 71-82.

Bumpass, L. L., & Lu, H. H. (2000). Trends in cohabitation and implications for children's family contexts in the United States. *Population Studies, 54*, 19-41.

Bumpass, L. L., Raley, K., & Sweet, J. A. (1995). The changing character of stepfamilies: Implications of cohabitation and nonmarital childbearing. *Demography, 32*, 1-12.

Bumpass, L. L., & Sweet, J. A. (1989). National estimates of cohabitation. *Demography, 26*, 615-625.

Bumpass, L. L., Sweet, J. A., & Cherlin, A. J. (1991). The role of cohabitation in declining rates of marriage. *Journal of Marriage and Family, 53*, 338-355.

Bumpass, L. L., Sweet, J. A., & Martin, T. C. (1990). Changing patterns of remarriage. *Journal of Marriage and Family, 52*, 747-756.

Burgess, E. W., & Locke, H. J. (1945). *The family: From institution to companionship*. New York: American Book Company.

Burstein, P., & Bricher, M. (1997). Problem definition and public policy: Congressional committees confront work, family, and gender, 1945-1990. *Social Forces, 75*, 135-169.

Burstein, P., Bricher, M., & Einwohner, R. L. (1995). Policy alternatives and political change: Work, family, and gender on the Congressional agenda, 1945-1990. *American Sociological Review, 60*, 67-83.

Burstein, P., & Wierzbicki, S. (2000). Public opinion and congressional action on work, family, and gender, 1945-1990. In T. L. Parcel (Ed.), *Work, family, and gender: Research informing policy* (pp. 31-66). Thousand Oaks, CA: Sage Publications.

Burt, M., Aron, L. Y., & Lee, E. (2001). *Helping America's homeless: Emergency shelter or affordable housing?* Washington, DC: Urban Institute Press.

Burtless, G., & Karoly, L. A. (1995). Demographic change, rising earnings inequality, and the distribution of personal well-being, 1959-1989. *Demography, 32*, 379-405.

Burton, L. M. (1990). Teenage childbearing as an alternative life-course strategy in multigenerational black families. *Human Nature, 1*, 123-143.

Burton, L. M. (1992). Black grandparents rearing children of drug-addicted parents: Stressors, outcomes, and social service needs. *The Gerontologist, 32*, 744-751.

Buss, D. M. (1994). *The evolution of desire: Strategies of human mating*. New York: Basic Books.

Buss, D. M., Shackelford, T. K., Kirkpatrick, L. A., & Larsen, R. J. (2001). A half-century of mate preferences: The cultural evolution of values. *Journal of Marriage and Family, 63*, 491-503.

Butler, J., Wacker, G., & Balmer, R. (2003). *Religion in American life: A short history*. New York: Oxford University Press.

Butterfield, F. (1997, February 3). 95 data show sharp drop in reported rapes. *The New York Times*, p. A1.

Butz, W. P., & Ward, M. P. (1979). The emergence of countercyclical U. S. fertility. *American Economic Review, 69*, 318-328.

Cain, M. (1983). Fertility as an adjustment to risk. *Population and Development Review, 9*, 688-702.

Caldwell, J. C. (1982). *Theory of fertility decline*. New York: Academic Press.

Calhoun, A. W. (1919). *A social history of the American family from 1865-1919*. New York: Barries and Noble.

Callendar, C., & Kochems, L. (1983). The North American berdache. *Current Anthropology, 24*, 443-470.

Camarillo, A. (1979). *Chicanos in a changing society: From Mexican pueblos to American barrios in Santa Barbara and Southern California, 1848-1940*. Cambridge, MA: Harvard University Press.

Cameron, T. (2003, September 6). A way but no will when it comes to foster care. *The New York Times*, p. A11.

Cancian, F. M. (1987). *Love in America: Gender and self-development*. Cambridge, England: Cambridge University Press.

Cancian, F. M. (2002). Defining "good" child care: Hegemonic and democratic standards. In F. M. Cancian, D. Kurz, A. S. London, R. Reviere & M. C. Tuominen (Eds.), *Child care and inequality: Rethinking carework for children and youth* (pp. 65-82). New York: Routledge.

Capaldi, D. M., & Patterson, G. R. (1991). Relation of parental transitions to boys' adjustment problems: 1. A linear hypothesis; 2. Mothers at risk for transitions and unskilled parenting. *Developmental Psychology, 27,* 489-504.

Carlson, M., McLanahan, S., & England, P. (2004). Union formation in fragile families. *Demography, 41,* 237-261.

Carrington, C. (1999). *No place like home: Relationships and family life among lesbians and gay men.* Chicago: University of Chicago Press.

Cate, R. M., & Lloyd, S. A. (1992). *Courtship.* Newbury Park, CA: Sage.

Cavan, R. S., & Ranck, K. H. (1938). *The family and the depression: A study of 100 Chicago families.* Chicago: University of Chicago Press.

Center for Law and Social Policy. (2006a). *Toward a decade of indifference: Administration ignores child care needs of working families.* Retrieved March 14, 2006, from http://www.clasp.org/publications/childcare_2007budget.pdf.

Center for Law and Social Policy. (2006b). *Update on the marriage and fatherhood provisions of the 2006 federal budget and the 2007 budget proposal.* Retrieved April 24, 2006, from http://www.clasp.org/publications/marriage_fatherhood_budget2006.pdf.

Chafe, W. H. (1972). *The American woman: Her changing social, economic, and political roles, 1920-1970.* New York: Oxford University Press.

Chalk, R., Gibbons, A., & Scarupa, H. (2002). *The multiple dimensions of child abuse and neglect: New insights into an old problem (research brief)* (No. 2002-27). Washington, DC: Child Trends.

Chambers, D. L. (1990). Stepparents, biological parents, and the law's perceptions of family after divorce. In S. D. Sugarman & H. H. Kay (Eds.), *Divorce reform at the crossroads* (pp. 102-129). New Haven, CT: Yale University Press.

Chao, R. (1994). Beyond parental control and authorization parenting style: Understanding Chinese parenting through the cultural norm of training. *Child Development, 65,* 1111-1119.

Chase-Lansdale, L., Brooks-Gunn, J., & Zamsky, E. (1994). Young multi-generational families in poverty: Quality of mothering and grandmothering. *Child Development, 65,* 373-393.

Chase-Lansdale, L., & Hetherington, M. E. (1990). The impact of divorce on life-span development: Short and long term effects. In P. B. Baltes (Ed.), *Life-span development, and behavior* (Vol. 10, pp. 105-150). Hillsdale, NJ.: Lawrence Erlbaum Associates.

Chase-Lansdale, P. L., Moffitt, R. A., Lohman, B. J., Cherlin, A. J., Coley, R. L., Pittman, L. D., et al. (2003). Mothers' transitions from welfare to work and the well-being of preschoolers and adolescents. *Science, 299,* 1548-1552.

Cherlin, A. (1978). Remarriage as an incomplete institution. *American Journal of Sociology, 84,* 634-650.

Cherlin, A. J. (1992). *Marriage, divorce, remarriage.* Cambridge, MA.: Harvard University Press.

Cherlin, A. J. (1999a). Going to extremes: Family structure, children's well-being, and social science. *Demography, 36,* 421-428.

Cherlin, A. J. (1999b, October 17). I'm O.K., you're selfish. *The New York Times Magazine,* 44-46.

Cherlin, A. J. (2000b). Toward a new home socioeconomics of union formation. In L. J. Waite, C. Bachrach, M. Hindin, E. Thomson & A. Thornton (Eds.), *Ties that bind: Perspectives on marriage and cohabitation* (pp. 126-144). Hawthorne: Aldine de Gruyter.

Cherlin, A. J. (2003, Fall). Should the government promote marriage? *Contexts, 2,* 22-29.

Cherlin, A. J. (2004). The deinstitutionalization of American marriage. *Journal of Marriage and Family, 66,* 848-861.

Cherlin, A. J., Burton, L. M., Hurt, T. R., & Purvin, D. M. (2004). The influence of physical and sexual abuse on marriage and cohabitation. *American Sociological Review, 69,* 768-789.

Cherlin, A. J., Chase-Lansdale, L., & McRae, C. (1998). Effects of parental divorce on mental health throughout the life course. *American Sociological Review.*

Cherlin, A. J., & Furstenburg, F. F., Jr. (1988). The changing European family: Lessons for the American reader. *Journal of Family Issues, 9* (291-297).

Cherlin, A. J., & Furstenburg, F. F., Jr. (1992). *The new American grandparent: A place in the family, a life apart.* Cambridge, MA.: Harvard University Press.

Cherlin, A. J., Furstenberg, F. F., Jr., Chase-Lansdale, P. L., Kiernan, K. E., Robins, P. K., Morrison, D. R., et al. (1991). Longitudinal studies of the effects of divorce on children in Great Britain and the United States. *Science, 252,* 1386-1389.

Cherlin, A. J., Kiernan, K. E., & Chase-Lansdale, L. (1995). Parental divorce in childhood and demographic outcomes in young adulthood. *Demography, 32,* 299-318.

Child Trends. (2005). *Facts at a glance* (No. 2005-02). Washington, DC: Child Trends.

Chipungu, S. S., & Bent-Goodley, T. B. (2004). Meeting the challenges of contemporary foster care. *Future of Children, 14* (Winter), 75-93.

Chodorow, N. (1978). *The reproduction of mothering: Psychoanalysis and the sociology of gender*. Berkeley, CA: University of California Press.

Clarkberg, M. (1999). The price of partnering: The role of economic well-being in young adults' first union experience. *Social Forces, 77*, 945-968.

Clearinghouse on International Developments in Child Youth and Family Policies. (2004). *Maternity, paternity, parental and family leave policies*. Retrieved March 14, 2006, from http://www.childpolicyintl.org/.

Cohen, P. N., & Bianchi, S. M. (1999). Marriage, children, and women's employment: What do we know? *Monthly Labor Review* (December), 22-31.

Cohen, R. (1971). Brittle marriage as a stable system: The Kanuri case. In P. Bohannan (Ed.), *Divorce and after* (pp. 205-239). Garden City, NY: Anchor Books.

Colapinto, J. (2000). *As nature made him: The boy who was raised as a girl*. New York: Harper Collins.

Coleman, J. S. (1988). Social capital in the creation of human capital. *American Journal of Sociology*.

Coleman, M., Ganong, L. H., & Fine, M. (2000). Reinvestigating remarriage: Another decade of progress. *Journal of Marriage and Family, 62*, 1288-1307.

Collier, J. F. (1997). *From duty to desire: Remaking families in a Spanish village*. Princeton, NJ: Princeton University Press.

Collins, R. (1971). A conflict theory of sexual stratification. *Social Problems, 19*, 3-21.

Coltrane, S. (1994). Theorizing masculinities in contemporary social problems. In H. Brod & M. Kaufman (Eds.), *Theorizing masculinities* (pp. 39-60). Thousand Oaks, CA.: Sage Publications.

Comstock, G., & Scharrer, E. (2001). The use of television and other film-related media. In D. G. Singer & J. L. Singer (Eds.), *Handbook of children and the media* (pp. 47-72). Thousand Oaks, CA: Sage Publications.

Conger, R. D., Jr., Elder, G. H., Lorenz, F. O., Conger, K. J., Simons, R. L., Whitbeck, L. B., et al. (1990). Linking economic hardship to marital quality and instability. *Journal of Marriage and Family, 52*, 643-656.

Connell, R. W. (1995). *Masculinities*. Cambridge, UK: Polity Press.

Connidis, I. A., & McMullin, J. A. (2002). Sociological ambivalence and family ties: A critical perspective. *Journal of Marriage and Family, 64*, 558-567.

Cook, K., O'Brien, J., & Kollock, P. (1990). Exchange theory: A blueprint for structure and process. In G. Ritzer (Ed.), *Frontiers of social theory: The new syntheses* (pp. 151-181). New York: Columbia University Press.

Cooney, T. M., & Uhlenberg, P. (1990). The role of divorce in men's relations with their adult children after mid-life. *Journal of Marriage and Family, 52*, 677-688.

Coontz, S. (1999). Working-class families 1870-1890. In S. Coontz, M. Parson, & G. Raley (Eds.), *American families: A multicultural reader*. New York: Routledge.

Coontz, S. (2005). *Marriage, a history: From obedience to intimacy, or how love conquered marriage*. New York: Viking.

Cooper, S. M. (1999). Historical analysis of the family. In M. B. Sussman, S. K. Steinmetz, & G. W. Peterson (Eds.), *Handbook of marriage and the family*, 2nd ed. New York: Plenum.

Cott, N. F. (1977). *The bonds of womanhood: "Woman's sphere" in New England, 1780-1835*. New Haven: Yale University Press.

Cott, N. F. (2000). *Public vows: A history of marriage and the nation*. Cambridge, MA: Harvard University Press.

Cowley, G. (1997, May 19). Gender limbo. *Newsweek*, pp. 64-66.

Cretney, S. (1993). *Step-parentage in English law*. Paper presented at the International Colloquium on Stepfamilies Today, Paris.

Crimmons, E. M., Saito, Y., & Ingegneri, D. (1997). Trends in disability-free life expectancy in the United States, 1970-90. *Population and Development Review, 23*, 555-572.

The crisis in foster care: New directions for the 1990s. (1990).). Washington, DC: Family Impact Seminar.

Curran, S. A. (2002). Agency, accountability, and embedded relations: "What's love got to do with it?" *Journal of Marriage and Family, 64*, 577-584.

D'Emilio, J., & Freedman, E. B. (1988). *Intimate matters: A history of sexuality in America*. New York: Harper and Row.

D'Onofrio, B. M., Turkheimer, E., Emery, R. E., Slutske, W. S., Heath, A. C., Madden, P. A., et al. (2005). A genetically informed study of marital instability and its association with offspring psychopathology. *Journal of Abnormal Psychology, 114*, 570-586.

Dao, J. (2005, October 11). Ohio court affirms grandparents' visiting rights. *The New York Times*, p. A14.

Darling, C. A., Kallen, D. J., & Van Dusen, J. E. (1984). Sex in transition, 1900-1980. *Journal of Youth and Adolescence, 13*, 385-399.

Das Gupta, M., & Bhat, P. N. M. (1997). Fertility decline and increased manifestation of sex bias in India. *Population Studies, 51*, 307-315.

Davis, J. A., Smith, T. W., & Marsden, P. (2003). *General social surveys, 1972-2002 cumulative codebook*. Chicago: National Opinion Research Center, University of Chicago.

Davis, J. A., Smith, T. W., & Marsden, P. (2004): *General social surveys, 1972-2004, cumulative file*. Ann Arbor, MI: Inter-University Consortium for Political and Social Research.

Davis, N. J., & Robinson, R. V. (1988). Class identification of men and women in the 1970s and 1980s. *American Sociological Review, 53*, 103–112.

Davis, N. J., & Robinson, R. V. (1998). Do wives matter? Class identification of wives and husbands in the United States. *Social Forces, 76*, 1063–1086.

Degler, C. N. (1980). *At odds: Women and the family in America from the Revolution to the present.* New York: Oxford University Press.

Deitch, C. H., & Huffman, M. L. (2001). Family-responsive benefits and the two-tiered labor market. In R. Hertz & N. L. Marshall (Eds.), *Working families: The transformation of the American home* (pp. 103–130). Berkeley: University of California Press.

DeLeire, T., & Kalil, A. (2002). Good things come in threes: Single-parent and multigenerational family structure and adolescent developmentr. *Demography, 39*, 393–413.

DeLeire, T., & Kalil, A. (2005). How do cohabiting couples with children spend their money? *Journal of Marriage and Family, 67*, 286–295.

Demos, J. (1970). *A little commonwealth: Family life in Plymouth Colony.* Oxford: Oxford University Press.

Di Leonardo, M. (1987). The female world of cards and holidays: Women, families, and the work of kinship. *Signs, 12*, 440–453.

Diamond, M., & Sigmundson, K. H. (1997). Sex reassignment at birth: Long-term review and clinical implications. *Archives of Pediatric and Adolescent Medicine, 151*, 298–304.

Diekmann, A., & Engelhardt, H. (1999). The social inheritance of divorce: Effects of parents's family type in postwar Germany. *American Sociological Review, 64*, 783–793.

Dill, B. T. (1988). Fictive kin, papers sons, and compadrazgo: Women of color and the struggle for family survival. *Journal of Family History, 13*, 415–431.

Dornbusch, S. M., Carlsmith, J. M., Bushwall, S. J., Ritter, P. L., Leiderman, H., Hastorf, A. H., et al. (1985). Single parents, extended households, and the control of adolescents. *Child Development, 56*, 328–337.

Douglas, W. (2003). *Television families: Is something wrong in suburbia?* Mahwah, NJ: Lawrence Erlbaum Associates.

Du Bois, W. E. B. (1903). *The souls of black folk.* Chicago: A. C. McClurg & Co.

Dunaway, W. (2003). *The African-American family in slavery and emancipation.* New York: Cambridge University Press.

Duncan, G. J. (1984). *Years of poverty, years of plenty.* Ann Arbor: Institute for Social Research, University of Michigan.

Duncan, G. J. (1991). The economic environment of childhood. In A. Huston (Ed.), *Children in poverty* (pp. 23–50). New York: Cambridge University Press.

Duncan, G. J., & Brooks-Gunn, J. (1997). Income effects across the life span: Integration and interpretation. In G. J. Duncan & J. Brooks-Dunn (Eds.), *The consequences of growing up poor* (pp. 596–610). New York: Russell Sage Foundation.

Duncan, G. J., & Rodgers, W. (1991). Has children's poverty become more permanent? *American Sociological Review, 56*, 538–550.

Dunifon, R., Kalil, A., & Danziger, S. K. (2003). Does maternal employment mandated by welfare reform affect parenting behavior? *Children and Youth Services Review, 25*, 55–82.

Dunifon, R., & Kowaleski-Jones, L. (2002). Who's in the house? Race differences in cohabitation, single parenthood, and child development. *Child Development, 73*, 1249–1264.

Easterlin, R. A. (1980). *Birth and fortune: The impact of numbers on personal welfare.* New York: Basic Books.

Eckholm, E. (2002, June 21). Desire for sons drives use of prenatal scans in China. *The New York Times*, p. A3.

Edin, K., & Kefalas, M. J. (2005). *Promises I can keep: Why poor women put motherhood before marriage.* Berkeley: University of California Press.

Eggebeen, D. J., & Hogan, D. P. (1990). Giving between generations in American families. *Human Nature, 1*, 211–232.

Eggebeen, D. J., Snyder, A. R., & Manning, W. D. (1996). Children in single-father families in demographic perspective. *Journal of Family Issues, 17*, 441–465.

Ehrenreich, B., Hess, E., & Jacobs, G. (1987). *Re-making love: The feminization of sex.* Garden City, NY: Anchor Books/Doubleday.

Ehrhardt, A. E. (1985). The psychobiology of gender. In A. S. Rossi (Ed.), *Gender and the life course.* New York: Aldine.

Eisenstadt v. Baird, 438 405 (U.S. 1972).

Elder, G. H. J. (1974). *Children of the great depression: Social change in life experience.* Chicago: University of Chicago Press.

Elder, G. H. J., Conger, R. D., Foster, M. E., & Ardelt, M. (1992). Families under economic pressure. *Journal of Family Issues, 13*, 5–37.

Elkin, F., & Handel, G. (1984). *The child and society: The process of socialization*, 4th ed. New York: Random House.

Ellwood, D. T., & Jencks, C. (2004a). The spread of single-parent families in the United States since 1960. In D. P. Moynihan, T. Smeeding, & L. Rainwater (Eds.), *The future of the family* (pp. 26–65). New York: Russell Sage Foundation.

Ellwood, D. T., & Jencks, C. (2004b). The uneven spread of single-parent families: What do we know? Where do we look for answers? In K. M. Neckerman (Ed.),

Social inequality (pp. 3–118). New York: Russell Sage Foundation.

Emerson, R. M. (1972). Exchange theory, part 2: Exchange relations and network structures. In J. Berger, J. Zelditch, & B. Anderson (Eds.), *Sociological theories in progress*. New York: Houghton Mifflin.

Emery, R. E. (1989). Family violence. *American Psychologist, 44*, 321–328.

Emery, R. E. (1999). *Marriage, divorce, And children's adjustment*, 2nd ed. Beverly Hills: Sage.

Emery, R. E., & Laumann-Billings, L. (1998). An overview of the nature, causes, and consequences of abusive family relationships: Toward differentiating maltreatment and violence. *American Psychologist, 53*, 121–135.

Engels, F. (1972). *The origin of family, private property, and the state*. New York: International Publishers.

England, P. (1994). Book review: Gender play: Girls and boys in school. *Contemporary Sociology, 23*, 282–283.

England, P. (2000). Marriage, the costs of children, and gender inequality. In L. J. Waite, C. Bachrach, M. Hindin, E. Thomson, & A. Thorton (Eds.), *Ties that bind: Perspectives on marriage and cohabitation* (pp. 320–342). New York: Aldine de Gruyter.

England, P. (2004). More mercenary mate selection? Comment on Sweeney and Cancian (2004) and press (2004). *Journal of Marriage and Family, 66*, 1034–1037.

England, P. (2005). Emerging theories of care work. *Annual Review of Sociology, 31*, 381–399.

England, P., Budig, M., & Folbre, N. (2002). Wages of virtue: The relative pay of care work. *Social Problems, 49*, 455–473.

England, P., & Farkas, G. (1986). *Households, employment, and gender: A social, economic, and demographic view*. New York: Aldine.

England, P., & Folbre, N. (1999). The cost of caring. *The Annals of the American Academy of Political and Social Science, 561*, 39–51.

English, D. J. (1998). The extent and consequences of child maltreatment. *The Future of Children, 8*(1), 39–53.

English, D. J., Widom, C. S., & Brandford, C. (2001). *Childhood victimization and delinquency, adult criminality, and violent criminal behavior: A replication and extension, final report (NCJ 192291)*. Washington, DC: National Institute of Justice.

Erikson, E. H. (1950). *Childhood and society*. New York, NY: W.W. Norton.

Eschbach, K. (1993). Changing identification among American Indians and Alaska natives. *Demography, 30*, 635–652.

Evans, M. (2004). A critical lens of romantic love: A response to Bernadette Bawin-Legros. *Current Sociology, 52*, 259–264.

Evans, M. D. R. (1986). American fertility patterns: A comparison of white and nonwhite cohorts born 1903–1956. *Population and Development Review, 12*, 267–293.

Farley, R., & Allen, W. R. (1987). *The color line and the quality of life in America*. New York: Russell Sage Foundation.

Federal Interagency Forum on Aging-Related Statistics. (2000). *Updated detailed tables: Population*. Retrieved October 25, 2003, from http://www.agingstats.gov/tables%202001/tables-population.html#Indicator%205.

Fergusson, D. M., Horwood, L. J., & Lynskey, M. T. (1997). Childhood sexual abuse, adolescent sexual behaviors, and sexual revictimization. *Child Abuse and Neglect, 21*, 789–803.

Fergusson, D. M., Horwood, L. J., & Ridder, E. M. (2005a). Partner violence and mental health outcomes in a New Zealand birth cohort. *Journal of Marriage and Family, 67*, 1103–1119.

Fergusson, D. M., Horwood, L. J., & Ridder, E. M. (2005b). Rejoinder. *Journal of Marriage and Family, 67*, 1131–1136.

Ferree, M. M., Lorber, J., & Hess, B. B. (2000). Introduction. In M. M. Ferree, J. Lorber & B. B. Hess (Eds.), *Revisioning gender* (pp. xv–xviii). Walnut Creek, CA: AltaMira Press.

Fine, G. A. (1987). *With the boys: Little league baseball and preadolescent culture*. Chicago, IL: University of Chicago Press.

Fischer, D. H. (1978). *Growing old in America*. New York: Oxford University Press.

Fisher, A. P. (2003). Still "not quite as good as having your own"? Toward a sociology of adoption. *Annual Review of Sociology, 29*, 335–361.

Fitch, C. A., & Ruggles, S. (2000). Historical trends in marriage formation. In L. J. Waite, C. Bachrach, E. Hindin, E. Thomson, & A. Thorton (Eds.), *The ties that bind: Perspectives on marriage and cohabitation* (pp. 59–88). New York: Aldine de Gruyter.

Flandrin, J.-L. (1985). Sex in married life in the early Middle Ages: The Church's teaching and behavioral reality. In P. Ariès & A. Benjin (Eds.), *Western sexuality: Practice and precept in past and present times* (pp. 114–129). Oxford: Basil Blackwell.

Folbre, N. (2001). *The invisible heart: Economics and family values*. New York: The New Press.

Fonow, M. M., & Cook, J. A. (2005). Feminist methodology: New applications in the academy and public policy. *Signs: Journal of Women in Culture and Society, 30*, 2211–2236.

Forrest, J. D., & Singh, S. (1990). The sexual and reproductive behavior of American women. *Family Planning Perspectives, 22*, 206–214.

Foucault, M. (1980). *The history of sexuality*. New York: Vintage Books.

Fox, R. (1967). *Kinship and marriage*. Harmondsworth, England: Penguin Books.

Frank, R. (2001, December 18). Child cares: To be a U.S. nanny, Ms. Bautista must hire a nanny of her own. *The Wall Street Journal*, pp. A1, A4.

Frazier, E. F. (1939). *The Negro family in the United States* (revised and abridged edition). Chicago, IL: University of Chicago Press.

Friedan, B. (1963). *The feminine mystique*. New York: W.W. Norton.

Friedberg, L. (1998). Did unilateral divorce raise divorce rates? Evidence from panel data. *American Economic Review, 88*, 608-627.

Fuller-Thomson, E., & Minkler, M. (2000). African American grandparents raising grandchildren: A national profile of demographic and health characteristics. *Health & Social Work, 25*, 109-118.

Fuller-Thomson, E., Minkler, M., & Driver, D. (1997). A profile of grandparents raising grandchildren in the United States. *The Gerontologist, 37*, 406-411.

Furstenburg, F. F., Jr., Brooks-Gunn, J., & Morgan, P. S. (1987). *Adolescent mothers in later life*. Cambridge, England: Cambridge University Press.

Furstenburg, F. F., Jr., & Cherlin, A. J. (1991). *Divided families: What happens to children when parents part*. Cambridge, MA: Harvard University Press.

Furstenburg, F. F., Jr., & Nord, C. W. (1985). Parenting apart: Patterns of childbearing after divorce. *Journal of Marriage and Family, 47*, 893-904.

Furstenburg, F. F., Jr., Sherwood, K. E., & Sullivan, M. L. (1992). *Daddies and fathers: Men who do for their children and men who don't*. New York: Manpower Demonstration Research Corporation.

Furstenburg, F. F., Jr., & Spanier, G. B. (1984). *Recycling the family: Remarriage after divorce*. Newbury Park, CA: Sage Publications.

Fussell, E., & Furstenburg, F. F., Jr. (2005). The transition to adulthood during the twentieth century. In R. A. Settersten, Jr., F. F., Jr. Furstenburg & R. Rumbaut (Eds.), *On the frontier of adulthood: Theory, research, and public policy* (pp. 29-75). Chicago: University of Chicago Press.

Fuwa, M. (2004). Macro-level gender inequality and the division of household labor in 22 countries. *American Sociological Review, 69*, 751-767.

Galinsky, E. (1992). *Work and family: 1992 status report and outlook*. New York: Families and Work Institute.

Galinsky, E. (2001). Toward a new view of work and family life. In R. Hertz & N. L. Marshall (Eds.), *Working families: The transformation of the American home* (pp. 168-186). Berkeley: University of California Press.

Galinsky, E., Bond, J. T., & Friedman, D. E. (1993). *The changing workforce: Highlights of the national study*. New York: Families and Work Institute.

Gamson, J. (1996). Must identity movements self-destruct? A queer dilemma. In S. Seidman (Ed.), *Queer theory/ sociology* (pp. 395-420). Cambridge, MA: Blackwell.

Gamson, J., & Moon, D. (2004). The sociology of sexualities: Queer and beyond. *Annual Review of Sociology, 30*, 47-64.

Ganong, L. H., & Coleman, M. (1999). *Changing families, changing responsibilities: Family obligations following divorce and remarriage*. Mahwah, NJ: Lawrence Erlbaum.

Ganong, L. H., & Coleman, M. (2004). *Stepfamily relationships: Development, dynamics, and interventions*. New York: Kluwer Academic/Plenum Publishers.

Gans, H. J. (1962). *The urban villagers: Group and class in the lives of Italian-Americans*. New York: The Free Press.

Gatz, M., Bengston, V. L., & Blum, M. J. (1990). *Caregiving families*, 3rd ed. Orlando, FL: Academic Press.

Gauthier, A. H., Smeeding, T. M., & Furstenburg, F. F., Jr., (2004). Are parents investing less time in children? Trends in selected industrialized countries. *Population and Development Review, 30*, 647-671.

Gelles, R. J., & Cornell, C. P. (1990). *Intimate violence in families*. Newbury Park, CA: Sage.

Gelles, R. J., & Straus, M. A. (1979). Determinants of violence in the family: Toward a theoretical integration. In W. R. Burr, R. Hill, F. I. Nye, & L. Reiss (Eds.), *Contemporary theories about the family* (Vol. 1, pp. 549-581). New York: The Free Press.

Gennetian, L. M., Duncan, G. J., Knox, V. W., Vargas, W. G., Clark-Kaufman, E., & London, A. S. (2002b). *How welfare and work policies for parents affect adolescents: A synthesis of research*. New York: Manpower Demonstration Research Corporation. Retrieved November 28, 2003, from www.mdrc.org/ Reports2002/ ng_adolescent/ng_adolsyn_full.pdf.

Geronimus, A. T. (1991). Teenage childbearing and social and reproductive disadvantage: The evolution of complex questions and the demise of simple answers. *Family Relations, 40*, 463-471.

Geronimus, A. T., & Korenman, S. (1992). The socioeconomic consequences of teen childbearing reconsidered. *Quarterly Journal of Economics, 107*, 1187-1214.

Gershuny, J., Bittman, M., & Brice, J. (2005). Exit, voice, and suffering: Do couples adapt to changing employment patterns? *Journal of Marriage and Family, 67*, 656-665.

Gerth, H. H., & Mills, C. W. (1946). *From Max Weber: Essays in sociology*. New York: Oxford University Press.

Ghimire, D. J., Axxin, W. G., Yabiku, S. T., & Thornton, A. (2006). Social change, premarital nonfamily experience, and spouse choice in an arranged marriage society. *American Journal of Sociology, 111*, in press.

Giddens, A. (1991). *Modernity and self-identity*. Stanford, CA: Stanford University Press.

Giddens, A. (1992). *The transformation of intimacy*. Stanford, CA: Stanford University Press.

Gilkes, C. T. (1995). The storm and the light: Church, family, work, and social crisis in the African-American experience. In N. Ammerman & C. Roof (Eds.), *Work, family, and religion in contemporary society* (pp. 177–198). New York: Routledge.

Gillis, J. R. (1985). *For better or worse: British marriages, 1600 to the present*. Oxford: Oxford University Press.

Gladwell, M. (2006, February 13 & 20). Million-dollar Murray. *The New Yorker*, 96–107.

Glass, J. L., & Estes, S. B. (1997). The family responsive workplace. *Annual Review of Sociology, 23*, 289–313.

Glendon, M. A. (1987). *Abortion and divorce in Western law*. Cambridge, MA: Harvard University Press.

Glendon, M. A. (1989). *The transformation of family law: State, law, and family in the United States and Western Europe*. Chicago: University of Chicago Press.

Glenn, E. N. (1983). Split household, small producer, and dual wage earner: An analysis of Chinese-American family strategies. *Journal of Marriage and Family, 45*, 35–46.

Glenn, E. N. (2000a). Creating a caring society. *Contemporary Sociology, 29*, 84–94.

Glenn, E. N. (2000b). The social construction and institutionalization of gender and race. In M. M. Ferre, J. Lorber, & B. B. Hess (Eds.), *Revisioning gender* (pp. 3–43). Walnut Creek, CA: AltaMira Press.

Glick, J. E., Bean, F. D., & Van Hook, J. V. W. (1997). Immigration and changing patterns of extended family household structure in the United States: 1970-1990. *Journal of Marriage and Family, 59*, 177–191.

Glick, J. E., & Van Hook, J. (2002). Parents' coresidence with adult children: Can immigration explain racial and ethnic variation? *Journal of Marriage and Family, 64*, 240–253.

Gold, S. J. (1993). Migration and family adjustment: Continuity and change among Vietnamese in the United States. In H. McAdoo (Ed.), *Family ethnicity* (pp. 300–314). Newbury Park, CA: Sage.

Goldin, C. (1977). Female labor force participation: The origin of black and white differences, 1870 and 1880. *Journal of Economic History, 37*, 87–108.

Goldscheider, F. K. (1990). The aging of the gender revolution: What do we know and what do we need to know? *Research on Aging, 12*, 531–545.

Goldscheider, F. K. (1997). Recent changes in the U.S. Young adult living arrangements in comparative perspective. *Journal of Family Issues, 18*, 708–724.

Goldscheider, F. K., & Bures, R. (2003). The racial crossover in family complexity in the United States. *Demography, 40*, 569–587.

Goldscheider, F. K., & Goldscheider, C. (1993). *Leaving home before marriage: Ethnicity, familism, and generational relationships*. Madison: University of Wisconsin Press.

Goldscheider, F. K., & Goldscheider, C. (1994). Leaving and returning home in 20th-century America. *Population Bulletin, 48* (4).

Goldscheider, F. K., & Waite, L. J. (1991). *New families, no families? The transformation of the American home*. Berkeley: University of California Press.

Goldstein, A. (2000, March 6). When wives bring home more bacon. *The Washington Post*, p. 18.

Goldstein, J. R. (1999). The leveling of divorce in the United States. *Demography, 36*, 409–414.

Goldstein, J. R., & Kenney, C. T. (2001). Marriage delayed or marriage forgone? New cohort forecasts of first marriage for U.S. women. *American Sociological Review, 66*, 506–519.

Goode, W., J. (1963). *World revolution and family patterns*. New York: The Free Press.

Goode, W. J. (1971). Force and violence in the family. *Journal of Marriage and Family, 33*, 624–636.

Goode, W. J. (1982). *The family*, 2nd ed. Englewood Cliffs, NJ: Prentice Hall.

Goodrich v. Department of Public Health, 440 309 (Mass. 2003).

Gordon, L. (1988). *Heroes of their own lives: The politics and history of family violence*. New York: Viking.

Gordon, M. M. (1964). *Assimilaton in American life*. New York: Oxford University Press.

Gottman, J. M. (1979). *Marital interaction: Experimental investigations*. New York: Academic Press.

Gottman, J. M. (1998). Toward a process model of men in marriages and families. In A. Booth & A. C. Crouter (Eds.), *Men in families: When do they get involved? What difference does it make?* (pp. 149–192). Mahwah, NJ: Lawrence Erlbaum Associates.

Gove, W. R., Style, C. B., & Hughes, M. (1990). The effect of marriage on the well-being of adults. *Journal of Family Issues, 11*, 4–35.

Greeley, A. M., Michael, R. T., & Smith, T. W. (1990). Americans and their sexual partners. *Society, 27*(July/August), 36–42.

Green, A. I. (2002). Gay but not queer: Toward a post-queer study of sexuality. *Theory and Society, 31*, 521–545.

Greenhouse, L. (2000, June 29). The Supreme Court: The Nebraska case; court rules that governments can't outlaw type of abortion. *The New York Times*, p. 1ff.

Greenstein, T. N. (2000). Economic dependence, gender, and the division of labor in the home: A replication and extension. *Journal of Marriage and Family, 62*, 322–335.

Gregory, R. G., Anstine, R., Daly, A., & Ho, V. (1989). Women's pay in Australia, Great Britain, and the United States. In M. H. Hartmann & B. O'Farrel (Eds.), *Pay equity: Empirical inquiries* (pp. 222-242). Washington, DC: National Academy Press.

Greven, P. J., Jr. (1970). *Four generations: Population, land, and family in colonial Massachusetts*. Ithaca, NY: Cornell University Press.

Griswold del Castillo, R. (1979). *The Los Angeles barrio, 1850-1890: A social history*. Los Angeles: University of California Press.

Griswold v. Connecticut, 381 479 (U.S. 1965).

Grubb, W. N., & Lazerson, M. (1988). *Broken promises: How Americans fail their children*. Chicago: University of Chicago Press.

Gutman, H. G. (1976). *The black family in slavery and freedom, 1750-1925*. New York: Pantheon Books.

Guzman, L., Lippman, L., Moore, K. A., & O'Hare, W. (2003). *How are children doing: The mismatch between public perception and statistical reality* (Research Brief No. 2003-12). Washington, DC: Child Trends.

Gwartney-Gibbs, P., & Stockard, J. (1989). Courtship aggression in mixed-sex peer groups. In Pirog-Good & J. E. Stets (Eds.), *Violence in dating relationships* (pp. 185-204). New York: Praeger.

Hagestad, G. (1985). Continuity and connectedness. In V. L. Bengtsen & J. F. Robinson (Eds.), *Grandparenthood* (pp. 31-48). Beverly Hills, CA: Sage.

Hajnal, J. (1965). European marriage patterns in perspective. In D. V. Glass & D. E. C. Eversley (Eds.), *Population in history: Essays in historical demography* (pp. 101-146). Chicago: Aldine.

Haldeman, D. C. (1991). Sexual orientation conversion therapy for gay men and lesbians: Scientific examination. In Gonsiorek & Weinrich (Eds.), *Homosexuality* (pp. 149-160). Newbury Park, CA: Sage.

Hall, D. H., & Zhao, J. Z. (1995). Cohabitation and divorce in Canada: Testing the selectivity hypothesis. *Journal of Marriage and Family, 57*, 421-427.

Hall, S. (1904). *Adolescence: Its psychology and its relations to anthropology, sociology, sex, crime, religion and education*. New York: Appleton.

Halpern, R. (1993). Poverty and infant development. In C. H. J. Zeanah (Ed.), *Handbook of infant mental health* (pp. 73-86). New York, NY: Guilford Press.

Hampton, R. L., Jenkins, P., & Vandergriff-Avery, M. (1993). Physical and sexual violence in marriage. In R. L. Hampton, T. P. Gulotta, & G. R. Adams (Eds.), *Family violence: Prevention and treatment* (pp. 169-197). Thousand Oaks, CA: Sage Publications.

Hampton, R. L., & Newberger, E. H. (1985). Child abuse incidence and reporting by hospitals: Significance of severity, class, and race. *American Journal of Public Health, 75*, 56-60.

Handler, J. (1995). *The poverty of welfare reform*. New Haven: Yale University Press.

Haney, L. (2002). After the fall: East European women since the collapse of state socialism. *Contexts, 1 (3)*, 27-36.

Hans, J. D. (2002). Stepparenting after divorce: Stepparents' legal position regarding custody, access, and support. *Family Relations, 51*, 301-307.

Hansen, K. V. (1989). Helped put in a quilt: Men's work and male intimacy in nineteenth-century New England. *Gender & Society, 3*, 34-54.

Harding, S., & Norberg, K. (2005). New feminist approaches to social science methodologies: An introduction. *Signs: Journal of Women in Culture and Society, 30*, 2009-2015.

Hareven, T. K. (1982). *Family time and industrial time*. Cambridge, England: Cambridge University Press.

Harjo, S. S. (1993). The American Indian experience. In H. McAdoo (Ed.), *Family ethnicity* (pp. 199-207).

Harknett, K., & McLanahan, S. S. (2005). Racial and ethnic differences in marriage after the birth of a child. *American Sociological Review, 69*, 790-811.

Harmon, A. (2005, March 20). Ask them (all 8 of them) about their grandson. *The New York Times*, pp. 1, 18.

Harrison, L. A., & Lynch, A. B. (2005). Social role theory and the perceived gender role orientation of athletes. *Sex Roles, 52*, 227-236.

Hartmann, H. I. (1976). Capitalism, patriarchy, and job segregation by sex. *Signs, 1*, 137-169.

Hartog, H. (2000). *Man and wife in America: A history*. Cambridge, MA: Harvard University Press.

Haskey, J. (2005). Living arrangements in contemporary Britain: Having a partner who usually lives elsewhere and living apart together (lat). *Population Trends, 122 (winter)*, 35-45.

Haskins, R. (2001). Giving is not enough: Work and work supports are reducing poverty. *The Brookings Review, 19 (3)*, 13-15.

Haub, C. (2006). *Hispanics account for almost one-half of U.S. population growth*. Retrieved February 22, 2006, from http://www.prb.org.

Haveman, R. H. (1996). *Earnings inequality*. Washington, DC: American Enterprise Institute.

Hawkins, A. J., Nock, S. L., Wilson, J. C., Sanchez, L., & Wright, J. D. (2002). Attitudes about covenant marriage and divorce: Policy implications from a three-state comparison. *Family Relations, 51*, 166-175.

Hays, S. (1996). *The cultural contradictions of motherhood*. New Haven, CT: Yale University Press.

Heath, S. (2004). Peer-shared households, quasi-communes and neo-tribes. *Current Sociology, 52*, 161-179.

Heclo, H. (1986). The political foundations of antipoverty policy. In S. Danziger & D. Weinberg (Eds.), *Fighting poverty: What works and what doesn't* (pp. 312-340). Cambridge, MA: Harvard University Press.

Heise, L., Ellsberg, M., & Gottmoeller, M. (2002). A global overview of gender-based violence. *International Journal of Gynecology and Obstetrics, 78* (Supplement), S5-S14.

Henrikson v. Gable, 412 N.W. 2nd 702 (Mich. app. 1987).

Hernandez, D. J. (1993). *America's children: Resources from family, government, and economy.* New York: Russell Sage Foundation.

Herskovits, M. J. (1990). *The myth of the Negro past* [reissued with an introduction by Sidney W. Mintz]. Boston: Beacon Press.

Hetherington, E. M., & Clingempeel, G. (1992). Coping with marital transitions. *Monographs of the Society for Research in Child Development, 57.*

Hetherington, E. M., Cox, R., & Cox, M. (1978). The aftermath of divorce. In J. Stevens & M. Mathews (Eds.), *Mother-child, father-child relations* (pp. 148-176). Washington, DC: National Association for the Education of Young Children.

Hetherington, E. M., & Jodl, K. M. (1994). Stepfamilies as settings for child development. In A. Booth & J. Dunn (Eds.), *Stepfamilies: Who benefits? Who does not?* (pp. 55-79). Hillsdale, NJ: Lawrence Erlbaum.

Hetherington, E. M., & Kelly, J. (2002). *For better or for worse: Divorce reconsidered.* New York: W. W. Norton.

Hetherington, E. M., & Stanley-Hagan, M. (2000). Diversity among stepfamilies. In D. H. Demo, K. R. Allen, & M. A. Fine (Eds.), *Handbook of family diversity* (pp. 173-196). New York: Oxford University Press.

Heuveline, P., & Timberlake, J. M. (2004). The role of cohabitation in family formation: The United States in comparative perspective. *Journal of Marriage and Family, 66,* 1214-1230.

Hewlett, S. A., & West, C. (1998). *The war against parents.* Boston: Houghton Mifflin.

Hill, M. S., & Yeung, W. J. (1999). How has the changing structure of opportunities affected transitions to adulthood? In A. Booth, A. C. Crouter, & M. J. Shanahan (Eds.), *Transitions to adulhood in a changing economy* (pp. 3-39). Westport, CT: Praeger.

Hill, S. A. (2005). *Black intimacies: A gender perspective on families and relationships.* Walnut Creek, CA: AltaMira Press.

Himes, C. L. (2002). Elderly Americans. *Population Bulletin, 56*(4).

Hirosima, K. (1997). Projection of living arrangements of the elderly in Japan: 1991-2010. *Genus, 53,* 79-111.

Hirsch, J. S. (2003). *A courtship after marriage: Sexuality and love in Mexican transnational families.* Berkeley: University of California Press.

Hochschild, A. (1989). *The second shift: Working parents and the revolution at home.* New York: Viking.

Hochschild, A. R. (1979). Emotion work, feeling rules, and social structure. *American Journal of Sociology, 85,* 551-575.

Hochschild, A. R. (1997). *The time bind: When work becomes home and home becomes work.* New York: Henry Holt and Company.

Hochschild, A. R. (2002). Love and gold. In B. Ehrenreich & A. R. Hochschild (Eds.), *Global woman: Nannies, maids, and sex workers in the new economy* (pp. 15-30). New York: Henry Holt.

Hofferth, S. (1984). Kin networks, race, and family structure. *Journal of Marriage and Family, 46,* 791-806.

Hoffman, K. L., Demo, D. H., & Edwards, J. N. (1994). Physical wife abuse in a non-Western society: An integrated theoretical approach. *Journal of Marriage and Family, 56,* 131-146.

Hoffman, S. D., Foster, M., & Furstenburg, F. F., Jr. (1993). Re-evaluating the costs of teenage childbearing. *Demography, 30,* 1-13.

Hogan, D. P., Hao, L., & Parish, W. L. (1990). Race, kin networks, and assistance to mother-headed families. *Social Forces, 68,* 797-812.

Holtzworth-Monroe, A. (2005). Male versus female intimate partner violence: Putting controversial findings into context. *Journal of Marriage and Family, 67,* 1120-1125.

Hondagnau-Sotelo, P., & Avila, E. (1997). "I'm here, but I'm there": The meanings of Latina transnational motherhood. *Gender & Society, 11,* 548-571.

Hong, L. K. (1999). Chinese marriages and families: Diversity and change. In S. L. Browning & R. R. Miller (Eds.), *Till death do us part: A multicultural anthology on marriage* (pp. 23-44). Stamford, CT: JAI Press.

Hoodfar, H. (1997). *Between marriage and the market: Intimate politics and survival in Cairo.* Berkeley: University of California Press.

Hotz, V. J., McElroy, S. W., & Sanders, S. G. (1996). The costs and consequences of teenage childbearing for the mothers and the government. *Chicago Policy Review, 1,* 55-94.

House panel leader jeered by elderly in Chicago. (1989, August 19). *The New York Times,* p. 8.

Howell, N. (1979). *Demography of the Dobe Kung.* New York: Academic Press.

Hua, C. (2001). *A society without fathers or husbands: The na of China* (A. Hustvedt, Trans.). New York: Zone Books.

Ihinger-Tallman, M., & Pasley, K. (1987). *Remarriage.* Newbury Park, CA: Sage Publications.

In re A. R. A., 919 P.2d 388 (Mont. 1996).

In re Dunn, 607 N.E.2d 81 (Ohio App.3 Dist. 1992).

Inglehart, R., Basáñez, M., Díez-Medrano, J., Halman, L., & Luijkx, R. (2004). *Human beliefs and values: A cross-cultural sourcebook based on the 1999-2002 values surveys.* Mexico City: Siglo Veintiuno Editores.

Ingraham, C. (1999). *White weddings: Romancing heterosexuality in popular culture*. New York: Routledge.

Ingrassia, M., & McCormick, J. (1994, April 25). Why leave children with bad parents. *Newsweek*, pp. 52-58.

Ishii-Kuntz, M. (2000). Diversity within Asian-American families. In D. H. Demo, K. R. Allen, & M. A. Fine (Eds.), *The handbook of family diversity* (pp. 247-292). New York: Oxford University Press.

Jacobs, J. A., & Gerson, K. (2004). *The time divide: Work, family, and social policy in the 21st century*. Cambridge, MA: Harvard University Press.

Jejeebhoy, S. J., & Cook, R. J. (1997). State accountability for wife beating: The Indian challenge. *Lancet, 349*, S110-112.

Jencks, C. (1994). *The homeless*. Cambridge, MA: Harvard University Press.

Joe, J. R., Sparks, S., & Tiger, L. (1999). Changing American Indian marriage patterns: Some examples from contemporary Western Apaches. In S. L. Browning & R. R. Miller (Eds.), *Till death do us part: A multicultural anthology on marriage* (pp. 5-21). Greenwich, CT: JAI Press.

Johnson, M. P. (1995). Patriarchal terrorism and common couple violence: Two forms of violence against women. *Journal of Marriage and Family, 57*, 283-294.

Johnson, M. P. (2005). Domestic violence: It's not about gender—or is it? *Journal of Marriage and Family, 67*, 1126-1130.

Johnson, M. P., & Ferraro, K. J. (2000). Research on domestic violence in the 1990s: Making distinctions. *Journal of Marriage and Family, 62*, 948-963.

Johnson, S. H., & Rendall, M. S. (2004). The fertility contribution of Mexican immigration to the United States. *Demography, 41*, 129-150.

Johnson, W. R., & Skinner, J. (1986). Labor supply and marital separation. *American Economic Review, 76*, 455-469.

Johnston, L. D., O'Malley, P. M., & Bachman, J. (2003). *Monitoring the future: National survey results on drug use, 1975-2002* (Volume 1, Secondary School Students). Bethesda, MD: National Institute on Drug Abuse.

Jones, J. (1985). *Labor of love, labor or sorrow: Black women and the family from slavery to the present*. New York: Basic Books.

Kalil, A., DeLeire, T., Jayakody, R., & Chin, M. (2002). *Living arrangements of single-mother families: Variations, transitions, and child development outcomes*. Retrieved 3 July, 2005, from http://www.src.uchicago.edu/prc/pdfs/kalil02.pdf.

Kalleberg, A. L. (2000). Nonstandard employment relations: Part-time, temporary, and contract work. *Annual Review of Sociology, 26*, 341-365.

Kalmijn, M. (1991). Shifting boundaries: Trends in religious and educational homogamy. *American Sociological Review, 56*, 786-800.

Kalmuss, D. (1984). The intergenerational transmission of marital aggression. *Journal of Marriage and Family, 46*, 11-19.

Kamerman, S. B., & Kahn, A. J. (1987). *The responsive workplace: Employers and a changing labor force*. New York: Columbia University Press.

Kane, A., & Lichter, D. T. (2006). *Reducing unwed childbearing: The missing link in efforts to promote marriage*. Retrieved April 29, 2006, from http://www.brookings.edu/es/research/projects/wrb/publications/pb/pb37.pdf.

Katz, J. (1976). *Gay American history*. New York: Harper and Row.

Katz, L. F., & Autor, D. H. (1999). Changes in wage structure and earnings inequality. In D. Card & O. C. Ashenfelter (Eds.), *Handbook of labor economics*, vol. 3a (pp. 1463-1555). New York and Oxford: Elsevier Science, North-Holland.

Katz, M. B. (1989). *The undeserving poor: From the war on poverty to the war on welfare*. New York: Pantheon Books.

Kaufman, J., & Zigler, E. (1987). Do abused children become abusive parents? *American Journal of Orthopsychiatry, 57*, 186-192.

Kaus, M. (1992). *The end of equality*. New York: Basic Books.

Kellam, S. G., Ensminger, M. E., & Turner, R. J. (1977). Family structure and the mental health of children. *Archives of General Psychiatry, 34*, 1012-1022.

Keller, S. (1991). The American upper class family: Precarious claims on the future. *Journal of Comparative Family Studies, 22*, 159-182.

Kempe, H. C., Silverman, F. N., Steele, B. F., Droegemuller, W., & Silver, H. K. (1962). The battered child syndrome. *Journal of the American Medical Association, 181*, 17-24.

Kendall, L. (1996). *Getting married in Korea: Of gender, morality, and modernity*. Berkeley: University of California Press.

Kendall-Tackett, K. A., Williams, L. M., & Finkelhor, D. (1993). Impact of sexual abuse on children: A review and synthesis of recent empirical studies. *Psychological Bulletin, 113*, 164-180.

Kennelly, I., Merz, S. N., & Lorber, J. (2001). What is gender? *American Sociological Review, 66*, 598-605.

Kertzer, D. I. (1991). Household history and sociological theory. *Annual Review of Sociology, 17*, 155-179.

Keshet, J. K. (1988). The remarried couple: Stresses and successes. In W. R. Beer (Ed.), *Relative strangers: Studies of stepfamily processes* (pp. 29-53). Totowa, NJ: Roman and Littlefield, 1988.

Kessler, R., House, J. G., & Turner, J. (1987). Unemployment and health in a community sample. *Journal of Health and Social Behavior, 28*, 51-59.

Kett, J. F. (2003). Reflections on the history of adolescence in America. *History of the Family, 8*, 345-479.

Kiernan, K. (2002). The state of European unions: An analysis of FFS data on partnership formation and dissolution. In M. Macura & G. Beets (Eds.), *Dynamics of fertility and partnership in Europe: Insights and lessons from comparative research.* Vol.1 (pp. 57-76). New York: United Nations.

Kiernan, K. E. (1992). The impact of family disruption in childhood on transitions made in young adult life. *Population Studies, 46*, 213-234.

King, V. (2003). The legacy of a grandparent's divorce: Consequences for ties between grandparents and grandchildren. *Journal of Marriage and Family, 65*, 170-183.

Kinsey, A. C., Pomeroy, W. B., & Martin, C. E. (1948). *Sexual behavior in the human male.* Philadelphia: W.B. Saunders.

Kitano, H. H. L., & Daniels, R. (1988). *Asian Americans: Emerging minorities.* Englewood Cliffs, NJ: Prentice Hall.

Kitano, H. L. (1988). The Japanese American family. In C. H. Mindel, R. W. Habenstein, J. & R. Wright, Jr. (Eds.), *Ethnic families in America: Patterns* (pp. 258-275). New York: Elsevier Science and Variations Publishing.

Kobrin, F. E. (1976). The fall of household size and the rise of the primary individual in the United States. *Demography, 13*, 127-138.

Koegl, P., Burnam, M. A., & Baumohl, J. (1996). The causes of homelessness. In J. Baumohl (Ed.), *Homelessness in America* (pp. 24-33). Phoenix, AZ: Oryx Press.

Koenig, M. A., Ahmed, S., Hossain, M. B., & Mozumder, A. B. M. K. A. (2003). Women's status and domestic violence in rural Bangladesh: Individual- and community-level effects. *Demography, 40*, 269-288.

Kohn, M. L. (1969). *Class and conformity: A study in values.* Homewood, IL: Dorsey Press.

Kohn, M. L., & Schooler, C. (1978). The reciprocal effects of the substantive complexity of work and intellectual flexibility: A longitudinal assessment. *American Journal of Sociology, 84*, 24-52.

Komarovsky, M. (1971). *The unemployed man and his family.* New York: Octagon Books.

Komter, A. (1989). Hidden power in marriage. *Gender and Society, 3*, 187-216.

Koss, M. P. (1988). Hidden rape: Sexual aggression and victimization in a national sample of students in higher education. In A. W. Burgess (Ed.), *Rape and sexual assault ii* (pp. 3-25). New York: Garland.

Kosterlitz, J. (2005). Inside the new Social Security accounts. *National Journal, 37*, issue 1/2, 21-23.

Kotlowitz, A. (1991). *There are no children here: The story of two boys growing up in the other America.* New York: Doubleday.

Kristof, N. D. (1996, February 11). Who needs love! In Japan, many couples don't. *The New York Times*, p. A1.

Lachs, M. S., & Pillemer, K. (2004). Elder abuse. *The Lancet, 364*, 1363-1272.

Lamb, M. E. (2002). Infant-father attachments and their impact on child development. In C. S. Tamis-LeMonda & N. Cabrera (Eds.), *Handbook of father involvement: Multidisciplinary perspectives* (pp. 93-117). Mahwah, NJ: Lawrence Erlbaum.

Lamont, M: (2000). *The dignity of working men: Morality and the boundaries of race, class, and immigration.* Cambridge, MA: Harvard University Press.

Land, K. C. (2005). *The 2005 FCD index of child well-being (CWI): Implications for policymakers.* Retrieved June 1, 2006, from http://www.soc.duke.edu/~cwi/policy_ brief_05.pdf.

Landale, N. S., & Fennelly, K. (1992). Informal unions among mainland Puerto Ricans: Cohabitation or an alternative to legal marriage? *Journal of Marriage and Family, 54*, 269-280.

Landry, B. (2000). *Black working wives: Pioneers of the new family revolution.* Berkeley: University of California Press.

Lansford, J. E., Deater-Deckard, K., Dodge, K. A., Bates, J. E., & Pettit, G. S. (2004). Ethnic differences in the link between physical discipline and later adolescent externalizing behaviors. *Journal of Child Psychology and Psychiatry, 45*, 801-812.

Lantz, H., Schultz, M., & O'Hara, M. (1977). The changing American family from the preindustrial to the industrial period: A final report. *American Sociological Review, 42*, 406-421.

Lareau, A. (2002). Invisible inequality: Social class and child rearing in black and white families. *American Sociological Review, 67*, 747-776.

Lareau, A. (2003). *Unequal childhoods: Class, race, and family life.* Berkeley: University of California Press.

Laslett, B. (1973). The family as a public and private institution: An historical perspective. *Journal of Marriage and the Family, 35*, 480-492.

Laslett, P., & Wall, R. (1972). *Household and family in past time.* Cambridge, England: Cambridge University Press.

Laumann-Billings, L., & Emery, R.E. (2000). Distress among young adults from divorced families. *Journal of Family Psychology, 14*, 671-687.

Laumann, E. O., Gagnon, J. H., Michael, R. T., & Michaels, S. (1994). *The social organization of sexuality: Sexual practices in the United States.* Chicago: University of Chicago Press.

Lawrence v. Texas, 539 (U.S. 2003).

Le Bourdais, C., & Juby, H. (2002). The impact of cohabitation on the family life course in contemporary North America: Insights from across the border. In A. Booth & A. C. Crouter (Eds.), *Just living together: Implications of cohabitation on families, children, and social policy* (pp. 107-118). Mahwah, NJ: Lawrence Erlbaum.

Le Bourdais, C., & Lapierre-Adamcyk, È. (2004). Changes in conjugal life in Canada: Is cohabitation pregressively replacing marriage? *Journal of Marriage and Family, 66,* 929-942.

Lee, S. M. (1998). Asian Americans: Diverse and growing. In *Population Bulletin* (Vol. 53). Washington, DC: Population Reference Bureau.

Lee, S. M., & Edmonston, B. (2005). New marriages, new families: U.S. racial and Hispanic intermarriage. *Population Bulletin, 60,* no. 2, 1-36.

Lehrer, E. L., & Chiswick, C. U. (1993). Religion as a determinant of marital stability. *Demography, 30,* 385-404.

Leone, J. M., Johnson, M. P., Cohan, C. L., & Lloyd, S. E. (2004). Consequences of male partner violence for low-income minority women. *Journal of Marriage and Family, 66,* 472-490.

Lever, J. (1976). Sex differences in the games children play. *Social Problems, 23,* 478-487.

Levin, I. (2004). Living apart together: A new family form. *Current Sociology, 52,* 223-240.

Levinson, D. (1988). Family violence in cross-cultural perspective. In V. B. Van Hasselt, R. L. Morrison, A. S. Bellack, & M. Hersen (Eds.), *Handbook of family violence* (pp. 435-455). New York: Plenum Press.

Levy, F. (1987). *Dollars and dreams: The changing American income distribution.* New York: Russell Sage Foundation.

Levy, F. (1998). *The new dollars and dreams: American incomes and economic change.* New York: Russell Sage Foundation.

Levy, F., & Michel, R. C. (1991). *The economic future of American families: Income and wealth trends.* Washington, DC: Urban Institute Press.

Lewis, O. (1965). *La vida: A Puerto Rican family in the culture of poverty, San Juan and New York.* New York: Random House.

Lewontin, R. (1995a, April 20). Sex, lies, and social science. *New York Review of Books,* 24-29.

Lewontin, R. (1995b, May 25). Sex, lies, and social science: An exchange. *New York Review of Books,* 43-44.

Lichter, D. T., McLaughlin, D. K., Kephart, G., & Landry, D. J. (1992). Race and the retreat from marriage: A shortage of marriageable men? *American Sociological Review, 57,* 781-799.

Lichter, D. T., McLaughlin, D. K., & Ribar, D. C. (2002). Economic restructuring and the retreat from marriage. *Social Science Research, 31,* 230-256.

Lichter, D. T., & Qian, Z. (2004). *Marriage and family in a multiracial society* (The American People: Census 2000). New York and Washington: Russell Sage Foundation and Population Reference Bureau.

Liem, J. H., & Liem, R. G. (1990). Understanding the individual and family effects of unemployment. In J. Eckenrode & S. Gore (Eds.), *Stress between work and family* (pp. 175-204). New York: Plenum Press.

Light, I. H. (1972). *Ethnic enterprise in America: Business and welfare among Chinese, Japanese, and blacks.* Berkeley, CA: University of California Press.

Liker, J. K., & Elder, G. H., Jr. (1983). Economic hardship and marital relations in the 1930s. *American Sociological Review, 48,* 343-359.

Lin, C., & Liu, W. T. (1993). Intergenerational relationships among Chinese immigrants from Taiwan. In H. McAdoo (Ed.), *Family ethnicity* (pp. 271-286). Newbury Park, CA: Sage.

Liss, L. (1987). Family and the law. In M. B. Sussman & S. K. Steinmetz (Eds.), *Handbook of marriage and the family* (pp. 767-794). New York: Plenum Press.

Liu, K., Manton, K. G., & Aragon, C. (2000). Changes in home care use by disabled elderly persons: 1982-1994. *Journal of Gerontology, 55B,* S245-S253.

Loeb, T. B., Williams, J. K., Vargas Carmona, J., Rivkin, I., Wyatt, G. E., Chin, D., et al. (2002). Child sexual abuse: Associations with the sexual functioning of adolescents and adults. *Annual Review of Sex Research, 13,* 307-345.

Lomnitz, L. A. (1977). *Networks and marginality: Life in a Mexican shantytown.* New York: Academic Press.

Lomnitz, L. A. (1987). *A Mexican elite family, 1820-1980: Kinship, class, and culture.* Princeton, NJ: Princeton University Press.

Lopoo, L., & Western, B. (2005). Incarceration and the formation and stability of marital unions. *Journal of Marriage and Family, 67,* 721-734.

Love, J. M., Harrison, L., Sagi-Schwartz, A., van Ijzendoorn, M. H., Ross, C., Ungerer, J. A., et al. (2003). Child care quality matters: How conclusions may vary with context. *Child Development, 74,* 1021-1033.

Loving v Virginia, 347 1 (U.S. 1967).

Luker, K. (1984). *Abortion and the politics of motherhood.* Berkeley, CA: University of California Press.

Lundquist, J. H. (2004). When race makes no difference Marriage and the military. *Social Forces, 83,* 731-757.

Lundquist, J. H., & Smith, H. L. (2005). Family formation among women in the U.S. military: Evidence from the NLSY. *Journal of Marriage and Family, 67,* 1-13.

Lüscher, K., & Pillemer, K. (1998). Intergenerational ambivalence: A new approach to the study of parent-child relations in later life. *Journal of Marriage and Family, 60,* 413-425.

Lye, D. N., & Klepinger, D. H. (1995). Childhood living arrangements and adult children's relations with their parents. *Demography, 32*, 261-280.

Lynd, R. S., & Lynd, H. M. (1929). *Middletown: A study in modern American culture*. New York: Harcourt, Brace, and World.

MacCallum, F., & Golombok, S. (2004). Children raised in fatherless families from infancy: A follow-up of children of lesbian and single heterosexual mothers at early adolescence. *Journal of Child Psychology and Psychiatry, 45*, 1407-1419.

Maccoby, E. E. (1990). Gender and relationships: A developmental account. *American Psychologist, 45*, 513-520.

Maccoby, E. E. (1992). Family structure and children's adjustment: Is quality of parenting the major mediator? In M. E. Hetherington & W. G. Clingempel (Eds.), *Coping with marital transitions*, Vol. 57 (pp. 230-238). Monographs of the Society for Research in Child Development.

Maccoby, E. E. (1998). *The two sexes: Growing up apart, coming together*. Cambridge, MA: Harvard University Press.

Maccoby, E. E. (2000). Parenting and its effects on children: On reading and misreading behavior genetics. *Annual Review of Psychology, 51*, 1-27.

Maccoby, E. E. (2003). The gender of child and parent as factors in family dynamics. In A. C. Crouter & A. Booth (Eds.), *Children's influence on family dynamics: The neglected side of family relationships*. Mahwah, NJ: Lawrence Erlbaum Associates.

Maccoby, E. E., & Mnookin, R. H. (1992). *Dividing the child: Social and legal dilemmas of custody*. Cambridge, MA: Harvard University Press.

Manegold, C. S. (1993, April 8). To Crystal, 12, school serves no purpose. *The New York Times*.

Manning, W., & Landale, N. S. (1996). Racial and ethnic differences in the role of cohabitation in premarital childbearing. *Journal of Marriage and the Family, 58*, 63-77.

Manning, W. D., & Smock, P. J. (1995). Why marry? Race and the transition to marriage among cohabitors. *Demography, 32*, 509-520.

Manning, W. D., & Smock, P. J. (2005). Measuring and modeling cohabitation: New perspectives from qualitative data. *Journal of Marriage and Family, 67*, 989-1002.

Manton, K. G., & Gu, X. (2001). Changes in the prevalence of chronic disability in the United States, black and nonblack population above age 65 from 1982 to 1999. *Proceedings of the National Academy of Sciences, 98*, 6354-6359.

Mare, R. D., & Winship, C. (1991). Socioeconomic change and the decline in marriage for blacks and whites. In C. Jencks & P. Peterson (Eds.), *The urban underclass* (pp. 175-202). Washington, DC: The Brookings Institution.

Markman, H. J., Whitton, S. W., Kline, G. H., Stanley, S. M., Thompson, H., St. Peters, M. et al. (2004). Use of an empirically based marriage education program by religious organizations: Results of a dissemination trial. *Family Relations, 53*, 504-512.

Marks, N. G., Lambert, J. D., & Choi, H. (2002). Transitions to caregiving, gender, and psychological well-being. *Journal of Marriage and Family, 64*, 657-667.

Marquardt, E. (2005). *Between two worlds: The inner lives of children of divorce*. New York: Crown.

Marsiglio, W. (1992). Stepfathers with minor children living at home: Parenting perceptions and relationship quality. *Journal of Family Issues, 13*, 195-214.

Marsiglio, W. (2004). *Stepdads: Stories of love, hope and repair*. Boulder, CO: Rowman and Littlefield.

Marsiglio, W., Amato, P. R., Day, R. D., & Lamb, M. E. (2000). Scholarship on fatherhood in the 1990s and beyond. *Journal of Marriage and Family, 62*, 1173-1191.

Martin, C., & Théry, I. (2001). The PACS and marriage and cohabitation in France. *International Journal of Law, Policy and the Family, 15*, 135-158.

Martin, L. G. (1989). The graying of Japan. *Population Bulletin, 44*, 1-43.

Martin, S. P. (2004a). *Growing evidence for a "divorce divide"? Education and marital dissolution rates in the U.S. since the 1970s*. Retrieved March 27, 2004, from http://www.russellsage.org/programs/proj_reviews/si/wpMartin02.pdf.

Martin, S. P. (2004b). Women's education and family timing: Outcomes and trends associated with age at marriage and first birth. In K. M. Neckerman (Ed.), *Social inequality* (pp. 79-118). New York: Russell Sage Foundation.

Martin, S. P., & Parashar, S. (2006). Women's changing attitudes toward divorce, 1974-2002: Evidence for an educational crossover. *Journal of Marriage and Family, 68*, 29-40.

Martin, T. C., & Bumpass, L. L. (1989). Recent trends in marital disruption. *Demography, 26*, 37-51.

Masheter, C. (1997). Healthy and unhealthy friendship and hostility between ex-spouses. *Journal of Marriage and Family, 59*, 463-475.

Mason, M. A., Harrison-Jay, S., Svare, G. M., & Wolfinger, N. H. (2002). Stepparents: De facto parents or legal strangers? *Journal of Family Issues, 23*, 507-522.

Massey, D. S., Charles, C. Z., Lundy, G. F., & Fischer, M. J. (2003). *The source of the river: The social origins of freshmen at America's selective colleges and universities*. Princeton, NJ: Princeton University Press.

Mattingly, M. J., & Bianchi, S. M. (2003). Gender differences in the quantity and quality of free time: The U.S. Experience. *Social Forces, 81*, 999-1030.

Mattingly, M. J., & Sayer, L. C. (2006). Under pressure: Gender differences in the relationship between free time and feeling rushed. *Journal of Marriage and Family, 68,* 205-221.

Maxwell, C. D., Garner, J. H., & Fagan, J. A. (2002). The preventive effects of arrest on intimate partner violence: Research, policy and theory. *Criminology & Public Policy, 2,* 51-80.

May, E. T. (1980). *Great expectations: Marriage and divorce in post-Victorian America.* Chicago: University of Chicago Press.

Mayer, S. E. (1997). *What money can't buy: Family income and children's life chances.* Cambridge, MA: Harvard University Press.

McCurdy, K., & Daro, D. (1994). *Current trends in child abuse reporting and fatalities: The results of the 1993 annual fifty state survey* (Working Paper No. 808). Chicago: National Committee to Prevent Child Abuse.

McDermott, M., & Samson, F. L. (2005). White racial and ethnic identity in the United States. *Annual Review of Sociology, 31,* 245-261.

McGue, M., & Lykken, D. T. (1992). Genetic influence on risk of divorce. *Psychological Science, 3,* 368-373.

McHale, S. M., & Crouter, A. C. (2003). How do children exert an impact on family life? In A. C. Crouter & A. Booth (Eds.), *Children's influence on family dynamics: The neglected side of family relationships* (pp. 207-220). Mahwah, NJ: Lawrence Erlbaum Associates.

McLanahan, S. (2004). Diverging destinies: How children are faring under the second demographic transition. *Demography, 41,* 607-627.

McLanahan, S. S. (1983). Family structure and stress: A longitudinal comparison of two-parent and female-headed families. *Journal of Marriage and Family, 45,* 347-357.

McLanahan, S. S. (1994). The consequences of single motherhood. *The American Prospect, 18*(Summer), 48-58.

McLanahan, S. S., & Sandefur, G. (1994). *Growing up with a single parent: What hurts, what helps.* Cambridge, MA: Harvard University Press.

McLaughlin, D. K., & Lichter, D. T. (1997). Poverty and the marital behavior of young women. *Journal of Marriage and Family, 59,* 582-594.

McLoyd, V. C. (1990). The impact of economic hardship on black families and children: Psychological distress, parenting and socioemotional development. *Child Development, 61,* 311-346.

McLoyd, V. C., Cauce, A. M., Takeuchi, D., & Wilson, L. (2000). Marital processes and parental socialization in families of color: A decade review of research. *Journal of Marriage and Family, 62,* 1070-1093.

McLoyd, V. C., & Smith, J. (2002). Physical discipline and behavior problems in African American, European American, and Hispanic children: Emotional support as a moderator. *Journal of Marriage and Family, 64,* 40-53.

McManus, P. M., & DiPrete, T. A. (2001). Losers and winners: The financial consequences of separation and divorce for men. *American Sociological Review, 66*(2), 246-268.

Mead, L. (1992). *The new politics of poverty: The nonworking poor in America.* New York: Basic Books.

Mellor, J. M. (2000). Filling in the gaps in long term care insurance. In M. H. Meyer (Ed.), *Care work: Gender, class, and the welfare state* (pp. 202-215). New York: Routledge.

Metraux, S., & Culhane, D. P. (1999). Family dynamics, housing, and recurring homelessness among women in New York City homeless shelters. *Journal of Family Issues, 20,* 371-396.

Meyer, D. R. (1999). Compliance with child support orders in paternity and divorce cases. In R. A. Thompson, P. R. Amato, & S. Garasky (Eds.), *The post-divorce family* (pp. 127-157). Thousand Oaks, CA: Sage Publications.

Michael, R. T., Hartmann, H. I., & O'Farrell, B. (1989). *Pay equity: Empirical inquiries.* Washington, DC: National Academy Press.

Milan, A., & Peters, A. (2003, Summer). Couples living apart. *Canadian Social Trends,* 2-6.

Mills, D. M. (1998). Stepfamilies in context. In W. R. Beer (Ed.), *Relative strangers: Studies of stepfamily processes* (pp. 1-28). Totowa, NJ: Rowman and Littlefield.

Min, P. (1993). Korean immigrants' marital patterns and marital adjustment. In H. P. McAdoo (Ed.), *Family ethnicity* (pp. 287-289). Newbury Park, CA: Sage.

Mintz, S. (2004). *Huck's raft: A history of American childhood.* Cambridge, MA: The Belknap Press of Harvard University Press.

Mintz, S., & Kellogg, S. (1988). *Domestic relations: A social history of American family life.* New York: The Free Press.

Mitterauer, M., & Sieder, R. (1982). *The European family.* Chicago: University of Chicago Press.

Modell, J. J. (1989). *Into one's own: From youth to adulthood in the United States.* Berkeley: University of California Press.

Modell, J. J., & Hareven, T. K. (1973). Urbanization and the malleable household: An examination of boarding and lodging in American families. *Journal of Marriage and Family, 35,* 467-479

Moffitt, R. (1990). The effect of the U.S. welfare system on marital status. *Journal of Public Economics, 41,* 101-124.

Money, J., & Tucker, P. (1975). *Sexual signatures: On being a man or a woman.* Boston: Little, Brown.

Moore, J. W., & Cuellar, A. B. (1970). *Mexican Americans.* Englewood Cliffs, NJ: Prentice Hall.

Morgan, S. P., McDaniel, A., Miller, A. T., & Preston, S. H. (1993). Racial differences in household and family structure at the turn of the century. *American Journal of sociology, 98,* 798-828.

Morrison, D. R., & Cherlin, A. J. (1995). The divorce process and young children's well-being: A prospective analysis. *Journal of Marriage and Family, 57,* 800-812.

Mortimer, J. T., & London, J. (1984). The varying linkages of work and family. In P. Voydanoff (Ed.), *Work and family: Changing roles of men and women* (pp. 20-35). Palo Alto, CA: Mayfield.

Mosley, J., & Thompson, E. (1995). *Fatherhood: Contemporary theory, research, and social policy.* Thousand Oaks, CA: Sage.

Nagel, J. (1995). American Indian ethnic renewal: Politics and the resurgence of identity. *American Sociological Review, 60,* 947-965.

Nagel, J. (1996). *American Indian ethnic renewal: Red power and the resurgence of identity and culture.* New York: Oxford University Press.

Najman, J. M., Behrens, B. C., Anderson, M., Bor, W., O'Callaghan, M., & Williams, G. M. (1997). Impact of family type and family quality on child behavior problems: A longitudinal study. *Journal of the American Academy of Child and Adolescent Psychiatry, 36,* 1357-1365.

Nakonezny, P. A., Shull, R. D., & Rodgers, J. L. (1995). The effect of no-fault divorce law on the divorce rate across the 50 states and its relation to income, education, and religiosity. *Journal of Marriage and Family, 57,* 477-488.

National Clearinghouse on Child Abuse and Neglect Information. (2003). *Foster care national statistics.* Retrieved November 6, 2003, from http://nccanch.acf.hhs.gov/pubs/factsheets/foster.pdf.

Newman, K. S. (1988). *Falling from grace: The experience of downward mobility in the American middle class.* New York: The Free Press.

Newman, K. S. (2003). *A different shade of gray: Midlife and beyond in the inner city.* New York: The New Press.

NICHD Early Childhood Research Network. (2003). Does amount of time spent in child care predict socioemotional adjustment during the transition to kindergarten? *Child Development, 74,* 976-1005.

Nicholas, D. (1991). Childhood in medieval Europe. In J. H. Hawes & N. Hiner (Eds.), *Children in historical and comparative perspective* (pp. 31-52). New York: Greenwood Press.

Nock, S. L. (1998). *Marriage in men's lives.* New York: Oxford University Press.

Nock, S. L., Wright, J. D., & Sanchez, L. (1999). America's divorce problem. *Society, 36,* 43-52.

Nova Scotia (attorney general) v. Walsh 83 (SCC 2002).

O'Brien, J. E. (1971). Violence in divorce prone families. *Journal of Marriage and Family, 33,* 692-698.

O'Connor, T. G., Caspi, A., DeFries, J. C., & Plomin, R. (2000). Are associations between parental divorce and children's adjustment genetically mediated? An adoption study. *Developmental Psychology, 36,* 429-437.

O'Hare, W. (1992). America's minorities—the demographics of diversity. *Population Bulletin, 47,* 4.

O'Neill, N., & O'Neill, G. (1972). *Open marriage: A new style for couples.* New York: Evans.

O'Neill, W. L. (1967). *Divorce in the progressive era.* New York: New Viewpoints.

Oda, T. (1991). Tradition and innovation of the Japanese family in an aging society: Focusing on family support of the elderly. In *Proceedings of the Nihon University International Symposium on family and the contemporary Japanese culture: An international perspective* (pp. 361-406). Tokyo: University Research Center, Nihon University.

Ogawa, N., & Retherford, R. D. (1993). Care of the elderly in Japan: Changing norms and expectations. *Journal of Marriage and Family, 55,* 585-597.

Ogawa, N., & Retherford, R. D. (1997). Shifting the costs of the elderly back to the families in Japan: Will it work? *Population and Development Review, 23,* 59-94.

Oliver, M., & Shapiro, T. M. (1995). *Black wealth/white wealth: A new perspective on racial inequality.* New York: Routledge.

Olson, J. S. (1979). *The ethnic dimension in American history.* New York: St. Martin's Press.

Ono, H. (2003). Women's economic standing, marriage timing, and cross-national contexts of gender. *Journal of Marriage and Family, 65,* 275-286.

Oppenheimer, V. K. (1970). *The female labor force in the United States, population monograph series, 5.* Berkeley: Institute of International Studies, University of California.

Oppenheimer, V. K. (1994). Women's rising employment and the future of the family in industrial societies. *Population and Developmental Review, 20,* 293-342.

Oppenheimer, V. K. (1998). A theory of marriage timing. *American Journal of Sociology, 94,* 563-591.

Oppenheimer, V. K. (2003). Cohabiting and marriage during young men's career-development process. *Demography, 40,* 127-149.

Oppenheimer, V. K., Blossfeld, H. P., & Wackerow, A. (1995). United States of America. In H. P. Blossfeld (Ed.), *The new role of women: Family formation in modern societies* (pp. 150-173). Boulder, CO.: Westview Press.

Oppenheimer, V. K., Kalmijn, M., & Lim, N. (1997). Men's career development and marriage timing during a period of rising inequality. *Demography, 34,* 311-330.

Oppenheimer, V. K., & Lew, V. (1995). American marriage formation in the 1980s: How important was women's economic independence? In K. O. Mason & A. M.

Jensen (Eds.), *Gender and family change in industrialized countries* (pp. 105-138). Oxford: Clarendon Press.

Orbuch, T. L., Veroff, J., & Hunter, A. G. (1999). Black couples, white couples: The early years of marriage. In E. M. Hetherington (Ed.), *Coping with divorce, single parenting, and remarriage* (pp. 23-43). Mahwah, NJ: Lawrence Erlbaum Associates.

Orloff, A. S. (1993). Gender and the social rights of citizenship: The comparative analysis of gender relations and welfare states. *American Sociological Review, 58*, 303-328.

Oropesa, R. S., Landale, N. S., & Kenkre, T. (2003). Income allocation in marital and cohabiting unions: The case of mainland Puerto Ricans. *Journal of Marriage and Family, 65*, 910-926.

Osgood, D. W., Ruth, G., Eccles, J. E., Jacobs, J. E., & Barber, B. L. (2005). Six paths to adulthood: Fast starters, parents without careers, educated partners, educated singles, working singles, and slow starters. In R. A. Settersten, Jr., F. F. Furstenburg, Jr., & R. Rumbaut (Eds.), *On the frontier of adulthood: Theory, research, and public policy* (pp. 320-355). Chicago: University of Chicago Press.

Oxford English Dictionary (1989). 2nd ed. Oxford: Clarendon Press.

Ozment, S. (1983). *When fathers ruled: Family life in reformation Europe*. Cambridge, MA: Harvard University Press.

Ozment, S. (2001). *Ancestors: The loving family in old Europe*. Cambridge, MA: Harvard University Press.

Pagnini, D. L., & Morgan, S. P. (1996). Racial differences in marriage and childbearing: Oral history evidence from the South in the early twentieth century. *American Journal of Sociology, 101*, 1694-1718.

Pahl, R., & Spencer, L. (2004). Personal communities: Not simply families of "fate" or "choice." *Current Sociology, 52*, 199-221.

Palkovitz, R. (2002). Involved fathering and child development: Advancing our understanding of good fathering. In C. S. Tamis-LeMonda & N. Cabrera (Eds.), *Handbook of father involvement: Multidisciplinary perspectives* (pp. 119-140). Mahwah, NJ: Lawrence Erlbaum.

Papernow, P. (1988). Stepparent role development: From outsider to intimate. In W. R. Beer (Ed.), *Relative strangers: Studies of stepfamily processes* (pp. 54-82). Totowa, NJ: Rowman and Littlefield.

Papernow, P. (1998). *Becoming a stepfamily: Patterns of development in remarried life*. Cleveland: Gestalt Institute of Cleveland Press.

Parish, W. L., Hao, L., & Hogan, D. P. (1991). Family networks, welfare, and the work of young mothers. *Journal of Marriage and Family, 53*, 203-215.

Parke, R. D. (1996). *Fatherhood*. Cambridge, MA: Harvard University Press.

Parreñas, R. S. (2002). The care crisis in the Philippines: Children and transnational families in the new global economy. In B. Ehrenreich & A. R. Hochschild (Eds.), *Global woman: Nannies, maids, and sex workers in the new economy* (pp. 39-54). New York: Henry Holt.

Parsons, T., & Bales, R. F. (1955). *Family, socialization, and the interaction process*. New York: The Free Press.

Pate, A. M., & Hamilton, E. E. (1992). Formal and informal deterrents to domestic violence: The Dade County spouse assault experiment. *American Sociological Review, 57*, 691-697.

Patterson, C. J. (2000). Family relationships of lesbians and gay men. *Journal of Marriage and Family, 62*, 1052-1069.

Pattillo-McCoy, M. (1999). *Black picket fences: Privilege and peril among the black middle class*. Chicago: University of Chicago Press.

Pattillo, M. (2005). Black middle-class neighborhoods. *Annual Review of Sociology, 31*, 305-329.

Pearlin, L. I., & McCall, M. E. (1990). Occupational stress and marital support. In J. Eckenrode & S. Gore (Eds.), *Stress between work and family* (pp. 39-60). New York: Plenum Press.

Pearlin, L. I., Pioli, M. F., & McLaughlin, A. E. (2001). Caregiving by adult children: Involvement, role disruption, and health. In R. H. Binstock & L. K. George (Eds.), *Handbook of aging and the social sciences*, 5th ed. (pp. 238-254). San Diego: Academic Press.

Pearsall, P. (1987). *Super marital sex: Loving for life*. New York: Doubleday.

Peplau, L. A. (1991). Lesbian and gay relationships. In J. C. Gonsiorek & J. D. Weinrich (Eds.), *Homosexuality: Research implications for public policy*. Newbury Park, CA: Sage.

Perry-Jenkins, Maureen, Repetti, R. L., & Crouter, A. C. (2000). Work and family in the 1990s. *Journal of Marriage and Family, 62*, 981-998.

Peterson, I. (2003, October 28). In home that looked loving, 4 boys' suffering was unseen. *The New York Times*, pp. A1, B8.

Pettit, B., & Western, B. (2004). Mass imprisonment and the life course: Race and class inequality in U.S. incarceration. *American Sociological Review, 69*, 151-169.

Pew Research Center. (2006). *Less opposition to gay marriage, adoption and military service*. Retrieved April 24, 2006, from http://people-press.org/reports/display.php3?ReportID=273.

Phillips, J. A., & Sweeney, M. M. (2005). Premarital cohabitation and marital disruption among white, black, and Mexican American women. *Journal of Marriage and Family, 67*, 296-314.

Phillips, R. (1991). *Untying the knot: A short history of divorce*. Cambridge, England: Cambridge University Press.

Pillemer, K., & Finkelhor. (1998). The prevalence of elder abuse: A random sample survey. *The Gerontologist, 28*, 51-57.

Pillemer, K., & Lüscher, K. (Eds.). (2003). *Intergenerational ambivalences: New perspectives on parent-child relations in later life*. Stamford, CT: Elsevier/ JAI Press.

Pillemer, K., & Suiter, J. J. (2002). Explaining mothers' ambivalence toward their adult children. *Journal of Marriage and Family, 64*, 602-613.

Pinker, S. (1997). *How the mind works*. New York: W.W. Norton.

Pleck, E. (1987). *Domestic tyranny: The making of American social policy against family violence from colonial times to the present*. New York: Oxford University Press.

Pleck, J. H. (1977). The work-family role system. *Social Problems, 24*, 417-427.

Podnieks, E. (1992). National survey on abuse of the elderly in Canada. *Journal of Elder Abuse and Neglect, 12*, 1-14.

Polachek, S. (1979). Occupational segregation among women: Theory, evidence, and a prognosis. In C. Lloyd (Ed.), *Women in the labor market* (pp. 137-157). New York: Columbia University Press.

Polgreen, L., & Worth, R. F. (2003, October 27). New Jersey couple held in abuse; one son, 19, weighed 45 pounds. *The New York Times*, pp. A1, B5.

Pollack, W. S. (1998). *Real boys: Rescuing our sons from the myths of boyhood*. New York: Henry Holt.

Pollard, M. S., & Morgan, S. P. (2002). Emerging parental gender indifference? Sex composition of children and the third birth. *American Sociological Review, 67*, 600-613.

Pollock, L. A. (1983). *Forgotten children: Parent-child relations from 1500-1900*. Cambridge, England: Cambridge University Press.

Popenoe, D. (1994). The evolution of marriage and the problem of stepfamilies: A biosocial perspective. In A. Booth & J. Dunn (Eds.), *Stepfamilies: Who benefits? Who does not?* (pp. 3-27). Hillsdale, NJ: Lawrence Erlbaum.

Popenoe, D. (1996). *Life without father*. New York: Free Press.

Population Problems Research Council. (2000). *The population of Japan: An overview of the 50 postwar years: Summary of the twenty-fifth national survey on family planning*. Tokyo: Mainichi Shimbun.

Population Reference Bureau. (2005). *World population data sheet*. Retrieved February 20, 2006, from http://www.prb.org/pdf05/05WorldDataSheet_Eng.pdf.

Port of Miami. (2006). *Cargo statistics*. Retrieved February 4, 2006, from http://www.miamidade.gov/portofmiami/port_statistics.asp.

Portes, A., Haller, W. J., & Guarnizo, L. E. (2002). Transnational entrepreneurs: An alternative form of immigrant economic adaptation. *American Sociological Review, 67*(2), 278-298.

Portes, A., & Jensen, L. (1989). The enclave and the entrants: Patterns of ethnic enterprise in Miami before and after Mariel. *American Sociological Review, 54*, 929-949.

Portes, A., & Sensenbrenner, J. (1993). Embeddedness and immigration: Notes on the social determinants of economic action. *American Journal of Sociology, 98*, 1320-1350.

Portes, A., Stepick, A., & Truelove, C. (1986). Three years later: The adaptation process of Cuban and Haitian refugees in South Florida. *Population Research and Policy Review, 5*, 83-94.

Press, J. E. (2004). Cute butts and housework: A gynocentric theory of assortative mating. *Journal of Marriage and Family, 66*, 1029-1033.

Presser, H. B. (1989). Can we make time for children? The economy, work schedules, and child care. *Demography 26*(523-543).

Presser, H. B. (1994). Employment schedules among dual-earner spouses and the division of household labor by gender. *American Sociological Review, 59*, 348-364.

Presser, H. B. (1999). Toward a 24-hour economy. *Science, 284*, 177-179.

Presser, H. B. (2000). Non-standard work schedules and marital instability. *Journal of Marriage and Family, 62*, 93-110.

Presser, H. B. (2004). Employment in a 24/7 economy: Challenges for the family. In A. C. Crouter & A. Booth (Eds.), *Work family challenges for low-income parents and their children* (pp. 83-105). Mahwah, NJ: Lawrence Erbaum Associates.

Preston, S. H., & Kono, S. (1988). Trends in the well-being of children and the elderly in Japan. In J. L. Palmer, T. Smeeding, & B. B. Torrey (Eds.), *The vulnerable* (pp. 277-307). Washington, DC: Urban Institute Press.

Preston, S. H., Lim, S., & Morgan, P. S. (1992). African American marriage in 1910: Beneath the surface of census data. *Demography, 29*, 1-15.

Preston, S. H., & McDonald, J. (1979). The incidence of divorce within cohorts of American marriages contracted since the Civil War. *Demography, 16*, 1-25.

Pryor, J., & Rodgers, B. (2001). *Children in changing families: Life after parental separation*. Oxford: Blackwell.

Ptacek, J. (1999). *Battered women in the courtroom: The power of judicial response*. Boston: Northeastern University Press.

Qian, Z., & Preston, S. H. (1993). Changes in American marriage, 1972 to 1987: Availability and forces of attraction by age and education. *American Sociological Review, 58,* 482–495.

Quadagno, J. S. (1994). *The color of welfare: How racism undermined the war on poverty.* New York: Oxford University Press.

Quadagno, J. S. (2005). *Aging and the life course.* New York, NY: McGraw-Hill.

Queen, S. S., Habenstein, R. W., & Quadagno, J. S. (1985). *The family in various cultures,* 5th ed. New York: Harper and Row.

Raley, R. K. (1996). A shortage of marriageable men? A note on the role of cohabitation in black-white differences in marriage rates. *American Sociological Review, 61,* 973–983.

Raley, R. K., & Bumpass, L. L. (2003). The topography of the divorce plateau: Levels and trends in union stability in the United States after 1980. *Demographic Research, 8,* 245–259.

Raley, R. K., Durden, T. E., & Wildsmith, E. (2004). Understanding Mexican-American marriage patterns using a life-course approach. *Social Science Quarterly, 85,* 872–890.

Raley, R. K., Frisco, M. L., & Wildsmith, E. (2005). Maternal cohabitation and educational success. *Sociology of Education* (78), 144–164.

Raley, S. B., Mattingly, M. J., & Bianchi, S. M. (2006). How dual are dual-earner couples? Documenting change from 1970 to 2001. *Journal of Marriage and Family, 68,* 11–28.

Rank, M. R., & Cheng, L. (1995). Welfare use across generations: How important are the ties that bind? *Journal of Marriage and Family, 57,* 673–684.

Rasmussen, B. B., Klinenberg, E., Nexica, I. J., & Wray, M. (Eds.). (2001). *The making and unmaking of whiteness.* Durham, NC: Duke University Press.

Rebhum, L. A. (1999). *The heart is unknown country: Love in the changing economy of Northeast Brazil.* Stanford, CA: Stanford University Press.

Reiner, W. (1997). To be male or female—that is the question. *Archives of Pediatric and Adolescent Medicine, 151,* 224–225.

Reinharz, S. (1992). *Feminist methods in social research.* New York: Oxford University Press.

Repetti, R. L. (2001). Searching for the roots of marital conflict in uxoricides and uxorious husbands. In A. Booth, A. C. Crouter, & M. Clements (Eds.), *Couples in conflict* (pp. 47–55). Mahwah, NJ: Lawrence Erlbaum.

Report cites heavy toll of rape among the young. (1994, June 23). *The New York Times,* p. A12.

Retherford, R. D., Sakamoto, S., & Ogawa, N. (1999). Values and fertility change in Japan. In R. Leete (Ed.), *Dynamics of values in fertility change* (pp. 121–147). Liège, Belgium: International Union for the Scientific Study of Population.

Rich, L. M. (2001). Regular and irregular earnings of unwed fathers: Implications for child support practices. *Children and Youth Services Review, 23,* 353–376.

Richardson, L. W. (1977). *The dynamics of sex and gender: A sociological perspective.* Boston, MA: Houghton Mifflin.

Richer, E., Frank, A., Greenberg, M., Savner, S., & Turetsky, V. (2003). *Boom times a bust: Declining employment among less-educated young men.* Retrieved July 18, 2003, from http://www.clasp.org/DMS/Documents/1058362464.08/Boom_Times.pdf.

Riley, N., & Gardner, R. W. (1997). *China's population: A review of the literature.* Liège, Belgium: International Union for the Scientific Study of Population.

Riley, N. E. (2004). China's population: New trends and challenges. *Population Bulletin,* Vol. 59, no. 2.

Rindfuss, R. R., Morgan, S. P., & Swicegood, G. (1988). *First births in America: Changes in the timing of parenthood.* Berkeley, CA: University of California Press.

Rindfuss, R. R., & VandenHeuvel, A. (1990). Cohabitation: A precursor to marriage or an alternative to being single? *Population and Development Review, 16* 703–726.

Risman, B. J. (1998). *Gender vertigo.* New Haven, CT: Yale University Press.

Roberts, N. A., & Levenson, R. W. (2001). The remains of the workday: Impact of job stress and exhaustion on marital interaction in police couples. *Journal of Marriage and Family, 63,* 1052–1067.

Roberts, R. E. L., Richards, L. N., & Bengston, V. L. (1991). Intergenerational solidarity in families: Untangling the ties that bind. *Marriage and Family Review, 16,* 11–46.

Robins, P. K., Spiegelman, R. G., Weiner, S., & Bell, J. G. (1980). *A guaranteed annual income: Evidence from a social experiment.* New York: Academic Press.

Robinson, J. D., & Skill, T. (Eds.). (2001). *Five decades of families on television: From the 1950s through the 1990s,* 2nd ed. Mahwah, NJ: Lawrence Erlbaum Associates.

Robinson, R. V. (1993). Economic necessity and the life cycle in the family economy of nineteenth-century Indianapolis. *American Journal of Sociology, 99,* 49–74.

Rodgers, J. L., Nakonezny, P. A., & Shull, R. D. (1997). The effect of no-fault divorce legislation on divorce rates: A response to a reconsideration. *Journal of Marriage and Family, 59,* 1026–1030.

Rodgers, J. L., Nakonezny, P. A., & Shull, R. D. (1999). Did no-fault divorce legislation matter? Definitely yes and sometimes no. *Journal of Marriage and Family, 61,* 803–809.

Rodgers, W. C., & Thornton, A. (1985). Changing patterns of first marriage in the United States. *Demography, 22,* 265-279.

Roe v. Wade, 410 113 (S. Ct. 1973).

Roschelle, A. R. (1997). *No more kin: Exploring race, class, and gender in family networks.* Thousand Oaks, CA: Sage.

Roseneil, S., & Budgeon, S. (2004). Cultures of intimacy and care beyond "the family": Personal life and social change in the early 21st century. *Current Sociology, 52,* 135-159.

Rosenfeld, M. J. (2001). The salience of pan-national Hispanic and Asian identities in the U.S. marriage markets. *Demography, 38,* 161-175.

Rosenfeld, M. J., & Kim, B.-S. (2005). The independence of young adults and the rise of interracial and same-sex unions. *American Sociological Review, 70,* 541-562.

Rosenmayr, L., & Kockeis, E. (1965). *Umwelt und familie alter menschen.* Berlin: Luchterland-Verlag.

Rossi, A. S. (1977). A biosocial perspective on parenting. *Daedalus, 106,* 1-31.

Rossi, A. S., & Rossi, P. H. (1990). *Of human bonding: Parent-child relations across the life course.* New York: Aldine de Gruyter.

Rossi, P. H. (1994). Troubling families: Family homelessness in America. *American Behavioral Scientist, 37,* 342-395.

Rothman, E. K. (1984). *Hands and hearts: A history of courtship in America.* Cambridge, MA: Harvard University Press.

Rubin, G. (1975). The traffic in women. In R. R. Reiter (Ed.), *Toward an anthropology of women* (pp. 157-211). New York: Monthly Review Press.

Rubin, L. B. (1976). *Worlds of pain: Life in the working-class family.* New York: Basic Books.

Rubin, L. B. (1992). *Worlds of pain: Life in the working-class family.* New York: Basic Books.

Rubin, L. B. (1994). *Families on the fault line.* New York: Harper Collins.

Ruddick, S. (1996). Reason's "femininity." In N. R. Goldberger, J. M. Tarule, B. M. Clinchy, & M. F. Belenky (Eds.), *Knowledge, difference, and power: Essays inspired by women's ways of knowing* (pp. 248-270). New York: Basic Books.

Ruggles, S. (1994). The transformation of American family structure. *American Historical Review, 99,* 103-128.

Ruggles, S. (1997). The rise of divorce and separation in the United States, 1880-1990. *Demography, 34,* 455-466.

Ryder, N. B. (1980). Components of temporal variations in American fertility. In R. W. Hiorns (Ed.), *Demographic patterns in developed societies* (pp. 15-54). London: Taylor and Francis.

Sandefur, G. D., & Liebler, C. A. (1997). The demography of American Indian families. *Population Research and Policy Review, 16,* 95-114.

Sandefur, G. D., & Tienda, M. M. (1988). *Divided opportunities: Poverty, minorities, and social policy.* New York: Plenum Press.

Santelli, J. S., Lindberg, L. D., Abma, J., McNeely, C. S., & Resnick, M. (2000). Adolescent sexual behavior: Estimates and trends from four nationally representative surveys. *Family Planning Perspectives, 32,* 156-165, 194.

Sarkisian, N., & Gerstel, N. (2005). Kin support among blacks and whites: Race and family organization. *American Sociological Review, 69,* 812-837.

Sassler, S. (2004). The process of entry into cohabiting unions. *Journal of Marriage and Family, 66,* 491-505.

Savin-Williams, R. C., & Esterberg, K. G. (2000). Lesbian, gay, and bisexual families. In D. H. Demo, K. R. Allen, & M. A. Fine (Eds.), *Handbook of family diversity* (pp. 197-215). New York: Oxford University Press.

Sawhill, I., & Chadwick, L. (1999). *Children in cities: Uncertain futures.* Washington, DC: Brookings Institution.

Sayer, L. C. (2005). Gender, time and inequality: Trends in women's and men's paid work, unpaid work and free time. *Social Forces, 84,* 285-303.

Sayer, L. C., & Mattingly, M. J. (2006). Under pressure: Gender differences in the relationship between free time and feeling rushed. *Journal of Marriage and Family, 68,* 205-221.

Scanzoni, J. H. (1972). *Sexual bargaining: Power politics in American marriage.* Englewood Cliffs, NJ: Prentice Hall.

Schaefer, R. T. (2007). *Sociology,* 10th ed. New York, NY: McGraw-Hill.

Schneider, D. M. (1980). *American kinship: A cultural account,* 2nd ed. Chicago: University of Chicago Press.

Schneider, D. M., & Smith, R. T. (1973). *Class differences and sex roles in American kinship and family structure.* Englewood Cliffs, NJ: Prentice Hall.

Schoen, R., Astone, N. M., Rothert, K., Standish, N. J., & Kim, Y. J. (2002). Women's employment, marital happiness, and divorce. *Social Forces, 81,* 643-662.

Schoeni, R., & Blank, R. M. (2000). *What has welfare reform accomplished? Impacts on welfare participation, employment, income, poverty, and family structure.* Retrieved November 28, 2003, from http://www.fordschool.umich.edu/research/papers/PDFfiles/00-016.pdf.

Schor, J. B. (1992). *The overworked American: The unexpected decline of leisure.* New York: Basic Books.

Schwartz, C. R., & Mare, R. D. (2005). Trends in educational assortative marriage from 1940 to 2003. *Demography, 42,* 621-646.

Schwartz, P., & Rutter, V. (1998). *The gender of sexuality.* Thousand Oaks, CA: Pine Forge Press.

Scott, J. W. (2000). Some reflections on gender and politics. In M. M. Ferree, J. Lorber, & B. B. Hess (Eds.), *Revisioning gender* (pp. 70-96). Walnut Creek, CA: AltaMira Press.

Seccombe, K. (2000). Families in poverty in the 1990s: Trends, causes, consequences, and lessons learned. *Journal of Marriage and Family, 62,* 1094-1113.

Sedlack, A. J. (1991). *National incidence and prevalence of child abuse and neglect: 1998 revised report.* Rockville, MD: Westat, Inc.

Sedlack, A. J., & Broadhurst, D. D. (1996). *Executive summary of the third national incidence study of child abuse and neglect.* Washington, DC: National Center on Child Abuse and Neglect, Administration for Children and Families, U. S. Department of Health and Human Services.

Seidman, S. (1991). *Romantic longings: Love in America.* New York: Routledge.

Seidman, S. (2003). *The social construction of sexuality.* New York: W. W. Norton.

Seidman, S. (Ed.) (1996). *Queer theory/sociology.* Cambridge, MA: Blackwell.

Seltzer, J. (1991). Relationships between fathers and children who live apart: The father's role after separation. *Journal of Marriage and Family, 53,* 79-101.

Seltzer, J. (2000). Families formed outside of marriage. *Journal of Marriage and Family, 62,* 1247-1268.

Serbin, L. A., Sprafkin, C., Elman, M., & Doyle, A. (1984). The early development of sex differentiated patterns of social influence. *Canadian Journal of Social Science, 14,* 350-363.

Settersten, R. A., Jr., Furstenberg, F. F., Jr., & Rumbaut, R. G. (Eds.). (2005). *On the frontier of adulthood: Theory, research, and public policy.* Chicago: University of Chicago Press.

Sexton, J. (1996, May 12). As reports of child abuse rise, officials split up more families. *The New York Times,* p. A 1.

Shelton, B. A., & Agger, B. (1993). Shotgun wedding, unhappy marriage, no-fault divorce? Rethinking the feminism-Marxism relationship. In P. England (Ed.), *Theory on gender/feminism on theory* (pp. 25-41). New York: Aldine de Gruyter.

Sherman, L., W., & Berk, R. A. (1984). *The Minneapolis domestic violence experiment.* Washington, DC: The Police Foundation.

Shilts, R. (1987). *And the band played on: Politics, people, and the AIDS epidemic.* New York: Penguin Books.

Shoemaker, N. (1991). Native American families. In J. H. Hawes & E. Nybakkin (Eds.): *A research guide and historical handbook* (pp. 291-317). New York: Greenwood Press.

Sigle-Rushton, W., & McLanahan, S. (2002). The living arrangements of new unmarried mothers. *Demography, 39.*

Silverstein, C. (1991). Psychological and medical treatments of homosexuality. In J. C. Gonsiorek & J. D. Weinrich (Eds.), *Homosexuality* (pp. 101-114).

Silverstein, M., & Bengston, V. L. (1997). Intergenerational solidarity and the structure of adult child-parent relationships in American families. *American Journal of Sociology, 103,* 429-460.

Simon, R. W. (2002). Revisiting the relationships among gender, marital status, and mental health. *American Journal of Sociology, 107,* 1065-1096.

Simon, R. W., & Nath, L. E. (2004). Gender and emotion in the United States: Do men and women differ in self-reports of feelings and expressive behavior? *American Journal of Sociology, 109,* 1137-1176.

Skocpol, T. (1991). Targeting within universalism: Politically viable strategies to combat poverty in the United States. In C. Jencks & P. Peterson (Eds.), *The urban underclass* (pp. 411-436). Washington, DC: The Brookings Institution.

Skocpol, T. (1992). *Protecting mothers and soldiers: The political origins of social policy in the United States.* Cambridge, MA: The Belknap Press of Harvard University Press.

Smart, C. (2000). Divorce in England 1950-2000: A moral tale. In S. N. Katz, J. Eekelaar, & M. Maclean (Eds.), *Cross currents: Family law and policy in the United States and England* (pp. 363-385). Oxford, England: Oxford University Press.

Smart, C., Neale, B., & Wade, A. (2001). *The changing experience of childhood: Families and divorce.* Cambridge: Polity Press.

Smeeding, T. M. (1990). Economic status of the elderly. In R. L. Binstock & L. K. George (Eds.), *Handbook on aging and the social services* (pp. 362-381). New York: Academic Press.

Smelser, N. J., Wilson, W. J., & Mitchell, F. (2001). *America becoming: Racial trends and their consequences.* Washingon, DC: The National Academies Press.

Smith-Rosenberg, C. (1975). The female world of love and ritual: Relations between women in nineteenth-century America. *Signs, 1,* 1-29.

Smith, A. (1776). *The wealth of nations.*

Smith, D. S. (1973). Parental power and marriage patterns: An analysis of historical trends in Hingham, Massachusetts. *Journal of Marriage and Family, 35,* 419-428.

Smith, D. S. (1979). Life course, norms, and the family system of older Americans in 1900. *Journal of Family History, 4,* 285-298.

Smith, J. P. (1994). *Marriage, assets, and savings.* Santa Monica, CA: RAND Corporation.

Smith, J. P., & Ward, M. P. (1985). Time-series growth in the female labor force. *Journal of Labor Economics, 3*, S59-90.

Smith, T. W. (1999). *The emerging 21st century American family*. University of Chicago: National Opinion Research Center.

Smock, P. J. (2000). Cohabitation in the United States: An appraisal of research themes, findings, and implications. *Annual Review of Sociology, 26*, 1-20.

Smock, P. J., & Gupta, S. (2002). Cohabitation in contemporary North America. In A. Booth & A. C. Crouter (Eds.), *Just living together: Implications of cohabitation on families, children, and social policy* (pp. 53-84). Mahwah, NJ: Lawrence Erlbaum.

Smock, P. J., & Manning, W. D. (2004). Living together unmarried in the United States: Demographic perspectives and implications for family policy. *Law and Policy, 26*, 87-117.

Smock, P. J., Manning, W. D., & Porter, M. (2005). "Everything's there except money": How money shapes decisions to marry among cohabitors. *Journal of Marriage and Family, 67*, 680-696.

Smolensky, E., Danziger, S., & Gottschalk, P. (1988). The declining significance of age in the United States: Trends in the well-being of children and the elderly since 1939. In J. Palmer, T. Smeeding, & B. Torrey (Eds.), *The vulnerable* (pp. 29-54). Washington, DC: The Urban Institute Press.

Snarey, J. (1993). *How fathers care for the next generation*. Cambridge, MA: Harvard University Press.

Snipp, C. M. (1989). *American Indians: The first of this land*. New York: Russell Sage Foundation.

Soldo, B. J., & Agree, E. M. (1988). America's elderly. *Population Bulletin, 43*.

Soldo, B. J., & Hill, M. S. (1993). Intergenerational transfers: Economic, demographic, and social perspectives. *Annual Review of Gerontology and Geriatrics, 13*, 187-216.

Sommers-Flanagan, R., Sommers-Flanagan, J., & Davis, B. (1993). What's happening on music television: A gender role content analysis. *Sex Roles, 28*, 745-753.

Sørenson, A. (1994). Women, family, and class. *Annual Review of Sociology, 20*, 27-47.

Sorenson, S. B., Upchurch, D. M., & Shen, H. (1996). Violence and injury in marital arguments: Risk patterns and gender differences. *American Journal of Public Health, 86*, 35-40.

South, S. J. (2001). Time-dependent effects of wives employment on marital dissolution. *American Sociological Review, 66*(2), 226-245.

Spain, D., & Bianchi, S. M. (1996). *Balancing act: Motherhood, marriage, and employment among American women*. New York: Russell Sage Foundation.

Spitze, G., & Logan, J. R. (1990). Sons, daughters, and intergenerational social support. *Journal of Marriage and Family, 52*, 420-430.

Stacey, J. (1990). *Brave new families*. New York: Basic Books.

Stacey, J. (2006). Gay parenthood and the decline of paternity as we knew it. *Sexualities, 9*, 27-55.

Stacey, J., & Biblarz, T. J. (2001). (How) does the sexual orientation of parents matter? *American Sociological Review, 66*(2), 159-183.

Stack, C. B. (1974). *All our kin: Strategies for survival in a black community*. New York: Harper and Row.

Starr, R. H. J. (1988). Physical abuse of children. In V. B. Van Hasselt, M. R., A. S. Bellack, & M. Hersen (Eds.), *Handbook of family violence* (pp. 119-155). New York: Plenum Press.

Statistics Canada. (2004). *Population and demography*. Retrieved August 2, 2004, from http://www.statcan.ca/english/Pgdb/popula.htm.

Steiner, G. Y. (1981). *The futility of family policy*. Washington, DC: The Brookings Institution.

Steinmetz, S. K. (1987). Family violence: Past, present, and future. In M. B. Sussman & S. K. Steinmetz (Eds.), *Handbook of marriage and the family* (pp. 725-765). New York: Plenum Press.

Stets, J. E. (1992). Interactive processes in dating aggression: A national study. *Journal of Marriage and Family, 54*, 165-177.

Stets, J. E., & Straus, M. A. (1989). The marriage license as a hitting license: A comparison of assault in dating, cohabiting and married couples. In M. A. Pirog-Good & J. E. Stets (Eds.), *Violence in dating relationships* (pp. 33-52). New York: Praeger.

Stevenson, B., & Wolfers, J. (2003). *Bargaining in the shadow of the law: Divorce laws and family distress*. Cambridge, MA: National Bureau of Economic Research.

Stevenson, R. W. (2003, November 6). Bush signs ban on a procedure for abortions. *The New York Times*, p. A1.

Stewart, S. D. (2005). Boundary ambiguity in stepfamilies. *Journal of Family Issues, 26*, 1002-1029.

Stiglitz, J. E. (1988). *Economics of the public sector*, 2nd ed. New York: W. W. Norton.

Stone, D. (2000, March 13). Why we need a care movement. *The Nation*, 13-15.

Stone, L. (1977). *The family, sex and marriage in England 1500-1800*. New York: Harper and Row.

Straus, M. A. (1979). Measuring intrafamily conflict and violence. *Journal of Marriage and the Family, 41*, 75-88.

Straus, M. A., & Gelles, R. J. (1986). Societal change and change in family violence from 1975 to 1985 as revealed by two national surveys. *Journal of Marriage and Family, 48*, 465-479.

Straus, M. A., Hamby, S. L., Boney-McCoy, S., & Sugarman, D. B. (1996). The revised conflict tactics scales (cts2): Development and preliminary psychometric data. *Journal of Family Issues, 17*, 283-316.

Straus, M. A., & Stewart, J. H. (1999). Corporal punishment by American parents. *Clinical Child and Family Psychology Review, 2*, 55-70.

Suarez, Z. E. (1993). Cuban exiles: From golden exiles to social undesirables. In H. McAdoo (Ed.), *Family ethnicity: Strength in diversity* (pp. 164-176). Newbury Park, CA: Sage Publications.

Sudarkasa, N. (1980). African and Afro-American family structure: A comparison. *The Black Scholar* (November–December), 37-60.

Sudarkasa, N. (1981). Interpreting the African heritage in Afro-American family organization. In H. P. McAdoo (Ed.), *Black families* (pp. 37-53). Beverly Hills, CA: Sage.

Sweeney, M. M. (2002). Two decades of family change: The shift in economic foundations of marriage. *American Sociological Review, 67*(1), 132-147.

Sweeney, M. M., & Cancian, M. (2004). The changing importance of white women's economic prospects for assortative mating. *Journal of Marriage and Family, 66*, 1015-1028.

Sweeney, M. M., & Phillips, J. A. (2004). Understanding racial differences in marital disruption. *Journal of Marriage and Family, 66*, 639-650.

Sweet, J. A., & Bumpass, L. L. (1987). *American families and households.* New York: Russell Sage Foundation.

Swidler, A. (2001). *Talk of love: How culture matters.* Chicago: University of Chicago Press.

Symons, D. (1979). *The evolution of human sexuality.* New York: Oxford University Press.

Tanner, M., Moore, S., & Hartman., D. (1995). *The work versus welfare trade-off: An analysis of the total level of welfare benefits by state.* Retrieved February 7, 1998, from www.cato.org/pubs/pas/pa-24-.html.

Tanner, N., & Zihlman, A. (1976). Women in evolution. *Signs, 1*, 585-608.

Tasker, F. (2005). Lesbian mothers, gay fathers, and their children: A review. *Journal of Developmental & Behavioral Pediatrics, 26*, 224-240.

Tasker, F., & Golombok, S. (1995). Adults raised as children in lesbian families. *American Journal of Orthopsychiatry, 65*, 203-215.

Tax Policy Center. (2006a). *Earned income tax credit projections, 2005-2006.* Retrieved April 24, 2005, from http://www.taxpolicycenter.org/TaxModel/tmdb/Content/PDF/T060070.pdf.

Tax Policy Center. (2006b). *Historical dependent care credits.* Retrieved April 25, 2006, from http://taxpolicy center.org/TaxFacts/TFDB/TFTemplate.cfm? Docid=180.

Tax Policy Center. (2006c). *Itemized deductions by AGI 2002.* Retrieved April 25, 2006, from http://taxpolicy center.org/TaxFacts/TFDB/TFTemplate.cfm? Docid=386.

Tax Policy Center. (2006d). *Projected income tax expenditure budget 2002-2008.* Retrieved April 25, 2006, from http://taxpolicycenter.org/TaxFacts/TFDB/TFT emplate.cfm?Docid=286.

The Clearinghouse on International Developments in Child Youth and Family Policies. (2004). *Table 1.12: Maternity, paternity, and parental leaves in the OECD countries 1998-2002.* Retrieved March 14, 2006, from http://www.childpolicyintl.org/.

Therborn, G. (2004). *Between sex and power: Family in the world, 1900-2000.* London: Routledge.

Thoits, P. A. (1986). Multiple identities: Examining gender and marital status differences in distress. *American Sociological Review, 51*, 259-272.

Thoits, P. A. (1992). Identity structures and psychological well-being: Gender and marital status comparisons. *Social Psychological Quarterly, 55*, 236-256.

Thompson, G. (2003, October 28). A surge in money sent home by Mexicans. *The New York Times*, p. A14.

Thompson, K. (Ed.). (1991). *To be a man: In search of the deeply masculine.* Los Angeles: Jeremy P. Tarcher, Inc.

Thompson, N. J., Potter, J. S., Sanderson, C. A., & Maibach, E. A. (1997). The relationship of sexual abuse and HIV risk behaviors among heterosexual adult female STD patients. *Child Abuse and Neglect, 21*, 149-156.

Thorne, B. (1992). Feminist rethinking of the family: An overview. In B. Thorne & M. Yalom (Eds.), *Rethinking the family: Some feminist questions*, rev. ed. (pp. 3-30). Boston, MA: Northeastern University Press.

Thorne, B. (1993). *Gender play: Girls and boys in school.* New Brunswick, NJ: Rutgers University Press.

Thornton, A., & Young-DeMarco, L. (2001). Four decades of trends in attitudes toward family issues in the United States: The 1960s through the 1990s. *Journal of Marriage and Family, 63*, 1009-1037.

Tolnay, S. E. (2004). The living arrangements of African American and immigrant children, 1880-2000. *Journal of Family History, 29*, 421-445.

Toshio, T. (1993). *U.S. child substitute care flow data for FY 92 and current trends in the state child substitute care populations* (VCIS research notes No. 9). Washington DC: American Public Welfare Association.

Treas, J., & Bengston, V. L. (1987). The family in later years. In M. B. Sussman & S. K. Steinmetz (Eds.), *Handbook of marriage and family* (pp. 625-648). New York: Plenum Press.

Tribe, L. (1990). *Abortion: The clash of absolutes.* New York: W.W. Norton.

Tronto, J. C. (1993). *Moral boundaries: A political argument for an ethic of care.* New York: Routledge.

Turner, C. F., Forsyth, B. H., O'Reilly, J. M., Cooley, P. C., Smith, T. K., Rogers, S. M., et al. (1998). Automated self-interviewing and the survey measurement of sensitive behaviors. In M. P. Couper, R. P. Baker, J. Bethlehem, C. Z. F. Clark, J. Martin, W. L. Nicholls II & J. M. O'Reilly (Eds.), *Computer assisted survey information collection*. New York: Wiley.

Turner, C. F., Ku, L. C., Rogers, S. M., Lindberg, L. D., Pleck, J. H., & Sonenstein, F. L. (1998). Adolescent sexual behavior, drug use, and violence: Increased reporting with computer survey technology. *Science, 280* May 8), 867–873.

Udry, J. R. (1994). The nature of gender. *Demography, 31*, 561–573.

Udry, J. R., Morris, N. M., & Kovenock, J. (1995). Androgen effects on women's gendered behavior. *Journal of Biosocial Science, 27*, 359–368.

Uhlenberg, P. (1979). Demographic change and the problems of the aged. In M. W. Riley (Ed.), *Aging from birth to death* (pp. 153–166). Boulder, CO: Westview Press.

Uhlenberg, P. (1980). Death and the family. *Journal of Family History, 5*, 313–320.

Uhlenberg, P. (2004). Historical forces shaping grand parent-grandchild relationships: Demography and beyond. *Annual Review of Gerontology and Geriatrics, 24*, 77–97.

Uhlenberg, P., & Hammill, B. G. (1998). Frequency of grandparent contact with grandchild sets: Six factors that make a difference. *The Gerontologist, 38*, 276–285.

Umberson, D. (1987). Family status and health behaviors: Social control as a dimension of social integration. *Journal of Health and Social Behavior, 28*, 306–319.

Umberson, D., & Chen, M. D. (1994). Effects of a parent's death on adult children: Relationship salience and reaction to loss. *American Sociological Review, 59*, 152–168.

Umberson, D., Wortman, C. B., & Kessler, R. C. (1992). Widowhood and depression: Explaining long-term gender differences in vulnerability. *Journal of Health and Social Behavior, 33*, 10–24.

U.S. Administration for Children and Families. (2004a). *AFCARS report, no. 9*. Retrieved April 25, 2006, from http://www.acf.hhs.gov/programs/cb/stats_research/afcars/tar/report9.htm.

U.S. Administration for Children and Families. (2004b). *Temporary assistance for needy families: Sixth annual report to Congress*. Retrieved April 24, 2006, from http://www.acf.hhs.gov/programs/ofa/indexar.htm.

U.S. Administration for Children and Families. (2005). *AFCARS report, no. 10*. Retrieved April 9, 2006 from http://www.acf.hhs.gov/programs/cb/stats_research/afcars/tar/report/.htm.

U.S. Bureau of Justice Statistics. (1995). *Violence against women: Estimates from the redesigned survey* (NCJ-154348). Washington, DC: U.S. Government Printing Office.

U.S. Bureau of Justice Statistics. (2000a). *Criminal victimization, 1999* (NCJ 182734). Washington, DC: U.S. Government Printing Office.

U.S. Bureau of Justice Statistics. (2000b). *Intimate partner violence* (NCJ 178247)). Washington, DC: U.S. Government Printing Office.

U.S. Bureau of Justice Statistics. (2003a). *Intimate partner violence, 1993–2001* (NCJ-197838). Washington, DC: U.S. Government Printing Office.

U.S. Bureau of Justice Statistics. (2003b). *Prisoners in 2002* (NCJ 200248). Washington, DC: U.S. Government Printing Office.

U.S. Bureau of Justice Statistics. (2005). *Prisoners in 2004*. Retrieved February 20, 2006, from http://www.ojp.usdoj.gov/bjs/pub/pdf/p04.pdf.

U.S. Bureau of Labor Statistics. (1988). *Labor force statistics derived from the Current Population Survey, 1948–1987*. Washington, DC: U.S. Government Printing Office.

U.S. Bureau of Labor Statistics. (2001). *Contingent and alternative employment arrangements, February 2001*. Retrieved July 9, 2003 from http://www.bls.gov/ newsrelease/conemp.nr0.htm.

U.S. Bureau of Labor Statistics. (2002). *Highlights of women's earnings in 2001*. Retrieved July 9, 2003, from http://www.bls.gov/cps/cpswom2001.pdf.

U.S. Bureau of Labor Statistics. (2003). *Household data annual averages*. Retrieved July 17, 2003, from http://www.bls.gov/cps/cpsaat6.pdf.

U.S. Bureau of Labor Statistics. (2005a). *Highlights of women's earnings in 2004*. Retrieved March 13, 2006, from http://www.bls.gov/cps/cpswom2004.pdf.

U.S. Bureau of Labor Statistics. (2005b). *National compensation survey: Occupational wages in the United States, July 2004 supplementary tables*. Retrieved March 11, 2006, from http://www.bls.gov/ncs/ocs/sp/ ncb10728.pdf.

U.S. Bureau of Labor Statistics. (2005c). *Women in the labor force: A databook*. Retrieved March 13, 2006, from http://www.bls.gov/cps/wlf-databook2005.htm.

U.S. Bureau of Labor Statistics. (2005d). *Work at home 2004*. Retrieved March 14, 2006, from http://www.bls.gov/news.release/homey.nr0.htm.

U.S. Bureau of Labor Statistics. (2005e). *Workers on flexible and shift schedules*. Retrieved March 14, 2006, from http://www.bls.gov/news.release/flex.toc.htm.

U.S. Bureau of Labor Statistics. (2006). *Employment projections*. Retrieved February 4, 2006, from http://www.bls.gov/emp/home.htm.

U.S. Bureau of the Census. (1975). *Historical statistics of the United States, colonial times to 1970*. Washington, DC: U.S. Government Printing Office.

U.S. Bureau of the Census. (1983). *America in transition: An aging society* (Current Population Reports, Series P23-128). Washington, DC: U.S. Government Printing Office.

U.S. Bureau of the Census. (1993a). *Marital status and living arrangements: March 1992* (Current Population Reports No. P20-468). Washington, DC: Government Printing Office.

U.S. Bureau of the Census. (1993b). *Population projections of the United States, by age, race, sex, and Hispanic origin: 1993 to 2050* (Current Population Reports Series No. P25-1104). Washington DC: U.S. Government Printing Office.

U.S. Bureau of the Census. (1999a). *Coresident grandparents and grandchildren*. Retrieved October 28, 2003, from http://www.census.gov/prod/99pubs/p23-198.pdf.

U.S. Bureau of the Census. (1999b). *Statistical abstract of the United States: 1999*. Washington, DC: U.S. Government Printing Office.

U.S. Bureau of the Census. (1999c). *Trends in premarital childbearing: 1930–1994* (Current Population Reports No. P23-97). Washington, DC: U.S. Government Printing Office.

U.S. Bureau of the Census. (1999d). *Who could afford to buy a house in 1995?* Retrieved February 9, 2006, from http://www.census.gov/prod/99pubs/h121-991.pdf.

U.S. Bureau of the Census. (2001a). *The foreign-born population in the United States*. Retrieved June 29, 2003, from http://www.census.gov/population/www/socdemo/foreign/cps2000.html.

U.S. Bureau of the Census. (2001b). *Historical living arrangements of children*. Retrieved October 17, 2003, from http://www.census.gov/population/socdemo/child/p70-74/tab02.pdf.

U.S. Bureau of the Census. (2001c). *Overview of race and Hispanic origin* (Census 2000 Brief). Washington, DC: U.S. Government Printing Office.

U.S. Bureau of the Census. (2001d). *Table A2. Family status and household relationship of people 15 years and over, by marital status, age, sex, race, and Hispanic origin: March 2000*. Retrieved October 25, 2003, from http://www.census.gov/population/socdemo/hhfam/p20-537/2000/tabA2.pdf.

U.S. Bureau of the Census. (2002a). *Age, sex, household relationship, race and Hispanic origin—poverty status of people by selected characteristics in 2001*. Retrieved October 25, 2003, from http://ferret.bls.census.gov/macro/032002/pov/new01_001.htm.

U.S. Bureau of the Census. (2002b). *The American Indian and Alaska native population: 2000*. Retrieved August 13, 2003, from http://www.census.gov/prod/2002pubs/c2kbr01-15.pdf.

U.S. Bureau of the Census. (2002c). *The Asian population: 2000* (Census 2000 Brief 01-16).

U.S. Bureau of the Census. (2002d). *Custodial mothers and fathers and their child support*. Retrieved November 13, 2003, from http://www.census.gov/prod/2002pubs/p60-217.pdf.

U.S. Bureau of the Census. (2002e). *Educational attainment of the population 25 years and over by sex, race, and Hispanic origin: March 2002. Table 7*. Retrieved August 13, 2003, from http://www.census.gov/population/socdemo/race/api/pp1-163/tab07.txt.

U.S. Bureau of the Census. (2002f). *Median income of families by selected characteristics, race, and Hispanic origin of householder: 2001, 2000, and 1999. Table 4*. Retrieved August 13, 2003, from http://www.census.gov/hhes/income/income01/inctab4.html.

U.S. Bureau of the Census. (2002g). *National population projections: I. Summary files*. Retrieved October 25, 2003, from http://www.census.gov/population/www/projections/natsum-T3.html.

U.S. Bureau of the Census. (2002h). *Poverty in the United States: 2001*. Retrieved July 9, 2003, from http://www.census.gov/prod/2002pubs/p60-219.pdf.

U.S. Bureau of the Census. (2002i). *Poverty thresholds from the Current Population Survey*. Retrieved July 9, 2003, from http://www.census.gov/hhes/poverty/threshld/thresh02.html.

U.S. Bureau of the Census. (2002j). *Table a-2. Percent of people 25 years old and over who have completed high school or college, by race, Hispanic origin, and sex: Selected years 1940 to 2002*. Retrieved August 13, 2003, from http://www.census.gov/population/socdemo/education/tabA-2.pdf.

U.S. Bureau of the Census. (2002k). *Table FINC-01. Selected characteristics of families by total money income in 2001*. Retrieved August 13, 2003, from http://ferret.bls.census.gov/macro/032002/faminc/new01_003.htm.

U.S. Bureau of the Census. (2003a). *Adopted children and stepchildren* (Census 2000 Special Reports, CENSR-6RV). Washington, DC: U.S. Government Printing Office.

U.S. Bureau of the Census. (2003b, June 2003). *America's families and living arrangements: 2000*. Retrieved October 4, 2003, from http://www.census.gov/prod/2001pubs/p20-537.pdf.

U.S. Bureau of the Census. (2003c). *Children's living arrangements and characteristics: March 2002*. Retrieved June 29, 2003, from http://www.census.gov/prod/2003pubs/p20-547.pdf.

U.S. Bureau of the Census. (2003d). *Custodial mothers and fathers and their child support: 2001*. Retrieved

June 5, 2006, from http://www.census.gov/prod/2003pubs/p60-225.pdf.

U.S. Bureau of the Census. (2003e). *Detailed poverty tables, table pov40: Age, sex, household relationship, by region and residence—ratio of income to poverty level.* Retrieved October 25, 2003, from http://ferret.bls.census.gov/macro/032003/pov/new40_001.htm.

U.S. Bureau of the Census. (2003f). *Educational attainment of the population 15 years and over, by age, sex, race, and Hispanic origin: March 2002.* Retrieved October 17, 2003, from www.census.gov/population/socdemo/education/pp1-169/tab01.pdf.

U.S. Bureau of the Census. (2003g). *Grandparents living with grandchildren: 2000.* Retrieved July 3, 2005, from http://www.census.gov/prod/2003pubs/c2kbr-31.pdf.

U.S. Bureau of the Census. (2003h). *Health insurance coverage in the United States: 2002.* Retrieved December 6, 2003, from http://www.census.gov/prod/2003pubs/p60-223.pdf.

U.S. Bureau of the Census. (2003i). *The Hispanic population of the United States.* Retrieved September 2, 2003, from http://www.census.gov/prod/2003pubs/p20-545.pdf.

U.S. Bureau of the Census. (2003j). *Historical income tables—families.* Retrieved July 9, 2003, from http://www.census.gov/hhes/income/histinc/incfamdet.html.

U.S. Bureau of the Census. (2003k). *Historical income tables—families, table f-13.* Retrieved February 10, 2006, from http://www.census.gov/hhes/income/histinc/f13.html.

U.S. Bureau of the Census. (2003l). *Historical poverty tables, table 4.* Retrieved July 9, 2003, from http://www.census.gov/hhes/poverty/histpov/hstpov4.html.

U.S. Bureau of the Census. (2003m). *Income in the United States: 2002.* Retrieved October 4, 2003, from http://www.census.gov/prod/2003pubs/p60-221.pdf.

U.S. Bureau of the Census. (2003n). *Interracial married couples: 1980 to present.* Retrieved September 2, 2003, from http://www.census.gov/population/socdemo/hh-fam/tabMS-2.pdf.

U.S. Bureau of the Census. (2003o). *Interracial married couples: 1980 to present.* Retrieved August 6, 2003, from http://www.census.gov/population/socdemo/hh-fam/tabMS-3.pdf.

U.S. Bureau of the Census. (2003p). *Marital status: 2000.* Retrieved February 22, 2006, from http://www.census.gov/prod/2003pubs/c2kbr-30.pdf.

U.S. Bureau of the Census. (2003q). *Married-couple and unmarried-partner households: 2000.* (Census 2000 Special Reports, CENSR-5). Washington, DC: U.S. Government Printing Office.

U.S. Bureau of the Census. (2003r). *Poverty in the United States: 2002.* Retrieved October 16, 2003, from http://www.census.gov/prod/2003pubs/p60-222.pdf.

U.S. Bureau of the Census. (2003s). *Poverty status of families in 2001 by family type, and by Hispanic origin type of householder. Table 15-2.* Retrieved August 13, 2003, from http://www.census.gov/population/socdemo/hispanic/pp1-165/tab15-2.pdf.

U.S. Bureau of the Census. (2003t). *PPL table 2A: Primary child care arrangement of children of employed mothers.* Retrieved October 25, 2003, from http://www.census.gov/population/socdemo/child/pp1-168/tab02A.pdf.

U.S. Bureau of the Census. (2003u). *Selected summary measures of age and income by Hispanic origin and race: March 2002, Table 1.* Retrieved August 13, 2003, from http://www.census.gov/population/socdemo/hispanic/pp1-165/sumtab01.pdf.

U.S. Bureau of the Census. (2003v). *Statistical abstract of the United States: 2002.* Washington, DC: U.S. Government Printing Office.

U.S. Bureau of the Census. (2003w). *Table C4. Children with grandparents by presence of parents, gender, race, and Hispanic origin for selected characteristics: March 2002.* Retrieved October 26, 2003, from http://www.census.gov/population/socdemo/hh-fam/cps2002/tabC4-all.pdf.

U.S. Bureau of the Census. (2003x). *Who's minding the kids? Child care arrangements: Spring 1999 detailed tables (PPL-168).* Retrieved October 16, 2003, from http://www.census.gov/population/www/socdemo/child/pp1-168.html.

U.S. Bureau of the Census. (2004a). *America's families and living arrangements: 2003.* Retrieved February 20, 2006, from http://www.census.gov/prod/2004pubs/p20-553.pdf.

U.S. Bureau of the Census. (2004b). *Educational attainment in the United States, 2003.* Retrieved November 23, 2005, from http://www.census.gov/prod/2004pubs/p20-550.pdf.

U.S. Bureau of the Census. (2004c). *The foreign-born population in the United States: 2003.* Retrieved January 29, 2006, from http://www.census.gov/prod/2004pubs/p20-551.pdf.

U.S. Bureau of the Census. (2004d). *Statistical abstract of the United States: 2004.* Washington, DC: U.S. Government Printing Office.

U.S. Bureau of the Census. (2005a). *Hispanic population in the United States 2004.* Retrieved February 20, 2006, from http://www.census.gov/population/www/socdemo/hispanic/ho04.html.

U.S. Bureau of the Census. (2005b). *Historical income tables—families, table f-2.* Retrieved February 5, 2006, from http://www.census.gov/hhes/www/income/histinc/f02ar.html.

U.S. Bureau of the Census. (2005c). *Historical poverty tables, table 3*. Retrieved June 1, 2006, from http://www.census.gov/hhes/www/poverty/histpov/hstpov3.html.

U.S. Bureau of the Census. (2005d). *Historical poverty tables, table 4*. Retrieved February 5, 2006, from http://www.census.gov/hhes/www/poverty/histpov/hstpov4.html.

U.S. Bureau of the Census. (2005e). *Income, poverty, and health insurance coverage in the United States: 2004*. Retrieved February 20, 2006, from http://www.census.gov/prod/2005pubs/p60-229.pdf.

U.S. Bureau of the Census. (2005f). *Living arrangements of children: 2001*. Retrieved February 20, 2006, from http://www.census.gov/prod/2005pubs/p70-104.pdf.

U.S. Bureau of the Census. (2005g). *Pov02. People in families by family structure, age, and sex, iterated by income-to-poverty ratio and race*. Retrieved February 5, 2006, from http://pubdb3.census.gov/macro/032005/pov/new02_000.htm.

U.S. Bureau of the Census. (2005h). *Poverty thresholds 2004*. Retrieved February 5, 2006, from http://www.census.gov/hhes/www/poverty/threshld/thresh04.html.

U.S. Bureau of the Census. (2005i). *Selected characteristics of families by total money income in 2004*. Retrieved February 20, 2006, from http://pubdb3.census.gov/macro/032005/faminc/new01_006.htm.

U.S. Bureau of the Census. (2005j). *State & county quickfacts: Miami-Dade County, Florida*. Retrieved February 20, 2006, from http://quickfacts.census.gov/qfd/states/12/120861k.html.

U.S. Bureau of the Census. (2005k). *Statistical abstract of the United States, 2004–2005*. Retrieved November 1, 2005, from http://www.census.gov/statab/www/minihs.html.

U.S. Bureau of the Census. (2005l). *Statistical abstract of the United States: 2006*. Washington, DC: U.S. Government Printing Office.

U.S. Bureau of the Census. (2005m). *Table ms-2, estimated median age at first marriage, by sex: 1890 to the present*. Retrieved December 6, 2005, from http://www.census.gov/population/www/socdemo/hh-fam.html#history.

U.S. Bureau of the Census. (2005n). *Table ms-2. Estimated median age at first marriage, by sex: 1890 to the present*. Retrieved January 31, 2006, from http://www.census.gov/population/socdemo/hh-fam/ms2.pdf.

U.S. Bureau of the Census. (2005o). *Who's minding the kids? Child care arrangements: Winter 2002*. Retrieved June 1, 2006, from http://www.census.gov/prod/2005pubs/p70-101.pdf.

U.S. Bureau of the Census. (2006a). *U.S. interim projections by age, sex, race, and Hispanic origin*. Retrieved January 29, 2006, from http://www.census.gov/ipc/www/usinterimproj/.

U.S. Bureau of the Census. (2006b). *We the people: American Indians and Alaska natives in the United States*. Retrieved February 23, 2006, from http://www.census.gov/prod/2006pubs/censr-28.pdf.

U.S. Centers for Disease Control and Prevention. (2004). *Trends in the prevalence of sexual behaviors*. Retrieved March 1, 2006, from http://www.cdc.gov/HealthyYouth/yrbs/pdfs/trends-sex.pdf.

U.S. Centers for Disease Control and Prevention. (2006). *Basic statistics*. Retrieved 2006 from http://www.cdc.gov/hiv/topics/surveillance/basic.htm.

U.S. Department of Health and Human Services. (2003a). *Child maltreatment 2001*. Retrieved November 7, 2003, from http://www.acf.hhs.gov/programs/cb/publications/cm01/chapterthree.htm.

U.S. Department of Health and Human Services. (2003b). *HHS releases data showing continuing decline in number of people receiving temporary assistance*. Retrieved November 28, 2003, from http://www.hhs.gov/news/press/2003pres/20030903.html.

U.S. Department of Justice. (2003). *Criminal victimization, 2002* (No. NCF 199994). Washington, DC: U.S. Government Printing Office.

U.S. House of Representatives. (1993). *1993 green book: Overview of entitlement programs*. Washington DC: U.S. Government Printing Office.

U.S. House of Representatives Committee on Post Office and Civil Service. (1994). *Hearings: Review of federal measurements of race and ethnicity*. Washington, DC: U.S. Government Printing Office.

U.S. National Center for Health Statistics. (1991). *Advance report of final marriage statistics, 1988* (Monthly Vital Statistics Report, 40, No. 4, Supplement). Washington, DC: U.S. Government Printing Office.

U.S. National Center for Health Statistics. (1993). *Annual summary of births, marriages, divorces and deaths: United States, 1992* (Monthly Vital Statistics Report 41 No. 12, 5e). Washington, DC.

U.S. National Center for Health Statistics. (1995). *Annual summary of births, marriages, divorces and deaths: United States 1994* (Monthly Vital Statistics Report 43 No. 13). Washington, DC: U.S. Government Printing Office.

U.S. National Center for Health Statistics. (1997a). *Annual summary of births, marriages, divorces and deaths: United States, 1996* (Monthly Vital Statistics Report 45 No. 12). Washington, DC: U.S. Government Printing Office.

U.S. National Center for Health Statistics. (1997b). *Characteristics of elderly nursing home residents:*

Data from the 1995 national nursing home survey (Advance Data from Vital and Health Statistics No. 289). Washington, DC: U.S. Government Printing Office.

U.S. National Center for Health Statistics. (1997c). *Fertility, family planning and women's health: New data from the 1995 national survey of family growth* (Vital and Health Statistics, Series 23, No. 19). Washington, DC: U.S. Government Printing Office.

U.S. National Center for Health Statistics. (1999). *Adoption, adoption seeking, and relinquishment for adoption in the United States.* Retrieved October 16, 2003, from http://www.cdc.gov/nchs/data/ad/ad306.pdf.

U.S. National Center for Health Statistics. (2002a). *Births: Final data for 2000* (National Vital Statistics Report, Vol. 50, No. 5). Washington, DC: U.S. Government Printing Office.

U.S. National Center for Health Statistics. (2002b). *Births: Final data for 2001* (National Vital Statistics Report, Vol. 51, No. 2). Washington, DC: U.S. Government Printing Office.

U.S. National Center for Health Statistics. (2002c). *Deaths: Leading causes for 2000* (National Vital Statistics Report, Vol. 50, No. 16). Washington, DC: U.S. Government Printing Office.

U.S. National Center for Health Statistics. (2002d). *The national nursing home survey: 1999 summary* (Vital and Health Statistics, Series 13, No. 152).

U.S. National Center for Health Statistics. (2004a). *Health, United States, 2004.* Retrieved July 2, 2005, from http://www.cdc.gov/nchs/data/hus/hus04trend.pdf#099.

U.S. National Center for Health Statistics. (2004b). *Teenagers in the United States: Sexual activity, contraceptive use, and childbearing, 2002* (Vital and Health Statistics, Series 23, No. 24).

U.S. National Center for Health Statistics. (2005a). *Births: Final data for 2003* (National Vital Statistics Report, Vol. 54 No. 54).

U.S. National Center for Health Statistics. (2005b). *Deaths: Leading causes for 2002* (National Vital Statistics Report, Vol. 53, No. 17). Washington, DC: U.S. Government Printing Office.

U.S. National Center for Health Statistics. (2005c). *Number and percent of births to unmarried women, by race and Hispanic origin: United States, 1940-2000.* Retrieved December 3, 2005, from http://www.cdc.gov/nchs/data/statab/t001x17.pdf.

U.S. National Center for Health Statistics. (2005d). *Sexual behavior and selected health measures: Men and women 15-44 years of age, United States, 2002* (Advance Data from Vital and Health Statistics, No. 362). Washington, DC.

U.S. National Institute of Justice. (1998). *Prevalence, incidence and consequences of violence against women: Findings from the national violence against women survey.* Washington, DC: U.S. Government Printing Office.

U.S. National Institute of Justice. (2000). *Extent, nature and consequences of intimate partner violence* (No. NCJ 181867).

U.S. National Institute of Justice. (2004). *When violence hits home: How economics and neighborhood play a role. (NCJ 205004).* Retrieved April 8, 2006, from http://www.ncjrs.gov/pdffiles1/nij/205004.pdf.

U.S. National Institute of Justice. (2006). *Extent, nature, and consequences of rape victimization: Findings from the national violence against women survey* (NCJ 210346). Retrieved April 8, 2006, from http://www.ncjrs.gov/pdffiles1/nij/210346.pdf.

U.S. National Research Council on Adolescent Pregnancy and Childbearing. (1987). *Risking the future: Adolescent sexuality, pregnancy and childbearing.* Washington, DC: National Academy Press.

U.S. Office of Juvenile Justice and Delinquency Prevention. (2004). *Explanations for the decline in child sexual abuse cases.* Retrieved April 8, 2006, from http://www.ncjrs.gov/pdffiles1/ojjdp/199298.pdf.

Vaughan, D. (1990). *Uncoupling: Turning points in intimate relationships.* New York: Vintage Books.

Veroff, J., Douvan, E., & Kulka, R. A. (1981). *The inner American: A self-portrait from 1957 to 1976.* New York: Basic Books.

Wainright, J. L., Russell, S. T., & Patterson, C. J. (2004). Psychosocial adjustment, school outcomes, and romantic relationships of adolescents with same-sex parents. *Child Development, 75,* 1886-1898.

Waite, L. J. (1995). Does marriage matter? *Demography, 32,* 483-507.

Waite, L. J., & Gallagher, M. (2000). *The case for marriage: Why married people are happier, healthier and better off financially.* New York: Doubleday.

Waite, L. J., & Joyner, K. (2001). Emotional satisfaction and physical pleasure in sexual unions: Time horizon, sexual behavior, and sexual exclusivity. *Journal of Marriage and Family, 63,* 247-264.

Waite, L. J., & Lehrer, E. L. (2003). The benefits from marriage and religion in the United States: A comparative analysis. *Population and Development Review, 29,* 255-275.

Waite, L. J., & Lillard, L. A. (1995). Til death do us part: Marital disruption and mortality. *American Journal of Sociology, 100,* 1131-1156.

Waldfogel, J. (1997). The effects of children on women's wages. *American Sociological Review, 62,* 209-217.

Waldfogel, J. (2006). *What children need*. Cambridge, MA: Harvard University Press.

Waller, W. (1938). *The family: A dynamic interpretation*. New York: Dryden.

Wallerstein, J. S., & Blakeslee, S. (1989). *Second chances: Men, women, and children a decade after divorce*. New York: Ticknor and Fields.

Wallerstein, J. S., & Kelly, J. B. (1980). *Surviving the breakup: How children and parents cope with divorce*. New York: Basic Books.

Wallerstein, J. S., Lewis, J. M., & Blakeslee, S. (2000). *The unexpected legacy of divorce*. New York: Hyperion.

Watkins, S. C., Menken, J. A., & Bongaarts, J. (1987). Demographic foundations of family change. *American Sociological Review, 52*, 346-358.

Webster, P. S., Orbuch, T. L., & House, J. S. (1995). Effects of childhood family background on adult marital quality and perceived stability. *American Journal of Sociology, 101*, 404-432.

Webster v. Reproductive health services, 109 3040 (S. Ct 1989).

Webster's third new international dictionary of the English language, unabridged. (1976). Springfield, MA: Merriam.

Weeks, J., Heaphy, B., & Donovan, C. (2001). *Same-sex intimacies: Families of choice and other life experiments*. London: Routledge.

Weinrich, J. D., & Williams, W. L. (1991). Strange customs, familiar lives: Homosexualities in other cultures. In J. C. Gonsiorek & J. D. Weinrich (Eds.), *Homosexuality: Research implications for public policy* (pp. 44-59). Newbury Park, CA: Sage Publications.

Weiss, J. (2000). *To have and to hold: Marriage, the baby boom, and social change*. Chicago: University of Chicago Press.

Weiss, R. S. (1975). *Marital separation*. New York: Basic Books.

Weiss, R. S. (1979). Growing up a little faster: The experience of growing up in a single-parent household. *Journal of Social Issues, 35*, 97-111.

Weiss, R. S. (1990). Bringing work stress home. In J. Eckenrode & S. Gore (Eds.), *Stress between work and family* (pp. 17-37). New York: Plenum Press.

Weitzman, L. J. (1985). *The divorce revolution: The unexpected social and economic consequences for women and their children in America*. New York: The Free Press.

Welter, B. (1966). The cult of true womanhood. *American Quarterly* (Summer), 151-174.

West, C., & Zimmerman, D. H. (1987). Doing gender. *Gender and Society, 2*, 125-151.

Westat Incorporated. (1981). *The national study of the incidence and severity of child abuse and neglect*. Washington, DC: National Center on Child Abuse and Neglect.

Weston, K. (1991). *Families we choose: Lesbians, gays, kinship*. New York: Columbia University Press.

White, L. (1990). Determinants of divorce: A review of research in the eighties. *Journal of Marriage and Family, 52*, 904-912.

White, L. (1994). Stepfamilies over the life course: Social support. In A. Booth & J. Dunn (Eds.), *Stepfamilies: Who benefits? Who does not?* (pp. 109-137). Hillsdale, NJ: Erlbaum Associates.

White, L., & Glibreth, J. G. (2001). When children have two fathers: Effects of relationships with stepfathers and noncustodial fathers on adolescent outcomes. *Journal of Marriage and Family, 63*, 155-167.

White, L., & Rogers, S. J. (2000). Economic circumstances and family outcomes: A review of the 1990s. *Journal of Marriage and Family, 62*, 1035-1051.

White, L. K., & Booth, A. (1985). The quality and stability of remarriages: The role of stepchildren. *American Sociological Review, 50*, 689-698.

Whitehead, B. D., & Popenoe, D. (2001). Who wants to marry a soul mate? In National Marriage Project (Ed.), *The state of our unions, 2001* (pp. 6-16): Retrieved February 12, 2004, from http://marriage.rutgers.edu/Publications/SOOU/NMPAR2001.pdf.

Whyte, M. K. (1990). *Dating, mating and marriage*. New York: Aldine de Gruyter.

Wilcox, W. B. (1998). Conservative protestant child rearing: Authoritarian or authoritative? *American Sociological Review, 63*, 796-809.

Wilcox, W. B. (2004). *Soft patriarchs, new men: How Christianity shapes fathers and husbands*. Chicago: University of Chicago Press.

Williams, W. L. (1986). *The spirit and the flesh: Sexual diversity in American Indian culture*. Boston, MA: Beacon Press.

Willson, A. E., Shuey, K. M., & Elder, G. H., Jr. (2003). Ambivalence in the relationship of adult children to aging parents and in-laws. *Journal of Marriage and Family, 65*, 1055-1072.

Wilson, K. L., & Portes, A. (1980). Immigrant enclaves: An analysis of the labor market experiences of Cubans in Miami. *American Journal of Sociology, 86*, 295-319.

Wilson, M., & Daly, M. (2001). The evolutionary psychology of couple conflict in registered and de facto marital unions. In A. Booth, A. C. Crouter, & M. Clements (Eds.), *Couples in conflict* (pp. 3-26). Mahwah, NJ: Lawrence Erlbaum.

Wilson, W. J. (1987). *The truly disadvantaged: The inner city, the underclass, and public policy*. Chicago: University of Chicago Press.

Wilson, W. J. (1996). *When work disappears*. New York: Knopf.

Wolf, D. A. (2004). Valuing informal elder care. In N. Folbre & M. Bittman (Eds.), *Family time: The social organization of care* (pp. 110-129). London: Routledge.

Wolfe, A. (1998). *One nation, after all.* New York: Viking.

Wolfers, J. (2003). *Did unilateral divorce laws raise divorce rates? A reconciliation and new results* (Working Paper No. 10014). Cambridge, MA: National Bureau of Economic Research.

Wolfinger, N. H. (1999). Trends in intergenerational transmission of divorce. *Demography, 36,* 415-420.

Wong, M. G. (1988). The Chinese American family. In C. H. Mindel, R. W. Habenstein, & J. W. Roosevelt (Eds.), *Ethnic families in America: Patterns and variations* (pp. 230-257). New York: Elsevier Science Publishing.

Woodhouse, B. (2002). Making poor mothers fungible: The privatization of foster care. In F. M. Cancian, D. Kurz, A. S. London, R. Reviere & M. C. Tuominen (Eds.), *Child care and inequality: Rethinking care-work for children and youth* (pp. 83-97). New York: Routledge.

Wright, L. (1994). One drop of blood. *The New Yorker,* pp. 46-55.

Wu, L. L., & Martinson, B. C. (1993). Family structure and the risk of premarital birth. *American Sociological Review, 59,* 210-232.

Wulczyn, F. H., & Goerge, R. M. (1992). Foster care in New York and Illinois: The challenge of rapid change. *Social Science Review, 66,* 278-294.

Xie, Y., Raymo, J. M., Goyette, K., & Thornton, A. (2003). Economic potential and entry into marriage and cohabitation. *Demography, 40,* 351-368.

Yamaguchi, K., & Wang, Y. (2002). Class identification of married employed women and men in America. *American Journal Sociology, 108,* 440-475.

Yanagisako, S. (1985). *Transforming the past: Tradition and kinship among Japanese Americans.* Stanford, CA: Stanford University Press.

Yanagisako, S. J., & Collier, J. F. (1987). Toward a unified analysis of gender and kinship. In J. F. Collier & S. J. Yanagisako (Eds.), *Gender and kinship: Essays toward a unified analysis.* Stanford, CA: Stanford University Press.

Yount, K. M. (2005). Resources, family organization, and domestic violence against married women in Minya, Egypt. *Journal of Marriage and Family, 67,* 579-596.

Zaretsky, E. (1986). *Capitalism, the family, and personal life* (revised and expanded edition). New York: Harper and Row.

Zelizer, V. (1985). *Pricing the priceless child: The changing social value of children.* New York: Basic Books.

Zeng, Y., Ping, T., Baochang, G., Yi, X., Onhua, L., Yongping, L. (1993). Causes and implications of the recent increase in the reported sex ratio at birth in China. *Population and Development Review, 19,* 283-302.

Zhou, M., & Bankston, C. L., III (1998). *Growing up American: How Vietnamese children adapt to life in the United States.* New York: Russell Sage Foundation.

Acknowledgments

Chapter 2: Figure 2.2, p. 66 from Donald J. Hernandez, Figure 4.1, "Children Aged 0-17 in Farm Families, Father-as-Breadwinner Families, and Dual Earner Families: 1790-1989." In *America's Children: Resources from Family, Government and the Economy.* © 1993 Russell Sage Foundation, 112 East 64th St., New York, NY 10021. Reprinted with permission.

Chapter 4: Figure 4.5, p. 131 Adapted from Alice S. Rossi and Peter H. Rossi, *Of Human Bonding: Parent-Child Relations across the Life Course.* Copyright © 1990 by Aldine Publishers. Reprinted by permission of Aldine Transaction, a division of Transaction Publishers.

Chapter 5: Quotation p. 167 from Nancy Landale & Katherine Fennelly, 1992. "Informal Unions Among Mainland Puerto Ricans: Cohabitation or an Alternative to Legal Marriage?" In *Journal of Marriage and the Family,* 54, p. 269-280. Copyright 2004 by the National Council on Family Relations, 3989 Central Ave. NE, Suite 550, Minneapolis, MN 55421. Reprinted by permission.

Quotation p. 173 From Alejandro Portes & Julia Sensenbrenner, 1993. "Embeddedness and Immigration: Notes on the Social Determinants of Economic Action." In *American Journal of Sociology,* 98:6 (1993) pp. 1329-1350.

Chapter 6: Quotation p. 192 From Richard Lewontin, 1995. "Sex, Lies, and Social Science: An Exchange." In *New York Review of Books,* May 25, 1999, p. 44. Used by permission.

Chapter 7: Figure 7.1, p. 227 from Francesca M. Cancian, 1987. *Love in America: Gender and Self-Development.* Reprinted by permission of Cambridge University Press.

Quotation p. 229 From Deanna L. Pagnini and S. Philip Morgan, 1996. "Racial Differences in Marriage and Child-bearing: Oral History Evidence from the South in the Early 20th Century." In *American Journal of Sociology,* 101:6 (1996) pp. 1694-1718.

Quotation p. 232 from Andrew Cherlin, 2004. "The Deinstitutionalization of American Marriage" In *Journal of Marriage and Family,* 66, pp. 848-861. Copyright 2004 by the National Council on Family Relations, 3989 Central Ave. NE, Suite 550, Minneapolis, MN 55421. Reprinted by permission.

Quotation p. 233 from Pamela J. Smock, Wendy D. Manning, & Meredith Porter, 2005. " 'Everything's There Except Money': How Money Shapes Decisions to Marry Among Cohabitors." In *Journal of Marriage and Family,* 67, pp. 689, 690. Copyright 2005 by the National Council on Family Relations, 3989 Central Ave. NE, Suite 550, Minneapolis, MN 55421. Reprinted by permission.

Quotation p. 233 From Barbara D. Whitehead and David Popenoe, 2001. "Who Wants to Marry a Soul Mate?" Adapted from the National Marriage Project (Ed.), The State of our Unions, 2001 (pp. 6-16): Retrieved February 12, 2004, from http://marriage.rutgers.edu/Publications/SOOU/NMPAR2001.pdf. © Copyright 2001 by the National Marriage Project. Reprinted with permission.

Quotation p. 242 from Wendy D. Manning & Pamela J. Smock, 2005. "Measuring and Modeling Cohabitation: New Perspectives from Qualitative Data." In *Journal of Marriage and the Family,* 67, p. 995. Copyright 2005 by the National Council on Family Relations, 3989 Central Ave. NE, Suite 550, Minneapolis, MN 55421. Reprinted by permission.

Chapter 8: Figure 8.3, p. 265 From Liana Sayer, "Gender, Time and Inequality: Trends in Women's and Men's Paid Work, Unpaid Work and Free Time" *Social Forces,* Vol. 84, Issue 1, September 2005, pp. 285-303. Copyright © 2005 by the University of North Carolina Press. Used by permission of the publisher.

Figure, p. 283 from Paul Burstein, R. Marie Bricher, Rachel L. Einwohner, 1995. "Policy Alternatives and Political Change: Work, Family, and Gender on the Congressional Agenda, 1945-1990." *American Sociological Review,* 60, No. 1. (February 1995) pp. 67-83, Fig 3. Used by permission of the American Sociological Association and the author.

Chapter 9: Quotation p. 292 From Catherine S. Manegold, "To Crystal, 12, School Serves No Purpose." *New York Times* April 8, 1993, p. A1. Copyright © 1993 by the New York Times Co. Reprinted with permission.

Figure 9.1, p. 311 from Suzanne M. Bianchi, John P. Robinson, and Melissa A. Milkie, Figure 4.1, "Primary Child Care of Mothers and Fathers, 1965-2000 (Average Weekly Hours)." In *Changing Rhythms of American Family Life,* © 2006 Russell Sage Foundation, 112 East 64th St., New York, NY 10021. Reprinted with permission.

Figure 9.4, p. 318 From Donald J. Hernandez, Figure 7.1, "Children, by Relative Income Levels 1939-1988." In *America's Children: Resources from Family, Government and the Economy.* © 1993 Russell Sage Foundation, 112

East 64th St., New York, NY 10021. Reprinted with permission.

Figure 9.5, p. 319 From Greg J. Duncan, 1991. "The Economic Environment of Childhood." In Althea C. Huston, ed., *Children in Poverty*. Reprinted with permission of Cambridge University Press.

Graph, p. 323 from Bruce Bradbury & Markus Jäntti, 1999. "Child Poverty across Industrialized Nations. *Innocenti Occasional Papers, Economic and Social Policy Series*, No. 71, Table 3.3: "Child Poverty Rates." Reprinted with permission of UNICEF International Child Development Centre, Florence, Italy.

Chapter 10: Figure 10.2, p. 340 From James A. Sweet and Larry L. Bumpass, Table 8.8, "Living Arrangements of Persons Aged 60 and Over, by Sex, 1940-1980." *American Families and Households*. Copyright © 1987 Russell Sage Foundation, 112 East 64th St., New York, NY 10021. Reprinted with permission.

Chapter 12: Figure 12.2, p. 414 From James A. Sweet and Larry L. Bumpass, Table 5.3, "Percent of Women Married 10-14 years Who Are No Longer In Intact First Marriages, by Sex, for Racial and Hispanic Groups, 1980." In *American Families and Households*. © 1987 Russell Sage Foundation, 112 East 64th St., New York, NY 10021. Reprinted with permission.

Figure 12.3, p. 421 From Judith A. Seltzer, 1991. "Relationships between Fathers and Children Who Live Apart: The Father's Role after Separation," *Journal of Marriage and the Family*, 53: 1, p. 86. Copyright © 1991 by the National Council on Family Relations, 3989 Central Ave., NE, Suite 550, Minneapolis, MN 55421. Reprinted with permission.

Chapter 13: Figure 13.1, p. 444 From Larry L. Bumpass, James A. Sweet and Andrew J. Cherlin, 1991. "The Role of Cohabitation in Declining Rates of Marriage." *Journal of Marriage and the Family*, 53:4, pp. 913-927. Copyright © 1991 by The National Council on Family Relations, 3989 Central Ave., NE, Suite 550, Minneapolis, MN 55421. Reprinted with permission.

Chapter 14: Graph, p. 488 From Tom Smith, "The Emerging 21st Century American Family." In *General Social Surveys: Social Change Report* No. 43, November 24, 1999. Reprinted by permission of National Opinion Research Center.

Photo Credits

Chapter 1: p. 2: ©Network Productions/The Image Works; p. 6: AP Images/Bob Edme; p. 10 top: © Viviane Moos/Corbis; p. 10 bottom: © Michael Newman/PhotoEdit; p. 14: © Frank Siteman/Stock Boston; p. 17: © Bob Daemmrich/Stock Boston; p. 24: © Ryan McVay/Photodisc Green/Getty Royalty Free; p. 26: Joel Gordon Photography

Chapter 2: p. 34: The Granger Collection; p. 37: The Marriage of Giovanni Arnolfini and Giovanna Cenami by Jan van Eyck © National Gallery Collection; By kind permission of the Trustees of the National Gallery, London/Corbis; p. 39: © Kaz Chiba/The Image Bank/Getty Images; p. 43: The Granger Collection; p. 47: North Wind Pictures; p. 50: © Lewis Wickes Hine/Corbis; p. 53: ©Ariel Skelley/Corbis; p. 54: Library of Congress; p. 59: © Hulton Archive/Getty Images; p. 63: © Bettmann/Corbis

Chapter 3: p. 78: © Stewart Cohen/Taxi/Getty Images; p. 81: Smithsonian American Art Museum; p. 85: ©Bob Daemmrich/The Image Works; p. 88: © Frank Siteman/Stock Boston; p. 95: © Colin Young Wolff/PhotoEdit; p. 97: © Tony Freeman/PhotoEdit; p. 100: © Carl Mydans/Time Life Pictures/Getty Images; p. 105: © Marc Benheim/Woodfin Camp & Associates

Chapter 4: p. 110: © Alison Wright/Corbis; p. 118: © Michael Newman/PhotoEdit; p. 121: © Simon Marcus/Corbis; p. 123: © Tony Freeman/PhotoEdit; p. 128: © Steven Rubin/The Image Works; p. 129: © Lawrence Migdale/Photo Researchers; p. 134: © Rob Levine/The Image Bank/Getty Images; p. 136: © Bob Daemmrich/Stock Boston

Chapter 5: p. 138: © Ronnie Kaufman/Corbis; p. 142: © Tony Metaxas/Asia Images/Getty Images; p. 145: © Mark Richards/PhotoEdit; p. 148: © Ryan McVay/Photodisc Red/Getty Royalty Free; p. 152: AP Images/Pat Sullivan; p. 153 top: AP Images/Eric Gay; p. 153 bottom: AP Images/Donna McWilliam; p. 156: © Rudi Von Briel/PhotoEdit; p. 161: © Steven Rubin/The Image Works; p. 165: © Bob Daemmrich/Stock Boston; p. 170: © Joe Raedle/Getty Images; p. 172: © David Butow/Corbis SABA; p. 173: © Spencer Grant/PhotoEdit; p. 175: © David Butow/ Corbis SABA

Chapter 6: p. 184: © Franco Vogt/Corbis; p. 187: © Archivo Iconografico, S.A./Corbis; p. 191: © Bettmann/Corbis; p. 193: © Ted Horowitz/Corbis; p. 195: © AFP/Getty Images; p. 205: © Gilles Peres/Magnum; p. 207: © Bryn Colton/Assignments Photographers/Corbis; p. 209: AP Images/Chitose Suzuki

Chapter 7: p. 214: © Brand X Pictures; p. 217: © David Young Wolff/PhotoEdit; p. 224: © William Gottlieb/Corbis; p. 230: © Randy Faris/Corbis Royalty Free; p. 234: © Ryan McVay/Stone/Getty Images; p. 236: © Tom Grill/Corbis Royalty Free; p. 239: © C. Devan/zefa/Corbis; p. 243: © Dex Images/Corbis; p. 252: © Lucidio Studio, Inc./Corbis Royalty Free

Chapter 8: p. 256: © Ryan McVay/ Photodisc Blue/Getty Royalty Free; p. 261: © William Taufic/Corbis; p. 263: © Mark Richards/PhotoEdit; p. 267: © Elie Brenager/Stone/Getty Images; p. 269: © Punchstock; p. 271: Kenneth Gabrielsen Photography; p. 277: © David Young Wolff/PhotoEdit; p. 284: © Taxi/Getty Images

Chapter 9: p. 290: Joel Gordon Photography; p. 295: AP Images/Jorge Rey; p. 297: © Stuart Nicol/Woodfin Camp & Associates; p. 300: © Bill Bachmann/The Image Works; p. 303: © Reuters/Corbis; p. 305: © William Campbell/Corbis Sygma; p. 310: ©Suzanne Arms/The Image Works; p. 313: © Jeffery Allan Salter/Corbis SABA; p. 324: © Steven Rubin/The Image Works; p. 322: © Dave Bartruff/Stock Boston

Chapter 10: p. 328: © Hunter Freeman 2000; p. 331: © Bob Daemmrich/Stock Boston; p. 336: © Alison Wright/Corbis; p. 339: ©Steven Rubin/The Image Works; p. 341: © Rhoda Sidney/Stock Boston; p. 344: © Jim West/The Image Works; p. 345 top: © Walter Hodges/Stone/Getty Images; p. 345 bottom: © Bob Daemmrich /The Image Works; p. 352: © Dennis O'-Claire/ Stone/Getty Images; p. 355: © Jeff Greenberg/The Image Works; p. 360: © Jose Luis Pelaez, Inc./Corbis

Chapter 11: p. 366: Joel Gordon Photography; p. 370: The Granger Collection; p. 371: © Ciniglio Lorenzo/Corbis Sygma; p. 379: © Yuri Dojc/The Image Bank/Getty Images; p. 380: © Rachel Epstein/PhotoEdit; p. 383: Gabe Palmer, Palmer Kane inc.; p. 385: AP Images/Nanine Hartzenbusch; p. 389: © Bob Mahoney/The Image Works; p. 396: © Richard Lord/The Image Works

Chapter 12: p. 400: © McGraw-Hill Companies, Inc./Jill Braaten, Photographer; p. 404: © Corbis; p. 408: © Jack Hollingsworth/Photodisc Green/Getty Royalty Free; p. 415: © Joyce Choo/Corbis; p. 419: © Bob Daemmrich/The Image Works; p. 425: © Jeff Greenberg/PhototEdit; p. 427: © Norbert Schaefer/Corbis

Chapter 13: p. 436: © C/B Productions/Corbis; p. 443: © Michael Krasowitz/Taxi/Getty Images; p. 447: © David Young Wolff/PhotoEdit; p. 450: © John Henley/Corbis; p. 452: © Penny Tweedie/Stone/Getty Images; p. 455: Illustrated by Eloise Wilkin, Golden Press, Western Publishing Company, Inc.; p. 458: April Saul; p. 462: © David Young Wolff/PhotoEdit

Chapter 14: p. 468: AP Images; p. 472: © Paul Conklin/PhotoEdit; p. 475: The New York Times; p. 478: Joel Gordon Photography; p. 480: © Steven Peters/Stone/Getty Images; p. 484: © Aaron Harupt/Stock Boston; p. 486: © LWA-Dann Tardif/Corbis; p. 489: © S.Villeger/Explorer/Photo Researchers; p. 491: © Bill Aaron/PhotoEdit; p. 494: © Dan Habib/The Concord Monitor/Corbis; p. 495 top: AP images/Winslow Townson; p. 495 bottom: AP Images/Victoria Arocho

Chapter 15: p. 500: © Jose Luis Pelaez, Inc./Corbis; p. 504: © Jeff Greenberg/PhotoEdit; p. 507: © Brooklyn Productions/The Image Bank/Getty Images; p. 509: © Cheryl Maeder/Taxi/Getty Images; p. 511: © Wil & Demi McIntyre/Photo Researchers

Name Index

Subject Index